ENCYCLOPEDIA OF WORLD WAR II

VOLUME I

Alan Axelrod

Consulting Editor
Col. Jack A. Kingston, U.S. Army (Ret.)

Facts On File
An imprint of Infobase Publishing

Encyclopedia of World War II

Copyright © 2007 by Alan Axelrod

Facts On File, Inc.
An imprint of Infobase Publishing
132 West 31st Street
New York NY 10001

ISBN-10: 0-8160-6022-3
ISBN-13: 978-0-8160-6022-1

Library of Congress Cataloging-in-Publication Data

Axelrod, Alan, 1952–
Encyclopedia of World War II / Alan Axelrod; consulting editor, Jack A. Kingston.
p. cm.
Includes bibliographical references and index.
ISBN 0-8160-6022-3 (alk. paper)
1. World War, 1939–1945—Encyclopedias. I. Kingston, Jack A. II. Title. III. Title:
Encyclopedia of World War Two. IV. Title: Encyclopedia of World War 2.
D740.A94 2007
940.5303—dc22   2006026155

Text design by Erika K. Arroyo
Cover design by Salvatore Luongo
Illustrations by Jeremy Eagle and Dale Williams

Printed in the United States of America

VB Hermitage 10 9 8 7 6 5 4 3 2 1

This book is printed on acid-free paper.

For Anita and Ian

Contents

VOLUME I

INTRODUCTION   vii

ENTRY LIST   ix

ENTRIES A–H   1

VOLUME II

ENTRIES I–Z   449

BIBLIOGRAPHY   893

INDEX   895

Introduction

The legendary American commander General George S. Patton, Jr., once observed that next to war, "all other human endeavor paled to insignificance." If we accept this judgment, we may begin to appreciate the magnitude of World War II, in which Patton played so prominent a role. It, after all, was the largest and bloodiest war in history.

Rare was the patch of the planet that was spared involvement in this war, at least at some time during 1939–45; however, the principal combatants were Germany, Italy, and Japan—the Axis powers—and France, Great Britain, the United States, the Soviet Union, and China—the Allies. The butcher's bill created by this conflict was unprecedented in extent and remains unequaled. Most authorities attribute 40 million to 50 million deaths—the vast majority of these civilians—directly to the war. The peak number of troops mobilized by all combatant nations was 72,928,000, and millions more civilians were committed to war-related industrial production (among these both free workers and slave laborers) and to partisan, guerrilla, and resistance activity.

World War II devastated Europe and Asia and left a world-shaping legacy in its turbulent wake. As a result of the war, the power of the Soviet Union was extended to many nations of eastern Europe, and communism also triumphed in China and established footholds in parts of Korea and Vietnam. The world experienced a profound shift in power and influence away from the old states of western Europe and toward the United States and the Soviet Union, which, through some five decades following the war, were the only global superpowers, each armed with another momen-

tous product of the war: nuclear (and, later, thermonuclear) weapons.

World War II is best understood as an extension of the earlier global cataclysm that was World War I (1914–18), which left many territorial issues unresolved even as it created a host of new cultural and economic incentives for war. The article entitled "Causes of World War II" and the articles treating France, Germany, Italy, Japan, and the United States in this encyclopedia provide discussion of the background against which World War II developed, including a straightforward summary of the causes of the war from the perspectives of each of the major combatant powers. While the economic and territorial causes of the war are relatively easy for a modern reader to grasp, the ideological dimensions are both more complex and yet more elemental.

Politically, the war was a contest involving three broad orientations:

1. The combination of German Nazism and Italian fascism (to which may be added Japanese militarism)
2. Soviet communism
3. Western democracy

Although the socioeconomic basis of Nazism, fascism, and Japanese militarism was fundamentally opposed to the communism of the Soviets, the German and Soviet dictators, Adolf Hitler and Joseph Stalin, began the war as unlikely allies. After Hitler betrayed the alliance by invading the Soviet Union in June 1941, Stalin made a new unlikely alliance, this time with the democratic powers, and thus the prewar ideological enmity between Soviet communism and Western democracy was held in abeyance for the purpose of defeating the common Axis enemy.

Yet the ideological dimension of World War II went far beyond politics to encompass racial mythologies held by Hitler and the Nazis as well as by the Japanese militarists (and to a far lesser degree, by the Italian Fascists), in which the aggressors saw themselves as a master "race" naturally and inexorably opposed to a number of lesser "races" (often defined as subhuman). These lesser races were properly subject to conquest, including economic exploitation for labor and other resources and even genocidal extermination—the latter most infamously exemplified in Nazi anti-Semitism, which gave rise to the "Final Solution" and the "Holocaust," both of which are treated in this encyclopedia, but also evident in Japan's brutal treatment of conquered peoples and defeated armies (see, for example, "Nanking [Nanjing], Rape of"). The mass persecution, torture, and murder of civilian populations were very much a part of World War II, both as a motive and a result, and these subjects are treated in this encyclopedia along with the more conventional military aspects of the war.

At somewhat more than a half million words, the *Encyclopedia of World War II* is intended to be comprehensive, but it makes no claim to being exhaustive. As Patton's assessment of war implies, discussion of World War II properly encompasses every aspect of human endeavor. Here, however, we have been guided by our sense of what subjects are most commonly sought by students and instructors at the high school and undergraduate levels, as well as by others with a nonspecialist interest in World War II. Beyond this, we do not claim to have definitively identified all that is important to the war anymore than we claim to have excluded absolutely all that is of only peripheral interest. We are confident, however, that each of the articles we have included will be useful, relevant, and interesting to the student, instructor, and general reader. Each article includes cross-references to related articles and concludes with suggestions for further reading. These suggestions constitute a specialized bibliography of World War II subjects; readers looking for general works on the conflict should consult the bibliography that concludes the encyclopedia.

Entry List

★

A

Aachen, Battle of
ABC-1 Staff Agreement
Acheson, Dean
Admiralty Islands, Battle of
African-American soldiers,
    sailors, marines, and airmen
airborne assault
aircraft, British
aircraft, French
aircraft, German
aircraft, Italian
aircraft, Japanese
aircraft, Polish
aircraft, Soviet
aircraft, U.S.
aircraft carriers
Alamein, Battles of
Alam el Halfa, Battle of
Albania
Aleutian Islands Campaign
Alexander, Harold
Algeria
Alsace-Lorraine
"Amerika" bomber
amphibious warfare
Anami Korechika
Anderson, John
Anderson shelter
Anschluss
antiaircraft weapons

antiarmor weapons
Anti-Comintern Pact
Antonescu, Ion
ANZAC
Anzio Campaign
appeasement policy
Arctic convoy operations
Ardennes, Battle of the (Battle
    of the Bulge)
armed neutrality
armor, British
armor, French
armor, German
armor, Italian
armor, Japanese
armor, Soviet
armor, U.S.
Arnim, Jürgen von
Arnold, Henry Harley ("Hap")
artillery, British
artillery, French
artillery, German
artillery, Italian
artillery, Japanese
artillery, Soviet
artillery, U.S.
Atlantic, Battle of the
Atlantic Charter
atrocities, German
atrocities, Japanese
attack aircraft

Attlee, Clement
Auchinleck, Claude John Ayre
Aung San
Auschwitz extermination camp
Australia
Australia, air force of
Australia, army of
Australia, navy of
Austria
Axis (Tripartite) Pact
Axmann, Artur

B

Bader, Douglas
Badoglio, Pietro
Balbo, Italo
Balck, Hermann
Baldwin, Stanley
balloon bombs
Baltic Sea, action on the
banzai charge
Barbie, Klaus
barrage balloon
Bataan, Death March
Bataan, fall of
battleships
bazooka
Belgium
Belorussia
Belzec extermination camp
Beneš, Edvard

Berchtesgaden
Bergen-Belsen concentration
    camp
Beria, Lavrenty
Berlin, Battle of
Bevin, Ernest
Biak Island, Battle of
Bidault, Georges
biological warfare
Bismarck, sinking of the
Bismarck Sea, Battle of the
blackout
Blackshirts
Blamey, Thomas
Blitz, the
Blitzkrieg
Bofors gun
bomber aircraft
Bonhoeffer, Dietrich
Bormann, Martin
Bose, Subbas Chandra
Bougainville Campaign
Boyington, Gregory "Pappy"
Bradley, Omar Nelson
Brauchitsch, Walther von
Braun, Wernher von
Brereton, Lewis
Britain, Battle of
British Borneo, action in
Brooke, Alan, first viscount
    Alanbrooke
Browning automatic rifle (BAR)
Buchenwald concentration
    camp
Buckner, Simon Bolivar, Jr.
Budenny, Semyon
Bulganin, Nikolay
Bulgaria
Buna, Battle of
Burma Campaign
Byrnes, James F.

C
Callaghan, Daniel Judson
Canada
Canada, air force of

Canada, army of
Canada, navy of
Canaris, Wilhelm
Cape Esperance, Battle of
Cape Matapan, Battle of (Cape
    Tainaron)
Carlson, Evans
Casablanca Conference
Cassino, Battles of
casualties in World War II
causes of World War II
Ceylon
Chamberlain, Neville
Channon, Henry (Chips)
Chennault, Claire
Chiang Kai-shek (Jiang Jieshi)
Chile
China, armed forces of
Chindits
Christison, Sir Alexander Frank
    Philip
Churchill, Sir Winston
Ciano, Count Galaezzo
civil defense
Clark, Mark
Clay, Lucius D.
Colmar Pocket
commandos
Commissar Order
concentration and
    extermination camps
Coningham, Sir Arthur
conscientious objectors
convoy system
Coral Sea, Battle of the
Corregidor, defense of
corvettes
Coventry air raid
Crete, action on
cruisers
cryptology
Cuba
Cunningham, Alan
Cunningham, Andrew
Cunningham, Winfield Scott
Czechoslovakia

D
Dachau concentration camp
Daladier, Édouard
Daluege, Kurt
Dambusters raid
Darlan, Jean-François
declarations of war
Dempsey, Miles
Denmark, invasion of and
    resistance in
Desert Rats
destroyer escorts
destroyers
Dieppe raid
Dietrich, Josef A. "Sepp"
Dimitrov, Georgi
Dirksen, Herbert von
Dissard, Marie Louise
dive bombers
Dobbie, William
Dodecanese Islands campaign
    of 1943
Dollfuss, Engelbert
Dollmann, Friedrich
Dönitz, Karl
Donovan, William
Doolittle, James Harold
    ("Jimmy")
Doolittle Tokyo Raid
Dowding, Hugh
Dresden air raid
Dulles, Allen
Dulles, John Foster
Dunkirk evacuation
Dutch East Indies, action in

E
Eaker, Ira
East Africa, action in
Eden, Anthony
Egypt, action in
Eichelberger, Robert Lawrence
Eichmann, Adolf
Einstein, Albert
Eisenhower, Dwight D.
embargo, U.S., on Japan

Enigma cipher and machine
Eniwetok Atoll, Battle of
espionage and counterespionage

F

Falkenhausen, Alexander von
Falkenhorst, Nikolaus
fascism
fifth column
fighter aircraft
Filipino Scouts
Final Solution
Finland campaign of 1944
flamethrower
Fletcher, Frank
flying boat
Flying Tigers
Foertsch, Hermann
Forrestal, James
Fortress Eben Emael
foxhole
France
France, air force of
France, army of
France, Battle of
France, navy of
Franco, Francisco (Francisco
    Paulino Hermenegildo
    Teódulo Franco Bahamonde)
Franco-Soviet pacts
Frank, Anne
Free French Forces
Freikorps
French foreign legion
French resistance and
    underground movements
Fritsch, Werner von
Fuchs, Klaus
Funk, Walther

G

Gamelin, Maurice-Gustave
Gaulle, Charles de
Gazala, Battle of
Geheimschreiber
Geiger, Roy

Geisler, Hans
Geneva Conventions
German-Japanese-Italian Pact
German resistance to Nazism
German-Soviet Non-Aggression
    Pact
Germany
Germany, air force of
Germany, army of
Germany, navy of
Gestapo
Gibraltar
Gideon Force
gliders
Goebbels, Joseph
Gomułka, Władysław
Gona, Battle of
Göring, Hermann
Gothic Line
Great Britain
Great Britain, air force of
Great Britain, army of
Great Britain, navy of
Greece, invasion of
Groves, Leslie
Guadalcanal campaign (Battle
    of Guadalcanal)
Guam, Battle of
Guderian, Heinz
Gustav Line

H

Hahn, Otto
Halsey, William "Bull"
Harris, Sir Arthur Travers
    "Bomber"
Heisenberg, Werner
Hess, Rudolf W.
Heydrich, Reinhard
Higashikuni, Naruhiko
Himmler, Heinrich
Hiranuma, Kiichiro
Hirohito
Hiroshima, atomic bombing of
Hitler, Adolf
Hitler Youth

Hoare, Samuel
Ho Chi Minh
Hodge, John
Hodges, Courtney
Hoepner, Erich
Hollandia, Battle of
Hollywood and World War II
Holocaust, the
Home Guard
Homma Masaharu
Honda Masaki
Hong Kong, fall of
Hopkins, Harry
Horii Tomitaro
Horthy de Nagybánya, Miklós
Hoth, Hermann
Hoxha, Enver
Hull, Cordell
Hump, the
Hungary

I

Iida Shojiro
Imamura Hitoshi
Imphal Offensive
incendiary bombs
India
Indian National Army
internment, Japanese-American
Iran
Iraq
Iron Guard uprising in Romania
island hopping strategy
Italian Campaign
Italy
Italy, air force of
Italy, army of
Italy, navy of
Iwo Jima, Battle of

J

Japan
Japan, air force of
Japan, army of
Japan, navy of
Japanese-American soldiers in
    World War II

jet aircraft
Jodl, Alfred
July Plot (to assassinate Hitler)

K
Kádár, János
kamikaze
Kasserine Pass, Battle of
Keitel, Wilhelm
Kenney, George
Kesselring, Albert
Kharkov, Battles of
Khrushchev, Nikita
Kimmel, Husband E.
Kimura Hoyotaro
King, Edward
King, William Lyon Mackenzie
Kinkaid, Thomas C.
Kleist, Paul Ludwig von
Kluge, Günther von
Koga Mineichi
Konev, Ivan
Konoye Fumimaro
Korea, action in
Kowerski, Andrezej
Kristallnacht ("Night of Broken
   Glass")
Krueger, Walter
Krupp munitions works
Kuribasyashi, Tadamichi
Kurita Takeo
Kursk, Battle of
Kwajalein Atoll, Battle of

L
landing craft
Latvia
Laval, Pierre
Leahy, William
Lebensraum
Lebrun, Albert
Leclerc, Jacques-Philippe
Leeb, Wilhelm von
Leigh-Mallory, Trafford
LeMay, Curtis

Lend-Lease Act
Leningrad, siege and relief of
Leyte, Battle of
Leyte Gulf, Battle of
Liberty Ships
Liddell Hart, Basil
List, Siegmund Wilhelm von
Lithuania
Litvinov, Maxim
Lucas, John
Lumsden, Herbert
Luzon, Battle of

M
MacArthur, Douglas
machine gun
Mackesy, Pierse
Macmillan, Harold
Madagascar, Battle of
MAGIC (Japanese code)
Maginot Line
Makin Island Raid
Malaya, fall of
Malinovsky, Rodion
Malmédy Massacre
Malta, siege of
Mandalay, Battle of
Manhattan Project
Mannerheim, Carl Gustav Emil
   von
Mannerheim Line
Manstein, Erich von
Manstein Plan
Manteuffel, Hasso-Eccard von
Mao Zedong
Mariana Islands campaign
Marshall, George Catlett
Marshall Islands campaign
Marshall Plan
Masaryk, Jan
Matapan, Battle of
Matsuoka Yosuke
Mauthausen concentration
   camp
McAuliffe, Anthony

McNair, Lesley
Meiktila, Battle of
Mein Kampf
Memel (Lithuania)
Mengele, Dr. Josef
Merrill, Frank D. W.
Mers-el-Kebir, Battle of
Messe, Giovanni
Messervy, Frank
Metaxas, Ioannis
MI5 (British military
   intelligence)
MI6 (British military
   intelligence)
Midway, Battle of
Mihailović, Draža
Mikolajczyk, Stanisław
mines, land
mines, naval
minesweeper
Mitscher, Marc
Model, Walther
Moelders, Werner
Molotov, Vyacheslav
Monckton, Walter
Montgomery, Sir Bernard Law
Morgenthau, Henry, Jr.
Morocco
Morrison shelter
mortar
Moscow, Battle of
Mosley, Oswald
Moulin, Jean
Mountbatten, Louis
Mount Suribachi
Mulberry harbor
Munich Conference and
   Agreement
Murphy, Audie
Mussolini, Benito
Mykikyina, Battle of

N
Nagasaki, atomic bombing of
Nagumo Chuichi

Nanking, Rape of
Narvik, Battles of
Navajo code talkers
naval war with Germany,
    undeclared (1940–1941)
Nazi Party (NSDAP)
Netherlands
Netherlands East Indies, action
    in
neutral nations
Neutrality Acts, U.S.
New Georgia Campaign
New Guinea Campaign
New Zealand, air force of
New Zealand, army of
New Zealand, navy of
Nimitz, Chester William
Noguès, Auguste
Norden bombsight
Normandy Landings (D-day)
North African Campaigns
Norwegian Campaign
Nuremberg Laws
Nuremberg War Crimes
    Tribunal

O
Oberth, Hermann
Oboe
O'Connor, Richard
Office of Strategic Services
    (OSS)
Okinawa Campaign
Operation Anvil/Dragoon
Operation Barbarossa
Operation Cobra
Operation Husky
Operation Market Garden
    (Battle of Arnhem)
Operation Overlord
Operation Sealion
Operation Torch
Oppenheimer, J. Robert
Orange (Japanese code)
Ozawa Jisaburo

P
Pact of Steel
Palestine
Papagos, Alexandros
Papen, Franz von
Paris, occupation and liberation
    of
Patch, Alexander McCarrell, Jr.
Patton, George Smith
Paulus, Friedrich
peace treaties ending World
    War II
Pearl Harbor, Battle of
Peenemunde (V-1 and V-2 base)
Peiper, Joachim
Peirse, Richard
Peleliu, Battle of
Percival, Arthur
Pétain, Henri-Philippe
Philippine Constabulary
Philippine Sea, Battle of the
Philippines, fall and reconquest
    of
Phony War
pillbox
Pius XI
Pius XII
Ploe ti raid
pocket battleships
Poland
Poland, air force of
Poland, army of
Poland, invasion of
Poland, navy of
Polish Home Army
Portal, Charles
Portugal
Potsdam Conference
prisoners of war
propaganda
PT boat
Puller, Lewis B. "Chesty"
PURPLE (Japanese diplomatic
    cipher)
Pyle, Ernie

Q
Q-ship
Quisling, Vidkun

R
Rabaul, Battles of
Raczkiewicz, Władysław
radar
Raeder, Erich
Rangers, U.S. Army
Rashid Ali el-Ghialani
refugees
Reichenau, Walther von
Remagen Bridge
resistance movements
Reynaud, Paul
Rhine crossings
Ribbentrop, Joachim von
Ridgway, Matthew
Riefenstahl, Leni
Rio Conference
Ritchie, Neil
River Kwai Bridge
River Plate, Battle of
Rokossovsky, Konstantin
Romania
Rommel, Erwin
Roosevelt, Franklin Delano
Rosenberg, Alfred
Rotterdam air raid
Rudel, Hans Ulrich
Rundstedt, Gerd von
Russian summer offensive of
    1943
Russian winter counteroffensive
    of 1941–1942
Russo-Finnish War (Winter
    War)

S
St. Nazaire Raid
Saipan, Battle of
Salerno, Battle of
Scapa Flow
Schacht, Hjalmar

Scheldt Estuary
Schellenberg, Walter
Schindler, Oskar
Schlabrendorff, Fabian
Schuschnigg, Kurt von
Schutzstaffel (SS)
Schweinfurt raids
Seeckt, Hans von
Selassie, Haile
Sevastopol sieges
Seyss-Inquart, Arthur
Shibasaki Keiji
ships, British
ships, French
ships, German
ships, Italian
ships, Japanese
ships, Soviet
ships, United States
Short, Walter
Sicherheitsdienst (SD)
Sicily Campaign
Sidi Rezegh, Battle of
Siegfried Line
Singapore, fall of
Sino-Japanese War
Sittang River Bridge, Battle of
Skorzeny, Otto
Slim, William Joseph
small arms and rifles, British
small arms and rifles, French
small arms and rifles, German
small arms and rifles, Italian
small arms and rifles, Japanese
small arms and rifles, Soviet
small arms and rifles, U.S.
Smith, Holland M. "Howlin-
   Mad"
Smith, Walter Bedell
Smuts, Jan Christiaan
Sobibór concentration camp
Somerville, James
SONAR
Sonderkommando Elbe
South Africa

Soviet Union
Soviet Union, air force of
Soviet Union, army of
Soviet Union, invasion of the
Soviet Union, navy of
Spaatz, Carl
Spain
Spanish civil war
Special Air Service (SAS)
Speer, Albert
Sperrle, Hugo
Spruance, Raymond
Stalin, Joseph
Stalingrad, Battle of
Stark, Harold
Stauffenberg, Claus von
Stavka (Soviet Supreme
   Command)
Stettinius, Edward
Stilwell, Joseph "Vinegar Joe"
Stimson, Henry L.
Strasser, Gregor and Otto
strategic bombing of Germany
strategic bombing of Japan
Streicher, Julius
Student, Kurt
Sturmabteilung (SA)
submarines
Sudetenland
Sun Li-jen
surrender documents of 1943–
   1945
Suzuki Kantaro
Sweden
Switzerland
Syria
Szilard, Leo

T
Tanaka Raizo
tank destroyers
Taranto, Battle of
Tarawa Atoll, Battle of
Tedder, Arthur
Teller, Edward

Ter Poorten, Hein
Terauchi Hisaichi
Thailand
theaters of World War II
Theresienstadt
Tibbets, Paul
Timoshenko, Semyon
Tito (Josip Broz)
Tobruk, Battles of
Todt, Fritz
Togo Shigenori
Tojo Hideki
Tokyo fire bombing
Tokyo war crimes trials
Toyoda Soemu
transport aircraft
treaties ending the war
Treblinka extermination camp
Tresckow, Henning von
Trier, Walter
Trott, Adam von
Truk Island, Battles of
Truman, Harry S.
Truscott, Lucian
Turing, Alan
Turkey
Turner, Richmond
Tuskegee Airmen

U
Ukraine campaign
Ultra
United Nations
United Nations Declaration
United States
United States Army
United States Army Air Corps
United States Army Air Forces
United States Coast Guard
United States Marine Corps
United States Marine Corps
   Women's Reserve
United States Merchant Marine
United States Navy
Ushijima Mitsuru

V

V-1 buzz bomb
V-2 rocket
Vandegrift, Alexander
Vasilevsky, Aleksandr
    Mikhailovich
V-E Day
Vella Lavella, Battle of
Versailles, Treaty of
Vichy government
Victor Emmanuel III
V-J Day
Voroshilov, Kliment

W

Waffen SS
Wainwright, Jonathan
Wake Island, Battle of

Wannsee Conference
Warsaw Ghetto Uprising
Warsaw Rising
Wavell, Archibald
Wehrmacht
Wei Li-huang
Weil, Simone
Western Desert Campaigns
Weygand, Maxime
Whittle, Frank
Wilson, Henry Maitland
    "Jumbo"
Wingate, Orde
wolf pack U-boat tactics
Women Accepted for Voluntary
    Emergency Service (WAVES)
Women Airforce Service Pilots
    (WASP)

women in World War II (United
    States)
Women's Army Corps (WAC)
Women's Auxiliary Ferrying
    Squadron (WAFS)
"wonder weapons"

Y

Yalta Agreement
Yamada Otozo
Yamamoto Isoruku
Yamashita Tomoyuki
Yugoslavia, invasion of

Z

Zhukov, Georgi Konstantinovich
Zog I

A

Aachen, Battle of

Aachen, near Germany's border with the Netherlands and Belgium, first distinguished in history as the capital of Charlemagne's empire, was the site of the first battle by U.S. forces on German soil and was the first German city to fall to the Allies. Located near the line of German fortifications known as the WEST WALL, Aachen was a prime gateway into Germany.

During September 12–15, 1944, COURTNEY HODGES's First U.S. Army attempted a penetration through the south side of Aachen. Repulsed, Hodges began an encirclement and, on October 2, launched a new assault, this time from the north as well as south. By October 16, Hodges completed his encirclement of the city and penetrated it generally. This resulted in days of costly street fighting, which finally produced the surrender of Aachen on October 21.

While Aachen was a major American triumph, it is also true that the German defense of the city, led by Col. Gerhard Wilck (under Gen. HERMANN BALCK), was highly effective in that it halted the advance of the First U.S. Army for more than five weeks. Hodges suffered nearly 8,000 casualties in operations in and around Aachen.

See also SIEGFRIED LINE.

Further reading: Astor, Gerald. *The Bloody Forest.* Novato, Calif.: Presidio, 2000; Rush, Robert S. *Hell in the Hurtgen Forest: The Ordeal and Triumph of an American Infantry Regiment.* Lawrence: University Press of Kansas, 2001; Whiting, Charles. *Battle of Hurtgen Forest.* New York: Da Capo, 2000; Whiting, Charles. *Bloody Aachen.* New York: Da Capo, 2000.

ABC-1 Staff Agreement

Concluded on March 27, 1941, at Washington, D.C. between naval and military representatives of the United States and Great Britain, the ABC-1 Staff Agreement established the practical basis of Anglo-American cooperation in the event that the United States entered the war. The document consisted of three major provisions:

1. An agreement that both powers would concentrate their efforts on defeating Germany as the most dangerous of the Axis powers
2. An agreement that the chiefs of staff of the British and the American militaries would work together as a single Combined Chiefs of Staff
3. An agreement that the U.S. Navy's Atlantic Fleet would begin assisting the Royal Navy in escorting Atlantic convoys as soon as the U.S. Navy was capable of doing so

Unlike the first two provisions, which would apply only after the United States actually entered the war, the third provision went into effect immediately, and the U.S. Navy, escorting Allied convoys, began what was, in effect, an undeclared naval war against Germany months before Pearl Harbor thrust the United States into both the Pacific and the Atlantic wars.

See also ARMED NEUTRALITY; ATLANTIC CHARTER; NAVAL WAR WITH GERMANY, UNDECLARED (1940–1941); and NEUTRALITY ACTS, U.S.

Further reading: Kemp, Peter. *Decision at Sea: The Convoy Escorts.* New York: Elsevier-Dutton, 1978; Matson, Robert W. *Neutrality and Navicerts: Britain, the United States, and Economic Warfare, 1939–1940.* London: Taylor & Francis, 1994; Rhodes, Benjamin D. *United States Foreign Policy in the Interwar Period, 1918–1941: The Golden Age of American Diplomatic and Military Complacency.* New York: Praeger, 2001.

Acheson, Dean (1893–1971) *U.S. diplomat instrumental in the Marshall Plan*

Although Dean Acheson served in government during World War II as assistant secretary of state from 1941 to 1945, he is most significant for his role in the United States' single greatest contribution to the postwar recovery and welfare of Europe, the MARSHALL PLAN. In 1947, Acheson, at the time undersecretary of state (in the office of Secretary of State GEORGE C. MARSHALL), laid out in broad form the principal points of the great relief, recovery, and redevelopment program, which not only rescued a devastated Europe, but saved much of it from being engulfed by the SOVIET UNION.

Acheson was educated at Yale University and at Harvard Law School. After serving as private secretary to Supreme Court Justice Louis Brandeis, Acheson joined a prestigious Washington law firm in 1921, then entered government service in the administration of FRANKLIN D. ROOSEVELT in 1933 as undersecretary of the treasury. During the war years, he served as an assistant secretary of state and, from 1945 to 1947, as undersecretary of state. In this post, Acheson was instrumental in engineering Senate approval of U.S. membership in the UNITED NATIONS.

In addition to his work in helping to design and promote the Marshall Plan, Acheson also profoundly influenced American postwar policy with his strong stance against the expansion of communism and his formulation of the so-called Truman Doctrine, including its leading theme of "containing" communism whenever and wherever its forcible expansion occurred. Acheson became secretary of state in the cabinet of HARRY S. TRUMAN in January 1949 and was instrumental in the creation of NATO, the North Atlantic Treaty Organization.

During the 1950s, despite his strongly anticommunist stance, Acheson became the target of the Red-baiting senator from Wisconsin, Joseph McCarthy, but remained in office until President Truman left the White House in 1953. Returning to the private practice of law, Acheson also continued to serve as a presidential adviser and was the author of several important firsthand histories, including the Pulitzer Prize–winning *Present at the Creation,* an account of his years as secretary of state.

Further reading: Acheson, Dean. *Present at the Creation: My Years in the State Department.* 1969; reprint ed., New York: W. W. Norton, 1987; Lamberton, John. *American Visions of Europe: Franklin D. Roosevelt, George F. Kennan, and Dean G. Acheson.* New York: Cambridge University Press, 1996.

Admiralty Islands, Battle of

The Admiralty Islands are located some 200 miles northeast of New Guinea and, captured by Australian forces early in World War I, became part of the Australian mandate of New Guinea in 1921. The islands were occupied by Japan in April 1942. The Japanese established air bases on them and used Seeadler Harbor at Manus Island as a fleet anchorage.

Pacific Allied theater commander Gen. DOUGLAS MACARTHUR needed to isolate and reduce the major Japanese base at Rabaul, chief town on New Britain Island, Papua New Guinea. To do this, he understood that the Japanese facilities on the Admiralty Islands would first have to be captured, and he assigned the U.S. Army's 1st Cavalry Division, supported by the 73rd Wing of the Royal Australian Air Force, to seize the islands. Commanded by Lt. Gen. WALTER KRUEGER, the 1st

Cavalry, covered by Australian air support, landed on Los Negros Island on February 29, 1944. After a week of fighting, the 1st Cavalry advanced to Manus Island, where it encountered extremely tenacious resistance from the large Japanese garrison there: two full infantry battalions and various naval units. Fighting, principally on Manus, continued throughout most of the spring before Krueger declared the islands secure on May 18, 1944. Losses to the 1st Cavalry Division were 326 men killed and 1,189 wounded. Japanese losses on Manus were probably about 2,000 killed.

Further reading: Rottman, Gordon I. *Japanese Pacific Island Defenses 1941–45.* London: Osprey, 2003; United States Army. *United States Army in World War II: War in the Pacific, Cartwheel, the Reduction of Rabaul.* Washington, D.C.: Government Printing Office, 1999.

African-American soldiers, sailors, marines, and airmen

During World War II, the U.S. armed forces were, for the most part, racially segregated. African-American soldiers, sailors, marines, and airmen were trained separately. They served in segregated units, usually commanded by white officers, although a small number of African Americans were commissioned during the war. At sea, black sailors were given segregated quarters, although modest experiments in integration were carried out. For the most part, African Americans served in support and labor units rather than in front-line combat units. In December 1942, President Roosevelt issued an executive order calling for African Americans to make up 10 percent of all personnel drafted for the services.

ARMY

During World War I, some 380,000 African Americans were enlisted or drafted into the army, 89 percent assigned to labor units and only 11 percent committed to combat. After the war, African-American membership in the army fell to just 5,000 enlisted men (2 percent of the service) and five officers. During World War II, black member-

ship in the army rose spectacularly; 900,000 African Americans served by war's end, mostly in support roles, including the famed Red Ball Express truck convoys run during the advance through France following the NORMANDY LANDINGS (D-DAY). Although black officers were few, there was one African-American brigadier general, Benjamin O. Davis, Sr.

ARMY AIR FORCES

In 1940, President FRANKLIN D. ROOSEVELT opened the UNITED STATES ARMY AIR CORPS in a limited way to black pilots, who were trained and who served in segregated units. The most famous of these were the TUSKEGEE AIRMEN, who served with distinction in the North African and Italian theaters but remained segregated throughout the war. Most African Americans served in labor roles. However, after the war, following President HARRY S. TRUMAN's 1948 Executive Order 9981, which mandated an end to segregation in the military and a universal policy of equal treatment and opportunity regardless of race, the U.S. Air Force (which had become an independent service in 1947) was far ahead of the other services in implementing the integration policy.

MARINES

Before World War II, the Marine Corps accepted no black enlistments. On the eve of World War II, President Roosevelt directed the commandant of the Marine Corps to take steps toward incorporating African Americans into the corps. A commission was created to study how black marines could best be used, but actual enlistments were not accepted until after the BATTLE OF PEARL HARBOR, December 7, 1941. A short time after this, a segregated training facility, Camp Johnson, was established outside Marine Corps Base Camp Lejeune in South Carolina. The first recruits arrived at Camp Johnson in August 1942 to make up the 51st Defense Battalion. Initially, they were trained by white drill instructors, but they were eventually replaced by black instructors.

The 51st Defense Battalion was brought to a strength of 1,400 and sent to the Pacific, first in the

Ellis Islands and then in the Marshalls. They remained posted there throughout the war. A second black unit, the 52nd Defense Battalion, was established in December 1943 and dispatched to Roi-Namur and then to the Marianas. The black marines were used almost exclusively as stewards and laborers, not as combat troops. In all, 19,000 African Americans served in the marines during World War II, most of them having been drafted. No black marine was commissioned an officer during the war.

NAVY

More than any other service during World War II, the U.S. Navy implemented steps toward racial integration. Black sailors had served in the sail navy during the 18th and 19th centuries, when the labor of handling sails required many hands. After the Civil War, as sails were replaced by steam and the number of hands required diminished, so did naval recruitment of African Americans. Those who did join were typically assigned to service positions, typically as "mess boys," stewards, and orderlies serving white officers. Segregation was enforced aboard ship in eating and sleeping areas. After the United States annexed the Philippines in 1898, black mess, steward, and orderly personnel were increasingly replaced by Filipinos, so that when the United States entered World War I in 1917, Filipinos outnumbered African Americans in the navy. The enlistment of Filipino volunteers declined beginning in the early 1930s, and African American enlistments rose proportionately—although black personnel were still confined to mess and steward positions, and segregation was enforced on board ships as well as in shore accommodations. In 1940, Walter White of the National Association for the Advancement of Colored People (NAACP), together with the black labor leader A. Phillip Randolph and activist T. Arnold Hill, wrote a letter to President Franklin D. Roosevelt protesting the strictures on black employment in the navy. In response, the president approved a plan in support of "fair treatment," but the navy failed to implement it, arguing that morale would suffer if blacks were assigned to nonservice posi-

tions. Only after World War II was under way did the NAACP again appeal to the administration, this time to Secretary of the Navy Frank Knox, to expand the role of African Americans beyond service positions. The conservative Knox declined to act, and the NAACP again appealed directly to the president. In June 1942, FDR personally prevailed on top naval command to adopt an expanded assignment policy. New guidelines were formulated that admitted African-American sailors to service in construction battalions, supply depots, air stations, shore stations, section bases, and yard craft. Although this represented an expansion well beyond mess and steward service, the new positions were overwhelmingly labor assignments and not combat postings.

President Roosevelt's December 1942 executive order mandating that African Americans represent 10 percent of the personnel in all the armed services created a dramatic increase in black enlistment in the navy. By July 1943, 12,000 blacks were being inducted monthly. By December 1943, 101,573 African Americans had enlisted, of whom 37,981 (37 percent) served in the Stewards Branch. The rest were boatswains, carpenters, painters, metalsmiths, hospital apprentices, firemen, aviation maintenance personnel, and members of the Shore Patrol. Few nonstewards were assigned sea duty. Nevertheless, by this time, the navy began selecting African Americans for commissioning as officers. The selectees were divided into line and staff officers.

In January 1944, the line officers began segregated 10-week training at Naval Training Center Great Lakes. Of these, 12 commissioned officers and one warrant officer were graduated—the first African-American officers in U.S. Navy history. This so-called Golden Thirteen were assigned to recruit training programs and small patrol craft and tugs.

The staff officer selectees were trained during the summer of 1944. Of the first class, two graduates were assigned to the Chaplain Corps, two to the Dental Corps, two to the Civil Engineer Corps, three to the Medical Corps, and three to the Supply Corps. By the end of the war, just 58 out of 160,000

African-American sailors had been commissioned as officers.

As for enlisted personnel, reform accelerated during 1944, after the death of Knox and his replacement as navy secretary by JAMES FORRESTAL. A political liberal and civil rights activist, Forrestal launched a trial integration program in which black sailors were assigned to general sea duty positions. As for shipboard segregation, the black sailors were placed exclusively on large auxiliary vessels (such as cargo craft and tankers) and constituted no more than 10 percent of the crew of any one ship. Some 25 ships were integrated in this way with no race relation problems reported. Before the war ended, Forrestal assigned African-American personnel to all auxiliary ships of the fleet, and, even more significantly, segregated training was ended. African-American recruits were assigned to the same training centers as whites.

See also UNITED STATES ARMY; UNITED STATES ARMY AIR FORCES; UNITED STATES MARINE CORPS; and UNITED STATES NAVY.

Further reading: Belknap, Michael R., ed. *Civil Rights, the White House, and the Justice Department, 1945–1968: Integration of the Armed Forces.* New York: Garland, 1991; Fletcher, Marvin E. *The Black Soldier and Officer in the United States Army, 1891–1917.* Columbia: University of Missouri Press, 1974.

airborne assault

In World War II, *airborne assault* referred to the deployment against the enemy of specially trained troops by parachute or GLIDERS. The introduction of airborne assault may be dated to 1922, when Red Army troops were first deployed by parachute. Later in the decade, Italy formed a company of military parachutists. By the end of the 1920s, the Soviet Union had created a battalion. France formed two companies of Infanterie de l'Air in 1938. Curiously, the German army, the WEHRMACHT, lacked enthusiasm for airborne assault. However, the air force, the Luftwaffe, acting in 1938, created the 7th Flieger Division, the largest unit of paratroopers and glider troops in any nation's army, under the command of Maj. Gen. KURT STUDENT.

It was elements of the 7th Flieger Division that staged the first airborne assault of World War II during the invasion of BELGIUM and the NETHERLANDS. This was a glider assault on Belgium's Eben Emael, a fortress that proved unassailable—except by airborne assault. The 7th Flieger Division, attached to the XI Air Corps, was deployed next against Crete in May 1941 and fought the first battle to be won by airborne troops alone. Nevertheless, the victory was purchased with losses so heavy that ADOLF HITLER himself forbade further airborne assaults. His elite airborne troops were henceforth used in a ground assault role only.

Despite Hitler's reservations, the British and the Americans (who had yet to enter the war) were both alarmed and impressed by Germany's execution of airborne assault. In response, Britain created the 1st Airborne Division in October 1941, which was followed in May 1943 by the 6th Airborne Division. Each of these units had two parachute brigades, a glider brigade, and divisional troops. Initially, the Royal Air Force provided transport using converted bombers. Toward the end of 1944, these were replaced by U.S.-built C-47 transports, called Dakotas by the British. In 1941, the United States began developing airborne assault as well, ultimately creating five divisions, the 11th, 13th, 17th, 82nd, and 101st. Each American division consisted of three parachute regiments and one glider regiment.

The first Allied airborne assaults took place during the NORTH AFRICAN CAMPAIGNS in 1942–43 and were carried out by the British 1st Airborne Division—initially by its 1st Parachute Brigade and then by elements of the entire division under Maj. Gen. G. F. Hopkinson. This division also participated in the SICILY CAMPAIGN and the ITALIAN CAMPAIGN during 1943. In February 1942, a company of the British 2nd Parachute Battalion dropped into Bruneval, France, where it successfully captured a new type of German RADAR installation. In November of that year, a force from the 1st Airborne Division made a pair of glider landings in Norway for the purpose of sabotaging a

German heavy water facility there in an effort to stem German development of an atomic weapon. The raid was unsuccessful.

During November 1943, the 2nd Independent Parachute Brigade Group, commanded by British Brig. Gen. C. H. V. Pritchard, participated in Italian operations, then, through 1945, as part of the 1st Airborne Task Force, fought in southern France and Greece. The British 6th Airborne Division, under Maj. Gen. Richard Gale, joined the U.S. 82nd (Maj. Gen. MATTHEW RIDGWAY) and 101st (Maj. Gen. Maxwell Taylor) Airborne Divisions in OPERATION OVERLORD in preparation for the NORMANDY LANDINGS (D-DAY) during June 1944.

After its initial drops, the 101st and 82nd Airborne fought as ground units until they were deployed, with the British 1st Airborne Division (Maj. Gen. Roy Urquhart), as the I Airborne Corps (Lt. Gen. "Boy" Browning), in OPERATION MARKET GARDEN (BATTLE OF ARNHEM) during September 1944. The I Airborne Corps was now part of the First Allied Airborne Army, under the overall command of Lt. Gen. LEWIS BRERETON. The 82nd Airborne (Brig. Gen. James Gavin) and the 101st (Taylor) achieved their objectives in Market Garden, but the 1st Airborne, dropping too far from its objectives, was badly defeated and suffered severe losses. Operation Market Garden failed. Nevertheless, lessons were learned from the failure, and in March 1945, when the XVIII U.S. Airborne Corps (Ridgway), consisting of the British 6th Airborne Division and the U.S. 17th Airborne Division, participated in Operation Varsity, a Rhine crossing, steps were taken to ensure accurate drops. Both divisions quickly achieved their objectives, and the operation was a success. Operation Varsity was, however, the last major airborne assault in Europe.

In the China-Burma-India theater, the Indian Army formed the 50th Indian Parachute Brigade in 1941. It fought extensively in the BURMA CAMPAIGN. The 44th Indian Airborne Division (later designated the 2nd Indian Airborne Division) was created in 1944 under the command of Maj. Gen. Eric Down. The unit made only a single airborne assault, at Elephant Point, Burma, in May 1945.

However, the brilliant Maj. Gen. ORDE WINGATE, commanding a special force of Chindits, made numerous small drops behind the Japanese lines in Burma. Also in Burma, the UNITED STATES ARMY AIR FORCE landed engineer squadrons (as part of the No. 1 Air Commando) by glider to build airstrips. The No. 1 Air Commando also operated P-51 Mustang fighters and L-5 light liaison aircraft in Burma, providing close air support and casualty evacuation.

In the Pacific theater, Maj. Gen. Joseph Swing commanded the 11th U.S. Airborne Division, which was the principal airborne assault unit in this theater. In February 1945, two 11th Airborne battalions dropped at Tagaytay Ridge, on Luzon in the Philippines, and, later in the month, the 503rd Parachute Infantry Regiment dropped on Japanese-held Corregidor. Shortly after this, the 1st Battalion 511th Parachute Infantry Regiment dropped just to the northeast of Tagaytay Ridge to make an assault on a Japanese prisoner of war camp. The unit liberated Allied prisoners held since the fall of the PHILIPPINES. Finally, in June 1944, elements of the 11th Airborne Division dropped on Luzon to cut off the Japanese withdrawal.

Despite the pioneering efforts in airborne assault by Italian, Soviet, and German forces, only the British and Americans made significant use of this mode of deployment during World War II. Italy eventually constituted two parachute divisions (each very much understrength) but used them exclusively in a ground role. The Soviets carried out a few small-scale airborne operations during 1943–44 but primarily used their parachute units as ground troops. The Germans, as noted, halted airborne assault operations very early in the war. The Japanese did create airborne assault units but used them only three times, landing at Menado and Palembang in the Dutch East Indies in 1942 and against American airfields at Burauen in the Philippines during December 1944. This was the last airborne assault of the war.

Further reading: Ambrose, Stephen E. *Band of Brothers: E Company, 506th Regiment, 101st Airborne from Normandy to Hitler's Eagle's Nest.* 2d ed. New York: Simon

& Schuster, 2001; Bandop, Mark A. *101st Airborne: The Screaming Eagles at Normandy.* St. Paul, Minn.: MBI, 2001; Flanagan, E. M., Jr. *Airborne: A Combat History of American Airborne Forces.* Novato, Calif.: Presidio Press, 2003; Quarrie, Bruce. *German Airborne Divisions: Blitzkrieg 1940–41.* London: Osprey, 2004; Quarrie, Bruce. *German Airborne Troops, 1939–45.* London: Osprey, 1983; Ruggero, Ed. *Combat Jump: The Young Men Who Led the Assault into Fortress Europe, July 1943.* New York: HarperCollins, 2003; Smith, Carl. *U.S. Paratrooper 1941–1945: Weapons, Armor, Tactics.* London: Osprey, 2000; Verier, Mike. *82nd Airborne Division: All American.* Hersham, U.K.: Ian Allan, 2002; Webster, David Kenyon. *Parachute Infantry: An American Paratrooper's Memoir of D-day and the Fall of the Third Reich.* Rev. ed. New York: Delta, 2002.

aircraft, British

When war clouds gathered in the 1930s, WINSTON CHURCHILL and a minority of others in the British government urged accelerated development and production of military aircraft as it became increasingly apparent that Germany, rearming in defiance of the TREATY OF VERSAILLES, was creating a large and advanced air force. The outbreak of war caught Britain with an undersized air force, and the nation consequently relied heavily on a variety of U.S.-supplied aircraft. However, the British aircraft industry also produced some of the most important planes of the war.

Among British bomber aircraft, the most significant were

Armstrong Whitworth Whitley V. Powered by two 1,145-horsepower RR Merlin X engines, the Armstrong Whitworth Whitley entered into Royal Air Force (RAF) service in March 1937. The first of the heavy RAF night bombers, the aircraft was a mediocre performer, with a top speed of 222 miles per hour and a service ceiling of 17,600 feet. Range was 1,650 miles. After 1942, it was used by the RAF exclusively as a trainer and glider tug. A total of 1,737 (all versions) were built. The Royal Navy's Fleet Air Arm operated the aircraft until 1945.

Avro Lancaster I. Becoming operational in March 1942, the Avro Lancaster was powered by four 1,460-horsepower RR Merlin XX engines and had a wingspan of 102 feet, a loaded weight of 68,000 pounds, a top speed of 308 miles per hour, and a ceiling of 24,500 feet. Its effective range was 1,600 miles. This military workhorse, produced in a quantity of 7,377, could carry a maximum bomb load of 22,000 pounds and was one of the great bombers of World War II, deserving a place beside such American aircraft as the B-17, B-24, and B-29. Lancasters were the most heavily used of British bombers, flying in excess of 156,000 operations and delivering 608,612 tons of bombs on target. Reflecting the monumental cost of the STRATEGIC BOMBING OF GERMANY, 3,249 Lancasters were lost in action.

Bristol Blenheim Mark IV. This bomber was developed from the Bristol model 142 civil transport, and when it first became operational (in the Mark I version) in 1937, it was actually faster than most RAF fighters. The Mark IV version, operational by 1939, had a top speed of 266 miles per hour, a service ceiling of 22,000 feet, and a range of 1,460 miles. With a wingspan of 56 feet 4 inches, it was powered by two 920-horsepower Bristol Mercury XV engines. Maximum bomb load was 1,325 pounds.

The Mark I version of the aircraft had the distinction of flying the first Allied operational mission of the war, a reconnaissance over Germany. Mark IV was used extensively as a light bomber and also as a fighter, a reconnaissance aircraft, and a close-support aircraft. The aircraft was crewed by three. A Mark V was developed, which increased the service ceiling to 31,000 feet and range to 1,600 miles. In other respects, however, its performance was disappointing, and the Mark V was used almost exclusively in the Far East.

Relatively slow by 1940s standards and with only light defensive armament, the Blenheims were especially vulnerable to fighter attack. They were withdrawn from the bomber role in 1943. About 6,200 (all versions) were built.

De Haviland Mosquito XVI. One of the war's great aircraft, the Mosquito was flown as a night fighter, fighter bomber, bomber, and reconnaissance plane. Crewed by two, it had a remarkable top speed of 425 miles per hour and a service ceiling of 36,000 feet. In bomber configurations, the XVI version carried no defensive armament but relied on its speed and maneuverability, which could outperform most fighters. Maximum range was 3,500 miles.

Affectionately dubbed the Mossie, the aircraft was first flown late in 1940 and became operational with the RAF in 1942. It served in Europe and Asia and proved so adaptable that it remained in service well after the war, until 1955. A total of 7,781 (all versions) were built.

The Mark XVI version was driven by two 1,680-horsepower Rolls Royce engines. Wingspan was 54 feet 2 inches, and maximum bomb load was 4,000 pounds.

Fairey Battle I. Introduced in 1940, the Fairey Battle I was a two-place light day bomber powered by a single Rolls-Royce Merlin II piston engine, which delivered 1,030 horsepower. With a 54-foot wingspan, it had a top speed of 241 miles per hour, a service ceiling of 23,500 feet, and a range of 1,050 miles. Armed with a forward-firing .303-inch fuselage-mounted Browning machine gun and a rear-facing .303-inch Vickers K machine gun, the aircraft could carry a 1,000-pound bomb load.

Deployed in France at the outbreak of the war in 1940, the Fairey Battle quickly proved inadequate as a day bomber and was withdrawn from such service very early in the war. However, it continued to operate with the RAF as late as 1949 as a trainer, target tug, and communications aircraft. Some 2,200 were built.

Handley Page Halifax VI. This four-engine bomber first flew in prototype in 1939, and the first Mark I version was delivered in 1940. The Mark VII entered production in 1944 and was powered by four 1,800-horsepower Hercules 100s and had a wingspan of 104 feet 2 inches. Maximum speed was 312 miles per hour with a service ceiling of 24,000 feet and a range of 1,260 miles. Maximum bomb load was 13,000 pounds. Although not nearly as well known as the Avro Lancaster, the Halifax was a highly successful heavy bomber, produced in a quantity of 6,176 (all versions).

Handley Page Hampden I. Powered by two 1,000-horsepower Bristol Pegasus XVIII engines, this medium bomber was designed beginning in 1933 and went into production in 1938. With a wingspan of 69 feet 2 inches and a maximum bomb load of 4,000 pounds, the aircraft could make 254 miles per hour and reach a service ceiling of 19,000 feet. Slow and vulnerable to fighters, it made its last bombing raid in September 1942 and was used mainly for training purposes thereafter. A total of 1,430 were built.

Short Stirling III. The Mark I version of this large four-engine bomber was delivered to the RAF in 1940. The first Mark IIIs were flying by 1942. Powered by four 1,650-horsepower Bristol Hercules XVI engines and with a wingspan of 99 feet 1 inch, this heavy bomber could deliver 14,000 pounds of bombs. However, it soon proved unpopular with aircrews because of its low ceiling (17,000 feet) and inadequate maneuverability near its maximum altitude. By 1943, the Stirling III was withdrawn from bombing missions and relegated to duty as a glider tug and transport. Some were adapted as Mark IVs and used as paratroop transports. Total production for all versions was 2,374.

Vickers Wellington III. First flown in prototype in 1936, the Mark I version of this medium bomber entered RAF service in 1938. It proved successful in a variety of roles, and 11,461 were produced before production ceased in October 1945. The Mark III version was powered by two 1,375-horsepower Bristol Hercules III or two 1,425-horsepower Hercules XI engines. Top speed was 255 miles per hour, service ceiling was 19,000 feet, and range was 1,540 miles. The aircraft could deliver a bomb load of 4,500 pounds. Defensive weapons included eight .303-inch machine guns, two in the nose, four in the tail turret, and two in fuselage positions.

At the beginning of World War II, the Wellington was the principal British bomber, and although it continued to fly bombing missions until the end of the war, it was largely supplanted in this role by heavier, four-engine bombers. The Wellington continued to be used very extensively for antisubmarine attacks and for transport duties.

The major British FIGHTER AIRCRAFT of World War II included

Bristol Beaufighter Mark 1. Powered by twin Bristol Hercules XVII fourteen-cylinder radial engines, rated at 1,725 horsepower each, this two-seat fighter had the advantage of long range (1,400 miles) and was used for a variety of missions, most notably as a night fighter. The prototype flew on July 17, 1939, and aircraft were delivered to the RAF beginning in October 1940. Equipped with the most advanced RADAR available at the time, the Beaufighter was armed with four 20-millimeter cannon and six to eight rockets. It could also carry a 500-pound bomb load or be modified for torpedo attack. The aircraft saw service in Europe as well as Asia and the Pacific, where the Japanese called it the Whispering Death because of its speed (323 miles per hour) over long range. Service ceiling was 28,900 feet and wingspan 57 feet 10 inches.

De Haviland Mosquito II. Whereas later versions of the Mosquito earned fame as bombers, the earlier versions were used primarily as twin-engine (two Merlin 23s at 1,635 horsepower each) fighters. Equipped with four 20-millimeter and 4 .303-inch machine guns, the Mosquito II had a top speed of 407 miles per hour and an operating radius of 800 miles.

Gloster Gladiator I. First flown in 1934 and acquired by the British military in 1937, the Gloster Gladiator was an evolutionary development of the earlier Gauntlet biplane fighter. From the beginning, however, its biplane design was obsolete among the latest generation of monoplane fighters, and the aircraft was badly outclassed by German fighters when it was deployed in the earliest battles of the war. All Gladiators in the two squadrons sent to France in 1940 were destroyed in 10 days of fighting. While the RAF soon abandoned the Gladiator as a fighter, the Royal Navy used it (as the Sea Gladiator) for AIRCRAFT CARRIER operations.

With a wingspan of 32 feet 3 inches, the Gladiator was powered by a single Bristol Mercury VIII AS engine, which developed 850 horsepower for a top speed of 257 miles per hour. Ferry range was 444 miles and service ceiling 33,500 feet. The fighter version of the aircraft was armed with four .303-inch Browning machine guns.

Gloster Meteor III. During the 1930s, the British aeronautical engineer FRANK WHITTLE developed a practical jet engine, and both the British and the Germans developed and flew JET AIRCRAFT before the war ended—although the novelty of the technology and a multitude of design and production problems kept the aircraft from being deployed in combat in significant numbers. The Meteor series has the distinction of being the only turbojet-powered aircraft flown in combat by the Allies during the war. Meteors were sent to shoot down German V-1 BUZZ BOMBS and V-2 ROCKETS and to engage German jets.

A prototype Meteor first flew in March 1943, and seven Meteor Is were first deployed in July 1944. Meteor IIIs commenced delivery in December 1944. Propelled by a pair of Derwent jets, each making 2,000 pounds of thrust, the Meteor III could reach 490 miles per hour at 30,000 feet (ceiling, 40,000 feet). Wingspan was 43 feet, range was 550 miles and armament consisted of four 20-millimeter cannon. The aircraft was not produced in great quantity during the war, but it continued to evolve afterward. By 1954, when it finally left service, 3,947 had been built.

Hawker Hurricane 1. Although less celebrated than the Supermarine Spitfighter, the Hawker Hurricane, not the Spitfire, was responsible for 80 percent of the German aircraft shot down in the BATTLE OF BRITAIN. Designed in 1935, the Hurricane was introduced into RAF service in 1937. At the beginning of the Battle of Britain, the RAF had 32 squadrons of Hurricanes versus only 19 squadrons equipped with Spitfires. Less agile than the Spitfire and slower than Germany's premier fighter, the Messerschmidt Bf109, the Hurricane was deployed against German bomber formations, whereas the Spitfires were used against German fighters.

At the start of the war, the RAF had 497 Hurricanes. Before the end of the war, the Hawker company delivered 10,030, the Gloster company 2,750, and the Canadian Car and Foundry Company 1,451. Powered by a single 1,030-horsepower Rolls-

Royce Merlin III 12-cylinder engine, the Hurricane had a wingspan of 40 feet and a top speed of 328 miles per hour at 20,000 feet. It was armed with eight wing-mounted .303-inch Browning machine guns.

Hawker Tempest V. Introduced in 1944, the Hawker Tempest V was a major evolutionary development from the Hawker Typhoon I. Featuring a thinner wing, a longer fuselage, and an all-round vision canopy, it was powered by an improved Sabre Mk2 engine, developed 2,000 horsepower, and could reach a top speed of 428 miles per hour. Wingspan was 41 feet, and ceiling was 37,000 feet. Operating radius was 740 miles. The Tempest was armed with four 20-millimeter cannon and could carry eight rockets or nearly 2,000 pounds of bombs. Some 1,418 Tempest Vs were built, including a number after the war had ended. Although introduced late in the conflict, the Tempest, thanks to its speed and maneuverability, was considered one of the best fighters of the war.

Hawker Typhoon I. This aircraft was used by the RAF mainly in a ground attack role rather than in air-to-air combat. Introduced in 1941, some 3,300 (all versions) were built before the end of the war. Powered by a single Sabre Mk2 engine developing 2,180 horsepower, the Typhoon had a top speed of 405 miles per hour and a ceiling of more than 30,000 feet. Wingspan was 41 feet 7 inches. The Typhoon was armed with four 20-millimeter cannon and could carry a bomb load of nearly 2,000 pounds or eight 127-millimeter rockets.

Supermarine Spitfire. Introduced in 1938 and produced in some 40 variants, the Supermarine Spitfire became the single most celebrated fighter aircraft of World War II. Driven by a Merlin Mk III engine making 1,030 horsepower, the version that first entered service had a top speed of about 360 miles per hour and was armed with eight .303-inch machine guns. The Spitfire XIV, introduced in 1944, had a ceiling of 40,000 feet and a top speed of 440 miles per hour and was responsible for shooting down more than 300 German V-1 buzz bombs. The XIV version and several earlier versions as well also had increased armament: two 20-millimeter can-

non were added either to the four .303-inch machine guns or to two .50-inch machine guns. Some versions also carried one 250- or 500-pound bomb under the fuselage and one 250-pound bomb under each wing. The Spitfire survived the end of the war and was used by the RAF for photoreconnaissance until 1954. Wingspan for all versions was 36 feet.

An aesthetically beautiful aircraft, the Spitfire incorporated a light-alloy monocoque fuselage and a single-spar wing with stressed-skin covering and fabric-covered control surfaces. The aircraft proved highly maneuverable and was more than a match for the best German fighters during the Battle of Britain, where it earned its first and most enduring glory. Some 20,334 Spitfires (all versions) were produced during the war, and a naval variant, the Seafire, was produced in a quantity of 2,556.

See also GREAT BRITAIN, AIR FORCE OF.

Further reading: Gunston, Bill, and Chris Westhorp. *The Illustrated Directory of Fighting Aircraft of World War II.* St. Paul, Minn.: MBI Publishing, 2000; Jane's Information Group. *Jane's All the World's Aircraft of World War II: Collector's Edition.* New York: HarperCollins, 1994; Mondey, David. *The Concise Guide to British Aircraft of World War II.* London: Book Sales, 2002; Wilson, Stewart. *Aircraft of World War II.* Fishwyck, Australia: Australian Aviation, 1999.

aircraft, French

Although the French had been early pioneers of military aviation and had developed important combat aircraft during World War I, few French designs played important roles in World War II. The most significant French bomber was the Liori et Olivier LeO 451. Introduced in 1937, this medium bomber, crewed by four, was driven by two 1,060-horsepower Gnome-Rhone 14N engines and could achieve a top speed of 298 miles per hour. Service ceiling was 29,530 feet, and range was 1,802 miles. The LeO 451 carried a bomb load of 3,086 pounds and was armed with a single 20-millimeter cannon and five 7.5-millimeter machine guns. Only 373 of these aircraft had been delivered to French forces before the armistice was signed with Germany on June 25, 1940. However, more were delivered to the Nazi-controlled Vichy French Air Force.

France produced two significant fighters early in the war. The Dewoitine D520 was introduced in 1940 and was capable of 329 miles per hour at 19,000 feet over a modest operating radius of 310 miles. The powerplant was a single Hispano-Suiza 910-horsepower engine. Wingspan was 33 feet 5 inches. In addition to a single 20-millimeter cannon, the D520 was armed with four machine guns. After Germany seized the unoccupied portion of France in November 1942, 246 Dewoitine D.520C1 fighters were captured, of which 182 were deemed airworthy. These were repainted and reequipped to serve as operational trainers for the LUFTWAFFE. During the Allied invasion of France in 1944, a few of these aircraft were recaptured and flown by Free French and Resistance pilots.

Introduced in 1939, the Morane-Saulnier MS 406 was powered by a single Hispano-Suiza 860-horsepower engine and had a top speed of 302 miles per hour at 16,000 feet. Operational radius was only 250 miles, wingspan was 34 feet 9 inches, and armament consisted of a single 20-millimeter cannon and a pair of machine guns. In terms of numbers, the MS 406 was the most important French fighter of the war, but it was both underpowered and underarmed, vastly outclassed by such German fighters as the Messerschmidt Bf109. In 1940, before the fall of France, 400 of the aircraft were lost, having scored only 175 kills. The Luftwaffe captured the surviving MS 406s and used them as trainers. German allies, including FINLAND, ITALY, and CROATIA, purchased some of the captured aircraft from Germany and used them in combat.

See also FRANCE, AIR FORCE OF.

Further reading: Gunston, Bill, and Chris Westhorp. *The Illustrated Directory of Fighting Aircraft of World War II.* St. Paul, Minn.: MBI Publishing, 2000; Jane's Information Group. *Jane's All the World's Aircraft of World War II: Collector's Edition.* New York: HarperCollins, 1994; Ketley, Barry. *French Aces of World War II.* London: Osprey, 1999; Wilson, Stewart. *Aircraft of World War II.* Fishwyck, Australia: Australian Aviation, 1999.

aircraft, German

German aircraft designs were consistently among the most advanced and successful of the war. Of all the nations, Germany was the first to begin to make significant use of JET AIRCRAFT, although these nevertheless came too late in the war and in insufficient quantity to have a decisive effect on the course of the air war. The Luftwaffe (German air force) had a few advocates for the production of large four-engine bombers, most notably the prewar chief of staff general Walther Wever. However, with his death in April 1936, the idea of a strategic role for the Luftwaffe also died, and the German air force instead adopted the basic doctrine that bombers should be used tactically to support the ground troops directly by striking targets on or near the battlefield. By the time the war began, German bombers were used strategically to bomb civilian targets, especially London and other English cities during the BATTLE OF BRITAIN. However, because of prevailing Luftwaffe doctrine, Germany, unlike the United States and Great Britain, produced no significant four-engine bombers. Abortive plans were made for the "AMERIKA" BOMBER, a spectacular aircraft of intercontinental range, but nothing came of the project.

The Stuka. Perhaps the most infamous of Germany's bombers was the single-engine Junkers Ju87, better known as the Stuka. Designed in the mid-1930s, the Stuka was a dive bomber, which deployed its 1,100-pound bomb load not from level flight but from low altitude, near the end of a sharp 80-degree dive. This ensured surgical accuracy of the strike. By 1942, it was even fitted with a single 4000-pound bomb, which was used against heavy tanks. After striking its target with bombs, the Stuka often circled around to strafe survivors with its three 7.9-mm machine guns. The aircraft was also fitted with sirens, so-called Jericho trumpets, which produced a truly terrifying scream during the high-speed dive. Thus, the weapon produced as much panic and terror as physical destruction.

Stukas were deployed with great effect in the INVASION OF POLAND, the BATTLE OF FRANCE, and the INVASION OF THE SOVIET UNION. However, after these early operations, the 238-mile-per-hour, poorly maneuverable Stuka proved increasingly vulnerable to fighter attack and was reconfigured in 1942 as the Ju87G-1, a dedicated antitank aircraft.

The Ju87B-2, best known of the Stuka iterations, was powered by a single 1,200-horsepower Jumo 211 Da engine and had a wingspan of 45 feet 3 1/3 inches, a service ceiling of 26,250 feet, and a range of 490 miles. It could be configured to carry a maximum of four individual bombs. About 5,700 Stukas were completed before production ended in 1944.

Germany's other significant bombers were twin-engine medium bombers and included the following.

Heinkel He111H-3. Crewed by four or five, the Heinkel first flew in early 1939. It was powered by two Junkers Jumo 211D-2 V-12 engines, each making 1,200 horsepower for a top speed, empty, of 258 miles per hour. Range was 745 miles and service ceiling 25,590 feet. The plane's wingspan was 74 feet 1 3/4 inches. It was heavily armed with 7.92-mm machine guns in the nose cap, in the dorsal position, in a ventral gondola, in waist windows, in a fixed forward-firing position, in the side of the nose (could be operated by the copilot), and in the tail. The plane also had a 20-mm cannon on a fixed mount in the front part of the ventral gondola. Bomb load was up to 4,410 pounds.

Dornier Do 17Z-1. Crewed by four, the Do17Z-1 was introduced in January 1939 and was driven by a pair of Bramo Fafnir 323P 9-cylinder radial engines making 1,000 horsepower each. Wingspan was 59 feet, top speed 263 miles per hour, and service ceiling 26,740 feet. Range was 721 miles. The aircraft was armed with three 7.92-mm machine guns, one manually aimed from a rear ventral hatch, one manually aimed to the rear from a dorsal position, and one fixed forward in the right windshield. The bomber could carry a 2,205-pound load internally. About 1,100 Dorniers (all versions) were produced before the type was phased out in 1942, having taken very heavy casualties in the BATTLE OF BRITAIN.

Junkers Ju88A-4. A very successful design, 14,676 were built in all versions. About 9,000 were configured as medium bombers. The rest were configured mostly as night fighters. The versatile aircraft was used throughout the war, beginning with operations in Poland in 1939 and against just about every enemy Germany fought. The Ju88A4 version was capable of operating as a level bomber, a dive bomber, and a torpedo bomber. Generally, the bomb load consisted of 10 50-pound bombs loaded internally with as many as four bombs of various types fixed to hard points under the wings. A pair of torpedoes could also be mounted under the wings. Wingspan was 65 feet 10 inches, and the plane was driven by a pair of 950-horsepower Junkers Jumo 211 F engines. Top speed was 292 miles per hour, ceiling 26,900 feet, and range 1,106 miles.

Dornier Do 217K/M. The Do 217 series of bombers became operational in March 1941 and represented a significant advance over the Do 17. In addition to serving as a level bomber, the Do 217 could be configured as a night fighter, a torpedo bomber, and a reconnaissance aircraft. By August 1943, the aircraft was also being used to carry antishipping missiles, and by September, it was delivering guided bombs against warships. Production reached 1,905 of all types, including some 1,366 level bombers. The Do 217K and M versions were crewed by four and powered by two 1,700-horsepower BMW 810D 14-cylinder radials (K) or two 1,750-horsepower Daimler-Benz DB603A inverted V12s (M). Top speed was 320 miles per hour, service ceiling 24,600 feet, and range 1,430 miles. Wingspan was 62 feet 4 inches, and, for the M version, armament consisted of four 7.92-mm and two 13-mm machine guns with a bomb load of 8,818 pounds; the K version added two underwing FX-1400 Fritz X radio-controlled bombs, two FX-1400 bombs, or two Hs 293 missiles.

Junkers Ju188E-1. Produced in reconnaissance (designated D) and bomber versions (designated E), the Ju188 series was crewed by five and first flew in 1940. About 1,100 were produced during the war. The Ju 188E was powered by two BMW 801G-2 18-cylinder two-row radials, each producing 1,700 horsepower for a top speed of 310 miles per hour. Service ceiling was 31,510 feet, and range was 1,211 miles. Wingspan was 72 feet 2 inches. Typically, the aircraft was armed with a single 20-mm cannon in its nose and three 13-mm machine guns, one in a dorsal turret, one manually aimed from the rear dorsal position, and one manually aimed from the rear ventral position; in some configurations, twin 7.92-mm machine guns were substituted for the last position. Typical bomb load was 6,614 pounds loaded internally, or two 2,200-pound torpedoes under the wings.

Heinkel He177A-5. This was the largest bomber Germany actually deployed, with a wingspan of 103 feet 1 ¾ inches and a bomb load capacity of 13,228 pounds. It was powered by two massive 3,100-horsepower Daimler-Benz DB610 coupled engines. This design feature was an innovative attempt to reduce drag, but it created severe reliability problems that often resulted in engine fires. Fully three-quarters of the preproduction prototypes crashed; 1,146 were produced, and while the 3,100-mile range was badly needed by the Luftwaffe, the airplanes were not very effective as strategic bombers. They were used with moderate effectiveness in an antitank role. Top speed was 295 miles per hour and service ceiling 26,500 feet. Armament consisted of one 7.92-mm machine gun manually aimed in the nose, one 20-mm machine gun manually aimed in the forward ventral gondola, two 13-mm machine guns in a front dorsal turret, one in the aft dorsal turret, and one 20-mm cannon in the tail position.

Arado Ar234B-2. Of greater historical than practical significance was the Arado Ar234B-2, the world's first jet bomber, which became operational at the end of November 1944, too late to have any impact on the course of the war. Powered by a pair of BMW 003A-1 jets, each developing 1,764 pounds of thrust, the Arado had a top speed of 461 miles per hour and could carry 4,409 pounds of bombs over a 1,000-mile range. Service ceiling was 32,810 feet. For defensive purposes, the Arado carried two 20-mm cannon. Only 210 were built.

German fighter designs were generally more successful and more innovative than its bomber designs. The two most important fighters were the Messerschmitt 109 series and the Focke-Wulf 190 series.

Messerschmitt 109. The Messerschmitt 109 first flew in October 1935, powered by British Rolls-Royce Kestrel engines. The aircraft entered Luftwaffe service in spring 1937 and received its baptism of fire in the Spanish civil war. By the beginning of World War II, the aircraft existed in a number of variants, and 1,000 were deployed against Poland in September 1939. The 109 was superior to most other fighters at the outbreak of the war but was fairly evenly matched with the British Spitfire and Hurricane in the Battle of Britain. It did have one very significant advantage over these rivals, however. Its fuel injection system allowed for a constant fuel flow even in negative-g conditions, which meant that a pilot could dive or shear away much more quickly than his opponents. This added significantly to the plane's survivability. Counterbalancing this advantage, however, was the 109's limited range—a 300-mile operating radius for the 109G. This gave the fighter precious little combat time over relatively remote targets such as those in England.

Some 109 variants had a cannon placed in the hollowed-out nose cap. In early models, this created an unacceptable level of vibration, which, however, was eliminated in later versions. Additionally, most of the fighters were fitted with two wing-mounted cannons and two machine guns mounted on the top of the nose cone that were synchronized to fire through the propeller arc. The 109G, introduced in 1942, was powered by a Daimler-Benz DB605 1,475-horsepower engine to a top speed of 387 miles per hour at 23,000 feet. Wingspan was 32 feet 6 ½ inches. The backbone of the Luftwaffe, some 30,000 109s were built before the end of the war.

Focke-Wulf Fw 190. Superior even to the formidable Messerschmitt 109 was the Focke-Wulf Fw 190, which made its first flight on June 1, 1939. It first saw action in the Battle of France in September 1941 and was markedly superior to the British Spitfire. Most Fw 190s were the A series, powered by a single BMW 801 2,100-horsepower radial engine. However, late in 1943, the D was deployed against U.S. bombers, powered by the Jumo 213 inline, liquid-cooled engine, which developed only 1,770 horsepower but had improved performance, producing a top speed of 426 miles per hour, 18 miles per hour faster than the A version. In all, some 20,000 Fw 190s of all types were built before the end of the war. Wingspan of the D type was 34 feet 5 ⅓ inches, and armament consisted of two 20-mm wing-mounted cannon and two 13-mm machine guns in the nose. Range was 520 miles and service ceiling 40,000 feet.

Messerschmitt Bf 110. The twin-engine Messerschmitt Bf 110 made its first flight in May 1936. With all-metal construction and a crew of three, the aircraft was powered by two Daimler Benz DB 601 engines, each making 1,100 horsepower and propelling the plane to a maximum speed of 336 miles per hour over a range of 680 miles. Wingspan was 53 feet 4 inches, and armament consisted of five machine guns and two 20-mm cannon. Formidable as all this seems, the aircraft performed poorly in the Battle of Britain. This prompted a redesign with the inclusion of RADAR, which transformed the Bf 110 into the Luftwaffe's finest night fighter. In all, nearly 6,000 Bf 110s were produced before the end of the war.

Jet and rocket-propelled fighters. Late in the war, in 1944, Germany introduced both jet- and rocket-propelled fighters. The Messerschmitt 163B was powered by a single Walter rocket motor developing 3,700 pounds of thrust and capable of reaching 590 miles per hour at 20,000 feet. Range, however, was extremely limited. Armed with two 30-mm cannon and 24 R4M rockets, the 163B had a wingspan of 30 feet 7 inches. Very few were produced. More significant, however, was the jet-powered Messerschmitt 262A, with two Junkers 004 jets, each making 1,980 pounds of thrust, mounted under the wings. Top speed was 540 miles per hour over a range of 420 miles. Armament was limited to four 30-mm cannon. The aircraft was designed primarily to attack Allied bombers, which it did very effectively. Had the aircraft been introduced earlier and in much greater numbers, its impact on the air war over Europe would have been profound.

See also GERMANY, AIR FORCE OF.

Further reading: Brown, Eric. *Wings of the Luftwaffe: Flying German Aircraft of the Second World War.* Shrewsbury, U.K.: Airlife, 2001; Donald, David, ed. *German Aircraft of World War II.* Minneapolis: Motorbooks International, 1996; Griehl, Manfred. *German Jets of World War II.* London: Arms & Armour, 1989; Gunston, Bill. *An Illustrated Guide to German, Italian and Japanese Fighters of World War II: Major Fighters and Attack Aircraft of the Axis Powers.* London: Salamander Books, 1980; Gunston, Bill. *World War II German Aircraft.* London: Book Sales, 1985; Kay, Antony L., and J. R. Smith. *German Aircraft of the Second World War.* Annapolis, Md.: United States Naval Institute, 2002; Shepherd, Christopher. *German Aircraft of World War II.* London: Sidgwick & Jackson, 1975.

aircraft, Italian

Like France, Italy, an early aviation pioneer, lagged behind Germany, Britain, and the United States in the design of military aircraft. Nevertheless, Italian designers were resourceful in compensating for deficiencies.

Savoia-Marchetti SM79. The Savoia-Marchetti SM79, Italy's most important bomber, produced in a quantity of 1,330, used wooden construction to conserve scarce wartime metals and was configured as a trimotor, a design that compensated for the low power (780 horsepower each) of its Alfa Romeo 126RC34 engines. As with all Italian military aircraft, weight was further reduced by stinting on both armor and defensive armament (light machine guns only), which proved to be fatal flaws.

The SM79 was crewed by four to five, had a wingspan of 69 feet, and carried a bomb load of 2,755 pounds. After it was generally replaced by the larger (wingspan 81 feet 4 inches; bomb load, 6,615 pounds) CRDA (Cant) Z1007bis early in the war, the SM79 was reconfigured as a torpedo bomber. In this role, it proved quite successful. Top speed for the SM79 was 267 miles per hour, service ceiling was 21,235 feet, and range was 2,050 miles.

CRDA Z1007bis. Crewed by five, the CRDA Z1007bis was a trimotor, like the SM79. Its Piaggio P.XIbis RC40 engines produced 1,000 horsepower each, propelling the bomber to a top speed of 280 miles per hour and a service ceiling of 26,575 feet. Range, however, was limited. Whereas the SM79 had a range of 2,050 miles, the larger and heavier Z1007bis was limited to 1,650 miles, though its bomb load, at 6,615 pounds, was more than twice that of the SM75. About 660 of this aircraft were built.

Fiat BR20M. In between Italy's two trimotors was the twin-engine Fiat BR20M, crewed by five or six and powered by 1,000-horsepower Fiat A.80 RC41 engines to a top speed of 267 miles per hour and a service ceiling of 24,935 feet. This medium bomber had a limited range of 1,243 miles but could carry more bombs than the three-engine SM79: 3,527 pounds. It was deployed in early raids against Britain in November 1940.

Italians flew five significant fighters during World War II, including one, the Macchi C202, that is considered a classic less for its performance than for its beautiful design. All Italian fighters were easily outclassed by the standard fighters of Britain and the United States.

Fiat CR 42. The CR 42 Falco (Falcon) was the last important biplane fighter of the World War II era. It was the product of the success of the CR 32 biplane in the Spanish civil war, and it entered flight testing in May 1938. Manufactured in greater numbers than any other Italian fighter, it was, of course, obsolete from its inception. Although it represented the pinnacle of biplane design—light on the controls and highly agile—it *was* a biplane, and, therefore, doomed to be outclassed by modern monoplane fighters. Nevertheless, it fought in Italy's first World War II campaign, against targets in southern France in 1940. The German LUFT-WAFFE also used the aircraft for night attack and as a trainer throughout the war. Belgian and Hungarian forces also flew the plane. During the BATTLE OF BRITAIN, Italy's Corpo Aero Italiano (Italian Air Corps) contributed bombers, reconnaissance aircraft, and the CR 42 to the effort. Wingspan was 31 feet, and the power plant was a single Fiat A74 engine, developing 840 horsepower. The CR 42 carried two 220-pound bombs and had a pair of 12.7-mm machine guns. Top speed was 266 miles per hour at 13,000 feet.

Fiat G50 (bis). Introduced in 1939 as the G50 and subsequently upgraded in the "bis" version, this fighter was underpowered and was out-gunned by Allied machines, yet it served in every theater in which the Italians fought, most extensively in North Africa. It was powered by a single Fiat A.74 R1C.38 radial engine rated at 840 horsepower. Top speed was 292 miles per hour at 16,405 feet, and wingspan was 36 feet ¼ inch. Armament included two .50-inch machine guns.

Macchi C200. Predecessor to the more famous C202, the C200 was driven by a Fiat AA74 870-horsepower radial engine to a top speed of 312 miles per hour at 14,700 feet. With two machine guns, it could carry a 600-pound bomb load and had a range of 270 miles.

Macchi C202. The C200 was introduced in 1939 and the C202 in 1941. It was an airplane with beautiful lines and saw extensive service in North Africa, where it performed better than any other Italian fighter, which is not to say that it could outperform the Allies. Like the C200, it had a wingspan of 35.1 feet, but it was powered by a single Mercedes-Benz DB601 engine, which delivered more than 1,175 horsepower, giving the C202 a top speed of 370 miles per hour at 16,500 feet. The C202 outgunned its predecessor, with four rather than two machine guns, but it carried the same 600-pound bomb load. Range was reduced from 270 to 240 miles.

Reggiane Re 2001 (Caproni). The last Italian fighter to be introduced in World War II, its predecessor, the Reggiane 2000, had been developed in 1938, but the Italian Regia Aeronautica (Air Force) judged it underpowered and did not buy it. Refitted with a 1,175-horsepower Daimler Benz Bd 601 engine and redesignated the Re 2001, it entered service in 1942 after Caproni completed a series of improvements required by the Regia Aeronautica. Only 237 were built before Italy withdrew from the war.

Although designed as an interceptor, the Re 2001 always flew as a fighter-bomber or as a night fighter. It had a top speed of 349 miles per hour and a ceiling of 36,000 feet. Range was an impressive 684 miles. Armed with four wing-mounted machine guns, it could carry either a 220-pound or

550-pound bomb, but, against naval targets, it even carried a 1,412-pound bomb.

See also ITALY, AIR FORCE OF.

Further reading: Apostolo, Giorgio, and Giovanni Massimello. *Italian Aces of World War II.* London: Osprey, 2000; Gunston, Bill. *An Illustrated Guide to German, Italian and Japanese Fighters of World War II: Major Fighters and Attack Aircraft of the Axis Powers.* London: Salamander, 1980; Gunston, Bill. *Japanese and Italian Aircraft.* London: Book Sales, 1985.

aircraft, Japanese

By the beginning of World War II, the Japanese military had developed a variety of advanced aircraft, both land based and carrier based. Like Germany, the Japanese emphasized the development of fighter planes and, in contrast to the British and Americans, devoted little or no attention to heavy bombers. Like Germany, Japan developed no heavy four-engine bomber.

The "Betty." The heaviest Japanese bomber—which by Allied standards was at best a medium bomber—was the Mitsubishi G4M, which the Allies (to facilitate identification) code named "Betty." Although this twin-engine aircraft flew from land-based airfields, the Betty was designed in 1937 for the Imperial Navy and made its first flight on October 23, 1939. Performance was exceptional—276 miles per hour with a range of 3,450 miles—and the Betty was employed against China during 1941 and against Royal Navy ships in Indo-Chinese waters. However, the great vulnerability of the Betty was its lack of armor, especially in critical crew areas and as protection for fuel tanks. As Allied fighter coverage increased during the course of the war, the Betty became an easy target. Its vulnerability was underscored on April 18, 1943, when, acting on decrypts of Japanese messages, U.S. aircraft targeted and shot down the Betty transporting Admiral YAMAMOTO ISORUKU, the Japanese supreme commander in the Pacific.

The Betty was powered by two 1360kW Mitsubishi MK4T Kasei 25 engines and had a wingspan of 82 feet. Its top speed was 276 miles per

hour with a service ceiling of about 30,000 feet and an impressive range of 3,450 miles. Typical armament consisted of three 7.7-mm manually aimed machine guns in the nose, dorsal, and ventral positions and one 20-mm manually aimed cannon in the tail. The internal bomb load was 2,205 pounds or one 17.7-inch torpedo. The plane was crewed by seven.

The Japanese Army Air Force operated three lighter medium bombers, the Mitsubishi Ki-21 (Allied code name "Sally"), the Nakajima Ki-49 Donryu ("Helen"), and the Mitsubishi Ki-67 Hiryu ("Peggy").

Mitsubishi Ki-21 ("Sally"). The Sally was ordered in 1936 and went into service three years later. The aircraft served on all Japanese fronts and was produced in a number of variants, with later models getting the benefit of the extra armor that the Betty lacked. Produced in a quantity of 2,055, the Sally may be considered the most important and certainly the most plentiful of Japan's World War II bombers. Nevertheless, it was obsolete by the beginning of the war.

The Sally was powered by two 1,500-horse-power Mitsubishi Ha-101 radial piston engines to a top speed of 302 miles per hour at 15,485 feet. Its service ceiling was 32,810 feet and its range 1,680 miles. The Sally had a wingspan of 73 feet 9 ¾ inches and a fuselage length of 52 feet, 5 ⅞ inches. Typical armament consisted of five 7.7-mm Type 89 machine guns in the nose, ventral, tail, port, and starboard beam positions as well as one 12.7-mm Type 1 machine gun in a dorsal turret. Maximum bomb load was 2,205 pounds, and the aircraft was crewed by five.

Nakajima Ki-49 Donryu ("Helen"). The Donryu ("Storm Dragon"), code named "Helen" by the Allies, was prototyped in 1939 and was produced in a quantity of 819. Throughout the war, the basic design was subject to several revisions in an effort to improve its overall mediocre performance, but to little avail. By 1944, following the Philippines campaign, the aircraft was generally consigned to KAMIKAZE missions.

Specifications for the most numerous Ki-49-IIa variant included a wingspan of 67 feet ⅛ inch and a fuselage length of 54 feet, 1 ⅝ inches. Top speed was 306 miles per hour at 16,405 feet, with a service ceiling of 30,510 feet and a range of 1,833 miles. The Ki-49-IIa was armed with one flexible 20-mm cannon in the dorsal position and one flexible 7.7-mm machine gun in the nose, ventral, beam, and tail positions. The Ki-49-IIb and Ki-49-III versions had one flexible 20-mm cannon in the dorsal position; one flexible 12.7-mm machine gun in the nose, ventral, and tail positions; and one flexible 7.7-mm machine gun in the port and starboard beam positions. The Ki-58 was equipped with five flexible 20-mm cannon and three flexible 12.7-mm machine guns. For all versions, a normal maximum bomb load was 1,653 pounds, but the aircraft was loaded with up to 3,527 pounds of bombs for suicide (kamikaze) missions. Except in kamikaze missions, the Helen was crewed by eight.

Mitsubishi Ki-67 Hiryu ("Peggy"). The Hiryu ("Flying Dragon"), or "Peggy," entered service late in the war, in 1944, and was produced in a number of variants in a quantity of 696. Relatively few were encountered in action by the Allies, which was a good thing, since the Peggy was certainly the best of Japan's medium bombers, highly capable of destroying ground targets and of deploying torpedoes against surface ships. Both the Japanese Army Air Force and the Imperial Navy adopted the aircraft, which was not only fast, but exceedingly maneuverable. Its powerplant consisted of two Mitsubishi Ha-104 18-cylinder air-cooled radial engines, rated at 1,900 horsepower for takeoff; later variants used two Mitsubishi Ha-214 18-cylinder air-cooled radials, rated at 2,400 horsepower for takeoff, or two Mitsubishi Ha-104 Ru 18-cylinder turbosupercharged air-cooled radials, rated at 1,900 horsepower for takeoff. Wingspan of all versions was 73 feet 9 ¹³⁄₁₆ inches, and fuselage length was 61 feet, 4 ⁷⁄₃₂ inches. Maximum speed of the aircraft was 334 miles per hour at 19,980 feet, with a service ceiling of 31,070 feet and a range of 2,360 miles. The final variant of the Peggy was armed with one flexible 12.7-mm machine gun in the nose and beam positions, twin flexible 12.7-mm machine guns in the tail turret, and one 20-mm cannon in the dorsal turret. Normal maximum bomb load was 1,764 pounds. For torpedo attack, the Peggy carried one 1,764-pound or one 2,359-pound torpedo. For suicide attack (kamikaze), the aircraft was loaded with up to 6,393 pounds of bombs. The crew consisted normally of six to eight and was reduced to three for suicide missions.

Whereas Japan produced no heavy bombers and few notable medium bombers, its Imperial Navy and Army did fly an extraordinary array of fighters, the most famous of which was the navy's Mitsubishi A6M Zero (code named "Zeke" by the Allies).

Mitsubishi A6M Zero ("Zeke"). Although hardly graceful in appearance, the Zero was fast and highly maneuverable with very good range. Early in the war, it outclassed anything the United States or other Allies could hurl against it, and it was, prior to the BATTLE OF MIDWAY in June 1942, the only carrier-based fighter in any combatant's inventory that was capable of outperforming and defeating land-based aircraft. In early encounters, American pilots learned quite rightly to fear the Zero.

The Imperial Navy issued highly advanced and demanding requirements for a new carrier fighter in October 1937. Whereas the Nakajima Company rejected the requirements as unrealistic, Mitsubishi forged ahead to design an all-metal low-wing monoplane, with a 780-horsepower Mitsubishi Zuisei 13 engine and (ultimately) a three-bladed propeller. In this configuration, the Zero met or exceeded all navy requirements, except for level speed. After Mitsubishi introduced the more powerful 950-horsepower Nakajima Sakae 12 engine, the Zero exceeded all requirements, and full-scale production began.

The aircraft was first deployed in small numbers in China during 1940. By the end of this year, Zeros had shot down 99 Chinese fighter aircraft, with the loss of only two Zeros—and these to ground fire, not the fire of their aerial opponents. At the beginning of the war in the Pacific, Japan had only 328 Zeros ready for combat. Despite these relatively small numbers, the aircraft was instrumental in Japan's string of early stunning victories, beginning with the BATTLE OF PEARL HARBOR up to the BATTLE OF THE CORAL SEA in May 1942. While this battle was a tactical victory for the Japanese, it was a strategic defeat, which ended the momentum of the Japanese juggernaut. This was followed by Japan's defeat at the Battle of Midway in June, which included the loss of four Japanese carriers, together with the Zeros (and other aircraft) they carried as well as many of the Imperial Navy's best pilots. This was not only the strategic turning point of the war, but spelled an end to the unchallenged reign of the Zero. The fighter was designed as an offensive weapon, with little armor and no self-sealing fuel tanks. Cast now into the defensive role, it proved increasingly vulnerable, especially as American aircraft improved and American pilots became more skilled. Despite this, Japanese designers continually worked throughout the war to refine the Zero, and it remained a mainstay of the Japanese naval air fleet until the surrender.

While the Zero was the most celebrated Japanese aircraft of World War II, the Allies experienced some confusion concerning nomenclature. The Allies code named the aircraft Zeke beginning in fall 1942, but misidentification of several variants also gave rise to the code names Ben, Ray, and Hamp. Eventually, all these were recognized as variants on the Zeke—yet, amid the confusion, that designation was largely rejected by U.S. military personnel, who universally adopted the English translation of the Japanese name for the aircraft, Reisen, Zero.

All Zero variants were single-seat, single-engine carrier-based fighters, featuring all-metal construction except for fabric-covered control surfaces and crewed by one pilot. Mitsubishi produced 3,840 Zeros, and Nakajima (under license) produced 6,528. The power plant for the A6M2 variant was one Nakajima NK1C Sakae 12 14-cylinder air-cooled radial, rated at 940 horsepower for takeoff. The A6M3 and A6M5 variants had one Nakajima NK1F Sakae 21 14-cylinder air-cooled radial, rated at 1,130 horsepower for takeoff, and the A6M6c and A6M7 variants had one Nakajima Sakae 31 14-cylinder air-cooled radial, rated at

1,130 horsepower for takeoff. The most powerful version, the A6M8, had one Mitsubishi MK8P Kinsei 62 14-cylinder air-cooled radial, rated at 1,560 horsepower for takeoff. Wingspan of the A6M2 Model 21 was 39 feet 4 $^7/_{16}$ inches; A6M3 Model 32, 36 feet 1 $^1/_{16}$ inches; A6M5 Model 52, 36 feet 1 $^1/_{16}$ inches; and A6M8 Model 64, 36 feet 1 $^1/_{16}$ inches. Fuselage length of the A6M2 Model 21 was 29 feet 8 $^{11}/_{16}$ inches; A6M3 Model 32, 29 feet 8 $^{11}/_{16}$ inches; A6M5 Model 52, 29 feet 11 $^7/_{32}$ inches; and A6M8 Model 64, 30 feet 3 $^{21}/_{32}$ inches. The A6M2 Model 21 made 331 miles per hour at 14,950 feet; the A6M3 Model 32, 338 miles per hour at 19,685 feet; the A6M5 Model 52, 351 miles per hour at 19,685 feet; and the A6M8 Model 64, 356 miles per hour at 19,685 feet. Service ceiling for the A6M2 Model 21 was 32,810 feet; the A6M3 Model 32, 36,250 feet; the A6M5 Model 52, 38,520 feet; and the A6M8 Model 64, 37,075 feet. The A6M2 Model 21 had a range of 1,930 miles; the A6M3 Model 32, 1,477 miles; the A6M5 Model 52, 1,194 miles; and the A6M8 Model 64, 1,194 miles. Typical armament for versions A6M2 through A6M5a included two fuselage-mounted 7.7-mm machine guns and two wing-mounted 20-mm cannon. The A6M5b had one fuselage-mounted 7.7-mm machine gun, one fuselage-mounted 13.2-mm machine gun, and two wing-mounted 20-mm cannon, while the A6M5c, A6M6c, and A6M7 versions had one fuselage-mounted 13.2-mm machine gun, two wing-mounted 20-mm cannon, and two wing-mounted 13.2-mm machine guns. The A6M8 had two wing-mounted 20-mm cannon and two wing-mounted 13.2-mm machine guns. For most versions, the normal bomb load was two 132-pound bombs under the wings. However, the A6M7 and A6M8 versions carried one 1,102-pound bomb under the fuselage. For suicide missions, all aircraft were loaded with one 551-pound bomb under the fuselage. A6M6c and A6M8 Zeroes could be loaded with eight 22-pound or two 132-pound air-to-air rockets. To extend range, drop tanks were used—one under-belly 72.6-gallon drop tank for all versions except the A6M7 and A6M8, which could carry two under-wing 77-gallon drop tanks.

Other Japanese naval fighter aircraft of note include the following.

Kawanishi N1K1-J Shiden ("George"). This was a land-based naval fighter, which first flew on December 27, 1942, and entered production the following year. A formidable opponent against U.S. carrier-based fighters and dive bombers, the George was afflicted with manufacturing and reliability problems. A particularly serious flaw was weak landing gear, which were finally modified in the final version of the aircraft, designated NIK2-J. Before the war ended, 1,435 George aircraft, of all variant types, had been produced.

The power plant for the George was one 1,990-horsepower Nakajima NK9H Homare 21 radial engine, the wingspan was 39 feet 4.4 inches, and the fuselage length was 29 feet 2 inches. The George had a top speed of 363 miles per hour at 19,357 feet. Its armament consisted of two 7.7-mm Type 97 machine guns in the nose and four wing-mounted 20-mm Type 99 cannon.

Kyushu J7W1 Shinden. While the Japanese name of the "George," Shiden, means "Violet Lightning," Shinden translates as "Magnificent Lightning." The Allies provided no English-language code name for this innovative fighter, which featured a canard wing forward of the main wing, two wing-mounted vertical stabilizers, and a rear-mounted pusher-type propeller arrangement. The prototype flew on August 3, 1945, just three days before the atomic bomb was dropped on Hiroshima. The aircraft, of course, never entered production or service. Its powerplant was a single Mitsubishi MK9D 18-cylinder air-cooled radial engine, rated at 2,130 horsepower for takeoff. Wingspan was 36 feet 5 $9/16$ inches and fuselage length, 31 feet 8 $5/16$ inches. Maximum speed for the Shinden was a stunning 466 miles per hour at 28,545 feet, with a service ceiling of 39,370 feet and a range of 529 miles. The aircraft was armed with four forward-firing 30-mm cannon in the nose, and there was provision under the wings for four 66-pound bombs or two 132-pound bombs.

Mitsubishi A5M ("Claude"). In this aircraft, Japan developed the world's first monoplane shipboard fighter. It was flown in prototype on February 4, 1935, and entered service in 1937, flying extensively in the SINO-JAPANESE WAR and in the early days of World War II itself. By the time production ended, 1,094 Claudes had been produced, including a two-seat trainer version, which prepared many pilots for the successor to the Claude, the great Zero.

The A5M variant was a single-seat carrier-based fighter, and the A5M4-K was a two-seat fighter trainer. The aircraft featured all-metal construction with fabric-covered control surfaces and (on later models) one Nakajima Kotobuki 41 nine-cylinder air-cooled radial, rated at 710 horsepower for takeoff. Later models of the aircraft had a wingspan of 36 feet 1 $3/16$ inches and a fuselage length of 24 feet 9 $27/32$ inches. Top speed in later models was 270 miles per hour at 9,845 feet, with a service ceiling of 32,150 feet and a range of 746 miles. Typical armament consisted of two fuselage-mounted 7.7-mm machine guns, or two fuselage-mounted 20-mm cannon, or one engine-mounted 20-mm cannon. The aircraft could carry two 66-pound bombs or one 35.2-gallon drop tank.

Mitsubishi J2M Raiden ("Jack"). The J2M Raiden—"Thunderbolt"—was code-named "Jack" by the Allies and was the Imperial Japanese Navy's first fighter expressly intended as a land-based interceptor. Like the army's Nakajima Ki-44 Shoki ("Tojo"), the Jack sacrificed maneuverability, the usual hallmark of the Japanese fighter, for speed and a high rate of climb. Indeed, navy planners had a difficult time accepting this compromise, and the development of the Jack was exceedingly troubled. Although design work began in 1938, a prototype was not completed until February 1942, and even after the navy accepted the interceptor in October, the plane was plagued by problems. By the time these were resolved, production of the aircraft had to give way to the high priority accorded production of the Zero, and only 476 Jacks were built before the war ended.

The Jack saw some service in the Philippines during September 1944, but it was used primarily against B-29s raiding the Japanese home islands. It was highly effective in this mission during the daytime, but, beginning in March 1945, when U.S.

strategists concentrated on incendiary raids by night and when the B-29s were regularly escorted by Iwo Jima–based P-47 Thunderbolts and P-51 Mustangs, the Jack became far less effective as an interceptor.

A single-seat, single-engine interceptor, the Jack had all-metal construction with fabric-covered control surfaces. Its powerplant in later models was one Mitsubishi Kasei 26a 14-cylinder air-cooled supercharged radial, rated at 1,820 horsepower for takeoff. In later models, the wingspan was 35 feet 5 $^3/_{16}$ inches, and the fuselage length 33 feet 7 $^{17}/_{32}$ inches. At its best, the Jack made 382 miles per hour at 22,310 feet and had a service ceiling of 36,910 feet and a range of 680 miles. Later models were equipped with four wing-mounted 20-mm cannon, and all models had two underwing racks to accommodate two 132-pound bombs.

Nakajima J1N Gekko ("Irving"). The Gekko— "Moonlight"—was the Imperial Navy's land-based, twin-engine, long-range escort fighter. It never fared well in its intended role, however, and was soon used for reconnaissance duty and then as a night fighter. In this latter role, it finally found its niche, although with the advent of the B-29 over Japan itself, the Gekko proved a far less effective contender.

Development of the Gekko began in 1938 in response to the navy's perceived need for a long-range escort in the Chinese theater during the Sino-Japanese War. A prototype flew in May 1941, but, as was so often the case with high-performance Japanese prototypes, the aircraft was plagued with problems; in October it was decided to reconfigure it for the reconnaissance mission. It served in this capacity until spring 1943, when some of the aircraft were converted as night fighters, incorporating two forward- and upward-firing 20-mm cannon in the observer's cockpit and two more that fired forward and downward. Against B-17 Flying Fortresses, the newly reconfigured Gekko proved quite effective, and authorization was given to build more of the night fighter variants.

The first J1N1-S Gekko Model 11, the purpose-built night fighter variant, rolled off the Nakajima assembly line in August 1943. This model either incorporated radar or a nose-mounted searchlight. The limited service ceiling, while sufficient for attacking B-17s, made the Gekko ineffective against B-29s. Before production ended in December 1944, 479 had been built.

A twin-engine, long-range escort fighter, reconnaissance aircraft, and night fighter (depending on the variant), the Gekko was constructed of metal with fabric-covered control surfaces. The night fighter variant was powered by two Nakajima Sakae 21 14-cylinder air-cooled radial engines, rated at 1,130 horsepower for takeoff. It had a wingspan of 55 feet 8 ½ inches and a length of 39 feet 11 $^{17}/_{32}$ inches. Top speed was 315 miles per hour at 19,160 feet, with a service ceiling of 30,610 feet and a range of 2,348 miles. The night fighter was armed with a pair of dorsal oblique-firing 20-mm cannon, and some aircraft also mounted one forward-firing 20-mm cannon in the nose. The Gekko could carry two 551-pound bombs, and all variants carried bombs when used for suicide attacks. The reconnaissance variant was crewed by three, and the night fighter by two.

Important fighter aircraft flown primarily by the Japan Army Air Force include the following.

Kawasaki Ki-45 Toryu ("Nick"). This twin-engine fighter was designed to operate over greater range than a single-engine plane. Although not designed for the role, the Nick was used mainly as a night fighter. Prototypes were produced in 1939, but flight trials were initially disappointing, especially in terms of speed, and the aircraft underwent many revisions before the required speed of 335 miles per hour was achieved in late 1940. The first production Nicks were not delivered until August 1942, and the aircraft was first used in combat in October in China. Crews welcomed its armor and highly survivable design, and in China it was deployed primarily against naval targets and for ground attack. In other theaters, the Nick was used increasingly for night missions.

Total output of the Nick reached 1,701 aircraft before production ended in July 1945. A twin-engine fighter and ground-attack aircraft, the Nick was of all-metal construction except for its fabric-covered control surfaces. In late models, the power plant was two Nakajima Ha-102 14-cylinder air-cooled radials, rated at 1,080 horsepower for take-off. Wingspan measured 49 feet 3 5/16 inches and length 36 feet 1 1/16 inches. Maximum speed of the aircraft was 335.5 miles per hour at 19,685 feet, with a service ceiling of 32,810 feet and a range of 1,243 miles. Late-model Nicks were armed with two nose-mounted 20-mm cannon, one 37-mm cannon in a ventral tunnel, and one rearward-firing 7.9-mm machine gun. Many Nicks were modified in the field with different configurations of armament. The crew consisted of a pilot and radio operator-gunner, who were accommodated in separate cockpits.

Kawasaki Ki-61 Hien ("Tony"). The Tony first saw combat in New Guinea in summer 1943 and was the first Japan Army Air Force fighter to incorporate both armor plating and self-sealing fuel tanks into its design from the outset. Previous fighters, most notably the Zero, sacrificed these in the interest of saving weight and thereby gaining performance, maneuverability, and range. Not only did the Hien ("Swallow") represent a departure from traditional design policy in this respect, it also looked very different from the blunt Zero and other fighters. Its sleek, streamlined profile much more closely resembled the German Bf-109, the Italian Macchi MC-202, or even the American P-51 Mustang. The profile had little or nothing to do with imitation, however, and was largely a function of the incorporation of a liquid-cooled engine, which meant that the forward end of the aircraft could feature a sleek nosecone instead of the blunt, open-ended cowling required by air-cooled radials.

As with the Kawasaki Ki-45 Toryu ("Nick"), the Tony, first prototyped in December 1941, went through many revisions and iterations before production was finally authorized. In the end, the Tony sacrificed a certain amount of maneuverability for high ceiling, high dive speeds, and armor protection. While the Tony proved to be a good fighter, it was chronically plagued by engine reliability problems, but by January 1945, 2,654 had been built. The aircraft operated in New Guinea and Rabaul as well as the Philippines, China, Formosa, Okinawa, and Japan itself, defending against

B-29 raids. A formidable opponent in a dogfight, the Tony nevertheless met its match in the P-51D Mustang.

A single-seat fighter, the Tony was of all-metal construction except for fabric-covered control surfaces. In later models, power was provided by a single Kawasaki Ha-140 12-cylinder inverted-V liquid-cooled engine, rated at 1,500 horsepower for takeoff. Wingspan was 39 feet 4 7/16 inches and length, 30 feet 5/8 inches. Late variants could reach 379 miles per hour at 19,685 feet, and service ceiling was 36,090 feet. Maximum range of the Tony was 995 miles. Later models were armed with two fuselage-mounted 12.7-mm machine guns and two wing-mounted 30-mm cannon, or four 20-mm cannon, two in the fuselage and two in the wings. Bomb load for all versions consisted of a pair of 551-pound bombs.

Kawasaki Ki-100 Goshikisen. The Allies first encountered the Ki-100 early in 1945 during attacks on the Japanese home islands. The plane was so new, introduced very late in the war, that Allied observers never got around to assigning it an English-language code name. Nevertheless, the new aircraft outperformed such U.S. carrier-based planes as the Hellcat and even held its own against the land-based P-51 Mustang. As shocking as the sudden appearance of the "new" aircraft was, the Ki-100 was not a radical new design, but was, rather, an extensive modification of the Ki-61, fitted with a larger air-cooled engine and a cut-down rear fuselage to improve the pilot's rear vision. Both these modifications were intended to create an effective high-altitude interceptor to meet the onslaught of the U.S. B-29s over the Japanese homeland. The new, more powerful engine enabled operation at more than 30,000 feet—customary B-29 territory—and the improved pilot visibility was indispensable to an interceptor operating among heavily armed Superfortresses and their Mustang escorts. Total production of the Ki-100, most of which commandeered Ki-61 airframes under construction, was no more than 393. A Ki-100-II, with an even more powerful turbosupercharged engine, was planned and prototyped, but the Japanese surrender came before production was started.

A single-seat fighter, the Ki-100 featured all-metal construction with fabric-covered control surfaces. It was driven by a single Mitsubishi Ha-112-II 14-cylinder air-cooled radial engine, rated at 1,500 horsepower for takeoff, and had a wingspan of 39 feet 4 $\frac{7}{16}$ inches and a length of 28 feet 11 $\frac{1}{4}$ inches. Top speed was 360 miles per hour at 19,685 feet, with a service ceiling of 36,090 feet and a range of 1,367 miles. Armament consisted of two fuselage-mounted 20-mm cannon and two wing-mounted 12.7-mm machine guns. There was provision for two underwing 44-gallon drop-tanks or two 551-pound bombs.

Nakajima Ki-27 ("Nate"). This low-wing cantilever monoplane with fixed landing gear first saw service in the Sino-Japanese War that began before World War II proper. Its introduction marked the transition of the Japan Army Air Force into a modern air arm, although the Ki-27 could not have competed with such European fighters as the Messerschmitt Bf-109 and the Hawker Hurricane. The prototype flew on October 15, 1936, and it went into production at the end of the following year. Total production during the war was 3,399. By 1944, the Ki27 was hopelessly obsolete as a fighter, but it continued to be used for advance flight training and, at the end of the war, loaded with some 1,102 pounds of bombs as a suicide aircraft.

A single-seat fighter, the Nate featured all-metal construction with fabric-covered control surfaces. Its powerplant (in late models) was a single Nakajima Ha-1b nine-cylinder air-cooled radial, rated at 710 horsepower for takeoff. Wingspan was 37 feet 1 $\frac{1}{4}$ inches and length 24 feet 8 $\frac{7}{16}$ inches. The Nate had a maximum speed of 292 miles per hour at 11,480 feet and a range of 1,060 miles. Typically, the Nate was armed with a pair of fuselage-mounted 7.7-mm machine guns and carried four 55-pound bombs or two 28.6-gallon drop-tanks.

Nakajima Ki-43 ("Oscar"). The Japanese name for the Nakajima Ki-43 ("Oscar"), Hayabusa, means "Peregrine Falcon," and, like its namesake, this aircraft was an extremely agile hunter, similar to the Zero but lighter, sleeker, and even more maneuverable, though rather slow and armed with nothing more than two fuselage-mounted machine guns. Early in the war, the Oscar figured as a very formidable opponent, but it was soon outgunned and generally outclassed by newer Allied fighters. Production reached 5,919 before and during the war.

A single-seat, single-engine fighter, the Oscar was of all-metal construction except for its fabric-covered control surfaces. The power plant in later models was one Mitsubishi Ha-112 14-cylinder air-cooled radial, rated at 1,300 horsepower for takeoff, the wingspan measured 35 feet 6 $\frac{3}{4}$ inches, and length was 29 feet 3 $\frac{5}{16}$ inches. The late models reached 358 miles per hour at 21,920 feet and had a service ceiling of 37,400 feet, with a range of 1,990 miles. Armament on later models was two 20-mm cannon, whereas earlier models had two machine guns only. Bomb load was two 66-pound or one 551-pound bombs or two 44-gallon drop-tanks.

Nakajima Ki-44 Shoki ("Tojo"). The Nakajima Ki-44 Shoki ("Tojo") was expressly designed as an interceptor. Shoki, its Japanese name, means "Devil Killer," and its mission was to intercept American bombers. As an interceptor design, the Tojo sacrificed maneuverability, much cherished in other Japanese fighters, for speed and rate of climb. The prototype flew in August 1940, and, after repeated modification, the aircraft was accepted by the Japan Army Air Force in September 1942. It was the fastest Japanese fighter aircraft. Before production ended in December 1944, 1,225 of the planes had been built.

A single-seat interceptor, the Tojo featured all-metal construction with fabric-covered control surfaces. In later models, the power plant was one Nakajima Ha-145 18-cylinder air-cooled radial, rated at 2,000 horsepower for takeoff. Wingspan was 31 feet $\frac{1}{16}$ inches and length, 28 feet 9 $\frac{7}{8}$ inches. The aircraft could hit 376 miles per hour at 17,060 feet and had a service ceiling of 36,745 feet, with a range of 1,056 miles. Late-model Tojos were armed with four 20-mm cannon, two in the fuselage and two in the wings, or two fuselage-mounted 20-mm cannon and two wing-mounted 37-mm cannons.

Nakajima Ki-84 Hayate ("Frank"). This is generally considered the best of the late Japanese fighters, and it saw desperate action in the culminating battles of the Pacific war, beginning with the Allied invasion of the Philippines and throughout the defense of the home islands. The Frank could out-climb, out-run, and out-maneuver both the U.S. P-51D Mustang and the P-47D Thunderbolt. Unfortunately for the Japanese, the aircraft was introduced quite late in the war, and it was built under conditions that tended to produce severe quality-control problems, which made the Frank unreliable. The prototype flew in April 1943, and the plane entered service at the beginning of 1944. Hard-pressed production facilities managed to turn out 3,415 of the aircraft before the end of the war.

A single-seat fighter/fighter-bomber, the Frank was initially produced with all-metal construction and fabric-covered control surfaces. Later models featured a wooden rear fuselage, wingtips, and control rods or lightweight alloys with carbon steel ribs, bulkheads, and cockpit section and sheet steel skinning. The Ki-106 version was made entirely of wood in an effort to conserve scarce metals. For most variants, the power plant was a single Nakajima Ha-45 (Army Type 4) 18-cylinder air-cooled radial engine, rated at 1,800 horsepower for take-off. Wingspan measured 36 feet 10 $^{7}/_{16}$ inches, length 32 feet 6 $^{9}/_{16}$ inches. Top speed was 392 miles per hour at 20,080 feet, and service ceiling was 34,450 feet. Range was 1,347 miles. Typical armament consisted of two fuselage-mounted 12.7-mm machine guns and two wing-mounted 20-mm cannon. The aircraft could carry two 551-pound bombs or two 44-gallon drop-tanks.

In addition to important bombers and land- and carrier-based fighters, the Japanese also operated seaplane fighters.

Kawanishi N1K Kyofu ("Rex"), Nakajima A6M2-N ("Rufe"), and Aichi E13A ("Jake"). The Rex was a seaplane variant of the Shiden, and the Rufe was a seaplane variant of the Zero. Several other seaplanes saw service with the Japanese forces, the most important of which was the Aichi E13A ("Jake"). Ordered in 1937 by the Imperial Navy as a reconnaissance floatplane, the E13A was prototyped the following year and began production in December 1940. Total production during the war was 1,418. In combat, the Jake was launched from the catapults of cruisers and seaplane tenders and was used not just for reconnaissance but for ground attack and against shipping. The aircraft saw action in China, and, launched from the cruisers *Tone, Chikuma,* and *Kinugasa,* it performed preattack reconnaissance of Pearl Harbor. The versatile aircraft was also used for bombing missions, long-range patrols, staff transport, and air-sea rescue, as well as suicide missions. Its major flaw was a lack of armor protection for crew and fuel tanks and inadequate defensive armament (a single 7.7-mm machine gun mounted in the rear cockpit). However, its endurance was an impressive 15 hours, which made it ideal for long-range reconnaissance.

A single-engine, three-seat, float reconnaissance seaplane, the Jake was built of metal construction with fabric-covered control surfaces. Its power plant was a single Mitsubishi Kinsei 43 14-cylinder air-cooled radial engine, rated at 1,060 horsepower for takeoff. Wingspan measured 47 feet 6 $^{7}/_{8}$ inches, and length 37 feet $^{7}/_{8}$ inches. The Jake's top speed was 234 miles per hour at 7,155 feet, and its service ceiling was 28,640 feet. Maximum range was 1,298 miles. Typical armament included one rearward-firing flexible 7.7-mm machine gun, and some aircraft were field-modified with the addition of a downward-firing ventral 20-mm cannon. The Jake carried a single 551-pound bomb or four 132-pound bombs or depth charges for antisubmarine warfare.

For the transport mission, the Japanese converted two of their bomber types and also flew the L2D ("Tabby"), which was a Douglas DC-3 (civilian version of the military's C-47), built under a license concluded in 1938.

Further reading: Collier, Basil. *Japanese Aircraft of World War II.* London: Sidgwick & Jackson, 1981; Francillon, René J. *Japanese Aircraft of the Pacific War.* New York: Putnam, 1970; Green, William. *Warplanes of the Second World War: Bombers.* Garden City, N.Y.: Doubleday,

1968; Green, William. *Warplanes of the Second World War: Fighters.* Garden City, N.Y.: Doubleday, 1968; Gunston, Bill. *Japanese and Italian Aircraft.* London: Book Sales, 1985; Mikesh, R. *Japanese Aircraft: Code Names and Designations.* Atglen, Penn.: Schiffer Publishing, 1993; Sakaida, Henry. *Japanese Army Air Force Aces 1937–1945.* London: Osprey, 1997.

aircraft, Polish

Like its other military forces at the outbreak of World War II, the Polish air force was gallant and determined but massively outnumbered, outgunned, and outclassed. During the BLITZKRIEG INVASION OF POLAND in September 1939, most of Poland's aircraft were destroyed on the ground. Nevertheless, Poland built one bomber and one fighter of note.

P.Z.L. P.37 LosB. This twin-engine medium bomber was powered by a 918-horsepower Bristol Pegasus XX engine. Top speed was 276 miles per hour, range was 1,615 miles, and bomb load was 4,850 pounds. Three 7.7-mm machine guns provided (wholly inadequate) defensive fire. With a wingspan of 58 feet 10 inches and a service ceiling of only 19,680 feet, the P.37 fell easy prey to German fighters. Only 108 were built.

PZL 11C. The PZL 11C was the principal Polish fighter. Its wingspan was 35 feet 2 inches, and it was driven by a single PZL-built Bristol Mercury 645-horsepower engine, which meant that it was perhaps the most underpowered fighter of the war. Top speed was 242 miles per hour at 18,000 feet. Armament consisted of four machine guns and two 12.3-kilogram bombs. Range was extremely limited: little more than 200 miles. The plane entered service in 1934, making it the oldest active fighter aircraft in Europe.

See also POLAND, AIR FORCE OF.

Further reading: Cynk, J. B. *Polish Aircraft 1893–1939.* London: Bodley Head, 1979; Koniarek, Jan, Don Greer, and Tom Tullis. *Polish Air Force 1939–1945.* Carrollton, Tex.: Squadron/Signal Publications, 1994; Peczkawski, Robert, and Bartlomiej Belcarz. *White Eagles: The Aircraft, Men and Operations of the Polish Air Force 1918–1939.* Mardens Hill, U.K.: Hikoki Publications, 2001.

aircraft, Soviet

That the German military aircraft industry entered World War II with innovative and devastatingly effective designs surprised no one, but little was expected of the Soviets. While it is true that some Soviet aircraft designs were obsolescent or even obsolete at the outbreak of war, the nation also produced a number of superb aircraft.

Ilyushin II-4. Among the bombers, only the major Soviet model is generally classified as a heavy bomber. The twin-engine Ilyushin II-4 was a superb aircraft, with more than 5,000 produced between 1937 and 1944, mostly during the final three years of production. The prototype design dates to 1935, and hard lessons learned during the Red Army invasion of Finland during 1939–40 resulted in improvements to armor protection. Nevertheless, later models of the aircraft replaced many metal parts with wood, which was easier to come by during the war. The II-4 served with the Red Army Air Force as well as with Soviet Naval Aviation, and it was naval pilots who flew the first Soviet air raids over Berlin on August 8, 1941. The aircraft served to the end of the war, although in the final months its age was showing, and it was relegated mainly to glider towing.

General specifications of the II-4 included two 1,100-horsepower M-88B radial piston engines, a wingspan of 70 feet 4 ¼ inches, and a top speed of 255 miles per hour. Service ceiling was 32,810 feet. Defensive armament consisted of 0.5-inch machine guns in the nose, in a dorsal turret, and in ventral positions. The II-4 carried up to 2,205 pounds of bombs or three 1,102-pound torpedoes and was crewed by four.

Like the Germans, the Soviets produced more light to medium bombers than heavy bombers. The three most important were the Tupolev SB-2, the Tupolev Tu-2, and the Petlyakov Pe-2.

Tupolev SB-2. Familiarly called the Katyusha, the Tupolev SB-2 was first flown on October 7, 1933. Intended as a high-speed bomber, it was at the time one of the Tupolev organization's most advanced designs, based on a heavy fighter airframe rather than a bomber. Construction was all metal and, in service during the Spanish civil war, its 255-mile-per-hour speed outflew many enemy fighters—until the appearance of the German Bf-109 fighter. A total of 6,656 SB-2s were built up to 1940, and some remained in service until 1943, despite heavy losses to the Bf-109s.

The SB-2 was driven by twin 850-horsepower M100 V-12 piston engines to a top speed of 255 miles per hour and a service ceiling of 27,885 feet. Its range was a modest 746 miles. Wingspan was 66 feet 8 ½ inches, and defensive armament consisted of two 0.3-inch machine guns in a nose turret, one in a dorsal turret, and one in the ventral position. Bomb capacity was 2,205 pounds, and the plane was crewed by three.

Tupolev Tu-2. First flown in October 1940, the Tupolev Tu-2 went into production beginning in 1942 and, with the Petlyakov Pe-2, emerged as the most important Soviet bomber of the war. This medium bomber had a maximum speed of 342 miles per hour and had a range of 1,243 miles. It was 45 feet 3 inches long with a wingspan of 61 feet 10 inches. Bomb load was an impressive 6,614 pounds. Along with the Petlyakov Pe-2, the Tupolev Tu-2 was used in large numbers during the war, and some of these aircraft remained in Soviet service during the postwar years, flying in the Korean War with North Korean forces. During the early 1960s, the Tu-2 continued to fly with the Chinese air force and with the air forces of other communist countries. Its general specifications included a power plant consisting of two Shvetsov Ash-82fn 1,850-horsepower 14 cylinder radial engines making a rop speed of 342 miles per hour over a range of 1,553 miles. Defensive armament was two 20-mm ShVAK cannon in wing roots and three 0.5-inch UBT machine guns, two in dorsal positions and one in the ventral position. As mentioned, the bomb load was 6,614 pounds. The aircraft was crewed by four.

Petlyakov Pe-2. This aircraft was produced in a light-bomber configuration and, like the Pe-3, in a fighter configuration. The Pe-2 is generally judged the most important light Soviet bomber of the war, and a total of 11,427 Pe-2s and Pe-3s were produced. By the time of the INVASION OF THE SOVIET UNION on June 22, 1941, only a few hundred Pe-2s had come off the assembly lines. As they reached the front in greater numbers, however, German fighter pilots despaired, because the fast and nimble aircraft was difficult to catch and destroy. The Pe-2 benefitted from continual improvements made in direct response to meetings with front-line pilots. By late 1942, more crew armor and better armament had been added. The ShKAS 7.62- mm dorsal and ventral guns were replaced by Berezin UBT 12.7-mm guns. A turret replaced the hand-held dorsal gun position, and the nose was redesigned to enhance bombardier protection and efficiency.

The final specifications for the aircraft included two 1,100-horsepower Klimov M-105R V-12 piston engines, which made a top speed of 335 miles per hour. Wingspan was 56 feet 3.5 inches, and service ceiling 28,900 feet. For a light bomber, range was excellent at 932 miles. Bomb load was 2,646 pounds, and the plane was crewed by three.

The Red Air Force suffered devastating losses during the opening weeks of the German invasion. Many planes were destroyed on the ground, while others, mostly obsolete or obsolescent, were shot out of the skies by superior German fighters. American and British aircraft were rushed to the Soviets to help make up for the losses, even as the Soviet aircraft industry went into high gear and began turning out some excellent fighters. Certainly, the early losses were devastating, but they also forced a rapid modernization of the Red air force, which threw impressive designs into the fray.

Lavochkin LaGG-3. First flown on March 30, 1940, the Lavochkin LaGG-3 was a refinement of the earlier, grossly underpowered LaGG-1. Built mainly of wood, the LaGG-3 was produced in great quantity (6,528) until mid-1942. Like its predecessor, it was still somewhat underpowered, and pilots grimly dubbed the wooden plane the "Guaranteed Varnished Coffin." Nevertheless, and despite its construction materials, it was remarkably durable and could survive very substantial battle damage. General specifications included a power plant consisting of the 1,050-horsepower Klimov M-105P liquid-cooled in-line engine, which made for a top speed of 357 miles per hour. Service ceiling was

31,825 feet, and maximum range was 404 miles. The aircraft had a wingspan of 32 feet 1 inch. Armament typically consisted of two 12.7-mm UBS machine guns mounted in the engine cowling and one ShVAK 20-mm cannon firing through the streamlined propeller hub. The LaGG-3 could carry six 3.23-inch rockets or 440 pounds of bombs.

Lavochkin La-5 and La-7. As the LaGG-3 was an evolutionary improvement on the LaGG-1, the La-5 and La-7, also from Lavochkin, developed from the LaGG-3. Like its predecessor, the La-5 was made chiefly of wood, but it was designed to accommodate the Shvetsov M-82F radial engine, which produced 1,330 horsepower and drove the plane to nearly 400 miles per hour, making it a match for the best German fighters. Production on the new aircraft began about July 1942, and it proved quite successful. In 1943, Lavochkin added a new power plant, the M-82FN direct-injection engine, which developed 1,630 horsepower and pushed the aircraft beyond 400 miles per hour. The modified plane was designated the La-5FN. Its general specifications included the 1,630-horsepower M-82FN radial engine for a top speed of 402 miles per hour and a service ceiling of 36,089 feet. Range was 475 miles, and wingspan was 32 feet 1 inch. Armament included a pair of 20-mm nose cannon and four 8.2-cm RS-82 rockets or 150 kilos of bombs.

The Lavochkin La-7 pushed the envelope even farther with yet another high-performance ASh-82FN engine, which made speeds of 423 miles per hour. The La-7 was introduced in 1944, when the Soviets had already achieved air supremacy over most of the vast eastern front. Except for the new engine, it was in other respects identical to the La-5FN.

MiG-3. Before the end of World War II and well into the postwar and cold war era, "MiG" would be one of the most widely recognized names in fighter aircraft design. It stands for Mikoyan-Gurevich, and the design team's MiG-3 earned a reputation for extraordinary performance—top speed of 398 miles per hour with a very rapid climb rate of nearly 4,000 feet per minute—that was tempered by the difficulty pilots had handling the machine and its inherently poor armament. Despite its high speed, it could barely hold its own against the German Bf-109.

The MiG-3 went into production in December 1940 and reached the front line fighter squadrons in April 1941. Production continued through December 1941, by which time it had reached some 3,120 aircraft. General specifications included a power plant consisting of a 1,350-horsepower Mikulin AM-35A liquid-cooled V-12 engine, which made 398 miles per hour. Wingspan was 33 feet 5 ½ inches, range 743 miles, and service ceiling 39,370 feet. Armament consisted of a single 12.7-mm machine gun and two 7.62-mm machine guns in the upper nose cowl. Some aircraft were also equipped with a pair of 12.7-mm machine guns mounted under the wings.

Yakovlev Yak series. The Yakovlev Yak series (Yak-1, Yak-3, Yak-7, and Yak-9) was so successful that a staggering 37,000 were produced during World War II, most of them Yak-9s. The Yak-1 first flew in January 1940, and the Yak-9 went into production in summer 1942. It was produced in several specialized variants, the most important of which were the Yak-9T, a ground-attack antitank version; Yak-9B, a fighter-bomber version; Yak-9D, a long-range fighter; Yak-9DD, a very-long-range fighter escort, and Yak-9U, the final evolutionary step of the type, which reached a speed of 435 miles per hour and could easily outperform the Bf-109 and, indeed, anything else the German could throw at it. General specifications of the Yak-9U included a 1,650-horsepower Klimov VK-107A V-12 piston engine, making 435 miles per hour. Wingspan was 32 feet 0.75 inches, and service ceiling was 39,040 feet. The fighter had a range of 541 miles. The Yak-9U was armed with one engine-mounted 20-mm MP-20 cannon and two 12.7-mm UBS machine guns. It could carry two 220-pound bombs on underwing racks.

Ilyushin Il-2. For the close air support or ground-attack role, the Red Air Force used the Lavochkin La-5 and La-7 fighters but also flew two more specialized aircraft, the Ilyushin Il-2 and the Sukhoi Su-2.

The Ilyushin Il-2 was produced in a remarkable quantity of 36,163, according to Soviet historians. The design dates to 1938, when it was conceived as a two-seat aircraft, but it was a lighter single-seat design that first flew, on October 12, 1940. The aircraft proved highly effective against German transport vehicles and tanks, although it was highly vulnerable to fighter attack. In February 1942, therefore, the two-seat design was resurrected, the second seat occupied by a rear-facing gunner who defended against air attack. A version of the aircraft survived World War II and was used in the Korean War. General specifications included a power plant consisting of one 1,700-horsepower Mikulin AM-38F liquid-cooled inline piston engine making a modest top speed of 251 miles per hour—adequate for ground attack. Wingspan was 47 feet 10 ¾ inches. Service ceiling was 19,500 feet, and range was 375 miles. Typical armament included two 37-mm machine guns and two 7.62-mm guns, all wing mounted; one 12.7-mm machine gun was fired from the rear cockpit. Bomb load consisted of up to 200 5.5-pound hollow-charge antitank bombs or eight RS-82 or RS-132 rockets.

Sukhoi Su-2. The Sukhoi Su-2 was produced from early in the war until about 1942 but was badly mauled by German fighters, despite the inclusion of a rear-facing defensive gunner. Late model specifications included one 1,520-horsepower Shvetsov M82 air-cooled radial piston engine, which made for a top speed of 302 miles per hour. Wingspan was 46 feet 11 inches, and service ceiling 28,870 feet. Armament consisted of four forward-firing 7.62-mm wing-mounted machine guns and one or two machine guns in a dorsal turret. The Su-2 could deliver 882 pounds of bombs.

Further reading: Gordon, Yefim, and Dmitry Khazanov. *Soviet Fighters and Bombers of WW II.* Osceola, Wis.: Motorbooks International, 1993; Gordon, Yefim, and Dmitry Khazanov. *Soviet Combat Aircraft of the Second World War: Twin-Engined Fighters, Attack Aircraft and Bombers.* Osceola, Wis.: Motorbooks International, 1999; Hardesty, Von. *Red Phoenix: The Rise of Soviet Air Power, 1941–1945.* Washington, D.C.: Smithsonian Books, 1991.

aircraft, U.S.

The UNITED STATES ARMY AIR FORCES (USAAF) (before 1941, the UNITED STATES ARMY AIR CORPS, USAAC) and the UNITED STATES NAVY and UNITED STATES MARINE CORPS flew a variety of aircraft during World War II. This entry surveys the most important of them.

ARMY AIR FORCES AIRCRAFT

Aircraft used primarily for close air support of troops were classified as Attack (designated "A") Aircraft. Although many fighter and medium bomber aircraft were used in close air support, only one USAAF plane was specifically designed for the role.

A-20 Havoc. This aircraft was delivered to the USAAF in a quantity of 7,230 from the Douglas Aircraft Company. The plane went into production at the close of the 1930s and was the first USAAF aircraft type to see action in Europe, arriving in the theater in 1942. The twin-engine craft was nicknamed the "Flying Pike" and had a top speed of 329 miles per hour, a service ceiling of 28,250, and a range of 1,060 miles. Production ended in 1944.

USAAF bomber aircraft were designated "B" and included the following.

B-17 Flying Fortress. The B-17 was the first U.S. bomber built for strategic bombing and the first U.S. four-engine monoplane bomber. The airplane was designed by Boeing, and a total of 12,731 were produced by Boeing and, under license, by Douglas and the Lockheed subsidiary Vega. The aircraft was designed before the war; during the war, it was produced in several iterations, the most successful of which was the B-17G, which was powered by four 1,200-horsepower Wright R-1820-97 engines that drove the 65,500-pound aircraft at 287 miles per hour and to a service ceiling of 35,600 feet. The Flying Fortress could deliver up to 8,000 pounds of bombs and had a fully loaded range of 2,000 miles. It was equipped with a multitude of defensive guns, which made it a most formidable target for fighters. The design and construction of the B-17, especially in the G iteration, which featured a strengthened rear fuselage, was greatly prized for its ability to withstand massive damage from enemy fighters and antiaircraft fire.

B-24 Liberator. The B-17 was a strikingly handsome airplane, whereas the boxy, lumbering B-24 looked rather awkward by comparison. Certainly, it did not command the same level of affection from the public or from air crews as did the B-17, but this Consolidated Aircraft design was actually built in greater numbers: 18,482 produced by five manufacturers. If the B-24 was massive in appearance, it was also a handful actually to fly. Handling the heavy craft was a difficult and fatiguing job, but the B-24 had two undeniable performance edges on the more agile B-17. It had a better maximum speed (300 miles per hour versus 287 miles per hour) and was capable of longer range (2,100 miles versus 2,000), although it is true that the B-17 was capable of considerably greater altitude: 35,600 feet versus 28,000 feet. Despite its limitations, the B-24 proved a highly durable workhorse, which, if anything, could take even more punishment than the B-17, thanks in no small measure to its mid-mounted, high-lift "Davis wing," which not only achieved 20 percent less drag than conventional airfoils of the time, but greatly added to the structural integrity of the aircraft.

B-25 Mitchell. Design work on the B-25 began at North American Aviation in 1938. Whereas the B-17 and B-14 were heavy bombers, the twin-engine B-25, named in honor of controversial military aviation and bomber advocate William "Billy" Mitchell, was a medium bomber, an extremely versatile aircraft that is considered one of the great bombers of World War II. The prototype flew in 1939, and by the time the war was over, more than 11,000 had been built, 9,815 for the USAAC and USAAF. It was first made famous by its highly unconventional use—launched from an AIRCRAFT CARRIER in the DOOLITTLE TOKYO RAID of 1942.

Top speed for the B-25 was 272 miles per hour, service ceiling was 24,200 feet, and maximum range was 1,350 miles with a 3,000-pound bomb load. The versatile B-25 airframe was adapted for use as a transport and as a reconnaissance plane.

B-26 Invader. Built by Douglas, the Invader entered service in 1944 as a very fast twin-engine bomber, with a top speed of 372 miles per hour and a service ceiling of 20,450 feet. It could carry a 4,000-pound bomb load over 892 miles.

B-26 Martin Marauder. The Martin Marauder shared with the Douglas Invader the same B-26 designation and, like the Douglas aircraft, was a twin-engine medium bomber. Unlike the Invader, however, the Martin Marauder was so difficult to master that it was branded a "Widow Maker" because it killed a number of novice pilots. However, by the time the Marauder entered full-time war service, the techniques for flying it safely and effectively had been perfected, and it proved to be a great airplane. More than 5,000 were delivered to the USAAF before production stopped in 1945. Top speed was 283 miles per hour, and the service ceiling was 19,800 feet. It could carry 4,000 pounds of bombs 1,100 miles.

B-29 Superfortress. The most advanced USAAF bomber and the most advanced bomber of its time was the B-29 Superfortress. Deployment of this bomber was restricted to the Pacific theater, where long range was a paramount requirement, and it was the only USAAF aircraft capable of delivering atomic weapons (which were much bigger and heavier than conventional ordnance), including those dropped on Hiroshima on August 6, 1945, and on Nagasaki on August 9. Designing the B-29 was an ambitious undertaking that began at Boeing in 1940. A prototype flew in 1942, but the aircraft was not put into combat service until the final two months of 1944. Two USAAF units were created expressly to fly the new bomber, the Twentieth Air Force and the Twenty-first Air Force.

Four engines drove the B-29 at 364 miles per hour to a service ceiling of 32,000 feet. This giant could carry a 20,000-pound bomb load over 4,200 miles. With a 141-foot wingspan and a 99-foot fuselage, it was by far the biggest bomber not just in the U.S. inventory but in the world at the time.

USAAF cargo and military transport aircraft are designated "C" and included the following airplanes.

C-46 Commando. The C-46 was designed by Curtiss-Wright in 1937 as a twin-engine commercial passenger plane. Shortly before the United

A North American B-25C Mitchell. This medium bomber provided excellent service during World War II and was the most widely exported U.S. bomber. *(San Diego Aerospace Museum)*

States entered World War II, the USAAC ordered a conversion for military transport, and before the war ended, 3,144 of the military version had been built. The C-46 did yeoman service flying THE HUMP during the harrowing Burma-China airlift. Top speed was 269 miles per hour, and the service ceiling was 27,600 feet. The C-46 could carry a payload of 10,000 pounds over 1,200 miles.

C-47 Skytrain. DWIGHT D. EISENHOWER listed four weapons he deemed indispensable to victory in World War II: the BAZOOKA, the jeep, the atomic bomb, and the C-47 Skytrain. Like the C-46, the C-47 began as a commercial aircraft, the spectacularly successful Douglas DC-3, which first flew in 1935. Before the war ended, 10,000 C-47s (in many configurations) were built for the USAAC and

USAAF. Many were flown by the Allies, especially the British, who called the C-47 the Dakota. This workhorse was used throughout the war to carry personnel and cargo, to tow gliders, and to drop paratroops. Especially valued was its ease of maintenance and its ability to fly into and out of even the most rudimentary of airstrips. The twin-engine C-47 flew at 230 miles per hour and had a service ceiling of 24,000 feet, a range of 1,600 miles, and a payload capacity of 10,000 pounds.

C-54 Skymaster. Another militarized commercial airliner, the Douglas C-54 Skymaster had been developed in the late 1930s as the four-engine DC-4. The first run of this model was entirely commandeered off the assembly line by the USAAF. By war's end, 1,163 were in military service as long-range transports, the primary overwater airlifters across the Atlantic and Pacific. A modified C-54 transported President Franklin D. Roosevelt to the YALTA CONFERENCE in 1945.

Top speed of the C-54 was 265 miles per hour, service ceiling was 22,000 feet, and range was 3,900 miles. The plane could carry 50 troops with complete equipment.

USAAF Fighter aircraft are designated either "P" (for pursuit) or, later, F (fighter).

P-38 Lightning. The twin-engine P-38 Lightning was designed by Lockheed and featured a distinctive twin-boom fuselage, which prompted opposing Luftwaffe pilots to dub it Der Gabelschwanz Teufel, the "Fork-Tailed Devil." Produced in prototype in 1939, it was delivered in a quantity of 9,923 by the end of the war. Interestingly, the P-38 was far more successful against Japanese fighters in the Pacific than against German fighters in the European theater. The fighter's twin engines drove the P-38 at 414 miles per hour to a service ceiling of 44,000 feet. Range was 450 miles.

P-39 Airacobra. Bell Aircraft Corporation's P-39 Airacobra was flown in prototype in 1939. The aircraft was used by the British and the Soviets as well as by the USAAF. Although designated a pursuit plane, the P-39 was actually used mainly for close air support, largely because most enemy aircraft outclassed it in a dogfight. Despite its speed, the P-39 was not highly maneuverable. The P-39 saw

some action in the Pacific, but it was used mostly in Europe before it was entirely replaced by the F-47 Thunderbolt early in 1944. Top speed was 399 miles per hour to a service ceiling of 38,500 feet. Range was 750 miles.

P-40 Warhawk. This Curtiss-Wright design achieved its greatest fame in service with the American Volunteer Group, better known as the FLYING TIGERS, a band of American civilian pilots serving under contract with the Nationalist Chinese Air Force against Japan. The P-40's distinctive profile, formed by the large air scoop that fed the supercharged engine, was adorned by the Flying Tigers with a row of tiger teeth, and it was in this battle dress that the plane became an icon of the war.

Although the P-40 was actually verging on obsolescence by the time the war began, it enjoyed the advantage of being ready for production and, shortcomings aside, was produced in a quantity of 13,700 before production ended in 1944. Top speed was 378 miles per hour, service ceiling was 38,000 feet, but range was limited to only 240 miles.

P-59 Airacomet. The P-59 Airacomet was developed by Bell Aircraft Corporation during 1941–42 and was the first U.S. jet aircraft. Only 30 were built, and it was never deployed in action. Its performance was actually inferior to the best piston-powered fighters of the time, and, worse, its design was inherently unstable. Top speed was 413 miles per hour, service ceiling 46,200 feet, and range was 525 miles.

P-61 Black Widow. The Northrup Company built the P-61 Black Widow as the USAAF's first night interceptor, a plane designed to shoot down enemy bombers at night. It was also the first aircraft specially built to accommodate RADAR. The plane's name came from its all-black color scheme. The P-61 first flew in 1942, and 732 were built. Driven by two engines, the P-61 was capable of 366 miles per hour and had a service ceiling of 31,000 feet. Maximum range was 3,000 miles.

P-63 Kingcobra. Bell Aircraft updated the P-39 Airacobra as the P-63 Kingcobra in 1942. Some 3,303 were built, but most went to the Soviet Red Air Force instead of to the USAAF. Top speed was

408 miles per hour with a service ceiling of 43,000 feet and a range of 390 miles.

F-47 Thunderbolt (originally designated P-47). The Republic F-47 Thunderbolt was built in greater quantity than any other World War II USAAF fighter: 15,579. Big and ugly, the P-47 was extremely durable and very powerful. It entered service in 1942 and began combat operations the following year, first with the Eighth Air Force out of bases in England, then also with units in the Pacific and with the Fifteenth Air Force in the Mediterranean theater.

The F-47 was designed specifically as an "air-superiority fighter," with the intention of dominating the skies. It did just this, achieving a spectacular 4.6 to 1 victory rate, which translated into 3,752 enemy aircraft downed. Highly versatile, the F-47 was also a fine close air support craft.

Although equipped with only a single engine, the F-47 was massive and could reach 467 miles per hour and climb to a service ceiling of 43,000 feet. Its range was a respectable 800 miles carrying 2,000 pounds in bombs and other ordnance.

F-51 Mustang (originally, P-51). Many pilots consider the F-51 Mustang the best all-around fighter of World War II. Produced by North American, the Mustang made its first flight in May 1943. Top speed was 437 miles per hour, and service ceiling was 41,900 feet. It also had enough range—950 miles—to escort bombers deep into enemy territory, and, in a dogfight, it could outmaneuver just about anything thrown against it. North American produced 14,490 Mustangs before the war ended.

F-82 Twin Mustang. In addition to the F-51, North American also produced the unique F-82 Twin Mustang as a very-long-range (2,240 miles) escort for bombers negotiating the great distances of the Pacific theater. The F-82 mated two P-51s joined by a center wing section and tailplane. Except for this, each fuselage was entirely independent and had its own engine and pilot. This oddity was never deployed in combat, but it has the distinction of being the last piston fighter acquired by the USAAF.

Gliders (designated "G") were used primarily to deploy airborne troops. Two were prominent.

Waco G-4 and *G-15 Hadrian.* The Waco Aircraft Company built almost 14,000 G-4s, which were made mostly of wood and carried 15 fully equipped troops (or four soldiers and a jeep, or a 75-mm howitzer and crew). The G-4 was replaced late in the war by the G-15 Hadrian, a more airworthy and sturdier craft that could carry 7,500 pounds and soar at about 120 miles per hour.

Trainer aircraft were indispensable to the task of turning out qualified combat pilots. USAAF trainers were designated "PT," primary trainer; "BT," basic trainer; and "T," trainer.

PT-16. The *PT-16,* a military version of the Ryan Model S-T, was the first monoplane the USAAC and USAAF used for training. Ordered in 1940, its production ended in 1942. Top speed was just 128 mile per hour, and service ceiling 15,000 feet.

PT-19. The PT-19 was manufactured by Fairchild and other companies under license beginning in 1940 but was soon replaced by the more capable PT-13 Kaydet.

PT-13 Kaydet. Built by Stearman Aircraft Company, the PT-13 Kaydet was one of the most successful military trainers ever built. The USAAC and USAAF acquired more than 5,000 of them. Top speed was 135 miles per hour, and the service ceiling was 13,200 feet.

BT-13. Basic training was the next step up from primary training. The *BT-13,* manufactured by Vultee Aircraft, Inc., was the most popular USAAF basic trainer during World War II. It made 180 miles per hour and had a service ceiling of 21,650 feet over a range of 725 miles.

T-6 Texan. The T-6 Texan was built by North American Aviation and first flew in 1938. It became the USAAF's advanced trainer during World War II, with more than 8,000 produced for the service. The Texan's top speed was 210 miles per hour, its service ceiling 24,200 feet, and its range 629 miles. It became a favorite with pilots, and a substantial number entered civilian service after the war as general aviation aircraft.

NAVY AND MARINE CORPS AIRCRAFT

The U.S. Navy and U.S. Marine Corps (USMC) flew some of the same planes as the USAAF, but the navy in particular had two special requirements: fighters that could take off and land on aircraft carriers, and seaplanes. The following are some of the best-known navy and USMC aircraft of World War II.

F2A Buffalo. The Brewster F2A Buffalo was the first monoplane fighter operated from an aircraft carrier. The rather unwieldy fighter was no match for Japanese aircraft and could achieve a top speed of no more than 300 miles per hour. After the navy abandoned it early in the war, the marines used it for land-based operations, mostly in the close air support role. Only 502 Buffalos were built.

TBD Devastator. While the Brewster Buffalo was the navy's first carrier-based monoplane fighter, the Douglas TBD Devastator was its first carrier-launched torpedo bomber. Built to carry a single heavy torpedo under the fuselage, it was a large aircraft powered by a 900-horsepower Pratt & Whitney R-1830 Twin Wasp radial engine, which made a speed of just over 200 miles per hour. A prototype flew in April 1935, and production began in 1937–39, so that the Devastator soon replaced prewar carrier-based biplanes.

In combat, the TBD's slow speed and inadequate defensive armament—one .30-caliber machine gun firing forward and another in the rear cockpit—made it very vulnerable to fire from enemy fighters and ships. At the BATTLE OF MIDWAY, only four of 41 TBDs escaped destruction.

TBF/TBM Avenger. The Grumman TBF Avenger was introduced in 1939 as a replacement for the TBD Devastator and proved so effective that General Motors also began to build the plane (designated TBM) under license in 1942. The large aircraft was equipped with an electrically powered gun turret and an internal bomb bay to accommodate four 500-pound bombs or a single aerial torpedo. Its crew included a pilot, radioman, and gunner. A total of 9,842 TBF/TBM Avengers were produced during the war. The TBM engine was a 1,900-horsepower Wright, and maximum takeoff weight was 17,895 pounds. Top speed was 276 miles per hour, ceiling 30,100 feet, and range 1,000 miles. The aircraft was armed with two 12.7-mm forward-firing machine guns, one 12.7-mm dorsal-mounted machine gun, and one 7.62-mm ventral-mounted machine gun; it could carry up to 2,000 pounds of ordnance.

F4U Corsair. The gull-wing F4U Vought Corsair went into production in 1942 and continued in production well after the war, ending its run in 1952, by which time 12,582 had been built. One of the most successful fighters of World War II, it enjoyed an 11 to 1 kill ratio against Japanese aircraft in the Pacific. The single engine developed a mighty 2,000 horsepower, and the gull wings not only reduced drag, but allowed for shorter landing gear to accommodate an oversized propeller. The wings could be folded over the canopy to save space on the hangar deck. Unfortunately, the big engine required considerable setback of the cockpit, which meant that visibility was poor during landing and takeoff. Also, the plane readily stalled at slow speed, and it also tended to bounce on landing, which made it difficult to engage the arresting hook. For these reasons, the F4U was restricted from aircraft carrier operations until late in 1944. In the meantime, it was extensively used on land by USMC pilots, including the celebrated GREGORY "PAPPY" BOYINGTON of the Black Sheep Squadron.

F4F Wildcat. The F4F Grumman Wildcat was ordered by the navy in 1938, and by the end of the war some 9,000 had been produced. By 1942, the F4F was being replaced by the F6F Hellcat for carrier operations, although USMC pilots continued to fly the Wildcat with great success. Capable of a top speed of 320 miles per hour, the F4F was armed with six 50-caliber machine guns.

F6F Hellcat. Grumman designed the F6F Hellcat as a replacement for the F4F Wildcat. The new plane benefitted from close study of captured Japanese fighters, and Hellcat pilots eventually achieved a spectacular 19 to 1 kill ratio. Some 12,275 F6Fs were produced between 1942 and 1945—a production rate of one plane per hour during every 24 hours, seven days a week. In hard numbers, the F6F destroyed 5,156 enemy aircraft, accounting for three-fourths of all U.S. Navy aerial kills in World War II. The Hellcat made 380 miles per hour at 23,000 feet and could reach a service ceiling of 37,300 feet. Armament was six 12.7-mm machine guns and a bomb load of 2,000 pounds.

F7F Tigercat. The F7F Grumman Tigercat was ordered in 1941 as the navy's first twin-engine fighter, although it did not fly until 1943. Highly maneuverable and reaching an impressive 400 miles per hour, the F7F had four .50-caliber machine guns and four 20-mm cannon. However, the Tigercat proved too heavy for regular carrier operations and was therefore turned over to the USMC in 1944 for service from shore bases.

F8F Bearcat. The F8F Grumman Bearcat appeared late in the war, in 1945, and was developed largely in response to KAMIKAZE attacks as well as to continue countering general Japanese fighters. The F8F was 20 percent lighter than the F6F and nearly 50 miles per hour faster, hitting 421 miles per hour. Part of the weight reduction was achieved by reducing armament from six to four .50-caliber machine guns. However, two wing pylons, each capable of carrying a 1,000-pound bomb, provided attack capability.

O2SU Kingfisher. The O2SU Vought Kingfisher was the most widely used navy float plane of the war. The aircraft was designed to be carried aboard BATTLESHIPS and CRUISERS. The planes were lowered into the water by a shipboard crane, which was also used to recover them. The O2SU was used on training, scouting, bombing, and other missions. Although most were employed in the Pacific theater, some were used in the Atlantic to hunt German SUBMARINES. The Kingfisher first flew in 1938 and reached a top speed of 170 miles per hour and a ceiling of 16,000 feet.

PBY Catalina. The Consolidated PBY Catalina was produced in great numbers for the U.S. Navy during World War II. Five U.S. and Canadian plants delivered 3,281 of these flying boats, which had begun life in the early 1930s. The PBY-5A was powered by two 1,200-horsepower Pratt & Whitney radial piston engines and had a maximum takeoff weight of 35,420 pounds, a wingspan of 104 feet, and a 63-foot length. Its top speed was a lumbering 179 miles per hour, but at 117 miles per hour it could cruise for 2,545 miles. Typical armament consisted of five 7.62-mm machine guns and as much as 4,000 pounds of bombs or depth charges.

PBM-3 Mariner. The PBM-3 Mariner from Martin was a large flying boat designed for long-range operations as a patrol bomber, convoy escort, and fleet operations scout. It was intended to replace the Consolidated PBY Catalina but ultimately supplemented rather than replaced it. About 1,000 were produced.

SBD Dauntless. The Douglas SBD Dauntless was effectively the U.S. Navy's standard carrier-based dive bomber from mid-1940 until November 1943, when the Helldivers began to replace it. In addition to its carrier use, the SBD Dauntless was flown extensively by the USMC.

Ordered in 1939, delivery began in 1940, and 5,936 were built by the time the aircraft was phased out late in 1944. A single 1,350-horsepower Wright engine lifted a maximum takeoff weight of 9,519 pounds to a top speed of 255 miles per hour and a ceiling of 25,200 feet. Range was 773 miles, and armament included two forward-firing 12.7-mm machine guns in addition to two 7.62-mm machine guns on flexible mounts. Up to 1,600 pounds of bombs could be carried under the fuselage, and another 650 pounds under the wings.

SB2C Helldiver. The Curtiss SB2C Helldiver was designed in 1938 as a scout-bomber to replace the SBD Dauntless. Improvements included a larger fuel capacity, 20-mm cannon, and an internal bomb bay to carry a 1,000-pound bomb. Design problems delayed initial production until June 1942, and then the aircraft was plagued by landing gear failure and a tendency to bounce, which interfered with tail-hook engagement on carrier landings. Eventually, however, the problems were resolved, and 5,500 were produced before the end of the war. The SB2C's single Wright engine developed 1,900 horsepower, enabling a maximum takeoff weight of 16,616 pounds. Top speed was 295 miles per hour, and ceiling was 29,100 feet. The SB2C had a range of 1,165 miles. Armament consisted of two 20-mm wing-mounted cannon and two 7.62-mm machine guns operated by a gunner in the rear cockpit. The bomb bay could accommodate a 1,000-pound bomb, and underwing racks could take an additional 1,000 pounds of ordnance.

Further reading: Dean, Francis H. *America's Hundred Thousand: U.S. Production Fighters of World War II.* Atglen, Penn.: Schiffer Publishing, 1996; Gunston, Bill. *The Illustrated Directory of Fighting Aircraft of World War II.* New York: Arco Publishing, 1988; Jarrett, Philip, and E. R. Hooten, eds. *Aircraft of the Second World War: The Development of the Warplane 1939–45.* London: Conway Maritime Press, 1997; Mondey, David. *American Aircraft of World War II.* London: Book Sales, 2002; Sharpe, Mike. *Aircraft of World War II.* Osceola, Wis.: Motorbooks International, 2000.

aircraft carriers

Aircraft carriers, large ships specially designed to carry, launch, and recover aircraft, revolutionized naval warfare during World War II and largely displaced BATTLESHIPS as the supreme naval weapon. With aircraft carriers, fleets could now fight each other "over the horizon," and the BATTLE OF THE CORAL SEA was history's first naval engagement in which the opposing ships never sighted one another; all combat took place in or from the air. Moreover, aircraft carriers served as floating air bases, from which air attacks could be launched against targets far beyond the range of land-based

U.S. carrier pilots get a premission briefing below decks. *(National Archives and Records Administration)*

aircraft. Traditionally, nations had projected military power with great ships. Now those ships, in turn, could project their power with aircraft.

The history of the aircraft carrier may be traced to November 1910, when an American civilian pilot, Eugene Ely, took off from a platform built on the deck of the U.S. CRUISER *Birmingham.* Ely successfully landed an airplane early the following year, on January 18, 1911, on a platform built on the quarterdeck of the battleship *Pennsylvania.* He used wires extended across the platform and attached to sandbags to serve as arresting gear, an innovation that, with many improvements, continues to be a key feature of carriers to this day, making it possible for aircraft to land in the comparatively short space of an aircraft carrier deck. The British were the first to contemplate introducing a carrier into war, converting a merchant vessel into the HMS *Argus* during World War I. However, the armistice was signed before the ship could be deployed. The example of the *Argus* did inspire both the United States and Japan to experiment with carriers. The U.S. Navy built a flight deck on a converted collier and launched its first carrier, the USS *Langley,* in 1922. Later that same year, the Japanese Imperial Navy launched the *Hosyo,* the first vessel designed and purpose-built as an aircraft carrier.

World War II, which saw the apotheosis of the aircraft carrier, was also the vessel type's first exposure to combat. Japan's devastating attack on Pearl Harbor, December 7, 1941, would have been impossible without aircraft carriers, and it dramatically demonstrated how a nation could project massive air power at great distances from its own land or bases. While the Japanese attack wreaked havoc on the U.S. Navy battleship fleet, the American carriers were out to sea and therefore escaped destruction. They would be vital in the Pacific war, and the combat theater that had been opened by means of the aircraft carrier would, in large measure, be concluded because of the aircraft carrier.

The Washington Naval Treaty of 1922, signed by the great powers as an arms control measure after World War I, allowed each of the major signatories to convert two of their existing capital ships to carriers of no more than 33,000 tons. Newly constructed carriers could displace no more than 27,000 tons. No carrier was permitted guns of more than 8 inches, about half the caliber of a modern World War II battleship. In fact, the conversions made by the United States (*Lexington* and *Saratoga*) and Japan (*Akagi* and *Kaga*) exceeded the treaty limit on displacement. The new carriers built by these nations during the 1930s (*Yorktown* and *Enterprise*, and *Hiryu* and *Soryu*) adhered to the 27,000-ton limit, however. Britain converted two World War I–era light battle cruisers, HMS *Courageous* and HMS *Glorious*, to carriers, then began construction on a new carrier, HMS *Ark Royal*, in 1935.

A new prewar naval treaty, concluded at London in 1936, placed more stringent size limitations on new carriers—23,000 tons maximum—but simultaneously removed all restrictions on the number of carriers a signatory might build. Britain's Royal Navy introduced the Illustrious class of 23,000-ton carriers. The United States did not build any more new carriers until the war had begun, an event that rendered the 1936 treaty restrictions moot. The U.S. Essex class displaced 27,500 tons, could carry more than 100 aircraft, and served as the main fleet carriers of the Pacific during the war. Also during the war, the United States began construction of the mammoth 45,000-ton *Midway*, with innovative armored flight decks. These ships were not completed before the war ended, however.

In addition to the principal carriers, the United States, Britain, and Japan also deployed light carriers, ranging from about 9,000 tons to 20,000 tons, which were designed for quick construction. These combatant nations also deployed escort carriers, displacing about 7,000 to 17,000 tons, intended to protect merchant convoys from submarine attack. While some light and escort carriers were designed from the keel up, many were converted from light cruisers (in the case of light carriers) and merchant hulls (in the case of escort carriers). Indeed, Britain's Royal Navy added flight decks to some tankers and grain transports, allowing them to serve as flight platforms without eliminating their original cargo role. These ships, few in number, were designated merchant aircraft carriers, or MACs.

The United States, Japan, and Britain had the major aircraft carrier fleets in the war. However, Germany, Italy, and Canada also possessed carriers. Even the Netherlands had a single ship.

U.S. CARRIER FLEET

LANGLEY (1922)
First U.S. carrier, converted from U.S.S. *Jupiter*, a collier
Displacement: 11,500 tons
Length: 542 feet
Beam: 65 feet
Draft: 18 feet 11 inches;
Top speed: 15 knots
Complement: 468; guns: four 5-inch guns and 55 AA guns.

Langley was converted to a seaplane tender during 1936–37 and, early in World War II, was assigned to American-British-Dutch-Australian forces assembling in Indonesia. She was sunk by Japanese air attack on February 27, 1942.

LEXINGTON and *SARATOGA* (both 1925)
Displacement: 36,000 tons (standard); 47,700 tons (full)
Complement: 2,951 (*Lexington*), 3,373 (*Saratoga* in 1945)
Length: 888 feet
Beam: 106 feet
Draft: 24 feet 1.5 inches
Aircraft: 75
Guns: eight 8-inch, 12 5-inch AA, and four 6-pounder saluting guns; *Saratoga* (in 1945): eight 5-inch AA, 24 40-mm AA Bofors, 16 20-mm AA
Power plant: G.E. turbines, electric drive, 4 screws. S.H.P.: 180,000, 16 boilers
Top speed: 33.25 knots

RANGER (1933)
Fleet carrier
Displacement: 14,500 tons
Complement: 1,788
Length: 769 feet
Beam: 80.1 feet

Draft: 19.7 feet
Aircraft: 86
Guns: eight 5-inch, 38 caliber dual-purpose and 40 smaller guns
Power plant: geared turbines, two shafts, S.H.P.: 53,500, six boilers
Top speed: 29.4 knots

ENTERPRISE and YORKTOWN (both 1936)
Fleet carriers
Displacement: 19,900 tons (standard); 25,500 tons (full)
Complement: 2,919
Length: 809.5 feet
Beam: 114 feet (maximum)
Draft: 28 feet (mean)
Aircraft: 89 (if necessary, could carry 100+)
Guns: eight 5-inch, 38-caliber dual-purpose; 16 1.1-inch AA machine guns, and 16 smaller machine guns
Power plant: geared turbines, four shafts, S.H.P.: 120,000, nine boilers
Top speed: 34 knots

HORNET (1940)
Fleet carrier
Displacement: 19,000 tons (standard); 29,100 tons (full)
Complement: 2,919
Length: 827.5 feet
Beam: 114 feet
Draft: 29 feet
Aircraft: 87 (if necessary, could carry 100+)
Guns: eight 5-inch, 38-caliber dual-purpose; 16 1.1-inch AA machine guns; 30 20-mm AA machine guns; and nine 0.5-inch machine guns
Power plant: geared turbines, four shafts, S.H.P.: 120,000, nine boilers
Top speed: 34 knots

WASP (1939)
Fleet carrier
Displacement: 14,700 tons; 20,450 ton, (full)
Complement: 2,367
Length: 741.3 feet

Beam: 80.9 feet
Draft: 28 feet
Aircraft: 80
Guns: eight 5-inch, 38-caliber; 16 1.1 inch AA; and 30 20-mm AA
Power plant: two-shaft Parsons turbines, S.H.P.: 75,000, six boilers
Top speed: 29.5 knots

SAIPAN and WRIGHT (both 1945)
Light carriers
Displacement: 14,500 tons; 20,000 tons (full)
Complement: 1,500
Length: 683 feet 7 inches
Beam: 76 feet 9 inches
Aircraft: 48
Guns: four 5-inch, 38-caliber; 40 40-mm AA; and 25 20-mm AA
Power plant: geared turbines, four shafts, S.H.P.: 120,000, Babcock & Wilcox boilers
Top speed: 33 knots

ESSEX CLASS (24 ships, 1940–1944)
Fleet carriers
Displacement: 27,100 tons; 33,000 tons (full)
Complement: 3,240
Length: 888 feet
Beam: 93 feet
Draft: 29 feet
Aircraft: 82 (if necessary, could carry 103)
Guns: 12 5-inch, 38 caliber; 72 40-mm AA quadrupled; 52 20-mm AA quadrupled
Power plant: geared turbines, four shafts, S.H.P.: 150,000, eight boilers
Top speed: 33 knots

INDEPENDENCE CLASS (9 ships, 1941–1943)
Light carriers
Displacement: 11,000 tons; 14,300 tons (full)
Complement: 1,569
Length: 618 feet
Beam: 71.5 feet
Draft: 20 feet
Aircraft: 45

Guns: two 5-inch AA; 16 40-mm AA Bofors; 40 20-mm AA Bofors
Power plant: geared turbines, four shafts. S.H.P.: 74,600, Babcock & Wilcox boilers
Top speed: 31.5 knots

COMMENCEMENT BAY CLASS (19 ships, 1944–1945)

Escort carriers
Displacement: 18,908 tons; 21,397 tons (full)
Complement: 1,066
Guns: two 5-inch, 36 40-mm, and 20 20-mm AA guns
Aircraft: 33
Power plant: geared turbines, two shafts, S.H.P.: 13,500
Top speed: 19 knots

SANGAMON CLASS (4 ships, 1940–1942)

Escort carriers (converted from oilers)
Displacement: 12,000 tons
Complement: 1,000+
Length: 556 feet
Beam: 75 feet
Draft: 30 feet
Aircraft: 34–36
Guns: one or two 5-inch, 51-caliber; eight 40-mm AA; 15 20-mm AA
Power plant: geared turbines, two shafts, S.H.P.: 13,500
Top speed: 18 knots

CASABLANCA CLASS (37 ships, 1943–1944)

Escort carriers
Displacement: 6,730 tons; 10,200 tons (full)
Complement: 800
Length: 498.6 feet
Beam: 80 feet
Draft: 19.7 feet
Aircraft: 40
Guns: one 5-inch, 38-caliber; 24 20-mm AA; some vessels added: eight 40-mm AA and 24 20-mm AA
Power plant: Skinner unaflow engines, two shafts, I.H.P.: 11,200
Top speed: 18 knots

BOGUE CLASS (10 ships, 1942–1943)

Escort carriers
Displacement: 7,800 tons (*Prince William*, 8,300 tons)
Complement: 650
Length: 494 feet (*Prince William*, 492 feet)
Beam: 65.5 feet
Draft: 23.4 feet
Aircraft: 21
Guns: one or two 5-inch, .51-caliber; 16 40-mm Bofors; 20 20-mm Oerlikon
Power plant: Westinghouse geared turbines, two shafts, B.H.P.: 8,500
Top speed: 16 knots

MIDWAY CLASS (3 ships, completed after the war)

Displacement: 45,000 tons; 55,000 (full)
Complement: 4,085
Length: 968 feet
Beam: 136 feet (maximum)
Draft: 32 feet 9 inches
Aircraft: 137
Guns: 18 5-inch, 54-caliber; 84 40-mm AA quadrupled; 82 20-mm AA
Power plant: Geared turbines, four shafts, S.H.P.: 200,000, 12 boilers
Top speed: 33 knots

BRITISH CARRIER FLEET

ARGUS (1917)
Britain's first carrier, a modified ocean liner
Displacement: 14,450 tons (standard); 15,750 tons (full)
Complement: 373
Length: 565 feet
Beam: 68 feet
Draft: 21 feet
Aircraft: about 20
Guns: six 4-inch AA; four 3-pounders; four machine guns; 10 Lewis guns
Power plant: Parsons turbines, four screws, S.H.P.: 20,000, 12 boilers
Top speed: 20.2 knots

EAGLE (1918)
Converted from a battleship
Displacement: 22,600 tons (standard); 26,500 tons (full)
Complement: 1,100
Length: 667 feet
Beam: 105.6 feet (maximum)
Draft: 24 feet (mean)
Aircraft: about 20
Guns: nine 6-inch, 50-caliber; five 4-inch AA; 36 smaller guns
Power plant: Brown-Curtis geared turbines, S.H.P.: 50,000, 32 small-tube boilers
Top speed: about 24 knots

HERMES (1918)
Britain's first ship designed expressly as an aircraft carrier
Displacement: 10,850 tons (standard); 12,950 tons (full)
Complement: 1,000
Length: 598 feet
Beam: 90 feet over flight deck
Draft: 18.75 feet (mean)
Aircraft: about 20
Guns: six 5.5-inch, 50-caliber; three 4-inch AA; 26 smaller guns
Power plant: Parsons all-geared turbines, S.H.P.: 40,000, two screws, Yarrow or Babcock boilers
Top speed: about 25 knots

FURIOUS (1916)
Converted from a cruiser
Displacement: 22,500 tons (standard); 28,450 tons (full)
Complement: 1,100
Length: 786.3 feet
Beam: 89.7 feet
Draft: 21.6 feet (mean); 25 feet (maximum)
Aircraft: 33
Guns: ten 5.5-inch AA; six 4-inch AA; 50 smaller guns
Power plant: Brown-Curtis all-geared turbines, four shafts, H.P.: 90,000, 18 boilers
Top speed: 31 knots

COURAGEOUS CLASS (2 ships, converted in 1924–1928)
Converted from cruisers
Displacement: 22,500 tons; about 26,500 tons (full)
Complement: 1,215
Length: 786.3 feet
Beam: 81 feet
Draft: 22.6 feet (mean), 26 feet (maximum)
Aircraft: about 45
Guns: 16 4.7-inch; four 3-pounders; 50 smaller guns
Power plant: Parsons geared turbines, four shafts, H.P.: 90,000, 18 boilers
Top speed: about 31 knots

ARK ROYAL (1937)
Fleet carrier
Displacement: 22,000 tons; about 27,720 tons (full)
Complement: 1,575
Length: 800 feet
Beam: 94.7 feet
Draft: 27.7 feet
Aircraft: about 65
Guns: 16 4.5-inch; 42 2-pounders; 32 .50-inch AA
Power plant: Parsons geared turbines, three shafts, S.H.P.: 102,000, six Admiralty three-drum boilers
Top speed: 31 knots

ILLUSTRIOUS CLASS (4 ships, 1939)
Fleet carriers
Displacement: 23,000 tons (standard); 25,500 tons (full)
Complement: 1,400
Length: 753,5 feet
Beam: 95.75 feet
Draft: 24 feet
Aircraft: about 45 (*Indomitable,* about 65)
Guns: eight 4.5-inch dual-purpose; various 40-mm and 20-mm AA
Power plant: Parsons geared turbines, three shafts, S.H.P.: 110,000 6 three-drum boilers
Top speed: 31 knots

IMPLACABLE CLASS (2 ships, 1942)
Fleet carriers
Displacement: 26,000 tons; 31,300 tons (full)
Complement: 1,800
Length: 766 feet 2 inches
Beam: 95 feet 9 inches
Draft: 29 feet 4 inches
Aircraft: about 70
Guns: 16 4.5-inch dual-purpose; 77 to 79 40-mm, 20-mm, and 2-pounder pompoms
Power plant: Parsons geared turbines, S.H.P. 110,000, four shafts. eight Admiralty three-drum boilers
Top speed: 32 knots

UNICORN (1943)
Light carrier
Displacement: 14,750 tons (standard); 20,300 tons (full)
Complement: 1,050
Length: 640 feet
Beam: 90 feet
Draft: 19 feet
Aircraft: 35
Guns: eight 4-inch; two multiple pompoms
Power plant: Parsons geared turbines, two shafts, S.H.P.: 40,000, four Admiralty three-drum boilers
Top speed: 24 knots

COLOSSUS CLASS (7 ships, 1943–1944)
Displacement: 13,190 tons (except *Theseus* and *Triumph*, 13,350 tons)
Complement: 840–854
Length: 694 feet 6 inches
Beam: 80 feet 3 inches
Draft: 23 feet
Aircraft: 39–44
Guns: four 3-pounders; 24 2-pound pompoms; 19 40-mm AA; various 40-mm and 20-mm AA
Power plant: Parsons geared turbines. two shafts, S.H.P.: 40,000, four Admiralty three-drum boilers
Top speed: 25 knots

ARCHER CLASS (23 ships, 1939–1940)
Escort carriers
Displacement: 14,500 tons
Length: 492 feet
Beam: 69.5 feet
Draft: 28.5 feet
Guns: 4-inch AA; 4-mm AA; Bofors machine guns; several 20-mm guns

NAIRANA CLASS (2 ships, 1943–1944)
Escort carriers
Displacement: 13,500 tons
Complement: 700–728
Length: 524 feet
Beam: 68 feet
Draft: 25 feet
Aircraft: 20
Guns: two 4-inch AA; 16 2-pounder pompoms; eight 40-mm AA; 16 20-mm AA
Power plant: Diesels, two shafts, B.H.P.: 10,700
Top speed: 16 knots

RULER CLASS (14 ships, 1942–1943)
Escort carriers
Displacement: 9,000 tons
Complement: 373
Length: 514 feet
Beam: 80 feet

JAPANESE CARRIER FLEET

HOSYO (*HOSHO*) (1921)
Experimental prototype
Displacement: 7,470 tons (standard); 10,000 tons (full)
Complement: 550
Length: 551 feet 6 inches
Beam: 59 feet
Draft: 20.4 feet
Aircraft (1942 configuration): 11 (could carry 26)
Guns (1941 configuration): eight double 25-mm AA
Power plant: two sets geared turbines, eight Kanpon boilers, S.H.P.: 30,000, two shafts
Top speed: 25 knots

AKAGI (1927)

Converted battleship

Displacement: 36,500 tons (standard); 41,300 tons (full)

Complement: 1,340

Length: 855.3 feet

Beam: 102.9 feet

Draft: 28.7 feet

Aircraft: 91

Guns: four 8-inch, 50-caliber in 2 twin mountings (as built); six 8-inch, 50-caliber in six single mountings (as built); 10 8-inch, 50-caliber in 10 single mountings (after reconstruction in mid-1930s); 12 4.7-inch, 45-caliber in six twin mountings (as built); 16 5-inch, 40-caliber in eight twin mountings (after reconstruction in mid-1930s); more than 25 25-mm (after reconstruction in mid-1930s); 30 13.2-mm machine guns

Power plant: geared turbines, S.H.P.: 133,000, four shafts

Top speed: 28.5 knots

KAGA (1928)

Converted battleship

Displacement: 38,200 tons (standard); 43,650 tons (full)

Complement: 2,016

Length: 812.6 feet

Beam: 108.75 feet

Draft: 31.3 feet

Aircraft: 90

Guns: four 8-inch, 50-caliber in two twin mountings (as built); six 8-inch, 50-caliber in six single mountings (as built); 10 8-inch, 50-caliber in 10 single mountings (after mid-1930s reconstruction); 12 4.7-inch guns in six twin mountings (as built); 16 5-inch guns in eight twin mountings (after reconstruction in mid-1930s); more than 25 25-mm (after reconstruction in mid-1930s); 30 3.2-mm machine guns

Power plant: geared turbines, D.H.P.: 91,000, four shafts

Top speed: 25 knots

RYUZYO (1933)

Light carrier

Displacement: 12,732 tons (standard); 14,000 tons (full)

Complement: 924

Length: 590.7 feet

Beam: 68.5 feet

Draft: 23.3 feet

Aircraft: 36

Guns: four double 5-inch; 12 double 25-mm AA

Power plant: Geared turbines, Kanpon boilers, S.H.P.: 65,000, two shafts

Top speed: 25 knots

SORYU (1937)

Fleet carrier

Displacement: 18,800 tons

Complement: 1,100

Length: 746.5 feet

Beam: 69.1 feet

Draft: 25 feet

Aircraft: 71

Guns: 12 5-inch AA; 28 25-mm; 15 13.2-mm machine guns

Top speed: 34 knots

HIRYU (1939)

Fleet carrier

Displacement: 20,250 tons

Complement: 1,100

Length: 745.1 feet

Beam: 73.3 feet

Draft: 25.9 feet

Aircraft: 73

Guns: 12 5-inch AA; 31 25-mm guns; 15 13.2-mm machine guns

Speed: 34 knots

SHOKAKU and *ZUIKAKU* (both 1939)

Fleet carriers

Displacement: 25,675 tons (standard); 32,000 tons (full)

Complement: 1,660

Length: 844.1 feet

Beam: 85.4 feet

Draft: 29.1 feet
Aircraft: 75–85
Guns: eight double 5-inch; 96 25-mm guns; six 28-barrel AA rocket launchers
Power plant: Geared turbines, four shafts, S.H.P.: 160,000
Top speed: 34 knots

ZUIHO (1940) and SHOHO (1942)
Light carriers
Displacement: 11,262 tons (standard); 14,200 tons (full)
Complement: 785
Length: 674.3 feet
Beam: 59.9 feet
Draft: 21.7 feet
Aircraft: 30
Guns: eight 5-inch guns in four twin mounts; eight 25-mm; 56 25-mm (by 1944); 12 13.2-mm; eight 28-barrel rocket launchers (by 1943)
Power plant: geared turbines, S.H.P.: 52,000, two shafts.
Top speed: 28 knots

TAIYO, (1941), UNYO (1942), and CHUYO (1942)
Light carriers
Displacement: 17,800 tons (standard)
Complement: 800
Length: 591.4 feet
Beam: 73.1 feet
Draft: 26.3 feet
Aircraft: 27
Guns: eight 5-inch AA (*Taiyo*, eight 4.7-inch); eight (later, 22) 25-mm; 10 13-mm
Power plant: Geared turbines, S.H.P.: 25,200, two shafts
Top speed: 21 knots

DYUNYO and HIYO (both 1942)
Fleet carriers
Displacement: 24,500 tons; 26,950 tons (full)
Complement: 1,224
Length: 719.7 feet
Beam: 87.7 feet

Draft: 26.9 feet
Aircraft: 53
Guns: 12 5-inch AA; up to 24 25-mm; six 28-barrel rocket launchers (from 1944)
Power plant: Geared turbines, S.H.P.: 56,000, two shafts
Top speed: 25 knots

CIYODA (1943) and CITOSE (1944)
Light carriers
Displacement: 11,190 tons
Complement: 800
Length: 631.7 feet
Beam: 68.3 feet
Draft: 24 feet
Aircraft: 30
Guns: eight 5-inch; 30 25-mm (65 25-mm in 1944); 12 13.2-mm
Top speed: 29 knots

TAIHO (1944)
Fleet carrier
Displacement: 29,300 tons (standard); 37,270 tons (full)
Complement: 2,150
Length: 855 feet
Beam: 90.1 feet
Draft: 30.6 feet
Aircraft: 60
Guns: 12 3.9-inch, 65-caliber; 71 25-mm, 60-caliber machine guns; 22 13-mm, 76-caliber machine guns
Power plant: geared turbines, S.H.P.: 180,000, four shafts
Top speed: 33 knots

UNRYU (1944), AMAGI (1944), KATSURAGI (1944), ASO (1944), IKOMA (1944), and KASAGARI (canceled)
Fleet carriers
Displacement: 17,250 tons (standard); 22,534 tons (full)
Complement: 1,459
Length: 745.1 feet
Beam: 72.2 feet
Draft: 25.9 feet

Aircraft: up to 70

Guns: 12 5-inch, 40-caliber in six twin mountings; six 4.7-inch, 45-caliber; 89 25-mm; 22 3.2-mm machine guns

Power Plant: Geared turbines, four shafts; *Unryu, Amagi,* S.H.P.: 152,000; *Aso, Katsuragi,* S.H.P.: 104,000

Top speed: *Unryu, Amagi,* 34 knots; *Aso, Katsuragi,* 32 knots

GERMAN CARRIER

Germany completed only one carrier before the war and halted construction of another. Neither was ever used in combat:

GRAF ZEPPELIN **(1938) and** *PETER STRASSER* **(never completed)**

Displacement: 19,250 tons

Length: 820.3 feet

Beam: 88.5 feet

Draft: 18.3 feet

Aircraft: 40

Guns: 16 5.9-inch; 10 4.1-inch AA; 22 37-mm AA

Power plant: geared turbines

Top speed: 32 knots

ITALIAN CARRIER

During 1941–43, the Italian navy converted a 1926 liner to a carrier. Work was suspended in 1943, and the ship was never used in combat.

AQUILA **(1943)**

Displacement: 23,350 tons (standard); 27,800 tons (full)

Length: 759 feet 2 inches

Beam: 96 feet 6 inches

Draft: 24 feet

Complement: 1,420

Aircraft: 36

Guns: eight 5.3-inch single-mounted; 12 65-mm single-mounted; 132 20-mm sextuple-mounted

Power plant: Belluzzo geared turbines, eight Thorneycroft boilers, four shafts, S.H.P.: 140,000

Top speed: 30 knots

CANADIAN CARRIERS

The Royal Canadian Navy operated two carriers during World War II.

WARRIOR **and** *MAGNIFICENT* **(both 1944)**

Light carriers

Displacement: 13,500 tons (*Warrior*), 14,000 tons (*Magnificent*)

Complement: 1,350

Length: 693.4 feet

Beam: 112.5 feet

Draft: 23 feet

Aircraft: 40

Guns: 24 2-pounders; 19 40-mm AA (Bofors)

Power plant: Parsons geared turbines, two shafts. S.H.P.: 40,000, four Admiralty 3-drum boilers

Top speed: 25 knots

Further reading: Belote, James H. *Titans of the Seas: The Development and Operations of Japanese and American Carrier Task Forces during World War II.* New York: HarperCollins, 1975; Brown, David. *Carrier Operations in World War II.* Annapolis, Md.: Naval Institute Press, 1998; Degan, Patrick. *Flattop Fighting in World War II: The Battles between American and Japanese Aircraft Carriers.* Jefferson, N.C.: McFarland, 2003; Kilduff, Peter. *U.S. Carriers at War.* Annapolis, Md.: United States Naval Institute Press, 1997; McGowen, Tom. *Carrier War: Aircraft Carriers in World War II.* Breckenridge, Colo.: 21st Century Books, 2001; Preston, Anthony. *Aircraft Carriers of World War II.* Rochester, U.K.: Grange Books, 1998.

Alamein, Battles of El

El Alamein was a small Egyptian settlement along the railroad that followed the coastline of the Mediterranean Sea. About 60 miles west of Alexandria, it was the scene of two important battles in the WESTERN DESERT CAMPAIGNS.

The first was a defensive stand by the Eighth British Army under General CLAUDE JOHN AYRE AUCHINLECK against ERWIN ROMMEL's Panzer Army Africa during July 1–4, 1942. Auchinleck succeeded in checking Rommel's advance at Ruweisat Ridge. Admirers of Auchinleck attribute this success to the

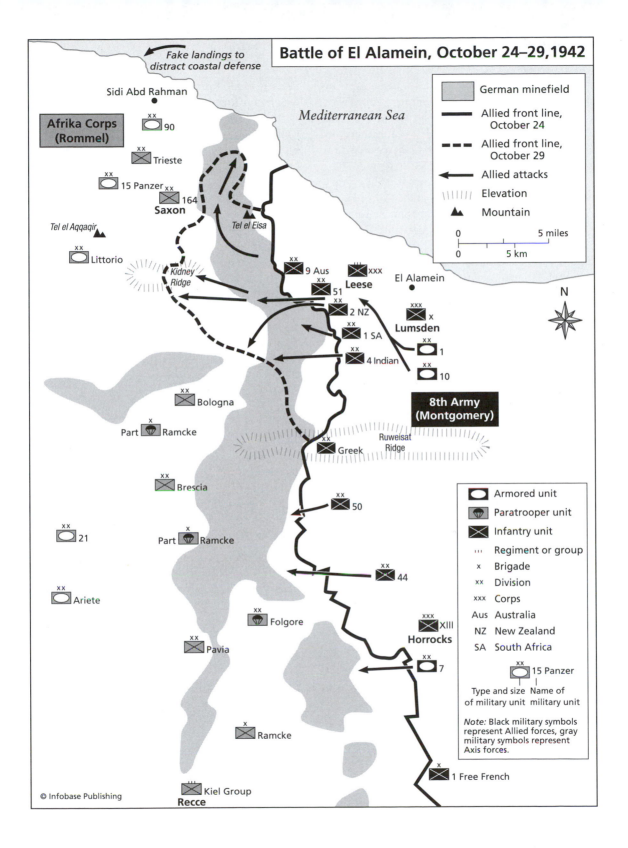

Battle of El Alamein, October 24–29, 1942

Fake landings to distract coastal defense

Afrika Corps (Rommel)

Sidi Abd Rahman

Mediterranean Sea

90

Trieste

15 Panzer

164

Saxon

Tel el Aqqaqir

Littorio

Tel el Eisa

Kidney Ridge

9 Aus

51

Leese

El Alamein

2 NZ

Lumsden

1 SA

1

4 Indian

10

Bologna

Part Ramcke

Brescia

21

Part Ramcke

Ariete

Folgore

Pavia

Ramcke

Kiel Group
Recce

8th Army (Montgomery)

Greek

Ruweisat Ridge

50

44

XIII
Horrocks

7

1 Free French

© Infobase Publishing

Legend

	German minefield
————	Allied front line, October 24
- - - -	Allied front line, October 29
←	Allied attacks
‖‖‖	Elevation
▲▲	Mountain

Scale: 0 — 5 miles / 0 — 5 km

N

	Armored unit
	Paratrooper unit
	Infantry unit
‖‖	Regiment or group
x	Brigade
xx	Division
xxx	Corps
Aus	Australia
NZ	New Zealand
SA	South Africa

15 Panzer

Type and size of military unit / Name of military unit

Note: Black military symbols represent Allied forces, gray military symbols represent Axis forces.

general's skillful determination, whereas his many detractors simply claim that Rommel's troops were exhausted and that the German withdrawal was strategic rather than an actual defeat. In either case, the first engagement at El Alamein resulted in a British defensive triumph.

The prize Rommel wanted was the Suez Canal, and he was determined to strike at the British Eighth Army again. In September 1942, he attacked at Alam Halfa but was again repulsed. After this, BERNARD LAW MONTGOMERY, the new commander of the Eighth, decided to seize the initiative and to attack Rommel. Montgomery wanted to take advantage of the fact that Rommel had temporarily assumed a defensive position west of El Alamein because he was short of fuel and other supplies. On the move, Rommel was a most formidable opponent, well deserving of his sobriquet "the Desert Fox," but in a situation of static defense, Montgomery reasoned, he was just as vulnerable as any other commander. Worse for Rommel, he had fallen ill and, on September 23, left his 15th Panzer Division to go on sick leave. (He would not return until October 25, two days after the Second Battle of El Alamein had begun.) Before he left, however, he prepared very strong defenses, the most important of which was a dense minefield consisting of some half a million antitank devices. Interspersed among this so-called Devil's Garden were many more antipersonnel mines. Additionally, well aware that the Italian units that now formed part of his force were markedly inferior and therefore vulnerable, Rommel ensured that they were stiffened ("corseted") by German units, which, he hoped, would put some iron into this most dubious of allies. Finally, Rommel gave great thought to the deployment of his defenses, carefully dividing his troops and tanks into six groups ideally placed to detect and repulse attacks from virtually any direction.

Formidable as Rommel had made his position, Montgomery enjoyed significant superiority of numbers: 195,000 troops versus 104,000, of which slightly more than half were Italians; 1,029 medium tanks versus 496; 1,451 antitank guns versus 800; 908 pieces of mobile artillery versus 500; and 530 aircraft versus 350, although an additional 150 were available from some distance. Montgomery

devised Operation Lightfoot to pierce Rommel's defenses from the north using four infantry divisions deployed across a 10-mile front. These units would also clear a route through the minefield to accommodate the next wave, the armored divisions of X Corps. This unit was to assume a defensive position at a place called Kidney Ridge, directly facing the panzers. Here the British tanks were to hold in order to fend off any German counterattack while the infantry pressed its offensive, which Montgomery called a "crumbling" process. Only after the infantry had prevailed would X Corps be ordered to assume offensive operations.

The brilliance of Montgomery's plan was that his attack fell precisely where it was least expected: on the most strongly defended German sector. To reinforce this element of surprise, Montgomery employed smaller units to make diversionary attacks in the more obvious sectors. Montgomery saw the battle as a three-stage contest, beginning with what he called a break-in, followed by a "dogfight," and then a break-out. He anticipated that the break-in, benefitting from surprise, would be over quickly, but that the dogfight would consume at least a bloody week of "crumbling."

Surprise was, in fact, achieved, but the break-in attack, beginning on the night of October 23–24, was slowed by the sheer depth of Rommel's defenses. As a result, X Corps armor did not pass beyond "Oxalic," the code name for the initial line of infantry advance, which was well short of the Kidney Ridge objective. Nevertheless, supporting units, including the 9th Australian Division and the 1st Armored Division, made excellent headway, the 1st Armored flanking the Kidney Ridge position. Rommel responded with intensive counterattacks, which were, at significant cost, contained. In the meantime, the grim and protracted process of infantry "crumbling" continued, supported by ceaseless Allied aerial and artillery bombardment. This relentless action was coordinated with the more mobile advance of the Australians, who continually drew off Rommel's best forces, leaving the weaker Italian units exposed and opening up a weak spot against which Montgomery planned to launch a second attack, code named Supercharge.

Viewed from the perspective of hindsight, it is obvious that the Second Battle of El Alamein was going very well for the British. However, at the time, progress fell well behind Montgomery's original optimistic timetable, and WINSTON CHURCHILL began to despair of its success, especially when Montgomery removed divisions from the front to use in the Supercharge attack. It was not until the night of November 1–2 that Supercharge was launched, north of Kidney Ridge, by the New Zealand Division and other infantry units. These forces quickly penetrated this weakened sector, Rommel's elite troops having had to engage the Australians. Now Montgomery was ready to unleash the full fury of his armored units, in the face of which Rommel understood he had been defeated.

Rommel sent a coded message to ADOLF HITLER on November 2 advising him that without fuel, he was in danger of being wiped out. He announced his intention to withdraw to Fuka. British ULTRA code-breaking intelligence intercepted Rommel's communications and allowed Montgomery to deploy units to intercept the retreat. However, Montgomery subsequently received a decrypt of Hitler's order in reply to Rommel, denying the German commander permission to withdraw. In obedience, Rommel accordingly attempted to organize a stand, but it was too late to halt all the retreating units. At dawn of November 4, the 51st Highland Division overran the hasty defenses of what was now a mixed retreat and a partial stand. Hitler, belatedly, released Rommel to withdraw his army in toto, and an epic pursuit across the Libyan desert got under way. Montgomery would claim some 30,000 prisoners of war for casualties to the Eighth British Army and associated units of 13,560 killed or wounded. The vaunted Panzer Army Africa was badly beaten and barely intact, the Italians were shattered, and the turning point in the Western Desert Campaigns had been reached. This persuaded the VICHY GOVERNMENT in North Africa to begin cooperating with the Allies.

Further reading: Bierman, John, and Colin Smith. *The Battle of Alamein: Turning Point, World War II.* New York: Viking, 2002; Bierman, John, and Colin Smith. *War Without Hate: The Desert Campaign of 1940–1943.* New York: Penguin, 2004; Bungay, Stephen. *Alamein.* London: Aurum, 2003; Latimer, Jon. *Alamein.* Cambridge, Mass.: Harvard University Press, 2002.

Alam el Halfa, Battle of

Commencing on August 31, 1942, a month after the German Panzerarmee Afrika was checked at the BATTLES OF EL ALAMEIN, Alam el Halfa was ERWIN ROMMEL's final attempt to break through to the Nile valley in continuation of his frustrated drive across Cyrenaica and western Egypt. Leading the British Eighth Army, Gen. SIR BERNARD LAW MONTGOMERY deployed his forces near Alam el Halfa, an east-west ridge astride Rommel's path of advance. On the first day of battle, three German armored divisions defeated British forces, turning the Eighth Army's southern flank. However, Montgomery rallied an extraordinary defense—considered by military historians a textbook example of the modern repulse—and, coordinating armor and infantry with air and artillery support, stopped Rommel at the ridge. By the fourth day of the battle, Rommel had been forced into retreat, redeploying his armor in a defensive line running north and south. The battle was over by September 7, by which time Rommel, checked again, had lost significantly more than the 1,750 casualties (killed and wounded) suffered by the Eighth Army.

Historically, the victory here is significant as an outstanding instance of ground-air coordination and the exploitation of intelligence. British breakthroughs in the decryption of the enemy's coded communication proved crucial to the triumph at Alam el Halfa. On August 15, 1942, Rommel, using the ENIGMA CIPHER, transmitted his plan of action—to effect a breakthrough to Cairo and the Nile—to ADOLF HITLER. Within 48 hours, Montgomery had a decrypted translation of this message. Learning that Rommel intended to move south around the end of the British line, then strike the British flank to cut off the Eighth Army from its base and supplies, Montgomery was able to deploy his forces at the Alam el Halfa ridge and check the German advance.

Further reading: Hinsley, F. H., and Alan Stripp, eds. *Codebreakers: The Inside Story of Bletchley Park.* New York: Oxford University Press, 2001; McCarthy, Peter, and Mike Syron. *Panzerkrieg: The Rise and Fall of Hitler's Tank Divisions.* New York: Carroll & Graf, 2002. Stewart, Adrian. *Eighth Army's Greatest Victories: Alam Halfa to Tunis 1942–1943.* London: Leo Cooper, 1999; Stewart, Adrian. *North African Victory: The 8th Army from Alam Halfa to Tunis, 1942–43.* London: Penguin UK, 2002.

Albania

Situated on the western Balkan Peninsula at the Strait of Otranto, the southern entrance to the Adriatic Sea, Albania was, at the outbreak of World War II, a monarchy with a population of a little more than 1 million. During the reign of Albania's King Zog I, Italy became increasingly influential in the country, and on April 7, 1939, the forces of Italy's Benito Mussolini invaded. Resistance was minimal, but two battalions plus a handful of tribal irregulars delayed the Italian advance for 36 hours, just long enough to allow Zog, his queen, and their infant son to flee the country. The royal family took up residence in exile in Britain for the duration of the war, although the British government did not recognize Zog as a head of state; in an attempt to discourage Italy from joining forces with Germany, Britain had, in fact, recognized Italy's annexation of Albania.

Italy's king, Victor Emmanuel III, was proclaimed king of Albania, and a fascist regime was installed in the Albanian capital, Tirana. Early in 1940, the British government supported an abortive Albanian revolt against the Italians. The revolt was led from Kosovo, a Yugoslav province. When Yugoslavia was invaded by the Germans in April 1941, however, Kosovo was transferred to Albanian control, and the revolt collapsed. It was renewed during late 1942 and early 1943 under college professor and communist activist Enver Hoxha, who, encouraged by Yugoslavia's (Josip Broz) Tito, formed a partisan movement. British Special Operations Executive (SOE) operatives coordinated with and supported partisan activities beginning in 1943. Thus, a resistance movement was in place when, in July 1943, Mussolini was overthrown. A general insurrection began. Two of the five Italian divisions occupying Albania obeyed the orders of the new Italian prime minister, Marshal Pietro Badoglio, and joined the partisans. The other three divisions either joined German units or dispersed, and by fall 1943, Albanian guerrillas had seized most of the equipment of the Italian garrison.

Albania was liberated from Italian occupation—only to be overrun by German forces, which instituted a regime of fierce reprisals against the partisans. This had the effect of terrorizing the civilian population, which largely withdrew its support from the resistance. The Germans, however, were more interested in neutralizing Albania than in dominating it. Mehdi Frasheri, a former governor of Jerusalem under the Ottoman Empire, formed a neutral government, which held sway over the cities and the coastal plain. The rest of the country fell prey to a variety of warlords and guerrilla leaders.

Enver Hoxha decided that the time was ripe to exploit the chaos and suppress the anticommunist traditionalist resistance known as the Balli Kombetar. This prompted the Germans to align with the resistance in order to exacerbate internal discord. Through the Tirana government, Germany helped to supply the Balli Kombetar with equipment and weapons. This incited the partisans to accuse the Ballists of collaboration with Germany. The result was outright civil war, which so destabilized Albania that by early 1944, Germany had regained dominion over the coast and the major cities. At this point in the war, the Allies understood that Albania could provide a means by which the German armies could retreat, intact, from Greece. Britain once again worked to encourage and aid Albanians to abandon internecine warfare and to harass the common enemy, the German army. To this end, Britain began supplying the principal Albanian factions with arms. Unfortunately, these were used not against the Germans but to perpetuate the civil war, which expanded. When the German army began its retreat through Albania in September 1944, the tribal leader Abas

Kupi, aided by members of the Balli Kombetar (who were on the run from communist forces), did harass retreating troops, but civil war made it impossible for British agents to incite all of northern Albania against them.

As World War II wound down, the communists gained ascendancy in Albania, and all British operatives were evacuated to Italy, together with Abas Kupi and the major leaders of the Balli Kombetar. Immediately after the surrender of Germany, Albania, under Hoxha, withdrew into extreme anti-Western isolation and remained politically and economically isolated under the dictatorship of the Albanian Communist Party as the People's Republic of Albania, which became, in 1976, the People's Socialist Republic of Albania.

Further reading: Fischer, Bernd Jurgen. *Albania at War, 1939–1945.* Lafayette, Ind.: Purdue University Press, 1999; Tomes, Jason. *King Zog of Albania: Europe's Self-Made Muslim Monarch.* New York: New York University Press, 2004; Vickers, Miranda, and James Pettifer. *Albania: From Anarchy to Balkan Identity.* New York: New York University Press, 2000.

Aleutian Islands Campaign

The Aleutians are a chain of 14 small islands and about 55 islets separating the Bering Sea from the main part of the Pacific Ocean. The chain extends in an arc that runs southwest then northwest for some 1,100 miles from the tip of the Alaska Peninsula to Attu Island, westernmost island of the chain. At the time of World War II, the Aleutians were part of the U.S. territory of Alaska and are today part of the state of Alaska.

In June 1942, Japanese forces occupied Attu and Kiska, which is the next of the larger islands to the southeast. The principal reason for this occupation was to draw U.S. assets of the Pacific Fleet away from the central Pacific in order to facilitate the planned Japanese attack on Midway Island. Secondarily, Japanese strategists had some fear that American forces might use the Aleutians as a forward base from which bombing raids or even an invasion might be launched against Japan. Thanks

to U.S. intelligence, which had broken the Japanese ULTRA codes, U.S. Pacific Fleet commander admiral CHESTER NIMITZ was apprised of the Japanese plan and quickly acted to send his most powerful forces to intercept and attack the Japanese fleet under Admiral YAMAMOTO ISORUKU in the vicinity of Midway and also formed Task Force 8 (also known as the North Pacific Force) to defend the Aleutians. Of necessity, this force was composed of older ships, some of which were even obsolescent, including five cruisers, 14 destroyers, and six submarines in addition to 85 USAAF aircraft, all under the command of Rear Admiral Robert Theobald. Opposing his force were elements of the Japanese 5th Fleet, under Vice Admiral Hosogaya Boshiro. These were divided into three groups: Rear Admiral Kakuta Kakuji's Mobile Force (built around two light carriers and a seaplane carrier), the Kiska Occupation Force, the Adak-Attu Occupation Force, and various supply ships, escorted by Hosogaya's flagship, the heavy cruiser *Nachi,* and two destroyers. For a time, a portion of the Midway Force was detached as a fourth group, the Aleutian Screening Force, but soon had to return to Midway. For both sides, the weather was often a more formidable foe than any human adversary. The islands were almost perpetually shrouded in fog and drenched in icy rain, both hazards to navigation and flight. Stiff storms were also a regular feature of life in the region.

In an effort to force Nimitz to divide his fleet, Kakuta's Mobile Force twice raided a U.S. base at Dutch Harbor, Unalaska Island, in the eastern Aleutians. Kakuta also raided U.S. destroyers in Makushin Bay but was repulsed. These actions induced Theobald to conclude that the Japanese intended to use the Aleutians as a base from which to invade the American mainland. As a result, he deployed his forces to intercept the Japanese supply transports, which thereby allowed Japanese troops to land on Attu (June 5, 1942) and Kiska (June 7) entirely unopposed. Indeed, the Americans were unaware of the landings until June 10. In response, U.S. bombers raided Kiska to little effect. Attu was beyond the bombers' range, and naval bombardment of the island proved largely ineffective.

On August 27, the Japanese began transferring most of the Attu garrison to Kiska, only to reoccupy and reinforce Attu in October. Whenever weather allowed, operations were conducted against these garrisons over a nine-month period, both by naval bombardment and by USAAF bombers operating from crude air strips constructed on Adak and Amchitka. These operations did remarkably little to cause attrition among the garrisons, but they did contain the Japanese forces on the islands, and in March 1943 the Americans were prepared to mount a major assault designed to drive the Japanese forces out.

An initial thrust fell short on March 26, when bad weather prevented crucial air support of the naval Battle of the Komandorski Islands. The battle did not dislodge the Attu garrison, but it did prevent the 2,630-man Japanese force from receiving reinforcements before 11,000 troops of the 7th U.S. Infantry Division landed on Attu on May 11, 1943. This assault is of historic tactical significance because air support was provided by an escort carrier—the first time in the war this vessel type was used for this purpose. Under the command of Colonel Yamazaki Yasuyo, the Japanese offered their customarily fierce resistance. Cornered and confined to the island's last high ground by May 29, they launched an all-out BANZAI CHARGE, so stunning that it quickly overran two command posts and a medical station before it was finally checked. After a final attack was crushed on May 30, most of the Japanese survivors committed suicide rather than submit to capture. Of the 2,630-man garrison, a mere 28 prisoners were taken. American casualties were 600 killed and 1,200 wounded.

In January 1943, Vice-Admiral THOMAS KINKAID succeeded Theobald as commander of

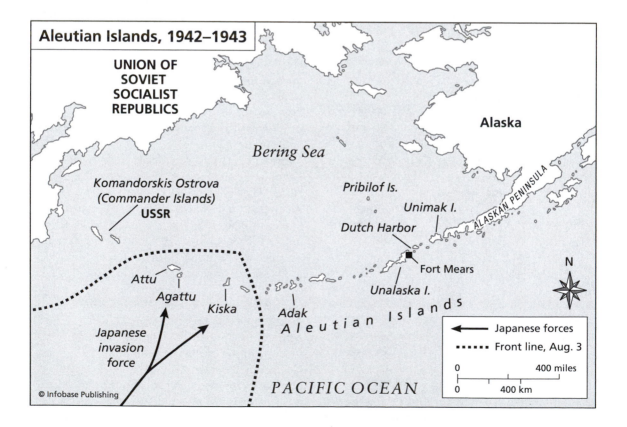

Aleutian Islands, 1942–1943

Task Force 8. With Attu retaken, he decided to attack Kiska, beginning by setting up a destroyer blockade and ordering aerial and naval bombardment of the garrison. However, during the foggy night of July 28–29, as navy ships refueled, 5,183 Japanese troops and civilians were stealthily evacuated. Despite aerial reconnaissance, the evacuation remained undetected, and, on August 15, 1943, 34,000 U.S. and Canadian troops were landed, unopposed, of course. Within a few days, they discovered that the island was deserted.

Regarded by many as a sideshow to the greater struggles in the Pacific theater, the Aleutian Campaign was a harsh and dangerous mission, in which the elements posed as great a danger as the enemy. For the Japanese, the campaign was a costly disaster that diverted assets better used elsewhere. Although invasion via the Aleutians was almost certainly never a real danger, it was nevertheless vitally important for American morale to rid U.S. soil of an invader. Moreover, the Aleutian Campaign served as a proving ground for amphibious assault tactics, which would be applied in more desperate combat farther south.

Further reading: Feinberg, Leonard. *Where the Williwaw Blows: The Aleutian Islands—World War II.* Longmont, Colo.: Pilgrims' Process, 2003; Garfield, Brian. *The Thousand-Mile War: World War II in Alaska and the Aleutians.* Fairbanks: University of Alaska Press, 1996; Mitchell, Robert J., Sewell T. Tyng, and Nelson L. Drummond, comps. *The Capture of Attu: A World War II Battle As Told by the Men Who Fought There.* Lincoln: University of Nebraska Press, 2000; Perras, Galen Roger. *Stepping Stones to Nowhere: The Aleutian Islands, Alaska, and American Military Strategy, 1867–1945.* Annapolis, Md.: United States Naval Institute, 2003.

Alexander, Harold (1891–1969) *Allied commander of the Mediterranean theater*

Harold Rupert Leofric George Alexander was born in London but was raised on the Ulster estate of his wealthy English-Irish family. Educated at Sand-

hurst, Britain's elite military academy, he earned renown for his service with the Irish Guards on the western front in World War I. Rising to divisional command by 1939, he was in charge of the rear guard at the DUNKIRK EVACUATION, and the success of that desperate operation owed much to his leadership. Posted to India after Dunkirk, it fell to Alexander to command the British withdrawal from Burma, another lifesaving action for which Alexander is generally given credit, although much of the success of the withdrawal was due to the brilliant and unconventional generalship of WILLIAM SLIM.

In 1942, Alexander was named to the theater command of the Middle East, replacing CLAUDE JOHN AYRE AUCHINLECK after the disaster of Tobruk. He was fortunate to have as his immediate field subordinate SIR BERNARD LAW MONTGOMERY, who had just taken over command of the Eighth British Army. The two commanders worked together very effectively, Alexander providing Montgomery with the logistical and strategic support necessary to turn the tide in North Africa by defeating the forces of ERWIN ROMMEL at the BATTLES OF EL ALAMEIN in the Tunisia campaign. This success allowed Montgomery's Eighth Army to link up with the newly landed U.S. forces of OPERATION TORCH.

The unified American and British forces were under the overall command of American general DWIGHT D. EISENHOWER, with Alexander assuming responsibility for the next phase of the Anglo-American effort in Sicily and mainland Italy. Alexander worked very effectively with Eisenhower, and, like him, was wholly committed to making the Anglo-American alliance an operational success. However, he often experienced friction with the egocentric Montgomery and, indeed, sometimes had trouble managing other subordinates, both British and American. Some considered his persona as a gentleman commander outmoded in a 20th-century war.

Late in 1943, Alexander was given command of the Mediterranean theater and successfully pushed for the liberation of Rome in June 1944. His inability to govern the actions of Fifth U.S. Army com-

British field marshal Harold Alexander (left) with U.S. major general Troy Middleton *(National Archives and Records Administration)*

mander MARK CLARK, however, contributed to the escape of most of the German army, which withdrew largely intact from Rome. This resulted in a heartbreaking impasse short of the Po River Valley, so that the final Allied push through Italy was not completed until April 1945, weeks before the war in Europe ended.

After the war, Alexander became governor general of Canada, serving in that office from 1946 to 1952. Created an earl in 1952, he became WINSTON CHURCHILL's minister of defence, serving from 1952 to 1954.

Further reading: Alexander, Harold. *The Alexander Memoirs, 1940–45.* London: Cassel, 1962; Nicolson, Nigel. *Alex: The Life of Field Marshal Earl Alexander of Tunis.* New York: Atheneum, 1973.

Algeria

Located in North Africa, Algeria, at the time of World War II, was a French colony of 6.6 million, about 1 million of whom were European. With the fall of France and the creation of the VICHY GOVERNMENT, General MAXIME WEYGAND became the Vichy delegate-general of Algeria in September 1940. Essentially dictator of the colony, Weygand, in conformity to Nazi and Vichy policy, acted against Jews by stripping them of their French citizenship. He also acted harshly against native nationalist Muslims. This had the effect of radicalizing hitherto moderate Muslims, thereby laying the foundation for the Algerian nationalist movement that would greatly erode France's hold on the colony during the postwar years and ultimately result in independence after a costly insurrection in 1962.

In December 1941, Weygand was replaced by General Alphonse Juin, who turned against Vichy to side with the Allies, whose forces occupied Algeria in November 1942, early in the NORTH AFRICAN CAMPAIGN. This proved especially fateful for the Algerian independence movement. Free French authorities reconstituted Algerian military units as part of the FREE FRENCH FORCES. This, in combination with the presence of the Allies in Algeria, emboldened Ferhat Abbas, one of the moderate Muslims radicalized during the Weygand regime, to present an independence manifesto to Governor General Marcel Peyrouton. He not only accepted the manifesto, but acknowledged the pressing need for change. However, in June 1943, the Committee for National Liberation appointed General Georges Catroux to replace Peyrouton. Although he introduced a number of liberal measures into the colonial government, he blocked the movement for immediate independence. Violent insurrection did not erupt during the war, but V-E DAY did unleash the pent-up rage of Algerian nationalists, who rose in armed protest.

During World War II itself, several native Tirailleur (sharpshooter) regiments fought in Europe against the invading Germans before the fall of France. Another two Tirailleur units fought on the side of the Allies during the campaign in North Africa.

Further reading: Curtis, Michael. *Verdict On Vichy: Power and Prejudice in the Vichy-France Regime.* New York: Arcade Books, 2003; Moorehead, Alan. *The Desert War: The North African Campaign, 1940–1943.* London: Sphere, 1968; Paxton, Robert O. *Vichy France.* New York: Columbia University Press, 2001; Stone, Martin. *The Agony of Algeria.* New York: Columbia University Press, 1997; Stora, Benjamin. *Algeria, 1830–2000: A Short History.* Ithaca, N.Y.: Cornell University Press, 2001.

Alsace-Lorraine

Located on FRANCE's border with GERMANY, Alsace-Lorraine encompasses two predominantly German-speaking regions (in German, Elsass and Lothringen), which have frequently been disputed between France and Germany. The provinces fell to France in the late 17th century and early 18th, but as a result of France's humiliating defeat in the Franco-Prussian War of 1871, all of Alsace and the northern portion of Lorraine (mainly Moselle) were annexed to the new German empire, the Second Reich, which emerged as a result of the war. Under German rule, the province was called Reichsland, the inhabitants were given the choice of remaining in the province or leaving for France (45,000 left), and the Second Reich set to work exploiting the rich coal fields of Lorraine, producing coke that fed the fires of Germany's great arms manufacturers. In Lorraine were forged many of the weapons with which World War I would be fought.

Germany's defeat in World War I resulted in France's recovery of Alsace and Lorraine, but the fall of France in 1940 meant that once again the territory would be annexed by Germany—this time to the Third Reich. The provinces were designated two *Gaue* (administrative districts) of the Reich, each governed by a *Gauleiter,* or manager, who answered directly to Berlin. In contrast to 1871, the French-speaking minority of Alsace-Lorraine were not asked to choose their nationality. Some 200,000 individuals were summarily evicted from the region and sent into occupied France with only such property as they could carry.

Different treatment was given to certain other groups within the two *Gaue.* Jews and others deemed by the Reich undesirable were deported to CONCENTRATION AND EXTERMINATION CAMPS, imprisoned, or summarily executed. French soldiers who had been born in the region and who had been made prisoners of war during the BATTLE OF FRANCE were, for the most part, conscripted into the WEHRMACHT. A significant number of pro-German soldiers thus conscripted were subsequently transferred from the Wehrmacht into the WAFFEN SS. Most of the rest of the region's inhabitants, though they spoke German, identified more readily with

France and certainly did not embrace Nazism. These individuals were subject to typical iron-fisted Nazi rule, and the resistance was never as active in the former Alsace-Lorraine as in central and southern France. This gave the German overlords a substantially free hand in exploiting the rich coking coal reserves of the region, which, as was the case before World War I, once again fed the furnaces of the German arms industry. After the German surrender in 1945, Alsace-Lorraine reverted to French control, and the region's inhabitants all became, quite automatically, French citizens once again.

Further reading: Engler, Richard E. *The Final Crisis: Combat in Northern Alsace, January 1945.* Bedford, Penn.: Aegis Consulting Group, 1999; Goodfellow, Samuel Huston. *Between the Swastika and the Cross of Lorraine: Fascisms in Interwar Alsace.* DeKalb: Northern Illinois University Press, 1999; Shaw, Michael. *History, People, and Places in Eastern France, Alsace, Lorraine, and the Vosges.* Bourne End, U.K: Spurbooks, 1979; Zaloga, Stephen J. *Lorraine 1944: Patton vs. Manteuffel.* London: Osprey, 2000.

"Amerika" bomber

In contrast to Britain and the United States, Germany never produced in quantity long-range heavy BOMBER AIRCRAFT. Nevertheless, the Reichsluftfahrtministerium, the Reich Aviation Ministry, in charge of aircraft production for the Luftwaffe from 1933 to the end of the war in 1945, sought to develop a very large, very-long-range bomber capable of a round-trip transatlantic mission to strike the United States from Germany. Early in the war, before the United States even became a combatant, the ministry requested design proposals from all the major German aircraft manufacturers. The goal was to create what was generally dubbed the "Amerika" bomber.

Messerschmidt, Focke-Wulf, and Junkers all submitted designs that were quite sound and quite conventional, similar to the heavy bombers of the United States and Great Britain. Focke-Wulf's Fw 300 was based on the existing Fw 200 Condor, a four-engine bomber often used as a transport and capable of a 2,210-mile range. Junkers's Ju 390 was a development from the Ju 290, an existing four-engine maritime patrol craft, transport, and bomber, capable of an impressive range of 3,843 miles. In contrast to these two companies, Messerschmidt presented the Me 264, an entirely new design. Like the other proposed craft, the Me 264 was driven by four engines and was designed to make a round-trip flight from Germany to New York City. One prototype was built, but the aircraft never went into production because the Reich Aviation Ministry announced its selection of the Ju 390. This aircraft was first prototyped in 1943 and had a range in excess of 6,000 miles. The largest aircraft ever built in Germany—112 feet, 2 inches long and with a wingspan of 165 feet, 1 inch—the prototype flew on October 20, 1943, and performed so well that the ministry ordered 26 of the craft. None, however, were produced before the "Amerika" project and the Ju 390 were cancelled in 1944.

Although ultimately abortive, the "Amerika" bomber project also elicited a number of proposals for highly forward-looking, radical designs. The aeronautical scientist Dr. Eugen Sänger was well known in German aviation circles for his speculative articles on rocket-powered aircraft. At the behest of the German government, he worked at a secret aerospace laboratory in Trauen to design and build an aircraft to be called *Silverbird.* Propelled by liquid-fuel rocket engines and piloted by a single aviator, the *Silverbird* was to be capable of great speed and of attaining low Earth orbit. For the "Amerika" program, Sänger modified the *Silverbird* design as an aircraft capable of supersonic flight in the stratosphere. Often called the *Sänger Amerika Bomber* and, alternatively, the *Orbital Bomber* and the *Atmosphere Skipper,* the aircraft design featured a flat fuselage, a very advanced lifting body design that allowed for short, wedge-shaped wings. This reduced drag and the structural hazards inherent in supersonic large-wing designs. As designed, the main rocket engine produced 100 tons of thrust and was flanked by a pair of smaller rocket engines. The pilot was housed in a pressurized cockpit. A single, centrally located bomb bay would have held just one 8,000-pound bomb, perhaps laced with nuclear material to create what today would be called a "dirty bomb" (not a true atomic weapon, but a bomb packed with conventional explosive and designed to scatter radioactive material to contaminate its target area). Because the aircraft would operate far beyond the range of any interceptors, it was fitted with no defensive armament.

Sänger imagined that his rocket plane would take off down a 1.9-mile-long rail, boosted by a rocket-powered sled developing 600 tons of thrust for 11 seconds. Assuming a 30° angle, the aircraft would attain an altitude of 5,100 feet at 1,149 miles per hour *before* its own main rocket engine would be fired for eight minutes. This would bring the craft to a speed of 13,724 miles per hour and loft it to an altitude in excess of 90 miles. At this point, the accelerating aircraft would descend due to gravity, but, in so doing, would encounter denser atmosphere at about 25 miles, which would cause it to skip back up, much as a stone does when it is skimmed across a lake. The flight would consist of a series of gradually shorter skips, until the plane would glide back into the lower atmosphere and, ultimately, to a landing, having covered, according to Sänger's calculations, 14,594 miles.

Sänger's project was cancelled in the summer of 1941, shortly after the German INVASION OF THE SOVIET UNION. The German military, it was decided, could not afford to expend time, effort, and cash on theoretical and experimental work. After the war, Sänger worked briefly for the French Air Ministry.

Further reading: Georg, Friedrich. *Hitler's Miracle Weapons: Secret Nuclear Weapons of the Third Reich and Their Carrier Systems;* Havertown, Penn.: Casemate, 2003; Herwig, Dieter, and Heinz Rode. *Luftwaffe Secret Projects: Ground Attack and Special Purpose Aircraft.* Leicester, U.K.: Aerofax Midland, 2003; Hyland, Gary, and Anton Gill. *Last Talons of the Eagle: Secret Nazi Technology Which Could Have Changed the Course of World War II.* London: Headline Books, 2000; Neufeld, Michael J. *The Rocket and the Reich: Peenemunde and the Coming of the Ballistic Missile Era.* New York: Free Press, 1994.

amphibious warfare

Military assault involving a combination of sea and land operations, usually with the object of invading enemy territory from the sea, amphibious warfare played a role of unprecedented importance during World War II. While the earliest amphibious assault recorded in Western history is the Battle of Marathon, 490 B.C.E., and the U.S. Army's first true amphibious operation was Winfield Scott's 1847 assault on Veracruz during the U.S.-Mexican War, it was not until World War II that the tactics and techniques reached maturity. The Allies brought the doctrine of amphibious warfare to an especially high state of development, both in the Atlantic (culminating in OPERATION OVERLORD, including the NORMANDY LANDINGS [D-DAY]) and the Pacific, where the intricate integration of air, sea, and land forces was the key element of victory. As fully developed, Allied amphibious warfare doctrine delivered large numbers of specially trained troops, together with equipment, vehicles, and other materiel via

Marines disembark during the Guadalcanal Campaign. *(National Archives and Records Administration)*

LANDING CRAFT onto the hostile beach, which, typically, had been "prepared" or "softened up" by naval and aerial bombardment. During the landing itself, naval and air elements provided supporting fire to suppress enemy resistance. In some cases, as in Overlord, airborne troops preceded the seaborne landings. These troops worked behind enemy lines to draw defenders away from the beaches and to disrupt lines of supply, reinforcement, and communications.

Early in the war, from 1939 to 1942, amphibious warfare was largely a matter of improvisation, but as the central importance of this assault mode became increasingly apparent, Allied strategists and tacticians rapidly produced a specialized doctrine, which divided assault forces into distinct functional components. The *assault formations* were the vanguard. They were "combat loaded" on their assault craft, their supplies and equipment stowed so they could be unloaded precisely in the order in which they were needed. Thus, the first elements of the invasion would be delivered complete and ready to fight from the moment they hit the beach. Behind the assault formations came the *follow-up formations,* whose equipment was "tactically loaded," that is, stowed in a way that compromised between combat loading and loading to maximize space aboard transport craft. Finally came the *build-up formations,* which could afford to deploy more slowly and, therefore, had their equipment loaded exclusively to make the most use of available transport space.

Assault formations, which were landed from landing craft or even smaller amphibious vehicles, were divided into "flights," each flight a complete military unit, which were in turn subdivided into "waves." It was deemed of critical importance to keep each wave together and to coordinate the landing of the waves in the proper, most effective tactical order. This ensured that troops would not be landed piecemeal, vulnerable to defeat in detail by the defenders.

After the assault formations had gained a toehold on the beach, the follow-up formations were deployed to supply the strength necessary to secure the beachhead. Once this was accomplished, the assault and follow-up formations began their push inland, and the build-up formations were deployed on the secure beachhead to begin the full-scale exploitation of the amphibious attack: the invasion proper.

While it was the Allies who brought amphibious warfare to near perfection during World War II, it was the Japanese, during the SINO-JAPANESE WAR (which preceded World War II and, ultimately, was absorbed into it), who first landed troops from specially designed ships at Tientsin in 1937. In contrast to Allied amphibious doctrine, which was led by the navy, Japanese doctrine was driven by the army, with the Imperial Navy playing very much a supporting role. Also key to Japanese amphibious warfare doctrine was the night landing. The Japanese saw amphibious assault less as invasion than as infiltration preparatory to invasion, and they prized the cover of darkness. In consequence, Japanese doctrine emphasized almost rigidly mechanical coordination of large elements to avoid confusion in a low-visibility environment. This proved a double-edged sword, because, while highly disciplined, Japanese amphibious formations lacked individual initiative and were therefore less able to cope with unexpected resistance or other exigencies.

Japan's theater of war, which encompassed the vast Pacific, required extensive amphibious operations. Germany's theater, more concentrated on the European continent, demanded fewer amphibious operations. Nevertheless, the April 1940 invasion of Norway showed that German forces were indeed capable of highly effective amphibious warfare. However, WEHRMACHT leaders never became comfortable with amphibious warfare and failed to integrate it into their doctrine. This may well explain the general hesitation to invade England early in the war. Similarly, the Soviet Red Army was slow to develop amphibious doctrine but, by late in the war, had formed and trained some 40 "naval infantry" brigades—perhaps 340,000 men—for amphibious warfare.

Notable amphibious warfare operations during World War II include, in the African and European theaters: the DIEPPE RAID of August 1942, the landings of the NORTH AFRICAN CAMPAIGN in

November 1942, the landings of the SICILY CAM-PAIGN in July 1943 (which made extensive use of amphibious vehicles), the landings preceding the BATTLE OF SALERNO in September 1943, and, of course, the D-day landings of Operation Overlord. Pacific amphibious assaults were many, the most notable coming at the GUADALCANAL CAMPAIGN and in the ALEUTIAN ISLANDS CAMPAIGN, the MARSHALL ISLANDS CAMPAIGN, the Philippines, and the OKINAWA CAMPAIGN. In the Pacific, it was the UNITED STATES MARINE CORPS that made the great advances in amphibious warfare, including the employment, beginning in January 1944, of a specialized HQ (headquarters) ship to coordinate assault operations. The marines also perfected new techniques of preparatory artillery fire, including bombardment from positions much closer inshore than before and the use of unoccupied islets as bases for artillery positions. Some landing craft were specially modified to fire rockets, which supplemented bombardment by naval guns. The marines also used specially trained underwater demolition teams to clear obstacles, both natural and artificial, thereby enabling landing craft to approach beaches much more closely and expanding the role of amphibious vehicles. Despite these advances, Pacific landings were almost invariably resisted fiercely, even suicidally. Typically, only badly wounded Japanese defenders were ever taken prisoner. The rest fought to the death. The final amphibious operation of the war actually took place after the Japanese surrender, when British troops landed unopposed near Port Swettenham, Malaya, to retake that former British possession.

Further reading: Alexander, Joseph H. *Storm Landings: Epic Amphibious Battles in the Central Pacific.* Annapolis, Md.: United States Naval Institute Press, 1997; Bartlett, Merrill L., ed. *Assault from the Sea: Essay on the History of Amphibious Warfare.* Annapolis, Md.: United States Naval Institute Press, 1993; Dwyer, John B. *Commandos From The Sea: The History of Amphibious Special Warfare In World War II and The Korean War.* Boulder, Colo.: Paladin Press, 1998; Speller, Ian, and Christopher Tuck. *Amphibious Warfare: Strategy and Tactics.* St. Paul, Minn.: MBI Publishing, 2001.

Anami Korechika (1887–1945) *Japanese general, vice minister of war, and militarist*

Anami was an important Japanese general, who, as vice minister of war in the cabinet of Prince KONOYE FUMIMARO, led the faction that elevated General TOJO HIDEKI to power as Japan's generalissimo in October 1941. In the field, Anami commanded the Eleventh Army in China and the Second Area Army in Manchukuo. When portions of the Second Area Army were transferred to New Guinea in November 1943, Anami took command there. He was appointed inspector general of the army in December 1944 as well as chief of the army's aviation department, then was made minister of war in the cabinet of SUZUKI KANTARO in April 1945. Unlike many of his military colleagues, Anami was not an uncompromising fanatic. Well aware that Japan had lost the war militarily, he struggled with what he saw as irreconcilable alternatives: continued war and certain total destruction versus a logical, humane peace, which, however, entailed a dishonorable surrender. His emotional and moral dilemma prompted him, on the one hand, to express sympathy for those who vowed to defy Emperor HIROHI-TO's decision to surrender, yet, on the other hand, to refuse to support any action against the decision. This lack of support ensured the failure of the attempted coup d'état by a cabal of junior officers, who, on August 14, 1945, raided the royal palace to find and destroy the emperor's recorded surrender message, which was to be broadcast the next day. As soon as he had confirmed the failure of the coup, Anami committed *seppaku,* the ritual suicide of the traditional Japanese warrior. The note he left explained that his death had been offered in expiation of the army's sins and failures. In the absence of Anami's leadership, the army quietly acquiesced in Japan's surrender.

Further reading: Edgerton, Robert B. *Warriors of the Rising Sun: A History of the Japanese Military.* Boulder, Colo.: Westview Press, 1999; Manning, Paul. *Hirohito: The War Years.* New York: Bantam, 1989; Toland, John. *The Rising Sun: The Decline and Fall of the Japanese Empire, 1936–1945.* New York: Modern Library, 2003.

Anderson, John (1882–1958) *British home secretary and civil defense advocate*

John Anderson (later Sir John Anderson, first viscount Waverley) was born at Eskbank by Dalkeith in Midlothian and was educated at the University of Edinburgh and Leipzig University. After service in World War I, Anderson entered the British government as chair of the Board of the Inland Revenue in 1919 and then as governor of Bengal, India, in 1932. He was elected to Parliament as member for the Scottish Universities in 1938 and served as home secretary in the cabinet of NEVILLE CHAMBERLAIN from late 1938 to 1940. Almost immediately upon assuming his cabinet post, and with war clouds rapidly gathering, Anderson proposed the design, manufacture, and distribution of domestic bomb shelters. The result was the ANDERSON SHELTER, which proved highly successful during THE BLITZ.

From 1943 to 1945, Anderson served as chancellor of the exchequer in the cabinet of WINSTON CHURCHILL. His most enduring contribution in this post was the introduction of the Pay-as-You-Earn (PAYE) system for income tax payment. Anderson was knighted in 1919 and raised to the peerage in 1952.

Further reading: Colvin, Ian Goodhope. *The Chamberlain Cabinet: How the Meetings in 10 Downing Street, 1937–9, Led to the Second World War; Told for the First Time from the Cabinet Papers.* London: Gollancz, 1971; Cross, Arthur, Fred Tibbs, and Mike Seaborne. *The London Blitz.* London: Dirk Nishen Publishing, 1987; Johnson, David. *The London Blitz: The City Ablaze, December 29, 1940.* New York: Stein & Day, 1982.

Anderson shelter

The Anderson shelter was a personal bomb shelter used by some 2.25 million London families during THE BLITZ. The shelter consisted of 14 sheets of corrugated iron or corrugated galvanized steel, which were assembled to form a shell 6 feet high, 4.5 feet wide, and 6.5 feet long. The structure was assembled in a 4-foot-deep pit dug in the family garden, then it was covered with at least 15 inches of earth.

A London family enters an Anderson shelter. *(Museum of the City of London)*

The idea of domestic air raid shelters is generally attributed to Home Secretary JOHN ANDERSON, who had responsibility for civil defense. On November 10, 1938, Anderson tasked William Paterson, an engineer, with designing a suitable shelter. Working with his business partner, Oscar Carl Kerrison, Paterson produced a blueprint for the shelter within a week of receiving the assignment. A week after this, he delivered a prototype. It is said that Anderson "tested" the prototype by jumping on it with both feet. However, he also turned the prototype and blueprints over to the Institution of Civil Engineers, which supplied expert evaluation by three engineers, David Anderson (no relation to John), Bertram Lawrence Hurst, and Sir Henry Jupp. This committee approved of the design, and the Anderson shelter went into production. By February 28, 1939, the first shelters were delivered to householders in Islington, North London. They were issued free to all households earning less than £250 annually and at a charge of £7 for those with higher incomes. Before production and issuance of the shelters was discontinued in mid-1941 due to a shortage of iron and steel, 2.25 million had been erected. They were of use only to families who had a garden in which to erect and bury them.

Although families did their best to make the shelters comfortable, even installing bunk beds in them, they were cold and subject to flooding. Yet they were quite effective during The Blitz, affording protection from everything except a direct hit.

Further reading: Bungay, Stephen. *The Most Dangerous Enemy: A History of the Battle of Britain.* London: Aurum Press, 2002; Cross, Arthur, Fred Tibbs, and Mike Seaborne. *The London Blitz.* London: Dirk Nishen Publishing, 1987; Johnson, David. *The London Blitz: The City Ablaze, December 29, 1940.* New York: Stein & Day, 1982; Nixon, Barbara Marion. *Raiders Overhead: A Diary of the London Blitz.* London: Scholar Gulliver, 1980.

Anschluss

The German word for "joining together" or "union," *Anschluss* describes the March 1938 political union of Austria with Germany that resulted when ADOLF HITLER unilaterally annexed Austria to the Third Reich. *Anschluss* was originally an initiative of an Austrian political party, the Social Democrats, who agitated for it from 1919 (after the Austrian government rejected it) through 1933, at which point Hitler's sudden elevation to power made the prospect of *Anschluss* look more like a German conquest of Austria, and even the Social Democrats withdrew their support for it. However, in July 1934, Austrian and German Nazis collaborated in an attempted coup d'état, which would have brought *Anschluss.* When the coup collapsed, a stern right-wing government ascended in Austria. Through authoritarian measures, lingering agitation for *Anschluss* was suppressed. However, in February 1938, Hitler invited Austrian chancellor Kurt von Schuschnigg to a meeting at Berchtesgaden, Hitler's Bavarian mountain retreat. There Hitler intimidated Schuschnigg into giving the Austrian Nazis a free hand. Returning to Austria, Schuschnigg repudiated his concessions to Hitler and determined to hold a plebiscite on national independence on March 13. Hitler, however, bullied Schuschnigg into canceling the plebiscite and resigning, with a final order to the Austrian army to refrain from resisting the Germans. When Austrian president Wilhelm Miklas then defiantly refused to appoint the Austrian Nazi ARTHUR SEYSS-INQUART to replace Schuschnigg as chancellor, Hitler's min-

ister HERMANN GÖRING ordered Seyss-Inquart to send a telegram requesting German military aid. This Seyss-Inquart refused to do. Undaunted, however, Göring arranged to have the telegram sent by a German agent stationed in Vienna. Thus armed with a fabricated request for "aid," Hitler invaded Austria on March 12. As Schuschnigg had ordered, no resistance was offered. Indeed, Austrians turned out to greet the German troops, which moved Hitler to annex Austria on the following day, March 13. In a gesture to legitimate the *Anschluss,* a thoroughly controlled plebiscite was held on April 10, which returned a 99.7 percent approval of the annexation. *Anschluss* was the first in a series of aggressive expansions that preceded and ultimately triggered World War II in Europe. As for Schuschnigg, he was imprisoned almost immediately after resigning and was not released until the war ended in May 1945.

Further reading: Lehr, David. *Austria Before and After the Anschluss.* Pittsburgh: Dorrance, 2000; Low, Alfred D. *The Anschluss Movement 1931–1938 and the Great Powers.* Boulder, Colo.: East European Monographs, 1985; Schuschnigg, Kurt. *The Brutal Takeover: The Austrian Exchancellor's Account of the Anschluss of Austria by Hitler.* London: Weidenfeld & Nicolson, 1971.

antiaircraft weapons

Air attack, including tactical attacks against ground troops, ground installations, and naval targets as well as strategic attacks against cities, factories, and other ostensibly civilian targets as well as major military installations, was a major component of combat in World War II. Accordingly, the warring powers made extensive use of a variety of antiaircraft weapons. The antiaircraft artillery (AAA) of this period consisted of conventional artillery, sometimes improved to achieve greater muzzle velocity and, therefore, to hurl projectiles higher, and improved ammunition. Some ammunition was not only designed to maximize velocity and, therefore, altitude, but also to explode in the air, broadcasting hundreds of large, jagged-edged metal fragments, or shrapnel. This meant that a fired round did not actually have to hit an enemy aircraft to destroy it—and a distant, fast-flying target was extremely difficult to hit—but that the aircraft had merely to fly through a shrapnel burst to be damaged, perhaps fatally. The German term for antiaircraft artillery was *Fliegerabwehrkanonen,* typically contracted to the word *flak.* This contracted term was adopted by the Allies as well, not used to describe the artillery pieces themselves, but the bursting shells fired against the aircraft. Flak was most effective when fired by many massed antiaircraft guns, which thus created a "field" of flak into which enemy bombers had to fly. The likelihood of inflicting damage was multiplied in such flak barrage fields. Allied air crews often spoke of flying through flak thick enough to walk across. While flak was intended first and foremost to disable or shoot down aircraft, it was also effective directly against aircrews. Because of weight considerations, it was impossible to equip bombers with "flak-proof" armor, and many airmen were wounded or killed by pieces of flak (that is, shrapnel) that penetrated the fuselage or entered through windshields, cockpit canopies, and so on. Allied airmen were issued "flak jackets," heavy-fabric body armor, which afforded a degree of protection to vital organs. In 1944 alone, flak accounted for 3,501 American planes shot down, compared with about 600 shot down by fighter aircraft during this period.

Sighting and aiming (often called by artillerists "laying") were critical to antiaircraft defense. Early in the war, sights consisted of simple arrangements of concentric rings, which yielded little accuracy. More sophisticated optical sights were developed as the war continued, as was a rudimentary computer called a "predictor." This electromechanical device could be made to follow a target, calculating its course and speed as well as the projectile's direction and velocity with the object of predicting the future position where the two would actually meet. The predictor generated information on bearing and elevation, which was fed to the gun via a pair of motors, which, in turn, automatically adjusted bearing and elevation. Because the predictor was bulky and required a large generator as well as careful calibration to align the guns to coincide with the alignment of the predictor, this device was generally installed on more-or-less permanently emplaced guns. In the field, with mobile artillery, manual sighting ("open sights") were generally more practical, despite their shortcomings.

The single greatest advance in directing antiaircraft fire was RADAR, which was especially effective at night and in conditions of low visibility. Combined with powerful, long-range antiaircraft artillery, radar greatly extended the range of AAA fire, allowing gunners to commence firing—effectively—much earlier in an attack.

Another aid to laying fire accurately was provided by the ammunition itself. Tracers were elements within the ammunition designed to burn through to the explosive and detonate the fuse if the (nonflak) round failed to hit a target. This provided an explosion clearly visible from the ground, which aided gunners in adjusting their aim for subsequent rounds. By igniting the round in the sky, the tracer also ensured that the shell would not fall back to Earth, hitting friendly targets.

The term *antiaircraft artillery* generally refers to antiaircraft cannon, firing more-or-less heavy shells. These were used mostly to defend against large bombers making strategic attacks against cities and other substantial installations. To defend against tactical attack by lighter aircraft, including fighters, ground-attack aircraft, and fighter-bombers, *light antiaircraft artillery* was employed. These were essentially large-caliber machine guns, capable of firing many rounds per minute. Their range was limited, but they were effective against aircraft coming in low for tactical bombing or strafing attacks. Typically, tracer rounds were inserted into the ammunition supply (often at every eighth round), so that the gunner could more easily follow, direct, and adjust his stream of fire.

GREAT BRITAIN

Early in the war, London and other British cities were subject to massive German air raids, and so Great Britain developed and deployed an array of antiaircraft artillery. The most common early weapon, first produced in 1936 by the Bofors arms firm of Sweden, was a 40-mm gun commonly called the BOFORS GUN. The Bofors was very widely used, and it was manufactured under license by Austria, Belgium, Finland, France, Hungary, Italy, Norway, and Poland as well as by Great Britain. Those nations whose manufacturers did not license it merely copied it. Officially designated by the British the QF 40-mm AA gun, it was typically mounted on a mobile platform. It could throw a shell to an altitude of 8,400 feet.

In the course of the war, the main British AAA weapon became the QF 3.7-inch Mk III, which fired a 28-pound shell to an altitude of 32,000 feet, much more effective against the high-altitude bombers that raided London and other cities. Even heavier was the QF 4.5-inch AA Mk II, which fired a 54-pound shell to an altitude of 42,000 feet and, with automated ammunition handling, could fire faster than hand-loaded weapons. The Mk II was so heavy that it also served in coastal defense as an antiship weapon.

The British used a variety of light AAA, including the Swiss 20-mm Oerlikon and the American Maxson Mount, but the British firm Polsten produced the nation's own 20-mm piece, which could fire at an impressive 450 rounds per minute. Inexpensive to manufacture, the Polsten was produced and issued in great quantity for defense against low-level air attack.

See also ARTILLERY, BRITISH.

FRANCE

France was caught critically short of AAA at the outbreak of the war. Its most important weapon was the 25-mm Hotchkiss gun, which was used against ground as well as air targets. Although its rate of fire was rapid, its range was short, and it was not available in sufficient numbers to defend against Germany's massive tactical deployment of ground-attack aircraft during the BATTLE OF FRANCE.

See also ARTILLERY, FRENCH.

GERMANY

German AAA was extensively developed during World War II. Light AAA consisted of a miscellaneous host of machine gun weapons, but heavy AAA, designed to defend against the ruinous com-

bined strategic assault of British and American heavy bombers, came in five important versions.

The 20-mm Flak series consisted of many variations with a variety of mounts, but all were rapid-fire weapons on a par with the British Polsten. The 37-mm Flak came in even more varieties than the smaller 20-mm Flak, including naval mounts, towed mounts, and self-propelled versions. The gun could also be permanently mounted in static locations.

Germany's heavier AAA weapons included the Flak 38, Flak 40, and Flak 88. The Flak 38 fired a 105-mm shell to a ceiling of 7,218 feet. Its rate of fire was 420 to 480 rounds per minute. Too heavy to be transported readily, it was used in advanced stationary positions. The Flak 40 was a 128-mm weapon introduced in 1942. It fired twelve 26-pound shells per minute to an altitude of nearly 35,000 feet. Heaviest of all was the Flak 88, a gun of extreme versatility, which was used against ships and tanks as well as aircraft. Many weapons historians consider it the premier artillery piece of World War II. It lofted a 20-pound shell to 37,000 feet and was renowned for its extreme accuracy.

See also ARTILLERY, GERMAN.

ITALY

Notoriously weak in armor and artillery, Italy nevertheless fielded four significant AAA weapons. Two 20-mm guns served the light AAA function. The 20-mm Breda had the advantages of light weight and mobility, whereas the 20-mm Scotti, more numerous, was heavier but also had a high rate of fire.

Italy's most important heavy AAA weapon was the Cannone DA 75/46 C.A. Modello 34, which fired a 14-pound shell to altitudes in excess of 27,000 feet. Like the Cannone DA 90/53, which followed it, the DA 75/46 was plagued by production problems, which kept the numbers deployed quite small. German forces, however, thought enough of the 75/46 that they readily took it into their AAA arsenal.

See also ARTILLERY, ITALIAN.

JAPAN

World War II Japanese military doctrine emphasized rapid, highly mobile conquest. As a result, the nation produced virtually no heavy artillery and precious little antiaircraft artillery of note, relying instead on a miscellany of naval weapons and weapons captured from the Allies. The American bombers that attacked the Japanese mainland during 1944 and 1945 encountered far less flak than their colleagues flying against Germany.

See also ARTILLERY, JAPANESE.

SOVIET UNION

The Soviet Union produced some fine artillery, including the 85-mm AA Gun Model 1939, the nation's most important AAA weapon. The Model 1939 fired a 20-pound shell to 34,000 feet. As a result of the BATTLE OF STALINGRAD and subsequent Red Army victories, huge numbers of German 88-mm guns fell to the Soviets. These were used extensively to supplement the Model 1939 for fixed AAA defense.

See also ARTILLERY, SOVIET.

UNITED STATES

The principal U.S. AAA weapon was the MI 90-mm gun, which could fire a 23-pound shell to an altitude of 39,000 feet at an astounding rate of 27 rounds per minute. Ammunition was typically fitted with altimeter or radar proximity fuses for greater effectiveness. Between this behemoth and the light AAA Maxson Mount was the medium MI 37-mm AA gun, which could fire 120 37-mm rounds per minute to an altitude of 18,000 feet.

The Maxson Mount, the main U.S. light AAA weapon, consisted of four .50-caliber Browning machine guns mounted on an electrically driven pedestal. With the four guns ganged in this fashion, the Maxson could pour a stream of fire at the withering rate of 2,400 rounds per minute, more intense than any other AAA weapon. Even a marginally competent gunner could achieve excellent results, provided the attack aircraft drew within range.

See also ARTILLERY, U.S.

Further reading: Hogg, Ian V. *Allied Artillery of World War Two.* Ramsbur, U.K.: Crowood Press, 1998; Hogg, Ian V., ed. *The American Arsenal: World War II Official Standard Ordnance Catalog of Artillery, Small Arms,* *Tanks, Armored Cars, Anti-aircraft Guns, Ammunition, Grenades, Mines.* London: Greenhill, 2002; Hogg, Ian V. *British and American Artillery of World War II.* London: Greenhill, 2002; Hogg, Ian V. *German Artillery of World War Two.* London: Greenhill, 2002; Hogg, Ian V. *Twentieth-Century Artillery: 300 of the World's Greatest Artillery Pieces.* London: Friedman/Fairfax, 2001; Müller, Werner. *German Flak in World War II 1939–1945.* Atglen, Penn.: Schiffer, 1998.

antiarmor weapons

The tank was developed during World War I as a proposed answer to the trench warfare stalemate on the western front. Not only could the vehicles—when they worked—traverse trenches, their armor was impervious to machine gun and rifle fire. Although tanks were neither sufficiently numerous nor sufficiently reliable to make a decisive impact on combat in World War I, their potential had been demonstrated, and, in the early phases of World War II, the Germans used greatly improved tanks to stunning effect in the early BLITZKRIEG invasions. Antiarmor, or antitank, weapons rapidly emerged as of great importance in World War II. They were of two broad types: antitank artillery and infantry antitank weapons. A third category, the tank destroyer, is, in fact, a fast, lightly armored tank and is therefore treated in ARMOR, FRENCH; ARMOR, GERMAN; ARMOR, ITALIAN; ARMOR, JAPANESE; ARMOR, SOVIET; and ARMOR, U.S.

BRITISH ANTITANK ARTILLERY

The British fielded three major antitank guns, the Ordnance, Q.F., 2 pdr, Ordnance, Q.F., 6 pdr, and Ordnance, Q.F., 17 pdr.

The Q.F. 2 pdr fired a two-pound, 40-mm round at 2,626 feet per second, which was capable of piercing 2.08 inches of armor at 500 yards. It had the advantage of being small and light and was usually towed by a small truck or jeep. Its great failing as a weapon was that it had been designed pursuant to 1934 specifications, when tank armor was relatively thin. By the time the war began, the gun was obsolescent, if not obsolete, as German tanks were very heavily armored. Nevertheless, the gun saw service throughout the war, especially in Far East theaters against Japanese tanks, which were much more lightly armored.

Two years after the Q.F. 2 pdr was ordered, work was begun on the design of a heavier weapon. However, the Q.F. 6 pdr was not deployed until late in 1941. Yet it was a case of better late than never. The new weapon (which would go through four iterations, from Mk. I through Mk. IV) had a muzzle velocity of 2,700 feet per second with a 6-pound projectile, which could penetrate 2.7 inches of armor at 1,000 yards. Although still outclassed by the heaviest of German tanks, the 6 pdr could handle a wide array of Axis armor.

By 1941, with the 6 pdr deployed, it was recognized that an even heavier antitank gun was required. The O.F. 17 pdr began production in August 1942 and became the standard British antitank gun by the final year of the war, 1945. The 17-pound projectile the large and heavy field gun fired was of 3-inch caliber and could penetrate more than 5 inches of armor at 1,000 yards. Even the most advanced German tanks could not stand up to it. Muzzle velocity was 2,900 feet per second. While the 17-pound gun proved to be one of the Allies' most effective antiarmor weapons, it had the disadvantage of being large, heavy, and awkward to move. At 6,444 pounds, it was almost three times the weight of the 2,471-pound 6 pdr.

FRENCH ANTITANK ARTILLERY

France fielded a number of 25-mm antitank guns, the first, Canon léger de 25 antichar SA-L mle 1934, was produced in 1934. This gun fired a 0.7-pound projectile through 1.57 inches of armor at 440 yards—performance that was quite inadequate against modern tanks. The Germans captured many of these guns during the BATTLE OF FRANCE, but even they found no use for them after 1942.

Much more impressive was the Canon de 47 antichar SA mle 1937. It fired a 47-mm, 3.8-pound shell through 3.15 inches of armor at 220 yards. The gun was good enough for the Germans to employ against the Allied NORMANDY LANDINGS (D-DAY) in 1944.

GERMAN ANTITANK ARTILLERY

German forces deployed three mainstream antitank guns, the 3.7-cm Pak 35/36, the 5-cm Pak 38, and the 7.5-cm Pak 40. In addition, relatively small numbers of innovative taper-bore guns were produced. These featured special tungsten-core projectiles, with outer flanges of much softer metal. The bore of the rifled barrel tapered, and as the shell moved out of the barrel, its flanges folded. This resulted in less loss of the gas produced by detonation and, therefore, an increase in muzzle velocity. The increased muzzle velocity, combined with the extremely dense tungsten core of the projectile, resulted in enhanced armor penetration.

Pak stands for *Panzerabwehrkanone*, "antitank gun," and the 3.7-cm Pak 35/36, first produced in the early 1930s, soon revealed its inadequacy against the heavier tanks of World War II. Muzzle velocity was 2,495 feet per second, projectile weight was three-quarters of a pound, and armor penetration at 400 yards was a mere 1.48 inches.

The 5-cm Pak 38, which went into production in 1939 and first saw service in summer 1940, figured importantly in the INVASION OF THE SOVIET UNION in 1941. Its 4.45-pound shell left the muzzle at 2,460 feet per second and could penetrate almost 4 inches of armor at 820 yards—quite effective against just about any Allied tank. The guns were produced in large quantities and in many versions, including one that was modified for antiaircraft use.

On the eve of the war, in 1939, German intelligence began learning of the heavy armor planned for the new generation of Soviet tanks. Accordingly, a gun even heavier than the Pak 38 was ordered. The 7.5-cm Pak 40 began production in 1940 and started to reach eastern front troops late in 1941. It fired a 15-pound projectile at a muzzle velocity of 2,460 feet per second and could pierce 3.86 inches of armor at 2,190 yards. At 500 yards, penetration increased to some 6 inches. The versatile gun could fire a wide range of ammunition and was readily towed.

The taper-bore weapons were never produced in great quantity, but their advantage was that they produced significantly increased muzzle velocities that drove the tungsten-core shells through many inches of armor. The extremely light 2.8-cm sPzB 41 threw a .27-pound shell through 2.205 inches of armor at 400 yards. The 4.2-cm Pak 41 had a three-quarter-pound projectile and could penetrate 2.835 inches of armor at 500 yards. The heavy 7.5-cm Pak 41 thrust a 5.5-pound round through 6.73 inches of armor at 500 yards. These were advanced weapons, but they were costly to produce. The tapered bore required engineering to extremely close tolerances, and the tungsten required for the ammunition was very scarce in wartime Germany.

JAPANESE ANTITANK ARTILLERY

Japan fielded only one antiarmor gun of note, the 47-mm Antitank Gun Type 1. It fired a projectile that weighed somewhat more than three pounds and could penetrate no more than two inches of armor at 1,000 yards. The limited penetration was offset somewhat by two advantages. The gun could be fired rapidly, at the rate of about 15 rounds per minute, and it was light, just 1,660 pounds. Japanese defensive doctrine during the Pacific campaign typically took little advantage of the gun's mobility. Japanese defenders usually dug these pieces into highly prepared static defenses, determined to die rather than retreat.

SOVIET ANTITANK ARTILLERY

The most important Soviet antitank guns were several versions of a 45-mm and a 76.2-mm piece. The M1942 45-mm gun fired a 3.151-pound projectile through 3.74 inches of armor at 330 yards, inadequate against the best German tanks. The M1942 76.2-mm gun, also called the ZiZ-2, was a highly maneuverable, relatively lightweight piece—3,770 pounds—that fired a 16.79-pound projectile through 3.86 inches of armor at 545 yards. The gun was widely used but, again, was barely adequate against the more advanced German tanks.

UNITED STATES ANTITANK ARTILLERY

The two most important U.S. Army antitank guns were the 37-mm M3 and the 3-inch M5. The first, developed in the late 1930s, was inspired by the German Pak 35/36, but with armor penetration of just one inch at 1,000 yards, it was no match against German tanks. Nevertheless, its light weight—just 912 pounds—was welcome in mobile and amphibious operations, and it was sufficiently versatile to have been produced in a quantity of 18,702 by the end of the war.

The heavier M5 antitank gun was introduced late in 1941, and while it proved to be a reliable weapon, it was heavy at 5,580 pounds and required a 6-by-6 truck for towing transport. It sent a 15.43-pound projectile at a muzzle velocity of 2,600 feet for armor penetration of 3.31 inches at a very impressive 2,000 yards.

INFANTRY ANTITANK WEAPONS

The most familiar infantry antitank weapon was the American BAZOOKA. This weapon was so effective that the Germans imitated it in the *Raketenpanzerbüchse,* or RpzB 43. This widely distributed weapon electrically fired an 88-mm rocket projectile to a maximum of 164 yards and could penetrate more than 6 inches of armor. Almost twice as heavy as the bazooka, it was also much longer and could not be shoulder fired. Nevertheless, it was highly effective against Allied tanks.

The Germans also fielded the *Panzerfaust,* or "tank devil," which was lightweight with a launching tube capable of projecting a hollow-charge grenade. Introduced in 1943, the *Panzerfaust* was a personal antitank weapon, operated by an individual soldier. The original model, *Panzerfaust* 30, had a range of about 30 meters (just over 30 yards); subsequently, a *Panzerfaust* 60 and *Panzerfaust* 100 were fielded. Over their short ranges, these weapons launched a finned grenade, which could penetrate (in later models) nearly eight inches of armor. Allied tanks were extremely vulnerable to such a weapon. The disadvantage of the *Panzerfaust* was that, although simple and cheap to produce, it could be used only once, and that was a major problem, as German raw materials resources dwindled after 1943.

The British counterpart of the American bazooka and German *Panzerfaust* was the Mk. 1 PIAT (Projector, Infantry, Anti-Tank). Although it resembled the bazooka and the *Panzerfaust,* it did not use an electric charge to ignite the charge in the projectile but, rather, a spring mechanism. The weapon fired a 3-pound finned grenade a maximum of 370 yards (practical range was closer to 110 yards), which was capable of piercing even heavy German armor. Although the weapon was an effective tank killer, the British Tommies did not much like it. It was a heavy load to carry at about 37 pounds, and it required two men to operate it.

Germany, Japan, and Britain fielded specially designed antitank rifles, while the United States produced antitank grenades that could be fired from the standard M1 rifle. The German rifles were all 7.92-caliber weapons, which fired armor-piercing rounds. Because these rounds could penetrate no more than an inch of armor at about 300 yards, the rifles were of very limited effectiveness against modern tanks. The Japanese Antitank Rifle Type 97 fired a 20-mm round, which could penetrate 1.18 inches of armor at 273 yards, barely sufficient to penetrate lightly armored tanks. Although the weapon was of little use against American Sherman tanks, the Japanese persisted in using it, and they even developed a grenade that could be launched from it. The British Boys Antitank Rifle fired a 13.97-mm round capable of penetrating 0.827 inches of armor at 330 yards. Long and heavy, the Boys could be carried and operated by one man, but they were most often mounted on a vehicle. Of no use against modern tanks, they were employed with success against such lightly armored vehicles as armored cars.

The U.S. Army did not devote resources to developing a weapon it considered of limited effectiveness. Instead, the Antitank Rifle Grenade M9A1 was designed to be fired from the standard-issue M1 rifle. Its range was a little over 100 yards, and its hollow-charge warhead had an impressive four-inch armor-piercing potential. The versatile grenade could also be launched from an M1 carbine using an M8 launcher attachment.

The British Grenade, Hand, Antitank, No. 75, more familiarly known as the Hawkins Grenade, could be thrown or laid as a mine to be detonated by the weight of a tank's treads. This grenade was intended to disable the treads. The Grenade, Hand,

Antitank, No 74 (ST) was better known as a sticky bomb because it was coated with an adhesive that stuck to the side of the tank when thrown. The drawback of this weapon was obvious: The adhesive would stick to anything, including the hand or glove of the would-be thrower.

The Soviets developed the RPG, the most successful of which was the RPG 1943. Despite the initials, which commonly denote rifle-propelled grenade, the RPG 1943 was hand thrown. What made it reasonably effective on lightly armored tanks was a fabric tail that deployed as the grenade was hurled. This tail ensured that the warhead end of the grenade would strike the target, thereby directing the blast toward—and, hopefully, through—the armor plate.

The Soviet RPG 1943 was inspired by the German *Panzerwurfmine,* an antiarmor hand grenade that incorporated four canvas fins that unfolded when the weapon was properly hurled. The fins stabilized the flight of the grenade and directed its hollow-charge warhead directly toward the target. A surprisingly powerful weapon, it was capable of penetrating most Allied armor plating.

Infantrymen devised and improvised other, less conventional, antitank weapons. The best known of these is the Molotov cocktail, named after Soviet foreign minister VYACHESLAV MOLOTOV and first used during the Spanish Civil War in 1936–39. The weapon, readily improvised, consisted of a glass bottle filled with gasoline (or other combustible liquid). An oil-soaked rag was tied around the bottle's neck, and, just before the bottle was thrown, the rag would be ignited; it would act as the fuse that touched off the gasoline when the bottle burst against its target. Of little effect against armor plate, the Molotov cocktail could be quite deadly if aimed at any openings in the tank, such as vision slits or engine louvers.

Japanese infantry troops sometimes made KAMIKAZE attacks against Allied tanks. They would load a backpack with about 20 pounds of high explosive to create a satchel charge. As the target tank approached, the soldier, backpack on his back, would dive under the tank and simultaneously pull a lanyard that would ignite a short time-delay fuse. As the tank rolled over the soldier, the backpack would ignite, destroying both the tank and the attacker. In a somewhat more humane version of this type of attack, the Soviets experimented with affixing a satchel charge to the back of a dog. A wooden rod projected from the top of the dog's back pack. The dog would be sent toward an approaching tank, which, when it rolled over the dog, would push the projecting rod. The rod was attached to an ignition device, which detonated the explosives—to the detriment of the tank as well as the dog. This antitank method was rarely used.

See also ARTILLERY, BRITISH; ARTILLERY, FRENCH; ARTILLERY, GERMAN; ARTILLERY, ITALIAN; ARTILLERY, JAPANESE; ARTILLERY, SOVIET; and ARTILLERY, U.S.

Further reading: Chamberlain, Peter. *Anti-Tank Weapons.* New York: Arco, 1975; Norris, John. *Anti-Tank Weapons.* London and New York: Brassey's, 1997; Quarry, Bruce, and Mike Spick. *An Illustrated Guide to Tank Busters.* Englewood Cliffs, N.J.: Prentice Hall, 1987.

Anti-Comintern Pact

The Anti-Comintern Pact was concluded on November 25, 1936, at Berlin between Germany and Japan. On November 6 of the following year, Italy joined Germany and Japan in the pact. Ostensibly a defensive alliance against the perceived menace of the Soviet-controlled "Communistic International," or Comintern, the document was also the formal basis of the Tokyo-Berlin-Rome Axis, the World War II ideological and military alliance among Germany, Japan, and Italy.

The Bolsheviks formed the Soviet Union in 1922 after the Russian civil war. Through the Communist International, or Comintern, the Soviet Union intended to operate as the center of world revolution, dedicated to the overthrow of capitalism everywhere. The Comintern created a high degree of instability throughout Europe, adding to the instability wrought by the politically and economically punitive TREATY OF VERSAILLES in Germany and its former World War I allies. In the 1930s, the Italian fascists and the German Nazis, as well as the Japanese militarists, sought to legitimate themselves, especially in the eyes of the Western democracies, by portraying themselves as united against Soviet expansion. The two Anti-Comintern Pacts defined, albeit vaguely, that unified front.

The 1936 document is brief enough to reproduce its entire substantive text:

The Imperial Government of Japan and the Government of Germany, In cognizance of the fact that the object of the Communistic International (the so-called Komintern) is the disintegration of, and the commission of violence against, existing States by the exercise of all means at its command;

Believing that the toleration of interference by the Communistic International in the internal affairs of nations not only endangers their internal peace and social welfare, but threatens the general peace of the world;

Desiring to cooperate for defence against communistic disintegration, have agreed as follows:

Article i
The High Contracting States agree that they will mutually keep each other informed concerning the activities of the Communistic International, will confer upon the necessary measures of defence, and will carry out such measures in close cooperation.

Article ii
The High Contracting States will jointly invite third States whose internal peace is menaced by the disintegrating work of the Communistic International, to adopt defensive measures in the spirit of the present Agreement or to participate in the present Agreement.

Article iii
The Japanese and German texts are each valid as the original text of this Agreement. The Agreement shall come into force on the day of its signature and shall remain in force for the term of five years. The High Contracting States will, in a reasonable time before the expiration of the said term, come to an understanding upon the further manner of their cooperation . . .

Supplementary Protocol to the Agreement Guarding against the Communistic International on the occasion of the signature this day of the Agreement guarding against the Communistic International the undersigned plenipotentiaries have agreed as follows:

(a) The competent authorities of both High Contracting States will closely cooperate in the exchange of reports on the activities of the Communistic International and on measures of information and defence against the Communistic International.

(b) The competent authorities of both High Contracting States will, within the framework of the existing law, take stringent measures against those who at home or abroad work on direct or indirect duty of the Communistic International or assist its disintegrating activities.

(c) To facilitate the cooperation of the competent authorities of the two High Contracting States as set out in (a) above, a standing committee shall be established. By this committee the further measures to be adopted in order to counter the disintegrating activities of the Communistic International shall be considered and conferred upon . . .

In signing on to the pact, Italy joined Germany and Japan to oppose the expansion of Soviet communism, thereby creating the kernel of the Axis that would oppose the Allies during World War II. The substantive text of 1937 follows:

The Italian Government; the Government of the German Reich, and the Imperial Government of Japan,

Considering that the Communist International continues constantly to imperil the civilized world in the Occident and Orient, disturbing and destroying peace and order,

Considering that only close collaboration looking to the maintenance of peace and order can limit and remove that peril,

Considering that Italy—who with the advent of the Fascist regime has with inflexible determination combated that peril and rid her territory of the Communist International—has decided to align herself against the common enemy along

with Germany and Japan, who for their part are animated by like determination to defend themselves against the Communist International,

Have, in conformity with Article II of the Agreement against the Communist International concluded at Berlin on November 25, 1936, by Germany and Japan, agreed upon the following:

Article 1
Italy becomes a party to the Agreement against the Communist International and to the Supplementary Protocol concluded on November 25, 1936, between Germany and Japan, the text of which is included in the Annex to the present Protocol.

Article 2
The three Powers signatory to the present Protocol agree that Italy will be considered as an original signatory to the Agreement and Supplementary Protocol mentioned in the preceding Article, the signing of the present Protocol being equivalent to the signature of the original text of the aforesaid Agreement and Supplementary Protocol.

Article 3
The present Protocol shall constitute an integral part of the above-mentioned Agreement and Supplementary Protocol.

Article 4
The present Protocol is drawn up in Italian, Japanese, and German, each text being considered authentic. It shall enter into effect on the date of signature.

Further reading: Martel, Gordon, ed. *The Origins of the Second World War Reconsidered: A.J.P. Taylor and the Historians.* 2d ed. New York: Routledge, 1999; Overy, Richard. *The Road to War.* New York: Penguin USA, 2000; Taylor, A. J. P. *The Origins of the Second World War.* New York: Touchstone, 1996.

Antonescu, Ion (1882–1946) *Romanian dictator during the World War II era*

As dictator of ROMANIA during World War II, Antonescu aligned his nation with the Axis. He was born in Pitesti, Romania, on June 15, 1882, and served in the Romanian army during World War I.

After the armistice, he remained in the army as military attaché in Paris and then in London. Returning to Romania, he became chief of the general staff in 1934, then minister of defense in 1937. After King Carol II created a new dictatorial government in 1938, Antonescu was dismissed as minister because he was associated with the Romanian fascist party known as the IRON GUARD. But in 1940, it was Antonescu and the Iron Guard who came into power following the June–September partition of Romania among the Axis powers and the Soviet Union.

Antonescu consciously emulated ADOLF HITLER in setting himself up as absolute dictator of the remaining portion of Romania, and he vowed allegiance to Germany. When his own Iron Guard instituted a reign of terror and corruption during 1940–41, Antonescu successfully suppressed the group, then recovered widespread public favor by instituting a program of domestic reform. He brought the country into World War II on the side of Germany, pouring massive numbers of troops into what became the lost cause of the Russian front.

There is no question that Antonescu was a fascist tyrant, yet he was substantially less brutal than Hitler or the leaders of other Axis regimes. Nevertheless, as Romanian war losses escalated and the civilian population suffered, support for Antonescu eroded, and the nation's new king, Michael, led a successful coup d'état against him in August 1944. Deposed, Antonescu was imprisoned, then tried by officials of the new communist regime in the Romanian Communist People's Court. Convicted of war crimes, he was executed near Jilava on June 1, 1946.

Further reading: Dragan, Iosif Constantin. *Antonescu: Marshal and Ruler of Romania, 1940–1944.* Timosoara, Romania: Europa Nova, 1995; Watts, Larry. L. *Romanian Cassandra.* Boulder, Colo.: East European Monographs, 1993.

ANZAC

ANZAC is an acronym for Australian and New Zealand Army Corps, a military formation created during World War I, in December 1914, by combining the Australian Imperial Force and New Zealand Expeditionary Force stationed in Egypt under the command of Lt. Gen. William Birdwood. It is believed that the acronym originated with Sgt. K. M. Little, a New Zealand clerk in Birdwood's headquarters, who needed something that would fit on a rubber stamp. Before the end of World War I, *Anzac* was used as a label for any Australian or New Zealand soldier.

A new Anzac Corps was formed during the World War II campaign in GREECE in 1941, and the acronym *ANZAC* was loosely applied to Australian and New Zealand forces throughout the war, while *Anzac* continued to serve as a familiar name for Australian and New Zealand troops, much as *G.I.* served for Americans.

Further reading: "Anzac," in *Oxford Companion to New Zealand Military History,* Ian McGibbon, ed. Oxford and New York: Oxford University Press, 2000.

Anzio Campaign

The ITALIAN CAMPAIGN proved to be far more difficult than Allied planners had imagined, and when the advance that followed the SALERNO landings stalled, it was decided to make a second landing on Italy's west coast in an effort to break through the Winter Line and speed up the capture of Rome. In conference at Marakesh, the Allies decided on Operation Shingle, sending Maj. Gen. JOHN LUCAS with elements of the VI Corps of the Fifth U.S. Army to land along a 15-mile beachhead near the resort town of Anzio, 30 miles south of Rome, on January 22, 1944. Units committed to the landings included the U.S. 3d Infantry Division; the British 1st Infantry Division and 46th Royal Tank Regiment; the U.S. 751st Tank Battalion, the 504th Parachute Infantry Regiment of the 82nd Airborne Division, and the 509th Parachute Infantry Battalion; two British Commando battalions; and three battalions of U.S. Army Rangers. The U.S. 45th Infantry Division and Combat Command A (CCA), a regimental-sized unit of the U.S. 1st Armored Division, were to land as reinforcements once the beachhead was established.

The landings were textbook perfect and encountered very little German resistance. Progress inland was rapid, with British and American units attaining their first day's objectives by noon. Before the end of the day, they had advanced three to four miles. Indeed, the Germans did not anticipate an amphibious assault at this time or place, but Lucas failed to move aggressively and thus lost the advantage gained by the element of surprise. Over the next week, his units busied themselves with consolidating their positions preparatory to the major breakout. This gave the Germans ample time to redeploy, and what had started with an easy landing would stretch agonizingly into a savage four-month campaign. Although Lucas would receive much blame, he was, in fact, acting on his understanding of the orders of Fifth Army commander Gen. MARK CLARK. Clark outlined two missions for VI Corps: to divert enemy strength from the south and to prepare defensive positions in anticipation of a violent German counterattack. He was further instructed to advance toward the Alban Hills and points east to link up with the rest of Fifth Army seven days after the landings. Lucas did not see his mission as immediately capturing the Alban Hills.

In support of the landings, some 2,600 Allied aircraft were available, as was a large naval flotilla, comprising ships from six nations. To preserve the element of surprise, the naval forces did not launch a major preinvasion bombardment.

German general ALBERT KESSELRING ordered a counterattack for January 28, but his subordinate commander, Eberhard von Mackensen, requested postponement until February 1, by which time the Fourteenth German Army in the area numbered some 70,000 troops. Lucas now raced to press the attack so that he could link up with Fifth Army forces in the south before the Germans counterattacked. However, thanks in no small measure to the vagueness of Clark's orders, Lucas had sacrificed the advantages of the surprise achieved by the landings. Kesselring had deployed a cordon around Lucas. Rangers under Col. William O. Darby made an initial attack on Cisterna. The 1st and 3rd Ranger Battalions were to spearhead the assault,

infiltrating the German lines to seize Cisterna until the 4th Rangers and 15th Infantry arrived. The German defenders, however, ambushed the Rangers. Of 767 men in the two battalions, only a half dozen returned to Allied lines. By January 30, Lucas had suffered 5,100 casualties, 3,000 American and 2,100 British. He was forced to relinquish the offensive and assume a defensive posture.

Yet the picture was not entirely bleak. Thanks to the Allies' having broken German ULTRA codes, Lucas had a remarkably thorough picture of Mackensen's plans and the German tank strength in the area. This allowed him to make a highly effective defense, which was very costly to the German counterattackers. Moreover, while Kesselring anticipated achieving a high degree of surprise with a counteroffensive near Aprilia, the Ultra decrypts tipped the Allies off, and the major operation was checked by February 20, just four days after it had been launched. Not only did the counteroffensive fail to push the Allied troops back, it cost the Germans 5,389 casualties.

Yet Lucas's superiors were persuaded that wars are not won by defensive operations, no matter how well executed, and, on February 22, Lucas was relieved and replaced by his deputy commander, the highly aggressive Maj. Gen. LUCIAN TRUSCOTT. He quickly beat back a renewed German assault on February 29, and it was now Kesselring's turn to readjust his objectives. He had hoped to wipe out the landings. He now knew this would not happen. Nevertheless, this tenacious commander maintained a stout perimeter around the Allies and kept their positions under almost continuous fire. What he could not prevent, however, was the steady reinforcement of VI Corps. Nevertheless, it was not until spring that Truscott felt sufficiently strong to make the final breakout.

On the morning of May 23, he opened an artillery barrage on the Cisterna front, followed by violent armor and infantry attacks along the entire line of German defenders. By that evening, the enemy's main line of resistance had been breached. Cisterna, long the nexus of German strength, fell on May 25, and on that same day, elements of VI Corps began the link up with the main body of the

Fifth Army—the union that was supposed to have taken place within one week of the Anzio landings.

The Anzio Campaign was concluded. During the campaign, the Allied VI Corps had suffered 29,200 combat casualties (4,400 killed, 18,000 wounded, 6,800 prisoners or missing) and 37,000 noncombat casualties. German losses were about 40,000, including 5,000 killed and 4,838 captured. They were losses the Germans could not replace.

There can be no doubt that the campaign failed in its immediate objectives of outflanking the German positions and thereby restoring mobility to the Italian campaign and speeding the capture of Rome. Lucas complained that he had never been provided forces adequate to his mission, and most recent historians agree, although most also believe that Lucas was, indeed, insufficiently aggressive. Costly and disappointing as it was, however, the Anzio Campaign did, in effect, monopolize the troops of the German Fourteenth Army for four months, preventing these forces from being deployed elsewhere. The campaign intensified a war of attrition the Germans simply could not afford.

Further Reading: Allen, William L. *Anzio: Edge of Disaster.* New York: Elsevier-Dutton, 1978; Blumenson, Martin. *Anzio: The Gamble That Failed.* New York: Cooper Square Press, 2001; Sheehan, Fred. *Anzio: Epic of Bravery.* Norman: University of Oklahoma Press, 1994.

appeasement policy

In May 1937, Neville Chamberlain replaced the retiring Stanley Baldwin as prime minister of Great Britain. Against the vigorous objections of a faction of Parliament led by Winston Churchill, the Baldwin government had maintained an essentially pacifist policy with regard to preparedness for war. At the same time, Great Britain was bound by a number of military treaties, chiefly with France, Czechoslovakia, and Poland, which could well draw Great Britain into war if any of those nations were attacked. Seeking a means of avoiding conflict, Chamberlain proposed a policy of "active appeasement" with regard to an increasingly vora-

cious Germany. Chamberlain's idea was to discover what Adolf Hitler wanted and then, if possible, to give it to him. In this way, Chamberlain hoped to conserve military resources to fight what his government considered the most immediate and serious war threats: from Italy and Japan, not from Germany.

On March 13, 1938, Hitler invaded Austria, his army receiving opposition from neither Italy (at the time perceived as a potential rival to Germany) nor from Austria itself. Hitler proclaimed *Anschluss,* the joining of Austria to Germany as a province of the German Reich, or government.

The easy success of *Anschluss* emboldened Hitler and put Germany in position to make its next move—into Czechoslovakia. Although he was intent on appeasing Hitler, Chamberlain warned him to negotiate with the Czechs. In response, Hitler blustered and stood firm. For his part, Chamberlain caved in. Hat in hand, as it were, he flew (in an age when executives of state rarely traveled by air) to Berchtesgaden, Hitler's Bavarian mountain retreat, and simply proposed to give Hitler all that he demanded. Almost taken aback by this bounty, Hitler demanded cession of the Sudetenland, the German-speaking region of Czechoslovakia. Chamberlain agreed, asking only that Hitler delay invasion until he could persuade Paris and Prague to go along with the plan.

British prime minister Neville Chamberlain returns from the Munich Conference. *(Author's collection)*

The French government was appalled by the proposal and appealed to President FRANKLIN D. ROOSEVELT, who was, however, unable to move Congress to alter U.S. neutrality. Thus rebuffed, France declined to stand alone against Germany and agreed to hand over the Sudetenland to Hitler. Pursuant to this agreement, Chamberlain organized the MUNICH CONFERENCE on September 29–30, 1938, which formalized the betrayal of the Czechs, ceding the Sudetenland to Germany in return for Hitler's pledge that he make no more territorial demands in Europe.

Chamberlain returned to London from the Munich Conference and announced the triumph of "active appeasement," declaring that he brought back from Hitler "peace for our time." The sense of relief was short lived. On March 16, 1939, Hitler effectively repudiated his pledge to take no more territory when he sent German army units to occupy Prague. The entire Czech nation suddenly ceased to exist, and Poland would be next. The appeasement policy not only failed to avert war, it made war inevitable by encouraging Hitler in his program of territorial aggression.

Further reading: Adams, R. J. Q. *British Politics and Foreign Policy in the Age of Appeasement, 1935–39.* Palo Alto, Calif.: Stanford University Press, 1994; McDonough, Frank. *Hitler, Chamberlain and Appeasement.* Cambridge: Cambridge University Press, 2002; Schmitz, David F., and Richard D. Challener, eds. *Appeasement in Europe: A Reassessment of U.S. Policies.* Westport, Conn.: Greenwood Publishing Group, 1990.

Arctic convoy operations

The Allies' merchant marine resources undertook some of the most arduous and dangerous missions of World War II, and none was more harrowing than the Arctic convoys that transported war materiel from ports in Great Britain and Iceland to the Soviets. Some 4.43 million tons of supplies were shipped by Arctic convoys, representing 22.7 percent of the supplies the USSR received under LEND LEASE. Losses were very high: 7.8 percent of ships bound for Soviet ports were sunk, as were 3.8 percent of those

returning. This loss rate was much higher than the rate for all other CONVOY routes. The first Arctic convoy sailed on August 21, 1944, from Scotland; the last convoy sailed on April 16, 1945.

The Arctic convoy routes connected Great Britain and Iceland with Soviet ports via the Norwegian and Barents Seas, but they were restricted by climate and geography, particularly the extent of ice fields. These same conditions, however, made it more difficult for submarines as well as surface raiders to attack convoys. Also, the long Arctic nights provided a welcome cloak of darkness. Counterbalancing these advantages was the necessity of hugging the Norwegian coast to avoid ice, which meant that convoys were thrust closer to German coastal forces stationed there. Escort vessels consisted mainly of a close escort of DESTROYERS and distant escort of CRUISERS. Most of these were Royal Navy ships, but the U.S. and Soviet navies also supplied escort ships. Air support was used but was severely limited by range and weather conditions.

All the convoys were dangerous, but Convoy PQ17, which sailed from Iceland on June 27, 1942, demonstrated just how disastrously dangerous this mission could be. Attacked by submarines and aircraft, 26 of the convoy's 37 ships were sunk with the loss of 3,850 trucks and vehicles, 430 tanks, and 2,500 aircraft. Thanks to efficient rescue and recovery, only 153 merchant seamen were lost—a remarkably small number, considering the number of ships sunk.

Further reading: Edwards, Bernard. *The Road to Russia: Arctic Convoys, 1942.* Annapolis, Md.: Naval Institute Press, 2003; Kemp, Paul. *Convoy: Drama in Arctic Waters.* London: Book Sales, 2003; Schofield, Brian Betham. *The Arctic Convoys.* London: Macdonald & Jane's, 1977; Smith, Peter C. *Arctic Victory: The Story of Convoy PQ18.* Manchester, U.K.: Crecy, 1995; Woodman, Richard. *Arctic Convoys 1941–1945.* London: Trafalgar Square, 1996.

Ardennes, Battle of the (Battle of the Bulge)

One of the key battles of World War II in Europe, the so-called Battle of the Bulge was the final German offensive of the war and came as a great surprise to the Allies, who widely assumed that the German armies had been beaten to the point that they were incapable of any offensive action. In sum, the battle began on December 16, 1944, when 25 German divisions attacked a thinly held portion of the Allied lines in the Belgian Ardennes Forest. Initially, the attack broke through the five green or recuperating U.S. divisions that had been assigned to what was considered a quiet sector, and the battle took its popular name from the bulge, or salient, the Germans achieved by penetrating nearly as far west as the Meuse River. The German plan was to cross the Meuse and divide Allied forces by penetrating all the way to Antwerp, Netherlands, the Allies' principal supply port. When Allied high command recognized the danger posed by the surprise offensive, reinforcements were rushed to the area, and the U.S. 101st Airborne and U.S. 10th Armored Division were ordered to hold Bastogne, completely encircled by the Germans, at all costs, until the main body of reinforcements could arrive. In bitter winter action, Bastogne was held, and elements of the U.S. First and Third Armies, supported by heavy British and U.S. air support (initially delayed by bad weather), managed to turn a potential Allied catastrophe into a decisive German defeat, after which, for the rest of the war, German forces were continually on the defensive and continually in retreat. It was the largest single battle fought by U.S. troops in Europe.

Some military historians look upon the Ardennes offensive as evidence of ADOLF HITLER's heedless desperation in the closing phase of the war. There is a certain merit in this view, but the offensive was also a brilliantly staged, bold, violent, and ruthless thrust, which came remarkably close to achieving its objective of splitting the Allied lines and capturing the Allies' most important supply port. Hitler's generals made highly effective use of the element of surprise and, even more, of the weather. By attacking during a prolonged winter storm, they ensured that the Allies' overwhelmingly superior air power would be useless, at least

in the important early stages of the offensive. It is unclear whether Hitler actually imagined that victory in this battle would reverse the course of his defeat. However, he had rational reason to hope that such a victory would so dispirit the Allies that they would negotiate a peace rather than demand unconditional surrender.

For purposes of this offensive, Hitler created the Sixth SS Panzer Army, consisting of four Panzer divisions under the command of JOSEF A. "SEPP" DIETRICH, an SS officer both fierce and trusted. From the northern Ardennes in the vicinity of Monschau, Dietrich would lead the *Schwerpunkt* (principal thrust) of a classic BLITZKRIEG offensive. Supplementing this principal thrust would be another new Panzer force, the Fifth SS Panzer Army, under HASSO-ECCARD VON MANTEUFFEL, assigned to attack in the center, and, in the south, the Seventh Army, under Lt. Gen. Erich Brandenberger. In all, German strength amounted to 30 divisions with grossly inadequate air support— about 1,000 fighters—from the badly depleted Luftwaffe (Brig. Gen. Dietrich Peltz's 2nd Fighter Corps).

As the Allies had deceived Hitler before and during the NORMANDY LANDINGS (D-DAY), so Hitler and his commanders prepared their massive offensive, code named "Wacht am Rhein" ("Watch on the Rhine," suggesting a defensive operation) in profound and highly effective secrecy, even deceiving and bypassing the German commander in chief, GERD VON RUNDSTEDT. This was understandable, because the realistic Rundstedt would doubtless have tried to veto a plan that seemed ultimately doomed to fail, even if successful in the short term. Even the commander Hitler chose to carry out the operation, WALTHER MODEL, thought the offensive too ambitious and suggested a modified operation he considered more feasible. Hitler listened but rejected the proposal out of hand.

The offensive included an AIRBORNE ASSAULT, which the Germans had not used since the very earliest days of the war, and a special unit, the 150th SS Brigade under OTTO SKORZENY, the bril-

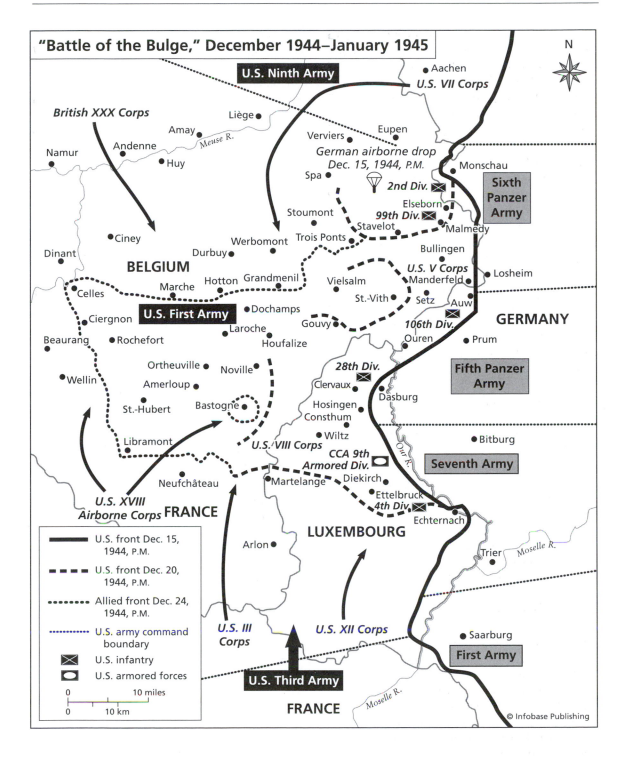

"Battle of the Bulge," December 1944–January 1945

N

U.S. Ninth Army

British XXX Corps

• Aachen
U.S. VII Corps

• Liège
Amay •
Verviers •
• Eupen
• Monschau

Andenne •
Namur •
• Huy

Meuse R.

Spa •
German airborne drop
Dec. 15, 1944, P.M.

Sixth Panzer Army

2nd Div.
Elseborn
99th Div.
Stavelot
• Malmedy

• Ciney
Stoumont •
Werbomont •
Trois Ponts

Dinant •
Durbuy •
• Bullingen

BELGIUM
Marche •
Hotton
Grandmenil
Vielsalm •
St.-Vith •
Manderfeld •
• Losheim

• Celles
U.S. First Army
• Dochamps
Gouvy •
Setz •
Auw

Ciergnon •
Laroche •
106th Div.
GERMANY

Beaurang •
Rochefort •
Houfalize •
Ouren •
• Prum

• Wellin
Ortheuville •
• Noville
28th Div.

Fifth Panzer Army

Amerloup •
Clervaux •
Dasburg •

St.-Hubert •
Bastogne •
Hosingen
Consthum
• Bitburg

Libramont •
U.S. VIII Corps
• Wiltz

Seventh Army

• Neufchâteau
CCA 9th
Armored Div.
Our R.

**U.S. XVIII
Airborne Corps** FRANCE
Martelange •
Diekirch
Ettelbruck
4th Div.
Echternach •

Arlon •
LUXEMBOURG
Trier •
Moselle R.

**U.S. III
Corps**
U.S. XII Corps
• Saarburg

First Army

U.S. Third Army
Moselle R.

FRANCE

© Infobase Publishing

— U.S. front Dec. 15, 1944, P.M.

- - - U.S. front Dec. 20, 1944, P.M.

•••••• Allied front Dec. 24, 1944, P.M.

•••••• U.S. army command boundary

⊠ U.S. infantry

⬭ U.S. armored forces

0   10 miles
0   10 km

liant special forces commander who had successfully pulled off the rescue of overthrown Italian dictator BENITO MUSSOLINI. The paratroops were to secure and hold key Meuse bridges in order to facilitate the German advance after it had broken through the Allied lines, and Skorzeny's command, which included English-speaking troops dressed in American uniforms and driving American vehicles, was to infiltrate and disrupt the American rear area. Unfortunately for the Germans, the airborne drops were poorly executed, the troops landing too widely dispersed to carry out their mission against the bridges. While Skorzeny's forces did cause significant confusion, they achieved little of tactical significance, and soldiers captured in American uniforms were summarily executed. Nevertheless, the very tip of Dietrich's 1st SS Panzer Division, Col. Joachim Peiper's armored *Kampfgruppe*, made an early lightning thrust deep into American-held territory, through Malmédy, Belgium (*see* MALMÉDY MASSACRE), west of which it was finally destroyed.

As Hitler took advantage of the weather, so he exploited Allied weakness in the Ardennes sector. U.S. Lt. Gen. COURTNEY HODGES, in command of the First Army (part of the Twelfth Army Group commanded by Gen. OMAR BRADLEY), had responsibility for Ardennes, but, acting in accordance with Bradley's instructions and those of higher Allied command, concentrated on the Aachen area with the object of capturing the vital Roer dams. The 80-mile Ardennes front was regarded as a quiet sector, which could be adequately defended by battle-weary units in need of rest and recuperation and by green units, which could benefit from gradual exposure to the line. In place at the time of the initial attack were the 99th and 106th Divisions from the First Army's V Corps, and the 28th and 4th Divisions from VIII Corps. The 9th Armored Division was held in reserve. Hodges and his superiors believed that careful intelligence would provide warning of any highly unlikely build-up of German forces in the area, affording sufficient time to reinforce the position, if necessary. However, the Germans were carrying out their build-up in such secrecy, amid absolute radio silence and under cover of weather that grounded Allied aerial reconnaissance, that neither Hodges, nor Bradley, nor British general SIR BERNARD LAW MONTGOMERY, overall commander of Allied ground forces, were aware of the gathering danger. The only clue came from ULTRA intercepts and decrypts, which revealed a build-up, but which the Allied commanders dismissed as a build-up being assembled to counter the next Allied offensive.

The attack, then, at 5:30 on the morning of December 16, came as a complete surprise. Worse, because German artillery had knocked out telephone lines, word of the attack reached Bradley's headquarters only after much delay and, even then, was misinterpreted as merely a local attack. Bradley's conclusions was overruled by the judgment of Supreme Allied Commander DWIGHT D. EISENHOWER, who ordered the 10th Armored Division of GEORGE S. PATTON's Third U.S. Army and the 7th Armored Division of the Ninth U.S. Army to reinforce the Ardennes line. This enabled the beleaguered 99th Division, reinforced by the 1st, 2nd, and 9th, to hold out against the attack in the north, while the 4th held the line against Brandenberger in the south. But between these, in the center, which had been hit hardest, resistance by the U.S. 28th and 106th Divisions collapsed. Two regiments of the 106th were captured, and a third division, reinforced by the 7th Armored Division, held St. Vith until December 22, when these units were ordered to withdraw to a position behind the Salm River. Despite this withdrawal, Allied high command deemed the village of Bastogne, with its important crossroads, too important to lose. The 101st Airborne and the 10th Armored Division were ordered to hold it, even as Manteuffel encircled it. Throughout the rest of the Ardennes offensive, Bastogne would form an Allied enclave within newly acquired German territory.

In the meantime, Ultra decrypts persuaded Eisenhower that the German objective was the Meuse. On December 19, accordingly, Eisenhower suspended the general Allied offensive and ordered Patton to turn his entire Third Army from its ongoing westward advance 90° to the north. His mission was to counterattack—massively—in the

Ardennes. The speed and efficiency with which Patton carried out this change in direction was one of the most remarkable tactical achievements of the entire war, and it spelled the beginning of the end of the German offensive. Patton would not only relieve the encircled 101st Airborne and 10th Armored Division, he would enable Hodges to realign his First U.S. Army and thereby transform his posture from one of defense to counterattack.

Dietrich's advance in the north was thwarted, but Manteuffel, in the central position, continued to drive on. Hitler gave permission to transfer the bulk of the attack to support Manteuffel, who reached the village of Foy-Notre Dame, a mere three miles east of the Meuse, on December 24. However, by December 22, the weather improved, allowing the Allies to call in air support, which they did—massively—flying 1,300 sorties on December 23 and some 2,000 on December 24. The effect was devastating on German supply lines, which had already been stretched to the breaking point. The Luftwaffe launched a truly desperate raid on Allied airfields on January 1, managing to destroy some 156 Allied aircraft, but at a staggering loss of more than 300 of its own craft. Already reeling, the Luftwaffe was now neutralized as an effective force in the war.

Manteuffel's advance to Foy-Notre Dame marked the farthest extent of the German "bulge." Pounded by Hodges from the north and drained by the continued resistance of encircled Bastogne, Manteuffel stalled. On January 3, Hodges's VII Corps attacked southward against Manteuffel, intending to crush him in a pincer action, of which Patton's Third Army formed the northward thrust. Once again, however, the weather intervened, bringing heavy snows that slowed the advance of both American armies, and it was not until January 16 that Hodges and Patton converged on Houffalize, by which time Manteuffel had withdrawn. Thus, an opportunity to destroy outright most of the German units committed to the offensive was lost. Nevertheless, the Americans inflicted some 100,000 casualties against an attacking force of 500,000, suffering, in turn, casualties almost as heavy. Yet there was no doubt as to the victor. The last German offensive had been crushed, and

whereas the Americans could make up their losses, the Germans could not. Hitler's gamble at the Ardennes had spent much of his irreplaceable last combat-worthy reserves and had exposed his Luftwaffe, already in extremity, to a blow that effectively destroyed it.

Further reading: Astor, Gerald. *A Blood-Dimmed Tide: The Battle of the Bulge by the Men Who Fought It.* New York: Dell, 1998; MacDonald, Charles B. *A Time for Trumpets: The Untold Story of the Battle of the Bulge.* New York: Morrow, 1984; Toland, John. *Battle: The Story of the Bulge.* Lincoln: University of Nebraska Press, 1999.

armed neutrality, U.S.

The U.S. NEUTRALITY ACTS of 1935, 1937, and 1939 ostensibly codified in law U.S. neutrality in the gathering European conflict. However, each act also incrementally aligned the "neutral" United States with the Allies and against Germany and Italy. Although in its original form the final Neutrality Act (1939) prohibited the arming of merchant vessels, Congress amended the act on November 17, 1941, after encounters with German U-boats and the torpedoing of the U.S. destroyer *Reuben James*. The amendment authorized the arming of merchant vessels and permitted these ships to transport cargoes directly to the ports of the belligerents. This amendment officially inaugurated a U.S. policy of armed neutrality—which, of course, proved short lived, since the Japanese attack on PEARL HARBOR on December 7, 1941, immediately thrust the United States into the war.

Even before passage of the amendment, the United States had clearly embarked on a de facto policy of armed neutrality, the first major feature of which was passage of the nation's first ever peacetime draft in September 1940. The ABC-1 STAFF AGREEMENT, concluded between British and American military and naval officials on March 27, 1941, stipulated that the U.S. Navy's Atlantic Fleet would begin assisting the Royal Navy in Atlantic convoy escort duty as soon as it was able. This may be seen as the effective commencement of armed neutrality. On April 10, 1941, the U.S. destroyer *Niblack* depth charged a German U-boat while rescuing the crew of a torpedoed Dutch freighter. This was the first hostile U.S. naval action against a vessel of the Axis powers. Between this event and Pearl Harbor, a low-intensity, undeclared naval war existed between the United States and Germany in the Atlantic (*see* NAVAL WAR WITH GERMANY, UNDECLARED [1940–1941]). On September 11, the U.S. freighter *Montana* was sunk en route to Iceland; on September 19, the armed U.S.-Panamanian freighter *Pink Star,* also bound for Iceland, was torpedoed and sunk; on September 27, the U.S.-Panamanian tanker *I. C. White* was sunk en route to South Africa; on October 16, the U.S. tanker *W. C. Teagle* and the U.S.-Panamanian freighter *Bold Venture* were sunk; on October 17, the destroyer *Kearny* was torpedoed and damaged with the loss of 11 American sailors; on October 19, the U.S. freighter *Lehigh* was sunk in the south Atlantic; on October 30, the U.S.-Panamanian armed tanker *Salinas* was damaged by German torpedoes; and on October 31, the U.S. destroyer *Reuben James* was sunk with the loss of 115 sailors. On November 24, U.S. Army troops were sent to occupy Dutch Guiana (Suriname) on the northeast Atlantic coast of South America. The objective was to protect the bauxite (aluminum ore) mines there.

Further reading: Kemp, Peter. *Decision at Sea: The Convoy Escorts.* New York: Elsevier-Dutton, 1978; Matson, Robert W. *Neutrality and Navicerts: Britain, the United States, and Economic Warfare, 1939–1940.* London: Taylor & Francis, 1994; Rhodes, Benjamin D. *United States Foreign Policy in the Interwar Period, 1918–1941: The Golden Age of American Diplomatic and Military Complacency.* New York: Praeger, 2001.

armor, British

The most important category of armored vehicle is, of course, the tank, and, during World War I, the British took the lead in developing this weapon. They continued work during the interwar years but, in a political climate of wishful pacifism, soon lost their pioneering advantage. As a result, the British tanks of World War II were markedly inferior to those of the Germans.

Vickers Light Tanks. Of all the British tanks, the Vickers Light Tank best exemplified the technical disparity between British and German armor. The basic design dated to the late 1920s, and many versions and variations were produced. But even the latest, the Mark VI, was a comparatively diminutive, lightly armored vehicle that was no match for even second-line German tanks.

The Mark VI series began production in 1936, and the Mark VIB was the principal light tank deployed by the British Expeditionary Force (BEF) to France in 1940. That so many of these vehicles were abandoned in the DUNKIRK EVACUATION was perhaps no great loss.

General specifications for the Mark VIC light tank included:

Weight: 5.2 tons
Length: 13 feet 2 inches
Width: 6 feet 10 inches
Height: 7 feet 5 inches
Power plant: six-cylinder, 88-horsepower Meadows engine
Armament: one Besa 7.92-mm gun and one Besa 15-mm gun
Top speed: about 35 miles per hour
Crew: three

The next Vickers design was the 1938 Light Tank Mark VII Tetrarch. The design, which featured four large independent road wheels on each side (the so-called Christie road wheel concept and suspension) and a large, two-man turret able to mount a large-caliber gun, was innovative. The performance of light tanks in the Spanish Civil War was generally disappointing and did not augur well for the Mark VII, the production of which was delayed until July 1940, too late to make an impact on the BATTLE OF FRANCE. Indeed, the fate of the light tank in that battle prompted the British government to cut back its orders of the Mark VII, which was used mainly with airborne troops during the NORMANDY LANDINGS (D-DAY) in 1944 and the D-day invasion in 1944 and the Rhine crossings in 1945. The Soviet Union received Mark VIIs as part of LEND-LEASE.

General specifications included:

Weight: 7.5 tons
Length: 14.12 feet
Width: 7.58 feet
Height: 6.96 feet
Power plant: one 165-horsepower Meadows 12-cylinder gasoline engine
Armament: one 40-mm gun or one 3-inch howitzer; one machine gun
Top speed: 39.74 miles per hour

Cruiser Tank A15E1, Mark 6 Crusader. During the first year of the war, British manufacturers scrambled to produce heavier tanks that could go up against their German opponents. The Cruiser Tank A15E1, Mark 6 Crusader was introduced in 1941 and was produced through 1943 in a quantity of about 5,300. It was powered by a Liberty aircraft engine and incorporated the Christie suspension used on the Mk VII Tetrarch. Rushed into production, the Crusader was still too lightly armored to be an adequate match against German firepower, and it had an unfortunately deserved reputation for mechanical unreliability. Nevertheless, the Crusader was one of the main British tanks used in the NORTH AFRICAN CAMPAIGN.

General specifications included:

Weight: 44,240 pounds
Length: 19 feet 8 inches
Width: 8 feet 8 inches
Height: 7 feet 4 inches
Armament: one 2-pounder gun and one machine gun
Top speed: 27 miles per hour
Crew: four

Cromwell series. The Cromwell series of tanks was put into production in 1943 in an ongoing effort to match the Germans. Armor was heavier, and the 75-mm gun used on the Mark VIII version was at last heavy enough to penetrate German armor—at least at relatively close ranges. The Cruiser Tank A27M, Mark VIII Cromwell emerged as the most important British tank by

the time of the Normandy Landings in 1944. Armor was heavy, and construction was welded rather than riveted, which gave the vehicle a high degree of survivability against heavy German firepower.

General specifications included:

Weight: 28 tons
Length: 20 feet 10 inches
Width: 9 feet 6.5 inches
Height: 8 feet 2 inches
Power plant: 600-horsepower Rolls-Royce Meteor V-12 gasoline engine
Armament: one 75-mm gun and one or two machine guns
Top speed: 40 miles per hour
Crew: five

Cruiser Tank A27L, Mark 8 Centaur. Contemporary with the Cromwell was the Cruiser Tank A27L, Mark 8 Centaur, which was similar to the Cromwell but used the Liberty aircraft engine instead of the Rolls-Royce Mercury. Centaurs were used mainly for training from 1942 to 1945. Specifications included:

Weight: 27.5 tons
Length: 20 feet 10 inches
Width: 9 feet 6 inches
Height: 8 feet 2 inches
Power plant: 395-horsepower Liberty
Armament: one 6-pounder and one or two machine guns
Top speed: 27 miles per hour
Crew: five

Cruiser Tank Challenger. Responding to an urgent need to mount a bigger gun—the 17-pounder—designers stretched the Cromwell and produced the ungainly looking Cruiser Tank Challenger. By the time the tank was put into service, the British army was accepting into service the American-built Sherman Firefly tank instead. Few Challengers, therefore, saw combat. Specifications included:

Weight: 32 tons
Length: 26 feet 4 inches
Width: 9 feet 6.5 inches
Height: 8 feet 9 inches

Power plant: 600-horsepower Rolls-Royce Meteor V-12 gasoline engine
Armament: one 17-pounder and one machine gun
Top speed: 32 miles per hour
Crew: five

British tanks designated "Cruisers" were designed for speed, whereas those designated "Infantry" were more heavily armored and were intended to be used in conjunction with infantry, so speed was less important. The distinction between the two tank types was, in fact, a dubious one, and no other combatant nation adopted it.

Matilda Infantry Tanks. The Mark I and Mark II Matilda infantry tanks were inexpensive Vickers designs, the first of which was delivered in 1936. Most of the Matildas—the name was intended to reflect the vehicle's ducklike gait and appearance—were lost during the Battle of France in 1940. Although slow, the Matildas were heavily armored and readily withstood fire from the German tanks used in France. They had some success in the North African Campaign, where their 2-pounder cannon had very good armor penetration. However, as the new German tanks introduced heavier armor and bigger guns, the Matilda was outclassed and was replaced by the adoption of such American-built tanks as the Lee, Grant, and Sherman.

Specifications included:

Weight: 11 tons
Length: 15 feet 11 inches
Width: 7 feet 6 inches
Height: 6 feet 1.5 inches
Power plant: 70-horsepower Ford V8
Armament: one 2-pounder gun and one machine gun
Speed: 8–15 miles per hour

Valentine Infantry Tank series. Another rush to production was the Valentine series of infantry tanks. Designed in 1938–39, the first Valentine tank was prototyped on February 14, 1940, Valentine's Day, and by the end of production in 1944, 8,275 Valentines had been built. They went through many major iterations and many modifications,

some performed in the field, and proved to be sturdy and reliable, especially after the initial riveted construction had been replaced by welding.

Specifications included:

Weight: 16–17 tons
Length: 17 feet 9 inches
Width: 8 feet 7.5 inches
Height: 7 feet 5.5 inches
Power plant: one AEC gasoline engine or an AEC or GM Diesel, developing 131 to 165 horsepower
Armament (Marks 8–10): one 6-pounder and one machine gun
Top speed: 15 miles per hour
Crew: three or four

Churchill Infantry Tank series. The first of the Churchill series of infantry tanks was delivered in mid-1941 and was beset by mechanical problems. Once these were resolved, however, the Churchill became the most familiar tank in the British inventory. It served as a platform for modification to suit a variety of specialty roles. In many ways a throwback to the era of trench warfare, the Churchill was lumbering but heavily armored and could accept a heavy gun. General specifications included:

Weight: 38.5–40 tons
Length: 24 feet 5 inches
Width: 10 feet 8 inches (most models)
Height: 8 feet 2 inches (most models)
Power plant: 350-horsepower Bedford twin six-cylinder
Armament: Varied, but up to one 95-mm cannon and two machine guns
Top speed: 15 miles per hour
Crew: five

Archer Tank Destroyer. The tanks of World War II were always tradeoffs among speed, armor, and firepower. A new breed of tank emerged, however. The tank destroyer sacrificed armor and speed for firepower. The weapon was specifically designed to kill other tanks, even if this meant exposing crews to return fire. The Germans built several tank destroyer types, but the British fielded only one, the Archer. It was converted from the Valentine chassis and had a large *rear-facing* turret that mounted a spectacular 17-pounder gun, capable of a high degree of armor penetration. The rear-facing configuration was necessary to maintain stability with such a long and heavy piece of ordnance. Also, this orientation was used to tactical advantage. The Archer was generally hidden in ambush, fired on its prey, then withdrew, its gun still pointing rearward.

General specifications included:

Weight: 38,840 pounds
Power plant: one 192-horsepower GM 6-71 six-cylinder diesel
Length: 21 feet 11 inches
Width: 9 feet 5 inches
Height: 7 feet 4.5 inches
Top speed: 20 miles per hour
Crew: four

Further reading: Buckley, John. *British Armour in the Normandy Campaign 1944.* London: Frank Cass, 2004; Chamberlain, Peter. *British and American Tanks of World War II.* New York: Arco, 1984; Chamberlain, Peter, and Chris Ellis. *British and American Tanks of World War Two: The Complete Illustrated History of British, American and Commonwealth Tanks, 1939–45.* New York: Sterling, 2000; Fletcher, David. *Great Tank Scandal; British Armour in the Second World War.* London: Stationery Office Books, 1989.

armor, French

France produced four important tanks that were used in World War II, three reflecting the thinking of World War I and one of an exceptional new design.

Hotchkiss light tanks. The Hotchkiss light tanks (H-35 and H-38/H-39) were intended to support cavalry units. They were, accordingly, light and relatively fast, with a top speed of 22.67 miles per hour. Armament consisted of a short-barreled 37-mm main gun and a 7.5-mm machine gun, wholly inadequate against modern tank armor. The Hotchkiss's own armor plating was very thin. Designed with little foresight and based mainly on

the state of tank design at the end of World War I, then deployed during the BATTLE OF FRANCE in piecemeal fashion rather than in potentially effective massed formations, the Hotchkiss light tanks were readily picked off. Captured by the Germans after the fall of France, they were used by second-line units only. Specifications included:

Weight: 26,680 pounds
Length: 13.85 feet
Width: 6.4 feet
Height: 7.05 feet
Armament: 37-mm main gun, 7.5-mm machine gun
Power plant: 120-horsepower Hotchkiss six-cylinder gasoline engine
Top speed: 22.67 miles per hour
Crew: two

Renault R-35. While the Hotchkiss was a "cavalry" tank, the Renault R-35 was an "infantry" tank, with somewhat more armor and a much lower maximum speed. It was the most numerous French light infantry tank during the time of the Battle of France, with more than 1,600 having been produced by 1940. Like the Hotchkiss, the Renault reflected the state of the art as of the end of World War I. It was prototyped in 1934 and went into production the following year. The tank mounted a long-barreled version of the 37-mm SA 38 L/33 cannon and also had a machine gun. The R-35 was not a standout as a performer, but it was neither better nor worse than most other tanks at the outbreak of war. Like other Allied tanks, it was quickly outclassed by newer German weapons, but the WEHRMACHT itself made use of captured Renaults against inferior opponents in the Balkans and, for a time in 1941, against the Russians as well. Specifications included:

Weight: 23,375 pounds
Length: 13 feet 9.25 inches
Width: 6 feet 0.75 inch
Height: 7 feet 9.25 inches
Armament: one 37-mm SA 38 L/33 cannon and one machine gun
Power plant: 85-horsepower Renault four-cylinder gasoline engine

Top speed: 12.42 miles per hour
Crew: two

SOMUA S-35 medium tank. The standout among French tanks was the SOMUA S-35 medium tank, which, in contrast to the other French tanks, looked forward rather than backward in its design. Turret and hull were cast and welded components rather than riveted plates. The armor was thick and shaped to deflect incoming rounds, a design feature that would later appear on the most advanced German tanks. Its eight-cylinder engine gave it a respectable top speed of 24.85 miles per hour, and it mounted a 47-mm SA 35 gun, one of the most potent in 1940 and still a decent contender by 1944, when the Germans fielded captured units.

An S-35 prototype was produced late in 1934, and by May 1940, the French army had more than 400 in service. Specifications included:

Weight: 42,997 pounds
Length: 17 feet 7.8 inches
Width: 6 feet 11.5 inches
Height: 8 feet 7 inches
Armament: one 47-mm SA 35 main gun
Power plant: 190-horsepower SOMUA V-8 gasoline engine
Top speed: 24.85 miles per hour
Crew: three

Char B1-bis heavy tank. The only significant French heavy tank was the Char B1-bis, which was the most backward-looking of the generally backward-looking French tanks. Its design dated to 1916–17, yet it was an excellent vehicle, overall—and one capable of mounting a 75-mm or even 105-mm gun. Unfortunately for the French, it was never used efficiently. Whereas the Germans developed superb tank tactics and doctrine, massing and coordinating firepower, the French tended to deploy their tanks in piecemeal and static fashion, making them relatively easy targets for attackers.

Specifications of the Char B1-bis included:

Weight: 41 tons
Length: 27.34 feet
Width: 6.5 feet

Height: 9.33 feet
Power plant: 240-horsepower Renault V-12 gasoline engine
Top speed: 17.4 miles per hour
Armament: one 75-mm or 105-mm gun and two 8-mm machine guns
Crew: seven

Further reading: Crawford, Steve. *Tanks of World War II.* Osceola, Wis.: Motorbooks International, 2000; Foss, Christopher. *The Encyclopedia of Tanks and Armored Fighting Vehicles: The Comprehensive Guide to over 900 Armored Fighting Vehicles from 1915 to the Present Day.* Berkeley, Calif.: Thunder Bay Press, 2002; Miller, David. *The Illustrated Directory of Tanks of the World.* Osceola, Wis.: Motorbooks International, 2000.

armor, German

Except for the Soviet T-34, German tanks were the most advanced and most formidable of World War II. The best of them were engineering masterpieces, a fact, however, that also limited their ultimate effectiveness as weapons. As German tanks became more complex, they became more difficult and time-consuming to manufacture. The most advanced models could not be produced in strategically sufficient quantities. Moreover, the complexity, the "overengineering," of the German tanks made field maintenance difficult and sometimes impossible. German tanks were reliable and had great durability, but when disabled by mechanical breakdown or battle damage, they often could not be readily made operational again.

The most famous and most numerous series of German tanks were the Panzerkampfwagenen, the Panzers. The Panzer program was instigated by HEINZ GUDERIAN, the father of German armor. Despite the success of British tanks in World War I, the conservative German military establishment of the early 1930s resisted the concept of armored warfare. In 1933, however, Guderian staged a demonstration of mobile tank warfare for ADOLF HITLER, who instantly grasped the potential of the weapon and authorized Guderian to develop tanks and a tank corps, giving both the highest priority.

Panzer I. The Panzer I was developed beginning in 1933 and was first deployed in the Spanish Civil War. By 1939 and the INVASION OF POLAND, it had been produced in a quantity of 1,445. Even for its time, the tank was small and light, crewed by just two men, a driver and a commander, and armed with nothing more than two light 0.3-inch machine guns. Lightly armed and thinly armored, the Panzer I was not used in great quantity during the BATTLE OF FRANCE, and by the end of 1941, these tanks were no longer used in front-line service at all, except for a version modified as a command tank, equipped inside with a small map table and extra radio equipment for use by Panzer unit commanders. Some other Panzer Is were converted for carrying either ammunition or an antitank gun, but even these were phased out well before the end of the war.

General specifications included:

Weight: 13,230 pounds
Length: 14 feet 6 inches
Width: 6 feet 9 inches
Height: 5 feet 8 inches
Power plant: one 100-horsepower Maybach NL38 TR six-cylinder gasoline engine
Top speed: 25 miles per hour
Armament: two 0.3-inch machine guns

Panzer II. The next development was the Panzer II, a three-man light tank designed in the mid-1930s and intended as an interim design while the Panzer III and Panzer IV medium tanks were under development. Although the Panzer II was used as a main battle tank in the invasions of Poland and France in 1939 and 1940, its longer-term purpose was primarily for training. About a thousand Panzer IIs took part in the Polish and French BLITZKRIEG operations. The tank was also used in the INVASION OF THE SOVIET UNION in 1941, but by that time it was certainly obsolescent, weak on armor as well as firepower.

The Panzer II chassis was used as the basis for such specialized vehicles as a fast reconnaissance tank and for Germany's first amphibious tank, complete with a propeller and intended for use in OPERATION SEALION, the planned invasion of England in 1940. Fitted with a pair of flamethrowers and christened Flammpanzer II, the Panzer II saw service as a flamethrower vehicle beginning in 1942. Some obsolete Panzer II models were also converted to self-propelled antitank guns, mounting captured Soviet 76-mm Marder I guns or German 75-mm Marder IIs. After the Polish occupation, the Panzer II sometimes carried a 105-mm Wespe.

General specifications of the Panzer II included:

Weight: 22,046 pounds
Length: 15 feet 3 inches
Width: 7 feet 6.5 inches
Height: 6 feet 7.5 inches
Power plant: one 140-horsepower Maybach six-cylinder gasoline engine
Top speed: 34 miles per hour
Armament: one 20-mm gun and one coaxial 0.3-inch machine gun

Panzer III. The Panzer III, a five-man medium tank, was also conceived in the 1930s and was formally accepted for service in 1939, at which time mass production commenced. Some of these tanks did see service in the invasion of Poland, but in the Soviet Union they met their match going up against the T-34. In response, a bigger gun was installed, but the real solution was the Panzer IV.

Despite its shortcomings, the Panzer III was the main German tank from 1940 to 1942, and some 15,000 were rolled off assembly lines before production ended in mid-1943. Even after this, the Panzer III continued to serve as the platform for a self-propelled gun, which was produced through war's end. Some models were modified as command tanks.

General specifications included:

Weight: 49,160 pounds
Length: 21 feet
Width: 9 feet 8 inches
Height: 8 feet 2.5 inches
Power plant: one Maybach 300-horsepower 12-cylinder gasoline engine
Top speed: 25 miles per hour
Armament: First models had a 37-mm gun; first combat models were fitted with a 50-mm

gun; later models received a 75-mm gun to counteract the firepower of the Soviet T-34. All models had two machine guns.

Panzer IV. Commencing production in 1936, the five-man Panzer IV medium tank was produced throughout World War II and was the principal German tank, production totaling some 9,000 units. The tank was variously and continuously modified during the war, but the basic chassis remained unchanged. Heinz Guderian relied heavily on the Panzer IV and repeatedly called for increased production. Hitler, however, always enamored of new weapons systems, diverted production to the Panzer V (Panther) and the Panzer VI (Tiger), huge, heavy, complex vehicles that required long production schedules. Shortages of the Panzer IV crippled German armored forces, but the tank itself was extremely formidable and, on a one-to-one basis, outgunned everything thrown against it.

General specifications included:

Weight: 55,115 pounds
Length: 23 feet
Width: 10 feet 9.5 inches
Height: 8 feet 9.5 inches
Power plant: one Maybach 300-horsepower 12-cylinder gasoline engine
Top speed: 24 miles per hour
Armament: short-barreled 75-mm gun, later replaced by a more powerful long-barreled 75-mm gun; two machine guns (one mounted coaxially and one as an antiaircraft mount)

Panzer V "Panther." The Panzer V "Panther" was a heavy tank, crewed by four and specifically designed to counter the excellent Soviet T-34. Its armor plating was thick and heavy, but, most important of all, sloped, so that rounds fired against it tended to ricochet off.

Production began at the end of 1942, and Hitler planned to turn out 600 of these mammoth vehicles per month. But the sheer complexity of the Panther made this impossible. In a good month, 300 rolled off the lines, and by the end of the war

some 4,800 had been produced. Worse, the tank was rushed into full production without adequate testing and trials. Mechanical failures were frequent and typically impossible to repair in the field. Once the problems had been addressed, the Panther emerged as the best German tank of the war, but its numbers were never sufficient to overcome the numerical advantages of Allied tank forces.

The Panther's baptism of fire came at the BATTLE OF KURSK (July 1943) in the Soviet Union—the greatest tank battle in history. However, the Panther also served in Normandy after the NORMANDY LANDINGS (D-DAY) and on most of the other fronts.

General specifications included:

Weight: 100,310 pounds
Length: 29 feet 0.75 inch
Width: 11 feet 3 inches
Height: 10 feet 2 inches
Power plant: one Maybach 700-horsepower 12-cylinder diesel engine
Top speed: 29 miles per hour
Armament: one long-barreled 75-mm gun and two machine guns (one coaxially mounted and one in an antiaircraft mount)

Panzer VI "Tiger." The Panzer VI Tiger tank was even more formidable than the Panther. It carried a spectacular 88-mm gun, Germany's most powerful, which could be used both as a heavy antiaircraft gun and as an antitank weapon. Two prototypes were rushed to completion in time for Hitler's birthday in April 1942. Between 1942 and August 1944, 1,350 Tigers were produced before production was shifted to the even heavier and more powerful Tiger II tank, the so-called King Tiger.

In addition to the standard Tiger with its 88-mm gun, a few tanks—no more than 10 in all—were produced to launch heavy rockets. Some Tigers were modified as gunless command tanks, which also mounted a winch so that they could be used for tank tow and recovery. Unfortunately for the Germans, this function was often needed because the complex Tigers frequently broke down. The tank's suspension wheels system, beautifully designed to carry the enormous weight of the vehicle, was complicated and, ultimately, delicate. Large stones and heavy mud fouled it, disabling the tank, especially in the Russian winter. Frozen and immobile, even a Tiger was vulnerable. Moreover, the Tiger was so large, complex, and expensive that relatively few could be produced—1,350 were built between August 1942 and August 1944—and while the Tiger outmatched any Allied opponent tank for tank, it was always vastly outnumbered. Finally, there was the issue of range. The Tiger was limited to 62 miles before it needed to refuel. This was a critical problem as German supply lines and fuel resources became increasingly strained.

Despite its serious drawbacks, the Tiger was a great, forward-looking design, which pointed the way to the tanks of the postwar era. It mounted a very potent gun matched to highly advanced optics. This gave the Tiger the ability to attack from long range, generally well out of the range of enemy tanks. And when it moved closer in, its heavy armor made it virtually impervious to the armor-piercing shells of the time.

General specifications of the Tiger included:

Weight: 121,250 pounds
Length: 27 feet
Width: 12 feet 3 inches
Height: 9 feet 3.25 inches
Power plant: one 700-horsepower Maybach 12-cylinder gasoline engine
Top speed: 24 miles per hour
Armament: one 88-mm gun and two machine guns (one coaxially mounted and one mounted above the front hull)

Panzer VI (Tiger II or King Tiger). As impressive as the Tiger was, a successor was on the drawing boards just as the Tiger went into production. The Panzer VI, called the Tiger II or King Tiger, would mount even more firepower and have more armor protection than the Tiger. Initially, designers thought of arming the King Tiger with a titanic 150-mm gun but settled instead on a long-barreled version of the 88-mm, which was more powerful than that used on the Tiger. Design work on the new tank was completed late in 1943, and produc-

tion began that December. At first, King Tigers were produced alongside the Tigers, but from August 1944, the King Tigers took over all assembly lines. This meant that the number of new tanks reaching the front lines was drastically reduced, and, by the end of the war, only 485 King Tigers had been built. Hitler's obsession with "wonder weapons" had succeeded in motivating the design of extraordinary tanks, but at a cost in reduced production that severely crippled the German war effort.

The King Tiger saw action against the Soviets in May 1944 and in France in August 1944. Its extremely heavy armor afforded a high degree of protection, but even its 700-horsepower engine could not push it above 24 miles per hour. Allied tanks could outmaneuver it and, working in concert, mass firepower against it. Worse, introduced late in the war, when Germany was increasingly on the defensive and the Allies had seized air superiority and even air supremacy, the massive King Tiger was almost impossible to hide and was therefore exposed to bombing attacks. Finally, like its predecessor, the King Tiger suffered the weaknesses of over-engineered complexity. When it broke down or was damaged, it was usually impossible to repair in the field. Like the Tiger, too, it consumed huge quantities of increasingly scarce fuel and had an operating range of just 68 miles.

General specifications included:

Weight: 153,660 pounds
Length: 33 feet 8 inches
Width: 12 feet 3.5 inches
Height: 10 feet 1.5 inches
Power plant: one 700-horsepower Maybach 12-cylinder gasoline engine
Top speed: 24 miles per hour
Armament: one long-barrel, high-muzzle-velocity 88-mm gun and two machine guns (one coaxially mounted and one mounted above the front hull)

If the Germans produced the most advanced tanks of the war, they also devoted more attention than any other combatant nation to the design and production of tank destroyers. These were essentially tanks that sacrificed varying degrees of armor protection and speed in order to carry heavy guns sufficiently powerful to penetrate the armor of enemy tanks.

Panzerjäger I. The first German tank destroyer was the Panzerjäger (Tank Hunter) I. Originally intended as a training vehicle, the Panzerjäger I began production in 1934. After the fall of CZECHO-SLOVAKIA, however, the Panzerjäger I was fitted with a Czech 4.7-cm antitank gun, along with a machine gun mounted in the same turret, and was pressed into service in 1940 as an antitank weapon.

General specifications of the Panzerjäger I included:

Weight: 13,288 pounds
Length: 13 feet 7 inches
Width: 6 feet 7.25 inches
Height: 6 feet 10.7 inches
Power plant: one 100-horsepower Maybach six-cylinder gasoline engine
Top speed: 24.8 miles per hour
Armament: one Czech 4.7-cm antitank gun and a machine gun

Marder II. Introduced next was the Marder II, which entered service in 1935 as a training vehicle. Like the Panzerjäger I, however, it was soon modified for the tank destroyer mission with the addition of a 7.5-mm Pak 40/2 antitank gun, the German army's standard antitank gun at the start of World War II. To accommodate the weight of the gun, the engine of the Marder had to be moved to the rear of the hull. The Marder II turret was fixed in the forward-firing position. The gun was aimed by steering and moving the tank. While the Marder II was far from being a flexible weapon, it proved durable and continued in production until 1944. It was one of the most widely used German self-propelled guns.

General specifications included:

Weight: 24,251 pounds
Length: 20 feet 10.4 inches
Width: 7 feet 5.8 inches
Height: 7 feet 2.6 inches
Power plant: one 140-horsepower Maybach HL 62 gasoline engine

Top speed: 24.8 miles per hour
Armament: one 7.5-mm Pak 40/2 antitank gun and one machine gun

Marder III. The Marder III, also called the Panzerjäger 38(t), was built on a Czech chassis intended for the Skoda TNHP-S tank and was produced in two variations, one that mounted a 7.62-cm Pak 36r gun and one that mounted the 7.5-cm Pak 40/3. The Marder III was fielded beginning in 1941 with the explicit purpose of countering the Soviet T-34, which overmatched the firepower of German tanks at the time.

General specifications of the Marder III included:

Weight: 24,251 pounds
Length: 15 feet 3.1 inches
Width: 7 feet 8.5 inches
Height: 8 feet 1.6 inches
Power plant: one 150-horsepower Praga AC gasoline engine
Top speed: 26 miles per hour
Armament: one 7.62-cm Pak 36r gun or one 7.5-cm Pak 40/3 gun; both variants mounted one machine gun

Hetzer. In March 1943, Germany's leading armor commander, Col. Gen. Heinz Guderian, called for a light tank destroyer to replace the Marder series, which was correctly considered a set of "interim solutions" for antitank warfare. In response, German designers developed the Hetzer, which was based on the Panzerkampfwagen 38(t) chassis. Designs were ready on December 17, 1943, and the first prototypes were produced in March 1944. The vehicle was manufactured by two Czech firms, BMM (Boehmish-Mährische Maschinenfabrik) and Skoda. Production started in April 1944, and by the end of the war in May 1945, 2,584 had been produced.

The Hetzer was characterized by an extremely low profile (6 feet 10.7 inches in height) and mounted a 75-mm Pak 39 L/48 antitank gun (or, in some versions, a 14-mm Flammenwerfer 41 flamethrower). Compact, economical to produce, and relatively easy to maintain in the field, the Hetzer was a highly effective tank destroyer.

General specifications included:

Weight: 31,967 pounds
Length: 20 feet 4.1 inches
Width: 8 feet 2.4 inches
Height: 6 feet 10.7 inches
Power plant: one 150-horsepower Praga AC/2800 gasoline engine
Top speed: 24.2 miles per hour
Armament: one 75-mm Pak 39 L/48 gun or one 14-mm Flammenwerfer 41 flamethrower; both versions also mounted one 7.92-mm machine gun

Jägdpanzer IV. Jägdpanzer IV was designed in early 1943 and prototyped in December of that year. It was designated Sturmgeschutz neuer Art mit 7.5cm PaK L/48 auf Fahrgestell PzKpfw IV (Sd.Kfz.162) and was also known as Jägdpanzer E 39, but was more commonly called Jägdpanzer IV. It incorporated the low silhouette that served the Hetzer so well, but was longer and heavier, capable of mounting the long-barrel version of the 7.5-cm Pak gun. Its armor was sloped to improve impact deflection. Like the Hetzer, the Jägdpanzer IV did not mount the gun in a turret, but on the front of the hull, so that directional aiming was accomplished mainly by steering the vehicle. Tank destroyer guns did not absolutely require the flexibility of a turret, because antitank tactics called for the vehicle to be hidden in ambush. Generally, the tank destroyer waited for its prey, then fired at will.

General specifications included:

Weight: 56,879 pounds
Length: 28 feet 1.8 inches
Width: 9 feet 7.4 inches
Height: 6 feet 5.2 inches
Power plant: one 265-horsepower Maybach HL 120 gasoline engine
Top speed: 22 miles per hour
Armament: one 7.5-cm PaK gun and one machine gun

Nashorn. The exigencies of combat on the Russian front moved German military planners to rush into production a number of improvised solutions to unanticipated problems. One of the most formidable and least anticipated of these problems was the Soviet T-34 tank. Powerful guns were required to destroy it, and it became necessary to find a rapid way to transport the formidable 88-mm PaK 43/1 L/71 gun. The new tank destroyer was called for in February 1942, and by November of that year, the vehicles began to arrive at the front. The design was originally called the Hornisse ("Hornet"), but on order of no less than Adolf Hitler, the name was changed to Nashorn—"Rhinoceros."

To conserve precious supplies of hardened armor plate, the hull of the vehicle was protected by unhardened plate. The Nashorn first served in quantity at the Battle of Kursk. It quickly proved its effectiveness when used as a standoff weapon— that is, out of the range of enemy guns. Close in, its high profile, necessary to accommodate the long 88-mm gun, made it vulnerable. As with the Hetzer and Jägdpanzer IV, the gun was mounted on the hull rather than in a turret.

General specifications included:

Weight: 54,000 pounds
Length: 27 feet 8.25 inches
Width: 9 feet 8 ⅛ inches
Height: 9 feet 7.75 inches
Power plant: one 265-horsepower Maybach HL 120 TRM1
Top speed: 25 miles per hour
Armament: one 88-mm Pak 43/1 L/71 gun and one 7.92-mm machine gun

Panzerjäger Tiger (P) "Elefant." The Panzerjäger Tiger (P) "Elefant" came into being in 1943 as an offshoot of the Tiger tank program. The Porsche firm competed with Henschel for the Tiger contract but lost the main contract to Henschel. By this time, Porsche had already built 90 chassis, which were converted into tank destroyers. Dubbed the "Elefant," this tank destroyer featured a unique power plant consisting of two gas generators that powered a pair of electric drive units. Thus, the engine may be described as gasoline-electric. The Elefants served on the Russian front, but, despite heavy armor and a very potent 8.8-cm

Stu.K. 43(L/71) or 43/2 gun, fared poorly because of a truly elephantine top speed of only 12.5 miles per hour and poor maneuverability.

General specifications included:

Weight: 143,300 pounds
Length: 26 feet 8 inches
Width: 11 feet 1 inch
Height: 9 feet 10 inches
Power plant: two Maybach HL 120 TRMs (combined horsepower, 590) driving two rear-mounted electric drive units
Top speed: 12.5 miles per hour
Armament: one 8.8-cm Stu.K. 43(L/71) or 43/2 gun

Jägdpanther. The Jägdpanther entered production in February 1944. In contrast to all the German tank destroyers that came before it, the Jägdpanther was purpose-built for its mission rather than converted from an existing tank chassis. The result was not only an excellent tank destroyer, but one that had few of the compromises characteristic of this vehicle type. Mounting a formidable 8.8-cm Pak 43 antitank gun, it was a great standoff weapon that could engage armored targets at long ranges from a static (ambush) position. But unlike the Jägdpanzer IV, it combined speed and heavy, sloping armor to allow it to work close in as well without rendering itself vulnerable. Fortunately for the Allies, only 382 of this most formidable weapon were produced before production facilities were captured in April 1945.

General specifications included:

Weight: 101,411 pounds
Length: 32 feet 5.8 inches
Width: 10 feet 8.7 inches
Height: 8 feet 10.9 inches
Power plant: one 700-horsepower Maybach HL230 gasoline engine
Top speed: 34.2 miles per hour
Armament: one 8.8-cm Pak 43/3 or 43/4(L/71) ball mounted in hull and one machine gun

Jägdtiger. The Jägdtiger was the tank destroyer version of the King Tiger tank. Instead of mounting its gun in a full-traverse turret, the massive 128-mm gun was ball mounted in a sloping superstructure rising from the hull. Crewed by six, the 167,551-pound vehicle was essentially a self-propelled gun, a piece of potent defensive artillery, intended to be moved where needed and then fired from a static position. Few were produced before the end of the war.

General specifications included:

Weight: 167,551 pounds
Length: 34 feet 11.4 inches
Width: 11 feet 10.7 inches
Height: 9 feet 8 inches
Power plant: one 700-horsepower Maybach HL230 gasoline engine
Top speed: 21.5 miles per hour
Armament: one 128-mm gun and one machine gun

Further reading: Carius, Otto. *Tigers in the Mud: The Combat Career of German Panzer Commander Otto Carius.* Mechanicsburg, Penn.: Stackpole, 2003; Chamberlain, Peter, and Hilary Doyle. *Encyclopedia of German Tanks of World War Two.* New York: Sterling, 1999; Fey, Will. *Armor Battles of the Waffen SS, 1943–45.* Mechanicsburg, Penn.: Stackpole, 2003; Green, Michael, Thomas Anderson, and Frank Schulz. *German Tanks of World War II in Color.* Osceola, Wis.: Motorbooks International, 2000; Raus, Erhard. *Panzer Operations: The Eastern Front Memoir of General Raus, 1941–1945.* New York: Da Capo, 2003; Wilbeck, Christopher. *Sledgehammers: Strengths and Flaws of Tiger Tank Battalions in World War II.* Bedford, Penn.: Aberjona Press, 2004.

armor, Italian

Italy fielded a small number of tanks during World War II and struggled to adapt the best of them to the harsh desert environment of the NORTH AFRICAN CAMPAIGN.

Fiat L 6/40 light tank. The Fiat L 6/40 light tank was typically classified as a tankette and was based largely on a prewar British model, the Carden Lloyd Mark VI. Initially, the diminutive tank was armed with a 37-mm gun in a sponson and twin machine guns in a turret. Most examples that actually saw combat service, however, either had a turret-mounted 37-mm gun and a coaxial machine gun or a turret-mounted Breda Model 35 20-mm cannon with a coaxially mounted Breda Model 38 8-mm machine gun. The tank was used principally for reconnaissance missions and was typically attached to cavalry units. Only 283 were produced between 1941 and February 1943.

General specifications included:

Weight: 14,991 pounds
Length: 12 feet 5 inches
Width: 6 feet 4 inches
Height: 6 feet 8 inches
Power plant: one 70-horsepower SPA 18D four-cylinder gasoline engine
Top speed: 26 miles per hour
Armament (late models): one Breda Model 35 20-mm cannon and one coaxially mounted Breda Model 38 8-mm machine gun

Fiat M 11/39 and M 13/40. The Fiat M 11/39 was prototyped in 1937, but by the start of the war, its hull was redesigned, offering riveted construction and heavier armor and redesignated the M 13/40. The tank was typically fitted with a 47-mm sponson-mounted main gun and, in the turret, twin 8-mm machine guns. Although both versions of the tank were quickly outclassed in desert warfare by Allied tanks, the British eagerly grabbed up whatever abandoned M 11/39s and M 13/40s they could get into running conditions.

General specifications included:

Weight: 30,865 pounds
Length: 16 feet 2 inches
Width: 7 feet 3 inches
Height: 7 feet 10 inches
Power plant: one 125-horsepower SPA TM40 diesel engine
Top speed: 20 miles per hour
Armament: one sponson-mounted 47-mm main gun and twin turret-mounted 8-mm machine guns

Fiat M 15/42. The most advanced of Italy's tanks was the Fiat M 15/42 medium tank, which was a modification of the M 15/41 fitted with a diesel engine and high-efficiency air filters designed

to cope with the desert sands that wreaked havoc on gasoline and diesel engines alike.

General specifications of the M 15/42 included:

Weight: 34,800 pounds
Length: 16 feet 7 inches
Width: 7 feet 4 inches
Height: 7 feet 11 inches
Power plant: one 192-horsepower SPA 15 TB M42 eight-cylinder diesel engine
Top speed: 25 miles per hour
Armament: one 47-mm turret-mounted main and two Modello 38 8-mm machine guns, one coaxially mounted and one mounted as an antiaircraft gun

Like its Axis partner Germany, Italy also fielded tank destroyers, tanklike vehicles that sacrificed thick armor, speed, and general flexibility to serve as mobile platforms for guns sufficiently large and powerful to deliver armor-piercing ordnance against enemy tanks. The two principal Italian tank destroyers were essentially self-propelled guns, designed to travel to a favorable firing position and engage the enemy from static ambush.

Semovente L.40 da 47/32. The Semovente L.40 da 47/32 was developed during the late 1930s and was little more than a track-mounted tank chassis bearing a 47-mm long-barrel antitank gun, built under license from the Austrian firm Böhler. The gun was mounted atop the vehicle superstructure, with little protection. About 280 of the tanks were produced by 1942, and they served effectively against relatively lightly armored British tanks in the North African desert.

General specifications included:

Weight: 14,330 pounds
Length: 13 feet 1.5 inches
Width: 6 feet 3.6 inches
Height: 5 feet 4.2 inches
Power plant: one 68-horsepower SPA 18D four-cylinder gasoline engine
Top speed: 26.3 miles per hour
Armament: one Böhler 47-mm antitank gun

Semovente M.41M da 90/53. The Semovente M.41M da 90/53 began production in 1941 and was produced in small quantity before the Italian surrender. Like the smaller and lighter L.40 da 47/32, it was little more than a tank chassis on which an exposed gun was mounted—in this case a formidable 90-mm long-barrel piece. This gun was sufficiently impressive that the Germans took special care to keep as many as possible out of Allied hands as the Italians fell apart during the North African Campaign.

General specifications included:

Weight: 37,479 pounds
Length: 17 feet 0.9 inch
Width: 7 feet 2.6 inches
Height: 7 feet 0.6 inch
Power plant: one 145-horsepower SPA 15-TM-41 eight-cylinder gasoline engine
Top speed: 22 miles per hour
Armament: one 90-mm long-barrel antitank gun

Further reading: Crawford, Steve, and Chris Westhorp. *Tanks of World War II.* Osceola, Wis.: Motorbooks International, 2000; Jowett, Philip S., and Stephen Andrew. *The Italian Army, 1940–45: Africa 1940–43.* London: Osprey, 2001; Jowett, Philip S. *Italian Army in World War II: Europe 1940–43.* London: Osprey, 2000.

armor, Japanese

With the exception of the remarkable Soviet T-34, Allied tanks, on a vehicle for vehicle basis, were generally inferior to German tanks. In the Pacific theater, however, the Allies, particularly the Americans, had the advantage. The Japanese militarists had created a formidable force in the Imperial Army, but they had largely neglected armor. As a result, they fielded only two major types of tanks, both outclassed by the American Sherman. The lack of emphasis on the tank is understandable, since the Japanese correctly envisioned fighting on Pacific jungle islands, not the open spaces of the European battlegrounds. What tank designs the military did order were light to medium, capable of being readily sealifted and landed.

Type 95 light tank (Ha-Go). The Type 95 light tank, the Ha-Go, was developed in 1933 by Mit-

subishi and was used throughout World War II. Light and durable, it could be readily landed during amphibious operations, and it performed well in the absence of roads and across marshy or monsoon-soaked ground. Its air-cooled, six-cylinder diesel performed well in Northern Manchuria as well as the Pacific jungles. Crewed by three or four, its small turret accommodated only a single man, so that, in addition to directing the driver, the commander had to load, aim, and fire the main 37-mm gun. Armor plating was very light, making the Type 95 extremely vulnerable to fire of all kinds. Although the Type 95 was a reasonable match for a U.S. M3 Stuart, it was readily outclassed by the Sherman.

General specifications included:

Weight: 7.4 tons
Length: 14 feet 4 inches
Width: 6 feet 9 inches
Height: 7 feet 2 inches
Power plant: one 120-horsepower Mitsubishi NVD 6120 six-cylinder diesel
Top speed: 25 miles per hour
Armament: two machine guns; one 37-mm main gun

Type 97 medium tank (Chi-Ha). The Type 97 medium tank, called the Chi-Ha, went into production in 1937, just in time for use in the SINO-JAPANESE WAR. Heavier than the Type 95, it was a medium tank of reasonably advanced design, but it was too heavy for the jungle terrain of the Pacific. It therefore did not enjoy great success in that principal theater of the Pacific war. Nevertheless, Mitsubishi produced about 3,000 of the vehicles mounting a 57-mm main gun as well as specialized versions used as tank recovery vehicles, flail mine clearers, bridge layers, and self-propelled gun mounts for antiaircraft guns. Very late in the war, the Imperial Navy even installed a 120-mm gun on some Type 97s.

General specifications of the Chi-Ha included:

Weight: 14.8 tons
Length: 18 feet 2 inches
Width: 7 feet 7 inches
Height: 7 feet 9 inches

Power plant: one 170-horsepower Mitsubishi 12-cylinder air-cooled diesel
Top speed: 25 miles per hour
Armament: one 57-mm Type 97 gun mounted in the turret; one 7.7-mm Type 97 machine gun mounted in the rear of the turret; one 7.7-mm Type 97 machine gun mounted in the hull

Further reading: Chamberlain, Peter. *Axis Combat Tanks.* New York: Arco, 1978; Crawford, Steve, and Chris Westhorp. *Tanks of World War II.* Osceola, Wis.: Motorbooks International, 2000; Jowett, Philip S. *Japanese Army 1931–45.* London: Osprey, 2002.

armor, Soviet

T-34. The single most important tank the Soviet Union produced during World War II was perhaps the greatest all-around tank of World War II. Indeed, a significant number of historians specializing in World War II weaponry believe that the T-34 was the greatest tank design *ever.* That it was essential to the Red Army victory is not a matter of opinion but a historical fact, and the T-34 achieved near-legendary status before the war was over.

While the formidable tanks the Germans introduced relatively late in the war were extraordinary engineering achievements, they failed to achieve what was accomplished with the T-34: balance among the competing priorities of armor protection, mobility, and firepower. Moreover, whereas the elaborately over-engineered German Panzers were almost impossible to maintain or repair in the field, the T-34 was not only reliable, but downright simple to maintain. And it was simple to maintain because it was, relatively speaking, simple to build. The super tanks of Germany were large, complex, and expensive—factors that sharply limited the quantities that could be produced. The straightforward T-34 was produced in a quantity of more than 35,000.

Like most Soviet weaponry, the T-34 was, in large measure, derivative of weapons systems developed in the West. Its design was based on the Christies "fast tank" developed by the British during the interwar period. But Soviet designers progressed far beyond the models they emulated, and the T-34 quickly evolved through a number of intermediate designs, prototypes, and limited-production examples. The hallmarks of the T-34 were its sturdy and flexible Christie-type suspension, its sloping hull and turret (which seemed to shed incoming rounds), and its fine 85-mm gun, which combined long barrel length with high muzzle velocity for accuracy and potency of fire. The Soviets mated the T-34 to a diesel engine both for durability and to reduce the risk of fire when hit. The diesel also endowed the T-34 with a longer operating range, which was essential on the vast battlefields of the eastern front.

The first T-34/76A was delivered to the Red Army in June 1940. Production was insufficient to allow fielding the new tank against the Germans during the opening phases of the INVASION OF THE SOVIET UNION. During 1941, about 2,800 of the tanks were turned out, but production soon accelerated. The tank itself could be built in just 40 hours. However, other component makers initially had difficulty keeping pace. Particularly critical was an early shortage of V-12 diesel engines and transmissions. But Soviet planners recognized the importance of the T-34 and rushed to build dedicated plants at Kharkov, Kirov, Stalingrad, Mariupol, Voroshilovgrad, Chita, Novo-Sibirsk, Chelyabinsk, Nizhni-Tagil, and, later, Gorki and Saratov. Once the T-34 made its debut in quantity in July 1941, the Germans were shocked. Accustomed to enjoying armored supremacy, the invaders now found that many of their tanks had become obsolete and certainly outgunned.

General specifications of the T-34 included:

Weight: 26 tons
Length: 19 feet 5.1 inches
Width: 9 feet 10 inches
Height: 8 feet
Power plant: one 500-horsepower V-2-34 V-12 diesel
Top speed: 34 miles per hour

Armament: one 85-mm main gun and two 7.62-mm machine guns, one coaxially mounted and one bow mounted

T-26. While the T-34 overshadowed the rest of Soviet armor, the Red Army fielded other important tanks. The T-26 light infantry tank was developed during the 1920s from the British Vickers light tank, and it went into production beginning in 1931. Over the next decade, the T-26 was built in many variations and in a quantity approaching 13,000 before production stopped in 1941 after the Germans had overrun the factories. Small, lightly armored, and undergunned, the T-26 was no match for the German tanks of the BLITZKRIEG, despite the valor of its crews.

General specifications included:

Weight: 17,600–20,900 pounds
Length (early models): 15 feet 2 inches
Width (early models): 11 feet 2.25 inches
Height (early models): 7 feet 11 inches
Power plant: one 91-horsepower GAZ T-26 eight-cylinder gasoline engine
Top speed: 17.4 miles per hour
Armament (typical): one 37-mm main gun and two 7.62-mm machine guns

T-28. The T-28 medium tank entered production in 1933 and emulated both German and British designs. The T-28 sported three turrets, a main turret mounting a short-barrel 3-inch main gun and two smaller turrets on either side, each mounting machine guns. All of this armament required a large, six-man, crew. The T-28 ended production early in the war, in 1941, because its very light armor made the tanks highly vulnerable. Moreover, their slab sides, as opposed to sloping sides, made them especially easy targets.

General specifications of the T-28 included:

Weight: 28 tons
Length: 24 feet 4.8 inches
Width: 9 feet 2.75 inches
Height: 9 feet 3 inches
Power plant: one 500-horsepower M-17V 12-cylinder gasoline engine
Top speed: 23 miles per hour

Armament (typical): one 3-inch short-barrel main gun and two 7.62-mm machine guns

BT-7. Design work on the BT (Bystrokhodniy Tank, "Fast Tank") series of tanks began in 1931, with the purchase from the United States of two Walter Christie tanks, which incorporated the Christie suspension system. By 1936, the BT-7 emerged and entered production. Thanks to its aircraft engine, the tank was fast at 53.4 miles per hour, but its speed was purchased at the expense of armor. Not only was its skin thin, the aircraft power plant had a fatal tendency to overheat. When the BT-7s faced German Panzers during summer 1941, they fared poorly, although this was by no means entirely a technological failing. At this point in the war, Soviet tank commanders had not mastered the art of effective deployment. Like the French, they tended to use tanks in piecemeal fashion, often firing from static positions. They had not yet developed formation tactics. About 2,000 BT-7s were built.

General specifications included:

Weight: 14 tons
Length: 18 feet 6.8 inches
Width: 7 feet 6 inches
Height: 7 feet 11.3 inches
Power plant: one 500-horsepower M-17T V-12 gasoline engine
Armament: one 45-mm M-1934 main gun and two 7.62-mm machine guns

T-35. Design work on what became the T-35 heavy tank began as early as 1930, and a prototype was produced in July 1932. It was an impressive monster, crewed by 11 and weighing in at 45 tons. Its main turret mounted a 76.2-mm gun, and it bristled with no fewer than four smaller turrets. Two, mounted right front and left rear, had 37-mm 1930 guns, and two, left front and right rear, had machine guns. Full-scale production commenced in 1935. The large crew complement necessitated the use of telephones for communication among crew members.

The T-35 first saw action during the war with FINLAND and also, during the German invasion of the Soviet Union, in and around Lvov and in defense of Moscow. Despite its intimidating appearance, the T-35 was not heavily armored, and that, along with its meager top speed of 18.6 miles per hour, rendered it highly vulnerable. It was used mainly as a self-propelled gun, to be fired from static, well-prepared positions. No more than 61 were produced between 1933 and 1939.

General specifications included:

Weight: 45 tons
Length: 31 feet 10.7 inches
Width: 10 feet 6 inches
Height: 11 feet 3 inches
Power plant: one 500-horsepower 17 V-12 gasoline engine
Top speed: 18.6 miles per hour
Armament (typical): one 76.2-mm main gun, two 37-mm 1930 guns, and two machine guns

KV-1. Despite the disappointing performance of the T-35, the Soviets did not give up on heavy tanks. The KV-1 heavy tank was designed in 1938 and was originally intended to mount a 3-inch main gun, but ultimately was given a 4.2-inch weapon. Three and even four machine guns were also fitted into the design. A modification known as the KV-2 accepted a 5.98-inch howitzer, but this necessitated a very high turret, which offered to the enemy a most inviting target. Armor was thick and heavy.

The KV-1 was an improvement over the T-35, to be sure, but it was plagued by automotive problems, including faulty clutches and transmissions. Nevertheless, the tank served effectively against heavy German vehicles.

General specifications included:

Weight: 43 tons
Length: 21 feet 11 inches
Width: 10 feet 10.7 inches
Height: 8 feet 10.7 inches
Power plant: one 600-horsepower V-2K V-12 diesel
Top speed: 21.75 miles per hour
Armament (typical): one 4.2-inch main gun and three or four machine guns

IS-2 and IS-3 heavy tanks. Aware that neither the T-35 nor the KV-1 were wholly successful heavy tanks, Soviet planners commissioned the IS (for "Iosif Stalin") heavy tank, dubbed the "Tank of the Victory." Design work began late in 1942 and built on the experience of the KV-1. Engineers focused on achieving much better mechanical reliability and mounting more powerful weapons. The IS-2 was the first production model and mounted a long-barrel 122-mm gun. In 1944, the more heavily armored IS-3 was fielded. This tank also featured a semicircular aerodynamic cast turret and a sophisticated fire control system, which allowed the tank commander to traverse the turret so that he could direct the gun faster. The IS-2 and IS-3 were used in the closing months of the European war, then went on to become the primary Soviet heavy tanks of the immediate postwar years. They were in service until the late 1960s.

General specifications of the IS-2 included:

Weight: 46 tons
Length: 32 feet 5.8 inches
Width: 10 feet 1.6 inches
Height: 8 feet 11.5 inches
Power plant: one 520-horsepower V-2 IS 12-cylinder diesel
Top speed: 23 miles per hour
Armament: one 122-mm M1943 D-25T L/43 gun, one 12.7-mm M1938 gun, and one 7.62-mm machine gun

Further reading: Bean, Tim, and Will Fowler. *Russian Tanks of World War II: Stalin's Armored Might.* Osceola, Wis.: Motorbooks International, 2002; Zaloga, Steven, Jim Kinnear, and Peter Sarson. *KV-1 and 2: Heavy Tanks 1939–1945.* Mechanicsburg, Penn.: Stackpole, 1996; Zaloga, Steven J., and Peter Sarson. *T-34 Medium Tank 1941–45.* London: Osprey, 1994.

armor, U.S.

M4 Sherman. Thanks to such officers as GEORGE SMITH PATTON, JR., who became the U.S. Army's premier tank officer and armor advocate in World War I, the United States came into World War II with a fairly well-developed doctrine for the use of tanks. While it did not have the most advanced tank designs—and, indeed, retained the obsolescent M3 Stuart light tank long after it had been clearly outclassed—the nation had the industrial capacity to produce and field many thousands of the tanks it did have. The most famous American tank of the war, the M4 Sherman was produced in greater quantity than any other tank of any other nation. Like the Soviet T-34 (*see* ARMOR, SOVIET), the Sherman, inferior to the best German tanks on a tank-for-tank basis, enjoyed three paramount combat qualities: it was highly mobile, highly reliable, and highly available.

Availability was, in fact, the decisive strength of the Sherman. Far simpler and therefore more reliable than German tanks, it was much more dependably available for service. Even more important were the numbers produced. A total of 49,324 Sherman tanks rolled out of 11 plants between 1942 and 1946. The vehicle was employed not only by the U.S. Army and Marine Corps but also by British, Canadian, and Free French forces, and it was used in North Africa, Sicily, Italy, and western Europe as well as the Pacific theater. Whereas the Germans produced some 1,835 Tiger and King Tiger tanks and 4,800 Panthers (most deployed against the Soviet T-34s on the eastern front), the Allies deployed more than 40,000 Shermans, which often were used in coordination with close air support targeting the German tanks. In general, thanks to the Sherman, the Allies enjoyed something approaching a 14 to 1 ratio against the Panthers and a staggering 50 to 1 ration against the most advanced Tigers and King Tigers.

Overwhelming superiority of numbers counterbalanced the one-on-one inferiority of the Sherman. In both armor and firepower, it was vastly outclassed by German tanks. Its 75-mm or 76-mm gun could not penetrate the front armor of the Tigers, even close in, while its thin armor rendered it vulnerable to the Tiger, even at considerable range. The Sherman's profile was also a weakness. Taller than the Tigers, it was difficult to conceal. The Sherman's gasoline-powered engine was another liability. Gasoline is far more explosively combustible than diesel fuel, and a direct hit on the Sherman

Major General George S. Patton, Jr. during prewar Louisiana Maneuvers, 1941, with Colonel Harry A. Flint and Brigadier General Geoffrey Keyes *(Patton Museum of Cavalry and Armor, Fort Knox, Kentucky)*

would often send it up in a fireball. The five-man tank crews nicknamed it "the Ronson," after a popular cigarette lighter that advertised its "lights-up-first-time-every-time" reliability. Quickly, Allied tank crews learned to use their single great advantage: numbers. They attacked German tanks only when they outnumbered them, so that they could outmaneuver their target and hit it from the side or from behind, the only angles from which the Sherman had a chance against its superior foe.

Shermans came in many variants and were often adapted to specialized applications, but their general specifications included:

Weight: 32.284 tons
Length: 24 feet 8 inches
Width: 8 feet 9.5 inches
Height: 11 feet 2.875 inches
Power plant: 400-horsepower Continental R974 C4 nine-cylinder radial gasoline engine
Top speed: 29 miles per hour
Armament (typical): 75-mm gun M3 M34 in turret; .50-caliber M2HB machine gun, flexible in turret; .30-caliber M1919A4 machine gun in AA mount; .30-caliber M1919A4

machine gun coaxial to the main gun; .30-caliber M1919A4 machine gun in ball mount in right bow

M3A1 Stuart. At the start of the war, the army fielded the M3 light tank, known as the Stuart, which had evolved from designs developed in the 1920s and 1930s. Based on U.S. observations during the German BLITZKRIEG, it was decided to add thicker armor to existing designs, which also necessitated revising suspension systems. The M3A1 therefore embodied responses to modern battlefield conditions, but it was essentially an already obsolescent tank. Nevertheless, it did not even begin full production until the United States entered the war at the end of 1941. Light, nimble, and reliable, the M3 Stuart was nevertheless thoroughly outgunned and outclassed by German adversaries. Its 37-mm main gun was of negligible combat value. The vehicle did prove far more useful in the Pacific, going against generally inferior Japanese light tanks.

General specifications of the M3 light tank included:

Weight: 12,927 tons
Length: 14 feet 10.75 inches
Width: 7 feet 4 inches
Height: 7 feet 6.5 inches
Power plant: one 250-horsepower Continental W-970-9A seven-cylinder radial gasoline engine
Top speed: 36 miles per hour
Armament: 37-mm main gun M5 M22 in turret, .30-caliber M1919A4 machine gun in AA mount, .30-caliber M1919A4 machine gun coaxial to main gun, .30-caliber M1919A4 machine gun in ball mount in right bow, and .30-caliber M1919A4 machine gun in each sponson

M24 Chaffee. Recognizing the inadequacy of the M3 Stuart and its 37-mm gun, the army developed the M24 Chaffee light tank, which was fielded late in 1943 but did not enter widespread service until late 1944. The tank mounted an impressive 75-mm gun and was highly mobile, with a top speed of 35 miles per hour.

General specifications included:

Weight: 18.37 tons
Length: 16 feet 4.5 inches
Width: 9 feet 8 inches
Height: 8 feet 1.5 inches
Power plant: two Cadillac Model 44T24 110-horsepower gasoline engines
Armament: one M6 75-mm main gun, one .30-caliber machine gun coaxial with main gun, one .30-caliber machine gun in bow, one .50-caliber machine gun in AA mount, and one M3 grenade launcher

M3 Grant. The immediate predecessor of the M4 Sherman medium tank was the M3 Grant medium tank. High in profile, the Grant was rushed into production and possessed neither stability nor speed (top speed was 26 miles per hour), but it did mount a powerful 75-mm main gun in addition to a 37-mm gun and three .30-caliber machine guns. Crews objected to its cramped quarters and stingy armor, and the tanks were rapidly withdrawn (except in the Pacific) as soon as the superior Shermans were ready to take their place.

General specifications included:

Weight: 27.24 tons
Length: 18 feet 6 inches
Width: 8 feet 11 inches
Height: 10 feet 3 inches
Power plant: one 340-horsepower Continental R-975-Ec2 radial gasoline engine
Top speed: 26 miles per hour

M26 Pershing. The United States fielded only a single heavy tank during World War II, the M26 Pershing, which did not enter service until 1945. Its 90-mm gun could meet the German Tiger and Panther on their own terms, and it featured heavy armor. While it was probably the best American tank used in the war, it was nevertheless underpowered, its 500-horsepower Ford engine inadequate to its heavily armored weight.

General specifications included:

Weight: 42 tons
Length: 20 feet 7 inches

Width: 8 feet 9.5 inches
Height: 11 feet 2.875 inches
Power plant: one 500-horsepower Ford GAF, V-8 gasoline engine
Top speed: 30 miles per hour
Armament: one 90-mm main gun, one .30-caliber machine gun coaxial with main gun, one .30-caliber machine gun mounted on the hull, and one 50-caliber machine gun in an AA mount

Like the Germans, the Americans fielded tank destroyers in addition to tanks. These were vehicles that sacrificed some maneuverability and armor in exchange for the ability to mount a heavy, usually long-barreled gun capable of a high degree of armor penetration at long range. Most tank destroyers also sacrificed speed, but the American vehicles were, in fact, very fast. They were generally employed as self-propelled guns, driven to an area affording concealment and fired in static ambush.

Gun Motor Carriage M10. The two most important American tank destroyers were the 3-inch Gun Motor Carriage M10 and the 3-inch Gun Motor Carriage M18. The M10 mounted the 76.2-mm M7 gun as well as a 12.7-mm Browning machine gun. The vehicle was built on an M4A2 tank chassis and had a thinly armored open-top turret. Its general specifications included:

Weight: 66,000 pounds
Length: 22 feet 5 inches
Width: 10 feet
Height: 8 feet 5 inches
Power plant: two 375-horsepower General Motors six-cylinder diesels
Top speed: 32 miles per hour
Armament: one 76.2-mm M7 main gun and one 12.7-mm Browning machine gun (mounted atop the open turret)

Gun Motor Carriage M18 Hellcat. Unlike the M10, which was designed atop the existing M4A2 chassis, the M18 was designed as a tank destroyer from the ground up, and it first saw service in 1943. Smaller and much lighter than the M10, the M18 Hellcat mounted the powerful 3-inch (76.2-mm gun) but achieved a top speed of 55 miles per hour, making it the fastest tracked vehicle of the entire war. The Hellcat proved the viability of the American tank destroyer concept and was used with great effect against Tigers and King Tigers.

General specifications included:

Weight: 37,557 pounds
Length: 21 feet 11 inches
Width: 9 feet 5 inches
Height: 8 feet 5.5 inches
Power plant: one 340-horsepower Continental R-975 C1 radial gasoline engine
Top speed: 55 miles per hour
Armament: one 76.2-mm M7 main gun and one 12.7-mm Browning machine gun (mounted atop the open turret)

Further reading: Baily, Charles M. *Faint Praise: American Tanks and Tank Destroyers During World War II.* North Haven, Conn.: Archon, 1983; Berndt, Thomas. *American Tanks of World War II.* Osceola, Wis.: Motorbooks International, 1994; Chamberlain, Peter. *British and American Tanks of World War II: The Complete Illustrated History of British, American and Commonwealth Tanks, Gun Motor Carriages and Special Purpose Vehicles, 1939–1945.* London: Arms & Armour, 1969; Forty, George. *United States Tanks of World War II in Action.* London: Blandford, 1986.

Arnim, Jürgen von (1889–1971) *German Panzer commander*

A career German military officer, Arnim, born into an old Prussian military family, fought in World War I and remained in the army during the interwar period, entering the armored branch during the 1930s and rising to command a panzer division by the start of OPERATION BARBAROSSA, the Nazi invasion of the Soviet Union, which was launched on June 22, 1941.

Arnim continued his rise, taking command of a panzer corps on the eastern front before being reassigned as commander in chief of the newly created Fifth Panzer Army in Tunis, North Africa, in November 1942. Arnim missed an opportunity

Jürgen von Arnim *(National Archives and Records Administration)*

to capitalize on ERWIN ROMMEL's success against U.S. forces at the BATTLE OF KASSERINE PASS during February 14–22, 1943, when he failed to support Rommel's offensive. He did launch an independent attack to the north of Rommel during February 26–28, but it came to little. Nevertheless, when Rommel, stricken with nasal diphtheria, was sent back to Germany to recuperate on March 6, Arnim assumed command of the Panzerarmee Afrika. It was he who directed the defense of Tunisia. Although he succeeded in keeping his forces intact following defeat at the Battle of Mareth during March 20–26, he lost contact with his supply lines, which were continually under Allied attack. Tunisia was overrun, and Arnim was captured on May 12. He spent the rest of the war as a prisoner, first in Britain and then in the United States. He lived as a private citizen for many years after the war.

Further reading: Atkinson, Rick. *An Army at Dawn: The War in North Africa 1942–1943.* New York: Henry Holt, 2003; Mellenthin, Vaughn. *Panzer Battles.* New York: Ballantine, 1976; Stolfi, R. H. S. *German Panzers on the Offensive: Russian Front and North Africa 1941–1942.* Atglen, Pa.: Schiffer, 2003.

Arnold, Henry Harley ("Hap")
(1886–1950) *commanding general of U.S. Army Air Forces*

Born in the Philadelphia suburb of Gladwyne, Pennsylvania, Henry "Hap" Arnold attended West Point and graduated in 1907 with a commission as second lieutenant in the infantry. He served in the Philippines during 1907–09, but soon became passionately interested in flying. Obtaining a transfer to the aeronautical section of the Signal Corps in April 1911, he received his flight instruction that June from none other than the Wright brothers, who were under U.S. Army contract.

Arnold proved to be a born aviator and in October 1912 won the Mackay Trophy for successfully completing the first reconnaissance flight in a heavier-than-air craft. Arnold hoped that this success would help to motivate U.S. Army interest in military aviation, but the tradition-bound army brass was unmoved, and Arnold was sent back to the infantry in April 1913. Three years later, he returned to the air service, where, promoted to captain in May 1916, he supervised the army's aviation training schools as the United States entered World War I in 1917. He supervised air training throughout America's involvement in the war, from May 1917 through 1919.

The postwar U.S. military was subject to massive demobilization and drastic reductions in funding. Nevertheless, Arnold continued to work toward developing the Army Air Corps. He was sent to the army's Command and General Staff School, from which he graduated in 1929 with the rank of lieutenant colonel and in 1931 was given command of the 1st Bomb Wing and the 1st Pursuit Wing at March Field, California. During July and August 1934, he led a flight of ten B-10 bombers on a round trip from Washington, D.C., to Fairbanks,

Alaska, winning a second Mackay Trophy for his demonstration of the endurance of the modern bomber.

Promoted to brigadier general, Arnold took command of 1st Wing, GHQ Air Force in February 1935 and was named assistant chief of staff of the Air Corps in December of that year. With the death of General Oscar Westover in September 1938, Arnold was promoted to the temporary rank of major general and named chief of staff of the Air Corps. He used his new authority to initiate programs to improve the combat readiness of the Air Corps, but he was severely hampered by a shortage of funds and a lingering reluctance on the part of military planners to develop a fully effective air arm. Nevertheless, his advocacy of air power did not go unrecognized. He was named acting deputy chief of staff of the army for air matters in October 1940 and chief of the Army Air Corps after it had been renamed the U.S. Army Air Forces in June 1941. Following this new appointment came a promotion to temporary lieutenant general, which was conferred shortly after the bombing of PEARL HARBOR and America's entry into World War II.

In March 1942, Arnold was named commanding general of Army Air Forces and the following year was promoted to the temporary rank of general. Arnold now served on the U.S. Joint Chiefs of Staff, which put him in a key position for the shaping of Allied strategy in the European as well as Pacific theaters. Arnold not only advocated and supervised the STRATEGIC BOMBING OF GERMANY, he created the Twentieth Air Force in April 1944 to carry out the STRATEGIC BOMBING OF JAPAN. Significantly, this unit reported directly to his command as a representative of the Joint Chiefs. This was a bold and savvy step toward the eventual (postwar) creation of a United States Air Force independent of the U.S. Army.

In December 1944, with generals DWIGHT D. EISENHOWER, DOUGLAS MACARTHUR, and GEORGE CATLETT MARSHALL, Arnold was elevated to the rank of general of the army—five-star general. He continued to command the Army Air Forces through the end of the war, retiring in March 1946. On September 18, 1947, thanks in large part to the foundation he had laid, the Army Air Forces became an independent service, and in May 1949, in recognition of the role he played as father of the U.S. Air Force, Arnold, although retired, was named first general of the air force. He died the following year on his ranch in Sonoma, California.

Further reading: Coffey, Thomas M. *Hap: The Story of the U.S. Air Force and the Man Who Built It, General Henry H. "Hap" Arnold.* New York: Penguin, 1982; Daso, Dik Alan. *Hap Arnold and the Evolution of American Airpower.* Washington, D.C.: Smithsonian, 2001.

Henry Harley "Hap" Arnold *(United States Air Force History Center)*

artillery, British

Artillery in World War II consisted mainly of seven major categories: self-propelled guns, heavy artillery, field artillery, heavy antiaircraft guns, light antiaircraft guns, rockets, and antitank guns.

SELF-PROPELLED GUNS

With their emphasis on mobile warfare (*see, for example,* Blitzkrieg), the Germans put more reliance on self-propelled guns than did any other combatant, including the British, who still relied mainly on traditional towed artillery.

The Bishop. In essence, self-propelled guns were major artillery pieces mounted on tank chassis. The only major British self-propelled guns were the Bishop and the Sexton. Both were soon replaced by the U.S. M7, called the Priest. The Bishop was rushed into production during the early stages of the North African Campaign, after the German Afrika Korps employed self-propelled guns against the British there. The Bishop was a poorly thought out conversion of the Valentine infantry tank chassis, which was modified to accept a 25-pound (87.6-mm) field gun. The army ordered 100 of the Bishops, which were sent to the Middle East as they were ready. About 80 were delivered to the Eighth British Army in July 1942.

From the beginning, there were problems. Because the gun was mounted in a large fixed superstructure, which limited traverse as well as elevation, range was severely limited and could only be maximized to its full 6,400 yards by driving the Bishop onto a dirt ramp prepared by the crew. Cramped quarters within the superstructure limited ammunition storage, necessitating a towed trailer to carry sufficient ammo. Indeed, crew accommodations were so cramped that one crew member had to perch outside on the engine cover during transit. Crews were happy to see the Bishop replaced early in the invasion of Italy, and the vehicle was used thereafter for training purposes only.

General specifications included:

Weight: 17,440 pounds
Length: 18 feet 6 inches
Width: 9 feet 1 inch
Height: 10 feet
Power plant: one 131-horsepower AEC six-cylinder diesel

Top speed: 15 miles per hour
Armament: one 25-pounder howitzer and one .303-caliber Bren machine gun

The Sexton. The unloved Bishop was replaced beginning in 1943 with the Sexton, which was similar to the U.S. M7 Priest. The Sextons were made in Canada by Montreal Locomotive, and production spanned 1943 to 1945. Roomier than the Bishop, the Sexton was also much more durable. The riveted construction of the Bishop was replaced by a welded superstructure at first, and later models had a cast nose.

The general specifications of the Sexton included:

Weight: 57,000 pounds
Length: 20 feet 1 inch
Width: 8 feet 11 inches
Height: 8 feet 1 inch
Power plant: one Wright Continental R-975-C11 radial air-cooled gasoline engine
Top speed: 25 miles per hour
Armament: one 25-pounder main gun and two .303-caliber Bren machine guns

HEAVY ARTILLERY

The single greatest feature of combat that distinguished World War II from World War I was mobility. On the western front, World War I had been a nightmare of static trench warfare. In contrast, World War II began with Blitzkrieg, the very essence of mobile warfare, and culminated both in Europe and the Pacific with an Allied counteroffensive conducted, for the most part, at top speed. It is little wonder, then, that the tank achieved preeminence in the ground war. However, heavy artillery was still a very important weapon. Heavy artillery was still essential to supporting infantry and even armor operations. Moreover, despite the war's mobility, there were still plenty of well-fortified strong points that would yield to nothing less than bombardment by heavy guns.

Marks IV Howitzer. The most important British heavy artillery pieces were its 7.2-inch howitzers, designated Marks I through V and Mark VI. Marks I through V were stop-gap weapons, converted from World War I–vintage artillery. Between the wars, the British had neglected artillery development, and when they discovered, at the outbreak of World War II, that their inventory of 8-inch howitzers provided insufficient range for the modern battlefield, they rushed into production a series of conversions, relining the 8-inch bores to 7.2 inches for an increase in muzzle velocity and range. The different Mark designations depended on the varying specifications of the barrel that was converted. Mark VI was the only new design, which featured a longer 7.2-inch barrel that boosted range and accuracy even further. By the end of 1944, the Mark VI guns had replaced virtually all the earlier conversions.

General specifications of the Mark VI howitzer included:

Caliber: 7.2 inches
Length: 20 feet 8 inches (versus 14 feet 3 inches for Marks I–V)
Weight: 29,120 pounds
Elevation: -2° to +65°
Traverse: 60°
Maximum range: 19,667 yards (versus 16,900 yards for Marks I–V)
Shell weight: 202 pounds

FIELD ARTILLERY

Ordnance, Q.F., 25-pdr., Mark 2. More readily transportable than heavy artillery, field artillery provided fire support for the infantry and other service arms. Whereas World War I relied mostly on heavy artillery, the demand for greater mobility in World War II made field artillery a well-established arm in the armies of all combatants. The British fielded one notable towed 25-pounder, designated Ordnance, Q.F., 25-pdr. The Mark 2 version of this weapon was considered a great field piece, its carriage was virtually indestructible, and the range of the gun itself was a substantial 13,400 yards.

General specifications included:

Caliber: 87.6 mm
Length: 94.5 inches
Weight: 3,968 pounds

Elevation: -5° to +40°
Traverse: 8° on carriage
Range: 13,400 yards
Shell weight: 25 pounds

HEAVY ANTIAIRCRAFT GUNS

Aircraft played an extensive role in World War II and were deployed against major targets, including cities. To defend important military installations, war plants, and cities, the combatant nations used heavy antiaircraft guns, which were capable of reaching the high altitudes of modern bombers. The British, whose cities were the targets of intensive German bombing campaigns, deployed three major types of heavy antiaircraft guns.

Ordnance, QF, 3-inch gun. The Ordnance, QF, 3-inch gun was a World War I design that had been upgraded early in World War II. It was manufactured in at least eight variants. The gun could be mounted in a static emplacement or on a four-wheel platform for limited towing. Like all antiaircraft guns, the 3-inch model was rigged with a system of pulleys that facilitated rapid aiming and target leading.

General specifications of the gun included:

Caliber: 3 inches
Weight: 17,584 pounds
Length of barrel: 11 feet 7.8 inches
Elevation: +90°
Traverse: 360°
Ceiling: 23,500 feet
Shell weight: 16 pounds

Ordnance, QF, 3.7-inch gun. The Ordnance, QF, 3.7-inch antiaircraft gun was developed after World War I as British military planners recognized the implications of more powerful and heavier bomber aircraft. At first, British gun crews continued to prefer the lighter 3-inch gun because it was "handier," more rapidly maneuverable, and far more easily emplaced. Eventually, however, the virtues of this more powerful weapon made themselves felt, and it became a mainstay of British antiaircraft defense.

General specifications included:

Caliber: 3.7 inches
Weight: 20,541 pounds

Length of barrel: 15 feet 5 inches
Elevation: +80°
Traverse: 360°
Ceiling: 32,000 feet
Shell weight: 28.56 pounds

Ordnance, QF, 4.5-inch gun. The largest British antiaircraft gun of World War II was the Ordnance, QF, 4.5-inch gun, which was adapted from a post–World War I naval gun intended for use on ships. For antiaircraft use, the gun was made transportable on a specially designed four-wheel carriage, but its great weight (37,128 pounds) always made it difficult to move. Originally, the gun was intended to defend dockyards and other shore-based naval facilities exclusively, but as early as 1941, it was deployed elsewhere as well.

General specifications included:

Caliber: 4.45 inches
Weight: 37,128 pounds
Length of barrel: 16 feet 8.25 inches
Elevation: +80°
Traverse: 360°
Ceiling: 42,600 feet
Shell weight: 54.43 pounds

LIGHT ANTIAIRCRAFT GUNS

Heavy antiaircraft (AA) guns were intended for use against strategic aircraft, principally the medium and heavy bombers that raided cities and other major installations. World War II also saw the widespread use of tactical aircraft for close air support. These medium and light bombers, dive bombers, and fighters, as well as specially designed attack aircraft, targeted troops, buildings, tanks, and other vehicles. Defending against them required light, highly mobile, and readily maneuverable antiaircraft guns capable of rapid fire. Since tactical aircraft attacked at much lower altitudes than strategic bombers, the guns' maximum ceiling was of less importance than it was with the heavy AA artillery.

The British fielded one important light AA piece, the Polsten. It was a simplified version of the Oerlikon gun reengineered by Polish designers but produced exclusively in the United Kingdom by the Sten Company ("Pol" Poland, and "sten" Sten). Light enough to be manhandled into position, readily transportable, and capable of being produced in vast numbers, the Polsten was used very effectively throughout the entire war.

General specifications included:

Caliber: 20 mm
Length of barrel: 85.75 inches
Weight: 121 pounds
Elevation: +85°
Traverse: 360°
Ceiling: 6,630 feet
Projectile weight: .2625 pound

ROCKETS

The rockets deployed in the field were not the complex technological marvels represented by the German V-1 BUZZ BOMB and V-2 ROCKET, but were revivals of a very ancient weapon of war. In and of themselves, field rockets or war rockets were inaccurate and mostly incapable of delivering the high-explosive punch of heavy artillery shells. However, mated to advanced launchers, rockets could be fired in great numbers and at terrifying speeds. This made up for their inherent inaccuracy and limited destructive power.

2-inch rocket. The British 2-inch rocket was developed in the 1930s as an antiaircraft weapon. The weapon was to be launched from the ground or from ships at low-flying incoming aircraft. As it rose, propelled by solventless cordite fuel, the rocket deployed a long trail of wire, which was designed to foul the propellers of enemy aircraft and bring them down. Not surprisingly, the system never worked, and the rockets were instead loaded with a small amount of high explosive and used as artillery.

3-inch rocket. Another rocket, this one of 3-inch diameter, was also developed during the 1930s as an alternative to the antiaircraft gun. The virtue of these inexpensive projectiles was that they could be launched in massive salvoes from a "Rocket Projector," 36 per salvo. While the 3-inch rocket was, in fact, rarely actually used against aircraft, it did prove to be a highly effective ground-attack weapon, especially against tanks. The 3-inch rocket weighed 54 pounds and traveled at 1,500 feet per second over 4,070 yards.

LILO. The LILO was a rocket system specially developed late in the war for use against the kind of fortified Japanese bunkers found on Pacific islands and on the Southeast Asian mainland. Such bunkers generally required bombardment by heavy artillery, but often they were located in places that were inaccessible to such artillery. The LILO was a single-fire rocket launcher designed to fire a rocket with a powerful 60-pound warhead at short range and directly against a bunker or other fortified target. The warhead was packed with high explosive, intended to penetrate concrete, earth, logs, or whatever other materials had been used to build the bunker. The typical Japanese bunker consisted of about 10 feet of earth plus logs. LILO rockets made short work of these.

The LILO launcher was a simple tube fitted with an electric triggering device. At short range, aiming was an easy matter, and the weapon was fitted with nothing more elaborate than an open sight. It was aimed by adjusting the height of its back legs. The system was transportable by two men, one to carry the launcher, the other to carry the rocket.

The Land Mattress was Britain's only purpose-designed ground-to-ground multiple-launch rocket weapon; the others had evolved from antiaircraft designs or were simply antiaircraft rocket systems used against ground targets. The Land Mattress launcher had 12, 16, 30, or 32 barrels from which 69.7-inch rockets, each carrying a 7-pound high-explosive warhead, could be launched in salvoes. Maximum range was 7,900 yards. Each salvo concentrated about 50 percent of its fire in an area about 240 yards square. The weapon could be reloaded very quickly, so that a battery of Land Mattress launchers could lay down a devastating blanket of fire.

ANTITANK GUNS

Unlike the Germans and the Americans, the British did not field tank destroyers against enemy armor, but instead relied on towed antitank artillery: 2-, 6-, and 17-pounder guns.

Ordnance, QF, 2-pounder. The Ordnance, QF, 2-pounder was developed during the mid-1930s and was by no means a bad weapon. However, it was an almost instantly obsolete weapon. Small, light, and compact, the gun lacked the armor penetration and range to be truly effective against modern tanks, especially German ones. Most of the British army's inventory of 2-pounders was abandoned on the beaches during the DUNKIRK EVACUATION in 1940.

General specifications included:

Caliber: 40 mm
Length: 6 feet 9.9 inches
Weight: 1,848 pounds
Traverse: 360°
Elevation: -13° to +15°
Range: 600 yards
Armor Penetration: 2.08 inches at 500 yards

Ordnance, QF, 6-pounder. The Ordnance, QF, 6-pounder went into development in 1938 but did not go into production until 1940–41, reaching some units in the field at the end of 1941. The 6-pounder proved highly effective until the introduction of the massive German Tiger tanks, whose heavy, sloping armor shed the 6-pound projectiles like water.

General specifications of the gun included:

Caliber: 57 mm
Length: 6 feet 8.95 inches
Weight: 2,471 pounds
Traverse: 90°
Elevation: -5° to +15°
Armor penetration: 2.7 inches at 1,000 yards

Ordinance, QF, 17-pounder. By 1941, it had become apparent to British planners that the enemy would field increasingly heavily armored tanks. Therefore, a new, heavier antitank gun was authorized. The Ordinance, QF, 17-pounder arrived in North Africa late in 1942 and, through the following months and years of the war, became a common presence on the battlefield. By the last year of the war, it was the British army's standard antitank gun. It was one of the most powerful antitank weapons of the war, and it sometimes served double duty as an all-around field gun.

General specifications included:

Caliber: 3 inches
Length: 14 feet 6.96 inches
Weight: 6,444 pounds
Traverse: 60°
Elevation: -6° to +16.5°
Armor penetration: 5.12 inches at 1,000 yards

Further reading: Dobinson, Colin. *AA Command: Britain's Anti-Aircraft Defences of World War II.* London: Methuen, 2002; Falvey, Denis. *A Well-Known Excellence: British Artillery and an Artilleryman in World War Two.* London and New York: Brassey's, 2002; Henry, Chris. *British Anti-tank Artillery, 1939–1945.* London: Osprey, 2004; Hogg, Ian V. *British and American Artillery of World War II.* London: Greenhill, 2002.

artillery, French

Artillery in World War II consisted mainly of seven major categories: self-propelled guns, heavy artillery, field artillery, heavy antiaircraft guns, light antiaircraft guns, rockets, and antitank guns. The French, however, fielded no self-propelled guns, heavy artillery, or rockets, but they did have some fine examples of the other categories.

FIELD ARTILLERY

Canon de 75 mle 1897 (French 75). The "French 75" was first fielded in 1897 and was officially designated the Canon de 75 mle 1897. The pride of the French military, it was often credited (by the French) for the final victory in World War I. Certainly, it was the first of the modern generation of artillery pieces. Two features distinguished it from previous guns. Its recoil mechanism was so efficient that it minimized the necessity to "re-lay" (adjust the aim) of the gun after firing. Its unique breech made loading and reloading much faster and more efficient. Together, these features greatly increased rate of fire.

There is no doubt that the French 75 was a remarkable weapon, but by the outbreak of World War II in 1939, the 1897 design was well past its prime and was far outranged by other guns. Nevertheless, the French used about 4,500 of the guns in their front lines, and many other nations came into the war with the weapon as well.

General specifications included:

Caliber: 75 mm
Length: 107.08 inches
Weight: 4,343 pounds
Elevation: -11° to +18°
Traverse: 6°
Range: 12,140 yards
Shell weight: 13.66 pounds

Canon de 105 mle 1913 Schneider (L13S). Somewhat newer than the French 75 was the Canon de 105 mle 1913 Schneider, first fielded in 1913. A French weapon based on a Russian design, the Schneider was also known as the L13S and proved itself admirably in World War I. Sturdy, handsome, and efficient, Schneiders were exported to many countries before World War II, and the Germans thought enough of them to make use of captured weapons throughout the war.

General specifications of the gun included:

Caliber: 105 mm
Length: 117.6 inches
Weight: 5,070 pounds
Elevation: 0° to +37°
Traverse: 6°
Range: 13,130 yards
Shell weight: 34.7 pounds

Canon de 105 court mle 1934 S and 1935 B. During the interwar period, even the French, like Britain reluctant to rearm or modernize its army, recognized that their vintage inventory of artillery was obsolescent. The Canon de 105 court mle 1934 S and 1935 B went into production in the mid 1930s. It was the 1935 model that was chosen for mass production, and it was an advanced design for the time. Its short barrel increased muzzle velocity and facilitated both transportation and laying, and its innovative carriage, which featured a split rail, maximized gun crew protection. Unfortunately, the gun was manufactured at a slow rate, and only 232 were in service during the BATTLE OF FRANCE. The Germans prized the examples they managed to capture.

General specifications included:

Caliber: 105 mm
Length: 69.3 inches
Weight: 3,587 pounds
Elevation: -6° to +50°
Traverse: 58°
Range: 11,270 yards
Shell weight: 34.62 pounds

HEAVY ANTIAIRCRAFT GUNS

During World War I, the French army responded to the need for antiaircraft defense not by developing new artillery, but by adapting the existing French 75 to the antiaircraft role. Versions of the modified gun were produced on the eve of the war in 1913 and during the war in 1915 and 1917. The major modifications were to the mount, which allowed for a 70° elevation and a 360° traverse, and to the fire controls, which, in the 1917 model, were moved to the carriage for greater convenience and efficiency. These three models, though antiquated by the outbreak of World War II, were all used during the war.

Canon de 75 mm contre aeronefs mle 17/34. A new modification of the 75, Canon de 75 mm contre aeronefs mle 17/34, was introduced in 1934 and featured a redesigned barrel, which improved performance by providing reduced time of flight of shells and increasing ceiling. At about this time, other versions, 1932, 1933, and 1936, were also produced, but all were based on the old French 75. Even with modifications, French heavy antiaircraft artillery was obsolete at the time of the the Battle of France.

General specifications for the 1932 model included:

Caliber: 75 mm
Length: 13 feet 3.5 inches
Weight: 8,377 pounds
Elevation: +70°
Traverse: 360°
Ceiling: 26,245 feet
Shell weight: 14.2 pounds

LIGHT ANTIAIRCRAFT GUNS

Two light, rapid-fire guns were in the French arsenal for defense against tactical air attack. In contrast to heavy antiaircraft guns, which were intended to defend cities and major installations from medium and heavy bomber attack—strategic bombing—the light guns were intended for use against smaller tactical aircraft, including light bombers, fighters, and ground attack aircraft. They were used to cover troops in the field.

25-mm Hotchkiss. The 25-mm Hotchkiss was introduced in 1932 on the initiative of the Hotchkiss armaments firm rather than at the request of the French army. The experience of World War I had persuaded the always backward-looking French military planners that modified French 75s were sufficient for heavy antiaircraft defense and that the 12.7-mm heavy machine gun was adequate for light antiaircraft defense. Hotchkiss company designers disagreed and offered the 1932 design on spec, as it were. Initially, the gun was rejected, only to be revived after French observers during the Spanish civil war saw a manifest need for a heavier light antiaircraft weapon. The Hotchkiss guns were accordingly ordered, with two models, a 1938 and 1939, being produced.

General specifications of the 1938 model included:

Caliber: 25 mm
Length: 59 inches
Weight: 1,874 pounds
Elevation: +80°
Traverse: 360°
Ceiling: 9,843 feet
Projectile weight: 0.64 pounds

37-mm Schneider. Like the Hotchkiss 25 mm, the 37-mm Schneider was initially rejected by the French army, which thought that the French 75 and the 12.7-mm machine gun were adequate for antiaircraft defense. Schneider continued to develop the gun in any case, and, as with the Hotchkiss, observation during the Spanish Civil War vividly demonstrated the need for tactical antiaircraft defense intermediate between a mere machine gun and heavy artillery. Unfortunately, very few of the guns had been produced by the time the Germans invaded, and the Schneider played a very small role in the war.

General specifications included:

Caliber: 37 mm
Length: unknown
Weight: 2,954 pounds
Elevation: +80°
Traverse: 360°
Ceiling: 9,843 feet
Projectile weight: 1.21 pounds

ANTITANK GUNS

Canon de 46 antichar mle 1937 and Canon de 47 antichar mle 1937. France produced two antitank guns, the Canon de 46 antichar mle 1937 and the Canon de 47 antichar mle 1937. Rushed through design and production based on French intelligence concerning the gauge of emerging German armor plate, the Canon de 46 was, perhaps surprisingly, an excellent weapon. It went into production in 1938 and was improved in the 47 version. After the fall of France, the Germans eagerly acquired the weapons and used them extensively.

General specifications included:

Caliber: 47 mm
Length: 8 feet 2 inches
Weight: 2,315 pounds
Elevation: -13° to +16.5°
Traverse: 68°
Range: 7,110 yards
Armor penetration: 3.15 inches at 220 yards
Projectile weight: 3.8 pounds

Further reading: Chant, Chris. *Artillery of World War II.* Osceola, Wis.: Motorbooks International, 2001; Jackson, Julian. *The Fall of France: The Nazi Invasion of 1940.* Oxford and New York: Oxford University Press, 2003; Sumner, Ian. *The French Army 1939–45: The Army of 1939–40 and Vichy France.* London: Osprey, 1998.

artillery, German

Artillery in World War II consisted mainly of seven major categories: self-propelled guns, heavy artillery, field artillery, heavy antiaircraft guns, light antiaircraft guns, rockets, and antitank guns.

SELF-PROPELLED GUNS

With their emphasis on mobile warfare (*see, for example,* BLITZKRIEG), the Germans put more reliance on self-propelled guns than did any other combatant. It is not surprising, then, that the German arsenal included a wide variety of self-propelled guns, which were essentially powerful artillery pieces mounted on a tank or a tanklike chassis, complete with treads.

sIG 33 auf Geschützwagen. Among the first of the German self-propelled guns was the sIG 33 auf Geschützwagen, which was converted from a light tank. The superstructure and hull of the tank were removed, and a 15-cm sIG 33 infantry howitzer was mounted on the chassis. The crew was shielded by the three-sided housing from which the gun projected, but the housing was open at the rear and on top. The gun did not traverse, but was directed by steering the tank chassis. Whereas tanks are designed to fire on the fly, self-propelled guns are fired from a static position. The gun is moved into position, stopped, then fired. Some 370 of this modification were produced during the war, from 1940 and the BATTLE OF FRANCE all the way through 1944.

General specifications included:

Weight: 25,353 pounds
Length: 15 feet 10.4 inches
Width: 7 feet 0.6 inches
Height: 7 feet 10.5 inches
Power plant: one 150-horsepower Praga six-cylinder gasoline engine
Top speed: 21.75 miles per hour
Armament: one 15-cm howitzer

Wespe (Wasp). At about the same time that the sIG 33 was developed, the Wespe (Wasp) was fashioned out of the outclassed PzKpfw II light tank. A 105-mm howitzer was mounted atop a tanklike hull on the light tank chassis. An open-top armor shield was supplied for the crew of five, and the vehicles saw extensive service on the eastern front. The weapon was highly favored for infantry support.

General specifications included:

Weight: 24,251 pounds
Length: 15 feet 9.4 inches

Width: 7 feet 5.75 inches
Height: 7 feet 6.6 inches
Power plant: one 140-horsepower Maybach six-cylinder gasoline engine
Top speed: 24.85 miles per hour
Armament: one 105-mm howitzer and one 7.92-mm MG34 machine gun

Hummel (Bumble Bee). The Hummel ("Bumble Bee"), officially designated Geschützwagen III/IV, was introduced in 1941 and combined components from two tank chassis, the Panzer III and Panzer IV, to create a platform for the long-barrel 5.9-inch howitzer. This was a formidable piece made more effective by the addition of mobility. It was used on all fronts, and it remained in production until the end of the war, some 666 rolling off assembly lines. The five-man crew was afforded an ample open-top armored shield, and the tank chassis and power plant provided sufficient motive force for the gun to keep pace even with a panzer unit.

General specifications included:

Weight: 52,911 pounds
Length: 23 feet 6.3 inches
Width: 9 feet 5 inches
Height: 9 feet 2.6 inches
Power plant: one 265-horsepower Maybach V-12 gasoline engine
Top speed: 26.1 miles per hour
Armament: one 5.9-inch howitzer and one 7.92-mm machine gun

Waffentrager. A radical new approach to the self-propelled gun was the Waffentrager, literally "Weapons Carrier," which was introduced in 1942. This vehicle carried a howitzer mounted in a turret. However, instead of being fired from the vehicle, the turret and gun were lowered into place on the ground, emplaced, and fired from there as the Waffentrager left, presumably to pick up another turret-and-gun assembly. It is not entirely clear why this vehicle and system were produced, since German war-fighting doctrine continued to stress mobility. However, while only eight weapons carriers were built, they were, in fact, used in combat.

General specifications for the Waffentrager included:

Weight: 37,479 pounds
Length: 19 feet 4.3 inches
Width: 9 feet 5 inches
Height: 7 feet 4.6 inches
Power plant: one 188-horsepower Maybach gasoline engine
Top speed: 28 miles per hour
Armament: one 10.5-cm howitzer

Karl series. Another unique self-propelled gun was the so-called Karl series. This vehicle mounted a monstrous 60-cm or 54-cm Karl siege howitzer, a mortarlike weapon intended for use against concrete fortifications and bunkers. The howitzers had been built in the late 1930s specifically to use against France's vaunted MAGINOT LINE but were instead used against Sevastopol defenses in Russia and against Warsaw in 1944. The projectiles the weapon fired were designed with delayed detonation, so that they would penetrate their target *before* exploding. The projectiles could penetrate between 8.2 and 11.5 feet of concrete at a range of between 5,000 and nearly 7,000 yards.

These massive guns were transported over long distances by rail, mounted between special railroad carriages, and for shorter distances they were transferred to purpose-built tracked carriages. The speed of the carriages is not recorded but was doubtless very slow.

General specifications of this weapon system included:

Weight: 273,373 pounds
Length (overall): 36 feet 7 inches
Power plant: one 1,200-horsepower 12-cylinder Maybach gasoline engine
Armament: one 54- or 60-cm Karl howitzer

Brummbär (Grizzly Bear). The Brummbär ("Grizzly Bear") was first fielded in 1943 as a self-propelled heavy assault howitzer to provide close infantry support. These vehicles advanced with the first waves of an infantry unit to provide devastating fire against enemy strong points, bunkers, and the like. They were highly effective in this role but, thinly armored, were quite vulnerable to antitank guns and tank destroyer fire.

General specifications included:

Weight: 62,170 pounds
Length: 19 feet 5.5 inches
Width: 9 feet 5.4 inches
Height: 8 feet 3.2 inches
Power plant: one 265-horsepower Maybach V-12 gasoline engine
Top speed: 24.85 miles per hour
Armament: one 5.9-inch howitzer and one or two 7.92-mm machine guns

Sturmtiger. The Sturmtiger was a self-propelled gun specifically intended for the kind of urban warfare the Germans encountered in the BATTLE OF STALINGRAD. Impatient with deadly house-to-house fighting, the Germans developed the Sturmtiger to simply blow away the houses—and anything else that got in the way. On a Tiger tank chassis and hull, the turret was replaced by a boxy superstructure through which a short, extremely wide–bore barrel penetrated. This was not a gun, but a rocket launcher (Raketenwerfer 61) modified to fire a rocket-propelled naval-style depth charge weighing 761 pounds, almost all of the weight representing the high-explosive charge. The rocket launcher could lob the depth charge 6,180 yards, and its detonation would certainly destroy anything it hit.

The Sturmtiger required a seven-man crew, with four dedicated to serving the launcher. Loading was assisted by an integrated crane mounted behind the superstructure. Only 10 Sturmtigers were actually produced, beginning in August 1944. They were never deployed effectively, however, and were either destroyed or captured, much to the fascination of Allied soldiers.

General specifications included:

Weight: 143,000 pounds
Length: 20 feet 7.25 inches
Width: 11 feet 8.6 inches
Height: 9 feet 4.2 inches
Power plant: one 650-horsepower Maybach V-12 gasoline engine
Top speed: 24.86 miles per hour

Armament: one 38-cm rocket projector and one 7.92-mm machine gun

Sturmgeschütz III. The Sturmgeschütz III was an armored mobile gun designed to follow infantry assaults to provide fire support and the kind of concentrated firepower required to neutralize strongpoints and destroy bunkers and other fortifications. The vehicle was developed before the outbreak of the war and was produced throughout the conflict in fairly large numbers. In addition to its application as a close infantry support weapon, it was also used as a tank destroyer.

General specifications of the vehicle included:

Weight: 52,690 pounds
Length: 22 feet 2.5 inches
Width: 9 feet 8 inches
Height: 7 feet 1 inch
Power plant: one 265-horsepower Maybach V-12 gasoline engine
Top speed: 24.85 miles per hour
Armament: one 75-mm gun and two 7.92-mm machine guns

HEAVY ARTILLERY

15-cm schwere Feldhabitze 18. Within Germany were two of the world's greatest manufacturers of heavy artillery, Krupp and Rheinmetall. The Nazi regime, tooling up for war as soon as it came to power in 1933, entered into a close working relationship with these firms, which eagerly furnished designs for the most advanced new guns. The two firms were avid competitors, but, in a kind of symbolic gesture, German military planners ordered in 1933 what would be the standard heavy field artillery piece, the 15-cm schwere Feldhabitze 18, from *both* companies. Rheinmetall furnished the gun, while Krupp supplied the carriage. This versatile gun would later be installed on a self-propelled carriage to become the Hummel ("Bumble Bee"), and it would also be used in fixed fortifications, most notably along the Atlantic Wall coastal defenses. The gun was used on every front throughout the entire war.

General specifications included:

Caliber: 149 mm
Length: 14 feet 6.8 inches

Weight: 13,898 pounds
Elevation: -3° to +45°
Traverse: 60°
Range: 14,570 yards
Shell weight: 95.9 pounds

15-cm Kanone 18. The new regime also ordered from Rheinmetall a new gun for divisional level artillery batteries, the 15-cm Kanone 18. It was a most impressive looking weapon, which could lob a 94.8-pound shell 26,800 yards. However, its barrel was so long that transportation over any distance required removing the barrel and placing it on its own carriage. This greatly compromised mobility, which was a prime requisite of Blitzkrieg doctrine. Another drawback was the gun's relatively slow two-round-per-minute rate of fire. These problems led to the discontinuation of production long before the war ended.

General specifications included:

Caliber: 149.1 mm
Length: 26 feet 10.8 inches
Weight: 41,226 pounds
Elevation: -2° to +43°
Traverse: 360° on platform or 11° on carriage
Range: 26,800 yards
Shell weight: 94.8 pounds

15-cm Kanone 39. Another marginally successful gun was the 15-cm Kanone 39, manufactured by Krupp. Performance was very good. The gun threw a 94.8 pound shell 27,010 yards, but, because the piece originally had been designed and built for Turkey, its ammunition was nonstandard in the German army. Large stockpiles of the Turkish-specification ammo existed at the beginning of the war, so these as well as about 40 of the guns were commandeered as heavy field pieces.

As with the Kanone 18, transportation was a weakness. Barrel, carriage, and a turntable had to be broken down and moved as three separate units. Fortunately, in the field, the turntable was not usually used, but this still meant that the gun had to be transported in two pieces. Well before the end of the war, the Kanone 39 was withdrawn from the field and installed in the Atlantic Wall defenses.

General specifications included:

Caliber: 149.1 mm
Length: 27 feet 0.8 inch
Weight: 40,305 pounds
Elevation: -4° to +45°
Traverse (turntable): 360°
Traverse (carriage): 60°
Range: 27,010 yards
Shell weight: 94.8 pounds

17-cm Kanone 18 and 21-cm Mörser 18. Krupp's 17-cm Kanone 18 and 21-cm Mörser 18 were among the very best heavy artillery pieces of World War II. The Kanone was a long-range artillery piece, whereas the Mörser ("mortar") was a shorter-range howitzer. Both featured the same carriage, which incorporated a brilliant double recoil design that minimized the need for re-laying the gun. This not only improved accuracy of fire but significantly increased the rate of fire. Moreover, although both versions of the gun were heavy, the design of the carriage facilitated rapid transport. An integral platform allowed for 360° traverse, which could be managed by a single gunner.

General specifications of the Kanone included:

Caliber: 172.5 mm
Length: 27 feet 11.8 inches
Weight: 51,533 pounds
Elevation: 0° to 50°
Traverse (platform): 360°
Traverse (carriage): 16°
Range: 32,370 yards
Shell weight: 149.9 pounds

General specifications of the Mörser included:

Caliber: 210.9 mm
Length: 21 feet 4.3 inches
Weight: 50,045 pounds
Elevation: 0° to 50°
Traverse (platform): 360°
Traverse (carriage): 16°
Range: 18,270 yards
Shell weight: 266.8 pounds

24-cm Kanone 3. Counterbattery fire is artillery fire directed against enemy artillery positions and emplacements. By definition, effective counterbattery fire must be long range—beyond the range, certainly, of the enemy battery that is being targeted. In 1935, the Rheinmetall firm began design work on such a long-range gun, the prototype of which was produced in 1938. The 24-cm Kanone 3 was a massive weapon with a double-recoil carriage (to minimize re-laying) mounting a 42-foot-long piece. Even with its well-designed carriage, the gun had to be broken down into six loads for transportation, and while it achieved long range (more than 41,000 yards), it was not produced in large numbers. Between eight and 10 were fielded.

General specifications included:

Caliber: 238 mm
Length: 42 feet 11.9 inches
Weight: 186,590 pounds
Elevation: -1° to +56°
Traverse (turntable): 360°
Traverse (carriage): 6°
Range: 41,010 yards
Shell weight: 335.78 pounds

35.5-cm Haubitze M.1. In 1935, German military planners commissioned from Rheinmetall a full-scale siege gun, the 35.5-cm Haubitze M.1. This massive gun had to be transported in six loads, plus one more transport to carry the gantry needed for the final assembly. The 35.5-caliber weapon fired a high-explosive projectile weighing 1,267 pounds or an anticoncrete projectile weighing 2,041 pounds. Range, however, was limited, at 22,800 yards, as was muzzle velocity, at 1,870 feet per second. Rate of fire was a leisurely one round per minute. Few of these giants were produced, and they were used exclusively on the eastern front.

General specifications included:

Caliber: 356.6 mm
Length: 33 feet 8.1 inches
Weight: 272,271 pounds
Elevation: +45° to +75°
Traverse (platform): 360°
Traverse (carriage): 6°
Range: 22,800 yards

Shell weight: 1,267.6 pounds (high-explosive round) or 2,041 pounds (anticoncrete round)

FIELD ARTILLERY

In contrast to heavy artillery, which has limited mobility or may, in fact, be fixed in place within permanent fortifications, field artillery is highly transportable. It is intended to support both infantry and armor operations. As such, the equipment must be light enough to advance with the troops and their machines.

10.5-cm leFH 18. If there was a standard German field artillery weapon, it was the family of 10.5-cm howitzers, which dated from World War I, though the weapon was updated just before and during World War II. By the mid-1930s, the standard model was the 10.5-cm leFH 18. The adjective that best describes the character of this weapon is *solid.* Conservative and conventional, it was overengineered in the typical German fashion so that it was virtually indestructible. The price of this durability was weight, an especially critical price for an army that, on the one hand, stressed mobility and, on the other, still depended heavily on horses to pull towed field artillery. Despite this drawback, the leFH 18 served throughout the war.

General specifications included:

Caliber: 105 mm
Length: 130.23 inches
Weight: 4,310 pounds
Elevation: -5° to 42°
Traverse: 60°
Range: 13,478 yards
Shell weight: 32.65 pounds

7.5-cm Feldkanone 16 nA. After World War I, the Treaty of Versailles severely limited the arms that Germany might retain. Among these was a stockpile of outmoded 7.7-cm field guns, which the interwar German army decided to modernize by rebarrelling for 7.5-cm shells. This modification increased muzzle velocity and range, bringing them up to modern standards. The 7.5-cm Feldkanone 16 nA was used early in World War II but was later relegated mostly to training, as newer, more powerful 105-mm weapons became available.

General specifications included:

Caliber: 75 mm
Length: 106.3 inches
Weight: 5,324 pounds
Elevation: -9° to +44°
Traverse: 4°
Range: 14,080 yards
Shell weight: 12.85 pounds

105-cm Kanone 18 and 18/40. During the 1920s, in covert contravention of the terms of the Treaty of Versailles, German military planners put out a call for a new long-range field artillery piece. The result, the 105-cm Kanone 18 and 18/40, married a Rheinmetall barrel to a Krupp carriage. The guns proved awkward and heavy in the field, so they were transferred early in the war to coastal defense duty.

General specifications included:

Caliber: 105 mm
Length: 214.96 inches
Weight: 14,187 pounds
Elevation: 0° to 48°
Traverse: 64°
Range: 20,860 yards
Shell weight: 33.38 pounds

HEAVY ANTIAIRCRAFT GUNS

World War II saw the development of two broad classes of antiaircraft artillery. Light antiaircraft guns were used in the field to defend troops, vehicles, and small installations against attack by tactical bombers and other ground-attack aircraft. Heavy antiaircraft guns targeted strategic bombers and protected cities, factories, and other major installations.

8.8-cm Flak (FliegerAbewehrKanone) 41 (the 88). The most famous German heavy antiaircraft gun was the 88, the 8.8 cm Flak (FliegerAbewehr-Kanone) 41. The modern 88 was designed in 1939 to 1941 to replace previous antiaircraft guns of this caliber. Built by Rheinmetall, the Flak 41 was initially plagued by mechanical problems, but once these were solved, it was a formidable weapon, capable of firing 25 flak rounds per minute to a ceiling of 48,230 feet. This made the gun useful against strategic as well as tactical attackers. More-

over, the weapon was flexible enough to double in an antitank role, if need be.

General specifications included:

Caliber: 88 mm
Weight: 27,780 pounds
Length: 21 feet 5.8 inches
Elevation: -3° to +90°
Traverse: 360°
Ceiling: 48,230 feet
Shell weight: 20.7 pounds (high explosive)

10.5-cm Flak 38 and Flak 39. While the Germans were justifiably proud of the 88 family of guns, they recognized long before the war began that defense against modern bombers required even heavier, more powerful weapons. In 1935, the 10.5-cm Flak 38 and Flak 39 were introduced. These guns had an all-electric control system and a powered loading system, which made them highly efficient. They were originally intended as field weapons, but their size prompted the Luftwaffe, which had charge of the Reich's antiaircraft defense, to appropriate them. Some were put in permanent emplacements, while others were mounted on railway carriages. The gun never achieved the renown of the 88, however, in part because it was far less numerous and in part because it did not perform as well as hoped, though it was a very good antiaircraft weapon.

General specifications included:

Caliber: 105 mm
Weight: 32,187 pounds
Length: 21 feet 9.7 inches
Elevation: -3° to +85°
Ceiling: 41,995 feet
Shell weight: 33.3 pounds

12.8-cm Flak 40. In 1940, design work was advanced on an even heavier antiaircraft gun, the 12.8-cm Flak 40. Originally intended as a mobile piece suspended between two four-wheel towed carriages, the gun was too big and too heavy to make long-distance transportation practical, and it was reserved for fixed installations to defend population centers. In some places, special flak towers were built for emplacement. These provided the best sighting for the guns, giving them the greatest range of traverse. Some guns were mounted on special railway carriages to provide a degree of mobility.

General specifications included:

Caliber: 128 mm
Weight: 59,524 pounds
Length: 25 feet 8.5 inches
Elevation: -3° to +87°
Traverse: 360°
Ceiling: 48,555 feet
Shell weight: 57.3 pounds

LIGHT ANTIAIRCRAFT ARTILLERY

2-cm Flak 30. The Germans developed a wide variety of guns to provide defense against tactical air attack. The first of these weapons was developed in 1935 by Rheinmetall. The 2-cm Flak 30 was the very first flak weapon, firing a high-explosive shell designed to burst in the air, sending thousands of deadly shrapnel fragments, which readily penetrated fuselages and control surfaces, damaging aircraft mechanically and also injuring or killing air crews. Early version of the weapon incorporated a complex sighting system, which, however, was eventually dropped as gunners realized that the rate of fire while tracking targets was far more important than one-on-one accuracy. The flak shell, after all, was not expected actually to hit its target, but would damage it or bring it down by exploding near it.

General specifications of the Flak 30 included:

Caliber: 20 mm
Length of piece: 90.6 inches
Weight: 992 pounds
Elevation: -12° to +90°
Traverse: 360°
Ceiling: 7,218 feet
Rate of fire: 280 rounds per minute
Projectile weight: 0.262 pound

2-cm Flak 38. At 280 rounds per minute, the Flak 30 was sluggish against fast-moving fighters and dive bombers. Recognizing a need to increase rate of fire, the Muser Company designed the 2-cm Flak 38. This weapon achieved a rate of fire of 420 to 480 rounds per minute. The projectiles

were relatively small, however, and German planners recognized that to inflict real damage on enemy attackers required even higher rates of fire. In 1940, therefore, they modified the carriage of the Flak 38 to accommodate four barrels, each firing at once, for a rate of fire of 1,800 rounds per minute. This proved to be a highly effective weapon.

General specifications for the Flak 38 included:

Caliber: 20 mm
Length: 88.7 inches
Weight: 926 pounds
Elevation: -20° to +90°
Traverse: 360°
Ceiling: 7,218 feet
Rate of fire: 420–480 rounds per minute
Projectile weight: 0.262 pound

3.7-cm Flak 36 and Flak 37. A series of 3.7-cm flak guns was developed in the 1930s and steadily improved, especially with regard to the sighting mechanism, which incorporated a sophisticated predictor to aid target leading. All skilled gunners understood that it was important to lead rather than track or follow a target; the trick was in judging just how far to lead it. Mechanical predictor units helped to simplify this job and guide the rate of target leading. Flak 36 and Flak 37 proved highly capable weapons, with 4,211 in service with the Luftwaffe by August 1944. The WEHRMACHT and the navy also used a version of the gun.

General specifications included:

Caliber: 37 mm
Length: 142.75 inches
Weight: 3,417 pounds
Elevation: -8° to +85°
Traverse: 360°
Ceiling: 15,748 feet
Rate of fire: 160 rounds per minute
Projectile weight: 1.41 pounds

3.7-cm Flak 43 and Flakzwilling 43. The next advance in the 3.7-cm flak weapons was the Flak 43 and the Flakzwilling 43. The Flak 43 was designed in 1942 but was not fielded until 1944. Its major advantage over previous 3.7-cm models was in rate of fire, which rose to 250 rounds per minute. Even at this rate, however, as Allied aircraft became faster and faster, it was difficult to score sufficient hits to bring an airplane down. The Flakzwilling added a second barrel to multiply the rate of fire, and it was this version that proved most popular with infantry gun crews. But by this time, the war was clearly being lost, and production of both versions of the new gun waned. Only 280 double-barreled Flakzwilling weapons saw service.

General specifications included:

Caliber: 37 mm
Length: 130 inches
Weight: 3,069 pounds
Elevation: -7.5° to +90°
Traverse: 360°
Ceiling: 15,748 feet
Rate of fire (Flak 43): 250 rounds per minute
Projectile weight: 1.41 pounds

5-cm Flak 41. The 5-cm Flak 41 was introduced in 1941 in an effort to address a gap in antiaircraft defenses between about 5,000 feet and 10,000 feet. Light antiaircraft guns were most effective below 5,000 feet, whereas heavy antiaircraft artillery were effective only above 10,000 feet. German military planners called for an intermediate-range weapon to fill the gap. The gun that resulted, however, not only failed to fill the gap but was generally ineffective at any altitude and severely limited above 10,000 feet. Underpowered, it produced a bright muzzle flash, which was visible even in bright daylight. This, of course, served to give away the position of the guns, rendering entire batteries vulnerable to counterattack. In the end, only about 60 of these weapons were produced.

Their general specifications included:

Caliber: 50 mm
Length: 184.5 inches
Weight: 6,834 pounds
Elevation: -10° to +90°
Traverse: 360°
Ceiling: 10,007 feet
Rate of fire: 180 rounds per minute
Weight of projectile: 4.85 pounds

ROCKETS

The Germans were infamous for developing two major strategic rocket systems, the V-1 BUZZ BOMB and the V-2 ROCKET, but they were also active in the development of tactical rockets. While far less accurate than traditional artillery, field rockets, or war rockets, as they are sometimes called, could be fired from multiple launchers at rapid rates, making up in quantity of fire what they lacked in precision of fire.

15-cm Wurfgranate 41. The 15-cm Wurfgranate 41 rockets came with two charges, either high explosive or smoke. They could be launched from the self-propelled Panzerwerfer 42, a half-track vehicle. Mobility was important in a rocket launcher, since the flash of multiple rocket firings quickly gave away the launcher's position, and shoot-and-run tactics could be essential to survival.

General specifications for the 15-cm Wurfgranate 41 Spreng (high explosive) included:

Length: 38.55 inches
Diameter: 6.22 inches
Weight: 70 pounds
Range: 7,715 yards

General specifications for the 15-cm Wurfgranate 41 w Kh Nevbel (smoke) included:

Length: 40.16 inches
Diameter: 6.22 inches
Weight: 79 pounds
Range: 7,500 yards

21-cm Wurfgranate 42. Pleased with the performance of the 15-cm rockets, German designers tried something larger, the 21-cm Wurfgranate 42. This rocket proved highly successful and could be launched from small, multitube towed launchers or from the Panzerwerfer 42 (modified to accept the larger-diameter rockets). American military planners carefully studied—and copied—captured units.

General specifications of the Wurfgranate 42 rocket included:

Length: 49.21 mm
Diameter: 8.27 inches

Weight: 241.5 pounds
Range: 8,585 yards

28-cm and 32-cm Wurfkörper. While the 15-cm and 21-cm Wurfgranate rockets were the most successful of Germany's tactical rocket weapons, the earlier and larger 28-cm and 32-cm Wurfkörper, though short in range, were also widely employed. Depending on the version used, these rockets deployed high-explosive warheads, incendiary warheads, or smoke effects. They could be launched from a variety of launchers, but most frequently used was the SdKfz 252, also known as a "Foot Stuka" or "Howling Cow." A low-profile half-track, the "Cow" was fitted with crude launchers affixed to its sides. The rockets could be launched individually or simultaneously.

General specifications of the 28-cm Wurfkörper Spreng (high-explosive) rocket included:

Length: 46.85 inches
Diameter: 11 inches
Weight: 181 pounds
Range: 2,337 yards

In 1942, a new, larger version of the Wurfkörper was introduced. At 32 cm in diameter, the new Wurfkörper had a longer range, created a more powerful explosion, and, thanks to an advanced propellent, generated less smoke and flash than previous rockets. This made it harder for an enemy to determine the location of the launcher.

The general specifications of the rocket included:

Length: 48.44 inches
Diameter: 11.8 inches
Weight: 277 pounds
Range: 4,975 yards

ANTITANK GUNS

Although the Germans deployed a number of tank destroyers, they also fielded four major types of towed antitank artillery.

Pak guns. Known as Pak guns—for *Panzerabwehrkanone*—there were three major caliber types: the 3.7-cm, the 5-cm, and the 7.5-cm. The 3.7-cm was designed early in the interwar period,

and production commenced in 1928. A modern design, the gun was nevertheless fitted to a carriage intended to be pulled by horses. First used during the Spanish civil war, the small gun proved highly effective against lightly armored vehicles. During the INVASION OF POLAND, it also served adequately. However, in the BATTLE OF FRANCE, against more heavily armored tanks, the velocity of the small shells proved inadequate. Nevertheless, the gun, which was even adapted for parachute deployment, served throughout the war.

General specifications included:

Caliber: 37 mm
Length: 5 feet 5.5 inches
Weight: 970 pounds
Traverse: 59°
Elevation: -8° to +25°
Range: 7,655 yards
Armor penetration: 1.48 inches at 400 yards
Weight of projectile: 0.78 pound

During 1939–40, the 5-cm Pak began production, in time for the INVASION OF THE SOVIET UNION, where it was the only German antitank gun effective against the mighty Soviet T-34 tank. Very widely used, the 5-cm Pak may be considered the German army's standard antitank gun.

Its general specifications included:

Caliber: 50 mm
Length: 10 feet, 5.5 inches
Weight: 2,341 pounds
Traverse: 65°
Elevation: -8° to +27°
Range: 2,900 yards
Armor penetration: 3.98 inches at 820 yards
Projectile weight: 4 pounds (high-explosive round)

Prior to the invasion of the Soviet Union, intelligence reached German war planners that the newest Soviet tanks were heavily armored. Fearing that the 5-cm Pak would be inadequate against Soviet armor, a 7.5-cm Pak was fielded in 1940. The new weapon rapidly became a favorite among antittank crews, and it was also sufficiently versatile to be used as an all-round field artillery piece.

General specifications included:

Caliber: 75 mm
Length: 12 feet 1.7 inches
Weight: 3,307 pounds
Traverse: 46°
Elevation: -5° to +22°
Range: 8,400 yards
Armor penetration: 3.86 inches at 2,190 yards
Projectile weight: 12.65 (high-explosive round)

Taper-bore guns. The Germans experimented with taper-bore antitank guns, which employed something called the Gerlich principle to produce high muzzle velocities capable of increased range and armor penetration. The Gerlich principle used shells with a soft flange at their base. These were fired through a bore that tapered from the bottom to the top, the flange folding as the shell moved through to the tapered end of the bore. This had the effect of creating a seal that prevented the explosive gases produced within the gun from escaping. Therefore, the shell was propelled by gas at much higher pressure, producing greater force and speed. It was a sound principle, but it required extremely precise manufacturing techniques and raw materials that were in increasingly short supply in Germany. The special shell had a tungsten core, and tungsten supplies were very scarce. While these guns were promising, Germany was never able to put them into significant mass production. Their potential can be gauged from the armor penetration figure for a 7.5-cm taper-bore gun: 6.73 inches of armor at 500 yards.

Further reading: Engelmann, Joachim. *German Artillery in World War II 1939–1945.* Atglen, Pa.: Schiffer Publishing, 1995; Engelmann, Joachim. *German Heavy Field Artillery in World War II: 1934–1945.* Atglen, Pa.: Schiffer Publishing, 1995; Engelmann, Joachim. *German Light Field Artillery: 1935–1945.* Atglen, Pa.: Schiffer Publishing, 1995; Engelmann, Joachim. *German Self-Propelled Artillery in World War II: Wespe 105mm Guns, Alkett Weapons Carrier, and Captured Vehicles.* Atglen, Pa.: Schiffer Publishing, 1992; Hogg, Ian V. *German Artillery of World War Two.* London: Greenhill Books, 2002.

artillery, Italian

Artillery in World War II consisted mainly of seven major categories: self-propelled guns, heavy artillery, field artillery, heavy antiaircraft guns, light antiaircraft guns, rockets, and antitank guns. The Italian army did not use rockets or dedicated antitank guns.

SELF-PROPELLED GUNS

Semovente da 149/40. The Italian army fielded several self-propelled guns, including some mounting 75-mm and 105-mm weapons. These were direct-fire guns, that is, artillery intended to be used at fairly close range against clearly visible targets. The Italian army also called for self-propelled heavy artillery, or indirect-fire weapons, which were intended to be fired at long-range targets, but the Italian arms industry was not equipped to develop a fully adequate weapon. What emerged was a kind of interim solution, the Semovente da 149/40, which featured a 149-mm long-barrel gun mounted on a modified Carro Armato M 15/42 tank chassis. The long gun was fitted to the chassis and was completely unprotected. The gun crew worked out in the open. Even given the range of the weapon, 25,919 yards, this degree of exposure was dangerous and limited the utility of the Semovente. Indeed, this consideration, stresses on the Italian economy, and, ultimately, the separate peace Italy concluded with the Allies prevented the gun from going into production beyond the prototype.

General specifications included:

Weight: 52,911 pounds
Length: 21 feet 7.8 inches
Width: 9 feet 10 inches
Height: 6 feet 6.7 inches
Power plant: one 250-horsepower SPA gasoline engine
Armament: one 149-mm long-barrel gun

HEAVY ARTILLERY

The military ambitions of Italy's premier BENITO MUSSOLINI drove a resolution to modernize Italy's arsenal of heavy artillery. The nation had invested extensively in such weapons during

World War I, but Mussolini and other Italian military planners recognized during the 1930s that these weapons were obsolescent at best and obsolete at worst.

Obice da 210/22 modello 35. The most important new heavy gun ordered was the Obice da 210/22 modello 35, a massive 210-mm howitzer, which was a masterpiece of artillery design. The gun was mounted on a modern split-trail carriage that featured two road wheels on each side. These were raised when the gun was in firing position, and the weight of the gun was taken by a firing platform beneath the main axle. Nominally, the gun could traverse 75°, but if placed so that the stakes that secured the split trail were raised, a 360° traverse was possible. The recoil mechanism was highly sophisticated, making for great accuracy and rapidity of fire. All that was wrong with this fine weapon was its relative complexity, which taxed the Italian arms industry beyond its capacity to keep pace with demand. The weapon was never deployed in sufficient numbers to make much impact, and when Italy bowed out of the Axis alliance in 1943, most of the existing modello 35s were sent with Hungarian units to the eastern front. Those that remained in Italy were eagerly seized by the Germans, who had great respect for the weapon.

General specifications included:

Caliber: 210 mm
Length: 16 feet 4.85 inches
Weight: 52,977 pounds
Elevation: 0° to +70°
Traverse: 75° nominal, 360° possible
Range: 16,850 yards
Shell weight: 222.7 pounds or 293.2 pounds

FIELD ARTILLERY

75-mm field guns. The Italian army employed a number of 75-mm field guns, none of which was very modern and one of which, the Cannone da 75/27 modello 06, was introduced in 1906. Despite its age, it was used throughout the Italian engagement in the war. Only slightly newer was another pre–World War I field piece, the Cannone da 75/27 modello 11, which was an improvement over the 06 in that its unconventional horizontal recoil mechanism performed quite well and minimized the need for re-laying after sustained firing. Despite their age, both guns were used extensively, particularly in the North African Campaign, where the Germans even employed them. Perhaps surprisingly, these field guns were also adapted for use from fixed fortifications and were, therefore, among the most versatile artillery pieces of the war.

General specifications for the modello 06 included:

Caliber: 75 mm
Length: 88.6 inches
Weight: 2,381 pounds
Elevation: -10° to +16°
Traverse: 7°
Range: 11,200 yards
Shell weight: 14 pounds

General specifications for the modello 11 included:

Caliber: 75 mm
Length: 83.93 inches
Weight: 4,190 pounds
Elevation: -15° to +65°
Traverse: 52°
Range: 11,200 yards
Shell weight: 14 pounds

Obice da 75/18 modello 35. In the 1930s, two more 75-mm field guns were introduced into the Italian army. The Obice da 75/18 modello 35 was designed specifically as mountain artillery. It was compact and could be broken down into eight separate components to facilitate transportation over difficult terrain. Elegantly designed, this small gun was highly effective for its specialized purpose. As with almost all Italian weapons, however, despite the thoughtful design, the nation's manufacturing capacity was simply insufficient to keep pace with need. This shortage was exacerbated on the eve of World War II when Mussolini, desperate for foreign currency, authorized the sale of many of these guns to the armies of other nations.

General specifications included:

Caliber: 75 mm
Length: 61.3 inches
Weight: 4,080 pounds
Elevation: -10° to +45°
Traverse: 50°
Range: 10,460 yards
Shell weight: 14.1 pounds

Cannone da 75/32 modello 37. The most modern of Italy's field guns was the Cannone da 75/32 modello 37. A long-barreled weapon, the gun had an impressive range of nearly 14,000 yards. It was designed to be pulled by motorized traction rather than horses, and its well-made split trail allowed for a 50° traverse. The weapon packed sufficient punch to be used effectively in an antitank role. As usual, the only problem was rate of production, which was never sufficient.

General specifications included:

Caliber: 75 mm
Length: 101.3 inches
Weight: 2,756 pounds
Elevation: -10° to +45°
Traverse: 50°
Range: 13,675 yards
Shell weight: 13.9 pounds

HEAVY ANTIAIRCRAFT GUNS

Antiaircraft guns (AA) were of two types. Light AA artillery was used against low-flying ground-attack aircraft and defended troops, vehicles, and structures. Heavy AA artillery was effective against high-altitude strategic bombers that attacked cities and other major facilities.

Cannone da 75/46 C.A. modello 34. Italy deployed two important heavy antiaircraft guns. The Cannonone da 75/46 C.A. modello 34 was a conventional 75-mm weapon mounted on a simple platform and fitted with crude but adequate fire control equipment. It could be transported easily but had a limited ceiling for the heavy AA application. As usual, the biggest drawback was the limited capacity of the Italian arms industry, which could not keep pace with orders for the gun.

General specifications included:

Caliber: 75 mm
Weight: 9,711 pounds
Length: 11 feet 3.8 inches
Elevation: +90°
Traverse: 360°
Ceiling: 27,230 feet
Shell weight: 14.33 pounds

Cannone da 90/53. Significantly heavier was the Cannone da 90/53, which could be fired from a fixed emplacement or from the platform of a heavy truck. The gun could fire a 22.77-pound shell to a ceiling of nearly 40,000 feet and was sufficiently versatile to be pressed into a heavy artillery role, if need be.

General specifications included:

Caliber: 90 mm
Weight: 19,371 pounds
Length: 15 feet 6.5 inches
Elevation: +85°
Traverse: 360°
Ceiling: 39,370 feet
Shell weight: 22.77 pounds

LIGHT ANTIAIRCRAFT GUNS

Italian forces employed a moderately heavy antiaircraft gun in the Cannone da 75/46 C.A. modello 34 and a heavy gun in the Cannone da 90/53, but they developed no truly intermediate weapon. Their two most important light antiaircraft guns were very light, both firing 20-mm projectiles.

Scotti. The Scotti was a 1930s design that fired a 0.276-pound projectile to a ceiling of only 7,005 feet, but it had the advantage of mobility and was reasonably effective against low-flying attack aircraft.

Its general specifications included:

Caliber: 20 mm
Length: 60.6 inches
Weight: 502 pounds
Elevation: -10° to +85°
Traverse: 360°
Ceiling: 7,005 feet
Rate of fire: 250 rounds per minute
Projectile weight: 0.276 pound

Breda. The Scotti was the standard light artillery piece of the Italian army, which also employed the 20-mm Breda, a 1934–35 design that traded a bit of the Scotti's rapid rate of fire for a 1,000-foot increase in ceiling. The Breda also had a much more sophisticated mount, which significantly improved accuracy. Indeed, the gun was held in sufficient esteem to be reserved mainly for defense of the Italian mainland.

General specifications included:

Caliber: 20 mm
Length: 51.2 inches
Weight: 678 pounds
Elevation: -10° to +80°
Traverse: 360°
Ceiling: 8,202 feet
Rate of fire: 200 to 220 rounds per minute
Projectile weight: 0.298 pounds

Further reading: Jowett, Philip S. *Italian Army in World War II: Europe 1940–43.* London: Osprey, 2000; Jowett, Philip S., and Stephen Andrew. *The Italian Army, 1940–45: Africa 1940–43.* London: Osprey, 2001; Knox, MacGregor. *Hitler's Italian Allies: Royal Armed Forces, Fascist Regime, and the War of 1940–1943.* Cambridge and New York: Cambridge University Press, 2000.

artillery, Japanese

Artillery in World War II consisted mainly of seven major categories: self-propelled guns, heavy artillery, field artillery, heavy antiaircraft guns, light antiaircraft guns, rockets, and antitank guns. Japan developed no heavy artillery of note.

SELF-PROPELLED GUNS

As they lagged behind the other major combatants in the development of armor (*see* ARMOR, JAPANESE), so Japan was slow to field self-propelled guns.

Type 4 HO-RO. The most important self-propelled gun Japan produced was the Type 4 HO-RO, a self-propelled short-range 150-mm howitzer. This was mounted on the chassis of a Type 97 medium tank in place of the tank's turret. The crew was afforded scant protection by the open-top

housing and the very thin armor around three sides of the gun's breech. Outmoded riveted construction (modern tanks and self-propelled guns used welded construction) also compromised the gun's survivability. Finally, Japanese industry simply was not tooled up to produce the Type 4 in quantity, and these guns were deployed piecemeal for infantry support only.

General specifications included:

Weight: about 30,000 pounds
Length: 18 feet 2 inches
Width: 7 feet 6 inches
Height: 5 feet 1 inch
Power plant: one 170-horsepower V-12 diesel
Top speed: 23.6 miles per hour
Armament: one 150-mm howitzer

FIELD ARTILLERY

75-mm Field Gun Type 38. The only notable field artillery the Japanese army used was the 75-mm Field Gun Type 38, a weapon of venerable design, dating back to a German Krupp 1905 prototype but upgraded in various ways, including by the adoption of a box trail (in place of the pole trail of the Krupp design), which increased elevation. The gun's barrel was balanced on its carriage more effectively, and the recoil mechanism was upgraded and improved. Nevertheless, the gun was at best obsolescent and was never even modified for vehicle traction. Through 1945, it was pulled by horses or mules. That an army as advanced as Japan's was saddled with so archaic a piece of field artillery is both remarkable and puzzling.

General specifications included:

Caliber: 75 mm
Length: 90 inches
Weight: 4,211 pounds
Elevation: -8° to +43°
Traverse: 7°
Range: 13,080 yards
Shell weight: 13.3 pounds

HEAVY ANTIAIRCRAFT GUN

In contrast to light antiaircraft guns, which are used in the field against ground attack by such tactical aircraft as fighters, attack planes, and light bombers, heavy antiaircraft guns target strategic bombers and protect civilian areas or large military facilities.

Type 88 75-mm antiaircraft gun. The principal Japanese heavy antiaircraft weapon was the Type 88 75-mm antiaircraft gun, which was introduced as early as 1928. At the time of its introduction, it represented the state of the art in heavy antiaircraft defense. By World War II, however, while it remained a good weapon, it was inadequate to defend against high-altitude B-17s and even less adequate against B-29s. It lacked sufficient ceiling to defend against planes of these types.

General specifications included:

Caliber: 75 mm
Weight: 6,056 pounds
Length: 10 feet 10.5 inches
Elevation: +85°
Traverse: 360°
Ceiling: 23,785 feet
Shell weight: 14.5 pounds

LIGHT ANTIAIRCRAFT GUN

As the Japanese army never developed a fully effective heavy antiaircraft gun, it failed also to field a fully effective gun for light, tactical antiaircraft defense.

Type 98 20-mm machine cannon. The Type 98 20-mm machine cannon was capable of firing a 0.3-pound projectile to a ceiling of nearly 12,000 feet, but its magazine held only 20 rounds, and the rate of fire was a mere 120 rounds per minute, about half the rate of most other light antiaircraft weapons. Although quite modern—it was introduced in 1938—the design of the gun was a compromise, since the weapon was intended to be used both for an antiaircraft application and as an antitank gun. Nevertheless, if a gunner could get on target, the Type 98 hit hard and was capable of inflicting serious damage.

General specifications included:

Caliber: 20 mm
Length: 57.5 inches
Weight: 593 pounds
Elevation: -10° to +85°
Traverse: 360°

Ceiling: 11,975 feet
Rate of fire: 120 rounds per minute
Projectile weight: 0.3 pound

ROCKETS

20-cm rockets. The Japanese made extensive use of artillery rockets, the most important of which were two 20-cm rockets, one developed by the army and the other by the navy. The army rocket was launched from a dedicated tube launcher (the Type 4), whereas the navy rocket was launched from a crude wooden trough.

The general specifications of the army rocket included:

Length: 38.75 inches
Diameter: 7.95 inches
Weight: 44.95 pounds
Velocity and range: Unknown

The general specifications for the navy rocket included:

Length: 41 inches
Diameter: 8.2 inches
Weight: 198.5 pounds
Velocity and range: Velocity unknown; range 1,970 yards

ANTITANK GUN

47-mm Type 1. Lagging in the development of armor weapons, the Japanese also fielded but a single significant dedicated antitank gun, the 47-mm Type 1. This weapon was introduced in 1941 to replace a grossly inadequate 37-mm weapon, which had been introduced in 1934. The larger gun had a rapid 15-round-per-minute rate of fire and could pierce two inches of armor at 1,000 yards. This made it effective against light Allied armor but not the heavier tank armor. Worse, the gun was deployed in very limited numbers.

General specifications included:

Caliber: 47 mm
Length: 8 feet 3.5 inches
Weight: 1,660 pounds
Traverse: 60°
Elevation: -11° to +19°

Projectile weight: 3.37 pounds
Armor penetration: 2 inches at 1,000 yards

Further reading: Daugherty, Leo J., III. *Fighting Techniques of a Japanese Infantryman: 1941–1945: Training, Techniques, and Weapons.* Osceola, Wis.: Motorbooks International, 2002; Jowett, Philip S. *Japanese Army 1931–45.* London: Osprey, 2002; Rottman, Gordon, and Ian Palmer. *Japanese Pacific Island Defenses 1941–45.* London: Osprey, 2003.

artillery, Soviet

Artillery in World War II consisted mainly of seven major categories: self-propelled guns, heavy artillery, field artillery, heavy antiaircraft (AA) guns, light antiaircraft guns, rockets, and antitank guns. The Red Army deployed no dedicated light antiaircraft guns but used its 85-mm weapons as well as heavy machine guns.

SELF-PROPELLED GUNS

During the opening weeks of the INVASION OF THE SOVIET UNION, the Germans destroyed or captured huge quantities of Soviet equipment. Seeking to make up their losses, the Soviets took a hard look at their arsenal and chose only the most effective weapons to produce anew on a mass scale.

SU-76. The ZIS-3 3-inch gun had proven itself a fine piece of field artillery and a very good antitank gun. It was now pressed into another role, as the armament of a new self-propelled gun, the SU-76. The ZIS-3 was mounted atop a hastily converted T-70 light tank chassis and body. The new vehicle rolled off assembly lines beginning late in 1942 and was deployed with the Red Army during 1943. By the time it reached the field in quantity, German armor plating had become heavier, and the ZIS-3 was no longer very effective as a tank killer. Soviet troops grew to dislike the weapon, at least until its application was changed from the antitank role to close infantry support.

General specifications included:

Weight: 23,810 pounds
Length: 16 feet

Width: 8 feet 11.5 inches
Height: 7 feet 1.4 inches
Power plant: two 70-horsepower GAZ six-cylinder gasoline engines
Top speed: 28 miles per hour
Armament: one 3-inch gun and one 7.62-mm machine gun

ISU-122 and ISU-152. The Red Army also fielded two heavy self-propelled guns, the ISU-122 and the ISU-152. The first was a conversion from a KV-2 heavy tank chassis. Protruding from the armored box mounted atop the tank's deck was a 122-mm howitzer and, atop the box, a 12.7-mm antiaircraft machine gun. The later ISU-152 was virtually identical, except that it mounted the 6-inch M 1937 howitzer.

General specifications for the ISU-122 included:

Weight: 102,361 pounds
Length: 32 feet 1.8 inches
Width: 11 feet 8.2 inches
Height: 8 feet 3.2 inches
Power plant: one 520-horsepower V-12 diesel
Top speed: 23 miles per hour
Armament: one 122-mm howitzer and one 12.7-mm machine gun in AA mount

HEAVY ARTILLERY

Red Army heavy artillery consisted mainly of 152-mm and 203-mm weapons, none of which were innovative, but all of which were serviceable, simple, and capable of being produced in quantity.

Model 1937 152-mm gun. The Model 1937 was typical of the Soviet 152-mm (6-inch) guns and had the following general specifications:

Caliber: 152.4 mm (6 inches)
Length: 16 feet 1.9 inches
Weight: 17,483 pounds
Elevation: -2° to +65°
Traverse: 58°
Range: 18,880 yards
Shell weight: 95.9 pounds

Model 1943 152-mm howitzer. In addition to 152-mm guns, the Soviets produced a series of

152-mm howitzers, which was considerably lighter, though they still had the range of a heavy artillery weapon. These howitzers, simple, sturdy, powerful, and produced in great quantity, were among the most effective artillery weapons of World War II.

General specifications of the Model 1943 included:

Caliber: 152.5 mm (6 inches)
Length: 13 feet 9.6 inches
Weight: 8,025 pounds
Elevation: -3° to 63.5°
Traverse: 35°
Range: 13,560 yards
Shell weight: 112.6 pounds

Model 1931 203-mm howitzer (B-4). The heaviest Soviet howitzer was the 203-mm Model 1931, also called the B-4. A very heavy gun at almost 40,000 pounds, the Model 1931 had a carriage that used tracks rather than wheels, which enabled it to be pulled across snow, soft ground, marsh, and other poor terrain. However, for transportation over long distances, the heavy weapon had to be broken down into as many as six loads.

The Model 1931 was a notable indirect fire weapon, capable of lobbing a 220-pound shell some 11 miles. Its great drawback, apart from its cumbersome weight, was its slow rate of fire: about one round every four minutes. This made barrage work impractical, but the gun was still highly useful for fire against strongpoints and well-prepared fortifications.

General specifications included:

Caliber: 203 mm (8 inches)
Length: 16 feet 8.3 inches
Weight: 39,022 pounds
Elevation: 0° to +60°
Traverse: 8°
Range: 19,712 yards
Shell weight: 220.46 pounds

FIELD ARTILLERY

Model 00/02 and 02/30 series. The major Soviet field artillery pieces were of 3-inch (76.2 mm) caliber and included the venerable Model 00/02 and 02/30 series, the first of which, produced in 1900 and 1902, dated from the czarist era and was used in both world wars. Many of the 00/02 series guns were modernized in 1930 (as the 02/30 series) with the addition of upgraded ammunition, propellants, and, in many cases, new barrels. This modernized weapon became the standard Red Army field piece of the interwar period.

Its general specifications included:

Caliber: 3 inches
Length: 90 inches
Weight: 2,910 pounds
Elevation: -5° to +37°
Traverse: 2.66°
Range: 13,565 yards
Shell weight: 14.11 pounds

Field Gun Model 1936 (76-36). Even before the outbreak of war, Red Army planners recognized that their field artillery was obsolescent, even obsolete, and in 1936 produced the Field Gun Model 1936, familiarly known as the 76-36. This was a strikingly modern design for its time, with a long, slender barrel that increased both muzzle velocity and range over the earlier model. Its new split-trail carriage provided an impressively wide angle of traverse, which made this gun far handier than the 00/02 and 02/30 models. The new gun also accepted antitank rounds and so had the capability of being used in the antiarmor role.

Its general specifications included:

Caliber: 3 inches
Length: 153.3 inches
Weight: 5,292 pounds
Elevation: -5° to +75°
Traverse: 60°
Range: 15,145 yards
Shell weight: 14.1 pounds

Field Gun Model 1942 (76-42 or Zis-3). While the Model 1936 was a fine gun, many examples of it had been lost to the Germans in the initial phases of the invasion of the Soviet Union. As a consequence, the urgent necessity of new production provided an opportunity to design new weapons.

Among the most impressive and important was the Field Gun Model 1942, also called the 76-42 or Zis-3. This gun holds the distinction of having been produced in greater quantity than any other gun in World War II, a number far into the thousands. The gun was extremely versatile, serving in the traditional infantry support role and also as an antitank weapon. Mounted on a suitable vehicle, it became a self-propelled gun. Soviet designers emphasized simplicity, which saved weight and made the gun easy to handle.

The gun's general specifications included:

Caliber: 3 inches
Length: 127.8 inches
Weight: 2,470 pounds
Elevation: -5° to +37°
Traverse: 54°
Range: 14,450 yards
Shell weight: 13.7 pounds

HEAVY ANTIAIRCRAFT GUNS

During the 1930s, the Red Army followed the lead of the forces of other nations in recognizing the need for a new class of heavy antiaircraft weapons, capable of defending against strategic bombers, which threatened cities and other large installations. The Soviets produced a series of 85-mm guns, culminating, on the eve of war, in the Model 1939 and continuing through the war itself.

Model 1939 antiaircraft gun. The 1939 model was an excellent weapon, with superb range and even very good mobility on its wheeled platform. The Red Army deployed this gun widely, and it served the strategic AA function as well as much of the tactical function usually reserved for light AA guns.

General specifications included:

Caliber: 85 mm
Weight: 9,303 pounds
Length: 15 feet 4.76 inches
Elevation: -3° to 82°
Traverse: 360°
Ceiling: 34,450 feet
Shell weight: 20.29 pounds

ROCKETS

The Red Army made extensive use of rockets, which they correctly saw as highly effective against personnel deployed across the kinds of vast battlefields that typically characterized the war on the eastern front.

M8 82-mm rocket. During the years between World War I and World War II, Soviet scientists devoted a great deal of work to developing effective propellants and produced, during the late 1930s, the M8 82-mm rocket, which could be launched from specially modified light tanks (such as the T-70) and was typically fitted with a high-fragmentation warhead that made these weapons especially devastating against massed troops. The M8 was so effective, in fact, that the Germans copied it.

Adapted from an original air-to-ground rocket, the M8 had the following general specifications:

Length: 26 inches
Diameter: 3.23 inches
Weight: 17.6 pounds
Range: 6,450 yards

M13 132-mm Katyusha. While the M8 was the first of the famous Soviet rockets of World War II, the most extensively used was the larger, 132-mm M13, which was called the Katyusha. The distinctive moan these missiles made in flight became so familiar to German troops that they dubbed the Katyusha "Stalin's organ." Whereas the M8s were generally launched from modified light tanks, the M13s were launched from simple rails mounted on heavy trucks. This made it possible to deploy them in massive numbers, which was the only effective way to use such an inaccurate weapon.

General specifications included:

Length: 55.9 inches
Diameter: 5.2 inches
Weight: 93.7 pounds
Range: 9,295 yards

M30 and M31 300-mm rockets. Experience with the M8 and M13 had persuaded the Soviets that the rocket was a devastatingly effective weapon, and Red Army planners reasoned that if 82-mm and 132-mm rockets were good, 300-mm rockets would be even better. By the end of 1942, the M30 and M31 300-mm rockets were in the field. They were launched from simple rail launchers mounted on trucks, and they carried high-explosive warheads. The improvement the M31 represented over the M30 was in the engine, which provided greater range (just how much greater is not known, because the range specifications for both weapons are unavailable).

General specifications for the M31 rocket included:

Length: 69.3 inches
Diameter: 11.8 inches
Weight: 201.7 pounds
Range: unknown, but initial velocity was 836 feet per second

ANTITANK GUNS

Armor played a huge, even decisive, role in the war on the eastern front, and antitank weapons were a high priority for the Red Army. The Soviets produced a series of 45-mm antitank guns and a more powerful series of 76.2-mm weapons.

45-mm antitank guns. The first 45-mm guns were produced in the 1930s, and they served in the RUSSO-FINNISH WAR to good effect, but during the German INVASION OF THE SOVIET UNION, it quickly became apparent that the 45-mm guns were of little use against the most modern German tanks, which were equipped with very heavy, sloping armor. In 1942, a redesigned 45-mm gun appeared, which had a much longer barrel than the weapons of the 1930s and which outperformed the earlier guns against armor, though it still left much to be desired.

General specifications of the Model 1942 gun included:

Caliber: 45 mm
Length: 9 feet 8.8 inches
Weight: 1,257 pounds
Traverse: 60°
Elevation: -8° to +25°
Projectile weight: 3.151 pounds
Armor penetration: 3.74 inches at 330 yards

M1942 76.2-mm antitank gun. Also produced during the 1930s was a series of 76.2-mm guns, which were followed by the M1942, introduced in 1942. This later model was one of the great artillery pieces of the war and could be used against tanks as well as other targets. Produced in massive numbers, it was deployed in massive numbers, so that Soviet gunners typically trained a great deal of fire on a single, concentrated target. The effect was devastating.

General specifications of the M1942 included:

Caliber: 76.2 mm
Length: 13 feet 8.5 inches
Weight: 3,770 pounds
Traverse: 60°
Elevation: -6° to +25°
Projectile weight: 16.79 pounds
Range: 14,586 yards
Armor penetration: 3.86 inches at 545 yards

Further reading: Bellamy, Chris. *Red God of War: Soviet Artillery and Rocket Forces.* New York and London: Brassey's, 1986; Foedrowitz, Michael, and David Johnston. *Soviet Field Artillery in World War II Including Use by the German Wehrmacht.* Atglen, Pa.: Schiffer, 2000; Markov, David R. *Soviet/Russian Armor and Artillery Design Practices: 1945 to Present.* Darlington, Md.: Darlington Productions, 1999; Zaloga, Steven J. *Red Army of the Great Patriotic War 1941–5.* London: Osprey, 1989.

artillery, U.S.

Artillery in World War II consisted mainly of seven major categories: self-propelled guns, heavy artillery, field artillery, heavy antiaircraft guns (AA), light antiaircraft guns, rockets, and antitank guns.

SELF-PROPELLED GUNS

The United States developed one important self-propelled gun on the eve of World War II and another during the conflict itself.

M7 Priest. The M7, nicknamed "The Priest" by British soldiers, who thought the housing for the antiaircraft machine gun mount looked like a pulpit, was produced just before American entry into World War II. Many examples were shipped directly from the assembly line to Great Britain as part of the LEND-LEASE ACT and so found their way into the war even before the United States entered the conflict.

During the interwar period, the venerable 105-mm howitzer had been mounted on half-track vehicles with some success. Designers reasoned that an even more effective platform would be an M3 tank chassis, and the gun was mounted on the front of the vehicle in a large, open armored superstructure. For antiaircraft defense, a 12.7-mm machine gun was mounted in a "pulpit," which provided a degree of protection to the gunner. The M7 served as a self-propelled gun through 1944, at which time many were converted into armored personnel carriers and were nicknamed "Kangaroos."

General specifications for the M7 Priest included:

Weight: 50,634 pounds
Length: 19 feet 9 inches
Width: 9 feet 6.25 inches
Height: 8 feet 4 inches
Power plant: one 375-horsepower Continental nine-cylinder radial gasoline engine
Top speed: 26 miles per hour
Armament: one 105-mm howitzer and one 12.7-mm machine gun in an antiaircraft mount

Carriage, Motor, 155-mm Gun, M40. During the war, the United States fielded a 155-mm self-propelled gun mounted on an M3 tank chassis called the M12 but soon began design work on another 155-mm gun, the long-barreled "Long Tom," which was mounted on an extensively modified M4A3 tank chassis and called the Carriage, Motor, 155-mm Gun, M40. It was not introduced in quantity until late in the war, during January 1945, but proved so effective that production continued after the war, and the M40 was used extensively in the Korean conflict during the 1950s. Although its World War II career was brief, it was among the very best self-propelled guns of the era.

General specifications included:

Weight: 82,000 pounds
Length: 29 feet 8 inches
Width: 10 feet 4 inches

Height: 9 feet 4 inches
Power plant: one 395-horsepower Continental nine-cylinder radial gasoline engine
Top speed: 24 miles per hour
Armament: one 155-mm gun

HEAVY ARTILLERY

M1 8-inch howitzer. The M1 8-inch howitzer was developed from World War I–era British and French guns of this caliber and was finally standardized in 1940, the year before the Untied States entered World War II. It was among the most efficient and powerful weapons of its kind and proved so durable that the U.S. Army still uses it. A superb carriage and recoil mechanism helped to make this a very accurate weapon.

Its general specifications included:

Caliber: 8 inches
Length: 17 feet 5.59 inches
Weight: 32,000 pounds
Elevation: -2° to +65°
Traverse: 60°
Range: 18,150 yards
Shell weight: 200 pounds

155-mm Gun M1. The 155-mm Gun M1 was designed during the late 1930s, using as its basis a World War I French design. The split-trail carriage was efficient and modern, as was the recoil mechanism, which made for a very stable platform. The gun was a very good all-round performer with excellent range for indirect fire.

Its general specifications included:

Caliber: 155 mm
Length: 24 feet 2 inches
Weight: 30,600 pounds
Elevation: -2° to +65°
Traverse: 60°
Range: 25,395 yards
Shell weight: 92.6 pounds

240-mm Howitzer M1. Shortly after World War I, American military planners recommended designing a large-caliber heavy howitzer, but the project languished during the interwar years until the deteriorating situation in Europe motivated completion of the work. The result was the 240-mm Howitzer M1, a massive weapon capable of lobbing a 360-pound shell 25,255 yards. The gun was transported on a six-wheeled carriage, with the barrel towed on a semi-trailer. Set-up of the 30-ton weapon was no easy task, and the gun had to be erected over a pit to take up the massive recoil. However, once set up, this monster was highly effective.

Its general specifications included:

Caliber: 240 mm
Length: 27 feet 7 inches
Weight: 64,525 pounds
Elevation: +15° to +65°
Traverse: 45°
Range: 25,255 yards
Shell weight: 360 pounds

Little David. Among the most notable pieces of heavy artillery in World War II was Little David, which, at 36 inches, was the largest-caliber weapon used in the war. It started out not as a gun, but as Bomb Testing Device T1, a ground-based launcher intended to test aircraft bombs. It occurred to someone that a testing device designed to lob heavy aerial bombs could easily be used as a super large–caliber howitzer. Indeed, Little David was more in the nature of a muzzle-loading mortar.

The plan, in early 1944, was to prepare Little David for use in what seemed the inevitable invasion of Japan. The weapon was to be directed against the heaviest of Japanese fortifications. The use of atomic weapons against Japan made the invasion unnecessary, and Little David was never used in combat.

General specifications of this oddity included:

Caliber: 36 inches
Length: 28 feet
Weight: 182,560 pounds
Elevation: +45° to +65°
Traverse: 26°
Range: 9,500 yards
Shell weight: 3,700 pounds

FIELD ARTILLERY

105-mm Howitzer M2A1. The United States fought World War I with many borrowed weapons, includ-ing in the areas of armor and artillery, and the army emerged from the war determined to begin design-ing its own standard artillery. In the isolationist interwar period, however, these plans languished until the late 1930s, when the deteriorating situa-tion in Europe finally prompted action. One of the results was the long-delayed emergence of the 105-mm Howitzer M2A1 and its carriage, designated M2A2. This weapon began production in 1939, became one of the great field pieces of World War II, and, in fact, has never been rendered obsolete.

The design of this howitzer is simple and sturdy, easy to produce in massive quantity (which it was) and easy to maintain in the field. Handy and durable, it was used in every U.S. theater of the war. There was nothing innovative or remarkable about the weapon, but it was thoroughly reliable and accurate.

General specifications included:

Caliber: 105 mm
Length: 101.35 inches
Weight: 4,260 pounds
Elevation: -6° to +65°
Traverse: 46°
Range: 12,500 yards
Shell weight: 33 pounds

HEAVY ANTIAIRCRAFT GUNS

3-inch Antiaircraft Gun M3. During the 1920s, the United States took what it believed would be a shortcut in developing heavy antiaircraft artillery by turning to existing equipment, namely the 3-inch coastal defense artillery that had long been in service. These were adapted to new mounts, one for static AA defense and the other a mobile plat-form. As it turned out, however, many more modi-fications were required than had been anticipated, including new rifling and an entirely redesigned breech mechanism. Instead of a shortcut, the new work consumed a great deal of time, especially in developing the machine tools necessary to work the guns to the exceedingly close tolerances required for the AA application. By the time the 3-inch Antiaircraft Gun M3 was fully ready in the mid 1930s, it had become apparent to designers that it was at best obsolescent. While the gun was used during the war, it was gradually withdrawn and replaced by the 90-mm Gun M1. The earlier weapon was relegated mainly to training use.

General specifications of the M3 included:

Caliber: 3 inches
Weight: 16,800 pounds
Length: 12 feet 6 inches
Elevation: +80°
Traverse: 360°
Ceiling: 31,200 feet
Shell weight: 12.8 pounds

90-mm Gun M1. The 90-mm Gun M1 was an all-new design that outperformed the 3-inch gun it replaced and that fired a much heavier shell to a much higher ceiling: 23.4 pounds to 39,500 feet versus 12.8 pounds to 31,200 feet. The new weapon also incorporated a wholly redesigned carriage, with a turntable, and included a power rammer and fuse setter, which greatly increased rate of fire. While the gun was widely admired, its high technology had the drawback of complexity, which slowed production and made maintenance more difficult. Nevertheless, by August 1945, 7,831 had been produced, most of these deployed for coastal AA defense.

General specifications included:

Caliber: 90 mm
Weight: 32,300 pounds
Length: 14 feet 9.2 inches
Elevation: +80°
Traverse: 360°
Ceiling: 39,500 feet
Shell weight: 23.4 pounds

LIGHT ANTIAIRCRAFT GUNS

Maxson Mount. The Maxson Mount was a unique American answer to the need for tactical AA defense. It was a carriage that combined four Browning M2 heavy machine guns of 12.7-mm caliber on a single mount, so that together a spectacular 2,300 round-per-minute rate of fire could be achieved. The rounds contained no explosive charge, and the Maxson Mount was aimed with a simple naval sight, but the rate of fire was nevertheless devastating against low-flying aircraft. The flexible Maxson Mount could be towed into posi-

tion, or it could be installed on half-tracks or other vehicles, and the use of tracer rounds greatly facilitated target leading.

General specifications included:

Caliber: 12.7 mm
Length: 65.1 inches
Weight: 2,396 pounds
Elevation: -5° to +85°
Traverse: 360°
Ceiling: 3,280 feet
Rate of fire: 2,300 rounds per minute (all four guns firing)

37-mm Antiaircraft Gun M1. Unlike some combatants, the United States fielded not only heavy AA artillery and light AA artillery, but also what might be classified as intermediate AA artillery. The 37-mm Antiaircraft Gun M1 fired heavier projectiles than a machine gun and had a much higher ceiling. It was effective against attack aircraft that flew well below strategic bomber altitudes but that remained above 5,000 feet. Many of these weapons were used by the United States, and even more were delivered to the Soviet Union under the provisions of Lend-Lease.

General specifications included:

Caliber: 37 mm
Length: 78.2 inches
Elevation: -5° to +90°
Traverse: 360°
Ceiling: 18,600 feet
Rate of fire: 120 rounds per minute
Projectile weight: 1.34 pounds

ROCKETS

The U.S. Army entered World War II without any field rocket weapons at all, but, observing the effectiveness of Soviet rockets, ordnance planners quickly developed several U.S. rockets, along with simple launchers.

M8 4.5-inch rocket. The most important American rocket was the M8, a 4.5-inch rocket with a high-explosive warhead. A total of 2.5 million of these fin-stabilized projectiles were produced during the war, and they were typically fired from multiple launchers, some mounting as many as 60 tubes. As with other rockets of the war, the M8 was quite inaccurate, but by massing fire, the effect could be devastating, especially at close range.

General specifications included:

Length: 33 inches
Diameter: 4.5 inches
Weight: 38.5 pounds
Range: 4,600 yards

ANTITANK GUNS

M3 37-mm towed gun. In addition to making very effective use of tank destroyers (*see* ARMOR, U.S.), the American army fielded two major antitank guns. The first, initially deployed in 1939, was the M3, a 37-mm towed gun that was obsolete upon its very introduction. Capable of penetrating no more than 2 inches of armor at 500 yards, it was thoroughly inadequate against modern German plate. Although it was deployed in the NORTH AFRICAN CAMPAIGN, it did not last long in Europe.

General specifications included:

Caliber: 37 mm
Length: 6 feet 10.5 inches
Weight: 912 pounds
Traverse: 60°
Elevation: -10° to +15°
Range: 500 yards
Armor penetration: 2 inches at 500 yards

3-inch M5 antitank gun. In late 1941, the army rushed into production a replacement for the woefully inadequate 37-mm M3 antitank gun. The 3-inch M5 was heavy and somewhat awkward, but it packed the kind of punch necessary to kill heavily armored German tanks. At 2,000 yards, its fire could pierce through 3.31 inches of armor plate. Popular with gun crews, the weapon was heavy and required the services of a 6 x 6 truck for towing. The gun was also adapted to a Sherman tank chassis as a self-propelled tank destroyer.

General specifications included:

Caliber: 3 inches
Length: 13 feet 2.4 inches
Weight: 5,850 pounds
Elevation: -5.5° to +30°

Traverse: 46°
Range: 2,000 yards
Armor penetration: 3.31 inches at 2,000 yards

Further reading: Crawford, Steve. *Artillery of World War II.* Osceola, Wis.: Motorbooks International, 2001; Gander, Terry. *Heavy Artillery of World War II.* Marlborough, U.K.: Crowood Publishing, 2001; Hogg, Ian V. *British and American Artillery of World War II.* London: Greenhill, 2002; Scheier, Konrad. *Standard Guide to U. S. World War II Tanks and Artillery.* Iola, Wis.: Krause, 1994.

ASDIC.   See SONAR.

Atlantic, Battle of the

The *Battle of the Atlantic* is a popular historical name (Britain's Prime Minister WINSTON CHURCHILL first began using the phrase in August 1940) for the long struggle—spanning the entire six years of World War II, from 1939 to 1945—to secure the Atlantic convoy routes, which were the lifeline for the European Allies. It was by no means a battle in the traditional military sense but, rather, a long series of numerous encounters, engagements, attacks, and campaigns. For the Allies, the overall objectives of the struggle were straightforward: blockade Axis Europe; secure sea movements, especially of vital convoys; and attain and maintain the ability to project military force overseas.

The first objective was achieved with relative ease, since the Allied navies far outnumbered German and Italian naval forces. Although Germany enjoyed very limited success with blockade-running operations, generally the Allied naval blockade was quite effective. It is also true, however, that the European Axis did not have to rely on the Atlantic for most of its supplies, since, through much of the war, Germany controlled many European overland routes and had conquered numerous manufacturing and agricultural centers.

The third objective depended largely on the development of AMPHIBIOUS WARFARE doctrine, techniques, and tactics, which had not fully matured until OPERATION OVERLORD and the NORMANDY

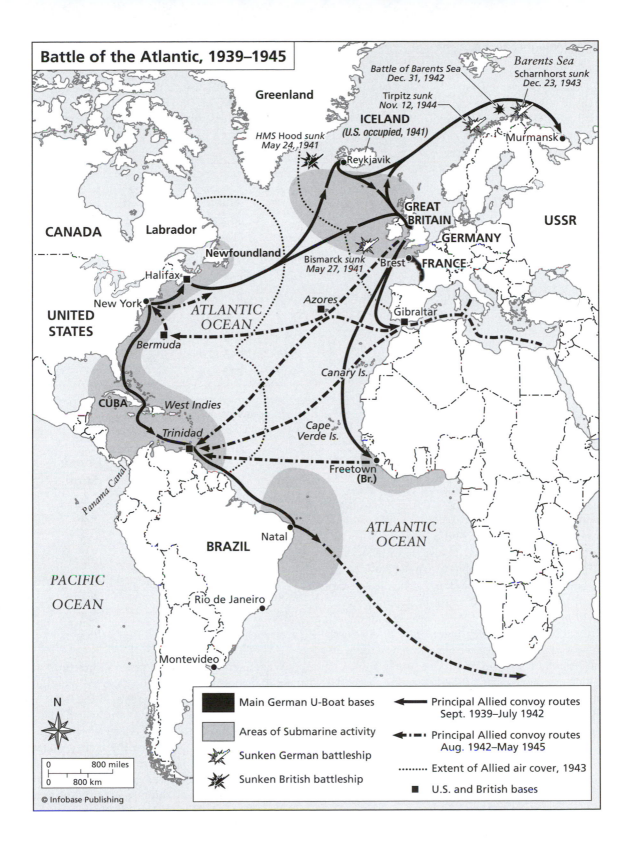

Battle of the Atlantic, 1939–1945

Greenland

Battle of Barents Sea
Dec. 31, 1942

Barents Sea

Tirpitz *sunk*
Nov. 12, 1944

Scharnhorst *sunk*
Dec. 23, 1943

ICELAND
(*U.S. occupied, 1941*)

Murmansk

HMS Hood *sunk*
May 24, 1941

Reykjavik

**GREAT
BRITAIN**

CANADA   Labrador

USSR

GERMANY

Bismarck *sunk*
May 27, 1941

Brest   **FRANCE**

Newfoundland

Halifax

*ATLANTIC
OCEAN*

Azores

Gibraltar

**UNITED
STATES**

New York

Bermuda

Canary Is.

CUBA

West Indies

Trinidad

*Cape
Verde Is.*

Freetown
(Br.)

Panama Canal

BRAZIL   Natal

*ATLANTIC
OCEAN*

*PACIFIC
OCEAN*

Rio de Janeiro

Montevideo

N

0		800 miles
0		800 km

© Infobase Publishing

■ Main German U-Boat bases	←	Principal Allied convoy routes Sept. 1939–July 1942
▨ Areas of Submarine activity	◄-·-	Principal Allied convoy routes Aug. 1942–May 1945
✺ Sunken German battleship	········	Extent of Allied air cover, 1943
✸ Sunken British battleship	■	U.S. and British bases

LANDINGS (D-DAY) of June 1944. By that time, the second objective, securing Allied sea movements, had been largely achieved, which also enabled achievement of the amphibious warfare objective.

That second objective, securing Allied sea movements, was, however, extremely difficult to attain. While the surface fleet of the Kriegsmarine, the NAVY OF GERMANY, was not large, its submarine (or U-boat) fleet was substantial, modern, and growing. It was the German U-boat that was the most destructive weapon in the Battle of the Atlantic, and the menace posed by submarine warfare largely dictated Allied operations in the battle.

Yet the U-boat did not immediately come to the fore in the Battle of the Atlantic. During the opening months of the war, after the INVASION OF POLAND in September 1939 and before the fall of France in June 1940, the Kriegsmarine operated against Allied shipping mainly using surface ships, including so-called pocket battleships (smaller than conventional battleships, but typically with even greater firepower) and cruisers, collectively called surface raiders. These vessels were augmented by smaller cruisers called auxiliary cruisers. This early phase of the Battle of the Atlantic largely consisted of German surface raiders harassing Allied shipping.

After the fall of France, Germany acquired French and Norwegian bases from which submarines could operate with little interference by the hitherto quite effective British naval blockade. Moreover, the German objective in the Battle of the Atlantic was no longer the catch-as-catch-can destruction of cargo and transport shipping or even battling the Royal Navy. With Great Britain cut off from the European continent, the objective was now to strangle and starve the nation by cutting off all Atlantic communication and supply routes. It quickly became apparent that submarines were the most effective weapon for this destruction, and the Battle of the Atlantic evolved into perhaps the most serious threat Germany posed. (Another important German vessel deployed in the Battle of the Atlantic was the merchant raider, better known as the Q-SHIP. Heavily armed warships disguised as civilian freighters, the Q-ships would sneak up on Allied merchant vessels and open fire.)

STATISTICAL COURSE OF THE BATTLE OF THE ATLANTIC

The overall course of the Battle of the Atlantic can be charted year by year by looking at tonnage lost:

Year	Allied Losses (Tons)	German U-Boat Losses (Tons)	German Surface Ship Losses (Tons)
1939	755,392	421,156	61,337
1940	7,805,360	3,801,095	277,028
1941	4,921,792	3,111,051	205,966
1942	7,790,697	6,546,271	325,086
1943	3,220,137	1,189,833	7,040
1944	1,045,629	N/A	N/A
1945	438,821	N/A	N/A

In terms of actual numbers of ships lost, the battle looked like this:

Year	Allied Losses to U-boats	U-boats Sunk
1939	50	9
1940	225	24
1941	288	35
1942	452	87
1943	203	237
1944	67	242
1945	30	151
Total	1,315	785

What accounts for the general direction of these statistics? German U-boats were plentiful and, early in the war, developed WOLFPACK U-BOAT TACTICS, by which several boats coordinated a single attack for greatly enhanced effectiveness. Moreover, by December 1941, when the United States entered the war, U-boats were already capable of operating as far as the Caribbean and the Gulf of Mexico and could attack shipping even off the East Coast of the United States. The effectiveness of the

U-boat increased alarmingly through 1942. However, by early 1943, several Allied technological and tactical advances began sharply to turn the tide against the U-boats, transforming the hunters into the hunted. SONAR technology (by which surface ships could detect U-boats underwater) was developed from earlier ASDIC technologies. Long-range bombers became available, thereby extending the range of antisubmarine patrol. Developments in RADAR technology greatly increased the effectiveness of these patrols. Tactically, the Allies perfected both the CONVOY SYSTEM and more effective means of escorting the convoys.

CHRONOLOGICAL COURSE OF THE BATTLE OF THE ATLANTIC

On the very first day of the war, September 1, 1939, German U-boats sank a British passenger liner, the *Athena,* and, two weeks later, a warship, HMS *Courageous.* On September 14, the British sank their first U-boat. During this first month, Germany also deployed two great surface raiders, *Admiral Graf Spee* and *Deutschland. Gneisenau* and *Scharnhorst* would follow in November. In the meantime, the British carrier *Royal Oak* was sunk on October 12 in its Scapa Flow anchorage, the principal home base of the Royal Navy.

On December 13, 1939, off the coast of Uruguay in the South Atlantic, the British cruisers *Ajax, Exeter,* and *Achilles* trapped the *Admiral Graf Spee* in the Battle of the River Plate. As a result of the engagement, the commander of the *Graf Spee* scuttled his ship rather than let it fall into British hands.

March 1940 saw the maiden voyage of the German surface raider *Atlantis,* which would sink 145,697 tons of Allied shipping—the most of any surface raider—before it was sunk in November 1941 by HMS *Devonshire.* During April 9–13, off Narvik, Norway (*see* NARVIK, BATTLES OF), the British battleship *Warspite,* in concert with the destroyers *Hardy, Hotspur, Havock, Hunter,* and *Hostile,* engaged a 10-ship German destroyer flotilla, sinking or forcing the scuttling of all the German combatants. In May, the Royal Navy managed one of the great rescues of the war, evacuating

trapped British forces from Dunkirk (*see* DUNKIRK EVACUATION), but on June 8, the Royal Navy suffered a sharp blow when the carrier HMS *Glorious* and two escort vessels were lost in action to *Scharnhorst* and *Gneisenau.*

Elsewhere, in July 1940, British ships fired on the French fleet at Oran, North Africa, after it refused to surrender. At about this time in the Mediterranean, British warships sank the *Giulio Cesare,* pride of the Italian fleet.

On September 2, 1940, U.S. president FRANKLIN D. ROOSEVELT issued an executive order transferring 50 obsolescent U.S. Navy destroyers to the Royal Navy in exchange for leases on various British bases. These ships would perform valuable convoy escort duty. However, on September 21, 11 British merchant ships were lost when German U-boats put into practice wolfpack tactics and attacked Convoy HX 72. Even worse came the next month, during the so-called Night of the Long Knives, October 17–18, when a wolfpack attacked Convoy SC 7, sinking 20 of 34 ships.

The first two months of 1941 brought more terrible destruction against Allied shipping. In January, *Scharnhorst* and *Gneisenau* renewed their attacks, and in February, the Germans staged the first coordinated assault on a convoy (HG 53), using aircraft, surface ships, and U-boats to sink 9 of 16 ships. In a single day, February 22, *Scharnhorst* and *Gneisenau* sank five British vessels.

March 9 saw the loss of five more British ships, and on March 15, German surface raiders and U-boats worked in concert to sink 13 ships and capture three tankers. However, at the Battle of Cape Matapan, March 27–28, 1941, British warships struck a devastating blow against the Italian fleet, sinking the cruisers *Pola, Fiume,* and *Zara* as well as two destroyers—without the loss of a single British vessel or sailor. More than 2,400 Italian sailors were drowned. Yet, during March 27–28, U-boats sank another 43 British ships. The ratification of the LEND-LEASE ACT by the United States Congress during this month promised to make up at least some of the British losses, but the record for April, 45 ships sunk, was grim, and the U.S. Navy, transferring ships from the Pacific to the Atlantic Fleet, began its UNDECLARED NAVAL WAR WITH GERMANY.

In May, while hunting the formidable German pocket battleship *Bismarck* and its companion, the cruiser *Prinz Eugen*, HMS *Hood* was sunk with the loss of all hands. Efforts to sink the *Bismarck* were redoubled after this catastrophe, and *Bismarck* was indeed sunk—a grave loss to the German surface fleet and a terrible blow to German morale. Despite this triumph, U-boats sank 58 ships this month. Nevertheless, during the summer, the effectiveness of U-boat attacks dipped as the Allies improved convoy tactics. It was the first glimmer of hope in the long struggle.

Although the United States would not enter World War II until December, increasing numbers of U.S. Navy destroyers began escorting convoys through waters adjacent to the North American continent. Germany's admiral KARL DÖNITZ ordered his U-boats to avoid attacking American vessels—he had no desire to provoke the United States into joining the war—but on September 4, 1941, U-652 fired on the destroyer USS *Greer*. This prompted President Roosevelt to authorize outright defense of convoys and brought the United States significantly closer to joining the battle. On October 16, the U.S. destroyer *Reuben James* was sunk with the loss of 115. In November, the British lost the carrier *Ark Royal* to a U-boat attack.

On December 11, just three days after the United States declared war on Japan following the attack on PEARL HARBOR, Germany declared war on the United States and immediately dispatched U-boats to prowl the waters of the American East Coast. This rapidly evolved into Operation Drumbeat, a concerted campaign against Allied shipping in American waters, inaugurated on January 13, 1942. Tankers were deemed first-priority targets, and 35 ships were sunk near the United States coast before the month ended. U.S. Navy air patrols began hunting for submarines, scoring their first kill off the East Coast on March 1. Nevertheless, Germany was committed to expanding operations in American waters and developed large submarines dubbed "milk cows," which performed underway replenishment of fuel and provisions for the

attack U-boats, thereby greatly extending patrol range and endurance. In May alone, U-boats sank 45 ships in the Gulf of Mexico.

Success in American waters notwithstanding, Admiral Dönitz decided in July to reconcentrate his U-boat fleet in the North Atlantic. Despite the deadly effectiveness of the U-boat campaign, Allied ships successfully landed U.S. and British troops in Northwest Africa, and the Allies also reinstated convoys to the Soviet Union. Determined to make up for losses and to ensure an uninterrupted flow of supplies and materiel, the United States inaugurated a crash program of ship building, launching LIBERTY SHIPS, specially designed to be built rapidly. Not only were the ships launched at an amazing rate, the pace of recruitment of sailors for the UNITED STATES MERCHANT MARINE was dazzling. The Allies also became increasingly aggressive in beating off attacks against convoys, as the Battle of Barents Sea on December 31, 1942, demonstrated. The Royal Navy cruisers *Jamaica* and *Sheffield* and the destroyers *Obdurate, Onslow,* and *Achates* engaged the German pocket battleship *Lutzow,* the cruiser *Hipper,* and seven destroyers, sinking one German destroyer for the loss of the *Achates,* but successfully driving off the attack on a convoy.

Disappointed in the performance of his surface fleet, ADOLF HITLER began 1943 by ordering the effective liquidation of his surface navy and greatly increased production of U-boats. Allied losses continued to mount, but, by April, it was becoming clear that these losses were beginning to level off even as U-boat losses increased. This was thanks mainly to new and improved escort tactics. Indeed, in May, Admiral Dönitz generally halted attacks on North Atlantic convoys because U-boat losses had reached unacceptable levels. Some historians believe that the Battle of the Atlantic essentially ended with this withdrawal, an assessment that sailors of the Allied merchant marine and German U-boat crews would certainly have disputed.

In September 1943, Royal Navy commandos were sent to sink the battleship *Tirpitz* using limpet mines. Although *Tirpitz* was damaged in this attack, it did not sink and would survive until November

1944, when Royal Air Force bombers finally destroyed it. On December 26, 1943, *Scharnhorst* was engaged by the Royal Navy's battleship *Duke of York* and the cruisers *Belfast, Norfolk, Sheffield,* and *Jamaica. Scharnhorst* was sunk with the loss of 1,927 sailors; the 36 crew members who were rescued became prisoners of war. In view of Hitler's abandonment of the surface navy, the loss of the *Scharnhorst* was the final blow for the German surface fleet.

During 1944 and through the opening months of 1945, the Battle of the Atlantic continued with far less intensity. One significant episode occurred on June 4, 1944, off the North African coast, when a U.S. Navy "hunter-killer group," consisting of the escort carrier *Guadalcanal* and five destroyers, attacked U-505, forcing it to surface. The German commander ordered his men to abandon ship and to scuttle the boat, but U.S. sailors boarded the vessel, disarmed its self-destruction device, and saved the U-505 from sinking. The first enemy prize taken by the U.S. Navy since the War of 1812, the U-505 was salvaged and eventually donated to the Museum of Science and Industry in Chicago. A more important prize than the submarine, however, were the code books recovered from it, which allowed American cryptanalysts to break the special code used to position U- boats. This intelligence allowed hunter-killer groups to home in on these locations and also to vector Allied convoy commanders away from them.

Although the Battle of the Atlantic did not fully end until Germany surrendered in May 1945, the role of the Atlantic fleets of the U.S. Navy and Royal Navy turned for a time almost exclusively to supporting OPERATION OVERLORD, the D-day invasion, in June 1944. Following this, most Allied Atlantic naval assets were deployed for ongoing convoy escort duty.

Further reading: Gannon, Michael. *Operation Drumbeat: The Dramatic True Story of Germany's First U-Boat Attacks Along the American Coast in World War II*. New York: Harper Perennial, 1991; Ireland, Bernard. *The Battle of the Atlantic*. Annapolis, Md.: Naval Institute Press, 2003; Morison, Samuel Eliot. *The Battle of the Atlantic: September 1939–May 1943*. New York: Castle Books, 2001; Pitt, Barrie. *The Battle of the Atlantic*. Boston: Little, Brown, 1977; Williams, Andrew. *The Battle of the Atlantic: Hitler's Gray Wolves of the Sea and the Allies' Desperate Struggle to Defeat Them*. New York: Basic Books, 2003.

Atlantic Charter

The United States was still officially neutral during August 9–12, 1941, when President FRANKLIN D. ROOSEVELT and British prime minister WINSTON CHURCHILL met aboard the cruiser USS *Augusta* in Placentia Bay, Newfoundland, and concluded an Anglo-American statement of common principles that became known as the Atlantic Charter. The two leaders signed the charter on August 14, 1941.

The Atlantic Charter enumerated eight principles of American and British aims in war as well as peace:

> The President of the United States of America and the Prime Minister, Mr. Churchill, representing His Majesty's Government in the United Kingdom, being met together, deem it right to make known certain common principles in the national policies of their respective countries on which they base their hopes for a better future for the world.
>
> First, their countries seek no aggrandizement, territorial or other;
>
> Second, they desire to see no territorial changes that do not accord with the freely expressed wishes of the peoples concerned;
>
> Third, they respect the right of all peoples to choose the form of government under which they will live; and they wish to see sovereign rights and self government restored to those who have been forcibly deprived of them;
>
> Fourth, they will endeavor, with due respect for their existing obligations, to further the enjoyment by all States, great or small, victor or vanquished, of access, on equal terms, to the trade and to the raw materials of the world which are needed for their economic prosperity;
>
> Fifth, they desire to bring about the fullest collaboration between all nations in the eco-

nomic field with the object of securing, for all, improved labor standards, economic advancement and social security;

Sixth, after the final destruction of the Nazi tyranny, they hope to see established a peace which will afford to all nations the means of dwelling in safety within their own boundaries, and which will afford assurance that all the men in all lands may live out their lives in freedom from fear and want;

Seventh, such a peace should enable all men to traverse the high seas and oceans without hindrance;

Eighth, they believe that all of the nations of the world, for realistic as well as spiritual reasons must come to the abandonment of the use of force. Since no future peace can be maintained if land, sea or air armaments continue to be employed by nations which threaten, or may threaten, aggression outside of their frontiers, they believe, pending the establishment of a wider and permanent system of general security, that the disarmament of such nations is essential. They will likewise aid and encourage all other practicable measures which will lighten for peace-loving peoples the crushing burden of armaments.

Franklin D. Roosevelt
Winston S. Churchill

The charter's principles were given broader scope when they were endorsed by 26 Allied nations in the UNITED NATIONS DECLARATION of January 1, 1942.

See also LEND-LEASE ACT and NEUTRALITY ACTS, U.S.

Further reading: Brinkley, Douglas, and David R. Facey-Crowther, eds. *The Atlantic Charter.* New York: St. Martins Press, 1994; Drakidis, Philippe. *The Atlantic and United Nations Charters: Common Law Prevailing for World Peace and Security.* Besançon, France: Centre De Recherche et d'information Politique et Sociale, 1995; Grenville, J. A. S. *The Major International Treaties 1914–1973: A History Guide with Texts.* New York: Stein & Day, 1974; Wilson, Theodore A. *The First Summit: Roosevelt and Churchill at Placentia Bay, 1941.* Lawrence: University Press of Kansas, 1991.

atrocities, German

Germany and Japan were by no means the only combatant nations that perpetrated atrocities during World War II. Viewed from the perspective of traditionally acceptable rules of warfare as well as from international law and formal convention, the British and Americans were guilty of massive atrocities when their massive bombing raids targeted civilians, and the Soviets operated concentration camps, called gulags, long before the regime of ADOLF HITLER built Germany's CONCENTRATION AND EXTERMINATION CAMPS. Nevertheless, throughout World War II, atrocities on an epic and horrific scale were matters of policy and routine for the forces of both Germany and Japan.

The most egregious of Nazi atrocities was, of course, the perpetration of the HOLOCAUST, the systematic murder of some 6 million Jews within the Reich and nations occupied by the Reich. Although Jews were the single greatest target of Nazi genocide, other groups were also singled out for deportation to concentration camps or execution. These included Slavs, certain categories of prisoners of war, Gypsies, political dissidents and "undesirables," homosexuals, and, in some cases, those judged physically or mentally subnormal. Although Hitler was careful to avoid issuing any written orders directing mass murder and other persecution of civilian populations, the historical evidence that these crimes were committed at his behest is overwhelming.

In addition to the systematic and outright persecution and genocide of civilian populations, German combat practices often involved atrocities. The bombing of Warsaw during the 1939 INVASION OF POLAND and the 1940 ROTTERDAM AIR RAID were deliberate military attacks on civilians intended to terrorize and thereby break the will of the nations to resist conquest. In fact, these tactics, terrible though they were, proved ineffective. Often, instead of crushing resistance, they tended to intensify it. The German COVENTRY AIR RAID (which, like Allied strategic bombing raids, targeted an industrial war production center and was not simply intended to induce terror) triggered vehement Allied reprisals against German civilian targets. No less a figure than the chief of the Luftwaffe, HER-MANN GÖRING, coined a new German verb to apply to the subsequent Allied air raids against German cities: *coventrieren*. It did not simply mean "to bomb" a target but literally meant "to Coventry" it.

On the ground, German troops and officers were greatly feared for their brutality, which was often as gratuitous as it was vicious and prodigal. This was especially the case on the eastern front, although not confined to it. Perhaps the most infamous instance of officially sanctioned atrocity was Hitler's so-called Commissar Order of 1941, which authorized the immediate execution of all Soviet political officers taken as prisoners of war. Another form of German atrocity was the practice of disproportionate reprisal. When partisan or other resistance was encountered in occupied areas—acts of sabotage, sniper activity, the assassination of German soldiers or officials—the German occupiers routinely responded by seizing and summarily executing large groups of individuals. If partisans killed one German officer, 10, 20, perhaps 100 individuals from the city or village in which the incident occurred would be rounded up and shot, typically in the presence of family members. Among the most notorious incidents of reprisal took place in the little Czech village of Lidice. After Czech partisans assassinated REINHARD HEYDRICH, the Nazi overlord of Czechoslovakia, the SCHUTZSTAFFEL (SS) arrested thousands, killing more than 2,000 Czechs and descending upon Lidice—population about 450—which they totally destroyed. All men were executed, the women were deported to Ravensbrück concentration camp, and the children (81 of them) were gassed in a death camp.

Generally speaking, Soviet prisoners of war (POW) held by the Germans were treated inhumanely, with abuse ranging from neglect and starvation to deliberate torture and murder. Nazi racial philosophy held that Slavs were subhuman and deserved no better treatment. Of the 5.7 million Soviet troops captured by the Germans during the war, as many as 3.3 million may have died in captivity. In contrast, western Allied prisoners were not customarily treated with gratuitous cruelty, although POW camp conditions were often grossly inadequate, with food and medical attention in critically short supply. The Luftwaffe, which had custody of captured Allied airmen, typically treated POWs more humanely than did camps operated by the WEHRMACHT. Nevertheless, the Germans perpetrated a number of notorious battlefield atrocities, including the following.

At Leparadis, France, in May 1940, British troops of the Royal Norfolk Regiment, pinned down and out of ammunition, surrendered to troops of the SS Totenkopf ("Death's Head") Division. On orders from their commander, Fritz Knoechlein, the SS men lined up 99 of the POWs and trained a machine gun on them. All but two died. After the war, Knoechlein was tried for this atrocity and hanged in January 1949.

Also in May 1940, at Wormhoudt, France, members of SS regiment Leibstandarte Adolf Hitler led 80 British POWs into a barn, then threw hand grenades in among them. As soldiers ran out of the barn, they were cut down by automatic weapons fire. Nevertheless, 15 survived to bear witness to the crime, although no one was ever tried for it.

In Kos, Greece, during October 1943, after capturing this Aegean island, German troops responded to an order from Hitler to summarily execute 102 Italian officers who had been fighting on the Allied side.

At Sagan, Silesia, Germany, in March 1944, 79 Royal Air Force (RAF) officers escaped from a Luftwaffe POW camp. Of this number, only three escaped to Britain; the rest were recaptured. Adolf Hitler personally ordered the execution of 50 of these men. After the war, 38 Germans were found guilty of this atrocity; 21 were hanged, and 17 sentenced to prison terms.

During the NORMANDY INVASION (D-DAY), members of the 12th SS Panzer Division (Hitler Jugend, "Hitler Youth") shot more than 130 of the Canadian troops they took prisoner. Some were executed individually, others cut down in groups.

The most notorious German battlefield atrocity occurred at Malmédy, Belgium, in December 1944 during the BATTLE OF THE ARDENNES (BATTLE OF THE BULGE). Troops of the 1st Panzer Division murdered 83 U.S. POWs.

As mentioned, in addition to battlefield atrocities, German military units frequently retaliated against civilian populations. In addition to the Lidice event, some of the most infamous of these atrocities include:

- At Kortelisy in Ukraine, during September 1942, SS members responded to partisan activity by enlisting the aid of Ukrainian police to kill every man, woman, and child in the village, about 2,900 persons.
- In Kalavryta, Greece, during December 1943, German troops rounded up all 696 men of the village and shot them to death, along with about 600 men from neighboring villages.
- After a partisan bomb killed some 90 SS police in Rome during March 1944, Adolf Hitler personally ordered reprisals in which more than 300 Romans were transported by truck to the Ardeantine Caves, where they were killed.
- In Ascq, France, during April 1944, the SS retaliated after saboteurs blew up railroad tracks on which troops of the 12th SS Panzer Division ("Hitler Jugend") were traveling. The Germans shot nearly 100 men from families whose houses were located near the sabotaged track.
- Troops of the 2nd SS Division ("Das Reich") descended on the village of Oradour-sur-Glane, France, in reprisal for partisan attacks. After assembling the villagers, the troops separated the men from the women and children, then shot the men as their families looked on. After this, the troops herded the women and children into a local church, locked the doors, and set the structure ablaze with hand grenades. A total of 642 died, two-thirds of them women and children.
- In the Saulx Valley, France, during August 1944, partisans, led by members of the British SPECIAL AIR SERVICE (SAS), ambushed a German staff car. In response, SS men arrested people from several of the valley's villages, killed 36 men, and set fire to all the buildings in the villages.
- In Putten, Holland, during September 1944, Dutch resistance operatives abducted a German lieutenant and held him hostage. Ultimately, the partisans released the officer, but the Germans nevertheless retaliated by arresting 589 men, and deporting them to Germany as slave laborers. Only 49 survived the war.
- At Bande, Belgium, during December 1944, German Security Service agents murdered 34 men in reprisal for the killing of three German soldiers.
- At De Woeste Hoeve, Holland, Dutch underground operatives attacked and severely wounded a German general during March 1945. The SS rounded up 116 villagers and shot them all. They then turned to prisoners they had already been holding. Total murders numbered 263. After the war, the British captured and tried Dr. Eberhardt Schongarth, the SS officer who had ordered the killings, and hanged him in 1946.

See also ATROCITIES, JAPANESE; NUREMBERG WAR CRIMES TRIBUNAL; STRATEGIC BOMBING OF GERMANY; STRATEGIC BOMBING OF JAPAN; TOKYO WAR CRIMES TRIALS.

Further reading: Rossino, Alexander B. *Hitler Strikes Poland: Blitzkrieg, Ideology, and Atrocity.* Lawrence: University Press of Kansas, 2003; Russell, Edward Frederick Langley. *The Scourge of the Swastika: A Short History of Nazi War Crimes.* London: Greenhill, 2002; Zillmer, Eric A. *The Quest for the Nazi Personality: A Psychological Investigation of Nazi War Criminals.* New York: Lea, 1995.

atrocities, Japanese

As observed in the discussion of German atrocities, Germany and Japan were certainly not the only combatant nations who perpetrated atrocities during World War II. The record of the SOVIET UNION is poor and often horrifying. The STRATEGIC BOMBING OF GERMANY by the United States and Great Britain and the STRATEGIC BOMBING OF JAPAN by the United States might well be defined as atrocities under international law and convention, because these programs deliberately targeted civilian populations. However, no combatant more routinely perpetrated battlefield atrocities—abuses committed against enemy soldiers—than the Japanese. And while no atrocity of World War II was of greater enormity than the Nazi HOLOCAUST, the Japanese also perpetrated war crimes against civilian populations in occupied countries. Collectively, these may have killed even more people than the atrocities committed by the forces of Hitler's Germany.

Whereas German war crimes and persecutions may be attributed in some part to Nazi racial mythology, which classified Jews, Slavs, Gypsies, and other groups as racially inferior and even subhuman, Japanese abuses may in significant part be ascribed to Bushido, the traditional warrior code of the Samurai, which defined surrender, not death, in battle as the greatest of disgraces. Bushido gave victors absolute power over those captured or conquered, who, having suffered the ultimate disgrace in surrendering rather than fighting to the death, were legitimately liable to whatever mistreatment the victor chose to mete out.

Although both the German and the Japanese officers and troops accused of war crimes were tried by Allied tribunals after the war, the Japanese atrocities are not nearly as well documented as those perpetrated by the Germans, and the numbers involved are widely disputed, some authorities claiming that Chinese civilian casualties during 1937–45 (and including those incurred during the SINO-JAPANESE WAR) numbered some 30 million killed. Many civilians died of neglect, starvation, and disease; many, however, were murdered outright or subjected to rape, torture, medical experimentation, and experimentation related to biological warfare. While German atrocities were committed against civilians on a genocidal scale comparable to that of the Japanese atrocities, German military commanders typically attempted to treat military prisoners of war (POW)

with a degree of honor, except in the case of Soviet POWs. In contrast, Japanese commanders, observing Bushido, deliberately abused, neglected, enslaved, and tortured prisoners of war, for example, the BATAAN DEATH MARCH. Less well known than the infamous Japanese POW camps were the prison ships on which the Japanese transported thousands of Allied prisoners. Conditions onboard were appalling, as prisoners were crammed into the cargo holds of decrepit and marginally seaworthy freighters and supplied with little food and water and no sanitary facilities. Many died of this treatment alone. As usual, guards were, in the main, sadistic and abusive. Because the prison ships were unmarked and appeared to Allied submarines and other warships and aircraft as nothing more or less than enemy freighters, they were frequently attacked and sunk, with the loss of most or all aboard.

The most infamous instances of Japanese atrocities include:

The RAPE OF NANKING, in which 250,000 to 300,000 Chinese civilians were killed, began in December 1937. Modes of murder included torture, immolation, burial alive, and beheading in addition to simple shooting. Among those killed in actual combat during the Japanese invasion of northern China, some were victims of BIOLOGICAL WARFARE agents.

At Tol Plantation, in Rabaul (on New Britain in the Solomon Islands chain), Japanese troops shot or bayoneted more than 100 Australian troops during February 1942 after they surrendered.

On Ballalae Island in the Solomons, between 1942 and the end of the war, 516 British POWs perished under forced labor. They had been transported from the FALL OF SINGAPORE to Ballalae to build an airstrip. This figure represents a 100 percent casualty rate.

In China's Kinso and Chekiang Provinces, Japanese troops exacted terrible reprisals against Chinese civilians after the capture (and summary execution) of three U.S. airmen who had crash landed after the successful

DOOLITTLE TOKYO RAID. During their hunt for other Doolittle raiders, Japanese troops killed thousands of Chinese and razed entire villages.

- On Ambon Island in the Dutch East Indies, Japanese troops beheaded more than 200 Australian and Dutch POWs during February 1943.
- In January 1943, following the valiant defense of WAKE ISLAND by U.S. Marines and civilian contractors, the finally victorious Japanese machine gunned 98 of the American contractors, who had been building the island's military facilities.
- During June 1945, at Kalagon, Burma (modern Myanmar), Japanese troops on the hunt for British-led Burmese guerrillas surrounded the village and bayoneted or shot to death more than 600 villagers.
- At Sandakan, North Borneo, during this same month, some 2,000 British and Australian POWs died. Most had been starved or marched to death, others succumbed to disease, and many were simply murdered. Here also, some 4,000 Javanese civilians died under Japanese enslavement as laborers.
- In July, at Loa Kulu, Borneo, Japanese soldiers murdered 140 men, then seized their wives and children, many of whom were thrown to their deaths down a deep mine shaft.
- In this same month, at Cheribon, Java, Japanese naval personnel herded 90 civilian prisoners onto the deck of a submarine, sailed, then submerged, leaving the men, women, and children to drown or to be attacked by sharks. A single badly injured survivor of a shark attack lived just long enough to report what had happened.
- Yet another war crime was the rape of thousands of so-called comfort women, women forced into sexual slavery to serve the sexual needs of Japanese troops at designated military "comfort stations." Most of these women were Korean, but they were transported to outposts on many fronts. Japanese warrior tradition held that sex before battle had talismanic or magical properties that could protect against injury or death.

See also NUREMBERG WAR CRIMES TRIBUNAL; TOKYO WAR CRIMES TRIALS.

Further reading: Chang, Iris. *The Rape of Nanking: The Forgotten Holocaust of World War II.* New York: Penguin, 1998; Daws, Gavin. *Prisoners of the Japanese: POWs of World War II in the Pacific.* New York: Perennial, 1996; Hicks, George L. *The Comfort Women: Japan's Brutal Regime of Enforced Prostitution in the Second World War.* New York: Norton, 1997; Pearson, Judith. *Belly of the Beast: A POW's Inspiring True Story of Faith, Courage, and Survival Aboard the Infamous WWII Japanese Hellship, the* Oryoku Maru. New York: New American Library, 2001; Tanaka, Yuki, and Toshiyuki Tanaka. *Hidden Horrors: Japanese War Crimes in World War II.* Denver: Westview Press, 1998.

attack aircraft

While the air arms of the major powers concentrated on developing BOMBER AIRCRAFT and FIGHTER AIRCRAFT, another important but less well developed category were attack aircraft, warplanes designed to support ground forces with what was variously called close air support, close ground support, or ground attack. The close air support concept was developed in the infancy of military aviation, during World War I, when aircraft were often used as "trench fighters," with the ability to break through the ground defenses that had transformed the western front into a bloody stalemate. However, the aircraft of World War I could not carry sufficient weapons to inflict decisive damage. Moreover, they were highly vulnerable to ground fire. During the interwar years, the Luftwaffe developed effective close air support tactics, which were honed and demonstrated during the Spanish Civil War (1934–36). The Junkers Ju-87 "Stuka" dive bomber became the ground attack aircraft par excellence of the BLITZKRIEG that opened World War II, and other nations either adapted current fighter designs and light bomber designs to the ground attack role or designed aircraft specifically for ground attack.

Ground attack consists of tactical bombing and strafing. Tactical bombing deploys relatively small bombs, often fragmentation weapons designed to broadcast shrapnel to kill or wound large numbers of personnel, in contrast to strategic bombing, which uses masses of large bombs, generally against major structures and population centers. Strafing is the use of extended machine gun or cannon bursts against ground targets, including personnel, vehicles, and even some structures. Ground attack generally requires highly skilled pilots capable of executing steep dives and low, slow attacks. The tactics expose aircraft to ground fire and also to counterattack by enemy fighter aircraft. Because of the nature of the ground attack mission, which requires aircraft capable of low, slow flight, opposing fighters generally have a performance advantage. Moreover, ground attack pilots, intent on their forward-looking mission below, are especially vulnerable to fighter attack from behind and above. This vulnerability was addressed in some ground attack aircraft by the inclusion of a rear-facing defensive machine gun manned by a gunner, who sat with his back to the pilot in a tandem cockpit.

For specific examples of attack aircraft, see Aircraft, British; Aircraft, French; Aircraft, German; Aircraft, Italian; Aircraft, Japanese; Aircraft, Polish; Aircraft, Soviet; and Aircraft, U.S.

Further reading: Gunston, Bill. *An Illustrated Guide to German, Italian and Japanese Fighters of World War II: Major Fighters and Attack Aircraft of the Axis Powers.* London: Salamander, 1980; Shores, Christopher F. *Ground Attack Aircraft of World War II.* London: Macdonald & Jane's, 1977; Smith, Peter Charles. *Stuka Spearhead: The Lightning War from Poland to Dunkirk 1939–1940.* London: Greenhill Books, 1998.

Attlee, Clement (1883–1967) *British prime minister at the end of World War II*

Clement Attlee replaced Winston Churchill as prime minister of the United Kingdom in July 1945, after leading his Labour Party out of the coalition with the Conservatives and achieving a large parliamentary majority. He served as prime minister until October 1951. Thus, Attlee was at the helm of British government as the war in the Pacific came to an end and during the immediate postwar years.

Born in London to a well-to-do solicitor, Attlee received an education that culminated in a law degree from Oxford. He began practicing in 1905 but left the law in 1909. Beginning in 1905, Attlee became involved in volunteer work in the slums of London, an experience that profoundly liberalized his social and political outlook. His new-found socialist leanings prompted him to join the Fabian Society in 1907 and the Independent Labour Party in 1908. Except for service in World War I, he lived and worked in the London's slums for the next 15 years, becoming mayor of the Cockney borough of Stepney in 1919 and gaining election to Parliament as the member from Limehouse in 1922. He was named undersecretary of state for war in the first Labour government in 1924 and in 1927 was appointed to the Indian Statutory Commission. Attlee broke with the administration of Ramsay MacDonald after MacDonald brought the Labour Party into coalition with the Conservative Party and the Liberal Party in 1931. Attlee succeeded George Lansbury as leader of the Labour Party in 1935 and aligned the party in opposition to fascism, but was reluctant to embrace rearmament. Nevertheless, Attlee fully supported the British declaration of war against Germany in 1939.

By refusing to join a coalition government under Conservative prime minister Neville Chamberlain, Attlee effectively forced Chamberlain's replacement by Winston Churchill, who appointed Attlee to his war cabinet as lord privy seal. In 1942, he was named deputy prime minister and secretary of state for Dominion affairs and in 1943 added lord president of the council to his duties. Attlee faithfully supported Churchill throughout the war, but, after victory over Germany, he led his party out of the coalition, presided over a major parliamentary sweep, and replaced Churchill as prime minister in July.

Attaining the prime minister's post at the end of the war, Attlee had virtually no influence over the course of combat. However, he was a primary architect of postwar Britain and oversaw the nationalization of the coal, railways, gas, and electricity industries as well as the creation of the National Health Service, among other social reforms. Despite his leftward leanings, Attlee was a strong proponent of defense and an opponent of Soviet expansion. Accordingly, he was a prime mover behind the creation of the North Atlantic Treaty Organization (NATO) in 1949 and readily committed British troops to the Korean War in 1950. While he oversaw the beginning of the end of the British Empire, including the creation of an independent India in 1947, Attlee also presided over a substantial rearmament program. After the Labour Party's defeat in 1955, Attlee resigned as party leader, was created an earl, and elevated to the House of Lords, in which he served until his death in 1967.

Further reading: Brookshire, Jerry H. *Clement Attlee.* London: Palgrave Macmillan, 1995; Burridge, Trevor. *Clement Attlee: A Political Biography.* New York: Random House, 1986; Swift, John. *Labour in Crisis: Clement Attlee and the Labour Party in Opposition, 1931–1940.* London: Palgrave Macmillan, 2001.

Auchinleck, Claude John Ayre (1884– 1881) *British commander in North Africa and the Middle East*

Auchinleck was the son of an army officer, and, destined from childhood for a military career, he was educated at Wellington and Sandhurst. On graduation, he was assigned as an officer in the Indian Army and saw service during World War I against Turkish forces in the Middle East. During the Great War, he rose rapidly through the ranks, becoming a lieutenant colonel by 1917. After the armistice, he was appointed to a teaching position at the Staff College, then returned to lead troops in India. He attended the Imperial Defence College in 1927 and was assigned to command the 1st Battalion, First Punjab Regiment, which he did during 1929–30. From 1930 to 1933, he taught at the Quetta Staff College, then, appointed to command

the Peshawar Brigade, he returned to India's Northwest Frontier during 1933–36 for combat against rebellious tribesmen.

In 1936, Auchinleck became deputy chief of the general staff at Indian Army headquarters in Simla, taking command of the Meerut District two years later. Promoted to major general in January 1940, he returned to England as commander of the ill-fated Anglo-French expeditionary force at NARVIK, Norway. Auchinleck supervised the successful evacuation of the force in June and was returned to India to command all British forces there. He was then named commander in chief of British forces in the Middle East in June 1941, but his failure to take the offensive soon lost him the confidence of Prime Minister WINSTON CHURCHILL. Having learned from Narvik the folly of operating precipitously with unprepared forces, Auchinleck repeatedly protested that he needed more time to forge an effective army. This argument was deeply undercut by the fall of TOBRUK in January 1942. Although Auchinleck was able to halt ERWIN ROMMEL's advance toward the Nile at the BATTLES OF EL ALAMEIN in June 1942, he was replaced in July by General HAROLD ALEXANDER and returned to India as commander in chief of operations there. As if to repudiate any aspersions cast on Auchinleck's prowess in high command, he was recognized in 1946 by a promotion to field marshal.

Further reading: Greenwood, Alexander. *Field-Marshal Auchinleck.* Durham, U.K: Pentland Press, 1991; Parkinson, Roger. *The Auk: Auchinleck, Victor at Alamein.* London: Hart-Davis MacGibbon, 1977; Warner, Philip. *Auchinleck, the Lonely Soldier.* London: Buchan & Enright, 1981.

Aung San (1914 or 1916–1947) *Burmese collaborator with the Japanese*

Aung San was the leader of the Dobama Asi-ayone ("We Burmans") Society, popularly known as the Thakin Society, a pre–World War II Burmese nationalist group made up of communist-leaning students mostly from Rangoon University. *Thakin* is the Burmese word for "master," commonly used by colonial Burmans in addressing Europeans; applying it to a nationalist society was a proclamation of the members' equality with the European "masters." As leader of the Thakin Society, Aung Sang was anti-British, focused exclusively on securing Burmese independence from Great Britain. He saw collaboration with the Japanese in World War II as a means of breaking free from colonial domination. However, late in the war, Aung San broke with the Japanese and aligned himself and his followers with the Allies.

Aung San was born into a family that had long been involved in the Burmese resistance against British rule. At Rangoon University, Aung San was secretary of the students' union and, with U Nu, led a mass students' strike in February 1936. Following BURMA's separation from India in 1937 and his own graduation in 1938, Aung San joined the Thakin Society, becoming its secretary general—leader—in 1939. The following year, having temporarily fled Burma, he was in China, seeking international support for the independence movement. There he was approached by Japanese agents, through whom he concluded an alliance whereby the Japanese government assisted him in forming a Burmese military force, dubbed the Burma Independence Army, which fought alongside the Japanese in their 1942 invasion of Burma.

From August 1942 to August 1943, Aung San led the Burma Independence Army with the rank of Japanese major general. Under him, the force steadily expanded and assumed administration of each occupied area. In 1943, the Japanese set up a puppet government under Ba Maw, in which Aung San was appointed minister of defense. However, Aung San became increasingly wary of the Japanese and began to doubt their promises of ultimate Burmese independence. More urgently, it became apparent to Aung San that the Japanese were destined to lose the war, and he saw that as they became increasingly desperate, Japanese officers treated Burmese forces with harsh contempt. In August 1944, therefore, he secretly formed the Anti-Fascist Organization (which later became the Anti-Fascist People's Freedom League), an organizing base for guerilla resistance against the Japanese

occupiers. In March 1945, Aung San made the break with Japan open by renaming his military forces the Burma National Army and formally declaring for the Allied cause.

Following the surrender of Japan in August 1945, British administrators sought to co-opt the Burma National Army by absorbing it into the regular army, but Aung San, a canny political leader, held back the most important leaders of the force and, with them, created the People's Volunteer Organization. To all appearances a veterans' association committed to social service, this group was actually a closely held political army, which was intended to displace the Burma National Army and to lead a renewed struggle for independence. In the meantime, Aung San became deputy chairman of Burma's Executive Council in 1946, effectively the Burmese prime minister, although still subject to the veto of a British governor. But this was the era of CLEMENT ATTLEE and the Labour Party, not WINSTON CHURCHILL and the Conservative-dominated coalition. Negotiations with Attlee produced an agreement on January 27, 1947, granting Burma independence within a year.

Aung San's party swept the elections for a constitutional assembly in April 1947, but the hardline Burmese communists had denounced him as a dupe and tool of British imperialism. Nevertheless, he assumed the office of prime minister, only to be assassinated in the Executive Council chamber by agents of his political rival, U Saw, on July 19, 1947. Six colleagues, including his brother, were also killed. U Saw was subsequently tried and executed.

Further reading: Aung San Suu Kyi, *Aung San.* Louth, U.K.: Granite Impex, 1990; Lintner, Bertil. *Aung San Suu Kyi and Burma's Unfinished Renaissance.* Santa Barbara, Calif.: White Lotus, 1991; Kin Oung, *Who Killed Aung San?* Santa Barbara, Calif.: White Lotus, 1993; Naw, Angelene. *Aung San and the Struggle for Burmese Independence.* Suthep, Thailand: Silkworm Books, 2002.

Auschwitz extermination camp

Oswiecim was one of many towns in southern Poland annexed to the German Reich after the fall of POLAND in 1939. Germans called it Auschwitz, and it was here, outside the town proper, that a complex of three particularly infamous Nazi extermination camps were built during 1940–42.

Auschwitz I, built in June 1940, was intended to hold Polish political prisoners. Auschwitz II, also known as Birkenau, was much larger and could accommodate more than 100,000 inmates; it opened in October 1941. Auschwitz III developed from a camp at Monowitz, a facility that supplied slave labor for a nearby I. G. Farben synthetic rubber and oil works. At Birkenau, gas chambers and crematoria were installed, primarily to murder and incinerate Jews as part of ADOLF HITLER's FINAL SOLUTION. It is reported that by 1944, more than 6,000 inmates were murdered each day. About a quarter million Hungarian Jews were killed here during a single six-week period. Birkenau was also the site of grotesque and sadistic medical "experiments" performed by DR. JOSEF MENGELE, known as the "Angel of Death."

A resistance movement developed within Auschwitz, though very few inmates managed to escape. Two who did in 1942 first carried to the world reports of the genocide. Three more escapees in 1944 carried even more horrific reports. A major revolt took place in October 1944, when slave laborers at a nearby armaments plant managed to convey explosives to some inmates. These were used to blow up a gas chamber, and in the resulting chaos 250 inmates escaped, only to be shot down. An additional 200 inmates, accused of complicity in the uprising, were also executed.

All three camps were liberated by advancing soldiers of the Red Army in January 1945. However, before their arrival, the WAFFEN SS began the demolition of the camp and "evacuated" all ambulatory inmates to Germany. They left behind the sick and dying—as well as mountains of corpses awaiting cremation. The Soviets hurriedly announced that Auschwitz had been the place of death for some 4 million. This was a gross exaggeration, but the reality was horrific enough: 1.2 million to 1.5 million killed, of whom at least 800,000 were Jews.

See also HOLOCAUST.

Further reading: Lengyel, Olga. *Five Chimneys.* Chicago: Academy Chicago, 1995; Levi, Primo. *Survival in Auschwitz: The Nazi Assault on Humanity.* New York: Touchstone, 1993; Matalon Lagnado, Lucette, and Sheila Cohn Dekel. *Children of the Flames: Dr. Josef Mengele and the Untold Story of the Twins of Auschwitz.* New York: Penguin, 1992; Mullter, Filip. *Eyewitness Auschwitz: Three Years in the Gas Chambers.* Chicago: Ivan R. Dee, 1999; Nomberg-Przuytyk, Sara. *Auschwitz: True Tales from a Grotesque Land.* Chapel Hill: University of North Carolina Press, 1985.

The sign over the entrance to Auschwitz proclaims: *WORK MAKES YOU FREE. (National Holocaust Museum)*

Australia

Constituting the world's smallest continent, Australia is a vast country that lies between the Pacific and Indian Oceans in the Southern Hemisphere. During World War II, its location was of supreme strategic importance, with the Netherlands East Indies and New Guinea directly to the north, and the Coral Sea Islands to the northeast. The Japanese eyed Australia as the greatest of Asian-Pacific prizes and believed that its conquest would certainly force the British and Americans into negotiating a favorable peace. Australia was a member of the British Commonwealth and was vigorous not only in its own defense, but in that of the entire Commonwealth. Royal Australian Air Force pilots flew in the

BATTLE OF BRITAIN, and the Royal Australian Navy contributed ships and personnel to the Mediterranean campaign during 1940–41, where they were instrumental in the victory at the BATTLE OF CAPE MATAPAN in March 1941. Australian troops were sent into the NORTH AFRICAN CAMPAIGN and fought in GREECE and CRETE.

At its peak, Australia mobilized 680,000 troops, and its modest industrial infrastructure geared up to produce both aircraft and munitions. However, once the Pacific war began with the attack on the United States at the BATTLE OF PEARL HARBOR on December 7, 1941, the thrust of Australian strategy immediately shifted to defense of the suddenly imperiled homeland. Not only did 15,000 Australians instantly become PRISONERS OF WAR (POWs) in the FALL OF SINGAPORE on February 15, 1942, but the city of Darwin, Australia, was bombed on February 19, and the Japanese, rolling up conquest after conquest, bore down on Port Moresby, New Guinea, stepping stone to a full-scale invasion of Australia. At this point, the principal Allied force in the Pacific, the United States, became Australia's major ally. Indeed, wartime alignment with America signaled a growing independence from Great Britain, and when Australian troops were recalled from the Middle East, Australian prime minister John Curtin defied British prime minister WINSTON CHURCHILL by committing the troops to the defense of Australia rather than dispatching them to Burma. On the U.S. side, it was to Australia that General DOUGLAS MACARTHUR traveled after his evacuation from the Philippines, and he established his first headquarters as supreme allied commander in Melbourne and then in Brisbane.

MacArthur was only the highest ranking of the many U.S. service personnel who poured into Australia. So many came that the Australian government created a Civil Construction Corps (CCC) as part of an Allied Works Council. Staffed by 53,500 men by 1943, the CCC built facilities for the American troops. Those too old to serve in the Australian armed forces, men aged 45 to 60, were liable to conscription into the CCC (some 16,000 CCC members were conscripts). The government also set up a Department of War Organization of Industry to regulate industrial production and assure that war materiel was always given top priority. Various civilian goods were subject to strict rationing, including tea, sugar, alcoholic beverages, tires, and gasoline. Strong legislation was enacted to combat incipient black marketeering. As U.S. forces continued to build up in Australia, the government was compelled to take the extraordinary step of releasing some 30,000 men from the army and 15,000 from the air force to serve as laborers to assist the CCC in necessary construction, including extensive building of port facilities. Even this drastic step left a shortage of laborers, and more than 10,000 Italian PRISONERS OF WAR (POWs) were put to work on Australian farms and elsewhere. In 1942, the Australian Women's Land Army was created, which sent some 2,000 women into the agricultural workforce.

Another important home front institution were civil defense and other ad hoc defense forces. The Volunteer Defence Corps (VDC) was initially composed of World War I veterans but soon took anyone who wished to serve as airfield defenders and coast watchers. The VDC guarded key homeland facilities, provided some counterespionage intelligence, and, after training, manned antiaircraft defenses. By 1944, the VDC consisted of about 100,000, and the duties they performed freed up thousands of military personnel for frontline service.

Civil defense included an extensive blackout policy, which was enforced by Air Raid Precaution (ARP) wardens. In the days when invasion loomed, much discussion was devoted to plans for evacuation from the cities. However, it was ultimately decided that people occupying and (as best they could) defending their own homes provided the most effective protection. A program of air raid shelter construction was instituted in major population centers.

The Australian armed forces are treated in detail in AUSTRALIA, AIR FORCE OF; AUSTRALIA, ARMY OF; and AUSTRALIA, NAVY OF. In general, these services fought alongside the Americans. The Royal Australian Navy participated in the important BATTLE OF THE CORAL SEA in May 1942. General Douglas

MacArthur prevailed upon Australian high command to abandon the idea of girding for a defensive war on the Australian homeland and instead take the offensive by fighting the Japanese in New Guinea. Thus, the Australian army was largely responsible for the Allied victory at Milne Bay, New Guinea, during August and September 1942, which marked the first step in the Allied seizure of the initiative on land against the hitherto triumphant Japanese. Australian troops were also instrumental in the long drive against the Japanese in southern New Guinea, forcing them back over the Kokoda Trail, a jungle track across the formidable Owen Stanley Mountains. While Australian troops engaged in a war of attrition against the Japanese throughout New Guinea, they played a decidedly subordinate role to American forces elsewhere.

Of the 680,000 men who served in the armed forces of Australia during World War II, 37,467 died (this included 23,365 battle deaths), and 39,803 were wounded. It was a heavy toll, but MacArthur's policy of offense, his insistence that the Australians bring the war to the Japanese in New Guinea rather than wait for an invasion of Australia, surely saved the Australian nation untold suffering. Apart from the loss of military personnel, Australia emerged from the war largely unscathed and, indeed, with a renewed nationalism, sense of achievement, and enhanced sense of independence from Britain.

Further reading: Barker, Anthony J., and Lisa Jackson. *Fleeting Attraction: A Social History of American Servicemen in Western Australia During the Second World War.* Crawley: University of Western Australia Press, 1996; Clark, Rosemary. *The Home Front: Life in Australia During World War II.* Melbourne: Australia Post, 1991; Gregory, Jenny. *On the Home Front: Western Australia and World War II.* Crawley: University of Western Australia Press, 1997; Johnston, Mark. *Fighting the Enemy: Australian Soldiers and Their Adversaries in World War II.* Cambridge and New York: Cambridge University Press, 2000; Ralph, Barry. *They Passed This Way: The United States of America, the States of Australia, and World War II.* Bloomington, Ind.: Kangaroo Press, 2000.

Australia, air force of

At the start of World War II, the Royal Australian Air Force (RAAF) consisted of just 164 aircraft, most of them obsolescent or downright obsolete. Early in the war, the British spurned an Australian offer of an expeditionary force of four bomber squadrons and two fighter squadrons and instead accepted Australian personnel into the British Empire Air Training Scheme, wherein experienced Australian military pilots helped train British and Commonwealth fliers. Also, Britain's Royal Air Force (RAF) accepted Australian aircrews for service, some in designated all-Australian units, but most dispersed throughout regular units of the RAF. RAAF personnel and units fought in Europe as well as the Middle East and Burma.

In the Far East, four RAAF squadrons served during the Malayan campaign. Two RAAF squadrons served in the DUTCH EAST INDIES. All these units flew either Hudson bombers or grossly inadequate Brewster Buffalo fighters. In the southwest Pacific, RAAF units were under the overall command of U.S. general DOUGLAS MACARTHUR. The RAAF had its first real success supporting the BATTLE OF THE BISMARCK SEA in March 1943 and continued to participate throughout the war. A total of 189,700 men and 27,200 women served in the RAAF during World War II.

Further reading: Odgers, George. *The Royal Australian Air Force: An illustrated History.* Brookvale, N.S.W., Australia: Child & Henry, 1984; Parnell, N. M. *Australian Air Force since 1911.* Sydney: Reed, 1976; Stephens, Alan. *High Fliers: Leaders of the Royal Australian Air Force.* Canberra: AGPS Press, 1996; Stephens, Alan. *The Royal Australian Air Force.* Oxford and New York: Oxford University Press, 2001.

Australia, army of

When World War II began in Europe in September 1939, the Australian Army consisted of 82,800 soldiers, of whom the overwhelming majority—80,000—were minimally trained militiamen. The 2,800 regulars included officers and noncommissioned officers as well as some coastal artillery personnel. Australia immediately contributed a division to the war in Europe, and it instituted simultaneously a program of voluntary enlistment for service overseas and a program of conscription for service in defense of the homeland (including Papua and New Guinea). Before the war with Japan, part of a division fought in Europe. After the fall of France, it became the nucleus of the 9th Division, which, with the 6th and 7th Divisions, became the 1st Australian Corps under Lt. Gen. Thomas Blamey, and fought in Egypt. Elements of the corps also fought in the Balkans, on Crete, and in Syria, as well as in the North African Campaign.

By August 1941, in anticipation of a Japanese threat, two 8th Division brigades were deployed to Malaya, and other 8th Division units were variously deployed in New Guinea and associated islands. The 7th Division had troops in Java, Ambon, New Britain, New Ireland, and the Solomon Islands. An independent company of Australian special forces troops was stationed on Timor. All of these units were overwhelmed by superior Japanese numbers early in the war.

In April 1942, Blamey hastened to reorganize the Australian Army for the defense of the Australian homeland, and by the middle of the year only an Australian Independent Company and militia units of the New Guinea Volunteer Rifles were actually fighting the Japanese in New Guinea. By November, these units were joined by the 6th and 7th Divisions and two additional militia brigades, all engaged in the New Guinea Campaign. It was not until February 1943 that Australian lawmakers legalized the use of conscripts in a defined area outside Australian territory. But Australian troops saw relatively little action until October 1944, when they followed behind American forces to conduct mop-up operations in Bougainville, New Britain, and New Guinea. Australian Army troops of the 7th and 9th Divisions did participate in the Borneo Campaign, specifically in assaults on Balikpapan, Tarakan, and Brunei. By the end of the war against Japan, 691,400 Australian men and 35,800 women had served in the army.

Further reading: Coates, John. *Bravery above Blunder: The 9th Australian Division at Finschhafen, Sattelberg and Sio.* Oxford and New York: Oxford University Press, 1999; Grey, Jeffrey. *The Australian Army.* Oxford and New York: Oxford University Press, 2001; Johnston, Mark. *At the Front Line: Experiences of Australian Soldiers in World War II.* Cambridge and New York: Cambridge University Press, 1996; Johnston, Mark, and Peter Stanley. *Alamein: The Australian Story.* Oxford and New York: Oxford University Press, 2004; Laffin, John. *The Australian Army at War, 1899–1975.* London: Osprey, 1982.

Australia, navy of

At the time of the outbreak of World War II in Europe, September 1939, the Royal Australian Navy consisted of two heavy cruisers and four light cruisers, five obsolete destroyers, and two vessels classified as sloops (smaller than destroyers). Two liners were converted as armed merchantmen for the Royal Australian Navy, and another three were converted for the British Royal Navy, but manned by Australians. Additionally, a number of civilian coastal vessels were hastily converted into minesweepers.

The destroyers were dispatched to the Mediterranean to serve with the Royal Navy fleet there. The light cruiser *Perth* joined British ships in the East Indies, and the heavy cruisers *Australia* and *Canberra* escorted Australian troop convoys. *Sydney,* a light cruiser, later fought in the Mediterranean, as did *Perth.* Other ships took part in action on Crete and the Battle of Cape Matapan. During 1940 and 1941, Australian vessels fought in Middle Eastern waters.

By the close of 1941, with the beginning of the war against Japan, the Australian ships were withdrawn to Australian or Singapore stations. Soon, they were effectively under the overall command of U.S. admiral Chester William Nimitz and Gen. Douglas MacArthur. Australian ships participated in the Battle of the Coral Sea in May 1942 and in the Battle of Savo Island during the Guadalcanal Campaign. Australian ships also supported other phases of the American assault on Guadalcanal. During the campaign to retake the

PHILIPPINES, the heavy cruiser *Australia* had the dubious distinction of being hit in the first Japanese KAMIKAZE attack. During the closing months of the war in the Pacific, most of the Australian fleet was used to support the Borneo Campaign and action in BURMA. Three Australian destroyers served with the British Pacific Fleet in action against the Japanese home islands. The Royal Australian Navy consisted of 45,800 men and 3,100 women during World War II.

Further reading: Odgers, George. *The Royal Australian Navy: An Illustrated History.* Brookvale, N.S.W., Australia: Child & Henry, 1982; Stevens, David. *The Royal Australian Navy.* Oxford and New York: Oxford University Press, 2001; Stevens, David. *The Royal Australian Navy in World War II.* London: Allen & Unwin, 1996.

Austria

Having entered World War I as the Habsburg Imperial and Royal Monarchy—the Austro-Hungarian Empire—the nation emerged from defeat in that conflict as a much diminished and dismembered Republic of Austria, 32,400 square miles in extent, with a population of 6.7 million. The Treaty of Versailles expressly barred Austria from union with Germany. However, by virtue of the ANSCHLUSS of March 1938, the nation was incorporated into ADOLF HITLER's Third Reich. When it happened, many Austrians warmly greeted *Anschluss.* In the course of World War II, however, as Germany and the rest of the Axis suffered increasing reverses, most Austrians began to feel that they were unwilling participants in a hopeless struggle.

Austria's federal chancellor, KURT VON SCHUSCHNIGG, was, at Hitler's behest, dismissed shortly after the *Anschluss* and replaced by a Nazi, ARTHUR SEYSS-INQUART, a puppet of the Third Reich. Austria was occupied by some 100,000 German troops, the SCHUTZSTAFFEL (SS) acted brutally to suppress all protest and opposition, and the Reich took steps to ensure that the region's rich natural resources, including iron ore, magnesite, and wood, would be wholly available to serve its needs. Also now available to the Reich was the Austrian military. On the eve of *Anschluss,* mobilization and conscription doubled that force from 60,000 to 120,000. The army included a motorized division, which had nothing but obsolete tanks. The Austrian air force had 90 obsolescent aircraft. Immediately after the *Anschluss,* the armed forces were required to take the same oath of personal loyalty to Hitler required of German military personnel. All but 125 men did so. The Federal Army of Austria was then wholly integrated into the WEHRMACHT—with the proviso that in no unit were Austrian troops to make up more than 25 percent of the force. Wartime conscription throughout Austria would greatly increase the number of Austrian men who served in the Wehrmacht and WAFFEN-SS. Austrian officers were given ample opportunity to rise within the German military, some 220 individuals attaining general officer rank before the end of the war.

Despite the apparently overwhelming scope and thoroughness of *Anschluss,* resistance groups formed throughout Austria from March 1938. The Austrian resistance maintained close links with the resistance within Germany itself. The resistance movement also established contacts with the Allies, and resistance members carried out acts of espionage and sabotage. It was the resistance that smoothed the way for the relatively easy separation from Germany and reestablishment of sovereignty that occurred after the German surrender.

Further reading: Keyserling, Robert H. *Austria in World War II: An Anglo-American Dilemma.* Montreal: McGill-Queen's University Press, 1990; Lehr, David. *Austria Before and After the Anschluss.* New York: Dorrance, 2000; Luza, Radomír. *Austro-German Relations in the Anschluss Era.* Princeton, N.J.: Princeton University Press, 1975.

Axis (Tripartite) Pact

Concluded on September 27, 1940, at Berlin among Germany, Italy, and Japan, the Axis, or Tripartite, Pact was the primary treaty creating the alliance of the three major Axis powers in World War II. The pact was concluded early in the war and at a time of high triumph for Germany, which had already invaded and conquered Poland, occupied France and created the puppet Vichy government in the unoccupied portion of the country, and appeared in position to defeat Great Britain as well. ADOLF HITLER, however, preferred to coerce the British to come to terms with his regime as he secretly prepared to violate the GERMAN-SOVIET NON-AGGRESSION PACT with an INVASION OF THE SOVIET UNION. Hitler did not want to fight a two-front war, and his foreign minister, JOACHIM VON RIBBENTROP, suggested to Hitler that a three-power agreement with Italy and Japan might just provide the leverage needed to move the stubborn Brits. Such a pact, Ribbentrop reasoned, would dissuade the ostensibly neutral, but by now clearly pro-British, United States from intervening in Europe and prompt it instead to turn its attention to the Pacific, where Japanese aggression presented a more immediate threat to its security. By formally bringing Japan into the Berlin-Rome Axis, the pact would threaten the Soviet Union with a two-front war, once Germany had invaded that country. Finally, with the United States and the Soviet Union distracted or threatened on other fronts, Great Britain would see itself as truly standing alone, and this would bring the British, at last, to the bargaining table.

As it turned out, the Axis Pact achieved none of these outcomes. Not only did it tend to reinforce and intensify pro-British U.S. policy, it failed to bring Japan into a war against the Soviet Union. It did, however, sharply define the adversaries in World War II. Article 2 clearly gave Japan license to expand into and dominate East Asia, and deftly, Article 4, while making reference to Germany's nonaggression pact with the USSR and thereby recognizing Russia as an ally, made it clear that the Soviets had no part in the Axis.

The substantive portions of the text of the pact follow:

The governments of Germany, Italy and Japan, considering it as a condition precedent of any lasting peace that all nations of the world be given each its own proper place, have decided to stand by and co-operate with one another in regard to their efforts in greater East Asia and regions of Europe respectively wherein it is their prime purpose to establish and maintain a new order of things calculated to promote the mutual prosperity and welfare of the peoples concerned.

Furthermore, it is the desire of the three governments to extend co-operation to such nations in other spheres of the world as may be inclined to put forth endeavours along lines similar to their own, in order that their ultimate aspirations for world peace may thus be realized.

Accordingly, the governments of Germany, Italy and Japan have agreed as follows:

ARTICLE 1
Japan recognizes and respects the leadership of Germany and Italy in establishment of a new order in Europe.

ARTICLE 2
Germany and Italy recognize and respect the leadership of Japan in the establishment of a new order in greater East Asia.

ARTICLE 3
Germany, Italy and Japan agree to co-operate in their efforts on aforesaid lines. They further undertake to assist one another with all political, economic and military means when one of the three contracting powers is attacked by a power at present not involved in the European war or in the Chinese-Japanese conflict.

ARTICLE 4
With the view to implementing the present pact, joint technical commissions, members which are to be appointed by the respective governments of Germany, Italy and Japan will meet without delay.

ARTICLE 5
Germany, Italy and Japan affirm that the aforesaid terms do not in any way affect the political status which exists at present as between each of the three contracting powers and Soviet Russia.

ARTICLE 6
The present pact shall come into effect immediately upon signature and shall remain in force 10 years from the date of its coming into force. At the proper time before expiration of said term, the high contracting parties shall at the request of any of them enter into negotiations for its renewal.

In faith whereof, the undersigned duly authorized by their respective governments have signed this pact and have affixed hereto their signatures.

Further reading: Martel, Gordon, ed. *The Origins of the Second World War Reconsidered: A.J.P. Taylor and the Historians.* 2d ed. New York: Routledge, 1999; Overy, Richard. *The Road to War.* New York: Penguin USA, 2000; Taylor, A. J. P. *The Origins of the Second World War.* New York: Touchstone, 1996.

Axmann, Artur (1913–1996) *founder of the Hitler Youth movement*

Born on February 18, 1913, in Hagen, Germany, Axmann studied law, became an early member of the Nazi Party (NSDAP), and, in 1928, established the first Hitler Youth group, in Westphalia. In 1932, the party summoned him to reorganize all Nazi youth cells throughout the country. The following year he was named chief of the Social Office of the Reich Youth leadership. From this post, Axmann put the Hitler Youth in the forefront of determining the nature and direction of state vocational training, and he put Hitler Youth groups to work on farms.

Axmann became an officer in the Waffen SS and fought on the western front until May 1940. In August, he succeeded Baldur von Schirach in the post of Reich youth leader of the Nazi Party. Returning to combat, he was gravely wounded on the eastern front in 1941, suffering the loss of an arm. Axmann returned to Germany and resumed personal leadership of the Reich Youth.

A thoroughly committed Nazi, Axmann was a member of Adolf Hitler's inner circle and was with Hitler in the infamous *Fuhrerbunker,* the shelter deep beneath the streets of Berlin from which the dictator directed the war in its final desperate days. Axmann escaped capture by the Red Army in April but was arrested in December 1945 by the Western Allies, after he was discovered organizing a Nazi underground movement. He was held until 1949, when he was tried by a Nuremberg de-Nazification tribunal, which sentenced him in May 1949 to a three-year three-month prison term. After serving his sentence, Axmann found employment as a salesman in Gelsenkirchen and Berlin. However, on August 19, 1958, a West Berlin de-Nazification court levied a heavy fine against Axmann of 35,000 marks (about $15,000), which represented some 50 percent of the value of property he owned in Berlin. Although it was the judgment of the court that he was guilty of indoctrinating German youth with National Socialism until the very end of the Third Reich, he was acquitted of actual war crimes.

Further reading: Kater, Michael H. *Hitler Youth.* Cambridge, Mass.: Harvard University Press, 2004; Koch, H. W. *The Hitler Youth.* New York: Cooper Square, 2000; Rempel, Gerhard. *Hitler's Children: The Hitler Youth and the SS.* Chapel Hill: University of North Carolina Press, 1991.

B

Bader, Douglas (1910–1982) *British aviator hero*

For Britons, standing alone against Germany during after the BATTLE OF FRANCE and during the BATTLE OF BRITAIN, Douglas Bader was one of the great heroic figures of the war and the embodiment of resistance against all odds. Born in London, the son of a soldier killed in World War I, Bader studied at Oxford and at the Royal Air Force (RAF) College in Cranwell. Commissioned an officer in the Royal Air Force in 1930, he was severely injured in a crash in 1931 and lost both his legs. Discharged from the RAF, he made a career with the Asiatic Petroleum Company. However, at the outbreak of World War II, he appealed for readmission to the RAF and, despite his double amputation, flew and fought as a pilot in the 222 Squadron, taking part in operations at DUNKIRK and scoring two kills there, shooting down a Messerschmitt Bf109 and a Heinkel He111. After this action, Bader was given command of 242 Squadron, a unit that had just suffered catastrophic 50 percent casualties. In an effort to rebuild morale, Bader radically reorganized the squadron, thereby incurring the wrath of higher command. His leadership was vindicated, however, when, in its first sortie during the Battle of Britain, on August 30, 1940, the 242 Squadron shot down a dozen German aircraft over the English Channel in the space of an hour, Bader personally downing a pair of Messerschmitt 110s.

Despite the results he achieved, Bader was repeatedly rebuffed by higher command over tactical issues, particularly his outspoken belief that RAF fighters should sortie out to intercept German planes before they reached Britain. This tactic was rejected on the grounds that it would take too long to organize properly. Others pointed out that Bader's overly aggressive tactics left RAF air bases exposed and vulnerable to Luftwaffe attack. Eventually, however, a version of Bader's tactics was adopted in the so-called Big Wing strategy, whereby large RAF fighter formations were deployed against German aircraft over the English Channel and even over northern Europe. This resulted in many kills, but did leave some prime homeland targets vulnerable. Nevertheless, Bader embraced the Big Wing and, during the summer of 1941, downed 12 German aircraft, for a total of 23—making him the fifth-highest-ranking ace in the RAF.

Bader's luck ran out on August 9, 1941, when he collided in midair with another aircraft over Le Touquet, France. He was able to parachute out of his plane, but his landing broke both of his prosthetic legs. Taken to a hospital, he enlisted the aid of a French nurse to escape but was caught, arrested, and sent to a prisoner of war camp. After several additional escape attempts, he was sent to a camp in Germany itself. There he spent the rest of the war.

Liberated after the German surrender, Bader was promoted to group captain but left the RAF in

1946 for a career as managing director of Shell Aircraft. In 1969, he become a member of the Civil Aviation Authority Board, published a memoir of the Battle of Britain in 1973, and was knighted in 1976.

Further reading: Bader, Douglas. *Fight for the Sky: The Story of the Spitfire and the Hurricane.* Garden City, N.Y.: Doubleday, 1973; Brickhill, Paul. *Reach for the Sky: The Story of Douglas Bader, Legless Ace of the Battle of Britain.* Annapolis, Md.: Naval Institute Press, 2001; Turner, John Frayn. *Douglas Bader: A Biography of the Legendary World War II Fighter Pilot.* Shrewsbury, U.K.: Airlife Publishing, 2002.

Badoglio, Pietro (1871–1956) *Italy's head of state after the removal of Mussolini*

After the downfall of BENITO MUSSOLINI as dictator of fascist Italy in 1943, the government devolved upon Marshal Pietro Badoglio, who concluded an armistice with the Allies in September 1943, even as his country continued to be occupied by the Germans, Italy's erstwhile ally. Badoglio was commissioned an artillery officer in the Italian Army in 1890 and saw action in the ill-fated Ethiopian campaign of 1896 and the Italo-Turkish War. He performed heroically in World War I, leading the capture of Monte Sabotino on August 6, 1916. Badoglio's command was defeated in the generally disastrous Battle of Caporetto on October 24, 1917, but his reputation survived intact, and, as a general, it was he who conducted the armistice talks on behalf of Italy.

After World War I, Badoglio was elevated to chief of the general staff, serving in this capacity from 1919 to 1921. Badoglio was generally oblivious to the rise of Mussolini and remained unmoved by Il Duce's epoch-making march on Rome in 1922. However, the following year, he embraced the Mussolini government and was appointed ambassador to Brazil, serving until Mussolini recalled him to Italy in May 1925 to serve once again as chief of staff. On May 26, 1926, he was promoted to field marshal. Badoglio was dispatched to Italian Libya as its governor from 1928 to 1934 and was

Marshal Pietro Badoglio *(Author's collection)*

created marquis of Sabotino. In 1935, he was assigned to command Italian forces in Ethiopia, led the capture of the Ethiopian capital, Addis Ababa, and served briefly there in 1936 as Italy's viceroy. This earned him the title of duke of Addis Ababa.

Badoglio differed sharply with Mussolini over Italy's preparations for entry into World War II during 1940. Disgusted by the defeat of the Italian Army in Greece, a disaster he laid at the feet of Mussolini, Badoglio resigned as chief of staff on December 4, 1940. To this day, it remains unclear whether Badoglio's objections were chiefly military or moral. Whatever the case, Badoglio began working covertly to bring about the ouster of Mussolini, which was accomplished on July 25, 1943.

With Il Duce's removal, Badoglio was appointed prime minister, and although he assured Italy's ally Germany that his nation would continue to prosecute the war, he made secret overtures to the Allies, ultimately negotiating an armistice on September 3. Just five days later, Italy's unconditional surrender to the Allies was announced, whereupon Badoglio officially dissolved the Fascist Party. On

October 13, Badoglio's Italy declared war on Germany. From this point until the end of the war, the Allied campaign against German-occupied Italy was arduous, bloody, and heartbreaking.

Badoglio resigned as prime minister in June 1944 in order to permit the formation of a new cabinet in liberated Rome. He retired to his estate in Grazzano Badoglio and lived out the remainder of his life as a private citizen.

Further reading: Badoglio, Pietro. *Italy in the Second World War*. Westport, Conn.: Greenwood, 1976.

Balbo, Italo (1896–1940) *Italian Fascist and air marshal*

Balbo, one of the pioneers of Italian aviation, became a leading Fascist early in the movement, and went on to become BENITO MUSSOLINI's air marshal, the architect of the Italian air force. Born near Ferrara, he was educated at the University of Florence and at the Institute of Social Science, Rome. During World War I, Balbo was commissioned as an officer in the Alpine Corps and after the war became a very early follower of Mussolini. It was he who led the BLACKSHIRTS in the October 1922 March on Rome, which catapulted Mussolini to power. Regarding Balbo both as a dashing and charismatic exponent of fascism and as a potential rival to himself, Mussolini was careful to define his role strictly in military terms, elevating him to general of militia in 1923 and then to undersecretary of state for air (1926), air minister (1929), and, finally, air marshal (1933).

Balbo was a champion of Italy's military air power as well as its commercial air prowess. He personally led a round-the-world flight, landing in various major cities, where he was generally greeted as a dashing hero of the skies. He proved to be not only a great promoter of Italian prestige as an air power, but a kind of ambassador of fascism. Mussolini may have become wary of Balbo's growing pro-British sympathies or of his growing appeal generally; in any case, Balbo was summarily removed from the limelight by his appointment as governor of Libya. Serving there very early in

World War II, he was shot down while flying over Tobruk, the victim of friendly fire. It is believed that he failed to render the correct recognition signals and that Italian gun crews assumed his was an enemy aircraft.

Although Balbo vigorously promoted Italian aviation, the nation's air arm never developed aircraft or tactics on a par with Germany, Britain, and the United States. In the end, Balbo was more public relations than substance, and the Italian air arm never became a significant force in World War II.

Further reading: Segrè, Claudio G. *Italo Balbo: A Fascist Life*. Berkeley: University of California Press, 1990; Taylor, Blaine. *Facist Eagle: Italy's Air Marshal Italo Balbo*. Woodbridge, U.K: Boydell & Brewer, 1996.

Balck, Hermann (1893–1982) *prominent German field commander*

According to some of his contemporaries, Hermann Balck was the most skilled, even the greatest, of Germany's field commanders in World War II. He was born in Danzig-Langfuhr, Germany, the son of a general, and entered Hanover Military College in February 1914. During World War I, he served with the 10th (Hanoverian) Jäger Regiment on the western front and remained in the army during the interwar period, becoming an enthusiastic advocate of motorized warfare, the tactics and technology that would enable the BLITZKRIEG program that was so devastatingly effective early in the war.

At the beginning of World War II, Balck commanded the 1st Security Regiment (Schutzanregiment) in the 1st Panzer Division, then became commanding officer of the 3rd Panzer Regiment, serving under HEINZ GUDERIAN in the invasion of France. On May 13, 1940, boldly exploiting a heavy air attack on Sedan, he raced his men across the Meuse River in storm boats, seized enough ground for a bridgehead, and set the divisional bridging train to work deploying pontoons for the waiting tanks. Decorated with the Knight's Cross for this action, he was promoted to colonel and sent to Greece on March 5, 1942, took Salonika on April 9, and was given command of the 11th Panzer Division. He then fought in the Soviet campaign, receiving Oak Leaves for his Knight's Cross on December 20, 1942, for action in the Caucasus. In November 1943, he was promoted to acting general in command of the 48th (Grossdeutschland) Panzer Corps.

In 1944, Balck was transferred to the western front as commanding general of Army Group G. After he failed to prevent the overwhelming advance of GEORGE SMITH PATTON's Third Army into Lorraine, ADOLF HITLER expressed his displeasure by relegating Balck to command of a sub-army, Armeegruppe Balck, against the Russians in Hungary in December 1944.

Failing to recapture Budapest from the Red Army, Balck was forced to retreat into Austria, where he surrendered on the day of Germany's formal capitulation, May 8, 1945. Held prisoner until 1947, he retired to Stuttgart.

Further reading: Mellenthin, Friedrich Wilhelm von. *German Generals of World War II: As I Saw Them.* Norman: University of Oklahoma Press, 1977; Thomas, Nigel. *The German Army in World War II.* London: Osprey, 2002.

Baldwin, Stanley (1867–1947) *prime minister who presided over British disarmament between the wars*

A Conservative, Baldwin served three terms as prime minister between 1923 and 1937 and was important in the years preceding World War II as a leading opponent of WINSTON CHURCHILL (at the time, a member of Parliament) on the subject of British rearmament and war preparation. The son of industrialist and railway baron Alfred Baldwin, Stanley Baldwin was educated at Harrow and Cambridge. After graduation, he became an executive in some of his father's industrial enterprises and was elected to the House of Commons in 1908, beginning a long political career that ended in 1937.

During World War I, Baldwin was parliamentary private secretary to Chancellor of the Exche-

quer Andrew Bonar Law in the cabinet of David Lloyd George, then served as financial secretary of the treasury from 1917 to 1921, when he became president of the Board of Trade. In October 1922, Baldwin became chancellor of the Exchequer in the Conservative government of Bonar Law. In this capacity, he negotiated the British World War I debt to the United States, reaching a settlement in 1923 that many Britons viewed unfavorably. Despite this controversy, King George V asked Baldwin on May 22, 1923, to form a government when Bonar Law fell ill. This first ministry ended on January 22, 1924, but, later that year, on November 4, Baldwin was returned to office after the downfall of the first Labour prime minister, Ramsay MacDonald. Baldwin resigned as prime minister following a Conservative electoral defeat on June 4, 1929. He returned to the government in 1931 as lord president of the council in the national coalition government of Ramsay MacDonald. It was during this period, in 1933, in response to the elevation of ADOLF HITLER as chancellor of Germany, that many in Britain first saw Nazism as an international threat. Resisting calls from some quarters for a program of British rearmament, Baldwin refused to take any position with regard to the situation in Germany. If anything, this complacency pleased most of the British public, beleaguered by the worldwide economic depression and wary of somehow instigating another war. Therefore, from June 7, 1935, to May 28, 1937, Baldwin once again served as prime minister.

The mounting evidence of fascist and Nazi aggression, including the Italian conquest of Ethiopia, the German reoccupation of the Rhineland in violation of the TREATY OF VERSAILLES, and German-Italian intervention in the Spanish Civil War, finally moved Baldwin to direct some efforts to strengthening the British military establishment. Yet, in contrast to Churchill, who repeatedly and eloquently sounded warning of the gathering storm, Baldwin deliberately demonstrated outward unconcern.

Despite Baldwin's attempts to maintain the status quo, the British public rose in outrage over the December 1935 agreement between British foreign secretary Sir SAMUEL HOARE and French premier PIERRE LAVAL to refrain from interfering in Italy's brutal conquest of Ethiopia. Yet even this crisis failed to move the mass of British public opinion in favor of war preparedness, and, indeed, the public's attention was soon far more absorbed in the romance between the new king, Edward VIII, and the American divorcée, Wallis Simpson. The prospect of marriage threatened the monarchy and prompted Baldwin to engineer Edward's abdication on December 10, 1936, a domestic diplomatic triumph that distracted the public from a failure to address the worsening international situation. On May 28, 1937, Baldwin, in poor health, resigned the ministry in favor of NEVILLE CHAMBERLAIN, was created earl, and spent the rest of his life in retirement.

Further reading: Watts, Duncan. *Stanley Baldwin and the Conservative Ascendancy.* London: Hodder Arnold H&S, 1996; Williamson, Philip. *Stanley Baldwin: Conservative Leadership and National Values.* Cambridge: Cambridge University Press, 1999; Young, Kenneth. *Stanley Baldwin.* London: Weidenfeld & Nicolson, 1976.

balloon bombs

Balloon bombs were something of a curiosity in World War II. As early as 1939, the British attempted to float balloons equipped with incendiary bombs over the German Black Forest. The idea was to start massive forest fires, which would deplete Germany's precious supply of timber. The balloons, however, did not even leave English air space, and when the wind suddenly changed direction, one of the balloons set fire to a farm in East Anglia.

It was the Japanese who made the most extensive use of balloon bombs. Helium-filled and fashioned out of bonded mulberry paper, they were approximately 91 feet in diameter, and they were released by the thousands during November 1944 and March 1945. Japanese climatologists predicted that prevailing winds would carry significant numbers of them over the western United States. They were maintained at the optimum drifting altitude by an ingenious mechanism, which would release

some of the balloon's helium if it floated too high and that would jettison a ballast sandbag if it went too low. Of the thousands deployed, some 200 landed in the American West and Alaska, as well as in Canada and as far south as Mexico. Explosives were suspended beneath each balloon, and detonations resulted in a total of seven deaths, including one woman in Helena, Montana, and six other people in Oregon. Small forest fires were also started but quickly extinguished. American civil defense authorities did not greatly fear the explosive devices, which were small and limited in the damage they could cause, but they were concerned that the Japanese would use the balloons to disseminate deadly bacteria in a desperate campaign of biological warfare. Initially, some officials suspected that the balloons that actually had landed carried biological weapons.

Further reading: Christopher, John. *Balloons at War: Gasbags, Flying Bombs and Cold War Secrets.* London: Tempus, 2004; Mikesh, Robert C. *Japan's World War II Balloon Bomb Attacks on North America.* Washington, D.C.: Smithsonian Books, 1990.

Baltic Sea, action on the

The Baltic Sea is an arm of the North Atlantic, which reaches from the latitude of southern Denmark nearly to the Arctic Circle and separates the Scandinavian Peninsula from the rest of continental Europe. Historically—as it was during World War II—the Baltic has been a strategic waterway, interconnecting many northern European nations. On September 1, 1939, during the INVASION OF POLAND, the Baltic became one of the war's very first battlegrounds, as German ships "visiting" the Baltic port of Gdansk (Danzig) opened fire on the Polish garrisons of the city. The German fleet made quick work of Poland's Baltic Navy, which consisted of only 15 warships, a few nevertheless managing to escape to Great Britain to fight throughout the war at the direction of the London-based Polish government-in-exile.

With the commencement of the RUSSO-FINNISH WAR in November 1939, the Baltic Red Banner

Fleet of the Soviet navy blockaded Finland's sea communications with Sweden and periodically bombarded the Finnish coast. After this, however, the Baltic fell silent until the German navy moved in during June 1941 to prepare for the INVASION OF THE SOVIET UNION. Some 48 minor German surface ships were transferred to the Baltic at this time, reinforcing the small German flotilla already there. Germany also built a naval base at Helsinki, from which it would direct naval action against the Soviets once the invasion began. Another key phase of German preparations was the extensive mining of strategic areas. These minefields caused serious Soviet losses.

After war broke out between Germany and the Soviet Union, the Baltic at first became the scene of numerous surface skirmishes and minor amphibious operations that took islands in the Gulf of Finland and the Gulf of Riga. Soviet forces staged a few amphibious raids on the Finnish mainland, behind German lines, but they were to little avail. In September 1941, Germany sent the great battleship *Tirpitz* at the head of a small Baltic fleet with the intention of blocking Soviet ships from escaping to Sweden after the anticipated fall of LENINGRAD. But because the city withstood the long siege against it, the *Tirpitz* and the rest of the fleet were withdrawn to duty elsewhere.

As for the Soviet Baltic fleet, it was substantial and far superior in numbers to anything the Germans ever dispatched to the area. The Soviet fleet included two obsolescent battleships, two cruisers, 19 destroyers, and 65 submarines in addition to various smaller vessels. Moreover, the Soviet navy operating in the Baltic controlled 656 combat aircraft. Poor command and organization combined with losses to German mines—five destroyers, three submarines, 10 smaller craft, and 42 merchant ships—seemed to paralyze the Soviet Baltic fleet during 1941, so that the force was little used. During 1942, however, the fleet's submarines sank 23 German and Finnish ships for the loss of 10 submarines. Five Swedish ships were also sunk. The Germans soon responded with antisubmarine nets laid across the Gulf of Finland, which excluded

Soviet submarines from the area until September 1944.

At the start of 1944, during January, the Soviet Baltic fleet did achieve a significant tactical and logistical triumph in sealifting and landing, by night, 44,000 Red Army troops from Leningrad to Oranienbaum. Thanks to this operation, Red Army forces were perfectly positioned to aid in lifting the German siege of Leningrad.

In March 1944, the Soviet Baltic fleet commenced minesweeping operations. Vessels came under heavy Luftwaffe attack, but by this point in the war, it was the Soviets, not the Germans, who enjoyed air superiority. Not only were the minefields cleared, but the Luftwaffe suffered heavy losses.

In September 1944, Finland changed allegiance from Germany to the Soviet Union. The Germans responded by attacking Suursaan, a Finnish island in the Gulf of Finland. Acting in concert now, the Soviets and Finns repulsed the attack. Shortly after this, the Soviet Baltic Red Banner Fleet carried out amphibious operations against the German-held islands in the Gulf of Riga.

The NORMANDY LANDINGS (D-DAY) prompted renewed German efforts in the Baltic. All available surface ships and a handful of submarines were dispatched to the Baltic in an effort to impede the advance of the Red Army. The Royal Air Force responded by dropping mines in the western Baltic, but the pocket battleships *Lützow* and *Admiral Scheer,* together with the heavy cruiser *Prinz Eugen,* got through to cover the retreat of German ground forces from the Baltic ports, which were now under siege by Soviet forces. It was a spectacular evacuation, which dwarfed the better-known DUNKIRK EVACUATION. By the end of the war in Europe in May 1945, a million German troops had been rescued, along with 1.5 million civilian refugees. Some 15,000 individuals were lost in the process, most of them victims of Soviet submarine attacks on the rescue ships. Amazingly, despite the many Soviet naval assets in the area, German ships continued to supply the many troops bottled up on the Courtland Peninsula. They did not surrender until the war was over.

Further reading: Chew, Allen F. *The White Death: The Epic of the Soviet-Finnish Winter War.* East Lansing: Michigan State University Press, 2002; Engle, Eloise, and Lauri Paananen. *The Winter War: The Soviet Attack on Finland 1939–1940.* Mechanicsburg, Pa.: Stackpole, 1992; Hiden, John, and Thomas Lane, eds. *The Baltic and the Outbreak of the Second World War.* Cambridge and New York: Cambridge University Press, 1992; Trotter, William R. *A Frozen Hell: The Russo-Finnish Winter War of 1939–40.* Chapel Hill, N.C.: Algonquin Books, 2000.

banzai charge

Banzai is a Japanese word derived from the traditional battle cry of the Japanese warrior, "*Tenno heika banzai,*" "Long Live the Emperor!" In World War II, *banzai* or a *banzai charge* was the term applied to an all-out infantry attack Japanese soldiers employed, en masse, against opponents, regardless of disparity in numbers. Typically, the banzai charge did not come at the beginning of an attack but was the last-ditch, even suicidal, response to imminent defeat. In many Pacific battles, and most notably at SAIPAN, banzai charges were as terrifying and costly as they were, in any tactical sense, futile. It was clear that the purpose of the banzai charge was to salvage military honor, in fulfilment of the Bushido, or ancient warrior code, rather than to achieve a tangible military advantage. For the traditional Japanese warrior—and, apparently, the majority of World War II Japanese soldiers—death in combat was infinitely preferable to surrender as a prisoner of war. The single-word exclamation *Banzai!* was also used as a victory cheer, *after* an objective had been achieved or a battle won.

Further reading: Cleary, Thomas. *Code of the Samurai: A Modern Translation of the Bushido Shoshinsu.* Rutland, Vt.: Tuttle Publishing, 1999; Harries, Meirion, and Susie Harries. *Soldiers of the Sun: The Rise and Fall of the Imperial Japanese Army.* New York: Random House, 1994.

Barbie, Klaus (1913–1991) *Gestapo chief in Lyon, France*

Dubbed the "Butcher of Lyon" because of his role in the deportation and execution of French Jews, resistance partisans, and others while he was chief of the Gestapo in Lyon from 1942 to 1944, Barbie proved highly adept at escaping postwar prosecution for his crimes and, with such figures as ADOLF EICHMANN, became a symbol for the pursuit of justice for, and remembrance of, the horrors of the HOLOCAUST. It is believed that Barbie was directly responsible for the deaths of approximately 4,000 and the deportation of an additional 7,500 persons.

Born in Bad Godesberg, Germany, Barbie became, like many German boys, a member of the HITLER YOUTH. Proving especially enthusiastic, he joined in 1935 the Sicherheitsdienst—the SD, or Security Service—of the SCHUTZSTAFFEL (SS). The SD was closely related to the GESTAPO, the Nazi secret police, and Barbie was seconded, or transferred, from the SD to the Gestapo while serving in the conquered Netherlands during the early phases of Germany's western European campaign. In 1942, he was promoted to chief of Gestapo Department IV in Lyon, France.

As Gestapo chief, Barbie was responsible for suppressing the work of the French Resistance and for carrying out the deportation (for transportation to CONCENTRATION AND EXTERMINATION CAMPS) of Jews and other "undesirables." Barbie was especially zealous and not only authorized the extensive use of torture of prisoners, but, during interrogations, typically administered the torture personally. He also ordered the execution of thousands accused of resistance activity or of supporting such activity. Among his victims were many women and children. Most infamously, Barbie was accused, after the war, of having personally ordered the deportation of 44 Jewish children, ages three to 13, together with their five teachers, to AUSCHWITZ, where they were all subsequently murdered. Barbie also arrested the French Resistance leader Jean Moulin, whom he and his men tortured with the utmost barbarity, forcing red-hot needles under his fingernails and breaking his knuckles by putting his fingers through the hinged side of a door and repeatedly slamming it shut. His wrists were broken with screw-levered handcuffs, and he was whipped and beaten. He refused to betray any of his resistance associates and finally slipped into a coma. In this state, Barbie exhibited him to other resistance leaders who were under interrogation at Gestapo headquarters. Indeed, Barbie kept Moulin on display in an office adjacent to his, his comatose body laid out on a chaise lounge. He soon died from his injuries. For his "work" with Moulin, Barbie was awarded—in person, by ADOLF HITLER—the Iron Cross, First Class, with Swords.

After the war, Klaus Barbie was arrested. Despite the western Allies' official policy of "denazification," Barbie was seen as a valuable intelligence asset and worked for the British in counterintelligence until 1947, when he was recruited by American counterintelligence agents to penetrate communist cells in the German Communist Party. American officials quietly shielded Barbie from prosecution for war crimes, and, with American aid, he avoided arrest in France in 1950 and was resettled in Bolivia with his wife and children. From 1951, he lived as a businessman in the South American country under the name Klaus Altmann. The "Nazi hunters" Beate and Serge Klarsfeld identified him in Bolivia about 1971, and a movement was begun to bring about his extradition to France. Extradition negotiations with the Bolivian government dragged on before he was finally extradited in February 1983. In August of that year, the United States made a formal apology to France for having aided in Barbie's escape.

Although postwar French military tribunals had twice sentenced Barbie to death, he was not brought to trial again until July 3, 1987. During this proceeding, Barbie expressed no remorse. Convicted of crimes against humanity, he was sentenced to life imprisonment and died on September 25, 1991, in prison of cancer.

Further reading: Beattie, John. *The Life and Career of Klaus Barbie: An Eyewitness Record.* London: Methuen, 1984; Dabringhaus, Erhard. *Klaus Barbie: The Shocking Story of How the U.S. Used This Nazi War Criminal As an Intelligence Agent.* New York: Acropolis Books, 1984; Murphy, Brendan. *The Butcher of Lyon: The Story of Infamous Nazi Klaus Barbie.* New York: HarperCollins, 1983; Ophuls, Marcel. *Hotel Terminus: The Life and Times of Klaus Barbie.* New York: Holiday House, 2004; Paris, Erna. *Unhealed Wounds: France and the Klaus Barbie Affair.* Berkeley, Calif.: Publishers Group West, 1986.

barrage balloon

Barrage balloons were unmanned, tethered, blimp-like, lighter-than-air craft employed as a defense against low-flying enemy aircraft. Their tethers were made of stout wire cable, which presented a significant hazard to airplanes flying low for strafing or dive bombing attacks. Both the Allies and the Axis used them, generally deploying them above vulnerable or valuable targets, including buildings and ships. They were especially widely deployed throughout Great Britain, including during the BATTLE OF BRITAIN, where they proved quite effective. During February–March 1941, barrage balloons were responsible for the loss of seven German aircraft. With the introduction of the unmanned V-1 buzz bomb, barrage balloons were even more effective, accounting for the loss of 231 of the missiles before the end of the war.

U.S. forces experimented with deploying barrage balloons in the Pacific at BOUGAINVILLE in November 1943, when they were flown above LANDING CRAFT. However, rather than protecting the landing craft, the balloons tended to betray the position of the vessels to Japanese reconnaissance flights, and their use was immediately discontinued.

Further reading: Slonaker, Arthur Gordon. *Recollections and Reflections of a College Dean: Including a Brief History of the 103rd Barrage Balloon Battery.* Parsons, W. Va.: McClain Printing, 1975; Wetzel, Frank R. *Victory Gardens and Barrage Balloons: A Collective Memoir.* Hallowell, Me.: Perry Publishing, 1995.

Bataan, Death March

After the FALL OF BATAAN during the Japanese conquest of the PHILIPPINES, approximately 2,000 defenders of Bataan managed to withdraw to CORREGIDOR; the rest, about 78,000 U.S. Army and Filipino troops, were left behind and became prisoners of the Japanese. The Japanese code of military conduct, founded on ancient warrior (Bushido) traditions, regarded surrender as dishonorable and therefore sanctioned, even encouraged, the abuse of prisoners in flagrant and unapologetic violation of the Geneva Conventions. The treatment of the Bataan prisoners was an especially horrific demonstration of this warrior code.

Japanese lieutenant general Homma Masaharu decided to transport the Bataan prisoners to a captured American camp, Camp O'Donnell, which became a Japanese prisoner of war camp. Accordingly, on April 9, 1942, the prisoners, who were in a state of semistarvation, having endured a long siege on half rations, were started out from Mariveles, on the southern end of the Bataan Peninsula, and were marched 55 miles to San Fernando, where they were put on trains to Capas, then marched an additional 8 miles to Camp O'Donnell.

The jungle climate was extremely hot and humid and the terrain difficult. Prisoners who faltered, collapsed, or otherwise fell behind were executed, typically by bayonet. Prisoners were frequently beaten, apparently at random. They were often denied food and water for days. During "rest periods," prisoners were typically forced to sit in the full sun without helmets or water. Sleep periods were a few hours long, the prisoners jammed into enclosures that allowed virtually no movement. Those who survived to reach the railhead at Capas were loaded into stifling boxcars.

The entire progress to Camp O'Donnell took more than a week to complete. Some 54,000 men reached the camp, 7,000 to 10,000 having died on the way, the rest having escaped into the jungle. Some of these men survived to fight alongside Filipino guerrillas.

Homma, overall commander of Japanese invasion forces in the Philippines, formally surrendered himself to U.S. forces in Tokyo on September 14, 1945, and was tried in December for war crimes. Subsequently remanded to the authority of a U.S. military commission in Manila, Philippines, he was tried there during January–February 1946 and convicted of having authorized the Bataan Death March and its attendant atrocities. He was executed on April 3, 1946.

Further reading: Bollich, James. *Bataan Death March: A Soldier's Story.* Gretna, La.: Pelican. 2003; Boyt, Gene. *Bataan: A Survivor's Story.* Norman: University of Oklahoma Press, 2004; Duggan, William J. *Silence of a Soldier: The Memoirs of a Bataan Death March Survivor.* Oakland, Or.: Elderberry Press, 2003; Dyess, William E. *Bataan Death March: A Survivor's Account.* Lincoln: University of Nebraska Press, 2002; Falk, Stanley L. *Bataan: March of Death.* New York: Jove Books, 1985; Knox, Donald. *Death March: The Survivors of Bataan.* New York: Harvest Books, 2002; Tenney, Lester I. *My Hitch in Hell: The Bataan Death March.* New York: Brassey's, 2000.

American prisoners on the Bataan Death March *(Library of Congress)*

Bataan, fall of

During the battle for the Philippines at the beginning of the war in the Pacific, Lt. Gen. Douglas MacArthur led his forces in an organized retreat to the Bataan Peninsula on the island of Luzon. Here, 67,500 Filipino troops (under MacArthur's command), together with 12,500 U.S. personnel and 26,000 civilians, made their last defensive stand against the Japanese onslaught in the hope and expectation of the imminent arrival of a U.S. relief force, which, in fact, never came.

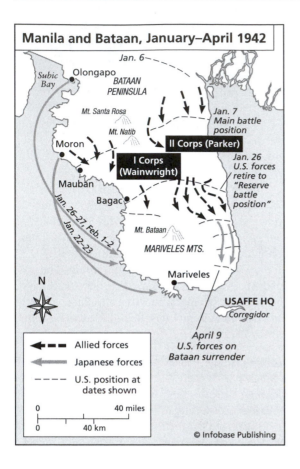

Manila and Bataan, January–April 1942

Subic Bay

Olongapo

BATAAN PENINSULA

Jan. 6

Mt. Santa Rosa

Mt. Natib

Moron

II Corps (Parker)

Jan. 7 Main battle position

I Corps (Wainwright)

Jan. 26 U.S. forces retire to "Reserve battle position"

Mauban

Bagac

Jan. 26-27, Feb. 1-2

Jan. 22-23

Mt. Bataan

MARIVELES MTS.

N

Mariveles

USAFFE HQ

Corregidor

April 9 U.S. forces on Bataan surrender

Allied forces

Japanese forces

U.S. position at dates shown

0   40 miles

0   40 km

© Infobase Publishing

After declaring the Philippine capital, Manila, an open city, MacArthur began the withdrawal to Bataan on December 24, 1941, and set up his headquarters at Corregidor, on the tip of the peninsula. On the face of it, at least as the Japanese saw it, the withdrawal to a narrow peninsula—25 miles long and 20 miles wide at its widest—was not only futile but a tactical error. The American and Filipino forces, after all, had entered a cul de sac, and the Japanese anticipated a quick and easy victory. What the Japanese commanders had not reckoned on was the rugged countryside, which made Bataan ideal defensive ground, and the fact that MacArthur had prepared for a siege by stockpiling ammunition, medical supplies, and provisions, though the latter were inadequate, and from the beginning the defenders were forced to subsist on meager half-rations.

The overall commander of the Japanese forces in the Philippines was Gen. Homma Masaharu. As he was about to launch his offensive against Bataan, he was compelled to withdraw his most experienced division for the invasion of the Dutch East Indies. This bothered Homma little, however, since he believed taking Bataan would require little effort. He assigned his Kimura Detachment and a raw unit, the 65th Brigade, to the task. They attacked on January 9, 1942, breaking through MacArthur's first line of defenders but becoming bogged down in the secondary line, to which two defending corps withdrew. Homma attempted a landing behind the American lines but was repulsed at heavy cost. After a month of fighting, on February 8, Homma aborted the offensive. He had lost 2,700 men killed and more than 4,000 wounded. The miserable jungle conditions had made another 13,000 too sick to fight. In effect, his entire attacking force had been neutralized.

On March 11, President Franklin D. Roosevelt ordered MacArthur to evacuate the Philippines with his family. With great reluctance, MacArthur left for Australia, and it fell to his second in command, Maj. Gen. Jonathan Wainwright, to resume the Bataan defense. Unless a relief force arrived, Wainwright knew his position was hopeless. Critically short on rations, his troops were near starvation. As the realization set in that no relief was to be sent, the morale of the debilitated defenders collapsed, and when Homma, reinforced, attacked again on April 3, 1942, the issue was a foregone conclusion. Ordered by MacArthur not to surrender, Wainwright mounted a counterattack, which, predictably, failed. Wainwright's front-line commander, Maj. Gen. Edward King, took it upon himself to order the surrender of his command rather than witness their fruitless slaughter. He capitulated to Homma on April 9. The fall of Bataan was complete—except for the infamous coda known as the Bataan Death March, the inhuman trek across 65 jungle miles from Mariveles to a prisoner of war camp at San Fernando.

Further reading: Astor, Gerald. *Crisis in the Pacific: The Battles for the Philippine Islands by the Men Who Fought*

Them. New York: Dell, 2002; Connaughton, Richard. *MacArthur and Defeat in the Philippines.* New York: Overlook Press, 2001; Johnson, Joseph Quitman. *Baby of Bataan: Memoir of a Fourteen-Year-Old Soldier in World War II.* Memphis, Tenn.: Omonomany, 2004; Morris, Eric. *Corregidor: The Nightmare in the Philippines.* New York: Random House, 1982.

battleships

As in World War I, the World War II battleship was a colossal, heavily armored, long-range, reasonably fast platform for massed naval artillery fire. In World War I, the battleship was without question the capital ship of the world's great navies, as it had been from about the mid-1860s. The battleship entered World War II enjoying that status, but, in the course of the war, it yielded in importance to AIRCRAFT CARRIERS, whose planes could project firepower more deeply, flexibly, and effectively than the artillery fire of the battleship. Indeed, aircraft and SUBMARINES rendered battleships increasingly vulnerable, so that they were sometimes combat liabilities, requiring extensive escort protection, rather than assets. By the end of World War II, the battleship was entering obsolescence. This fact aside, battleships remained impressive and formidable presences throughout the war, combining size, mighty guns, and heavy armor. The World War II battleship could hit targets more than 20 miles away, which made them valuable not only against other ships but especially in providing prelanding and preinvasion bombardment in amphibious operations.

The World War II battleship traces its lineage directly to the British HMS *Dreadnought* of 1906. This quantum leap forward in battleship design introduced steam-turbine propulsion and an artillery complement that did away with medium guns altogether and mounted only 10 to 12-inch guns. Although big and heavy, the *Dreadnought* was immensely seaworthy, capable of making better than 20 knots. As the era of World War II approached, the *Dreadnought*-class battleship evolved into the even more formidable "superdreadnought," which mounted guns of 16-inch and even 18-inch caliber.

A superdreadnought might displace as much as 40,000 tons, but the Washington Naval Treaty of 1922, an international attempt at arms limitation, limited new battleships to 35,000 tons. Designers made the best of this limitation by focusing their efforts on attaining speed without sacrificing the dreadnought-style heavy guns and heavy armor. The posttreaty generation of battleships was capable of making better than 30 knots, easily matching the speed of modern CRUISERS.

On the eve of World War II, the great powers abrogated the Washington Naval Treaty, and began building ever larger ships. Germany built two *Bismarck*-class vessels, each displacing 52,600 tons, while the Japanese built the world's largest battleships, the 72,000-ton *Yamato* class. The new U.S. battleships, of the *Iowa* class, displaced 45,000 tons. While the big-gun policy still dominated battleship design, these weapons were liberally supplemented with antiaircraft defense in the form of rapid-fire 5-inch guns and myriad automatic guns in the 20-mm to 40-mm category mounted strategically throughout the ship.

During World War II, the British Royal Navy fleet included 20 battleships (including two smaller battleships, often called battle cruisers). France entered the war with two battleships. Germany had two very large battleships, the *Bismarck* and the *Tirpitz,* and five smaller battleships, known as pocket battleships. Italy entered the war with six battleships. Japan had a dozen battleships, of which 10 were operational during the war, including the *Yamato* and *Musashi,* by far the largest battleships ever built. The United States entered the war with 15 pre-1921 battleships and two built in the 1930s. The BATTLE OF PEARL HARBOR resulted in sinking or severely damaging eight of these vessels. During the war, between 1942 and 1944, five ships of the *Iowa* class were added to the American battleship fleet. The Soviet Union had no battleships.

Although battleship design varied, the USS *Iowa* may be taken as an example of the state of the art during World War II. During the war years, its general specifications included:

Displacement, light: 45,231 tons
Displacement, full: 57,271 tons

Dead weight: 12,040 tons
Length, overall: 888 feet
Length, waterline: 860 feet
Beam, extreme: 109 feet
Beam, waterline: 108 feet
Maximum navigational draft: 38 feet
Draft limit: 37 feet
Maximum speed: 35 knots
Power plant: Eight boilers, four geared turbines, four shafts, 212,000 shaft horsepower
Armament: nine 16-inch guns, 20 6-inch guns, 60 40-mm antiaircraft mounts, and 60 20-mm antiaircraft mounts
Aircraft: The ships could launch and recover three Vought Kingfisher floatplanes
Crew: 1,921 officers and sailors

Each major combatant's battleships are discussed further in France, Navy of; Germany, Navy of; Great Britain, Navy of; Italy, Navy of; and Japan, Navy of.

Further reading: Dulin, Robert O., Jr. *Battleships: Allied Battleships of World War II.* Annapolis. Md.: Naval Institute Press, 1980; Garzke, William H., Jr., and Robert O. Dulin, Jr. *Battleships: United States Battleships, 1935–1992.* Annapolis, Md.: Naval Institute Press, 1995; Hore, Peter. *Battleships.* London: Lorenz Books, 2004; Skulski, Janusz. *The Battleship Yamato.* Annapolis, Md.: Naval Institute Press, 1989; Whitley, M. J. *Battleships of World War Two: An International Encyclopedia.* Annapolis, Md.: Naval Institute Press, 1999; Worth, Richard. *Fleets of World War II.* New York: Da Capo, 2002.

bazooka

During the early 1930s, the U.S. Army began experimenting with a variety of close-range antitank weapons for use by the infantry. Initially, the hope was to develop an antitank rifle, but when these efforts proved unsatisfactory, weapons specialists at the Aberdeen (Maryland) Proving Grounds began working with shaped-charge warheads. This ammunition was developed and stockpiled on the eve of American entry into World War II, but what was still lacking was the actual weapon to fire these rounds. Early in 1942, conventional mortar tubes were modified to fire the shaped-charge projectile. The result was codified in the Rocket Launcher M1, which went into production later in the year. It was almost immediately christened the bazooka, because it resembled a folk musical instrument, a kind of primitive trombone, that had been popularized by 1930s radio comedian Bob Burns.

The bazooka is a very simple weapon that can be fired by a single soldier, although it is preferable to serve the weapon with two: a gunner (who aims and fires) and a loader (who prepares and loads the ammunition). The weapon is nothing more than a steel tube, 60 mm in diameter and open at both ends. The ammunition is a small, fin-stabilized, rocket-propelled grenade, which the loader inserts into the rear of the tube while the gunner rests the weapon on his shoulder. The trigger is an electric switch that closes a circuit, passing an electric current that ignites the ammunition's rocket stage.

The original M1 bazooka consisted of a one-piece tube and a trigger mechanism powered by two batteries located inside the wooden shoulder rest. A small lamp on the left side of the shoulder rest indicated the on-off status of the weapon. The weapon was fitted with a two-piece iron sight and fired a projectile 55 cm in length, capable of penetrating more than 100 mm of armor. In addition to the standard armor-piercing rounds, smoke and incendiary warheads were also available. Beginning in 1943, Bazooka M1A1 replaced the M1 model. Key improvements included a more accurate sight and a distinctive funnel-shaped muzzle, which protected the gunner from the backblast of the exiting projectile. The next year, Bazooka M9 replaced M1A1. The new weapon consisted of a two-piece tube manufactured out of light metal. Because it could be broken into its two constituent pieces, it was more conveniently portable. The batteries, which had proven to be somewhat unreliable, were replaced by a small generator, and the gunsight was greatly improved. The wooden shoulder stock was replaced by a metal one. The Germans captured a bazooka during the Tunisia Campaign in 1943 and used it as the basis for the design of their own infantry antitank weapon, the *Raketenpanzerbüchse.*

Specifications for the M1A1 included:

Caliber: 60 mm
Length: 4 feet 6.5 inches
Weight: launcher, 13.25 pounds; ammunition, 3.4 pounds
Range: 650 yards
Muzzle velocity: 270 feet per second
Armor penetration: 119.4 mm

Further reading: Chamberlain, Peter. *Anti-Tank Weapons.* New York: Arco, 1974; Gander, Terry. *Anti-Tank Weapons.* Ramsbury, U.K.: Crowood Press, 2000; Norris John, and James Marchington, eds., *Anti-Tank Weapons.* New York: Brassey's, 2003.

Belgium

At the time of World War II, Belgium was a constitutional monarchy with 8.2 million people. It had been devastated in World War I, despite its declared neutrality and, at the outbreak of World War II, again proclaimed itself a neutral. However, the Belgian government also declared its resolute intention to defend itself against attack and invasion from whatever quarter. Initially, to assert both its neutrality and sovereignty, Belgian Army troops were deployed along the French as well as German frontiers. However, during November 1939 and January 1940, invasion alerts made it clear that France presented no threat, and all troops were transferred to the German border. British-supplied intelligence put the Belgian forces on heightened alert, and the invasion, code named by the Germans Fall Gelb, was not a surprise when it came on May 10, 1940. The Belgians even entertained a reasonable hope of repelling the invaders. Their most formidable fortress, Eban Emael, which guarded the Albert Canal, was considered a great bulwark against invasion and was judged to be almost certainly impregnable. What the Belgians had not considered, however, was an AIRBORNE ASSAULT, which was made on May 10 and which reached the fort from above, where it was, in fact, quite vulnerable. The fall of the fort allowed the main body of German invaders to cross into Belgian territory, and the nation's armed forces, some 600,000 men, were rapidly overwhelmed.

King Leopold and his principal ministers met to discuss the situation. The ministers advised the king to flee to France and to continue the struggle in exile. Leopold, however, resolved to remain in Belgium and share the fate of his troops. He negotiated a surrender on May 28, then withdrew to his palace in a self-imposed internal exile. Breaking with their king, the principal ministers traveled to France and there proclaimed Leopold unable to reign because he was a prisoner. A parliament in exile was held at Limoges on May 31, and the rift between king and government deepened. When the BATTLE OF FRANCE ended in the fall of France, the ministers returned to Belgium in the hope of patching up relations with the king. Leopold refused to see them, and asserted that the war between Germany and Belgium had come to an end. Leopold's aim was to negotiate with the occupiers, avoid further bloodshed, and salvage in the process some degree of independence.

On November 19, 1940, Leopold met with ADOLF HITLER at BERCHTESGADEN and sought guarantees of independence. Hitler refused any definitive answer, and Leopold returned to Belgium, refusing to recognize or communicate with the leaders of the Belgian government-in-exile now located in London. In the meantime, popular support for the king declined, and, in June 1944, German authorities deported him to the Reich.

In the absence of any real government, the German occupiers then annexed to the Reich the frontier cantons of Eupen, Malmédy, and St. Vith. Prior to World War I, these had been part of Germany and had been ceded to Belgium by the terms of the TREATY OF VERSAILLES. As for the rest of Belgium, it was grouped together with the French departments of Nord and Pas-de-Calais under a WEHRMACHT military government called the *Militärverwaltung* under the administrative direction of Eggert Reeder. In July 1944, this military administration was replaced by a German-run civil administration, the *Zilverwaltung.*

Under Reeder, the occupation was typically brutal. Suppression of the underground (*see* RESISTANCE MOVEMENTS) was vigorous, and, in general, a policy of reprisals for partisan attacks was instituted, with 100 civilian hostages to be executed for every German soldier or official killed by partisans. Hitler, in July 1940, ordered Reeder to make some accommodations to garner the support of the Germanic Flemish population but to treat the French-speaking Walloons more harshly. However, Reeder had to work with a minimum of manpower, and he also had to take steps to secure from all Belgians a level of industrial productivity to aid the German war effort. These requirements led to a number of accommodations. Nevertheless, friction and conflict frequently developed between Belgian civil servants, who had assumed much authority in the absence of a government, and military administrators.

Among Belgium's economic elite, including its bankers and industrialists, the drive to cooperate with the occupiers was strong. There was profit to be made from feeding the German war machine. Nevertheless, these elite groups also sought to maintain a degree of economic independence from Germany.

Finally, in addition to civil servants and economic elites, another group was a powerful force in occupied Belgium: the Catholic Church. The military occupiers adopted a mostly hands-off policy where the clergy was concerned and also relegated the conduct of the educational system to the church.

The Belgian underground was a strong presence in the country. In the beginning, organized resistance grew from a core of those who had masterminded anti-German activities during World War I. As the possibility of ultimate German defeat became increasingly real, the Belgian resistance movement grew rapidly, some, though not all of it, organized by the Belgian Communist Party. Belgian resistance was not organized solely to sabotage German war efforts. A great deal of the underground was dedicated to developing and maintaining intelligence networks to supply the Allies with information and also with developing networks, lines, and safe houses to aid in the escape of downed Allied airmen.

Somewhat less significant were the Belgian armed forces in exile. They were very small in

number, amounting only to about 3,000 men, of whom only some 1,600 had arms and equipment. A Belgian battalion was organized at Tenby, Wales, and participated in Allied efforts to liberate Belgium. Some 300 Belgians also served in small commando units and in units of the SPECIAL AIR SERVICE (SAS). In terms of numbers, about 40,000 colonial troops in the Belgian Congo remained under Allied control throughout the war and served in Africa. After the liberation of Belgium, they constituted more than half the 75,000-man new Belgian army that was quickly formed to fight in the closing months of the war.

In addition to resistance groups in Belgium, there were pro-German collaborationist factions, the most important of which were Flemish nationalists, who secured government positions under the Nazis. Even among the Walloons, a group known as the Légion Wallonie, though French speaking, enthusiastically espoused Nazi ideology and served not only in collaboration with the SCHUTZSTAFFEL (SS) within Belgium but also against the Soviets on the eastern front.

In general, even Belgians who neither resisted nor collaborated with the German occupiers suffered the same privations the populations of other occupied countries endured, including severe shortages of food, fuel, and clothing. The process of liberation caused many civilian casualties and much damage, as Allied bombers attacked railway junctions, bridges, factories, and other facilities essential to the German war effort. Some 70,000 Walloons were held as prisoners of war throughout the conflict, and Belgium's Jewish population did not escape the horrors of the HOLOCAUST. Immediately after the occupation, German authorities instituted anti-Jewish laws and ordinances, which restricted civil rights, confiscated property and businesses, and banned Jews from most professions. Beginning in 1942, all Jews were required to wear a yellow Star of David. Many Belgian Jews were arrested and consigned to forced labor, mostly in the construction of military fortifications in northern France, but also in clothing and armaments factories and Belgian stone quarries. Between 65,000 and 70,000 Jews lived in Belgium, mostly in the major cities of Antwerp and Brussels. Most of these Jews were from Poland and had found refuge in Belgium after World War I. Because many Belgians aided Jews and resisted attempts to arrest them, and because Belgian civil servants generally refused to cooperate with deportation orders, more than 25,000 Jews managed to avoid deportation. Nevertheless, between 1942 and 1944, German military police deported almost 25,000 Jews from Belgium via intermediate camps at Breendonk and Mechelen to AUSCHWITZ, where most were killed. Fewer than 2,000 of those deported survived the Holocaust.

As mentioned, popular support for King Leopold waned early in the war and, concomitantly, support for the government in exile grew. By 1941, most Belgians recognized the exiled ministers as the legitimate Belgian government.

The liberation of Belgium began late in summer 1944, and most of the country had been liberated by early September of that year. Because King Leopold had been deported by the Germans in June 1944, his brother, Prince Charles, was quickly installed as regent. Hubert Pierlot, prime minister before the war and head of the government in exile, returned to Belgium once again as its prime minister until he resigned in February 1945 and was replaced by Achille van Acker, a socialist. Leading problems for the new government, aside from feeding and caring for the population, were how to deal with collaborators and what to do with the king. The first problem was never resolved to everyone's satisfaction, and, as for the king, no agreement was reached between him and van Acker concerning his return to the throne. He spent the rest of his life in Swiss exile, failing in the 1950s in a bid to regain power.

Further reading: de Bruyne, Eddy, and Marc Rikmenspoel. *For Rex and for Belgium: Leon Degrelle and Walloon Political & Military Collaboration 1940–45.* Solihul, U.K.: Helion, 2004; Cook, Bernard A. *Belgium: A History.* New York: Peter Lang, 2002; Eisner, Peter. *The Freedom Line: The Brave Men and Women Who Rescued Allied Airmen from the Nazis During World War II.* New York: William Morrow, 2004; Files, Yvonne De Ridder.

The Quest for Freedom: Belgian Resistance in World War II. McKinleyville, Calif.: Fithian Press, 1991.

Belorussia

Before it became the independent nation of Belarus in 1991, Belorussia—White Russia—was the smallest of the three Slavic republics of the Soviet Union, covering an area of 80,153 square miles. Belorussia was bordered on the northwest by LATVIA and LITHUANIA and by Russia on the northeast and the east. Its southern border was Ukraine. Before the GERMAN-SOVIET NON-AGGRESSION PACT was concluded, Belorussia had been divided between Poland and the Soviet Union, of which it was the Belorussian Soviet Socialist Republic (SSR). Pursuant to the pact and after the German INVASION OF POLAND, the western region was annexed to the Soviet Union. The capital city, Minsk, was in the Belorussian SSR. The total population of Belorussia was 8 million as the war commenced, consisting of a White Ruthenian (or Belorussian) majority and three principal minorities: Poles, Jews, and Russians. In addition to Minsk, Grodno, Bialystok, and Pinsk were the major cities. Sophisticated industrial and commercial centers, they were culturally and economically influenced by the Jewish minority. Beyond the cities was a swampy and thickly forested hinterland populated by the Belorussian agricultural peasantry.

Because of its location on the Soviet Union's western border, Belorussia suffered the first terrible impact of the German BLITZKRIEG, and the region was occupied by German forces for three full years. The conquerors incorporated Belorussia into what they called Reich Commissariat Ostland and immediately set about establishing ghettos into which Belorussian Jews were herded and held until they could be sent to CONCENTRATION AND EXTERMINATION CAMPS. The RESISTANCE MOVEMENT was extensive in Belorussia, with partisans highly active. Their objective was not only to make life difficult for the invaders of Belorussia, but, because the region was the principal communication and supply conduit between Germany and the interior of the Soviet Union, the partisans also focused on disrupting the entire ongoing invasion operation. For their part, the Germans fully recognized the stakes Belorussia represented. They responded fiercely and brutally to partisan attacks, exacting disproportionate reprisals against the civilian population for every attack. Many Belorussians were killed or deported to the Reich to work as slave labor in German war production factories.

As if conditions were not bad enough in Belorussia, the eastern portion of the republic entered World War II having already suffered a decade of ravage by the Soviets, who waged an undeclared but massively brutal war against Belorussian nationalists and who violently enforced the collectivization of farms. This history worked against Belorussia when it was reoccupied by the Red Army during January–July 1944. As the Nazi oppressors were pushed out, the Soviet "liberators" resumed the program of forced Sovietization and purges that had been interrupted by the outbreak of war. The Belorussian SSR was one of the Soviet republics for which JOSEPH STALIN managed to secure separate United Nations membership following World War II. This, however, was of no benefit to Belorussia itself, which had, in fact, no real independence, nor did the central Soviet government acknowledge Belorussia's war losses. Most likely to conceal the terrible toll taken by the agents of Sovietization, the government never officially calculated Belorussian casualties. Most historians believe civilian deaths were approximately 2 million, that is, a staggering 25 percent of the Belorussian population.

Further reading: Cholawsky, Shalom. *Jews of Bielorussia During World War II*. New York: Harwood Academic Publishers, 1997; Glantz, David M., and Harold S. Orenstein. *Belorussia 1944: The Soviet General Staff Study*. London: Frank Cass, 2001; Gross, Jan Tomasz. *Revolution from Abroad: The Soviet Conquest of Poland's Western Ukraine and Western Belorussia*. Princeton, N.J.: Princeton University Press, 2002; Munoz, Antonio, and Oleg V. Romanko. *Hitler's White Russians: Collaboration, Extermination and Anti-Partisan Warfare in Byelorussia, 1941–1944*. Chicago: Europa Books, 2003.

Belzec extermination camp

Belzec began as a labor camp in April 1940, on the Lublin-Lvov railway line, about 100 miles southeast of Warsaw. In November 1941, construction was started to convert Belzec to a death camp. As built, the camp's extermination section consisted of a wooden building housing three gas chambers for administering lethal doses of carbon monoxide. Later, this building was replaced by a brick-and-concrete structure housing six gas chambers. Belzec began full-scale operations on March 17, 1942.

The camp was small, only about 1,220 yards in circumference, and this space was divided into two sections, each surrounded by a barbed wire fence. One section was divided into a small area containing the administration buildings and a barracks for Ukrainian guards. The larger section included a railway siding, where the incoming "deportees" were separated by sex and age, and the barracks, where they were stripped and robbed of their personal property. This section also contained huts for Jewish workers employed by the SCHUTZSTAFFEL (SS) to assist in the process of mass extermination. The second section of the camp contained the gas chambers and the mass burial pits. The extermination area was hidden from the view of the rest of the camp by leafy branches intertwined in the barbed wire fencing.

At the height of operations, the camp's six gas chambers killed 1,200 persons at a time. Before the camp ended operations and was razed in December 1942, it is estimated that some 600,000 Jews and at least 12,000 Gypsies were murdered here.

See also CONCENTRATION AND EXTERMINATION CAMPS; FINAL SOLUTION; and HOLOCAUST, THE.

Further reading: Arad, Yitzhak. *Belzec, Sobibor, Treblinka: The Operation Reinhard Death Camps*. Bloomington: Indiana University Press, 1999.

Beneš, Edvard (1884–1948) *Czech president forced to cede the Sudetenland to Germany*

One of the founders of modern CZECHOSLOVAKIA after World War I, Beneš capitulated to ADOLF

Hitler's demands during the 1938 Sudetenland crisis and the larger Czech crisis that followed. Beneš was educated in Prague as well as in Paris and Dijon, an experience that nurtured in him a strong identification with western Europe. He was a professor at the Prague Commercial Academy and the Czech University of Prague in the years before World War I. During this period, Beneš became an admirer and adherent of the Czech nationalist Tomáš Masaryk, who sought to liberate both the Czechs and Slovaks from the Austro-Hungarian Empire. During World War I, Beneš followed Masaryk to Switzerland, then moved to Paris, where, with Masaryk and the Slovak nationalist Milan Štefánik, he created a propaganda organization that evolved into the Czechoslovak provisional government on October 14, 1918, the eve of collapse of the Austro-Hungarian Empire. With the armistice in November 1918, Beneš and the others were fully prepared to install the government of a new Czechoslovak state.

In the new government, the urbane Beneš became foreign minister, a post he held until 1935 and in which he served as head of the Czech delegation to the Paris Peace Conference in 1919, which drafted the Treaty of Versailles and founded the League of Nations. Beneš was an enthusiastic champion of the doomed league, serving as its council chairman for six terms. He was fearful that a union between Austria and Germany, in the offing from the end of World War I, would ultimately swallow up Czechoslovakia, and he worked toward establishing a favorable balance of power in eastern Europe. In 1921, Beneš negotiated treaties with Romania and Yugoslavia, forming with them the so-called Little Entente. The original purpose of the alliance was to keep Hungary in check, but when France joined in 1924, it became an alliance against Germany and, to some degree, against the Soviet Union as well. As the German threat loomed larger and larger under the Nazi regime, Beneš in 1935 signed a mutual assistance pact between Czechoslovakia and the Soviet Union.

Masaryk resigned as Czechoslovakia's president in 1935, and Beneš was elected to replace him. He entered office at a time of worsening relations with Poland and Germany. When Hitler demanded the autonomy of the largely German-speaking Czech Sudetenland region, Beneš agreed, in the hope that doing so would appease Hitler (*see* Appeasement policy). Of course, it did not, and Germany was, with the acquiescence of Britain and France (the latter in direct contravention of the Little Entente alliance), entirely relinquished the Sudentenland in September 1938. Almost immediately following this, Poland occupied the disputed Teschen area, and Germany soon swallowed up the rest of Czechoslovakia whole.

Beneš resigned as president on October 5, 1938, and went into exile. With the outbreak of war, he created in France a Czechoslovak national committee, the seed of a government in exile, which he was compelled to move to London in 1940 as France fell. Shortly before V-E day, on April 3, 1945, Beneš returned the exiled government to Czech soil, then personally entered Prague on May 16 as head of the only eastern European government allowed to return from exile after the war. Any sense of triumph Beneš may have felt, however, was tempered by his awareness of the necessity of compromising with the Soviet Union. Beneš was in poor condition to negotiate. Fatigued from the stresses of the war and his exile, his health deteriorated and, in 1947, he suffered two strokes. On February 25, 1948, the Soviets acted through Beneš's own Communist prime minister, Klement Gottwald, who compelled Beneš to accept a Communist-dominated cabinet. Nevertheless, he refused to sign a new Communist constitution and instead resigned on June 7, 1948. He died in September, shortly after the suicide of Jan Masaryk, his lifelong friend and the son of his political idol and mentor, Tomáš Masaryk.

Further reading: Beneš, Edvard, and Milan Hauner. *The Fall and Rise of a Nation: Czechoslovakia 1938–1941.* Boulder, Colo.: East European Monographs, 2004; Korbel, Josef. *Twentieth-Century Czechoslovakia: The Meanings of Its History.* New York: Columbia University Press, 1977.

Berchtesgaden

Berchtesgaden is a town in southern Bavaria on the border with Austria. Although Berchtesgaden itself is nestled in a deep valley, it lent its name to ADOLF HITLER's retreat, officially known as the Berghof, on the Obersalzberg, 1,640 feet above the town. Also perched on the Obersalzberg were chalets occupied by HERMANN GÖRING and MARTIN BORMANN, among other top-ranking Nazis. To all appearances a large holiday retreat, the Berghof was often used by Hitler for important conferences, including that with Austrian chancellor KURT VON SCHUSCHNIGG in February 1938, compelling him to accept *ANSCHLUSS,* and the meeting with Britain's prime minister NEVILLE CHAMBERLAIN in September 1938, in which Hitler presented his demands with regard to Czechoslovakia. A network of bunkers and air raid shelters existed under the Berghof, and a private elevator, its shaft cut through solid rock, connected it with Hitler's sanctum sanctorum, "Eagle's Nest," at the very top of the mountain. The Berghof proper was destroyed in an Allied air raid in April 1945, and the building's ruins were razed in 1952. A stand of trees was planted on the site. Eagle's Nest survived the bombing and is now a teahouse, which may be visited by tourists.

Further reading: Van Capelle, H. *The Eagle's Nest: Hitler at Berchtesgaden.* Lanham, Md.: National Book Network, 1989.

Bergen-Belsen concentration camp

Officially, the Germans listed this facility, near Hanover, as a *Krankenlager,* a sick camp or medical camp. It was, in fact, created as an internment camp in April 1943, but by July was a fully developed concentration camp. It differed from other such camps, however, in that it was divided into two sections. One was used for the incarceration of political prisoners and Jews of foreign nationality, who were being held, in effect, as hostages. The other section was a conventionally horrific concentration camp.

By early 1945, Bergen-Belsen became a holding facility for many thousands of prisoners who had become too sick or weak for forced labor but who were, for various reasons, not "selected" for extermination. Soon, the camp was disastrously overcrowded by some 60,000 inmates. This condition gave rise to a typhoid epidemic, in which approximately 18,000 prisoners died in March 1945 alone. SS-Hauptsturmführer Josef Kramer, Bergen-Belsen's third commandant, was also its most infamous. He became known as the Beast of Belsen. His answer to the typhoid epidemic was simply to starve the prisoners. He reasoned that typhoid was spread by feces and that if prisoners did not eat, they would not defecate. The most famous victim of typhoid in Bergen-Belsen was ANNE FRANK, the young author of a diary that would gain her worldwide posthumous fame after her father published it in 1947.

The camp was liberated by the British in April 1945. They found 38,500 living inmates (of whom about 28,000 subsequently died), mass graves holding some 40,000 bodies, and mountains of an estimated 10,000 unburied dead.

See also CONCENTRATION AND EXTERMINATION CAMPS; FINAL SOLUTION; and HOLOCAUST, THE.

Further reading: Herzberg, Abel J. *Between Two Streams: A Diary from Bergen-Belsen.* London and New York: I. B. Tauris, 1997; Levy, Isaac. *Witness to Evil: Bergen-Belsen, 1945.* London: Peter Halban in association with the European Jewish Publication Society, 1995.

Beria, Lavrenty (1899–1953) *chief of the NKVD, the Soviet secret police*

As chief of the People's Commissariat of Internal Affairs (NKVD), the Soviet secret police, Beria was a trusted deputy of JOSEPH STALIN both before and during World War II. Ruthless and treacherous, he was, aside from Stalin himself, also the most powerful and feared individual in the wartime Soviet Union.

Like Stalin, Beria was a native of Georgia. He joined the Communist Party in 1917, participating in the revolutionary movement in Azerbaijan and Georgia, then becoming a member of the secret police (Cheka) in 1921. He rose rapidly through the ranks of the Cheka, becoming its chief for Georgia and, simultaneously, attaining very high Communist Party rank. In 1931, he became party boss of Georgia and, the following year, of all the Transcaucasian republics. During Stalin's Great Purge of 1936–38, Beria executed the dictator's orders and generally oversaw arrests, interrogations, and other aspects of purge operations. Having earned Stalin's trust and admiration, he was brought to Moscow in 1938 as deputy to Nikolay Yezhov, chief of the NKVD. In fact, Stalin had brought in Beria to replace Yezhov, who was arrested and executed shortly after Beria's arrival. Beria assumed his new office and served as NKVD head until his own death by execution in December 1953.

During the immediate prewar years, Beria personally instigated and led a purge of the police bureaucracy and established a network of labor camps—gulags—throughout the Soviet Union. Untold legions of Soviet citizens were consigned to these, often on the slightest suspicion. During the opening months of the war, in 1939–40, when the Soviet Union was effectively allied with Germany, Beria introduced security troops into territories incorporated into the Soviet Union, including eastern Poland, Lithuania, Latvia, Estonia, Bessarabia, and southern Finland. On Beria's orders, hundreds of thousands were arrested in these regions, including Polish army officers, who were executed en masse in the Katyn Forest.

Beria quickly earned a reputation not simply as a ruthless leader of the secret police, but as a sadist, who personally beat and tortured prisoners during interrogations and who ordered the abduction of young women for his sexual gratification. It is believed that his own wife had consented to marry him only after being forcibly abducted.

Beria was named a deputy prime minister of the Soviet Union in February 1941 and, during World War II, was appointed to a high position within the State Defense Committee, with responsibility for the Soviet Union's internal security (counterespionage and political control and enforcement) as well as the management of slave labor for certain aspects of war production. Beria

Soviet KGB chief Lavrenty Beria with Joseph Stalin's daughter, Svetlana. Stalin is seen in the background. *(Library of Congress)*

ordered and carried out the deportation of nationalities Stalin considered suspect, including Chechens. Kalmucks. Crimean Tatars, and Volga Germans. Throughout the war, he policed and intimidated the high command of the Soviet army to ensure these officers' absolute loyalty to Stalin. Early in the war, in July 1941, Stalin even delegated Beria to approach ADOLF HITLER's Bulgarian envoy with a proposal for a separate peace. This overture proved abortive.

As the war progressed and the Red Army turned the tide toward victory during 1943–44, Beria used purges and other terror tactics to consolidate control over conquered territories. He recruited, indoctrinated, and trained Communist cells within territory seized from the Germans and used these as the core of the Communist regimes that would be established in these areas immediately after the war. Establishing the local apparatus of secret police units was always a high priority, as was ensuring that these units answered directly to Moscow.

Beria was made a marshal of the Soviet Union in 1945 and, after the war, in 1946, was elevated to the highest executive policy-making committee, the Politburo. After the Politburo became the Presidium in 1952, Beria retained his position on it. The death of Stalin in March 1953 made Beria one of four deputy prime ministers and the head of the

Ministry of Internal Affairs, which encompassed both the secret police and the regular police. Soon after the dictator's death, however, Beria tried to use his position as the head of the secret police to elevate himself to sole dictator of the nation. He soon was confronted by a powerful and committed anti-Beria bloc, consisting of Georgy M. Malenkov, VYACHESLAV M. MOLOTOV, and Nikita S. Khrushchev at the uppermost level. Suddenly, the Soviet power structure turned against Beria, who was arrested, summarily stripped of his government and party posts, and, in a show trial, found guilty of being an "imperialist agent" and of conducting "criminal antiparty and antistate activities." He was executed on December 23, 1953, in Moscow.

Further reading: Beria, Sergo. *Beria, My Father: Inside Stalin's Kremlin.* London: Gerald Duckworth & Company, 2003; Conquest, Robert. *Inside Stalin's Secret Police: NKVD Politics, 1936–1939.* New York: Macmillan, 1985; Knight, Amy. *Beria.* Princeton, N.J.: Princeton University Press, 1995.

Berlin, Battle of

The capital of Germany, Berlin had a powerful political appeal as a target and objective in the final phases of the war in Europe. While it was certainly a major Germany city, it was in many ways throughout the war no longer the functioning capital, since ADOLF HITLER spent most of his time at BERCHTESGADEN and at various field headquarters. The Supreme Allied Commander, DWIGHT D. EISENHOWER, did not consider Berlin a key military objective and made the decision to allow the city to fall to the Soviet Red Army while the forces of the western Allies turned south into Bavaria. (Eisenhower's decision was also motivated by his understanding of the diplomatic situation; at the YALTA CONFERENCE, WINSTON CHURCHILL and FRANKLIN ROOSEVELT had promised JOSEPH STALIN that, all other things being equal, Berlin would be a Red Army objective.) Yet it is undeniably true that Berlin was a moral and symbolic prize of enormous importance, both to the Nazi regime and the victorious Allies. It is also true that Hitler had returned

to Berlin from his western front headquarters on January 15, 1945, only to find himself held hostage by relentless bombing raids, which drove him into his massively fortified bunker beneath the Reich chancellery building. Thus, an advance on Berlin was an advance directly against Adolf Hitler.

The First Belorussian Front ("front" was the Soviet equivalent of an Allied "army group"), under Marshal GEORGI KONSTANTINOVICH ZHUKOV, and the First Ukrainian Front, under Marshal IVAN KONEV, advanced on the Oder River, about 35 miles east of Berlin early in February 1945. Zhukov reached Küstrin, on the Oder, first, and he favored an immediate advance against Berlin. Stalin ordered a delay, however, preferring to attack with overwhelming numbers. This was a mistake, because at the time, the forces defending this approach to Berlin were badly depleted, nothing more than the remnants of the Third Panzer Army and the Ninth Army now cobbled together in Army Group Vistula. The delay, however, was hardly fatal to the Soviet offensive since Germany could no longer muster a sufficient force to exploit it. Moreover, Konev began an advance across the Oder to the Neisse River, targeting the Fourth Panzer Army

Red Army soldiers raise the Hammer and Sickle over Berlin. *(National Archives and Records Administration)*

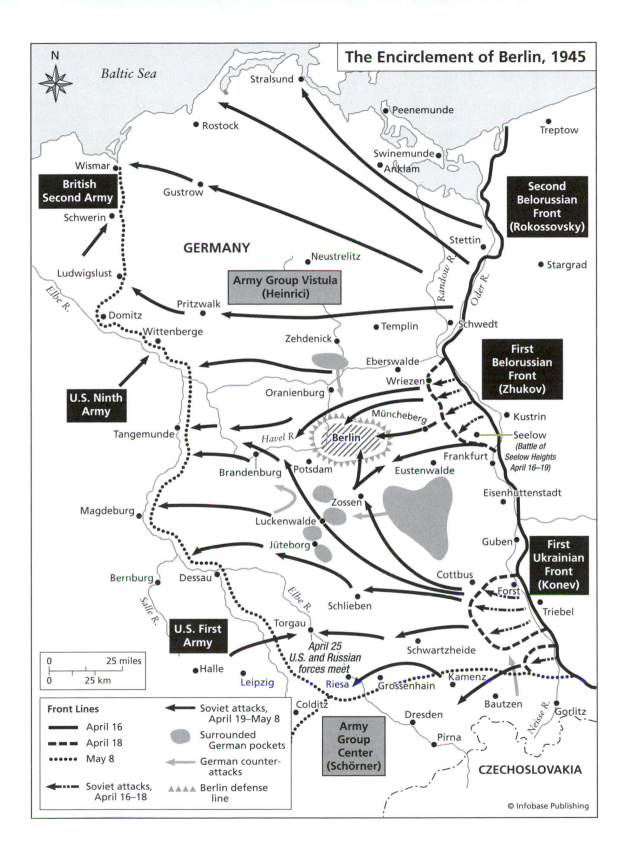

The Encirclement of Berlin, 1945

positions there and creating a new threat to Berlin, this one from the south. That the German situation was indeed hopeless did not, however, deter Hitler from ordering that Berlin would be defended "to the last man and the last shot." He deployed troops, including at this point overaged men and underaged boys, in four concentric rings around the city. The first was about 20 miles from central Berlin; the second some 10 miles from the center; the third positioned along the S-Bahn, the city's suburban rail system; and the fourth, called the Z-ring (Z for *Zitadelle*, Citadel), within the center of the city itself, surrounding the government buildings and the *Füherbunker* beneath the chancellery.

What finally moved Stalin to order the Zhukov-Konev advance renewed was not the German situation, but the speed with which the Americans and British were advancing from the west. On March 31, Stalin informed Zhukov that he would have the honor of taking Berlin, and he accordingly ordered him to regroup and immediately resume his advance. His advance would be in concert with Konev, who would protect and support Zhukov's left flank as well as advance against Dresden. A third Red Army group, the Second Belorussian Front, under Marshal Konstantin Rokossovsky, was sent to the lower Oder River, where it would support Zhukov's right flank. Taken together, these three army groups mustered 2.5 million men, 6,250 tanks and other armored vehicles, and 7,500 aircraft, most of them attack planes well suited for close air support.

Depleted and exhausted as the German army was, it resisted the attack on Berlin with great determination. Zhukov began his assault at dawn on April 16, concentrating his attack at Seelow Heights, west of the Oder. In an effort to confuse and blind the defenders, Zhukov massed concentrations of antiaircraft searchlights, directing these into the German positions. The effect, however, was also to reduce visibility for the Russians. Chaos ensued among the attackers, and the assault proved abortive. Zhukov regrouped and launched a new assault with six armies (including two armies consisting solely of armor) on April 17. These troops

also were forced to withdraw. The next day brought a new assault, which pushed the German lines back but created no breakthrough, whereupon Stalin personally intervened with an order to break off the attack from the east and wheel around to the north, resuming the assault from there. Simultaneously, Konev, having crossed the River Neisse on April 16, was ordered to advance his two tank armies against Berlin from the south. Rokossovsky, already positioned to the northeast with his Second Belorussian Front, was assigned to assist Zhukov in his southbound attack. The German capital lay now within the jaws of a great pincer.

As for Hitler, he was within the grasp of a desperate delusion. Ordering the Ninth German Army to stand fast on the Oder in the belief that he might somehow win this battle and counterattack, he took the pressure off Konev and effectively invited the marshal into the capital. On April 20, Adolf Hitler's birthday, Konev's armor reached Jüterbog, the German army's major ammunition depot. After taking this objective, Konev advanced to the communications center at Zossen. In the meantime, in the *Füherbunker*, Hitler gave to all those of the Nazi inner circle permission to leave Berlin as best they could before the last roads were closed. He told them that he would remain in the city to the end.

On April 21, Zhukov reached the outermost defensive ring. By April 25, Zhukov had linked up with Konev, and the Red Army now completely encircled the German capital. Hitler scrambled to organize a relief force, but the Ninth German Army, itself separately encircled, was in the last extremity, and the Twelfth German Army, approaching Berlin from the west, was a shell of its former self, far too depleted to make any difference in the battle. The troops that now manned the city's inner defensive rings were a mixture of veterans who had fallen back from the attack on the outermost ring and a collection of HITLER YOUTH and old men, some not even armed. Nevertheless, fighting progressed from street to street. On April 29, Lt. Gen. Karl Weidling, commandant of the capital's defenses, reported that all ammunition would be exhausted by the next day. With no relief from the outside possible, the city fell. On April 30, Red Army troops stormed the Reichstag, seat of German government. Unknown to them, inside the *Füherbunker,* Adolf Hitler and his new bride, Eva Braun, took their own lives.

Still, the street fighting continued. On May 1, Lt. Gen. Hans Krebs, chief of the German general staff, fruitlessly—and foolishly—bargained for surrender terms. The Soviets would accept nothing less than unconditional surrender. Lt. Gen. Weidling gave them precisely that on May 2.

No accurate casualty figures exist for the Battle of Berlin. Estimates vary widely. Red Army losses are put at anywhere from some 78,000 killed in action to 305,000 killed. Most authorities believe German losses were approximately 325,000 killed, including soldiers and civilians. There are no estimates of wounded.

Further reading: Bahm, Karl. *Berlin 1945: The Final Reckoning.* Osceola, Wis.: Motorbooks International, 2002; Beevor, Antony. *The Fall of Berlin 1945.* New York: Penguin, 2003; Read, Anthony, and David Fisher. *The Fall of Berlin.* New York: Da Capo, 1995; Ryan, Cornelius. *Last Battle: The Classic History of the Battle for Berlin.* New York: Simon & Schuster, 1995.

Bevin, Ernest (1881–1951) *British minister of labor during World War II*

During World War II, this British union leader and statesman served as minister of labour and national service in the cabinet of WINSTON CHURCHILL and as foreign secretary under CLEMENT ATTLEE. He was born into relative poverty and had no formal education after age 11, when he helped to support his family and himself with a series of menial jobs, culminating in a position as a delivery man for a mineral water company in Bristol. During this period, he became involved in the labor movement and in 1905 was appointed secretary of the Bristol Right to Work Committee. Five years later, he organized a carters' branch of the Dockers' Union in Bristol, and by 1919 he was that union's assistant general secretary. In 1921, Bevin engineered the amalgamation of a number of unions into the Transport and General Workers' Union, of which he served as general secretary until 1940, by which time it had become the largest trade union in the world. Beginning in 1925, Bevin served as a member of the general council of the Trades Union Congress (TUC), achieving election as TUC chairman in 1937. Bevin entered the national spotlight in 1926 as the prime organizer of the British general strike of May 3–12. He was also a key figure in resolving and settling the strike.

With the onset of the Great Depression at the end of 1929, Bevin was a strong voice of criticism directed against the Labour Party government (1929–31) of Prime Minister Ramsay MacDonald, who consistently failed to introduce emergency measures to relieve unemployment. When MacDonald assembled a coalition ministry in 1931, Bevin refused to support it. In contrast to MacDonald and STANLEY BALDWIN after him, Bevin was an outspoken advocate of British rearmament to back a firm stand against the gathering and growing threat of Nazi Germany and fascist Italy. This record led Churchill to appoint Bevin, who was not a member of Parliament at the time, minister of labour and national service in May 1940. Most significantly, Bevin was included in the War Cabinet as of September 1940.

Bevin proved to be one of Churchill's most effective cabinet appointments. The working man and woman responded to him enthusiastically, and he proved to be a skilled leader, whose authority, under the Emergency Powers Act of 1940, was unprecedented in extent. Bevin had total control over the country's labor force, of which some 7 million had been marshaled for war industries by 1943.

After Attlee replaced Churchill as prime minister and formed a Labour Party government on July 26, 1945, Bevin became foreign secretary. In this post, he advocated a strong stance against Soviet expansion, arguing against British recognition of new Soviet puppet governments in the Balkans. His advocacy of the Brussels Treaty alliance of the United Kingdom, France, Belgium, the Netherlands, and Luxembourg and of the Organization for European Economic Cooperation, both in 1948, provided a strong platform for his support of the North Atlantic Treaty in 1949, creating NATO. Illness forced Bevin to resign from the cabinet on March 9, 1951, but shortly before his death, he was named lord privy seal.

Further reading: Bullock, Alan. *Ernest Bevin: A Biography.* Tunbridge Wells: Politicos, 2002; Tames, R. *Ernest Bevin.* London: Newbury, 1974; Weiler, Peter. *Ernest Bevin.* London: Palgrave Macmillan, 1993.

Biak Island, Battle of

During the New Guinea Campaign, elements of the 41st U.S. Division under Maj. Gen. Horace Fuller landed on Biak (an island off the northern coast of Dutch New Guinea) on May 27, 1944. Their objective was to take this important Japanese air base and seize it for basing U.S. aircraft to support the campaign to retake the Philippines. The Japanese garrison of 11,400 made a typically tenacious stand and, despite a U.S. naval cordon around the island, managed to land 1,200 reinforcements. The rugged terrain of the island favored the defenders.

Anticipating little resistance on Biak, the often impetuous Gen. Douglas MacArthur had prematurely announced victory on the island when he learned that Biak had yet to be taken. Embarrassed and also deeply dissatisfied with the slow progress of the American advance on Biak, MacArthur relieved Fuller and replaced him with Lt. Gen. Robert Lawrence Eichelberger on June 14. Under new leadership, the 41st Division began quickly rolling up the defenders, except for holdouts at Ibdi (the so-called Ibdi Pocket), who held off the attackers until July 28. Although victory was now announced again, mop-up operations continued on Biak until August 17.

American forces lost 400 killed and 2,000 wounded, with another 7,000 disabled by endemic tropical diseases, including typhus and a fever of mysterious origin that was never identified. Japanese losses exceeded 5,000 killed. Some 800 were taken prisoner. Others slipped off into the dense jungle, and a very few holdouts continued to resist as late as January 1945.

Further reading: Bernstein, Marc D. *Hurricane at Biak: MacArthur Against the Japanese, May–August 1944.* Philadelphia: Xlibris, 2000; Catanzaro, Francis Bernard. *With the 41st Division in the Southwest Pacific: A Foot Soldier's Story.* Bloomington: Indiana University Press, 2002; Taaffe, Stephen. *MacArthur's Jungle War: The 1944 New Guinea Campaign.* Lawrence: University Press of Kansas, 1998.

Bidault, Georges (1899–1983) *French resistance leader*

With Jean Moulin, Georges Bidault was the central leader of the French resistance and underground movements following the fall of France. In postwar France, he served two terms as prime minister and three as minister of foreign affairs.

Born in Moulins, Bidault received his early formal education at an Italian Jesuit school. He served in the French Army just after World War I and participated in the occupation of the Ruhr in 1919. After military service, he attended the Sorbonne, from which he received degrees in history and geography in 1925. A Roman Catholic activist, he founded in 1932 *L'Aube (Dawn),* a Catholic leftist daily, and wrote the paper's foreign affairs column until the outbreak of war in 1939. As a high-profile leftist, Bidault was a target for German authorities immediately after the fall of France. He was arrested in 1940 and imprisoned in Germany. Released and returned to France in 1941, Bidault became active in the resistance movement and was a charter member of the National Council of Resistance when it was formed by Jean Moulin in May 1943. With the death of Moulin the following month, Bidault became head of the council. By 1944, the Gestapo discovered Bidault's involvement in the council, but he managed to stay one jump ahead of his pursuers and even found opportunity to create the Mouvement Républicain Populaire, a Christian-Democratic Party.

Bidault was an ardent supporter of the wartime Free French government-in-exile of Charles de Gaulle and was appointed foreign minister in the provisional government in 1944. In this capacity, he signed the Franco-Soviet alliance of December and voiced his support of the YALTA AGREEMENT in 1945. In the immediate postwar years, Bidault concluded key economic agreements with Belgium, the Netherlands, and Luxembourg and, on behalf of France, signed the Charter of the United Nations.

In 1946, Bidault was head of the provisional government, then once again served as foreign minister during 1947–48. Although his leftist sympathies at first favored wide latitude toward the Soviet bloc, the 1948 Communist takeover in Czechoslovakia persuaded him of the need for both western European economic union and a defense alliance. He thus became a proponent of the North Atlantic Treaty Organization (NATO).

Bidault served a second term as prime minister in 1949–50 and was minister of defense in 1951–52 and foreign minister in 1953–54. Bidault steadily drifted to the right, breaking with de Gaulle over the issue of Algerian independence (de Gaulle moved toward it, Bidault opposed), and founded in 1958 a new, *right*-wing Christian-Democratic Party. Bidault, now a member of the National Assembly, became increasingly militant on the subject of Algerian independence and, in 1961, founded a national council of resistance, which advocated terrorism in France as well as Algeria to halt the movement toward independence. Reverting to his wartime ways, Bidault went underground and labeled the de Gaulle government illegitimate and illegal. For his incitement to terrorism, Bidault was charged in absentia with conspiracy and formally stripped of parliamentary immunity from arrest. A fugitive now, he fled France in 1962, settling in Brazil from 1963 to 1967, but returning to France in 1968 after the suspension of his arrest warrant. In that most turbulent political year, he founded a new right-wing organization, the Mouvement pour le justice et la liberté, but found that he had become a largely marginalized figure, although his Christian-Democratic Party made him its honorary president in 1977.

Further reading: Demory, Jean-Claude. *Georges Bidault: 1899–1983*. Paris: Julliard, 1995; Schoenbrun, David. *Soldiers of the Night: The Story of the French Resistance*. New York: Dutton, 1980.

biological warfare

Biological warfare (BW) did not figure among the horrors of World War II on any large scale. Only two combatant nations are known to have used it, Poland and Japan. In 1943, the Polish Home Army, a resistance organization, disseminated typhoid (by means of infected lice) and managed to kill several hundred German troops and agents of the GESTAPO. Far more extensive were Japanese BW efforts. During the interwar period, in the 1930s, the Japanese Imperial Army created two units devoted to BW. The mission of Unit 100 was to create and deploy biological agents for small-scale sabotage purposes, while the mission of the far more notorious Unit 731, known as the Ishii Detachment after its commander, Lt. Col. Ishii Shiro, was to develop BW on a large scale. Unit 731 was created in Manchukuo, Japanese-occupied Manchuria, in 1936 and operated under the cover designation Kwantung Army Epidemic Prevention and Water Supply Unit. The unit's location gave it an available pool of Chinese victims on which to test various BW weapons. These included a porcelain bomb designed to deliver plague-infected fleas, live and unharmed, against chosen targets. The unit's Ha bomb was designed to disseminate anthrax or tetanus among soldiers on the battlefield. Essentially modified antipersonnel ordnance, the bomb exploded, broadcasting infected shrapnel over a wide area. Injuries created by the shrapnel would cause infection. Another version of the device, known as the Uji bomb, was designed for use against civilians as well as food animals. Some hundreds or perhaps thousands of Chinese prisoners were used as guinea pigs to test these weapons and biological agents.

Although the Japanese worked intensively on BW, they used it only very tentatively. Unconfirmed reports suggest that a suicide unit contaminated the Khalka River with typhus, paratyphus, and cholera during combat against Soviet troops in August 1939. In October 1940, the Japanese disseminated cholera, typhus, and plague at the Chinese port of Ningpo. Aircraft dropped plague-infested fleas and grain on the city of Changteh in 1941, which triggered a number of epidemics. Worse was the so-called

China Incident, in which Japanese forces used the bacteria causing anthrax, dysentery, cholera, typhoid, plague, and paratyphoid against the forces of CHI-ANG KAI-SHEK in Chekiang and Kiangsi Provinces in 1942. The numbers of Chinese deaths are unknown but apparently were very large. However, some 10,000 Japanese soldiers were also infected. During this same period and also in action against Chiang Kai-shek, 3,000 Chinese prisoners of war may have been given food laced with typhoid and paratyphoid bacteria and were then returned to their units. It is not known whether these individuals became sick or whether they infected others.

The Western Allies continually feared that the Japanese would use BW against them. Indeed, there was a plan to use plague-infected fleas against U.S. forces that had captured SAIPAN, but the transport carrying the BW team and their biological agents was sunk before it reached the island. On the continental United States, there were fears that Japanese BALLOON BOMBS would detonate over the country, broadcasting various BW agents to infect the civilian population. Thousands of balloon bombs were indeed launched, and some 200 reached North America; none carried BW agents.

Further reading: Barenblatt, Daniel. *A Plague upon Humanity: The Hidden History of Japan's Biological Warfare Program.* New York: Perennial, 2005; Gold, Hal. *Unit 731 Testimony.* Rutland, Vt.: Tuttle, 1995; Harris, Sheldon H. *Factories of Death: Japanese Biological Warfare 1932–45 and the American Cover-Up.* New York: Routledge, 1995; Williams, Peter, and David Wallace. *Unit 731: Japan's Secret Biological Warfare in World War II.* New York: Free Press, 1989.

Bismarck, sinking of the

The *Bismarck,* at 42,000 tons, was the fastest, newest, most powerful BATTLESHIP in the NAVY OF GERMANY and the pride of the German fleet. As with the rest of the German surface fleet early in the war, the role of the *Bismarck* was seen mainly as that of a commerce raider, its mission to attack British convoys. No less a figure than WINSTON CHURCHILL put the highest priority on the sinking of the *Bismarck,* not just to protect the vital convoys, but to destroy a mighty symbol of the Nazi war-making machine.

On May 20, 1941, an intelligence officer in ostensibly neutral Sweden informed the Stockholm-based British naval attaché of a conversation he had had at a cocktail party with a Norwegian official. He had learned that two very large German warships had been sighted steaming toward the Denmark Strait. Royal Navy command immediately assumed these were the *Bismarck* and the heavy cruiser *Prinz Eugen.* Acting on the tip, HMS *Norfolk,* a cruiser on patrol in the Denmark Strait, sighted the ships on May 24. They were immediately engaged by the Polish destroyer *Piorun.* The light battleship (or battle cruiser) HMS *Hood* and the battleship HMS *Prince of Wales* soon joined the battle. Tactically, the British vessels were at a disadvantage, because the angle at which they had intercepted the German vessels prevented them from bringing all guns to bear. Worse, the *Hood* and *Prince of Wales* divided their fire between the *Bismarck* and *Prinz Eugen.* The *Bismarck,* under the highly skilled command of Admiral Günther Lütjens (1889–1941) and Captain Ernst Lindemann (1894–1941), directed all of its fire against the *Hood.* A 42,000-ton battleship laid down during World War I and completed in 1920, the *Hood* was a fleet flagship. Less than 10 minutes after the battle had begun, her inadequate armor having been penetrated by a shell that detonated an ammunition magazine, the *Hood* exploded and, within two minutes, sank. All but three of its crew of more than 1,400 men, including Group Commander Admiral Lancelot Holland (1887–1941), died. The *Prince of Wales,* which had sailed before final fitting had been completed (there were civilian contractors on board), was not fully operational and was now also damaged. Its captain broke off the engagement, and, fortunately for his ship, the *Bismarck* had also been damaged, a torpedo hit from an airplane launched from the AIRCRAFT CARRIER *Victorious* having opened up a fuel leak. The *Bismarck,* therefore, did not give chase to the *Prince*

The *Bismarck* under final attack *(National Archives and Records Administration)*

of Wales, but headed for repair facilities at Brest. The *Prinz Eugen* sailed to the west.

Shocked and enraged by the loss of HMS *Hood,* the British admiralty, again at the personal urging of Churchill, deployed all available forces to the area in search of the *Bismarck.* Fortunately for the hunters, the *Bismarck* briefly broke radio silence, which allowed the British ships to get a fix on it. In a spectacular blunder, however, the pursuers misplotted the *Bismarck*'s bearings and sent the British Home Fleet, under the command of Admiral Lord John Cronyn Tovey (1885–1971), in exactly the opposite direction from the *Bismarck*'s flight. Nevertheless, at 10:30 on the morning of May 26, a Catalina flying boat of the Coastal Command sighted the ship. The carrier HMS *Ark Royal* launched torpedo bombers, which made an attack that disabled the *Bismarck*'s steering gear. This rendered it a sitting duck when the next morning, May 27, the battleships HMS *Rodney* and *King George V* opened up on it. It was the cruiser *Dorchester* that finished off the *Bismarck* with a torpedo attack,

though some of the 115 men who survived (out of a crew of 2,222) claimed that Captain Lindemann (who, with Lutjens, perished in the attack) ordered the ship scuttled. Evidence recovered in a 1989 salvage dive suggests this was indeed the case. The German surface navy never recovered from the loss of the *Bismarck,* and it prompted ADOLF HITLER personally to direct that capital surface ships be confined to home waters to avoid another loss of such demoralizing magnitude.

Further reading: Ballard, Robert D., and Rick Archbold. *The Discovery of the Bismarck: Germany's Greatest Battleship Surrenders Her Secrets.* New York: Warner Books, 1990; Burkard, Freiherr Von Mullenheim-Rechberg. *Battleship Bismarck: A Survivor's Story.* Annapolis, Md.: Naval Institute Press, 1990; Forester, Cecil Scott. *Last Nine Days of the Bismarck.* Boston: Little, Brown, 1959; Herzog, Ulrich E. *The Battleship Bismarck.* Atglen, Pa.: Schiffer, 1990; Kennedy, Ludovic. *Pursuit: The Chase and Sinking of the Battleship Bismarck.* Annapolis, Md.: Naval Institute Press, 2000).

Bismarck Sea, Battle of the

Thanks to U.S. Navy Ultra decrypts, Allied forces learned well in advance of the movement on February 28, 1943, of 7,000 Japanese reinforcements to Lae and Salmaua on New Guinea's northeastern coast. Fully alerted, the Americans moved large numbers of aircraft into forward positions, and, on March 2, fighters and bombers of the Fifth U.S. Air Force attacked the Japanese troop convoy. One Japanese transport was sunk, and two more were severely damaged. At dawn on March 3, Australian aircraft and more U.S. bombers attacked again. Some of the planes had been equipped for skip bombing, a special antiship technique by which bombs, dropped at low altitude over the water, skip over the surface, making contact with the target vessel below the waterline. Other of the attacking aircraft concentrated on strafing. The skip bombing proved devastatingly effective. Of 37 500-pound bombs dropped in the first wave of the March 3 attack, 28 hit their targets. The disabled ships were then vulnerable to successive waves of attack from the air throughout the day. With nightfall, U.S. PT boats were deployed, so that by daybreak on March 4, only six destroyers had escaped destruction. U.S. bombers sank two of these. Of the 7,000 troops in the convoy, only 950 reached Lae. Many others were fished out of the water by the surviving destroyers. Total Japanese fatalities numbered 3,660.

Further reading: Cortesi, Lawrence. *Battle of the Bismarck Sea.* New York: Leisure Books, 1977; McAulay, Lex. *Battle of the Bismarck Sea.* New York: St. Martin's Press, 1991.

blackout

To a degree unprecedented in history, combat in World War II was directed against civilian populations, and this was especially the case with air raids, such as the Blitz. Advances in avionics (aircraft instrumentation), radar, and radio-guided direction finding made nighttime air raids not only feasible but common. Brightly lit cities made excellent targets. Even in rural areas, lights were readily spotted from the air. To reduce vulnerability, cities in the war zones instituted strict blackout policies, which restricted or eliminated the use of street lighting and required citizens to provide opaque blackout curtains and shades for all their windows. Automobile headlamps were fitted with slitted covers to reduce light emission to an absolute minimum. Even in the United States, which had escaped air raids, blackout curtains and shades were installed in public buildings. In some locations—for example, New York's famed Grand Central Station—windows were permanently blacked out with paint. Periodically, throughout American cities, air raid drills were conducted, largely to familiarize Americans with rapid blackout procedures.

Blackout policies were introduced not only to help defend against nighttime air raids, but, in coastal locations, to combat the menace of attack from the sea. German submarines lying off the East Coast of the United States often targeted merchant ships that were silhouetted against the bright lights of coastal cities.

In the United States as well as in the cities of Europe and Asia, blackout regulations were enforced by air raid wardens and other officials. Sanctions for violations of blackout policies, orders, and ordinances ranged from a stern lecture to fines to incarceration.

Further reading: Fountain, Nigel. *The Battle of Britain and The Blitz: Voices from the Twentieth Century.* London: Michael O'Mara Books, 2003; Harris, Mark Jonathan. *Homefront: America During World War II.* New York: Putnam, 1984; Harrison, Tom. *Living Through the Blitz.* New York: Random House, 1989; Heacock, Nan. *Battle Stations! The Homefront in World War II.* Ames: Iowa State University Press, 1992; Johnson, David. *The London Blitz.* Lanham, Md.: National Book Network, 1984; Nixon, Barbara Marion. *Raiders Overhead: A Diary of the London Blitz.* San Diego, Ca.: Gulliver, 1980; Pender, R. Allen. *The Sojourners: Life on the American Homefront During World War II.* Bloomington, Ind.: Authorhouse, 2002.

Blackshirts

In Italy, *Blackshirts,* or *Camicie Nere,* was a catch-all term for any of the numerous armed squads loyal to Benito Mussolini's fascists (*see* fascism). All wore black shirts as part of their uniforms.

Blackshirts entered on the scene early, when so-called Action Squads were organized beginning in March 1919 to intimidate, attack, and destroy the leftist organizations rising in Italy after World War I, including those of the socialists (the most numerous) as well as communists and even the more centrist republicans. Against their political rivals, the Blackshirt squads used tactics that ran the gamut from intimidation and bullying humiliation to outright violence, ranging from beatings to murders. On October 24, 1922, Mussolini presided over a large fascist convention in Naples, which amounted to the mustering of what had become a paramilitary organization. Mussolini rallied the Blackshirts in the infamous March on Rome, which catapulted Mussolini to power. Once he had assumed dictatorial authority, Mussolini transformed the Blackshirts on February 1, 1923, from a collection of private squads to a national militia, the Voluntary Fascist Militia for National Security. The uniform of this body was, of course, the black shirt, but it was also worn by other, nonmilitary members of the fascist party (especially on official or celebratory occasions) and even by supporters of fascism who were not themselves party members, as well as by private individuals who wished to exhibit their patriotism. The Blackshirts rapidly dissolved after the fall of Mussolini in 1943.

In Britain, Sir Oswald Mosely founded the British Union of Fascists in 1932. His intention to emulate Mussolini was shown in the uniforms he and his followers adopted, black shirts, and the British fascists were typically referred to as Blackshirts. At their height in 1934, the British Blackshirts numbered about 34,000. The party was forcibly disbanded at the outbreak of the war, and Mosely and others were arrested and interned in May 1940.

Finally, in Germany, members of the Schutzstaffel (SS), the Nazi elite, were often informally called Blackshirts, again because of their uniforms. Members of the Sturmabteilung (SA), or Storm Troopers, were often called Brownshirts after *their* uniforms.

Further reading: Boxer, Andrew. *The Rise of Italian Fascism.* Hooksett, N.H.: Collins Educational, 2000; De Grand, Alexander, *Italian Fascism: Its Origins and Development.* 3d ed. Lincoln: University of Nebraska Press, 2000; Shermer, David R. *Blackshirts: Fascism in Britain.* New York: Ballantine, 1971; Thurlow, Richard. *Fascism in Britain: From Oswald Mosley's Blackshirts to the National Front.* New York: St. Martin's Press, 1998.

Blamey, Thomas (1884–1951) *commander of ANZAC*

Blamey was the often contentious and controversial commander of the Australian Corps, or ANZAC. A staff officer during World War I, Blamey saw no combat, resigned his commission after the armistice, and served as chief of police of the Australian state of Victoria, a service for which he was knighted in 1935. With the outbreak of World War II, Blamey was named commander in chief of Australian ground forces in 1939, an appointment that ignited widespread controversy and protest because he had been exclusively a staff officer (and not a combat leader) in the last war and had been in retirement for virtually all the interwar period. The high emotions were not the product of jealousy, but rather reflected a feeling among the Australian officer corps that Blamey's appointment reflected poorly on them, as if the government had no confidence in the ability of the currently serving command. Assuming his office under a cloud, therefore, Blamey responded defensively, jealously guarding his authority, refusing to delegate tasks that should have been delegated, and, in consequence, greatly diluting his effectiveness.

Appointed commander of the Australian Corps (later ANZAC) in February 1940, Blamey directed the early battles in Libya and Egypt with considerable success (*see* North African Campaign). He was also in command of early action in Greece during April–May 1941, and directed the evacuation of Allied forces from Crete. After serving briefly as deputy commander in chief of Middle East forces under Claude John Ayre Auchinleck, he returned to Australia, where he was appointed commander in chief of Australian Military Forces and Allied land commander in the South-West Pacific Area (SWPA) in March 1942. This put him under SWPA supreme commander DOUGLAS MACARTHUR.

Service with MacArthur was not a happy experience for Blamey. During the struggle for NEW GUINEA, MacArthur ordered Blamey to take personal command of Allied land forces in New Guinea. MacArthur's objective in this was to ensure that the Japanese advance to Port Moresby via the Kokoda Trail was blocked. However, when the campaign for BUNA nearly ended in disaster at the end of 1942, MacArthur judged that Blamey had moved too slowly to be effective in personal command. Accordingly, he ordered him back to his headquarters in Australia at the beginning of 1943. MacArthur then assumed direct command of the U.S. component of the SWPA.

After what amounted to dismissal by MacArthur, Blamey was an Allied commander almost in name only. Worse, beginning in October 1944, Blamey was generally and severely criticized for action against Japanese troops who had already been cut off by MacArthur. These battles, fought exclusively by the Australians under his command, were called unnecessary, and it was true that Blamey acted with neither government approval nor the backing of MacArthur. A cry among public and politicians was raised calling for Blamey's resignation. He weathered the criticism and even secured from the Australian government a retroactive approval of his highly questionable late campaigns. Indeed, after the war, in 1950, he received promotion to field marshal (the only Australian to achieve this rank). Nevertheless, Blamey was among the least capable of the major Allied commanders, and his leadership of Australian ground forces significantly diminished the effectiveness of the Australian component in the South Pacific, especially toward the end of the war.

Further reading: Carlyon, Norman D. *I Remember Blamey.* South Melbourne, Australia: Macmillan, 1980; Gallaway, Jack. *The Odd Couple: Blamey and MacArthur at War.* Queensland, Australia: University of Queensland Press, 2000; Hetherington, John Aikman. *Blamey, Contro-* versial Soldier: A Biography of Field Marshal Sir Thomas Blamey, GBE, KCB, CMG, DSO, ED. Canberra, Australia: Australian War Memorial and the Australian Government Publishing Service, 1973; Hetherington, John Aikman. *Blamey; The Biography of Field-Marshal Sir Thomas Blamey.* Melbourne, Australia: Cheshire, 1954; Horner, D. M. *Blamey: The Commander-in-Chief.* St. Leonards, Australia: Allen & Unwin, 1998.

Blitz, the

Shortened by the British from the German BLITZKRIEG, "lightning war," the Blitz was the name Britons applied to Germany's nighttime air raids against London and other English cities during August 1940 to May 1941. Intended to demoralize the British population and undermine the nation's will to continue to make war, the Blitz killed about 43,000 civilians and injured some 139,000. Infrastructure damage was severe, and many houses and apartment buildings were destroyed. Moreover, defending against the air raids and coping with their results monopolized a great deal of manpower and other resources. The German Luftwaffe lost about 600 bombers during the Blitz, which represented only some 1.5 percent of the sorties flown. While this loss ratio was low, it did not purchase the hoped-for result. By targeting cities, the Luftwaffe missed its opportunity to destroy Royal Air Force (RAF) bases and destroy British aircraft on the ground. Nor did the terror campaign succeed in undermining British morale.

The term *Blitz* is also often applied to the 1944 raids against London and other cities (including some in Belgium and the Netherlands), using the Nazis' so-called vengeance weapons, the V-1 BUZZ BOMB and V-2 ROCKET. Some 10,000 V-1s were launched against Britain, 7,488 of which crossed the English Channel, of which 3,957 were shot down before reaching their targets. Of the 3,531 that made it through, 2,419 hit London; a few hit Southampton and Portsmouth, and one hit Manchester. The V-1s claimed the lives of 6,184 Britons and injured 17,981. Between September 8, 1944, and March 27, 1945, 1,054 V-2 rockets hit England, of which 517 fell on London, killing some 2,700.

The Blitz began just as the Battle of Britain was turning against the Germans. Originally, the raids had been conceived as preparation for an invasion of Britain (Operation Sealion), but the Luftwaffe failed to achieve air supremacy. The original objective of the air raids, which had been to destroy infrastructure and to destroy the RAF, changed by October 1940 to terror against civilians. While the raids took a terrible toll, they ensured that the RAF would be preserved to continue to fight—a strategic error that ultimately doomed the Luftwaffe. Furthermore, the terror tactics were interpreted by such neutral nations as the United States as examples of atrocity and served to increase American sympathy for the British cause.

Early in the Blitz, British ground-based antiaircraft defenses were largely ineffective. Although radar had been developed and was in use, systems to link antiaircraft artillery with radar (ground-controlled interception radar) were still under development. Few of the RAF's night fighter aircraft were equipped with radar at this time. Ground-based searchlights were in ample supply, but the chances of catching a German bomber in a beam and shooting it down were slim, especially when bombers flew at altitudes above 12,000 feet. Early advances in electronic warfare did allow British technicians to jam some of the radio beams the bombers used to find their targets, and this jamming technology improved rapidly.

During the early phase of the Blitz, which lasted through mid-November, an average of 200 planes, including some Italian aircraft, bombed London nightly. Fighter-bombers raided by day. In addition to London, Coventry, Southampton, Birmingham, Liverpool, Bristol, and Plymouth were heavily attacked. Beginning on February 19, 1941, and extending through May 12, 46 air raids were concentrated on port cities in a renewed effort to disrupt British shipping. During this period, Plymouth, Portsmouth, Bristol, Avonmouth, Swansea, Merseyside, Belfast, Clydeside, Hull, Sunderland, and Newcastle were targeted.

Although the British people bravely withstood the onslaught, defenses continued to prove heart-breakingly inadequate, and relief did not come until May 1941, when the Luftwaffe, stretched thin by the demands of the Invasion of the Soviet Union, had to withdraw many of its resources from Britain. By this time, too, night defenses had been greatly improved, as had radar technology. The Blitz simply petered out.

Further reading: Fountain, Nigel. *The Battle of Britain and the Blitz: Voices from the Twentieth Century.* London: Michael O'Mara Books, 2003; Harrison, Tom. *Living Through the Blitz.* New York: Random House, 1989; Johnson, David. *The London Blitz.* Lanham, Md.: National Book Network, 1984; Nixon, Barbara Marion. *Raiders Overhead: A Diary of the London Blitz.* San Diego, Calif.: Gulliver, 1980.

Blitzkrieg

Blitzkrieg, a German word meaning "lightning war," is an attack doctrine, tactic, and strategy intended to overawe defenders with rapid, violent, and, above all, highly mobile action coordinated among armor, mechanized infantry, massed firepower, and air power, with special forces units acting to disrupt the defenders' communication and supply, thereby increasing confusion during the onslaught. While always advancing, the simultaneous object of Blitzkrieg is to disable and paralyze the enemy's capacity to coordinate defenses effectively. If defenses are *disabled*, the attacker need not be delayed by a costly campaign aimed at *destroying* defenses, and thus the attack may be accelerated with maximum penetration.

Although the term *Blitzkrieg* is still used to describe any exceptionally vigorous mobile assault, its application in World War II is chiefly to Germany's opening campaigns of the war, against Poland, France, Belgium, the Netherlands, and then the Soviet Union. Some historians have also applied the term to the rapid and devastating advance of the Third U.S. Army under George Smith Patton, Jr., following the Normandy landings (D-day) and Operation Cobra.

As executed by German forces early in the war, Blitzkrieg was aimed at thrusting through a relatively narrow front using armor, motorized artillery, and aircraft, especially the Stuka dive bomber. This created a point of attack, or *Schwerpunkt* ("strong point"), a gap in which defenders were fatally weakened. Before this gap could be repaired, wide, rapid sweeps by massed tanks followed, along with mechanized infantry (mainly specially trained so-called shock troops). This further disrupted the enemy's line of defense, creating areas in which defenders were trapped, immobilized, and cut off from one another. Their only option at this point was surrender. Although Blitzkrieg depended on extreme violence, its speed, which neutralized rather than destroyed a defender, actually spared casualties on both sides. The tactic was seen as an alternative to the far more destructive war of stalemate that had developed along the western front in World War I.

The doctrine of blitzkrieg may be traced to two pre–World War II German commanders. In World War I, General Oskar von Hutier (1857–1934) executed the newly formulated German infiltration tactics, based largely on British and French tactics, in the capture of Riga on September 3, 1917. Violent, highly coordinated, and swift, the attack on Riga demoralized and overwhelmed the defenders, and this approach to combat was dubbed "Hutier tactics." During the interwar period, HANS VON SEECKT, head of the Reichswehr (the German army as it was reformed and much reduced by the TREATY OF VERSAILLES), used the precedent of Hutier tactics to formulate the foundation of Blitzkrieg doctrine. During World War II itself, the chief architect and greatest exponent of blitzkrieg was General HEINZ GUDERIAN. The actual term *Blitzkrieg* was not invented by the German military, but was probably the coinage of a journalist and was as widespread outside Germany as within it. The term was truncated as THE BLITZ to describe the German terror bombing of London and other British targets early in the war. This campaign, however, was strictly an air war and bore no tactical resemblance to Blitzkrieg.

Further reading: Corum, James S. *The Roots of Blitzkrieg: Hans von Seeckt and German Military Reform.* Lawrence: University Press of Kansas, 1994; Deighton, Len. *Blitzkrieg: From the Rise of Hitler to the Fall of Den-* *mark.* London: Book Sales, 2000; Pallud, Jean-Paul. *Blitzkrieg in the West.* London: After the Battle, 1991; Zaloga, Steven J. *Poland 1939: The Birth of Blitzkrieg.* New York: Praeger, 2004.

Bofors gun

The Bofors gun was a generic name for any 75-mm lightweight, highly transportable howitzer that resembled the Bofors 75-mm Model 1934 weapon manufactured by AB Bofors, a Swedish arms maker. Indeed, many nations purchased the original Bofors weapon prior to and during World War II. (Sweden, a neutral in the war, was free to deal with all belligerents.) The original Bofors was a beautifully crafted, very sturdy artillery weapon mounted on wheels and designed to be pulled by a vehicle, horse, or the troops themselves. It was designed expressly as a "mountain gun," readily transported across difficult terrain, but it was used elsewhere as well. As a howitzer, it could be made to fire for range with a relatively flat trajectory, or it could be adjusted for a steeper, mortar-like trajectory.

The specifications for the Model 1934 include:

Caliber: 75 mm
Length: overall, 1.8 meters (70.87 inches); barrel only, 1.583 meters (62.32 inches)
Weight: 2,046 pounds
Elevation: -10° to +50°
Traverse: 8°
Muzzle velocity: 1,493 feet per second
Maximum range: 10,171 yards
Projectile weight: 14.53 pounds

Further reading: Murray, Williamson R., and Allan R. Millett, eds. *Military Innovation in the Interwar Period.* New York: Cambridge University Press, 1998.

bomber aircraft

This article discusses the development and employment of bomber aircraft during World War II. *For discussion of specific aircraft, see* AIRCRAFT, BRITISH; AIRCRAFT, FRENCH; AIRCRAFT, GERMAN; AIRCRAFT,

ITALIAN; AIRCRAFT, JAPANESE; AIRCRAFT, POLISH; AIR-
CRAFT, SOVIET; and AIRCRAFT, U.S.

By the outbreak of World War II in September
1939, the typical bomber would be classified as a
medium bomber, with two engines, monoplane
design, and all-metal construction (save for control
surfaces, which were often fabric covered). Most of
these aircraft carried a bomb load of 1,000 to 4,500
pounds, and the best medium bombers had a range
of about 2,500 miles. In contrast to the other combatants, the United States and Great Britain developed heavy bombers, with four engines, in addition
to the medium bombers. These were capable of
reaching higher altitudes, carrying heavier bomb
loads, and attaining greater range.

Germany entered the war with twin-engine
bombers such as the Heinkel He111 and the Dornier Do17 and with the single-engine dive bomber
the Junkers Ju87, popularly called the Stuka. Within
a short time after the start of the war, the Ju88, a
twin-engine medium bomber, would become available and would serve throughout the war as Germany's most versatile bomber.

Germany's ally, Italy, flew the three-engine
Savoia-Marchetti SM79 as its main bomber at the
beginning of the war. In contrast to the German
machines, the SM79 was mostly built of wood. It
was soon replaced by the Cant Z1007, another trimotor aircraft, which proved successful as a torpedo bomber.

The bombers of Germany's early opponents,
Poland and France, were wholly outclassed by the
German planes. Although Poland's P.Z.L. P37 Los
was technologically comparable to the German
planes, it was never mass produced, and only 36 of
the aircraft were in service at the time of the INVA-
SION OF POLAND. The French air arm was equipped
with obsolete, slow bombers, and although the
new Lioré et Olivier LeO451 was rushed into production in 1939 and was, in fact, the fastest
bomber of its time, France fell before many had
been produced.

Great Britain entered the war with a mixture of
obsolescent twin-engine medium bombers (such
as the Bristol Blenheim) and the downright obsolete single-engine Fairey Battle. However, the Ger-

The U.S. B-17 was the most celebrated bomber
of World War II. *(National Archives and Records
Administration)*

mans had nothing to compare with the British
heavy bombers, including the Armstrong Whitworth Whitley, the Handley Page Hampden, and
the Vickers-Armstrong Wellington. The latter
would become one the Royal Air Force's most
important strategic bombers.

The Soviet Union, at the beginning of the war,
flew few bombers except for ground attack and
ground support.

The United States, which trailed other nations
in many areas of military aviation at the beginning
of World War II, was the first to fly an all-metal,
truly modern heavy bomber, the B-17 Flying Fortress, which, after passing through several iterations, emerged as a tremendously durable,
survivable aircraft capable of carrying a heavy
bomb load, of absorbing a great deal of damage,
and of defending itself with an array of guns. Following the B-17, which was introduced in 1935,
was the B-24 Liberator in 1939, another large, four-
engine heavy bomber. America also produced fine
medium bombers, including the Douglas DB7, the
B25 Mitchell, the B26 Martin Marauder, and the
Douglas A26 Invader.

Great Britain, in 1941, introduced two new
four-engine heavy bombers, the Short Stirling and
the Handley Page Halifax, which were followed
early the next year by the Avro Lancaster, the most

advanced and, ultimately, most successful night heavy bomber of World War II. Although Anglo-American air doctrine strongly advocated strategic bombing (*see* STRATEGIC BOMBING OF GERMANY *and* STRATEGIC BOMBING OF JAPAN), which called for four-engine heavy bombers, Great Britain also introduced in 1943 the remarkable de Haviland Mosquito. Made largely of wood to save weight, this beautiful aircraft had no defensive armament and relied wholly on its 400-mile-per-hour speed and high degree of maneuverability to evade harm. In fact, the nimble Mosquito had the lowest casualty record of any bomber in the war.

Whereas Germany had entered the war with some of the most advanced aircraft designs, and while German designers continued to produce outstanding FIGHTER AIRCRAFT, including JET AIRCRAFT, they lagged behind Britain and the United States in bomber design during the course of the war. As for heavy bombers, with a few relatively insignificant exceptions and experiments, Germany failed to enter this arena effectively. German designers started a number of innovative and highly advanced projects, including the Heinkel He177, which employed a very complex and mechanically unreliable system of pairs of coupled engines, and the Arado AR234, which not only carried a 3,308-pound bomb load, but was the world's first jet-propelled bomber. These, however, barely progressed beyond the prototype stage and certainly never entered the war in any militarily significant way.

In the Pacific theater, the Japanese, like the Germans, concentrated development on medium bombers and close-air support bombers. Because so much of the Pacific war was naval, the Japanese also devoted a good deal of attention to torpedo bombers. Japanese designers also recognized that the key to the success of land-based bombers was range, and early on, they produced the Mitsubishi G4M (Allied codename Betty), which traded armor for weight in order to achieve a range of 3,765 miles.

American designers also produced a bomber specifically designed for the Pacific war, the spectacular B-29 Superfortress, which dwarfed all other four-engine aircraft of the time and had a 3,250-mile range, even with a 5,000-pound bomb load. Operating at high altitude, it featured a pressurized cabin for enhanced crew comfort and efficiency, and it was the only Allied aircraft capable of carrying the atomic bomb. Discounting the Germans' stab at a jet bomber, the B-29 was by far the most advanced bomber aircraft of the war.

If World War II spurred the technological development of bombers, it also necessitated the development of bombing doctrine and tactics. Germany honed its doctrine and tactics in the Spanish civil war of the mid-1930s, concentrating on the tactical use of bombers, targeting troops as well as civilians and providing close-air support for ground attack. The BLITZKRIEG employed these bomber tactics, especially dive bombing techniques, by which specially designed aircraft (most notably the Stuka) would deploy bombs at low altitude while recovering from a very steep dive in order to achieve levels of accuracy impossible with conventional horizontal bombing.

The British entered the war without a bombing doctrine and with precious few tactics. During the disastrous BATTLE OF FRANCE, British airmen learned the consequences of having developed no effective close-air support tactics, and they quickly improvised a repertoire of these when it came to the NORTH AFRICAN CAMPAIGN. In addition to individual close-air support bombing tactics, Britain's air chief marshal ARTHUR TEDDER developed a unique use of massed bomber formations for close-air support known as Tedder's Carpet. This required bombers to lay down a carpet of napalm and high-explosive ordnance ahead of attacking troops. While this was a great advantage to the advancing attackers, it required flawless timing and precision to avoid potentially catastrophic friendly fire incidents.

In contrast to the Germans and Japanese, who concentrated on developing and refining the techniques of tactical bombing, the British and Americans developed the doctrine of strategic bombing and the techniques to execute it. Advanced bombsight equipment, especially the top-secret American-invented NORDEN BOMBSIGHT, greatly aided the offensive component of strategic bombing.

What had to be developed were effective defensive techniques, for the big bombers were highly vulnerable to fighter attack and to attack by heavy antiaircraft guns. The Anglo-American airmen practiced close formation flying to better leverage the firepower of the defensive guns carried by the heavy bombers, and they worked closely with fighter escorts. The British added the defensive element of darkness, flying virtually all their missions at night. This provided a significant degree of protection, of course, but also limited the effectiveness of bombing. American bombers flew virtually all their missions during the day, so they could employ precision bombing techniques. While these were more effective at hitting selected targets (war materiel production facilities, for example), flying in the daylight over the enemy's homeland exposed the bombers to extremely high risk.

In the Pacific, new and very daring strategic bombing techniques were developed, especially by Maj. Gen. CURTIS LeMAY. One of the great advantages of the B-29 (which was used exclusively in the Pacific theater) was its high service ceiling. However, the results of high-altitude bombing were consistently disappointing over the Japanese homeland. Beginning in January 1945, therefore, LeMay ordered his B-29s stripped of all defensive armament except for the tail gun. This allowed the plane to achieve better-than-maximum speed and to accept better-than-maximum bomb load. He further ordered bomb loads to be mostly incendiary, on the assumption that Japanese cities were built principally of wood and paper. Finally, he ordered night attacks from very low altitudes: about 6,000 feet. Although the absence of defensive armament rendered the planes vulnerable to fighter attack, and the low altitude made them vulnerable to all manner of antiaircraft ground fire, the night provided some cover, and the enhanced speed provided some safety. Certainly, the low-altitude deployment of incendiaries proved devastatingly effective, inflicting far more damage than the atomic bombs that would be dropped on Hiroshima and Nagasaki. Moreover, the "Fire Raids" caused so much devastation so quickly, and the stripped-down B-29s moved so fast, that the attack-

ers' survivability was actually enhanced. Counterintuitive as LeMay's tactics were, they actually saved the lives of Allied airmen while rendering their work more effective.

Further reading: Ardery, Philip. *Bomber Pilot: A Memoir of World War II.* Lexington: University Press of Kentucky, 1996; Astor, Gerald. *The Mighty Eighth: The Air War in Europe as Told by the Men Who Fought It.* New York: Dell, 1998; Chant, Christopher. *An Illustrated Data Guide to World War II Bombers.* New York: Chelsea House, 1997; Donald, David. *Bombers of World War II.* New York: MetroBooks, 1998; Gunston, Bill. *The Illustrated Directory of Fighting Aircraft of World War II.* Osceola, Wis.: Motorbooks International, 2000; Tillman, Barrett, and Robert L. Lawson. *U.S. Navy Dive and Torpedo Bombers of World War II.* Osceola, Wis.: Motorbooks International, 2001; Werrell, Kenneth P. *Blankets of Fire: U.S. Bombers over Japan During World War II.* Washington, D.C.: Smithsonian, 1996.

Bonhoeffer, Dietrich (1906–1945) *German theologian and opponent of Hitler*

Bonhoeffer was a prominent German theologian and opponent of ADOLF HITLER whose activities in connection with a plot to overthrow Hitler resulted in his execution. While imprisoned by the Nazis, he wrote *Letters and Papers from Prison,* which were published posthumously in 1951 and are regarded as one of the great professions of moral conviction of modern times.

Bonhoeffer was the son of a prominent professor of psychiatry and neurology, in later life an opponent of the Nazi's infamous T4 (euthanasia) program. Instead of becoming a scientist, like his father, Dietrich Bonhoeffer studied theology at the Universities of Tübingen and Berlin and became greatly interested in combining sociology with theology in understanding the evolution of religion. Ordained, Bonhoeffer served as assistant pastor of a German-speaking congregation in Barcelona, Spain, during 1928–29, then studied for a time in New York, returning to Germany in 1931 as a lecturer at the University of Berlin. After Hitler was named chancellor in 1933, Bonhoeffer became a vocal opponent of Nazism and Nazi-led anti-Semitism. He left Germany during 1933–35 to serve as pastor of two German-speaking congregations in London but returned to Germany as a leading activist for the Confessing Church, a focus of anti-Nazi protest. He took a pragmatic approach to fighting the Nazi doctrine of identifying Jews racially, holding that Jews who converted to Christianity were indeed Christian. Although Bonhoeffer opposed anti-Semitism, he was not an unambiguous advocate of the toleration of practicing Jews.

After the Confessing Church was proscribed by the government of the Third Reich in 1937, Bonhoeffer continued to teach its precepts covertly and wrote important works of theology. He also developed an essentially pacifist philosophy.

About 1938, Bonhoeffer's brother-in-law Hans von Dohnanyi, a prominent jurist, introduced him to a group seeking to overthrow Hitler. Soon, Bonhoeffer was clearly targeted by the government as a subversive. When the American theologian Reinhold Niebuhr arranged sanctuary for Bonhoeffer in the United States, Bonhoeffer came to New York and stayed for a mere two weeks before returning to Germany, explaining to Niebuhr that he would have no right to participate in the reconstruction of Christian life in Germany after the war if he refused to share "the trials of this time with my people." In 1940, publicly charging the Christian church with silent acquiescence in Nazi persecutions, Bonhoeffer and von Dohnanyi began helping Jews emigrate to Switzerland. Remarkably, Bonhoeffer found cover for his resistance work by taking a job with the Military Intelligence Department. During the war, in May 1942 in the guise of performing official government work, Bonhoeffer flew to neutral Sweden to communicate to the British government a secret proposal for a negotiated peace. The Allies, however, were willing to accept nothing less than unconditional surrender, and, his subversion. discovered, Bonhoeffer was arrested by the GESTAPO on April 5, 1943.

Imprisoned, Bonhoeffer was caught in the dragnet that was cast after the failure of the attempt by a cabal of WEHRMACHT officers to assassinate

Hitler on July 20, 1944. During the investigations that followed the attempt, documents implicating Bonhoeffer in the conspiracy led to his execution. While incarcerated, Bonhoeffer wrote *Letters and Papers from Prison,* a remarkable meditation on modern spirituality, morality, and the role of an activist church. His life, death, and writings have stood as a challenge to all those who profess religious faith, especially in a time of government-decreed immorality and injustice.

Further reading: Bethge, Eberhard. *Dietrich Bonhoeffer: A Biography.* Minneapolis: Augsburg Fortress, 2000; Bonhoeffer, Dietrich. *Letters and Papers from Prison.* New York: Touchstone, 1997.

Bormann, Martin (1900–1945?) *Hitler's private secretary*

ADOLF HITLER's private secretary, Martin Bormann was one of the most powerful men in the NAZI PARTY (NSDAP) and the Nazi regime. Crude and uneducated (he was a school dropout), Bormann typified Nazi leadership at its most brutal.

Bormann was born in Halberstadt and, after serving briefly in World War I, trained as an estate manager in Mecklenburg, then managed a farm. He was a vociferous advocate of the union of all German-speaking people and joined the extremist right-wing FREIKORPS. In 1924, he was convicted as an accomplice to a political murder but was released in 1925 after serving a year. After his release, he joined the NSDAP and quickly rose to prominence, becoming the director of the Nazi press in Thuringia in 1926, then (from 1928) an officer in the STURMABTEILUNG (SA), or Storm Troopers. In 1933, he was appointed chief of staff to the deputy führer, RUDOLF W. HESS and in November of that year, was elected as a Nazi delegate to the Reichstag.

After the war began, on May 12, 1941, Hitler personally appointed Bormann to succeed Hess as chief of the party chancellery, effectively head of the administrative bureaucracy of the Nazi Party. Bormann proved himself a master of intrigue, who deftly exploited conflicts within the Nazi Party as well as the many weaknesses of Hitler's personality to insinuate himself into the very highest levels of German government. As some saw it, Bormann became effectively a kind of shadow Führer. Certainly, he exercised a high degree of control over national legislation as well as appointments and promotions within the party. Most important of all, Bormann had absolute control over who gained access to Hitler. He was the keeper of the dictator's schedule and appointments calendar, and by manipulating these, he shaped Hitler's picture of reality, effectively insulating him from dissident counsel and, increasingly, from bad news concerning the course of the war.

Bormann was more than a bureaucratic climber. He was an ardent Nazi who enthusiastically promoted Nazi concepts of racial superiority and the necessity of persecuting and exterminating Jews, Slavs, and others deemed undesirable. He was also one of the prime architects of the exploitation of these "undesirables" as slave labor and presided over the vast expansion of slave labor programs during the war.

In September 1944, Hitler appointed Bormann to head the Volkssturm, the citizen militia desperately recruited during the closing months of the war to defend—to the death—the homeland. As the Soviet Red Army was completing the invasion of Berlin (see BERLIN, BATTLE OF), Hitler appointed Bormann party minister and accorded him the personal "honor" of witnessing his last testament as well as his marriage to Eva Braun. Hitler committed suicide in his Berlin bunker on April 30, 1945. During the night of May 1–2, Bormann apparently left the bunker in an effort to escape to the new German government convening at Flensburg. He never arrived, and it is now believed that he was either killed or committed suicide in or near Berlin. However, in the absence of conclusive evidence of his death, Allied authorities indicted Bormann in absentia on charges of war crimes on August 29, 1945. Subsequently tried in absentia by the NUREMBERG WAR CRIMES TRIBUNAL (along with other Nazi leaders), he was convicted and sentenced to death on October 1, 1946.

As was the case with Hitler and some other Nazi leaders, rumors persisted after the war that Bormann had succeeded in escaping Berlin and was living in hiding. During the 1960s, it was widely believed that he made his home in Paraguay. These rumors were largely put to rest in 1973 when a German forensic anthropologist, after examining a pair of skeletons unearthed during construction excavation in West Berlin, concluded that one was definitely that of Martin Bormann. On April 11, 1973, the West German government officially declared Bormann dead.

Further reading: Bormann, Martin. *Bormann Letters.* New York: AMS Press, 1954; Kilzer, Louis. *Hitler's Traitor: Martin Bormann and the Defeat of the Reich.* Novato, Calif.: Presidio Press, 2000; Lang, Jochen von. *The Secretary: Martin Bormann, the Man Who Manipulated Hitler.* New York: Random House, 1979; McGovern, James. *Martin Bormann.* New York: Morrow, 1968; Whiting, Charles. *Hunt for Martin Bormann.* New York: Ballantine, 1973.

Bose, Subbas Chandra (1897–ca. 1945)
Indian collaborator with Japan

Also known by the Hindi byname Netaji ("Respected Leader"), Subbas Chandra Bose was an advocate of Indian liberation from British rule who sided with Japan during World War II in the belief that defeating the Western powers would promote the cause of independence. Born in Cuttack, Orissa, India, Bose was a child of privilege, his father a prominent attorney. He enrolled at Presidency College in Calcutta, only to be expelled in 1916 for his highly vocal advocacy of independence. He then enrolled at the Scottish Churches College, from which he graduated in 1919. Upon graduation, Bose went to England, where he studied at Cambridge in preparation for a career in the Indian civil service. After passing the necessary examinations in 1920, Bose applied for candidacy in the civil service, but, as the nationalist cause heated up, he withdrew his candidacy in April 1921 and returned to India. He sought the counsel of nationalist leader Mohandas K. Gandhi, who advised him to apprentice himself to the Bengali nationalist Chitta Ranjan Das. Under Ranjan Das's tutelage, Bose became a teacher and journalist as well as the commandant of the Bengal Congress volunteers. This led to his imprisonment in December 1921. Subsequently, in 1924, Bose was named chief executive officer of the corporation of Calcutta, under Das, who served as mayor. Bose's increasingly high profile resulted in his deportation to Burma (Myanmar). He was allowed to return to India in 1927, only to discover that the Bengal Congress and its nationalist activities had largely disintegrated after the death of Das. However, when Gandhi stepped in to fill the void, Bose became president of the revived Bengal Congress and was again twice arrested and imprisoned. Released in 1934, he was forced into European exile, during which he published *The Indian Struggle, 1920–1934*, a plea to the leaders of Europe on behalf of Indian nationalism.

Bose returned to India in 1936 and was immediately imprisoned for a year. Elected president of the Indian National Congress in 1938, he broke with Gandhi over industrialization (which the agrarian Gandhi opposed) and, in 1939, defeated Gandhi's handpicked candidate for reelection to the presidency of the congress. Yet without Gandhi's support, Bose found he had little power, and he soon resigned from the Indian National Congress to found the radical Forward Bloc. Imprisoned yet again in July 1940, he went on a hunger strike, vowing to starve himself to death. Fearful of creating a martyr, British authorities released Bose, who, on January 26, 1941, evaded police and slipped out of India to make his way, by April, to Germany. There he became associated with a newly formed Special Bureau for India, and, beginning in January 1942 with other Indian expatriates, he made proindependence, anti-British broadcasts over German-sponsored Azad Hind Radio, which were beamed throughout India.

In spring 1943, after the Japanese had invaded and occupied much of Southeast Asia and were menacing British India, Bose was transported by German and Japanese submarines and by Japanese aircraft to Tokyo. On July 4, he announced himself leader of the Indian Independence Movement in East Asia and, with the aid and cooperation of the Japanese military, formed and trained an army of 40,000 Indian men and women recruited from throughout Japanese-occupied Southeast Asia. On October 21, 1943, Bose proclaimed a provisional independent Indian government, and he accompanied what he called his Indian National Army (Azad Hind Fauj), attached to Japanese forces, in an advance on Rangoon. With Japanese forces, his Indian National Army then invaded India on March 18, 1944, but, defeated in battle, was forced to retreat. Despite this, Bose maintained the Indian National Army as an army of liberation in exile, based in Burma and subsequently Indochina. The surrender of Japan, however, brought about the immediate collapse of his army, and in August 1945, after Japan accepted unconditional surrender, Bose fled from Southeast Asia. It is believed—but has never been confirmed—that Bose died in a Japanese hospital at Taipei, Taiwan, from injuries sustained in an airplane crash.

Further reading: Bose, Sisr K. *A Beacon across Asia: A Biography of Subhas Chandra Bose.* New Delhi: Orient Longman, 1973; Wolpert, Stanley. *A New History of India.* Oxford and New York: Oxford University Press, 1999.

Bougainville Campaign

Bougainville is the largest of the Solomon Islands and is located near the northern end of the Solomons chain in the southwestern Pacific. With the island of Buka and the Kilinailau, Tauu, Nukumanu, Nuguria, and Nissan Island groups, Bougainville is now a province of Papua New Guinea. The island is 75 miles long and varies in width from 40 to 60 miles. Its topography is ruggedly volcanic, the Emperor Range reaching 9,000 feet at the northern end of the island. Another, lower range, the Crown Prince Range, occupies the southern half of the island. Bougainville is surrounded by coral reefs.

From November 1943 to August 1945, Bougainville was the target of a U.S. campaign to eject the Japanese garrison stationed there. Having achieved success in the NEW GUINEA CAMPAIGN and the NEW GEORGIA CAMPAIGN, American forces closed in on the major Japanese base at RABAUL. Bougainville was the final Japanese line of defense protecting Rabaul from U.S. forces progressing up the Solomon chain. Recognizing Bougainville's critical importance, the Japanese rushed to reinforce it by sending in 37,500 men of the Seventeenth Japanese Army commanded by Lt. Gen. Hyakutake Haruyoshi. However, most of these men were deployed to the southern end of Buin and to offshore islands. This left Empress Augusta Bay vulnerable to a landing by U.S. Marines on November 1, 1943, after the 3rd New Zealand Division had taken the Treasury Islands nearby. The marines set up a perimeter and immediately began construction of airstrips. In the meantime, at sea, the Battle of Empress Augusta Bay commenced on November 2. U.S. naval forces sank a Japanese cruiser and a destroyer. Simultaneously, the Fifth U.S. Army Air Force bombed Japanese airstrips and provided close air support for the marines.

Despite these initial successes, American forces were menaced by the powerful naval force of V. Adm. Kurita Takeo based at Rabaul. U.S. Adm. WILLIAM A. "BULL" HALSEY seized the offensive and attacked Kurita's fleet before it had gotten under way from Rabaul. It was a bold gamble, since it put Halsey's two-carrier task force squarely within range of the formidable air arm at Rabaul. Indeed, Halsey expected that the carriers might be sunk, but land-based aircraft defended them so vigorously that they escaped unscathed, even as their aircraft battered Kurita's fleet, forcing its withdrawal to Truk.

By the time the sea battle was in its final stages, the marines on Bougainville had completed sufficient airstrips to launch intensive air raids against Rabaul, forcing the Japanese to withdraw from this key base. The defeat of Rabaul allowed a rapid build-up of American forces on Bougainville. Japanese counterattacks were readily repulsed. Under Maj. Gen Oscar Griswold, U.S. ground forces, now numbering 62,000 men, repulsed one final Japanese counteroffensive by March 27, 1944. Bougainville largely fell silent, and Griswold enlarged his perimeter before withdrawing after his force was relieved by Australian II Corps. This relief was completed by December 1944. However, the Allies had at this time grossly underestimated remaining Japanese strength on Bougainville. They believed only 12,000 to 25,000 troops were present, whereas, in fact, some 40,000 remained. These troops offered renewed fierce resistance to the Australians before they were defeated.

Further reading: Gailey, Harry A. *Bougainville, 1943–1945: The Forgotten Campaign.* Lexington: University Press of Kentucky, 2003; McGee, William L. *The Solomons Campaigns, 1942–1943: From Guadalcanal to Bougainville—Pacific War Turning Point.* St. Helena, Calif.: BMC Publications, 2001.

Boyington, Gregory "Pappy" (1912–1988)
most celebrated aviator in the U.S. Marine Corps

Boyington commanded USMC Squadron 214, consisting mostly of novice pilots shunned by the veterans and therefore known as the "Black Sheep" squadron. At age 31, Boyington stood out among these youngsters as an "old man" and was therefore dubbed "Pappy."

Boyington was a dynamic commander, and he was an even more accomplished combat pilot. He flew his land-based F4U Corsair to victories against 14 Japanese aircraft in the mere 32 days of his squadron's first combat tour. Boyington led the Black Sheep Squadron in combat during the Battle of GUADALCANAL, Battle of NEW GEORGIA, Battle of New Britain, and Battle of RABAUL before he was shot down and made a prisoner of war on January 3, 1944. Liberated by the Allies on August 29, 1945, Boyington received the Medal of Honor and retired from the Marine Corps with the rank of colonel in 1947.

In 1958, Boyington published a memoir, *Baa Baa Black Sheep,* which helped ensure his fame. In 1976, NBC television premiered *Baa Baa Black Sheep,* loosely based on the memoir. Dropped at the end of 1977, the show was briefly revived during 1977–78 as *Black Sheep Squadron.*

"Pappy" Boyington, USMC air ace *(United States Marine Corps History Center)*

Further reading: Boyington, Gregory "Pappy." *Baa Baa Black Sheep.* 1958. Reprint. New York: Bantam, 1990; Gamble, Bruce. *Black Sheep One: The Life of Gregory "Pappy" Boyington.* Novato, Calif.: Presidio Press, 2000).

Bradley, Omar Nelson (1893–1981)
American commander of the Twelfth Army Group in Europe

Bradley played a key role in the Allied reconquest of Europe as commander of the Twelfth Army Group following the NORMANDY LANDINGS (D-DAY). The front-line war correspondent ERNIE PYLE called the homely Bradley, whose unadorned field uniform was in drab contrast to the beribboned spit-and-polish of GEORGE SMITH PATTON, JR., the "GI general," a label that stuck and that made Bradley one of the most recognizable and popular Allied figures of the war.

Bradley was born in Clark, Missouri, grew up in nearby Moberly, and graduated from the U.S. Military Academy at West Point in 1915 with a commission as second lieutenant in the infantry. From 1915 to 1918, he served on posts in the American West and was promoted to major in 1918 but did not serve overseas during World War I. After that war, in 1919, Bradley was appointed military instructor at South Dakota State College, then served as an instructor at West Point from 1920 to 1924. He attended Infantry School at Fort Benning, Georgia, in 1925, and was subsequently posted to Hawaii from 1925 to 1928. Earmarked for higher command, Bradley graduated from the Command and General Staff School at Fort Leavenworth in 1929 and was assigned as an instructor at the Infantry School during 1929–33. After attending and graduating from the prestigious U.S. Army War College in 1934, Bradley was assigned to West Point as tactical officer, serving in that post from 1934 to 1938; he was promoted to lieutenant colonel in 1936.

In 1938, Bradley received an appointment to the Army General Staff and was promoted to brigadier general in February 1941. For the next year, he served as commandant of the Infantry School before being assigned, beginning in February 1942, to command the 82nd Division and then the 28th Division. Bradley served briefly as deputy to top U.S. European theater commander DWIGHT D. EISENHOWER from January to March 1943, until Eisenhower assigned him to replace Patton as commander of II Corps. Patton had replaced the incompetent Lloyd R. Fredendall and transformed II Corps, which had suffered a humiliating defeat at the BATTLE OF KASSERINE PASS, into a first-rate unit. Bradley went on to lead II Corps through the final stages of the Tunisia Campaign and into the SICILY CAMPAIGN. In August 1943, he was transferred to England to work with Eisenhower and others in planning the invasion of France.

At the start of 1944, Bradley was named commander of First Army and assigned the right-wing position in the D-day landing. In July after the initial assault, Bradley planned and led the Saint-Lô breakout at Normandy, and in August he was assigned to lead Twelfth Army Group, consisting of the First Army (under COURTNEY HODGES) and the Third Army (Patton). This was the greatest field command ever given to any U.S. general. Bradley was responsible for the entire southern wing of the mammoth Allied advance across France, and his forces amounted to 1.3 million men.

Bradley endured—and, indeed, contributed to—considerable friction with the notoriously difficult British commander BERNARD LAW MONTGOMERY, and he was also severely criticized for his nearly catastrophic delay in appreciating the magnitude of the German ARDENNES offensive. Nevertheless, in March 1945, Bradley was promoted to general and continued to command Twelfth Army Group through final operations in Germany.

Bradley's reputation as the "GI general" contributed to his postwar appointment by President HARRY S. TRUMAN as head of Veterans Administration. In February 1948, he succeeded Eisenhower as army chief of staff and, the following year, was named the first chairman of the new Joint Chiefs of Staff. In 1950, in recognition of his service and role in the war, he was promoted to general of the army, the rank held by DOUGLAS MACARTHUR and by Eisenhower. Bradley retired from the army in 1953, having published his enormously popular World War II memoir, *A Soldier's Story*, in 1951. His full autobiography, *A General's Life*, appeared posthumously in 1983.

Further reading: Bradley, Omar Nelson. *A Soldier's Story*. New York: Random House, 1999; Bradley, Omar Nelson, with Clay Blair. *A General's Life: An Autobiography*. New York: Simon & Schuster, 1983.

Brauchitsch, Walther von (1881–1948)
commander in chief of the Wehrmacht early in World War II

Brauchitsch was commander in chief of the WEHRMACHT from February 1938 to December 1941. He had rendered distinguished service during World War I as a member of the general staff, and

when the TREATY OF VERSAILLES mandated the abolishment of the general staff, Brauchitsch continued to serve on the *Truppenamt*, the clandestine proxy for the outlawed body. Trained as an artillerist, Brauchitsch was instrumental in the development of the 88-mm gun, the celebrated German 88, considered by many to be the most important artillery weapon of the war. By 1936, Brauchitsch had been promoted to the well-deserved rank of lieutenant general, and he was a natural candidate to replace Werner Freiherr von Frtisch (1880–1939), who had been removed as commander in chief in 1938 on a fabricated charge of homosexuality. Field Marshal WILHELM KEITEL, head of the German Armed Forces High Command, personally chose Brauchitsch not only because of his demonstrated competence but because he was politically naive, just the type of malleable figure ADOLF HITLER wanted as commander in chief. In fact, Brauchitsch personally regarded the NAZI PARTY (NASDAP) as repugnant, but Hitler soon found a means of manipulating Brauchitsch and, through him, subordinating the Wehrmacht to his political will. Brauchitsch wanted a divorce in order to remarry, but he was unable to meet his current wife's demands for a financial settlement. From Hitler, he borrowed the necessary 80,000 marks and was thereafter personally bound to the dictator.

Brauchitsch voiced objections to Hitler's plans for the invasion of Austria (ANSCHLUSS) and CZECHOSLOVAKIA, but declined to resist these war plans in any affirmative, active way. When General Ludwig Beck (1880–1944) asked him to persuade the entire general staff to resign if Hitler persisted in pressing his designs on Czechoslovakia, Brauchitsch replied that he would let events take their course. Similarly, Brauchitsch was well aware of a conspiracy among a number of officers to overthrow Hitler and the Nazi regime. When in September 1938, they attempted to persuade him, as commander in chief, to take charge of a coup, he replied that he himself would do nothing, but that he would not stop anyone else from acting. When the coup died aborning, Brauchitsch turned a deaf ear to all further appeals from Beck and others to use the army to overthrow Hitler before the dictator plunged the nation into war.

Brauchitsch said nothing when Hitler invaded Poland (*see* POLAND, INVASION OF), but in November 1939, he did attempt to persuade Hitler that Germany could not win a protracted European war. Hitler vented his full wrath on Brauchitsch, who emerged thoroughly cowed from his meeting with Hitler. Despite his own misgivings, however, Brauchitsch managed the logistics of the western BLITZKRIEG offensive brilliantly. Although Hitler rewarded him with a marshal's baton, signifying promotion to the rank of field marshal, he repeatedly ignored his military advice, including a plea to reverse the order that halted the German advance short of DUNKIRK and thereby allowed the trapped British Expeditionary Force (BEF) to be evacuated. Despite this disappointment, Brauchitsch was elated by the speedy victory over France, and he allowed himself to believe that victory over Russia would be similarly quick.

Although he found it distasteful, Brauchitsch obeyed Hitler's directive that he sign and implement the "Commissar Order" and the "Order for Guerrilla Warfare," documents that effectively authorized the mass liquidation of Soviet prisoners of war and civilians. What he found far harder to accept was Hitler's subsequent decision to divert panzer divisions of Army Group Center north to Leningrad and south to the Caucasus instead of concentrating on the objective of capturing Moscow. Spreading the invasion forces so thinly, Brauchitsch understood, would doom the Moscow operation. As usual, however, Brauchitsch proved himself incapable of making vigorous protest, although he noted his objections in tepid memos to Hitler.

Brauchitsch soon reaped the consequences of his habitual fence-sitting. When, inevitably, the invaders failed to take Moscow, Hitler laid the entire blame on Brauchitsch, who promptly suffered a heart attack. This gave Hitler ample excuse to relieve the field marshal as commander in chief on December 19, 1941, and the ailing Brauchitsch retired. Hitler now seized direct, personal control of the Wehrmacht.

In retirement, Brauchitsch continued to act without spine. When the July 20, 1944, attempt to assassinate Hitler failed, Brauchitsch rushed into print with an article condemning the plot and lauding the politically motivated appointment of HEINRICH HIMMLER as commander in chief of the Home Army. Beyond this, Brauchitsch denounced a number of fellow officers. His pronouncements ensured that he would be charged as a war criminal by the NUREMBERG WAR CRIMES TRIBUNAL after the war. His behavior during his arraignment was yet another demonstration of a deficiency of character. He simply perjured himself, claiming that he never received money from Hitler to remarry and that he had no foreknowledge of Hitler's war aims during 1938–41. He also testified that he had been ignorant of atrocities committed in Poland and that he had no inkling that the Commissar Order had resulted in genocide. After his arraignment, Brauchitsch was sent to a prisoner of war camp in New South Wales, then was returned to Germany in 1948 for trial. He succumbed to a fatal heart attack before the proceedings began.

Further reading: Barnett, Correlli. *Hitler's Generals.* New York: Grove Press, 2003; Galante, Pierre. *Operation Valkyrie: The German Generals' Plot against Hitler.* New York: Harper & Row, 1981; Mauch, Christof. *The Shadow War against Hitler.* New York: Columbia University Press, 2002; Shirer, William L. *Rise and Fall of the Third Reich.* New York Simon & Schuster, 1990; Thomsett, Michael C. *The German Opposition to Hitler: The Resistance, the Underground, and Assassination Plots, 1938–1945.* Jefferson, N.C.: McFarland, 1997.

Braun, Wernher von (1912–1977) *creator of Germany's rocket weapons*

As the father of Germany's V-2 ROCKET—with the V-1 BUZZ BOMB one of the two "vengeance weapons" ADOLF HITLER deployed against civilian populations in England, the Netherlands, and Belgium— Wernher von Braun was also the father of modern rocket science. After surrendering to the Americans in the closing days of the war, Braun went on to direct the major phase of the U.S.' development of rockets and missiles as weapons and for the purposes of space exploration.

Born of an aristocratic family in Wirsitz, Germany, Braun early on showed a great interest in science, particularly astronomy, which his parents encouraged. Nevertheless, Braun proved to be an indifferent student and was deficient in particular in physics and mathematics, the core subjects of rocketry. In 1925, however, the young man experienced an epiphany when he read Hermann Oberth's (1894–1989) *Die Rakete zu den Planetenräumen* (*The Rocket into Interplanetary Space*), a visionary book many consider to be the foundation of all modern rocket science. Unable to decipher Oberth's mathematics, Braun threw himself into the subject and soon leaped to the head of his class in mathematics as well as physics. On graduation, he was accepted for enrollment at the prestigious Berlin Institute of Technology and, while a student there, he joined the German Society for Space Travel in 1930. He became a protégé and friend of Oberth, whom he assisted in early experiments with liquid-fuel rocket motors.

After graduating from the institute in 1932, he enrolled in Berlin University and continued his work with the German Society for Space Travel. Up to this time, Braun had not envisaged rockets being used as weapons. However, with the society acutely short of funding, he accepted a research grant from the ordnance department of the Reichswehr (the 100,000-man German army allowed under terms of the TREATY OF VERSAILLES). Under the sponsorship of Capt. Walter R. Dornberger, the ordnance department officer in charge of solid-fuel rocket research, Braun began liquid-fuel rocket research at the Kummersdorf Army Proving Grounds outside of Berlin. He integrated this work—on 300- and 660-pound-thrust rocket engines—into his doctoral thesis and in 1934 received a Ph.D. in physics from the University of Berlin.

Braun was never content with theory and, early on, put his calculations to practical tests. By December 1934, he had gathered a small and brilliant working group around him and was launching rockets to altitudes greater than 1.5 miles. The military, keenly aware of the potential value of Braun's work, saw to it that civilian research was prohibited. The space travel society was banned, and Braun became a military scientist. He was moved to a new, much larger testing and development facility at Peenemünde, a town on the Baltic Sea, and while Dornberger (now a colonel) was named military commander of the facility, Braun became its technical director. In rapid succession, he gave practical demonstrations of liquid-fuel rocket-propelled aircraft as well as engines for the jet-assisted takeoff of conventional aircraft. With the advent of war, Braun and his colleagues turned their attention to the development of a long-range ballistic missile and a supersonic antiaircraft missile. Work on the latter, called the Wasserfall, was largely suspended so that A-4 development could be accelerated. Renamed the V-2—Vengeance Weapon 2—by JOSEPH GOEBBELS's Ministry of Propaganda, the missile, which first flew in October 1942, was put into full production beginning in May 1944.

Wernher von Braun *(NASA Photo)*

The V-2 caused significant destruction, especially during the Blitz in London, but was deployed too late in the war to be decisive. Braun, a member of the Nazi Party (NSDAP) and without question "guilty" of having developed a terror weapon intended for use against noncombatant civilians, could have been tried as a war criminal by the Nuremberg War Crimes Tribunal after the Allied victory. Instead, he and the entire Peenemünde-based rocket development team surrendered to U.S. troops and offered their service to the United States. A few months after their surrender, Braun and some 100 other scientists and technicians were installed at the U.S. Army Ordnance Corps test site at White Sands, New Mexico. Any question of war crimes or Nazi affiliation took a backseat to the conditions of the developing cold war, and American officials believed it crucially important to keep German rocket technology out of Soviet hands.

Braun and his team continued to test and work on captured V-2s at White Sands. In 1952, Braun was appointed technical director and, subsequently, chief of the army's ballistic weapons program, headquartered at the Redstone Arsenal in Huntsville, Alabama. Here Braun directed development of the first generation of U.S. ballistic missile weapons, the Redstone, Jupiter-C, Juno, and Pershing missiles. Naturalized a U.S. citizen in 1955, Braun directed the team that successfully launched *Explorer I*, the first U.S. Earth-orbiting satellite on January 31, 1958. After the creation of the National Aeronautics and Space Administration (NASA), Braun was made director of NASA's George C. Marshall Space Flight Center in Huntsville. Here he led the development of the Saturn space launch vehicles, the most powerful and advanced rocket boosters ever built. He left the Marshall center in March 1970 to become NASA's deputy associate administrator for planning in Washington, D.C., resigning two years later to enter the private sector as vice president of the Fairchild aerospace company. Braun founded the National Space Institute in 1975, with the object of generating public support for space research.

Further reading: Braun, Wernher von. *History of Rocketry and Space Travel.* New York: Crowell, 1966; Neufeld, Michael J. *The Rocket and the Reich: Peenemunde and the Coming of the Ballistic Missile Era.* New York: Free Press, 1994; Piszkiewicz, Dennis. *Wernher von Braun: The Man Who Sold the Moon.* New York: Praeger, 1998; Stuhlinger, Ernst. *Wernher von Braun Crusader for Space: A Biographical Memoir.* New York Krieger, 1995.

Brereton, Lewis (1890–1967) *U.S. commander of the Middle East Air Forces (Ninth Air Force)*

Brereton commanded the Middle East Air Forces, which later became the Ninth U.S. Air Force. He authorized the controversial strategic raids on the oilfields of Ploesti, Romania (*see* Ploesti raid), then in August 1944, assumed command of the First Allied Airborne Army.

Born in Pittsburgh, Pennsylvania, Lewis Hyde Brereton graduated from St. John's College, Annapolis, Maryland, and entered the U.S. Naval Academy in 1907. He graduated from Annapolis in June 1911 but resigned his commission as an ensign to become a second lieutenant in the Coast Artillery Corps of the U.S. Army on August 17, 1911. After serving for a year with the Coast Artillery, he transferred in September 1912 to the Aviation Section, Signal Corps, and received flight instruction at the Signal Corps Aviation School, San Diego, California, earning his wings on March 27, 1913. Three years later, in July 1916, he transferred to the 2nd Field Artillery in the Philippines but was reassigned in January 1917 to the 2nd Aero Squadron in the Philippine Islands in January 1917. Just two months later, he was assigned as chief signal officer in the Office of the Aviation Section, Washington, D.C. After the United States' entry into World War I, he was sent overseas in October 1917 and, in March 1918, was assigned to command the 12th Aero Squadron. Brereton led missions in the Toul and Luneville sectors and participated in the attack at Vaux in July 1918. On the fifth of that month, he was appointed chief of aviation, I Army Corps, and commanded the Corps Observation Wing during the St. Mihiel offensive. In October 1918, Brereton was named operations officer on the staff of the chief of air service of the American Expeditionary

Forces, serving in this post through the armistice, when he was appointed chief of staff, Headquarters Air Service of the Third Army.

Brereton returned to the United States in February 1919 as chief of the Operations Division, Training and Operations Group, in Washington, D.C. In December 1919, he returned to France as air attaché at the U.S. embassy in Paris. Three years later, in August 1922, he was assigned to Kelly Field, Texas, first as commanding officer of the 10th School Group, then as assistant commandant of the Advanced Flying School, and, finally, as director of attack training and president of the board on attack aviation.

In September 1924, Brereton was assigned as an instructor at the Air Corps Tactical School, Langley Field, Virginia, then in June 1925 became commanding officer of the 2nd Bombardment Group at Langley. Two years later, in August 1927, he enrolled in the Command and General Staff School at Fort Leavenworth, Kansas, graduating the following June. After this, he received an appointment as commanding officer of the 88th Observation Squadron at Post Field, Fort Sill, Oklahoma, and also served as air service instructor at the Field Artillery School.

Brereton was sent to Panama in August 1931, where he was commanding officer of France Field and the 6th Composite Group, then commanding officer of the Panama Air Depot and air officer of the Panama Canal Department. In July 1935, he became an instructor at the Command and General Staff School, Fort Leavenworth, Kansas, serving here until June 1939, when he was transferred to Barksdale Field, Louisiana, as base commander. He was subsequently assigned to command the 17th Bombardment Wing, General Headquarters Air Force, stationed at Savannah, Georgia. From here, he was transferred in July 1941 to command the Third Air Force at Tampa, Florida.

At the outbreak of World War II, Brereton was assigned command of the Far East Air Force (FEAF) in the Philippine Islands. A complete breakdown in communications with the headquarters of DOUGLAS MACARTHUR prevented Brereton from receiving orders when the Japanese began invading the Philippines in December 1941. As a result, most of Brereton's B-17s, based on Luzon, were destroyed on the ground along with most of the rest of FEAF forces there. Brereton did what he could to lead the desperate defense of the Philippines but soon evacuated. In January 1942, he was named air commander in chief of the Allied Air Forces on the staff of British general Sir ARCHIBALD WAVELL, stationed in Java, in addition to his new duties as commander of the Fifth Air Force. In March 1942, he was tasked with organizing and commanding the new Tenth Air Force in India, then was designated commander of the Middle East Air Force, which later became the Ninth Air Force. In August 1944, Brereton was assigned command of the First Allied Airborne Army and served in this capacity in the European theater until the German surrender in May 1945.

After the war ended in Europe, Brereton returned to the United States, where he was assigned to USAAF headquarters at Washington. In July 1945, he was transferred to command of the Third Air Force at Tampa, Florida, and in January of the next year, he took command of the First Air Force, based at Mitchell Field, New York. The very next month, however, Brereton was assigned to the office of the secretary of war, Washington, D.C. Serving in this high post until July 1947, Brereton was assigned to the Military Liaison Committee of the Atomic Energy Commission, also based in Washington. Brereton returned to air force headquarters in June 1948 as secretary general of the Air Board, then retired from the now-independent U. S. Air Force on September 1, 1948, with the rank of lieutenant general.

Further reading: Brereton, Lewis H. *The Brereton Diaries: The War in the Air in the Pacific, Middle East, and Europe, 3 October 1941–8 May 1945.* New York: Da Capo Press, 1976.

Britain, Battle of

Following the fall of France in the BATTLE OF FRANCE, ADOLF HITLER contemplated launching OPERATION SEALION, the cross-channel invasion of

Britain's Hawker Hurricane was more numerous in the Battle of Britain than the more famous Supermarine Spitfire. *(Author's collection)*

England. Encouraged by the claims of Luftwaffe chief HERMANN GÖRING, Hitler believed that bombing raids on principal English cities and industries would, at the very least, prepare the way for the invasion and, even more important, might well render the invasion unnecessary by bringing Britain to its knees.

At Hitler's disposal were the forces of the Luftwaffe now based on French and Belgian airfields. The available forces amounted to approximately 2,679 aircraft, including 1,015 medium bombers, 350 Stuka dive bombers, 930 fighters, and 375 heavy fighters. These included some of the most advanced aircraft of the war at this time. To oppose these forces, the British Royal Air Force (RAF) could muster no more than about 600 Hurricane and Spitfire fighters. Outnumbered as they were, these were excellent planes, and they were manned by superbly trained, highly skilled, and extraordinarily motivated pilots under the command of the venerable air chief marshall HUGH DOWDING.

The battle, the first in history fought entirely in the air, unfolded in three successive, albeit overlapping, phases, beginning on July 10, 1940, with a heavy German air raid. This signaled the start of the battle's first phase, which was directed at destroying the southern ports from Dover west to Plymouth. This area was the most likely site for invasion landings, and Hitler sought to neutralize

its defenses. Almost every day, German medium bombers, escorted by fighters, crossed the English Channel and bombed ships as well as port installations. On August 15, the first phase of the battle reached its point of greatest intensity when approximately 940 German aircraft attacked in the south as well as in the north. The RAF managed to shoot down 76 of the German planes, losing 34 fighters in the exchange. The Germans also destroyed 21 British bombers on the ground.

Overlapping the first offensive phase was the second, which targeted airfields, aircraft factories, and radar installations. The objective was to achieve air supremacy by attacking Britain's airfields (and the aircraft there) and aircraft production as well as its highly advanced radar capability. In the space of two weeks, from August 24 to September 6, the Luftwaffe destroyed or severely damaged 466 Hurricane and Spitfire aircraft; 103 British pilots were killed and 128 wounded, representing a quarter of the RAF's entire fighter pilot strength. Yet the cost to the attackers was so heavy as to be a pyrrhic victory. The Germans lost more than twice the number of planes the British lost and more than twice the number of pilots. Worse, Hitler directed his bombers to cease their attacks on RAF facilities and aircraft factories and, beginning on September 7, to bomb civilian targets. The first objective was the air defenses of London, which was raided by some 300 German airplanes in a daylight mission. On September 15, more than 400 bombers attacked the British capital in what would be the largest daylight raid on London, with 56 of the bombers downed by RAF fighters or ground-based antiaircraft fire.

Göring was badly shaken by his losses on September 15 and concluded that daylight raids were too costly. This led to the opening of the third and final phase of the Battle of Britain, the exclusive concentration on night bombing. Historians generally identify September 7 as the beginning of THE BLITZ. For its first week, the Blitz included daylight and nighttime raids, but from September 16 on, only night raids were carried out. The Blitz portion of the Battle of Britain proceeded continuously, without intermission, for 57 nights. On average each night, 200 bombers dropped both incendiary and high-explosive ordnance on London. The worst night was that of October 15, when 480 bombers dropped 386 tons of high explosive and 70,000 incendiary bombs on the city. They were met by six squadrons of British night fighters and the massed fire of some 2,000 antiaircraft guns.

There is no question that the 57-night Blitz was devastating. More than 43,000 British civilians were killed, and some 200,000 were wounded. Property damage was staggering; ultimately, about 20 percent of London was destroyed. Food production was diminished, but no major food crisis was created. Nevertheless, the Blitz was futile. Hitler had made a disastrous and unrecoverable mistake in diverting the raids from the RAF facilities and factories, which turned out Spitfires and Hurricanes at an incredible rate. When Göring was forced to abandon daylight raids, he effectively conceded victory to the RAF. Although the Battle of Britain would not end until November 3, the Germans had lost it back in September.

Between July and November, the RAF lost 915 fighters, 481 pilots killed, missing, or taken prisoner, and 422 pilots wounded. The RAF claimed 2,698 kills against the Germans, but documented German aircraft losses amounted to 1,733—still a crippling number.

After the November 3 raid on London, the Battle of Britain proper ended, but the Blitz continued as the Luftwaffe turned to raids on industrial centers, especially the COVENTRY AIR RAID (500 bombers dropped 600 tons of ordnance on the night of November 14) and Birmingham (hit mercilessly from November 19 to November 22). London was struck again on December 29, mainly in a massive incendiary attack that triggered more than 1,500 uncontrollable blazes. All through the winter of 1940–41, raids hit port cities, and on May 10, 1941, London was hit by an incendiary attack that was the worst and last of the Blitz. In the more than 2,000 fires started, some 3,000 were killed or injured. Defenders shot down 16 German bombers, the most shot down during any nighttime raid.

Rather than see his air force destroyed, Hitler broke off the Blitz after the May 10 raid and redirected the bulk of the Luftwaffe to the eastern front war against the Soviet Union. Operation Sealion, the invasion of Britain, would never be carried out.

Further reading: Bishop, Patrick. *Fighter Boys: The Battle of Britain, 1940.* New York: Viking, 2003; Bungay, Stephen. *The Most Dangerous Enemy: A History of the Battle of Britain.* London: Aurum Press, 2002; Clayton, Tim, and Phil Craig. *Finest Hour: The Battle of Britain.* New York: Simon & Schuster, 2002; Wellum, Geoffrey. *First Light.* New York: Wiley, 2003.

British Borneo, action in

Located southeast of the Malay Peninsula in the Greater Sunda group of the Malay Archipelago, Borneo is the world's third-largest island. It is encircled by the South China Sea, the Sulu Sea, the Celebes Sea, the Makassar Strait, and the Java Sea. During World War II, Borneo was part of the British and Dutch Empires. The largest part of the island, today known as Kalimantan, was Dutch, and combat there is discussed in ACTION IN NETHERLANDS EAST INDIES. British colonies on Borneo included North Borneo (as well as Labuan Island), Brunei, and Sarawak. Borneo presents a challenging tropical climate and a formidable terrain consisting largely of mountains lushly covered in rain forest.

The island's situation, at the intersection of so many major seas and sea routes, made it strategically critical. Moreover, the Japanese saw Borneo as a staging area and stepping stone to an invasion of Australia. Although the British, as well as their Dutch allies, fully recognized the importance of Borneo, neither possessed the resources to defend it adequately at the outbreak of the war in the Pacific. For the Japanese, Borneo was such a key objective that they launched an assault against it in the very first month of the war, December 1941. Realizing the futility of attempting to defend all of British Borneo, the relatively few Anglo-Indian troops stationed there concentrated exclusively on the defense of Kuching airfield in Sarawak. However, they also took the important step of destroying the oilfields at Sarawak and in Seria, Brunei, with the purpose of depriving the Japanese attackers of this extraordinarily valuable resource.

The Japanese landings on Borneo took place on December 16. A single Indian battalion made a stand but was soon forced to withdraw into the Dutch portion of Borneo. There the battalion continued to fight as long as it could hold out but eventually surrendered.

While British Borneo was quickly taken by the Japanese, the Chinese population (some 50,000) leagued with the native Dyaks in an uprising against the occupiers in October 1943. The rebels actually succeeded in capturing the important port town of Jesselton before they were overwhelmed by a Japanese counterattack. The Japanese treated the rebels as insurgents, and those not killed in battle were, for the most part, executed.

Also in October 1943, Australian special forces troops (COMMANDOS belonging to Special Operations Australia [SOA]) landed on the coast of British Borneo to gather intelligence and to organize, arm, and train the local population. In March and April 1945, more SOA operatives were parachuted into the interior of Sarawak, where they continued to organize, arm, and train the locals so they could conduct actions preparatory to major landings by the 9th Australian Division. These landings took place in June and targeted Labuan and Brunei Bay. Resisting their attack were elements of the substantial 31,000-man Japanese garrison deployed throughout British Borneo. The landing forces never progressed far inland. However, the SOA troops and the native guerrillas they trained continued to press the fight against the Japanese stationed in the interior.

British Borneo was so isolated from the action in the rest of the Pacific theater that the guerillas continued to fight the Japanese for at least two months after Japan had surrendered in August 1945. The last Japanese soldiers to surrender did not do so until October 1945.

Further reading: Ooi, Keat Gin. *Rising Sun Over Borneo: The Japanese Occupation of Sarawak, 1941–1945*. London: Palgrave Macmillan, 1999; Webster, Donovan. *The Burma Road: The Epic Story of the China-Burma-India Theater in World War II*. New York: Farrar, Straus & Giroux, 2003.

Brooke, Alan, first viscount Alanbrooke
(1883–1963) *Chief of the British Imperial Staff*

Born at Bagnères-de-Bigorre, France, Brooke was educated in French schools and then at the Royal Military Academy in Woolwich. He was an officer in the Royal Artillery during World War I and, in the interwar years, rose rapidly as a staff officer and as director of military training in the War Office during 1936–37. His particular expertise was in the all-important developing field of mechanized warfare.

At the outbreak of World War II, Brooke commanded II Army Corps in France. He performed with brilliance, courage, and cool efficiency during the retreat to Dunkirk and was chiefly responsible for covering the DUNKIRK EVACUATION of the British Expeditionary Force (BEF) during May 26–June 4, 1940. Once back in England, Brooke was assigned to command the home forces, but in December 1941, Prime Minister WINSTON CHURCHILL named him chief of staff. He would hold the position throughout the war, until 1946.

Like the American general DWIGHT DAVID EISENHOWER, Brooke craved a key field command, but, like Eisenhower, he was destined to serve in a staff capacity. He not only headed the Imperial General Staff ably but, as chairman of the Chiefs of Staff Committee, performed the often difficult and delicate task of representing the frequently divergent views of the staff to the prime minister and to the Joint Chiefs of Staff of the U.S. forces. Quietly, he exercised an important influence on the shaping of Allied strategy in Europe.

During the war, Brooke worked well with Eisenhower, the Supreme Allied Commander, Europe, but after the war he published portions of his wartime diary that were frankly critical not only of Eisenhower, but of U.S. military strategy in the European conflict. The material provoked a lively controversy. The Crown honored his wartime service by creating him baron Alanbrooke of Brookeborough in 1945 and first viscount Alanbrooke the following year.

Further reading: Bryant, Arthur. *The Turn of the Tide; A History of the War Years Based on the Diaries of Field-*

marshal Lord Alanbrooke, Chief of the Imperial General Staff. Garden City, N.Y.: Doubleday, 1957; Fraser, David. *Alanbrooke.* New York: Atheneum, 1982.

Browning automatic rifle (BAR)

One of the most important infantry weapons of World War II, the BAR was introduced in World War I and modified, as the M1918A2, in 1940. It was this version that was used in World War II combat. The new model could be fired only in two automatic modes, slow (300 to 450 rounds per minute) or fast (500 to 650 rounds per minute). Because the U.S. Marine Corps preferred to use the weapon in semiautomatic mode, none of the 1940 modified BARs were used by the corps. The original World War I model of the BAR lacked the later version's buffer spring in the butt and was, therefore, fatiguing for the shooter. Introduced in the 1940 variant, the buffer spring not only increased shooter endurance, it also improved accuracy by reducing recoil. Nevertheless, the BAR was a large weapon, and it was often mounted on its own detachable folding bipod.

During World War II, the army infantry squad, consisting of nine men, was tactically organized around a single BAR. The marine squad consisted of 13 men divided into three fire teams, each of which was organized around a BAR.

Specifications for this air-cooled, gas-operated, magazine-fed, shoulder-type infantry weapon include:

Caliber: .30 (30–06)
Muzzle velocity: 2,800 feet per second
Capacity: 20-round detachable box magazine
Weight: 18.5 pounds
Length: 47 inches
Rate of fire: 550 rounds per minute
Effective range: 600 yards

Further reading: Department of the Army. *Operator's and Organizational Maintenance Manual, Including Repair Parts and Special Tools List: Rifle, Caliber .30, Automatic, Browning, M1918A2, W/E (1005–674–1309).* Washington, D.C.: U.S. Government Printing Office, n.d.

Buchenwald concentration camp

One of the largest CONCENTRATION AND EXTERMINATION CAMPS in Germany proper, Buchenwald was located in Thuringen, on the northern slope of Ettersberg, a mountain five miles north of Weimar. In addition to the main camp, Buchenwald encompassed 130 satellite camps and extension units.

Buchenwald was established well before World War II, on July 16, 1937, and originally housed just 149 inmates, mostly political detainees and criminals. The camp was officially named Buchenwald by HEINRICH HIMMLER, head of the SCHUTZSTAFFEL (SS) on July 28, 1937. By 1939, during the INVASION OF POLAND, the camp was divided into three parts: a "large camp," which housed prisoners who had some seniority; a "small camp," to quarantine new prisoners; and a "tent camp," to receive Polish prisoners. Additionally, the camp included the SS barracks and the camp factories. Buchenwald was commanded by SS-Standartenfuhrer Karl Koch from 1937 to 1941 and by SS-Oberfuhrer Hermann Pister from 1942 to 1945.

The camp grew quickly. From the original 149 in July 1937, the population swelled to 2,561 by the end of the year. Most of these were identified as political prisoners. As the Nazi regime cracked down on various groups identified as "asocial elements," Buchenwald received even more prisoners. By July 1938, there were 7,723; 2,200 more, all Jews, came from Austria on September 23, 1938. Following *KRISTALLNACHT*, November 9–10, 1938, the camp received another 10,000 Jews, so that by the end of the month the population passed 18,000. However, by the end of the year, most of the Jewish prisoners were released, bringing the camp population to 11,000.

The commencement of the war sharply increased the number of arrests throughout the Reich. Thousands of new political prisoners arrived at Buchenwald, along with thousands of Poles. By 1943, armament factories were built near the camp, which now served to house slave labor. By the end of 1944, there were 63,048 prisoners, and by February 1945, 86,232. In all, from July 1937 to March 1945, 238,980 prisoners from 30 countries passed through Buchenwald and its satellites. Of this number, 43,045 were murdered or died from neglect and abuse.

As mentioned, the first major influx of Jewish prisoners came after *Kristallnacht.* At Buchenwald, Jews were singled out for the harshest treatment. Most were put to work 14 to 15 hours a day at the infamous Buchenwald quarry. At this point, ADOLF HITLER's object was not to kill Jews, but to force them to emigrate from Germany. Therefore, during the winter of 1938–39, 9,370 Jews were released from Buchenwald after their families (and Jewish and international organizations) had arranged for their emigration.

After the commencement of war, the influx of Jewish prisoners increased, and there were no further releases. Buchenwald was used to house Jewish prisoners from Germany as well as from the "Protectorate" of Bohemia and Moravia. By September 1939, the Jewish prisoners numbered some 2,700.

On October 17, 1942, an order was issued for the transfer of all Jewish prisoners held within the Reich proper to AUSCHWITZ EXTERMINATION CAMP. All of Buchenwald's Jews, except for 204 deemed essential workers, were transferred. Two years later, Hungarian Jews began coming to Buchenwald from Auschwitz. Most of these were forced into labor at the armament factories. Beginning on January 18, 1945, Auschwitz and other camps in the east were being evacuated as Red Army troops advanced. Thousands were now transferred to Buchenwald. Among the Auschwitz evacuees were several hundred children and youths, who were consigned to a special barracks, "Children's Block 66," erected in the tent camp. This block housed more than 600 children and youths, most of whom survived. Even at this late date, however, Jewish prisoners at Buchenwald were often used for grotesque medical experiments.

Resistance cells among the prisoners formed from the very beginning of Buchenwald's existence. German Communist Party prisoners formed one such cell in 1938 with the purpose of planting members in the most important posts available to inmates. Until the end of 1938, the criminal inmates managed most of the camp's internal administration, but when authorities discovered that the criminals were conspiring with some SS personnel in schemes of corruption and theft (stealing from other inmates), inmate influence began to pass to the political prisoners. Under these conditions, some clandestine activities became possible, and by the war years, many resistance cells had developed, mostly based on the nationality of the prisoners. In 1943, a more inclusive underground movement, including Jews, was formed. Called the International Underground Committee, it directed sabotage carried out in the armament plants employing Buchenwald prisoners. Underground members also smuggled arms and ammunition from the plants into the camp. There was, however, never any large-scale uprising at the camp until very nearly the day the camp was liberated by U.S. forces.

As units of the U.S. Army approached, authorities began evacuating the Jewish prisoners from Buchenwald on April 6, 1945. On April 7, thousands more of various nationalities were evacuated from the main camps and the satellite camps. A total of 28,250 were evacuated. Of this number, 7,000 to 8,000 were murdered or died during evacuation. The evacuation was not completed because resistance members holding administrative posts sabotaged SS evacuation orders. By April 11, most of the SS guards had fled, and the remaining prisoners did not wait for the approaching American army before they rose up and, using smuggled weapons, seized control of the camp, killing the few dozen SS men who had stayed behind. Thus, on April 11, 1945, Buchenwald earned the distinction of having liberated itself. Some 21,000 prisoners, including about 4,000 Jews and 1,000 children, greeted U.S. troops when they arrived. During the NUREMBERG WAR CRIMES TRIBUNAL in 1947, 31 Buchenwald staff members were tried; two of this number were sentenced to death, and four to life imprisonment.

See also HOLOCAUST, THE.

Further reading: Clark, J. Ray. *Journey to Hell: The Fiery Furnaces of Buchenwald.* Chapel Hill, N.C.: Pentland Press, 1996; Hackett, David A. *Elusive Justice: War Crimes and the Buchenwald Trials.* Denver: Westview, 2004; Hackett, David A. *The Buchenwald Report.* Denver: Westview Press, 1997; Werber, Jack, and William B. Helmreich. *Saving Children: Diary of a Buchenwald Survivor and Rescuer.* Somerset, N.J.: Transaction Publishers, 1996.

Buckner, Simon Bolivar, Jr. (1886–1945)
U.S. Army commander in the Pacific theater

Buckner was commander in the Pacific theater during the tough and little-heralded ALEUTIAN ISLANDS CAMPAIGN and served as commander of the Tenth U.S. Army in the OKINAWA CAMPAIGN. A front-line general, he was killed by a Japanese artillery shell on June 18, 1945, three days before Okinawa was finally taken. Holding the rank of lieutenant general, he was the highest-ranking U.S. officer killed in World War II combat.

Buckner was born at Munfordville, Kentucky, the son of Confederate Lt. Gen. Simon Bolivar Buckner. Destined from birth for a military career, Buckner enrolled at Virginia Military Institute and studied there from 1902 to 1904 before entering West Point, from which he graduated in 1908. He served in U.S. postings as well as in the Philippines and even flew briefly with the U.S. Army Air Service. He was not sent to France during World War I but remained in the states as a teacher and trainer. Between the wars, he taught infantry tactics at West Point from 1919 to 1923, then completed the advanced infantry course at Fort Benning in 1924. He then attended the Command and General Staff School at Fort Leavenworth, remaining there as an instructor until 1928. From here, he enrolled in the Army War College (AWC). After graduating in 1929, he taught at the AWC until 1932, when he served for a year as instructor of tactics at West Point. He was appointed commandant of cadets in 1933 and served in this capacity until 1936.

Promoted to colonel in 1937, Buckner served with the 66th Infantry Regiment, then took command of Fort McClellan, Alabama; the command coincided with command of the 22nd Infantry Regiment and District D of the Civilian Conservation Corps. Buckner was elevated to chief of staff, 6th Division, then in 1940 was tapped to head the Alaskan Defense Command with the rank of brigadier general.

Buckner was a vigorous and proactive commander who lobbied the Joint Chiefs of Staff for resources to defend Alaska against what he feared would be Soviet aggression after the conclusion of the GERMAN-SOVIET NON-AGGRESSION PACT. Buckner's forces were in a reasonably high state of preparedness when, after the BATTLE OF PEARL HARBOR, the Joint Chiefs suddenly grasped the importance of Alaska and promoted Buckner to major general. He rapidly built up forces there and, in a brilliantly ambitious move, directed construction of the Alcan Highway, connecting Alaska with the lower 48 states and creating a critically important transportation and communication artery.

In June 1942, after eluding U.S. naval units, Japanese forces occupied the Aleutian islands of Kiska and Attu. This was largely a diversionary move to draw U.S. forces away from the central and south Pacific so that the Japanese fleet could better attack MIDWAY. In and of itself, Japanese occupation of these two remote islands had little direct military significance. However, the effect on U.S. morale was powerful. American continental territory had been invaded. Buckner led assaults on Attu and Kiska in 1943. Attu was recaptured on May 29 after 18 days of unexpectedly fierce combat. This prize retaken, Buckner jumped off for Kiska, only to find that the Japanese had withdrawn. For his achievements in the Aleutians, Buckner was promoted to lieutenant general.

Buckner was next assigned to command the newly created Tenth U.S. Army. He led this force, which included not only army personnel but Gen. ROY GEIGER's III Amphibious Corps, a marine unit, into the Okinawa campaign during April–June 1945. Buckner adopted a conservative strategy, which proved so slow and costly that his colleagues in the navy and marines leveled harsh criticism against him. No one, however, questioned his boundless battlefield courage. A front-line commander, he continually exposed himself to fire and was killed by an artillery burst on June 18, 1945. Okinawa fell to the United States just three days later.

Buckner was buried in the Tenth Army Cemetery on Okinawa. Subsequently, his remains were returned to Kentucky, where he was buried beside his father. In 1954, he was posthumously promoted to general.

Further reading: Buckner, Simon Bolivar, and Joseph Warren Stilwell. *Seven Stars: The Okinawa Battle Diaries of Simon Bolivar Buckner, Jr. and Joseph Stilwell.* Lubbock: Texas A&M University Press, 2004; Garfield, Brian. *The Thousand-Mile War: World War II in Alaska and the Aleutians.* Fairbanks: University of Alaska Press, 1996; Rottman, Gordon, and Howard Gerrard. *Okinawa 1945: The Last Battle.* London: Osprey, 2002.

Budenny, Semyon (1883–1973) *Soviet Red Army marshal*

A veteran of the Russian civil war (1918–20), Budenny was one of the Red Army's marshals during World War II. Born in Kozyurin, near Rostov-on-Don, Budenny was of peasant stock and, like many poor Russian young men, sought opportunity in the Imperial Russian Army, which he joined in 1903, serving in East Asia. During the Russian Revolutions of 1917, he threw in his lot with the Bolsheviks and was named chairman of the divisional soviet of soldiers in the Caucasus. With the outbreak of the civil war, he organized a cavalry unit to fight the counterrevolutionary Whites in the northern Caucasus in 1918, then formally joined the Communist Party the following year. As commander of the 1st Cavalry Army during 1919–24, Budenny enjoyed success against White forces and Polish forces. He was appointed to command the entire north Caucasian military district in 1922, though he also retained direct command of the 1st Cavalry Army.

In 1924, Budenny was elevated to inspector of the Red Army cavalry and served in that post until 1937, when he was named commander of the Moscow military district. He graduated from the prestigious Frunze Military Academy in 1932 and was promoted to marshal of the Soviet Union. In 1938, he was admitted as a member of the Presidium of the Supreme Soviet and became a full member of the party's Central Committee the following year. In 1940, he was promoted from command of the Moscow military district to the post of first deputy commissar for defense. This put him in position for a key command after the German INVASION OF THE SOVIET UNION in 1941. He was dispatched to the southwestern front and charged with defending against German advances into Ukraine. No Red Army senior commander was more trusted than Budenny, whose troops were the cream of the Soviet land forces. Moreover, the marshal enjoyed significant superiority of numbers on this front. Nevertheless, he was outgeneraled by German BLITZKRIEG tactics and was enveloped first at Uman and then at Kiev. These were disasters virtually unprecedented in military history. Under Budenny, the Red Army lost a million and a half men, killed or taken prisoner. The number of wounded is not known. Utterly routed, the Red Army yielded Ukraine, rich in agricultural, mineral, and industrial resources, to the invader.

In September 1941, Budyenny was relieved as commander of the southwestern front and was replaced by SEMYON TIMOSHENKO. He was, however, retained in the senior ranks of the Red Army and given command of the Reserve Front. Later in the war, he was returned to his old area of expertise and assumed command of the Soviet cavalry.

Full blame for the catastrophic failure of the defense of the Ukraine cannot be laid at the feet of Semyon Budenny, who was to a considerable degree constrained by the hold-fast orders of JOSEPH STALIN. Perhaps it was awareness of this that spared Budenny the fate of other generals who suffered serious, but much less extensive, defeats: the firing squad. Indeed, far from incurring censure, Budenny continued to enjoy Stalin's favor and was settled, after the war, into his former post as inspector of the cavalry in 1953. Even years after Stalin's death, in 1958, Budenny was honored when he was named Hero of the Soviet Union, the nation's highest military award. That he was reduced in 1961 from full membership in the Central Committee of the Communist Party to the status of candidate member was more the result of shifting Soviet politics in the post-Stalin era than criticism of Budenny's war record.

Further reading: Clark, Alan. *Barbarossa.* New York: Perennial, 1985; Glantz, David M. , and Jonathan M. House. *When Titans Clashed: How the Red Army Stopped Hitler.* Lawrence: University Press of Kansas, 1998; Overy, Richard. *Russia's War.* New York: Penguin, 1998.

Bulganin, Nikolay (1895–1975) *deputy premier of the Soviet Union*

Bulganin was among the coterie of Soviet leaders whose World War II experience elevated them to major roles in the postwar Soviet Union. Born in Nizhny Novgorod, Bulganin was an early member of the Bolsheviks and entered the Cheka (secret police) as an officer in 1918. He was later detailed to manage a state-run electrical equipment factory in Moscow, a position in which he distinguished himself. In contrast to many Soviet industrial administrators, Bulganin was innovative and efficient. In 1931, he was named chairman of the Moscow Soviet, then served as premier of the Russian Republic from 1937 to 1938, when he was named chairman of the state bank of the Soviet Union. With the outbreak of World War II, JOSEPH STALIN tapped Bulganin for the post of deputy premier of the Soviet Union. He was made a full member of the Central Committee of the Communist Party in 1939. After the German INVASION OF THE SOVIET UNION, Bulganin entered Stalin's inner circle and, in 1944, was named a member of the State Defense Committee, Stalin's war cabinet. From this point until the end of the war, Bulganin was effectively Stalin's deputy for war-related matters. After the war, in 1947, he returned to the post of deputy premier of the Soviet Union and was also named to succeed Stalin himself as minister of the armed forces, a position that carried the military rank of marshal of the Soviet Union.

In 1948, Bulganin was elevated to full membership in the Politburo of the Central Committee. After Stalin's death on March 5, 1953, Bulganin became deputy premier and minister of defense in the government of Stalin's successor, Georgy M. Malenkov. A canny politician, Bulganin turned on Malenkov when Nikita S. Khrushchev made his move to succeed him. This put Bulganin in position, on February 8, 1955, to become chairman of the Council of Ministers of the USSR, effectively the nation's premier.

Bulganin became virtually inseparable from Khrushchev but again proved disloyal by siding with the "antiparty group" that attempted to topple Khrushchev from his party leadership position in June 1957. The group was suppressed and its leaders purged from the Central Committee and its Presidium in July, but Bulganin managed to remain premier until March 27, 1958, and a member of the Presidium until September 5, 1958. At last, as 1958 came to a close, he was ousted, stripped of his marshal's rank, and consigned to a low-level party position. The final blow came in 1961, when he lost his membership on the Central Committee.

Further reading: Taubman, William. *Khrushchev: The Man and His Era.* New York: Norton, 2003; Zubok, Vladislav, and Constantine Pleshakov. *Inside the Kremlin's Cold War: From Stalin to Khrushchev.* Cambridge, Mass.: Harvard University Press, 1997.

Bulgaria

At the outbreak of World War II, Bulgaria, located in the Balkans and bounded by Romania on the north, the Black Sea on the east, Turkey and Greece on the south, Macedonia to the southwest, and Yugoslavia on the west, had a population of 6,341,000. Its king, Boris III (1894–1943), struggled in the early months of the war to keep his nation neutral. Bulgaria had lost territory in World War I, and it relied heavily on German trade. These were powerful incentives to join the Axis. Moreover, although the Bulgarian people identified with the Soviets as Slavs, the officer corps of the Bulgarian Army had a strong pro-German bias. The conclusion of the GERMAN-SOVIET NON-AGGRESSION PACT in August 1939 tended to reconcile even the Russophile Bulgarians to the possibility of alignment with Germany.

With the conclusion of the Treaty of Craivoa on September 7, 1940, Bulgaria belatedly received the return of some of the territory lost in World War I. This served further to align the country with Germany, which pushed King Boris III to sign on to the Axis (Tripartite) Pact. The people were especially receptive at this point because the Germans let it be known that Joseph Stalin's foreign minister, Vyacheslav Molotov, had announced to his German counterpart, Joachim von Ribbentrop, the Soviet Union's intention to forcibly make of Bulgaria a political satellite. In addition, the Bulgarians balked at the prospect of British intervention in Greece. At last, Boris announced to the German government that he intended to commit Bulgaria to the Axis, but he remained indefinite as to precisely when. Contemplating the impending invasion of the Soviet Union, Adolf Hitler was especially anxious to make Bulgaria friendly.

But it was the German invasion of Greece that finally motivated Boris's prime minister, Bogdan Filov, to sign the Axis Pact on March 1, 1941. This allowed German troops to traverse Bulgaria on their way to Greece. On March 5, Great Britain responded by severing diplomatic relations with Bulgaria, but that country held off declaring war against Britain until December 13, 1941, at which time it also declared war on the United States. The country refrained from declaring war against the Soviet Union.

Boris did not actually intend to fight and, indeed, was fully aware that his armed forces were in no condition to conduct a modern war against modern opponents. Moreover, Bulgarian peasant conscripts would mutiny before they would fight at any distance from their homes. Boris was also deeply concerned that affiliation with the Axis would stir fascists within Bulgaria to rise up against him and to replace the monarchy with a fascist republic. Nevertheless, Boris dispatched troops to participate in the German invasion of Yugoslavia, an action that garnered him a large portion of Yugoslav Macedonia, at least on an administrative basis, pending the successful conclusion of the war. Nominally, Bulgaria also received Greek Macedonia and western Thrace. The Bulgarians instituted such a harsh administration in these areas that their populations rose up in revolt in September 1941, and it was only with great effort that the widespread rebellion was crushed.

As an ally, Bulgaria contributed little to the German war effort. Bulgarian troops participated minimally in the invasions of Yugoslavia and Greece, but Boris steadfastly refused to commit troops, even on a purely voluntary basis, to the war against the Soviets. He also declined, in the summer of 1943, to use his troops against Yugoslav and Albanian partisans. On the sea, the nation's few warships participated in convoy escort missions, but nothing more. Internally, however, the Bulgarian government did make a number of concessions to German demands, including, in December 1940, passage of a Defense of the Nations Act, which forbade gentiles to engage in sexual relations with Jews, which barred Jews from land ownership, and which banned Jews from a wide variety of professions. Nevertheless, Boris resisted pressure to begin the deportation of Jews, and, thanks to this, some 55,000 Bulgarian Jews survived the war.

On August 28, 1943, Boris III suddenly died shortly after a rancorous meeting with Hitler. Many believed the 49-year-old king had been poisoned because he had begun, quite clearly, to maneuver the nation out of the Axis and out of the war. A regent assumed the role of head of state, and although the regency also favored removal from the war, its leaders proved feckless. Premier Filov was replaced on September 14 by Dobri Bozhilov, who did attempt to negotiate a separate peace with the Allies but never committed to them because he feared Nazi reprisals (as had occurred in Italy and Hungary).

Shortly after the death of Boris, the people of Bulgaria at last began to experience the war firsthand. Food shortages became critical by 1943, and on November 19, 1943, Sofia was attacked. On March 30, 1944, much of the population of that city fled to refuge in the country. Yet resistance movements did not become widespread in Bulgaria. There was more popular support for the anti-German Fatherland Front, largely in reaction to Allied bombing and the successful advance of the Red Army. On September 8, 1944, Konstantin Muraviev, Bulgaria's new prime minister, yielded to

Soviet pressure and declared war against Germany. With this, the Red Army crossed into Bulgaria, and on the very next day, the Fatherland Front staged a bloodless coup in Sofia. Outside the city, the left-wing takeover was anything but bloodless. The Fatherland Front conducted a brutal purge.

The Fatherland Front had affected the army as well. Gone were the pro-German officers. Now, approximately 339,000 Bulgarian troops eagerly joined the Red Army as an adjunct to the Third Ukrainian Front (Soviet army groups were called "fronts"). These troops participated in battles in the Balkans, Hungary, and Austria. Some 32,000 of these troops were killed. By the end of the war, Bulgaria had been transformed into a communist country.

Further reading: Bar-Zohar, Michael. *Beyond Hitler's Grasp: The Heroic Rescue of Bulgaria's Jews.* Holbrook, Mass.: Adams Media, 2001; Crampton, R. J. *A Concise History of Bulgaria.* Cambridge and New York: Cambridge University Press, 1997; Littlejohn, David. *Foreign Legions of the Third Reich: Poland, the Ukraine, Bulgaria, Rumania, Free India, Estonia, Latvia, Lithuania, Finland and Russia.* San Jose, Calif.: R. James Bender, 1987.

Buna, Battle of

Gen. Douglas MacArthur's plan to defend Australia against impending Japanese invasion was not to hunker down in Australia itself, but to take the battle to New Guinea, which he correctly saw as the necessary staging area for any assault on Australia. Thus, the New Guinea Campaign was a defense by means of offensive, and the Battle of Buna, a village on the northeastern coast of Papua, was a key phase of the campaign. Here, during July 1942, the Japanese had established a beachhead, and here, beginning in November 1942, two Allied divisions attacked.

The 7th Australian Division attacked the fortified Japanese perimeter at its northwestern end, near the village of Gona, while the 32nd U.S. Division marched toward Buna village and its associated mission at the southeastern end. Simultaneously, elements of this unit attacked the two airstrips at Cape Endaiadere nearby. Gen. MacArthur was confident of a quick victory, which was even announced—very much prematurely—in the Allied press. However, intelligence had been wildly off the mark in its underestimate of Japanese strength at the perimeter. Moreover, the 32nd was green and entirely unfamiliar with jungle warfare. As the assault stalled and casualties multiplied, MacArthur dispatched Gen. Robert Lawrence Eichelberger to Buna, charging him to take the village "or not come back alive." It was vintage MacArthur, which meant that the do-or-die order had been delivered in all literal sincerity.

Eichelberger was appalled by the conditions he saw at the front. The Americans were thoroughly demoralized, starving, and ravaged by malaria. He acted quickly by relieving and replacing most of the senior commanders, establishing reliable logistics and lines of supply, and ordering up fresh reinforcements as well as armor. Under Eichelberger, the reinvigorated 32nd took Buna on December 14. However, the nearby mission held out until January 2, 1943. That same day, Cape Endaiadere fell to the Americans. MacArthur was delighted, but to Eichelberger's dismay, he tended to discount as a "mopping up operation" the additional three weeks of costly battle that were required to clear the beachhead completely of this most tenacious enemy.

Thanks to Eichelberger, MacArthur's reputation, Allied morale, and the New Guinea Campaign were all saved at Buna. The cost to the 32nd U.S. Division was staggering. Of 10,825 troops deployed, 9,688 became casualties, most falling ill with malaria and other jungle diseases. This 90 percent casualty rate did provide a valuable lesson in jungle warfare by underscoring the preeminence of logistics in prolonged tropical campaigns.

Further reading: Chwialkowski, Paul. *In Caesar's Shadow: The Life of General Robert Eichelberger.* Westport, Conn.: Greenwood Press, 1993; Eichelberger, Robert L. *Dear Miss Em: General Eichelberger's War in the Pacific, 1942–1945.* Westport, Conn.: Greenwood Press, 1972; Eichelberger, Robert L. *Our Jungle Road to Tokyo.* New York: Viking Press, 1950; Mayo, Lida. *Bloody Buna:*

The Campaign That Halted the Japanese Invasion of Australia. Newton Abbot, U.K.: David & Charles, 1975; Shortal, John F. *Forged by Fire: Robert L. Eichelberger and the Pacific War.* Columbia: University of South Carolina Press, 1987; Vader, John. *New Guinea: The Tide Is Stemmed.* New York: Ballantine, 1971.

Burma Campaign

The Burma Campaign spanned the entire breadth of the war in the Pacific, from December 1941 to August 1945. While British and American forces participated in the campaign, and while the major force, the British Fourteenth Army, was under the command of British general SIR WILLIAM JOSEPH SLIM, most of the fighting on the Allied side was done by colonial troops and troops of other nations, including Indians as well as Burmese, Chinese, Chins, Gurkhas, Kachins, Karens, Nagas, and native soldiers from British East Africa and British West Africa. The bulk of the campaign was fought by an Indian army under British command.

The Japanese sought occupation of Burma to guard the flank of their forces in Malaya and those advancing to effect the capture of Singapore. Once these objectives had been achieved, Japan saw Burma as strategically important for three reasons. First, the so-called Burma Road was a major supply route into China. Second, Burma would figure as the westernmost anchor of the new, greatly expanded Japanese Empire. Third, Burma was an essential staging area or stepping stone for a massive invasion of British-held India. The Japanese also exploited Burma for political purposes by granting it ostensible independence in August 1943 to demonstrate that Japan intended to liberate Southeast Asia from European colonial domination in what it called the Greater East Asian Co-Prosperity Sphere.

The British were especially anxious to retake Burma because they had lost it in ignominious military defeat. However, the China-Burma-India theater (CBI) was always at the bottom of the Allies' list of priorities, and adequate forces were not made available. British planners hoped that a prolonged and costly land battle could be avoided

by naval action and an amphibious campaign to take the Burmese capital of Rangoon. Rangoon would serve the British as a springboard from which to retake Singapore, while it would simultaneously serve the Americans as a staging area from which to launch operations to clear the Burma Road into China. Yet plans for an amphibious assault never materialized because the CBI was at the end of the line for the distribution of landing craft, which, throughout the war, were in extremely high demand and short supply. Instead, by default, the retaking of Burma was achieved through an arduous and long overland campaign.

On December 14, 1941, Japanese forces attacked and occupied Victoria Point and its airfield at the southern tip of Burma. Japanese possession of the airfield here meant that the British could not fly reinforcements from India to Malaya. Next to fall, during January 1942, were Tavoy, Kawkareik, and Moulmein, all north of Victoria Point. The 17th Indian Division, under British Maj. Gen. John Smyth, planned to retake these positions by fighting from behind the natural barriers of the Salween, Bilin, and Sittang rivers, but, on February 23, Smyth found himself outflanked by the 33rd Division under Lt. Gen. Sakurai Shozo, who was rapidly advancing on Rangoon. In desperation, Smyth ordered the demolition of the Sittang bridge, which did delay Shozo's advance, but which also left 5,000 Indian soldiers isolated and cut off, to be captured by the Japanese, and resulted in the loss of artillery and other equipment. For this disaster, Smyth was relieved and replaced by Lt. Gen. HAROLD ALEXANDER. Shozo took Rangoon on March 8 and also nearly bagged Alexander and the Burma Army. They were saved only by the rigidity of one of Shozo's subordinate commanders, who insisted on adhering to earlier orders to enter Rangoon. To do so, he had to withdraw from the position blocking Alexander, who was thereby allowed to lead his army, intact, to safety.

Chinese reinforcements advanced into Burma as far south as Toungoo, only to be repelled by the Japanese 56th Division. The Chinese troops, of the 38th Chinese Division, assisted the 1st Burma Division, which had been cut off at Yenangyaung. After

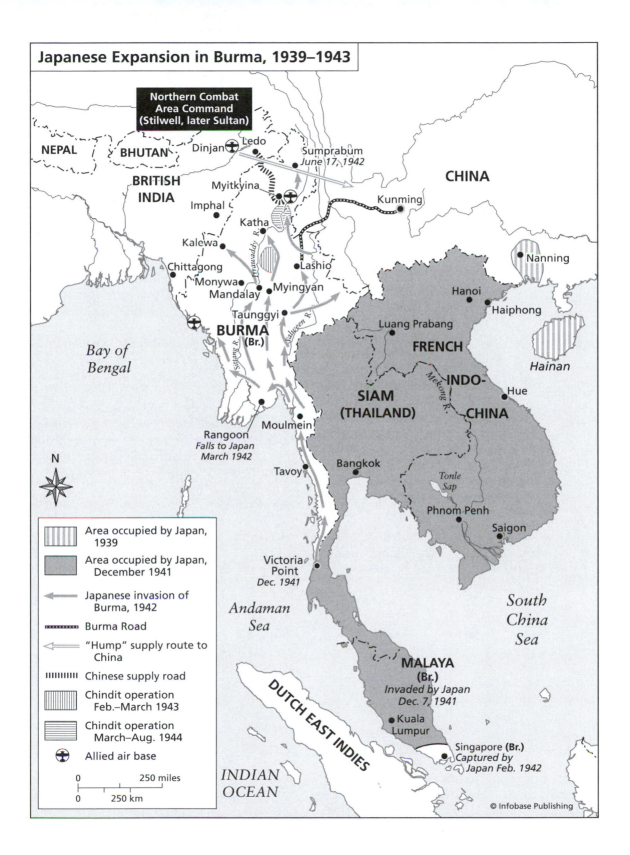

Japanese Expansion in Burma, 1939–1943

Northern Combat Area Command (Stilwell, later Sultan)

NEPAL

BHUTAN

BRITISH INDIA

CHINA

Dinjan
Ledo
Sumprabum
June 17, 1942
Myitkyina
Kunming
Imphal
Katha
Nanning
Kalewa
Chittagong
Lashio
Hanoi
Monywa
Myingyan
Haiphong
Mandalay
Luang Prabang
Taunggyi
FRENCH
BURMA (Br.)
INDO-
Hue
Bay of Bengal
SIAM (THAILAND)
CHINA
Hainan
Moulmein
Bangkok
Tonle Sap
Rangoon
Falls to Japan March 1942
Tavoy
Phnom Penh
Saigon
N
Victoria Point
Dec. 1941
Andaman Sea
South China Sea

Irrawaddy R.
Salween R.
Sitang R.
Mekong R.

Legend

	Area occupied by Japan, 1939
	Area occupied by Japan, December 1941
←	Japanese invasion of Burma, 1942
•••••	Burma Road
←	"Hump" supply route to China
ⅢⅢⅢ	Chinese supply road
	Chindit operation Feb.–March 1943
	Chindit operation March–Aug. 1944
✈	Allied air base

MALAYA (Br.)
Invaded by Japan Dec. 7, 1941

DUTCH EAST INDIES

Kuala Lumpur

Singapore (Br.)
Captured by Japan Feb. 1942

INDIAN OCEAN

0 250 miles
0 250 km

© Infobase Publishing

rescuing the Burmese, the Chinese continued their retreat through Imphal and into India. Also in retreat, beginning in March, was all that remained of the British forces in Burma. Slim led this so-called Burcorps in the longest fighting retreat in British military history, spanning March to May 1942, and ending in India.

As the Allies retreated, the Japanese continued to advance. The Japanese 18th and 56th Divisions reached the Chinese frontier by the end of April 1942, and the town of Sumprabum fell on June 17. On May 4, Akyab and its airfields on the Bay of Bengal were captured. Amid these disasters, ARCHIBALD WAVELL, recently appointed commander in chief of India, launched an operation intended to retake Burma. In December 1942, however, the 14th Indian Division was defeated in its attempt to recover Akyab. The Indians tried again, and again failed, then turned against Donbaik, from which they were also repulsed in March 1943. Months of fighting had gained the Anglo-Indian forces nothing.

In the meantime, in northern Burma, Brig. Gen. ORDE WINGATE launched the Chindit raids on February 13. Supplying his troops by air, he managed to penetrate the Japanese lines, although he lost a third of his force of 3,000 in the process. Nevertheless, this bold and effective action, set against so many defeats, greatly heartened the British and other Allies, and Wingate became a master of guerrilla-style tactics supplied by air. It was a valuable set of lessons in jungle warfare.

In March 1943, Lt. Gen. Kawabe Masakazu assumed command of the Japanese Fifteenth Army, and, in August, Burmese independence (under strict Japanese control) was proclaimed. For their part, in October, the Allies reorganized the CBI by forming the South-East Asia Command (SEAC) under Slim. A brilliant, resourceful, and aggressive commander, Slim planned what he hoped would be a comprehensive counteroffensive against the many Japanese advances. In Arakan, a long, narrow strip of land along the eastern coast of the Bay of Bengal in southern Burma, British Lt. Gen. Sir Alexander Frank Philip Christison would take XV Corps south against Akyab. Simultaneously, American Lt. Gen. JOSEPH A. "VINEGAR JOE" STILWELL would lead U.S. and U.S.-trained Chinese forces (Northern Area Combat Command) in coordination with forces under CHIANG KAI-SHEK to occupy Myitkyina, a northern Burmese stronghold of the Japanese. The objective of this advance, which would also be supported by CHINDITS under British commander Orde Wingate, was to allow the completion of the Ledo Road, an alternative supply route into China intended to replace the Burma Road, which the Japanese now controlled. Coordinated with these two operations was a third, on the Assam front in central Burma. The 17th and 20th Indian Divisions, commanded by Lt. Gen. Geoffrey Scoones, advanced on reconnaissance patrols deep into Japanese-held country.

The Japanese responded by creating a new army in Arakan, the Twenty-eighth, and, in northern Burma, the Thirty-third. Operation Ha-Go was launched in Arakan to surround the Allied forces there. It supplemented the IMPHAL OFFENSIVE, a plan to invade India from Burma. To the profound shock of the Japanese, however, both operations were defeated, the failure of the Imphal Offensive in March 1944 proving to be the worst defeat in Japanese military history to that time.

Just to the north of the Assam front, Stilwell led two Chinese divisions and the American volunteer rangers code named Galahad but better known as Merrill's Marauders (see FRANK DOW MERRILL). Even as the Japanese were suffering defeat in their Imphal Offensive, in March 1944, Stilwell pushed them out of the Hukawng Valley. By hard persuasion, Stilwell managed to wring from the grasp of Chiang Kai-shek another five Chinese divisions, and he called on Wingate's Chindits to disrupt Japanese communication to his south. After very bitter fighting, Stilwell secured the airfield at Myitkyina on May 17.

In January 1945, West African colonials attacked and captured Buthidaung, then overran a key Japanese communications center at Myohaung on January 25. The 25th Indian Division landed on the island of Akyab during this month, only to find that the Japanese had already withdrawn. This cleared the way for a steady Allied advance through

Arakan, which was secured early in the year, thereby enabling the construction of airstrips to support an all-out assault on Rangoon.

The campaign to retake Rangoon was William Slim's masterpiece. He deployed his forces with the aplomb of a magician thoroughly versed in the art of deception by misdirection. In mid-January, Slim sent the 19th Indian Division across the Irrawaddy River toward Mandalay, which it approached from the north. The 2nd British and 20th Indian Divisions, as well as the 7th Indian Division, crossed the river elsewhere during February, pulling off the longest opposed river crossing of the war, crossing points where the river's width varied from 1,000 to 4,500 yards. While these crossings were being effected, the 20th Division suddenly veered southward and cut rail and road routes to Rangoon. Slim sent the 2nd Division eastward to approach Mandalay from the south, even as the 19th Division actually attacked and took it from the north on March 20, stunning the thoroughly confused Japanese defenders.

Yet Slim was also surprised. He had expected the Japanese, as usual, to make a suicidal stand rather than see Mandalay, full of symbolic as well as strategic import, fall. Instead, Lt. Gen. Kimura Hyotaro withdrew and regrouped. Slim responded deftly. He was not seduced by taking Mandalay. He understood that a truly decisive battle would have to destroy the Japanese presence, not merely take even so important a city. Therefore, Slim deployed south of Mandalay and fought Kimura at Meiktila, central Burma. The battle lasted four weeks, during February through March, and resulted in a Japanese defeat and withdrawal on March 28. This opened the way to Rangoon, except for a brief (and fierce) Japanese stand at Pyawbwe. By April 29, Slim's 17th Division was on the edge of Pegu, just 50 miles from Rangoon. Heavy rains delayed the final push, and when the Anglo-Indian forces arrived in the capital, they were unopposed. The Japanese had pulled out.

During the summer, Japanese forces executed a long fighting retreat. The Japanese Twenty-eighth Army hammered fiercely against the British divisions arrayed along the Mandalay-Rangoon road, but because Japanese battle plans had been intercepted, the British were able to put themselves wherever the Japanese wanted to be, and the Twenty-eighth Army suffered some 17,000 casualties in the space of 10 July days, whereas the British lost just 95 men. It was almost certainly the most lopsided victory of the entire war.

After the Allies retook Rangoon, the Burma Campaign was essentially won, except that the Japanese continued to fight—fiercely, in the case of the Twenty-eighth Army, but more sporadically elsewhere. It was August 28, 1945, two weeks after Emperor Hirohito had broadcasted his surrender message to the people of Japan, before preliminary surrender documents were signed in Burma.

At the beginning of the Pacific war, the Japanese had taken Burma at comparatively slight cost: 2,000 dead in Burma, another 3,500 in Malaya. With this, the Japanese effectively began the dismantling of the British Empire, although they themselves were destined to lose their conquests by the summer of 1945.

Further reading: Astor, Gerald. *The Jungle War: Mavericks, Marauders and Madmen in the China-Burma-India Theater of World War II.* New York: Wiley, 2004; Dupuy, Trevor N. *Asiatic Land Battles: Allied Victories in China and Burma.* New York: Franklin Watts, 1963; Hogan, David W. *India-Burma (The U.S. Army Campaigns of World War II).* Carlisle, Pa.: Army Center of Military History, 1991; Webster, Donovan. *The Burma Road: The Epic Story of the China-Burma-India Theater in World War II.* New York: Farrar, Straus & Giroux, 2003.

Byrnes, James F. (1879–1972) *director of war mobilization under President Roosevelt and secretary of state under Truman*

During World War II, Byrnes served in the administration of Franklin D. Roosevelt (FDR) as director of war mobilization (1943–45)—in which capacity he was popularly dubbed "assistant president for domestic affairs"—and, in the cabinet of Harry S. Truman, as secretary of state (1945–47). Born in Charleston, South Carolina, Byrnes was a self-educated lawyer who became a public prosecutor in 1908, then gained election to the U.S. House of Representatives in 1911, serving until 1925. In 1931, he was elected to the Senate and became especially powerful during the Roosevelt administration, personally shepherding through that legislative body the great bulk of the New Deal legislation. Although FDR frequently consulted with Byrnes, the southerner was innately a social conservative and often broke with the president over issues he considered too radical. However, as U.S. involvement in World War II loomed during 1939–41, it was Byrnes who once again was responsible for garnering Senate support for the president's defense-preparedness measures.

In 1941, Byrnes left the Senate when he was appointed to the United States Supreme Court. He left the Court, however, after only a year to accept appointment in 1942 as director of economic stabilization and, subsequently, head of the Office of War Mobilization. This was a tremendously powerful office, and Byrnes was directly responsible for overseeing the production, procurement, and distribution of all civilian and military goods, the allocation of manpower, and the institution of measures for economic stabilization during the war emergency. No other government official, save the president himself, wielded more actual authority than Byrnes during the war years.

An intimate adviser to Roosevelt, Byrnes accompanied him to the YALTA Conference in February 1945, resigning soon afterward. Following FDR's sudden death in April 1945, President Truman recalled Byrnes to government service and asked him to accept appointment as secretary of state. In this capacity, Byrnes accompanied Truman to the POTSDAM CONFERENCE. Byrnes took an uncompromising hard line on such issues as obtaining from the Axis nations unconditional surrender as the only acceptable basis for ending World War II and on using the atomic bomb against Japan. Originally inclined to embrace the Soviet Union as a bosom ally, Byrnes was soured on the prospect of postwar cooperation between East and West by his experiences at Potsdam, especially over the issue of German reunification. During the cold war that set in almost immediately after the Axis surrender, Byrnes adopted an uncompromisingly anticommunist stance and called for an extensive U.S. military presence to be established in Western Europe to checkmate the expansion of the Soviet sphere. Byrnes's increasing conservatism clashed with the liberalism of Truman, prompting Byrnes's resignation as secretary of state in 1947.

Although Byrnes enjoyed a distinguished career in the national government, he never came close to achieving his most cherished ambition, which was to be elected to the presidency. In 1951, he was elected governor of South Carolina and was reelected in 1955. By this time, however, the realities of social reform had passed Byrnes by, and his later political career was marred by his insistent defense of racial segregation in public schools.

Further reading: Messer, Robert L. *The End of an Alliance: James F. Byrnes, Roosevelt, Truman, and the Origins of the Cold War.* Chapel Hill: University of North Carolina Press, 1982; Robertson, David. *Sly and Able: A Political Biography of James F. Byrnes.* New York: Norton, 1994.

C

Callaghan, Daniel Judson (1892–1942)
U.S. rear admiral hero of Guadalcanal

A UNITED STATES NAVY rear admiral who led a task force of five cruisers and 10 destroyers in support of U.S. landings at the Battle of GUADALCANAL, Callaghan received the Medal of Honor posthumously for his actions on November 13, 1942. He was one of the heroes of this most important battle.

Callaghan was born in San Francisco and was educated in Catholic schools, including St. Elizabeth's in Oakland and the College of St. Ignatius, a high school. He went on to the U.S. Naval Academy, Annapolis, in 1911 and graduated 38th in a class of 193. He served as commander of an 8-inch turret on the cruiser *California,* then was engineering officer on the destroyer *Truxton,* which he subsequently commanded. After serving as engineering officer on the cruiser *New Orleans* in 1916, he was transferred to the Atlantic upon America's entry into World War I and assigned to convoy duty. During the interwar years, Callaghan served as fire-control officer on the battleship *Idaho,* then had assignments on the battleships *Colorado, Mississippi, Pennsylvania,* and *California,* becoming gunnery officer on the staff of the U.S. fleet commander.

In 1936, Callaghan was executive officer of the heavy cruiser *Portland* and distinguished himself sufficiently to merit appointment as naval aide to President FRANKLIN D. ROOSEVELT. Callaghan accepted the honor of the appointment, although he left seagoing duty with considerable reluctance. In his capacity as naval aide, Callaghan did manage to promote the fitting out of the fleet's ships with modern and highly effective 40-mm Bofors antiaircraft cannon. However, with war clouds gathering, Callaghan at last prevailed upon the president to release him for sea duty, and he thus secured command of the heavy cruiser *San Francisco.*

In 1942, Callaghan, promoted to rear admiral, was assigned as chief of staff to Vice Admiral Robert Ghormley, who headed the newly created Southwest Pacific Command. When Ghormley was replaced by Admiral WILLIAM A. "BULL" HALSEY, Callaghan, at his own request, was returned to command of the *San Francisco.* In early November 1942, with the heavy cruiser as his flag ship, he was put in command of a task force charged with escorting a large transport and supply convoy in support of the massive amphibious assault on Guadalcanal. Early on the afternoon of November 12, 32 Japanese torpedo bombers swooped in on the American combat ships, intending to knock them out so that some 30,000 Japanese reinforcements could be landed unopposed on Guadalcanal. Callaghan then participated in a combined task force sent to head off the approaching Japanese invasion force. What followed on the night of November 13, 1942, was a naval battle that has been described by eyewitnesses as the "most furious" action of the entire Pacific war. The outnumbered American task force succeeded in turning back the Japanese reinforcements in action off Savo Island. However, Callaghan was killed on the bridge of his flagship. For his leadership, he was posthumously awarded the Medal of Honor.

Further reading: Frank, Richard B. *Guadalcanal: The Definitive Account of the Landmark Battle*. New York: Penguin, 1992; Newcomb, Richard F. *The Battle of Savo Island*. New York: Owl,

Canada

At the time of World War II, Canada was a British Dominion and therefore obligated to commit troops and resources to the British war effort. At the outbreak of the conflict, it did so with dutiful resignation, but little enthusiasm. Canadian casualties in World War I had been heavy (60,000 killed, some 172,000 wounded), and the new war also exacerbated the long-standing bitter division between the French Canadian minority and the Anglophone majority. Canadian Prime Minister W. L. MACKENZIE KING had the extremely difficult task of leading a fearful, disheartened, and divided nation into war. He did this, initially, by pledging a war of "limited liability," in which compulsory service would be necessary, but in which no conscript would be sent overseas. Canada maintained this more-or-less temporizing policy for the first 10 months of the war. After France fell in the BATTLE OF FRANCE, however, the desperate nature of the conflict suddenly hit home among Anglophones and French Canadians alike. The war was now perceived as a contest for survival, and Canada committed itself wholeheartedly.

Whereas early war production lifted the United States out of the Great Depression beginning early in 1940, materiel orders came late to Canada, but once they did, the hard-hit nation enjoyed an economic rebirth, with a doubling of the gross national product by the middle of the war and a virtual end to unemployment. Throughout the war, Canada served as a major manufacturing center, but, even more important, it was an agricultural powerhouse and a great source of iron, steel, oil, and synthetic rubber. By 1945, Canada was fourth among the

Allies in war production, and it accounted for one-seventh of the war production of the entire British Empire. A little less than a third of this production was used by Canadian forces; the rest was contributed freely to the other Allies. This boon was of critical importance to the perpetually strapped British. As for the Canadian government, it saw war production as a means of providing full employment and rescuing the nation from the grip of the depression, as well as helping to ensure victory. The result was that in contrast to virtually all the other belligerent nations, including even the United States, the standard of living for Canadians sharply improved during World War II, and the government even managed to hold inflation to a manageable rate.

As in the case of AUSTRALIA, the war brought Canada closer to the United States than even to Great Britain. However, whereas this closeness was in large measure military in the case of Australia and America, a function of the nature of the Pacific war, it was far more a matter of economics for Canada and its southern neighbor. Canada's rapidly expanding wartime economy brought a meteoric rise in trade between the two nations, especially U.S. exports to Canada. Even Canadian-made munitions and materiel often incorporated components imported from the United States. The result for Canada was an exploding trade deficit with the United States, an issue that King and President FRANKLIN D. ROOSEVELT addressed in the Hyde Park Declaration of April 20, 1941. Within the compass of just six paragraphs, the two heads of state agreed to provide one another with the materiel each was most capable of producing. In cases where Canada required U.S.-made components for equipment required by the United Kingdom, these could be acquired by the U.K. under the already existing provisions of the LEND-LEASE ACT.

While Canada often cooperated closely with the British in military action abroad, it was with the United States that Canada forged its closest military ties for continental defense. Motivated by the fall of France, Prime Minister King met with President Roosevelt in August 1940 to draft what became the plan for a Permanent Joint Board of Defense. The board included plans for allowing U. S. troops into Canada's maritime provinces to repel any German threat, and U.S. Army engineers were sent into Canada to build the 1,523-mile-long Alaskan International Highway (also called the Alaska Military Highway or the Alcan Highway) during March to November 1942 as an emergency war measure to provide an overland military supply route to Alaska. American service personnel also manned Canadian-based weather stations and laid an oil pipeline in the far north. Royal Canadian Air Force personnel and aircraft were dispatched to Alaska and based there after the Japanese invaded the Aleutian Islands, and a U.S.-equipped Canadian infantry brigade participated in the ALEUTIAN ISLANDS CAMPAIGN during 1943. U.S.-Canadian defense cooperation also went beyond the continent, as Canada and the United States collaborated in fighting the BATTLE OF THE ATLANTIC beginning in 1941.

In general, U.S.-Canadian relations strengthened during World War II, and this good feeling extended far into the postwar years. The Canadian government did take pains to ensure that the U.S. military presence in Canada was strictly controlled and that it would end with the conclusion of the war. As if to settle its military accounts, Canada, after the war, insisted on paying the United States for all fixed military installations it had built in the country. The exigencies of cold war defense, however, would soon bring back a U.S. military presence, and the two countries entered into a long period of close cooperation in early warning and other nuclear age continental defense systems.

Further reading: Chartrand, Rene, and Ronald Volstad. *Canadian Forces in World War II.* London: Osprey, 2001; Cohen, Stan. *The Forgotten War: A Pictorial History of World War II in Alaska and Northwestern Canada.* Missoula, Mont.: Pictorial Histories Publishing Company, 1993; Douglas, William A. B., and Brereton Greenhous. *Out of the Shadows: Canada in the Second World War.* Toronto: Dundurn Press, 1995; Dziuban, Stanley W. *United States Army in World War II: Special Studies Military Relations Between the United States and Canada*

1939–1945. Washington, D.C.: United States Government Printing Office, 1991; Esberey, Joy E. *Knight of the Holy Spirit: A Study of William Lyon Mackenzie King.* Toronto: University of Toronto Press, 1980; Granatstein, J. L. *Mackenzie King: His Life and World.* Toronto: McGraw-Hill Ryerson, 1977; Steveneson, Michael D. *Canada's Greatest Wartime Muddle: National Selective Service and the Mobilization of Human Resources During World War II.* Montreal: McGill-Queen's University Press, 2002; Woolner, David B. *The Second Quebec Conference Revisited: Waging War, Formulating Peace: Canada, Great Britain, and the United States in 1944–1945.* New York: St. Martin's Press, 1998.

Canada, air force of

At the outbreak of the war, the Royal Canadian Air Force (RCAF) was a puny service consisting of 2,750 enlisted airmen and 298 officers in addition to 1,000 reservists. Its inventory of aircraft numbered just 270, of which 37 were combat ready. Around this unpromising nucleus, the British government, on September 26, 1939, asked the Canadians to create the British Empire Air Training Scheme (BEATS). BEATS was tasked to train a total of 20,000 military pilots and 30,000 aircrew primarily to be integrated into the British Royal Air Force (RAF). The plan must have seemed outrageous in 1939, but the RCAF grew rapidly, and BEATS proved to be Canada's greatest contribution to the Allied air war; some historians judge it to be Canada's most important contribution to the war effort as a whole.

In 1940, the RCAF trained 240 pilots, 112 navigators, and 168 other aircrew. By the next year, these numbers had risen spectacularly to 9,637 pilots, 2,884 navigators, and 4,132 other aircrew. In 1943, the peak year for BEATS, the RCAF turned out 15,894 pilots, 8,144 navigators, 6,445 bombardiers, and 8,695 other aircrew. By September 30, 1944, when the program ended, the RCAF had trained 116,417 pilots, navigators, bombardiers, and other aircrew. Australia, which also participated in BEATS, had trained 23,262 men by this time, New Zealand 3,891, South Africa 16,857, and Southern Rhodesia 8,235.

While BEATS was Canada's most significant contribution to the air war, the RCAF also flew many operational missions, sending overseas 94,000 officers and men in 48 squadrons. Many RCAF personnel were seconded to RAF squadrons, but, in response to unremitting RCAF pressure on the British, many were also formed into Canadian squadrons. Eventually, the RCAF had several fighter wings and one bomber group. Canadian fighter pilots served in the BATTLE OF BRITAIN, over MALTA, in the NORTH AFRICAN CAMPAIGN, and in continental Europe. Canadian pilots flew transport missions out of Burma, and they manned a Catalina floatplane squadron in Ceylon. Canadian-based RCAF fliers provided not only for home defense, but flew fighter support for U.S. forces in Alaska.

In Europe, Canadians flew many strategic bombing missions beginning in June 1941. Until well into 1943, the Canadians were relegated to aging Wellington heavy bombers, which they flew from a remote base in Yorkshire. The age of the aircraft and the extra flying time required by their basing contributed to a high rate of loss, especially between March and June of 1943. By January 1944, however, more efficient command and new equipment—Lancasters and Halifaxes—brought significant improvement. The Canadians' bomber group, Group 6, consisting of eight squadrons, flew 41,000 operations in which 126,000 tons of ordnance were dropped, accounting for a little more than 12 percent of the total bombs dropped by Britain's Bomber Command. Group 6 lost 3,500 killed. Among Canadians serving in other squadrons of Bomber Command, 4,700 were killed. Total RCAF losses in World War II were 17,101 killed.

See also CANADA, ARMY OF and CANADA NAVY OF.

Further reading: Blyth, Kenneth K. *Cradle Crew: Royal Canadian Air Force, World War II*. Manhattan, Kans.: Sunflower University Press, 1997; Chartrand, Rene, and Ronald Volstad. *Canadian Forces in World War II*. London: Osprey, 2001; Cohen, Stan. *The Forgotten War: A Pictorial History of World War II in Alaska and Northwestern Canada*. Missoula, Mont.: Pictorial Histories Publishing Company, 1993; Douglas, William A. B., and Brereton Greenhous. *Out of the Shadows: Canada in the Second World War*. Toronto: Dundurn Press, 1995; Greenhous, Brereton, Stephen J. Harris, William Johnston, and Wil Rawlings. *The Crucible of War, 1939–1945: The Official History of the Royal Canadian Air Force*. Toronto: University of Toronto Press, 1994.

Canada, army of

At the outbreak of World War II, the Canadian Army consisted of a "Permanent Force" of just 4,261 officers and men. Additionally, a Canadian militia mustered 51,000 mostly ill-trained men. Equipment was virtually nonexistent: two light tanks, 82 Vickers machine guns, 10 Bren guns, five mortars, and four antiaircraft guns. By the end of the war, the army of Canada had expanded to a well-equipped force of 730,159 men and women.

As explained in the entry on CANADA, it was a very reluctant and divided nation that Prime Minister MACKENZIE W. L. KING led into war. For the first 10 months of the war, King pursued a policy of what he called "limited liability," by which no conscripts would be sent to overseas duty. Two volunteer divisions were raised initially, elements of the first of which, the Canadian 1st Division, shipped out for England in December 1939. Enlistments, however, were slow and light: fewer than 35,000 between October 1939 and May 1940, despite a depression-plagued economy. With the fall of France following the BATTLE OF FRANCE, however, enlistments skyrocketed; during June and July, 60,000 rushed to enlist. By the end of 1940, 122,000 had voluntarily joined up. In 1941, there were 94,000; in 1942, 130,000; in 1943, 77,000; and in 1944, 75,000.

By 1942, the First Canadian Army, in Europe, consisted of two corps with three infantry and two armored divisions as well as two armored brigades. By 1943, a home-based force was also fully deployed, consisting of three divisions charged with the defense of the Atlantic and Pacific coasts. King was gratified at the size of the force, but he was also concerned that it would generate huge casualty figures. Yet casualties were light during the first three years of combat, and although Canadians participated in Dunkirk and in the Dunkirk Evacuation, their involvement was peripheral, so even this fiasco created few casualties. Indeed, the real problem during the first three years of the war was the discontent of the Canadian public, which demanded action from the army.

Under political and public pressure, troops were sent to Hong Kong in September 1941. They arrived late in November and were involved in defending against a Japanese attack on December 8. The battle ended in surrender on December 25, the nearly 2,000 Canadians engaged having suffered 40 percent casualties before the rest surrendered. Canadian participation in the Dieppe Raid on August 19, 1942, produced even higher casualties: 2,752 captured or killed out of 4,963 engaged. On the brighter side, however, Canadian troops also played important roles in Operation Husky (in the Sicily Campaign) and the Normandy landings (D-day). After Sicily, the 1st Canadian Division and 1st Canadian Armored Brigade fought in the Italian Campaign, landing at Reggio Calabria on September 3, 1943, where they were soon joined by 5th Canadian Armored Division and the 1st Canadian Corps HQ. All were attached to the British Eighth Army and participated in some of the most bitter fighting in the slow but relentless Allied advance up the Italian Peninsula. In all, some 93,000 Canadian troops fought in Italy, of whom 5,399 were killed, 19,486 wounded, and 1,004 captured, a stunning 25 percent casualty rate.

Participating in the D-day landings were the 3rd Canadian Division and the 2nd Canadian Armored Brigade. The landing on Juno Beach was lightly opposed, but the mostly green Canadians were mauled by a counterattack from the 25th SS Panzer-Grenadier Regiment on June 7, 1944. Over the next several days, however, the Canadians rallied and progressed rapidly through the Falaise-Argentan pocket and into Dieppe, Boulogne, and Calais, thence into Belgium. At the Scheldt Estuary, they engaged in a bloody battle but cleared the objective by November 3, having incurred 6,367 killed or wounded.

Although the Canadians generally served as part of larger Allied forces, in February 1945, Gen. Henry Crerar was assigned command of no fewer than 13 Allied divisions, including British, U.S., Dutch, and Polish units, the largest force any Canadian army officer had ever led. He was assigned to clear the territory west of the Rhine, a mission he accomplished by the beginning of March. The First Canadian Army (transferred from Italy after a period of rest) crossed the Rhine on March 23. Canadian forces now liberated the northeastern and western Netherlands, then took up occupying positions along the coast of Germany as far east as the Elbe River. By the time of the German surrender, the Canadians in Europe had lost 11,336 killed. Total army casualties in all theaters were 42,666 killed (including 37,476 direct battle deaths) and 53,174 wounded.

Further reading: Chappell, Mike. *The Canadian Army at War*. London: Osprey, 1985; Chartrand, Rene, and Ronald Volstad. *Canadian Forces in World War II*. London: Osprey, 2001; Cohen, Stan. *The Forgotten War: A Pictorial History of World War II in Alaska and Northwestern Canada*. Missoula, Mont.: Pictorial Histories Publishing Company, 1993; Copp, Terry. *Fields of Fire: The Canadians in Normandy*. Toronto: University of Toronto Press, 2003; Douglas, William A. B., and Brereton Greenhous. *Out of the Shadows: Canada in the Second World War*. Toronto: Dundurn Press, 1995; Granatstein, J. L. *The Generals: The Canadian Army's Senior Commanders in the Second World War*. Toronto: Stoddart, 1994; Nicholson, Gerald W. L. *The Canadians in Italy 1943–1945*. London: Queen's Printer, 1966; Reid, Brian A. *No Holding Back: First Canadian Army and the Drive Toward Falaise, 1944*. Montreal: Robin Brass Studio, 2004.

Canada, navy of

As was true of the Canadian army and air force, the Royal Canadian Navy (RCN) was an inconsiderable force at the outbreak of World War II. Manned by 1,990 officers and enlisted personnel (plus 1,700 naval reservists), the RCN fleet consisted of four modern destroyers and two obsolescent ones in addition to four minesweepers. In February 1940, the Canadian government let contracts for the construction of 64 Corvettes; before the end of the war, a total of 122 would be built in Canada. These small vessels, the minimum crew of which was 47, were sent to sea as soon as they were built. They were immediately attached to Atlantic convoys and given the mission of antisubmarine warfare, defending the convoys against U-boat attack. Officers and crews were quickly and inadequately trained, but they made it their business to pick up what they could on the job. The ships were poorly armed, and they often lacked RADAR.

Despite the odds stacked against them, by mid-1941, the men and ships of the RCN assumed total responsibility of escorting North Atlantic convoys from Halifax, Nova Scotia, to the waters of Newfoundland, where other Allied escort ships took over. The RCN coordinated with the Royal Canadian Air Force, which provided air cover for this portion of the North Atlantic journey. Unfortunately, the RCN proved incapable of pulling off the miracles unrealistically expected of it. In assessing convoy losses to U-boat action during November–December 1942, the British Royal Navy concluded that four-fifths of convoy vessels sunk had been sunk while under escort by the RCN. For this reason, the RCN escort groups were relieved in the North Atlantic and transferred to the much less dangerous England-Gibraltar route, which allowed crews to acquire more skill and experience.

In March 1943, the retrained RCN escorts, their vessels equipped with the latest radar and antisubmarine warfare weaponry and detection devices, were reassigned to the Northwest Atlantic Command, given escort and antisubmarine warfare responsibility west of 47° west and as far south as 29° north. The service quickly redeemed itself, sinking 22 of the 33 German U-boats sunk by the Allies here after March 1943.

By 1944, the RCN was operating armed merchant cruisers in the Mediterranean and the Pacific, and also during the NORMANDY LANDINGS (D-DAY). The days following the landings, RCN destroyers patrolled the English Channel. Also by 1944, the RCN crewed two aircraft carriers (their aircrews were British, however) and two heavy cruisers. By the end of the war, the RCN had expanded its fleet to 365 ships, making it the third-largest among the Allied navies. In battle, 2,024 officers and men lost their lives, and 24 ships were sunk.

Further reading: Douglas, Sarty, and W. A. B. Douglas. *No Higher Purpose: RCN in WW II 1939–43.* St. Catherines, Ontario: Vanwell Publishing, 2004; Foster, Tony. *Heart of Oak: A Pictorial History of the Royal Canadian Navy.* Toronto: General Publishing Company, 1985; Graves, Donald E. *In Peril on the Sea: The Royal Canadian Navy and the Battle of the Atlantic.* Montreal: Robin Brass Studio, 2003; MacPherson, Ken. *Minesweepers of the Royal Canadian Navy 1938–1945.* Charlottesville, Va.: Howell Press, 1997; Milner, Marc. *The U-Boat Hunters: The Royal Canadian Navy and the Offensive against Germany's Submarines.* Annapolis, Md.: Naval Institute Press, 1994.

Canaris, Wilhelm (1887–1945) *leading figure of German espionage who was also an agent of the anti-Nazi underground*

Canaris was born in Aplerbeck, near Dortmund, and, from earliest childhood, manifested an aptitude for spying. All who knew him reported his absolute, insistent need to know what everyone around him was doing, and he was nicknamed Kieker, "Snoop."

After education in the public schools, Canaris enrolled in the Imperial Naval Academy at Kiel in 1905 and, in World War I, served as an officer aboard the light cruiser *Dresden.* He was taken prisoner by the British at the Battle of the Falkland Islands in December 1914 and made a spectacular escape from Quiriquina Island near Valparaiso, Chile, making his way over the Andes, through Argentina, and via a Dutch steamer to Rotterdam, from which he returned to Germany to a hero's welcome. His feat earned Canaris recruitment by the German intelligence service, which sent him on an espionage mission to Spain. Recalled to Berlin in 1916, Canaris was trained as a U-boat commander and served in the Mediterranean during 1917. Recalled again to Berlin in 1918, he was assigned to intelligence work until the armistice in November 1918.

Between the wars, Canaris was essentially a naval spy for the Weimar government, then served from 1931 to 1932 as chief of staff of naval operations in the Kiel area. From 1932 to 1934, he commanded the obsolete battleship *Schlesien,* until he was appointed head of German intelligence, the Abwehr, beginning on January 1, 1935. Immediately, he became aware of the attempts of HEINRICH HIMMLER, head of the German internal security (Reichssicherheithauptamt), and REINHARD HEYDRICH, chief of political espionage (Sicherheitsdienst), to take over the Abwehr, and he moved quickly to ingratiate himself with both men. It was for Canaris the beginning of a double life, as he operated to placate the Nazi insiders even as he fought to keep the Abwehr independent of the party. But this was hardly his only goal. During the 1930s, Canaris built the Abwehr into perhaps the most effective intelligence service in the world, specializing in espionage, sabotage, and counterespionage and placing agents in sensitive posts in all major capitals and in many industrial establishments, especially defense-related plants in the United States. Promoted to admiral in September 1935, he soon met with ADOLF HITLER and earned his absolute confidence. By the eve of World War II, in 1939, Canaris had developed German counterintelligence to such a thorough degree that virtually all British agents had been flushed out of Germany. The Abwehr was also instrumental in preparation for ANSCHLUSS (the invasion of Austria), the annexation of the SUDETENLAND, and the INVASION OF POLAND.

Canaris's work had been important in the Polish invasion, but reports of SCHUTZSTAFFEL (SS) and GESTAPO atrocities soon prompted Canaris to confront WILHELM KEITEL, Hitler's chief of staff, who informed him that Hitler had personally authorized such actions. It was apparently at this moment, at the beginning of the war, that Canaris resolved to work secretly against the Hitler regime. In England and Norway, Canaris subtly but effectively compromised and undercut German intelligence, although his spies in Switzerland continued to supply valuable information to the regime. His American agents also supplied valuable information about U.S. war production capacity, which, however, Hitler refused to believe. Canaris's agents also worked through the embassies and consulates of ostensibly neutral SPAIN to infiltrate the Allied countries.

As the war continued, Canaris increasingly compromised and distorted the intelligence he fed to Hitler. Although, for example, his agents had penetrated the movement to oust BENITO MUSSOLINI from power in Italy, Canaris concealed the information in the hope that the fall of Italy would bring about the collapse of the entire Axis. Inevitably, it became increasingly apparent to Hitler and his advisers that Canaris was, at the very least, ineffective. On February 19, 1944, Hitler dismissed Canaris as head of the Abwehr and replaced him with WALTER SCHELLENBERG. Apparently, however, Canaris was not yet suspected of outright disloyalty. He was named chief of the Department of Economic Warfare in Potsdam, a post from which he resumed his covert operations against the regime and began to work with the German underground, the so-called Black Orchestra, in plotting the outright overthrow of Hitler. Although he did not directly participate in the July 29, 1944, assassination attempt against Hitler, he was among the thousands of military officers and others who were rounded up following the incident. Sentenced to death, Canaris received a reprieve from Himmler, who had him sent to a concentration camp in Flossenberg instead. This reprieve came to an end in March 1945, when Hitler personally ordered the admiral's execution. On April 9, 1945, Canaris, stripped naked, was hanged as a traitor and would-be assassin, his corpse left unburied to rot.

Further reading: Hohne, Heinz. *Canaris: Hitler's Master Spy.* New York: Cooper Square, 1999; Kahn, David. *Hitler's Spies: German Military Intelligence in World War II.* New York: Da Capo, 2000; Schellenberg, Walter. *The Labyrinth: Memoirs of Walter Schellenberg, Hitler's Chief of Counterintelligence.* New York: Da Capo, 2000.

Cape Esperance, Battle of

The Battle of Cape Esperance was one of many naval battles spawned by the GUADALCANAL CAMPAIGN. On the night of October 11–12, 1942, a U.S. Navy task force commanded by R. Adm. Norman Scott fought a Japanese force under R. Adm. Goto Aritomo. Its mission was to pin down U.S. Marines onshore with suppressing fire while two Japanese seaplane carriers landed reinforcements. Thanks to advances in available U.S. RADAR technology, namely a new type of surface radar, Scott was able to surprise Aritomo's group. Unfortunately, the seaplane carriers did manage to land their reinforcements, but at great cost: One Japanese heavy cruiser and one destroyer were sunk, while another heavy cruiser was severely damaged. Goto died in the battle, and the next day U.S. aircraft sank another two destroyers.

The cost to the U.S. Navy was one destroyer sunk and damage to three other vessels. The beleaguered marines, however, were thrilled by the effective support they had received from the navy, and, for the navy, Cape Esperance was an important victory, which not only boosted morale at a time when most of the news from the Pacific was bad, but also demonstrated the effectiveness of the navy's night-fighting capability.

Further reading: Cook, Charles O. *The Battle of Cape Esperance: Encounter at Guadalcanal.* Annapolis, Md.: Naval Institute Press, 1992; Poor, Henry V. *The Battles of Cape Esperance, 11 October 1942 and Santa Cruz Islands, 26 October 1942.* Washington., D.C.: U.S. Government Printing Office, 1994.

Cape Matapan, Battle of

On the night of March 28, 1941, British and Italian ships fought at Cape Matapan (now Cape Taínaron), in the Mediterranean, off southern Greece. The battle was the fruit of British intelligence, which, as early as September 1940, had broken the Italian naval code. ULTRA intelligence, derived from this decryption, enabled Allied code breakers to decipher a message on March 25, 1941, revealing that Italian warships were planning to attack British convoys transporting troops and supplies from Egypt to Greece. Informed of this intelligence, Royal Navy Adm. ANDREW CUNNINGHAM, commander in chief of the Mediterranean, diverted a pair of decoys from the danger zone and laid an ambush for the Italian fleet using four cruisers and nine destroyers, which were positioned southwest of Gavdo Island. Then, on the night of March 27, Cunningham sailed with a battle squadron built around the aircraft carrier *Formidable*. Air reconnaissance from the carrier spotted three Italian groups, including one led by the *Vittorio Veneto*, the battleship that was the pride of the Italian fleet. Cunningham targeted *Vittorio Veneto* and its escorts, coordinating an assault by the cruisers and by *Formidable*'s aircraft. The planes scored several torpedo hits and also succeeded in stopping the Italian cruiser *Pola*. However, neither ship was sunk, and the outcome of the first engagement remained inconclusive.

On the next night, calculating that the Italians' fastest ships had been damaged or disabled, Cunningham decided to press a night attack with his own slower vessels. RADAR returns indicated that *Pola* was severely damaged, so Cunningham concentrated on finding it. As he searched, his squadron encountered the Italian cruisers *Zora* and *Plume*, escorted by two destroyers. These four vessels had been sent back to aid the stricken *Pola*, Italian Adm. Angelo Iachino having assumed that the principal British force had yet to leave Alexandria, Egypt. It was a fatal error, which Cunningham was quick to exploit. At Cape Matapan, he fell upon the two cruisers and their escorts, sinking them all, along with *Pola*. The only major ship to escape was *Vittorio Veneto* and her escort vessels.

Further reading: Porch, Douglas. *The Path to Victory: The Mediterranean Theater in World War II.* New York: Farrar, Straus & Giroux, 2004; Pack, S. W. C. *Night Action off Cape Matapan.* London: Allan, 1972.

Carlson, Evans (1896–1947) *U.S. Marine leader of Carlson's Raiders*

Carlson became famous in World War II as the leader of Carlson's Raiders, a UNITED STATES MARINE CORPS guerrilla unit in the Pacific. He was born in Sydney, New York, and ran away from

Evans Carlson *(United States Marine Corps)*

took the raiders into battle in August 1942, leading them in a surprise attack on MAKIN ISLAND in the Gilberts. This was followed by a month-long operation behind Japanese lines on GUADALCANAL in November. As a result of these operations, Carlson emerged as one of the great heroes of World War II. His courage was extraordinary, but so was his leadership, which relied on building teamwork within his unit, which ran contrary to the traditional strict military adherence to chain of command. Operations were always subject to thorough discussion, in which Carlson would solicit comment and suggestion from all ranks. This—and the fact that Carlson's Raiders were handpicked—contributed to the high morale and tremendous effectiveness of the raiders. Carlson used a Chinese phrase to describe his approach to guerrilla command, calling his raiders the Kung-Ho—"Work Together"—Battalion. That phrase became popularized as Gung-Ho and was soon adopted by marines and others to describe a marine who was both heedlessly courageous and fanatically committed to battle. While this interpretation of the phrase was surely inspired by Carlson and his men, fearless in operations behind the lines, it did not do justice to Carlson's "work together" command philosophy. Today, that approach continues to influence the training and operation of America's elite and unconventional forces (such as Seals, Delta Force, and so on).

Continuous combat in jungle environments damaged Carlson's health, as did untreated or inadequately treated wounds. He served throughout the war but was forced into retirement in 1946 with the rank of brigadier general.

Further reading: Blankfort, Michael. *The Big Yankee: The Life of Carlson of the Raiders.* Nashville: Battery Press, 2004; Daugherty, Leo J. *Fighting Techniques of a U.S. Marine: 1941–1945: Training, Techniques, and Weapons.* Osceola, Wis.: Motorbooks International, 2000; Frank, Richard B. *Guadalcanal: The Definitive Account of the Landmark Battle.* New York: Penguin, 1992.

home to join the army when he was only 16. He served in France during World War I as assistant adjutant general on the staff of General John J. Pershing, with the rank of captain. After the armistice, Carlson continued to serve on Pershing's staff in Germany as part of the army of occupation. He left the army in 1920, a year after returning to the United States, only to enlist as a private in the marines in 1922. Within a year, he was commissioned a second lieutenant.

As a marine, Carlson served in China from 1927 to 1929 and again in 1937, this time as an observer of the Chinese armies during the SINO-JAPANESE WAR. For about a year, he was attached to Chinese guerrilla units behind Japanese lines. After returning to the United States, he wrote and lectured on the dangers of Japanese expansionist ambitions in Southeast Asia and warned the nation that Japan was a potential and formidable enemy.

In 1941, Carlson was named to command the 2nd Marine Raider Battalion (Carlson's Raiders), a unit he trained based on his Chinese experience. He

Casablanca Conference

The Casablanca Conference was held from January 12 to January 23, 1943, at Casablanca, Morocco, between President FRANKLIN D. ROOSEVELT and Prime Minister WINSTON CHURCHILL, together with their top military aides, advisers, and chiefs. The objective of the conference was to plan the ongoing and future military strategy of the Western Allies. Although JOSEPH STALIN was invited, he did not attend.

The principal topics for discussion included agreeing definitively on the next step to come after the conquest of North Africa. The leaders concluded that Sicily would be the Allies' next objective. Also under discussion was the deployment of forces in the Pacific theater and, in the Far East, how scarce resources could best be apportioned. Finally, and after much debate, it was also agreed to continue the intensive STRATEGIC BOMBING OF GERMANY.

While the focus of the Casablanca Conference was almost entirely military in nature, Roosevelt and Churchill also covered ongoing, top-secret research on the atomic bomb, and they pondered the delicate situation of competing claims for the leadership of the Free French war effort against the Axis. Perhaps the most consequential agreement the two Allies

reached was that neither would accept anything short of "unconditional surrender" from Germany, Italy, and Japan. In the eye of history, this policy proved controversial. Some historians believe that anti-Nazi factions in Germany might have succeeded in overthrowing ADOLF HITLER and then negotiated a substantially earlier peace, had they not been disheartened by apparent Allied vindictiveness and intransigence. Other historians believe that under the circumstances, unconditional surrender constituted the only acceptable, effective terms. Accepting anything less would have been to recapitulate the tragic prewar errors of APPEASEMENT.

Further reading: Alldritt, Keith. *The Greatest of Friends: Franklin D. Roosevelt and Winston Churchill, 1939–1945.* New York: St. Martin's, 1995; Kimball, Warren F. *Forged in War: Roosevelt, Churchill, and the Second World War.* Chicago: Ivan R. Dee, 1997; Meacham, Jon. *Franklin and Winston: An Intimate Portrait of an Epic Friendship.* New York: Random House, 2003; Stafford, David. *Roosevelt and Churchill: Men of Secrets.* Woodstock and New York: Overlook, 1999.

U.S. general George S. Patton Jr. was military host of the Casablanca Conference. He is shown here with President Franklin D. Roosevelt at Casablanca on January 17, 1943. *(Patton Museum of Cavalry and Armor, Fort Knox, Kentucky)*

Cassino, Battles of

Cassino is a town a mile west of Monte Cassino, a rocky hill about 80 miles south of Rome, atop which was a Benedictine monastery. During World War II, the Germans fortified both the town and the commanding hill. It was, in fact, an obvious strategic choice; the town and its hill provided a formidable defensive position and had been the scene of battles and sieges since antiquity. To complete the advance on Rome. MARK CLARK's Fifth U.S. Army had to break through the GUSTAV LINE, the well-prepared defensive line that spanned the Italian peninsula at this position. The series of battles in and around Cassino would prove heartbreaking in their cost.

The first battle began on January 4, 1944. In the course of it, the monastery atop the hill, which the Allies believed was occupied by Germans and part of the German defenses, was destroyed by Allied bombers on February 15. In fact, the Germans did not occupy the monastery until after it had been reduced to rubble, which proved to be highly effective for creating defensive positions, providing even better cover than the intact building. Accordingly, more air attacks were ordered in, and the ruins were intensively bombed on March 15.

Clark had overall command of the Fifth U.S. Army proper, but, in the field, British general HAROLD ALEXANDER directed the battle, which included, in addition to American and British troops, soldiers from India, Canada, Australia, South Africa, Poland, Belorussia, and New Zealand. Three assaults were launched against the monastery hill: January 17–25, February 15–18, and March 15–25. All failed. Neither the city nor the hill was seized.

The Fourth Battle of Monte Cassino was fought by the II Polish Corps under General Wladyslaw Anders from May 11 to May 19. The first assault, during May 11–12, resulted in heavy Polish losses, but it did succeed in allowing the British Eighth Army, commanded by Gen. Sir Oliver Leese, to break through German lines in the Liri River valley just below the monastery. The Poles then mounted a second assault from May 17 to May 19, in concert with French Moroccan troops. The latter, accustomed to mountain warfare, proved especially valuable, and, at great cost, the German 1st Parachute Division was at last dislodged from its defenses surrounding the monastery. Exhausted and depleted, the Poles and Moroccans nevertheless nearly enveloped the retreating German paratroops, but many of them were able to withdraw intact. By the morning of May 18, a reconnaissance team from the Polish 12th Podolian Uhlans Regiment occupied the monastery ruins and raised the Polish flag over them.

The brutally won prize of Monte Cassino gave the Allies the high ground and cleared the last great obstacle to the final advance on Rome. The series of battles were, in the end, a strategic victory for the Allies, who nevertheless suffered some 54,000 casualties, killed or wounded, compared with losses for the Germans amounting to about 20,000. As if the terrible toll in lives were not sufficiently tragic, the destruction of the ancient monastery was certainly unnecessary. Despite Allied intelligence to the contrary, the German defenders of Monte Cassino and the town of Cassino did not occupy the monastery. Only after it had been reduced to rubble did the German soldiers take up defensive positions. It would not be until 1969 that the Americans admitted the bombing had been an error.

Further reading: Hapgood, David, and David Richardson. *Monte Cassino: The Story of the Most Controversial Battle of World War II.* New York: Da Capo, 2002; Lamb, Richard. *War in Italy 1943–1945: A Brutal Story.* New York: Da Capo, 1996; Parker, Matthew. *Monte Cassino: The Hardest-Fought Battle of World War II.* New York: Doubleday, 2004.

casualties in World War II

In terms of human life, World War II was the most destructive armed conflict in history. The total number of military personnel deployed during the war was approximately 120,908,000. The total military dead of all causes was approximately 20,280,000. The total military wounded in action was approximately 47,980,000. But the war took an even greater toll on civilian populations. Overall, civilian deaths directly ascribable to the war (including victims of bombing, murder, and genocide, as well as the privation, starvation, and disease directly caused by the war) are estimated at from 30 million to 55 million.

The following is a breakdown of military casualties by combatant nation.

Nation	Mobilized*	Dead (all causes)	KIA**	WIA***
Germany	9,200,000	3,250,000	2,850,000	7,250,000
Japan	6,095,000	2,565,878	1,555,308	326,000
Italy	4,000,000	380,000	110,823	225,000
Romania	600,000	300,000	169,882	n/a
Hungary	350,000	200,000	147,435	89,313
Finland	250,000	82,000	79,047	50,000
Austria	800,000	280,000	n/a	350,117
Bulgaria	450,000	18,500	6,671	21,878
USSR****	12,500,000	8,668,400	6,329,600	14,685,593
China*****	5,000,000	2,220,000	n/a	1,761,335
Yugoslavia+	500,000	305,000	n/a	425,000
Poland+	1,000,000	597,320	123,178	766,606
U.K.	4,683,000	403,195	264,443	369,267
Australia	680,000	37,467	23,365	39,803
Canada	780,000	42,666	37,476	53,174
India	2,150,000	48,674	36,092	64,354
New Zealand	157,000	13,081	10,033	19,314
South Africa	140,000	8,681	6,840	14,363
U.S.A.	16,353,659	407,318	292,131	671,801
France	5,000,000	245,000	213,324	390,000
Greece++	414,000	88,300	17,024	42,290
Belgium	800,000	22,651	8,460	55,513
Norway	25,000	3,000	1,598	364
Netherlands	500,000	7,900	6,344	2,860
Denmark	15,000	6,400	1,800	2,000
Czechoslovakia	180,000	n/a	6,683	8,017
Brazil	200,000	n/a	943	4,222
Philippines	105,000	n/a	27,258	n/a
British Colonies	n/a	n/a	6,877	6,972

*Maximum number of troops mobilized

**Killed in Action (battle deaths)

***Wounded in Action

****Recent historical research, still under way, suggests that these figures, staggering as they are, may have been grossly underreported.

*****Includes casualties from 1937 to 1945.

+Troops mobilized include regulars only, but casualty figures include regulars and partisans.

++Troops mobilized include regulars and partisans, as does military dead of all causes; KIA and WIA include regulars only.

Civilian deaths are impossible to break down accurately. Estimates follow.

Germany (bombing deaths): 593,000 (includes 56,000 foreign workers and 40,000 Austrians)

Germany (victims of crossfire in the west): 10,000

Germany (victims of Soviet fire and retribution in the east): 619,000

Japan: 658,595

Hungary: 290,000

Romania: 200,000

Austria: 170,000

Italy: 152,941

Bulgaria: 10,000

Finland: 2,000

USSR: 7,000,000–12,000,000

Poland: 5,675,000 (including 3 million Jews, amounting to approximately half the total of 6 million Jews killed in the HOLOCAUST)

Yugoslavia: 1.2 million or more

France: 350,000

Greece: 325,000

Czechoslovakia: 215,000

Netherlands: 200,000

U.K.: 65,000

Philippines: 91,000

Belgium: 76,000

Norway: 7,000

U.S.A.: 6,000 (of whom 5,638 were members of the Merchant Marine)

Civilian property losses may be summarized as follows.

Germany: 39 percent of dwellings destroyed or severely damaged in the 49 largest cities

Japan: 40 percent of dwellings destroyed in the 66 largest cities

Great Britain: 30 percent of dwellings destroyed or severely damaged

Poland: 30 percent of dwellings destroyed or severely damaged

Yugoslavia: 20 percent of dwellings destroyed or severely damaged

France: 20 percent of dwellings destroyed or severely damaged

Netherlands: 20 percent of dwellings destroyed or severely damaged

Belgium: 20 percent of dwellings destroyed or severely damaged

Other catastrophic civilian losses include:

Japan: 80 percent of merchant marine sunk

France: 70 percent of merchant marine sunk

Belgium: 60 percent of merchant marine sunk

Norway: 50 percent of merchant marine sunk

Netherlands: 40 percent of merchant marine sunk

Further reading: Clodfelter, Michael. *Warfare and Armed Conflicts: A Statistical Reference to Casualty and Other Figures, 1500–2000,* 2d. ed. Jefferson, N.C.: McFarland, 2002.

causes of World War II

The proximate cause of World War II may be found in the aggressively expansionist policies of ADOLF HITLER's Germany (rationalized under the conceptual policy of LEBENSRAUM), BENITO MUSSOLINI's Italy, and imperialist Japan. Behind these policies lay a complex of economic, political, nationalist, racial, and even mythological forces. Most of this complex was embodied in a conflict between political ideologies, particularly FASCISM and Nazism on the one hand versus communism on the other; another ideological dynamic was capitalist democracy (as embodied in the Western democracies) versus totalitarianism (as embodied in the fascist and Nazi powers). Had Hitler not betrayed the GERMAN-SOVIET NON-AGGRESSION PACT he concluded with JOSEPH STALIN, it is likely that the democratic versus totalitarian dynamic would have trumped the natural ideological opposition of fascism-Naziism versus communism. But the German INVASION OF THE SOVIET UNION made uneasy allies of the western democracies and communist Russia. Hitler's pact with Stalin was, for Hitler, a matter of temporary convenience. Not only was Hitler ideologically opposed to communism, he was motivated by racial beliefs—the racial mythology at the heart of Nazism—that made the

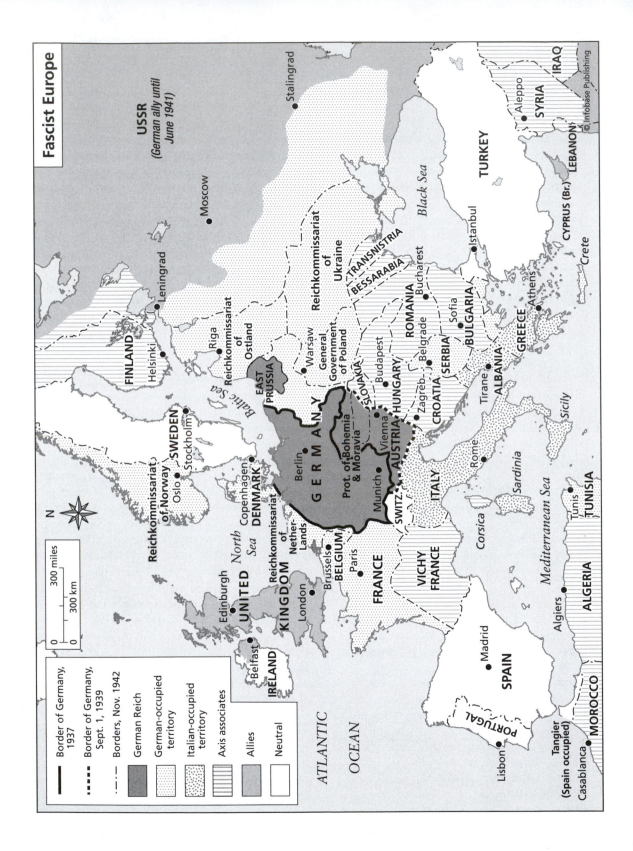

Fascist Europe

Border of Germany, 1937 (solid line)
Border of Germany, Sept. 1, 1939 (dashed line)
Borders, Nov. 1942 (dash-dot line)

German Reich
German-occupied territory
Italian-occupied territory
Axis associates
Allies
Neutral

ATLANTIC OCEAN

N

300 miles
300 km
0

IRELAND
Belfast
Edinburgh
UNITED KINGDOM
London
North Sea
Brussels
BELGIUM
Paris
FRANCE
VICHY FRANCE
SPAIN
Madrid
PORTUGAL
Lisbon
Tangier (Spain occupied)
Casablanca
MOROCCO
ALGERIA
Algiers

Reichkommissariat of Norway
SWEDEN
Oslo
Stockholm
Copenhagen
DENMARK
Reichkommissariat of Nether-Lands
Baltic Sea
GERMANY
Berlin
Munich
SWITZ.
ITALY
Rome
Corsica
Sardinia
Mediterranean Sea
Tunis
TUNISIA

FINLAND
Helsinki
Leningrad
Riga
Reichkommissariat of Ostland
EAST PRUSSIA
Warsaw
General Government of Poland
Prot. of Bohemia & Moravia
Vienna
AUSTRIA
SLOVAKIA
HUNGARY
Budapest
Zagreb
CROATIA
SERBIA
Belgrade
ALBANIA
Tirane
GREECE
Athens
Sicily
Crete

USSR
(German ally until June 1941)
Moscow
Stalingrad
Reichkommissariat of Ukraine
TRANSNISTRIA
BESSARABIA
ROMANIA
Bucharest
BULGARIA
Sofia
Black Sea
Istanbul
TURKEY
CYPRUS (Br.)
SYRIA
Aleppo
LEBANON
IRAQ

© Infobase Publishing

conquest of the Slavs a kind of racial duty and national destiny. Nazi racial mythology held that the Slavic "race" was inherently inferior to the German, or Aryan, race.

For Japan, race was also an issue. Since virtually the first extensive contact between the Western powers and the nations of Asia, Asians had been the economic, political, and cultural victims of white Christian racism. Western imperialism with regard to the East was rationalized in large measure by a Western assertion of cultural, moral, religious, and racial superiority. Asia was widely subjugated and colonized. Although Japan made compromises with the Western powers beginning in the mid-19th century, it remained one of the few Asian nations that was never conquered or colonized. However, contact with the West resulted in a blending of Japanese and Western traditions. Particularly powerful was the synergy of Western military doctrine, tactics, and equipment with Japanese warrior traditions. By the beginning of the 20th century, Japan was becoming a formidable industrial power and, as the Russo-Japanese War (1904–05) stunningly demonstrated, had already become a major military power. After Japan's victory over Russia, the Japanese military assumed an increasingly important role in Japanese government. Industry and militarization proceeded apace. Yet modernization did not produce greater social tolerance. As Japan became more powerful economically and militarily, it sought expansion of its empire, and it sought, in effect, redemption of Asia from white Western Christian imperialism. The racial dimension of Japan's desire for empire did not preclude its own treaty of convenience with the West: the Axis (Tripartite) Pact with Nazi Germany and fascist Italy.

Broadly speaking, these are the economic, political, nationalist, racial, and mythological forces that contributed to the outbreak of the war. Another key causal dimension is historical. Most historians view the period between World War I and World War II not as a peace but as a truce, and an uneasy one at that. World War I created economic disaster and unresolved national, ethnic, and quasi racial hatreds. It ended with the Treaty of Versailles, which imposed on Germany nationally humiliating and economically ruinous terms, creating the desperate conditions in which a charismatic dictator could readily find acceptance for a political, cultural, and mythic program that promised national and racial regeneration. Moreover, the Great War had created such general devastation that the putative victors suffered as much as the vanquished. The collective sentiment prevailing among the Western democracies was antiwar. This gave Hitler and the Japanese militarists the leeway they needed to establish the early phases of their expansionist programs, including rearmament and actual conquest, virtually unopposed.

If World War I caused general hardship and political instability in Europe, it also changed the political structure of much of the rest of the world beyond Europe by substantially undermining the old colonial order and stimulating a wide variety of nationalist and independence movements. Between the wars, much of the world oscillated violently among competing political ideologies. There was continual crisis, crisis that was greatly exacerbated by economic collapse. Although many national economies failed to recover from World War I, some nations prospered during the 1920s. However, by the beginning of the 1930s, economic depression was a worldwide phenomenon, reaching even the United States, which, otherwise politically stable, sought generally to isolate itself from the upheavals of Europe and Asia. Isolationism precluded American intervention, moral or otherwise, in the rise of Nazism, fascism, and Japanese imperialism.

By the 1930s, then, the Western democracies, beleaguered by economic depression and fearing a new world war, were largely demoralized, afflicted by a kind of collective political malaise and a willfully blind complacency. In contrast, the dictatorships, fascist, Nazi, communist, and militaristic, were increasingly suffused with an intoxicating mythology of conquest and national rebirth. Hitler's early expansionist moves—the remilitarization of the Rhineland (in defiance of the Treaty of Versailles), Anschluss (the annexation of Austria), the annexation of the Czech Sudetenland, and, ultimately, the absorption of all Czechoslovakia—were met not by western democratic opposition, but by an APPEASEMENT POLICY, which, far from appeasing Hitler, encouraged further aggressive expansion. Japan's imperialist ventures, most notably the conquests wrought by the SINO-JAPANESE WAR, brought economic opposition from the United States. President FRANKLIN D. ROOSEVELT imposed an embargo on the export to Japan of war materiel and raw industrial materials. He saw these economic steps as viable alternatives to war. However, they actually provoked Japan into attacking the United States at the BATTLE OF PEARL HARBOR.

Finally, all these events took place despite the existence of an international deliberative body created by the Treaty of Versailles. The League of Nations was supposed to provide international arbitration and mediation as alternatives to war. The failure of the United States to join the league virtually ensured its doom from the beginning. Weak from the start, the League of Nations soon became quite powerless to stop the forces of war.

In addition to these broad forces, the following specific events and factors contributed to create the conditions in which war became virtually inevitable.

Reichstag Fire. When the German parliament building, the Reichstag, burned on February 27, 1933, Adolf Hitler blamed the arson on a Dutch Communist. In reality, the man was mentally incompetent and had almost certainly been hired by the Nazis themselves to commit the arson. Hitler seized on the event to declare a state of emergency and to make widespread arrests. He presented himself to German voters as the only person in Germany capable of restoring stability to the nation. Nevertheless, in March 1933, the Nazis failed to capture a majority of Reichstag seats, whereupon Hitler secured directly from that body the absolute powers of a dictator. This led to the arrests of more anti-Nazis and the passage of an Enabling Act, which gave Hitler unlimited emergency powers for a five-year period. The act was subsequently renewed.

Hitler's Anti-Semitic Policies. Hitler's anti-Semitism served him in his rise to power in Germany by providing a scapegoat against which he could direct collective national hatred and anxiety. Anti-Semitism was soon revealed, however, as more than a means of scapegoating; it was an absolute doctrine of Nazi belief, and the drive to persecute and ultimately murder not only German Jews, but all European and even world Jewry, became a cause of war. Hitler and his fellow Nazis needed war in order to carry out the program of genocide that became THE HOLOCAUST.

Anti-Comintern Pact. Concluded on November 25, 1936, the Anti-Comintern Pact between Germany and Japan was the first step toward creating the wartime Axis. Italy signed on to the pact in 1937. Ostensibly a pledge of mutual defense against communist aggression, it was, in fact, a military alliance against the Soviet Union.

Spanish Civil War. As the entry on the SPANISH CIVIL WAR explains, this very bloody 1936–39 conflict between left- and right-wing factions over control of Spain's government was a kind of surrogate war between the Western democracies and the Soviet Union on the one side and fascist Italy and Nazi Germany on the other. It drew the battle lines of the much bigger war to come, and it gave Hitler's Luftwaffe in particular an opportunity to practice and hone the all-important aerial component of BLITZKRIEG.

Japan's Greater East Asia Co-Prosperity Sphere. Throughout the 1930s, Japan's militarists were driven by a need to acquire control over what they called the Southern Resources Area, which encompassed Malaya, the Philippines, Indochina, and the Dutch East Indies. Japanese politicians dubbed this the Greater East Asia Co-Prosperity Sphere and attempted to rationalize their aggressive wartime conquest of this vast region as the reclamation by and for Asians of territory usurped by the West. In reality, the Greater East Asia Co-Prosperity Sphere was the empire that Japanese rulers and militarists believed was theirs by divine right. In a less metaphysical vein, this Southern Resources Area contained most of the raw materials required by industry and the military, as well as an abundant supply of food and labor. Possession of the territory would make Japan autonomous and inordinately powerful.

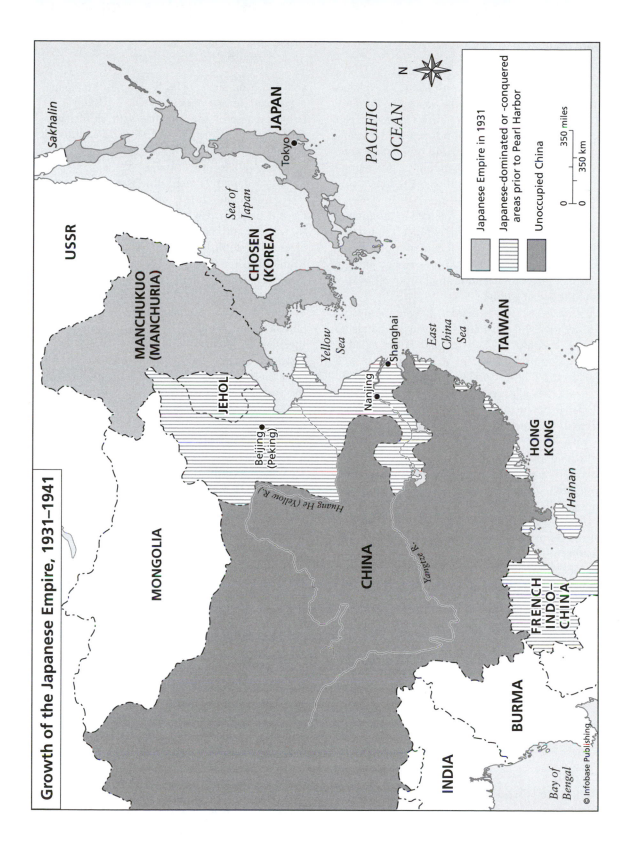

Growth of the Japanese Empire, 1931–1941

Japanese Empire in 1931

Japanese-dominated or -conquered areas prior to Pearl Harbor

Unoccupied China

350 miles
350 km

N

Sakhalin

USSR

JAPAN

Tokyo

PACIFIC OCEAN

MANCHUKUO (MANCHURIA)

CHOSEN (KOREA)

Sea of Japan

JEHOL

Yellow Sea

Shanghai

East China Sea

TAIWAN

Nanjing

Beijing (Peking)

Huang He (Yellow R.)

Yangtze R.

CHINA

HONG KONG

Hainan

MONGOLIA

FRENCH INDO-CHINA

BURMA

INDIA

Bay of Bengal

© Infobase Publishing

U.S. Trade Embargos Against Japan. As explained in the entry U.S EMBARGO ON JAPAN, the Roosevelt administration's attempts to curb Japanese expansionism not by armed opposition but through embargoes on war materiel and other staples succeeded not in pacifying Japan, but in provoking it to attack the United States directly, thereby bringing America into World War II.

Russo-Finnish War. As explained in the entry on the RUSSO-FINNISH WAR, this conflict resulted from the Soviet Union's territorial demands on Finland. It served to align Finland with Germany and give German forces a vital additional route of invasion into the Soviet Union.

Danzig, the Polish Corridor, and the Polish Crisis. In addition to Germany's prewar demands for Czech cession of the Sudetenland, Hitler called for the cession of the free city of Danzig (Gdansk) as well as the "Polish Corridor" that connected Danzig with Poland proper. The Treaty of Versailles had declared the historically German city of Danzig a free city and then compounded this by designating a narrow strip of territory as the Polish Corridor, which not only severed Danzig from Germany, but, Germans felt, flagrantly violated their national sovereignty. Poland's rejection of Germany's suggestion, in October 1938 that Danzig and the Polish Corridor be ceded prompted Hitler to plan the INVASION OF POLAND, which was executed on September 1, 1939, thereby beginning World War II in Europe as Britain and France honored agreements to defend Poland against German aggression.

See also NAZI PARTY (NSDAP).

Further reading: Dowswell, Paul. *The Causes of World War II.* London: Heinemann, 2003; Duignan, Peter, and L. H. Gann. *World War II in Europe: Causes, Course, and Consequences.* Palo Alto, Calif.: Stanford University Press, 1995; Eubank, Keith. *World War II: Roots and Causes.* New York: Houghton Mifflin, 1992; Ross, Stewart. *The Causes of World War II.* London: Hodder Wayland, 2003.

Ceylon

At the time of World War II, Ceylon (Sri Lanka), an island in the Indian Ocean, was a British colony and had been since 1818. It escaped the Japanese juggernaut of the opening weeks of the war and remained one of the very few sources of natural rubber still controlled by the Allies. In addition, its position in the Indian Ocean made it a vital transportation link to British India.

When Japan entered the war in December 1941, Australian troops were rushed to garrison Ceylon until British troops could arrive to reinforce the island. Early in 1942, the British Eastern Fleet was established there, and, in March 1942, Prime Minister WINSTON CHURCHILL assigned V. Adm. Geoffrey Layton as commander in chief of the island, giving him absolute authority over the military as well as civilians there (some 6 million Sinhalese and Tamils). His mission was to prepare the island's defenses. However, no sooner did he arrive in Ceylon than a Japanese carrier striking force under V. Adm. NAGUMO CHUICHI sailed into the Indian Ocean to attack. The British Eastern Fleet, under Adm. JAMES SOMERVILLE, sailed to the defense, as Nagumo launched bombing raids against Ceylon from his carriers. While he targeted Ceylon, V. Adm. OZAWA JISABURO led a smaller Japanese force in a raid into the Bay of Bengal, destroying 23 merchant vessels (20 in a single day) and bombing two Indian towns. The surface actions of Nagumo and Ozawa were coordinated with Japanese submarine attacks against shipping off India's west coast.

Somerville's resources were uneven in quality. He had three aircraft carriers, two of which were new, but his five battleships were obsolescent and slow. He decided that the most effective way to check Nagumo was to make a preemptive attack, planned for the night of April 1, 1942. When Nagumo's fleet failed to materialize, however, Somerville was forced to retire to a base on Addu Atoll in order to refuel and replenish water supplies. While he was doing this, he sent an aircraft carrier (*Hermes*), two cruisers (*Dorsetshire* and *Cornwall*), and an Australian destroyer to Ceylon for repair and escort duties. Thus, Somerville was hardly prepared to launch his preemptive attack when the opportunity suddenly arose on April 4. Learning that Nagumo had been sighted, Somerville sailed from

Addu Atoll but arrived too late to preempt Nagumo's raid on Ceylon.

On April 5, the Japanese targeted Colombo, the colonial capital, as well as Colombo's harbor. A British destroyer and an armed merchant cruiser were quickly sunk, and 27 British airplanes were destroyed. Next, Japanese aircraft sank the *Dorsetshire* and *Cornwall* as they attempted to steam out of Colombo harbor. Somerville quickly grasped the terrible reality: His carrier-based aircraft were obsolete and far outclassed by the Japanese. Realizing that he could not protect his elderly battleships, he sent them to Kilindini, in British East Africa, then set about trying to create a desperate diversion using the rest of his inferior fleet. As luck would have it, Nagumo suffered a failure of reconnaissance and was unable to locate the rest of Somerville's ships. On April 9, he did launch an air raid against Trincomalee, a Ceylonese port, which resulted in the sinking of the aircraft carrier *Hermes* and the Australian destroyer *Vampire,* but, grievous as these losses were, they could have been much worse. Ceylon lay exposed to further attack and invasion, yet these never came to pass. The Japanese withdrew, and no further fighting took place on Ceylon for the rest of the war.

Further reading: Banks, Arthur. *Wings of the Dawning, 1939–1945: The Battle for the Indian Ocean.* London: Harold Martin & Redman, 1997; Jackson, Ashley. *War and Empire in Mauritius and the Indian Ocean.* London: Palgrave Macmillan, 2001.

Chamberlain, Neville (1869–1940) *British prime minister and proponent of appeasement*

British prime minister from May 28, 1937, to May 10, 1940, Neville Chamberlain wanted to avoid another world war and embarked upon a disastrous Appeasement Policy in an attempt to stem the ambitions of Adolf Hitler and, at the very least, buy time for Britain to prepare defenses against fascist Italy, which the prime minister considered the more immediate threat. Born in Birmingham, the son of statesman Joseph Chamberlain, young

Neville was sent to Andros Island in the Bahamas to manage his father's sisal plantation. With this practical training in business behind him, he returned to Birmingham and became a successful industrialist. In 1915, he was elected the city's lord mayor and in December 1916, during World War I, joined the coalition government of Prime Minister David Lloyd George as director general of national service. Frustrated by the limited scope of authority in this position, Chamberlain resigned in August 1917 and, the following year, entered Parliament as a Conservative. Chamberlain was Britain's postmaster general during 1922–23, paymaster general of the armed forces in 1923, minister of health in 1923 and from 1924 to 1929, then again in 1931, and, finally, chancellor of the exchequer during 1923–24 and from 1931 to 1937. He became prime minister on May 28, 1937, assuming the reins of a government that desperately wished to avoid war, even as Benito Mussolini and Adolf Hitler were becoming increasingly aggressive in voicing their expansionist designs.

Chamberlain was more fearful of the extravagantly bellicose Mussolini than of Hitler, and he was especially anxious to drive a wedge between the Italian fascist and the German Nazi. In an effort to appease Mussolini, he agreed, on April 16, 1938, to recognize Italian control over Ethiopia, despite the pleas of Ethiopian emperor Haile Selassie. He also insisted on absolute British neutrality with regard to the Spanish civil war (1936–39), in which both Italy and Germany were involved. Finally, in an effort to demonstrate Britain's peaceful intentions, Chamberlain authorized the abandonment of Britain's naval bases in Ireland. Although Chamberlain argued that this was largely a symbolic gesture, many in British politics, chief among them Winston Churchill, protested this as a show of weakness and a serious diminishment of Britain's defenses.

But it is for Chamberlain's attempts to appease Hitler—"active appeasement," the prime minister termed his policy—that he is most infamously remembered. Three times in September 1938, Chamberlain traveled to Germany, hat in hand, as it were, in the hope of preventing a new world war, which threatened to begin over Hitler's demand that Czechoslovakia cede to Germany the German-speaking SUDETENLAND. Such was Chamberlain's anxiety to avoid war that he quickly concluded with Hitler the Munich Agreement of September 30, persuading French premier ÉDOUARD DALADIER to agree, with the British government, to allow the cession of the Sudetenland and to withdraw from any agreement to defend Czechoslovakia. From the Czech point of view, Chamberlain had, quite simply, sold the nation out. As most of the British people saw it, however, he had performed a last-minute miracle, bringing what he called "peace with honour" and "peace for our time."

With the hindsight of history, of course, Chamberlain's policy of "active appeasement" seems craven, and the Munich Agreement a tragedy. However, neither was the product of cowardice or naïveté. Chamberlain believed that Britain was ill-prepared to go to war, and he hoped that the Munich Agreement would buy sufficient time to rearm the nation. Immediately after concluding the Munich Agreement, the prime minister ordered a crash program of rearmament in preparation for war. And when, in abrogation of the Munich Agreement, Hitler marched beyond the Sudetenland to seize all of Czechoslovakia during March 10–16, 1939, Chamberlain repudiated active appeasement. He declared the absolute Anglo-French guarantee to defend Poland, Romania, and Greece in the event of attack. In April, Chamberlain ordered general military conscription, the first peacetime conscription in the history of Britain.

Even these preparations for war, belated as they were, were frustrated by the stunning conclusion of the GERMAN-SOVIET NON-AGGRESSION PACT on August 23, 1939. Chamberlain had planned to include the Soviet Union in Britain's mutual assistance agreement with France. Chamberlain did rush to conclude an assistance pact with Poland the very day after the German-Soviet pact was announced, and he made good on this agreement upon the INVASION OF POLAND on September 1, 1939. On September 3, Chamberlain secured from Parliament a declaration of war.

Chamberlain did not prosecute the war vigorously in its opening weeks, a period known as the "phony war" or, in Chamberlain's own phrase, a "twilight war," but he did courageously take into his war cabinet his most vociferous critic, Winston Churchill, who was named first lord of the admiralty. Nevertheless, the course of the war quickly went from bad to worse, and when British operations in Norway failed in April 1940 (*see* NARVIK, BATTLES OF), support for Chamberlain among his fellow Conservatives collapsed. Even as German armies swept into Belgium and the Netherlands, Chamberlain resigned on May 10. Churchill, now prime minister, quickly assembled a coalition government, in which Chamberlain stayed on as lord president of the council. He was, however, a stricken man, broken in health, and stepped down on September 30, 1940. Within weeks, Neville Chamberlain was dead.

Further reading: Caputi, Robert J. *Neville Chamberlain and Appeasement.* Selinsgrove, Pa.: Susquehanna University Press, 2000; Dilks, David. *Neville Chamberlain: Volume 1, 1869–1929.* Cambridge: Cambridge University Press, 1984; Dutton, David. *Neville Chamberlain.* London: Arnold Publishers, 2001; Feiling, Keith. *The Life of Neville Chamberlain.* North Haven, Conn.: Shoe String Press, 1970; McDonough, Frank. *Neville Chamberlain, Appeasement and the British Road to War.* London: Palgrave-Macmillan, 1998.

Channon, Henry (Chips) (1897–1958)
leading British profascist and chronicler of the right wing

Born in Chicago and educated in America and France, Channon was an intensely conservative personality who despised his native country, moved to Britain after World War I (initially to study at Christ College, Oxford, then to live permanently), and became a profascist figure in the Conservative government. Channon, who came to be called "Chips" because he had shared quarters during college with a friend known as "Fish," inherited fortunes from his father and grandfather and was therefore independently wealthy. He made a name for himself as the editor of the *British Gazette,* a right-wing paper opposed to the general strike of 1926, and he became a minor novelist and historian. He was also an avid diarist, whose diaries, published posthumously, chronicle the world of the right-wing well-to-do between the wars and during World War II.

Channon's marriage in 1933 to Honor Guinness, daughter of the second earl of Iveagh, catapulted him to membership in the House of Commons. Here he was a strong voice against communism and an ardent supporter of Spain's fascist leader. General FRANCISCO FRANCO. Channon opposed NEVILLE CHAMBERLAIN's policy of neutrality in the Spanish civil war, believing Britain should actively support Franco, but he was an enthusiastic supporter of Chamberlain's APPEASEMENT POLICY, not so much because he hoped it would bring "peace for our time," but because he thought that ADOLF HITLER could thereby be maneuvered into attacking the Soviet Union.

In 1938, Chamberlain appointed Channon parliamentary private secretary to Rab Butler, one of Chamberlain's junior ministers. Channon remained in government throughout World War II, albeit in minor posts.

Further reading: Channon, Henry. *Chips: The Diaries of Sir Henry Channon.* London: Phoenix, 2000; Overy, R. J., and Andrew Wheatcroft. *The Road to War.* New York: Penguin, 2000.

Life magazine cover featuring Claire Chennault. *(Author's collection)*

Chennault, Claire (1890–1958) *Creator and commander of the famed Flying Tigers in China*

Chennault recruited, organized, and commanded the American Volunteer Group (AVG), better known as the FLYING TIGERS, a group of intrepid American fighter pilots who flew, as soldiers of fortune, for the Chinese Air Force in World War II and proved highly effective against far superior Japanese forces. After the AVG was absorbed into the UNITED STATES ARMY AIR FORCES (USAAF), Chennault was assigned to command the newly created U.S. Fourteenth Air Force.

Chennault was born in Commerce, Texas, and joined the army infantry as a first lieutenant in 1917. Two years later, he transferred to the Signal Corps for flight training. After earning his wings, he was assigned as the commander of a pursuit squadron. Operating in the infancy of American military aviation, Chennault became an avid student of fighter strategy and tactics. He attended the Air Corps Tactical School in 1931, becoming, after graudation, an instructor there until 1936. He emerged from his study an advocate of the strategic importance of fighters, a doctrine that was vehemently opposed by the so-called bomber mafia of the interwar years. UNITED STATES ARMY AIR CORPS planners relied on the bomber not only as the major air weapon, but as the *only* air weapon of strategic importance. Fighter development as well as fighter doctrine were relegated to supporting roles, and, discouraged, Chennault retired from the army in 1937, having achieved no higher rank than captain.

In the year of his retirement, with the SINO-JAPANESE WAR in progress, Mme. Chiang Kai-shek, the influential wife of Nationalist China's generalissimo CHIANG-KAI-SHEK, recruited Chennault to organize and train the American Volunteer Group—the Flying Tigers. Their aircraft were obsolescent P-40s, markedly inferior to Japanese fighter aircraft. Chennault recognized this but used the shortcomings of the P-40 to his advantage, choosing and training AVG pilots who were willing to learn and to develop superior tactics that would more than compensate for the limitations of their aircraft. The result was a cadre of splendid, creative, and courageous aviators.

The AVG operated out of bases in China from December 1941 to July 1942, when it officially became the 23rd Fighter Squadron of the U.S. Army Air Forces. During this period, the Flying Tigers shot down 299 Japanese aircraft with a loss of 32 planes and 19 pilots. Although some recent historians believe these figures are variously inflated, none disputes the overall success of the AVG against numerically and technologically superior Japanese aircraft. Under Chennault, fighter planes proved their strategic value by substantially retarding Japanese offensive progress in China.

Chennault returned to USAAF service in April 1942 with the rank of colonel and was soon promoted to brigadier general. In July, with the absorption of the AVG into the USAAF, he was named commanding general of all army air forces in China. In March of the following year, he was named to command of the Fourteenth Air Force, which specialized in ground attack and other support of General JOSEPH A. "VINEGAR JOE" STILWELL's operations in the China-Burma-India (CBI) theater. Chennault never shook the hard-won habits of a military maverick. Now part of the military establishment, he nevertheless repeatedly frustrated his superiors by circumventing the chain of command to work directly with Chiang Kai-shek. Nevertheless, in a chronically undermanned and

undersupplied Allied theater, Chennault produced results, and he retained command of the Fourteenth Air Force through the entire war, retiring after Japan's surrender in 1945.

In the postwar years, Chennault organized the Chinese National Relief and the Civil Air Transport to assist Chiang Kai-shek in the fight against the Chinese communists. Although he had left U.S. service, the USAF honored Chennault's service and achievements by promoting him to the honorary grade of lieutenant general just nine days before he succumbed to cancer in 1958.

Further reading: Byrd, Martha. *Chennault: Giving Wings to the Tiger.* Tuscaloosa: University of Alabama Press, 2003; Ford, Daniel. *Flying Tigers: Claire Chennault and the American Volunteer Group.* Washington, D.C.: Smithsonian Books, 1995; Scott, Robert T., Jr. *Flying Tiger: Chennault of China.* Cutchogue, N.Y.: Buccaneer Books, 1992.

Chiang Kai-shek (Jiang Jieshi) (1887–1975) *leader of Nationalist China during World War II*

As head of state of Nationalist China, Chiang Kai-shek was a major, albeit often difficult, ally of the United States and Great Britain against Japan, which had been waging war against China since the start of the SINO-JAPANESE WAR in 1937, a conflict that melted into World War II. Born into a merchant and farmer family in Chekiang (Zhejiang), Chiang graduated from the Paoting (Baoding) Military Academy in 1906, then continued his military education in Japan during 1907–11. He served in the Japanese army from 1909 to 1911 and learned much from this experience. Like many other young Chinese intellectuals of the period, Chiang became a revolutionary, determined to modernize China by bringing about the overthrow of the corrupt and backward Manchu dynasty. While he was in Japan, in 1911, Chiang heard news of widespread revolution at home. He returned to China and participated in the more-or-less desultory combat that overthrew the tottering Manchus. No sooner was the dynasty toppled, however, than

Yüan Shih-k'ai (Yuan Shìkài), officially president, manifested a desire to become the new Chinese emperor. During 1913–16, Chiang participated in the fight to overthrown Yüan.

For more than a year, during 1916–17, Chiang slipped out of the spotlight and became involved, in Shanghai, with the Green Gang (Ch'ing-pang [Qing-bang]), a secret society that, in the chaotic aftermath of revolution, engaged in nefarious financial manipulations. However, Chiang emerged again in 1918, this time as a lieutenant to Sun Yat-sen, leader of the Nationalist Party, or Kuomintang (Guomin-dang). Sun's goal was to unify China, and toward

this end, he began to reorganize the Nationalist Party according to the Soviet model. Chiang visited the USSR in 1923, where he closely observed the Red Army. On his return to China, he was named commandant of a military academy, which he ran according to Soviet principles. The Nationalists embraced the Chinese Communists, welcoming them into the party. But after Sun's death in 1925, the Communist faction grew increasingly strong and threatened to take over the Nationalists.

Backed by the students of his academy, the so-called Whampoa Army, Chiang emerged as the most powerful of Sun Yat-sen's heirs apparent. He

Chiang Kai-shek in conference with Franklin Roosevelt and Winston Churchill. At the right is Chiang's charming, politically savvy wife, Soong Mei-ling, known to the world as Madame Chiang Kai-shek. *(National Archives and Records Administration)*

acted against the rising Communist tide and, in 1927, broke with them and expelled them from the Nationalist Party. In the meantime, he made progress toward reunifying China under the Nationalist banner, with himself as de facto head of state. He had defeated and suppressed most of the warlords who vied for power, and in 1928, entered Peking (Beijing) with his army. It was in Nanking, however, that Chiang established the capital of the Nationalist government and became recognized as the legitimate head of the new Chinese state.

Chiang embraced Western culture and trade. His 1930 marriage into the powerful Soong family, which had many Western ties, reinforced his Western leanings, and his wife, Mei-ling, beautiful, charming, intelligent, and extraordinarily canny, made an appealing ambassador to the West. A progressive, Chiang led an ambitious program of social reform, although comparatively little of it was actually put into practice because of continual threats from the warlords and the Communists. Even worse were the war clouds looming from the direction of Japan. In 1931, that empire seized Manchuria and seemed clearly poised to use this province as a stage from which to launch a general invasion of the rest of China. Beleaguered by the Communists, Chiang refused to resist the Japanese, concentrating instead on defeating the Communists. This proved to be an elusive goal, and, in the meantime, the Japanese position grew stronger.

At last, in 1937, the SINO-JAPANESE WAR began, leaving Chiang no choice but to turn from opposing the Communists to forging an uneasy alliance with them against the mutual enemy invading the nation. China struggled alone against the Japanese until the end of 1941, when the United States and Britain declared war on Japan. Now China was a major ally in the fight against the Axis. Although this conferred a certain prestige on Chiang Kai-shek and the Nationalists, his regime had become increasingly corrupt and was losing touch with the people. Although Chiang mustered large armies during World War II, they were poorly equipped, were poorly led, and were riddled with defeatism. Moreover, Chiang continually interfered with American and British commanders in the China-Burma-India theater. Still, he remained a faithful ally, and, for his Nationalists, the war, terrible though it was, served as a kind of reprieve, a suspension in the steady advance of the Communists under the visionary leadership of Mao Zedong (Mao Tse-tung).

Almost immediately after the surrender of Japan, civil war erupted anew in China. By 1949, Chiang Kai-shek retreated to Taiwan, where he established a Nationalist government supported by the United States. On the continent, China was finally unified—under Mao's Communist regime. In 1955, the United States concluded an agreement guaranteeing the security of Taiwan against Communist incursion. By the early 1970s, as President Richard Nixon sought détente with Mao's China, the American connection to Taiwan became increasingly tenuous. Chiang did not live to see the United States break diplomatic relations with Taiwan in 1979 when it established full diplomatic ties with the People's Republic on the mainland.

Many historians ascribe Chiang's defeat at the hands of the Communists to his strategy during World War II. Chiang refrained from using his armies to stage concerted counteroffensives against the Japanese invaders. He harassed the invaders, to be sure, but he bided his time, relying on the United States and the British to bring about Japan's defeat. He thus sought to preserve his army intact to fight what he knew would be a Communist onslaught as soon as the war was over. This innately conservative plan had the unanticipated consequence of making Chiang seem passive and weak. His unwillingness to fight vigorously against the invaders made him lose face with many of his long-suffering countrymen. The Communists offered an alternative, and the majority seized it.

Further reading: Bagby, Wesley M. *The Eagle-Dragon Alliance: America's Relations with China in World War II.* Newark: University of Delaware Press, 1992; Crozier, Brian. *The Man Who Lost China: The First Full Biography of Chiang Kai-shek.* New York: Scribner, 1976; Fenby, Jonathan. *Chiang Kai Shek.* New York: Carroll & Graf, 2004; Lattimore, Owen. *China Memoirs: Chiang Kai-Shek and the War against Japan.* Tokyo: University of

Tokyo Press, 1991; Sainsbury, Keith. *The Turning Point: Roosevelt, Stalin, Churchill, and Chiang Kai-shek, 1943: The Moscow, Cairo, and Teheran Conferences.* Oxford and New York: Oxford University Press, 1986.

Chile

During World War II, Chile presented something of a paradox among South American nations. Although it was the most liberal of those states and was, in spirit, strongly pro-Allied, Chile, while endorsing the anti-Axis resolutions of the RIO CONFERENCE, initially refused to sever diplomatic relations with the Axis countries. As a result, LEND-LEASE ACT agreements were never concluded between the United States and Chile, and the Chilean government found itself under continual pressure to act against the German agents who freely operated in the country, reporting on Allied shipping through the region.

It was not until January 20, 1943, that the Chilean Senate agreed to sever relations with the principal Axis powers, but the senate stood fast in its refusal to declare war on Germany. Chile did declare against Japan on February 12, 1945, and was a signatory to the UNITED NATIONS DECLARATION.

Further reading: Francis, Michael J. *The Limits of Hegemony: United States Relations with Argentina and Chile During World War II.* South Bend, Ind.: University of Notre Dame Press, 1977; Mount, Graeme. *Chile and the Nazis: From Hitler to Pinochet.* Toronto: Black Rose Books, 2002.

China, armed forces of

Since the beginning of the 20th century, China had been in a chronic state of civil war, fought over by competing warlords as well as by the two largest factions, the Nationalists (Koumintang, or KMT), under the leadership of CHIANG-KAI-SHEK, and the Communists, led mainly by MAO ZEDONG. As a result, the nation was especially vulnerable to invasion by the Japanese, which led to the SINO-JAPANESE WAR. Beginning in 1937, that conflict was absorbed into World War II in December 1941.

During the period of World War II, a fragmented China had many armed forces, including individual forces maintained by each major political regime (especially the Nationalists and the Communists), and provincial forces, which ranged from fairly well-organized and well-armed militias to mere gangs of outlaws. Finally, the Japanese occupiers of Manchuria (Manchuoko) organized their own Chinese-manned forces against the Allies.

NATIONALIST FORCES

As chairman of the National Military Council, Chiang Kai-shek exercised direct and effectively absolute control over the Central Armies, which consisted of about 300,000 men when the Sino-Japanese War began in 1937. These troops had been trained during the 1930s by German advisers Chiang had engaged. Of this number, about 80,000 were organized into an elite corps known as the Generalissimo's Own. They were equipped with up-to-date German-made weapons. Although the Central Armies were the best of China's conventional military forces, and the Generalissimo's Own the best of the best, they were all generally inferior to the Japanese forces and, for that matter, the forces of the West.

The Nationalists also tenuously commanded the loyalty of a less organized, less well-equipped coalition of heterogeneous forces, amounting by 1937 to some 1.2 million. Thus, Chiang Kai-shek had perhaps 1.5 million men to field against the Japanese invaders, which, though outnumbered, were far better equipped, trained, and led. The result was that perhaps as many as 1 million of the 1.5 million men of the Nationalist armies became casualties in the first year of the Sino-Japanese War. Chiang Kai-shek instituted conscription to make up his losses, and he also incorporated more regional forces as they became available. However, between 1937 and 1939, the Japanese advanced rapidly through central and southern China. After 1939 and during the major phases of World War II, the Japanese ended their offensive and concentrated on operations to cut off China from communication with the outside. Their object was now to win the war here through attrition rather than outright conquest.

Beginning in the summer of 1941 and before the Burma Road was cut off by the Japanese early in 1942 (*see* BURMA CAMPAIGN), Chiang Kai-shek's forces received American munitions and supplies under the terms of the LEND-LEASE ACT. After the closure of the Burma Road and until the completion of the Ledo Road under the direction of U.S. commander JOSEPH A. "VINEGAR JOE" STILWELL in January 1945, China was supplied solely by Allied airlift over the notoriously hazardous Himalayan HUMP route. However, the bulk of these airlifted supplies went not to indigenous Chinese forces, but to U.S. forces operating in China. The inequity of supply operations created a good deal of friction between U.S. troops and their Chinese allies.

What little the Nationalist forces had in the way of modern equipment, including armor, artillery, mechanized transport, and aircraft, was destroyed by the Japanese during 1937–38. Early in World War II proper, the gap in air power was addressed valiantly, albeit inadequately, by the small American Volunteer Group, or FLYING TIGERS, under the leadership of American military maverick CLAIRE CHENNAULT. As if the material deficiency of the Nationalist forces did not present difficulty enough, the leadership and administration of the forces were corrupt at every level. Particularly abhorrent were Chinese conscription practices, which amounted to wholesale abduction and created much ill will among the people. It seemed that as the army increased in size, it declined in effectiveness. By 1941, the Nationalist army had swelled to 5.7 million, and during 1937–45, some 14 million were drafted. It is estimated that between 1937 and 1945, about 1.3 million Nationalist and Nationalist-associated troops were killed and another 1.8 million wounded. As great as these numbers are, it is also true that Chiang Kai-shek tended to hold his forces back, using them mainly to harass the Japanese rather than confront them in all-out offensives. Most historians believe that this was purposeful policy on Chiang's part, an effort to preserve as much of his army for what he knew would be a postwar showdown with his very temporary ally, the Chinese Communist Party.

COMMUNIST FORCES

The Japanese invasion forced a military alliance between the Nationalists and the Communists, in which the Communists ostensibly agreed to be commanded by Nationalist officers and, ultimately, by Generalissimo Chiang Kai-shek. The Nationalists, accordingly, designated the bulk of Communist forces, which were in northern China, as the Eighteenth Group Army, consisting of three divisions. In 1938, another unit, the New Fourth Army, was organized in the region of the lower Yangtze River. This organizational scheme was largely for the benefit of public show, however. In actuality, while both the Nationalists and Communists wanted to defeat the Japanese, they operated quite independently of one another. Indeed, although both called the New Fourth Army by the same name, the larger force the Nationalists had dubbed the Eighteenth Group Army, the Communists themselves referred to as the Eighth Route Army. In addition to these two forces, the Communists also controlled local and militia forces.

Generally speaking, the Communist armies were less well equipped than the Nationalists, which meant that they were very poorly equipped indeed, but they were better led and had a far higher level of morale and commitment to the cause. By the end of the war, in August 1945, regular Communist forces mustered about 1 million men, while the local and militia forces, mostly under Communist control, consisted of at least 2 million and maybe somewhat more. The militia and local forces, however, consisted strictly of part-time soldiers and were used as second-line troops, supplying logistics prior to combat and repair and recovery afterward.

JAPANESE-CONTROLLED FORCES

In Japanese-occupied regions, administrators were quick to establish puppet governments and collaborationist military forces. From the Japanese point of view, these forces were notoriously unreliable, their loyalties and their numbers quite fluid. At their peak, it is possible that collaborationist forces amounted to 1.8 million men, but the Japanese found that they could make little military use of them. They required direct and continual supervision, and they could not be counted on to carry out missions assigned to them. Nevertheless, maintaining even relatively ineffective puppet forces allowed the Japanese at least to neutralize a substantial body of potential enemies: If the soldiers could not be counted on to fight *for* the Japanese, neither would they fight *against* them. Moreover, the existence of these puppet forces also tended to throw the Nationalists, Communists, and Allied armies off balance. The collaborationist forces represented the continual possibility of a new, vast army the Japanese might suddenly deploy. The fact is that this eventuality never materialized, and the collaborationist forces saw little action.

Further reading: Bagby, Wesley M. *The Eagle-Dragon Alliance: America's Relations with China in World War II.* Newark: University of Delaware Press, 1992; Dorn, Frank. *The Sino-Japanese War, 1937–41: From Marco Polo Bridge to Pearl Harbor.* New York: Macmillan, 1974; Dupuy, Trevor N. *Asiatic Land Battles: Allied Victories in China and Burma.* New York: Franklin Watts, 1963; Puyu Hu. *A Brief History of Sino-Japanese War (1937–1945).* Taipei, Taiwan: Chung Wu Publishing, 1974.

Chindits

Chindit is a corruption of the Burmese *chinthe,* the word describing the winged stone lions that guard Buddhist temples and that were adopted as the insignia of these Long Range Penetration (LRP) troops who fought under the command of Brig. Gen. Orde Wingate during the Burma Campaign. Chindits fought far behind enemy lines, relying for supply on air drops and also relying on close-air support in place of conventional artillery support. As long-range penetration troops, the Chindits specialized in attacking the enemy from the rear and so made full use of the tactics of extreme mobility and surprise. A small, elite force, the Chindits were never expected to deal knockout blows, but, by continually threatening the enemy

where it least expected attack, they forced the Japanese to continually redeploy frontline troops to the rear, thereby rendering the rest of their forces vulnerable to conventional attack from conventional Allied forces. Wingate frequently spoke of his mission as forcing the Japanese to "drop their fists." The genius of Chindit deployment was that it was always coordinated with conventional forces, so that Chindit raids were not mere gestures intended to disrupt and demoralize, but guerrilla- or Commando-style components of full-scale conventional attack.

The Chindits comprised the 13th Kings Liverpool Regiment, the 32nd Gurkha Rifles, the No. 142 Commando Company, and the 2nd Burma Rifles. Wingate organized these forces not into the customary battalions, but into eight self-contained, autonomous columns, further divisible into four patrols of four sections. When necessary, Wingate abandoned even this unconventional organizational scheme and reorganized ad hoc to suit the mission.

The two major Chindit operations included:

Operation Longcloth. Launched in February 1943, the operation was aimed at destroying railroad lines in northern Burma. One important line was indeed cut, but an attempt to destroy the Mandalay-Lashio line resulted in intense fighting, which prompted Wingate to order his columns to disperse and make their way back, individually and as best they could, to Allied lines. Of 3,000 men engaged, 2,182 returned, each having traveled some 1,000 miles on foot, mostly through dense jungle. While Operation Longcloth was at best only a partial tactical success, the British public hailed it as a triumph, and Winston Churchill recalled Wingate to London so that he could take him to the Quebec Conference in August 1943. There, he sold President Franklin D. Roosevelt and his military advisers on the concept of long-range penetration. This resulted in enthusiastic backing for new Chindit and other LRP forces.

Operation Thursday. Deploying 20,000 men, including Chindits and other LRP troops, Wingate coordinated with Chinese forces under U.S. general JOSEPH A. "VINEGAR JOE" STILWELL to counter the IMPHAL OFFENSIVE, a major Japanese thrust into India via Burma. Wingate was tasked with attacking the 18th Japanese Division from the rear in order to sever its communications, causing this unit to "lower its fists," so that Stilwell could attack frontally with great effect. Wingate was determined not only to accomplish this mission, but also to bring up his reserves to attack the Fifteenth Japanese Army as well, thereby turning a diversionary mission into a full-scale offensive. This bold plan was aborted when Wingate was killed in a plane crash on March 24. His successor, the far more conservative Walter Lentaigne, shifted the focus of Operation Thursday back to supporting Stilwell, and, in fact, the Chindits themselves came under Stilwell's direct command in May 1944.

Without the leadership of Wingate, the Chindits were not used effectively. Stilwell employed them as he needed them, which was essentially as a conventional force. The result was heavy casualties, and the by-now legendary Chindit Special Force was disbanded in February 1945.

Further reading: Bidwell, Shelford. *The Chindit War: Stilwell, Wingate, and the Campaign in Burma, 1944.* New York: Macmillan, 1980; Calvert, Michael. *Chindits: Long Range Penetration.* London: Pan Macmillan, 1974; Chinnery, Philip D. *March or Die: The Story of Wingate's Chindits.* Shrewsbury, U.K.: Airlife Publishing, 1997; Cochrane, Stewart. *Chindit.* Philadelphia: Xlibris, 2000; Rooney, David. *Wingate and the Chindits: Redressing the Balance.* New York: Sterling, 1994.

Christison, Sir Alexander Frank Philip
(1893–1993) *Britain's excellent senior commander in Rangoon and Southeast Asia*

During World War II, Christison commanded the British forces at Rangoon, where he proved highly effective against the Japanese. By the end of the war, he was the highest-ranking British officer in

Southeast Asia, and the honor of accepting the surrender of all Japanese forces in the theater fell to him on September 3, 1945.

Christison served in World War I and, on the eve of World War II, during 1937–38, was commanding officer of the duke of Wellington's regiment, then from 1938 to 1940, commanding officer of the Quetta Brigade, India. In 1940, he was named commandant of Staff College, Quetta, then became commander of the 15th Division in 1941. He transferred to command of the XXXIII Indian Corps, Burma, in 1942, and to the XV Indian Corps, Burma, in 1943. He commanded this unit through 1945, when he took command of the Fourteenth Army, also in Burma. Simultaneously, Christison was named commander in chief, Allied Land Forces South East Asia.

After accepting the Japanese surrender, Christison served as military governor of the Dutch East Indies. During 1946–47, he was commander in chief of the Northern Command and of the Scottish Command, as well as governor at Edinburgh Castle. In 1947, he was appointed aide-de-camp general to the king, a post he held until his retirement from the army in 1949. Christison went on to become secretary of the Scottish Education Department in the 1950s and 1960s. He lived to the remarkable age of 100.

Further reading: Allen, Louis. *Phoenix: Burma: The Longest War 1941–1945.* London: Cassell, 2000; Webster, Donovan. *The Burma Road: The Epic Story of the China-Burma-India Theater in World War II.* New York: Farrar, Straus & Giroux, 2003.

Churchill, Sir Winston (1874–1965) *prime minister of Britain and the Allies' single greatest war leader*

One of the giants of British history, world history, and the 20th century, Winston Churchill was prime minister of Great Britain through most of World War II and led the transformation of his nation's darkest days into what he himself called its "finest hour." He also became one of the war's most distinguished historians.

Prime Minister Winston Churchill, with Franklin Roosevelt and their military advisers, at the Casablanca Conference, February 1943. *(National Archives and Records Administration)*

The son of Lord Randolph Churchill (descended from the first duke of Marlborough) and Jennie Jerome, an American, Winston Churchill was packed off to Harrow School, where he compiled a miserable academic record and, after graduation, eschewed the university education that befitted his aristocratic station. Instead of enrolling at Oxford or Cambridge, as was expected of him, he chose Sandhurst, the British military academy, from which he graduated in 1894 with a commission in the 4th Hussars. Almost at the outset of his military career, Churchill took a two-month leave in 1895 to cover unrest in Cuba as a war correspondent.

This assignment completed, he returned to his regiment and was dispatched with it to India, where he served in the Malakand expedition to the Northwest Frontier during 1897. While on active duty, he continued to write as a war correspondent and published the first of his many distinguished historical works, *The Malakand Field Force*.

In 1898, while serving in Lord Horatio Kitchener's expedition into the Sudan, Churchill rode in the charge of the 21st Lancers at the Battle of Omdurman and, afterward, published a two-volume account of the British army's Sudanese experience in *The River War*, which appeared in 1899, the same year in which Churchill resigned his army commission to enter politics. Defeated in his first bid for Parliament, he took up journalism once again, sailing to South Africa on assignment for the *Morning Post* to cover the Second Boer War. Always eager to put himself in danger, Churchill was captured by the Boers but managed an escape so daring that he instantly became a world celebrity. This feat also made him a popular hero at home, and in 1900 he was elected to Parliament as a Conservative.

Already well received as a writer, Churchill now earned a reputation as an eloquent speaker and brilliant debater. Yet he could not remain tied down to the Conservatives for very long, and in 1904, he suddenly declared himself a Liberal. Churchill's timing proved impeccable, as the Liberals came to power in 1905, and Churchill, already a shining star, was named undersecretary of state for the colonies. He was elevated to the cabinet three years later, as president of the Board of Trade and, in 1910, was appointed home secretary. But it was in his next appointment, in 1911, as first lord of the admiralty, that Churchill was given his first great opportunity to excel. Working closely with First Sea Lord Admiral Lord Fisher of Kilverstone, he crafted and championed an ambitious program to modernize the Royal Navy in preparation for what Churchill correctly saw as a coming world war. As a result of his efforts, Churchill felt boundless confidence in the Royal Navy at the outbreak of World War I. Acting on this confidence, he planned, in 1915, a daring but tragically unrealistic amphibious assault on the Turkish-held Dardanelles, control of which would open a supply line to Britain's ally Russia. It was one thing to have confidence in great ships, but half the execution of an amphibious operation takes place on land, and it was this piece of the operation that had been poorly conceived and was destined to be even more ineptly executed. The Gallipoli assault ended in a blood-drenched disaster, which worsened as the land campaign developed and failed. In disgrace, Churchill was removed as first lord of the admiralty and relegated to a minor cabinet post.

Winston Churchill had every reason to believe that his political career had been ended by Gallipoli. In an effort to comfort himself, he took up painting, which would become both a solace and a passion for the rest of his life. Yet while Churchill despaired, there were many others who had not ruled him out but recognized the value of his boldness, courage, and resolve. These were manifest in his decision to leave the government and accept field command of the 6th Royal Scots Fusiliers. With this unit, Churchill fought in France until May 1916, when he returned to England.

In July 1917, Churchill's friend, political ally, and new prime minister, David Lloyd George, returned him to government in the cabinet post of minister of munitions. Churchill threw himself into this work with boundless energy and quickly succeeded in increasing munitions production so dramatically that an actual shell surplus was achieved before the war ended. While Churchill gloried in the traditions of arms, he was also a technological visionary, with a strong belief in the potential of new weapons systems. He became an ardent champion of armored warfare—the tank—which he believed was just the weapon needed to break the stalemate of the western front. The heavily armored all-terrain vehicle could defy machine gun fire, mow down barbed wire and other obstacles, and roll over trenches. Churchill's vision for the tank far exceeded what was technologically feasible in 1917–18, but the weapon did figure importantly in the late stages of the war, and it would certainly become a major weapon in the next war.

In 1918, Churchill left munitions to become secretary of state for war and air, serving in this capacity until 1921, when he was again named secretary of state for the colonies. In this post, he negotiated key treaties in the Middle East and also hammered out the 1921 agreement creating the Irish Free State, which signaled the end of centuries of bitter conflict between England and Ireland. Yet these advances meant little when Lloyd George's government fell in 1922, for Churchill lost his office as well as his seat in Parliament.

The collapse of the Liberal government prompted Churchill to realign himself with the

Conservatives, and it was under the Conservative banner that he was returned to Parliament in 1924, joining the cabinet of Prime Minister STANLEY BALDWIN in what was effectively the number-two post in British government: chancellor of the exchequer, roughly the equivalent of the American secretary of the treasury. Once again, however, Churchill met with disaster. In 1925, one year after he took office, Churchill returned Britain to the gold standard, an act that drastically deepened the depression following the end of the Great War. When the economic hardship he himself had exacerbated triggered the general strike of 1926, Churchill responded not with sympathetic understanding but mean-spirited condemnation. The breach this created with British labor would never be healed.

Churchill stepped down in 1929 and for the next decade held no cabinet office—though he remained very much in the public eye, first as a vehement critic of Baldwin's proindependence policy for India, then as an even fiercer critic of Baldwin's refusal to acknowledge the growing menace of "Hitlerism" and his consequent failure to rearm Britain. Churchill warned that Germany was spoiling for a new world war, and he advocated putting Britain on a full war footing, with special attention paid to developing a program that would match Germany's growing air power. Churchill believed that the Germans would attack Britain from the air in an attempt to bring the nation to its knees and ripen it for invasion. When Baldwin stepped down in 1938, Churchill became the leading opponent of Prime Minister NEVILLE CHAMBERLAIN'S APPEASEMENT POLICY. Churchill vigorously argued that a dictator could not be appeased and that, moreover, sacrificing Czechoslovakia's SUDETENLAND was immoral, cowardly, and, perhaps worst of all, strategic folly. With an eye for the broad strokes of strategy, Churchill pointed out that Czechoslovakia's position at what was effectively the nexus of the European continent made it the keystone of middle Europe. Moreover, its coal fields and arms industry were of tremendous value to any power.

Chamberlain forged ahead with appeasement, but Churchill refused to back down. When the prime minister returned from the MUNICH CONFERENCE (September 29–30, 1938), having given ADOLF HITLER the Sudetenland and claiming, as a result, to have achieved "peace for our time," Churchill called the affair a "total and unmitigated defeat." Wishful thinking nevertheless prevailed among most Britons, and Chamberlain was widely regarded as a hero. Events, fast approaching, would, of course, prove Churchill right.

After the INVASION OF POLAND in September 1939 and the consequent commencement of World War II, Chamberlain immediately acted for what he believed was the good of the nation and offered Churchill his former post as first lord of the admiralty. Churchill jumped at the opportunity and, with characteristic aggressiveness, proposed an immediate assault on Norway to dislodge the Germans there. Like the Gallipoli Campaign of World War I, the BATTLE OF NARVIK was a fiasco, and the British assault on Norway was quickly aborted. But this time, it was Chamberlain, not Churchill, who took the fall. He resigned, and Churchill replaced him as prime minister. Rather than brood on the Norway disaster, he threw himself into the business of defending Britain and, indeed, the entire free world.

Churchill turned to the United States, resolutely neutral in 1940, and began to develop a warm personal relationship with President FRANKLIN D. ROOSEVELT, wooing him into a de facto alliance through such measures as the LEND-LEASE ACT. Despite this, the war continued to go very badly for Britain, as France faltered and collapsed in the BATTLE OF FRANCE. In June 1940, the British army was beaten back and, up against the English Channel, very nearly annihilated, saved only by the brilliant DUNKIRK EVACUATION. Later in the summer, the BATTLE OF BRITAIN commenced as the German Luftwaffe conducted a massive bombing campaign against Britain's cities, especially London. With invasion apparently imminent, Churchill stirringly prepared his people to resist with all that they had. He made inspirational speeches that successfully glorified sacrifice and hardship, and the combination of his personal character and rhetorical skill fired the courage of the nation. Fortunately—and to the shock of Nazi Germany—it was the Royal Air Force (RAF) that emerged victorious in the Battle of Britain, staving off invasion.

As effective as Churchill was in building consensus, morale, and an unshakeable sense of mission, he was also fully engaged in every aspect of the actual conduct of the war. Nevertheless, unlike Hitler and BENITO MUSSOLINI, who imposed their will on their military commanders, usually to the detriment of sound strategy, Churchill forged an effective partnership with the military. He did insist that British forces assume the offensive as quickly as possible, that they take the battle to the enemy, and he diverted an entire armored division, one of only two in Britain, to fight the armies of Hitler and Mussolini in the Middle East. But aside from this broad stroke of strategic policy, Churchill listened to his military professionals, bought into their plans, and showed them the highest degree of loyalty and confidence. He also proved flexible with regard to JOSEPH STALIN and the SOVIET UNION. An ardent foe of communism, Churchill nevertheless forged a strong alliance with the Soviet Union after it had been invaded by Germany, pledging to prosecute the war to the end and to make no separate peace. When the United States entered the war after the Japanese attack on PEARL HARBOR on December 7, 1941, Churchill quickly took a strong hand in fashioning a three-way alliance among the United States, U.S.S.R., and Britain.

The most controversial item of Churchill's strategic policy in World War II was doubtless his insistence on avoiding an invasion of the European mainland until what he called the "soft underbelly of Europe" had been breached by clearing North Africa and the Mediterranean of the enemy. He did not want to face another Dunkirk disaster, but he did want to institute vigorous offensive operations. Most U.S. commanders believed the soft underbelly approach was timid and wasteful of resources and that a direct invasion from the west—even as the Soviets fought from the east—would end the war sooner. Roosevelt, however, ultimately agreed with Churchill and committed large American forces to North Africa. It was not until summer 1943 that the Allies invaded Sicily and then mainland Italy, having fought the first part of the "European" war in North Africa. And it would not be until June 6, 1944, that the NORMANDY LANDINGS (D-DAY) would usher in the main Allied offensive in Europe.

To be sure, Churchill's "soft underbelly" strategy dominated much of the war, but his strategic influence diminished once the Normandy campaign was under way. Indeed, as Allied victory came firmly into sight, Churchill increasingly turned a wary eye toward the Soviets, seeing in them a grave postwar threat. It was not merely his hatred of communism that motivated his fears, but his detestation of all manner of totalitarian regimes. To resist Stalin, Churchill advocated a drive by the western Allies directly into Berlin to prevent the city's occupation by the Soviets. Both President Roosevelt and his successor, President HARRY S. TRUMAN, however, backed Supreme Allied Commander DWIGHT D. EISENHOWER, who believed it far more important to destroy the last German resistance in the west. Berlin, he argued, was a political, not a military, objective, and he did not want to squander casualties on it.

In a tactical sense, Eisenhower's plan was sound, but Churchill, as usual, looked beyond the tactical range to see the overall strategic consequences of an action. Indeed, he looked beyond World War II itself and to a world that, in his own phrase, would be divided by an "iron curtain," with the democracies on one side and the totalitarian communist regimes on the other. Thus, in some significant ways, Churchill was disheartened by the final conditions of the Allied victory in Europe. Worse, he received what any other man would have felt as a crushing blow. In July 1945, with Germany defeated but Japan still in the war, he was replaced as prime minister by CLEMENT ATTLEE.

During the postwar years, Churchill was returned to office in 1951 and was honored with a knighthood. In July 1953, he suffered a stroke but continued in office until April 1955, when he was succeeded by ANTHONY EDEN. He spent the last decade of his life painting and seeing to the publication of the last of his great literary works, the four-volume *History of the English Speaking Peoples* (1956–58). Indeed, had he not been a statesman, Churchill would nevertheless be remembered as a great journalist and historian. He produced a prodigious body of biographical and historical writings, including a monumental six-volume history of World War II, published during 1948–54, which earned him the Nobel Prize for literature in 1953. If anything, however, he treasured even more the honorary United States citizenship conferred on him in 1963 by President John F. Kennedy and the Congress, to date the only such honor ever rendered by this country.

Further reading: Churchill, Winston S. *The Second World War,* 6 vols. New York: Mariner Books, 1986; Gilbert, Martin. *Churchill: A Life.* New York: Owl Books, 1992; Gilbert, Martin. *Winston Churchill's War Leadership.* New York: Vintage, 2004; Meacham, Jon. *Franklin and Winston: An Intimate Portrait of an Epic Friendship.* New York: Random House, 2003.

Ciano, Count Galaezzo (1903–1944) *Fascist Italy's foreign minister who turned against Mussolini*

Count Galeazzo Ciano rose to prominence in the fascist government of Benito Mussolini after he married Mussolini's daughter Edda in 1930. It was Ciano who helped propel Italy into World War II after the fall of France. However, Ciano also took a leading role in the ouster of Mussolini, for which he ultimately paid with his life.

Born in Livorno, Italy, Ciano early on became a follower of Mussolini and participated in the 1922 march on Rome, which catapulted the fascists to power. After pursuing law studies at the University of Rome, Ciano worked as a journalist, then entered the Italian diplomatic corps. He was posted to Rio de Janeiro and Buenos Aires, and he served as consul general in Shanghai and as Italy's minister to China. He made a politically advantageous marriage to Edda Mussolini in 1930, which brought him appointment as chief of the press bureau (1933), undersecretary of state for press and propaganda (1934), and, finally, membership on the

Fascist Grand Council, the inner party that made all policy decisions.

Handsome and dashing, Ciano cut the kind of romantic figure that was especially appealing to fascists. In Italy's war of conquest against Ethiopia, Ciano led a bomber squadron during 1935–36. After the war, he was named minister of foreign affairs on June 9, 1936, and was likely being groomed by Mussolini as his heir apparent and successor.

If anything, Ciano was more aggressive than Mussolini. He urged the Duce to conclude an alliance with Germany, although he distrusted Adolf Hitler, especially after the invasion of Poland in September 1939, which was undertaken without first consulting Italy per the terms of the alliance Ciano had concluded with his German counterpart, foreign minister Joachim von Ribbentrop. Acting on his misgivings, he now advised Mussolini not to declare war, but to adopt a policy of noninterference and nonbelligerence. However, when France fell and Germany seemed unstoppable, Ciano counseled Mussolini to enter the war. Both he and Mussolini anticipated a quick general German victory, and both believed Italy could make painless territorial gains.

It did not take long for Ciano to change his mind yet again. Italy never fared well in the war, and as Axis defeats accumulated in North Africa during 1942, Ciano conspired with other prominent fascists in promoting the idea of Italy's making a separate peace with the Allies. Mussolini, growing increasingly suspicious of his son-in-law, dismissed him along with his entire cabinet on February 5, 1943. Ciano was given a "safe" appointment as ambassador to the Vatican. This, however, was not enough to neutralize Ciano's influence as more and more fascists turned against Mussolini. Ciano was in the vanguard of those who, at the meeting of the Fascist Grand Council during July 24–25, 1943, voted for the removal of Mussolini. Unfortunately for Ciano, the new government formed under Marshal Pietro Badoglio charged Ciano with corruption and embezzlement. Ciano fled Rome to avoid prosecution but was seized by pro-Mussolini partisans and Germans as he made his way through northern Italy. He was imprisoned, and after Hitler set up Mussolini as his puppet in German-controlled northern Italy, Mussolini ordered the execution of Ciano as a traitor. On January 11, 1944, at Verona, he was shot in the back by a firing squad. Mussolini's daughter never forgave her father for the act.

Ciano kept extensive and highly revelatory diaries of the inside workings of the fascist regime from 1937 to 1943. Recovered after the war, they were translated into English and published in 1946.

Further reading: Ciano, Edda Mussolini. *My Truth.* New York: Morrow, 1977; Ciano, Galeazzo. *Diary, 1937–1943.* New York: Enigma, 2002; Moseley, Ray. *Mussolini's Shadow: The Double Life of Count Galeazzo Ciano.* New Haven, Conn.: Yale University Press, 2000.

civil defense

Civilian populations have always suffered in wartime, but World War II brought a historically unprecedented level of suffering, as civilian populations became the target of all manner of attack, especially from the air. All the major combatant nations developed systems of civil defense—that is, systems intended to afford passive protection of civilians, to maintain communications and government administration, and to repair and reconstruct infrastructure and industry. World War II civil defense systems encompassed programs of training and preparation; public warning systems; systems by which the public reported attacks, damage, approaching aircraft, and so on; and systems for the coordination of police and fire services.

FRANCE

At the outbreak of World War II, French civil defense operations were administered by the Ministry of War, which established liaison with a network of antiaircraft stations set up throughout the country to defend towns. These stations were manned chiefly by civilian volunteers who were members of the Association des Volontaires de la Défense Passive. Towns were grouped into sectors, which were in turn subdivided into blocks (*ilots*), each of which was supervised by a volunteer chief (*chef*). In addition to providing for antiaircraft defense, French civil defense authorities declared compulsory in November 1938 the possession of gas masks, but by the outbreak of war, on September 1, 1939, only a third of the required masks were available and had been distributed.

Thousands of French citizens volunteered to sandbag the architectural and artistic treasures of Paris as a protection against air raid, and authorities enacted draconian measures to prevent looting, including the death penalty for anyone actually caught in the act. Authorities recruited women workers to fill places vacated by men who had been conscripted or had volunteered for military service. Large numbers of children were evacuated from Paris, and, indeed, many adult Parisians fled the city as well.

GERMANY

Before the war and even during its early months, Germany neither planned nor established extensive systems of civil defense. The assumption was that victory would be achieved so quickly through vigorously offensive means that passive defense was almost unnecessary. However, with typical Teutonic thoroughness, authorities classified Germany's towns according to their value for war production. In 106 first-priority cities and towns, air raid shelters were constructed during the 1930s. In a second tier of 201 towns, the government provided nothing more than certain emergency measures. In all other towns, civil defense was regarded as an entirely local matter.

The one area in which Germany acted early, pursuant to a law of June 26, 1935, was antiaircraft defenses for all major cities, towns, and military-related installations. An all-volunteer Reich's Air Defense League (*Reichsluftschutzbund*) was created to help harden cities against air raids, but shelter building was grossly inadequate. Antiaircraft artillery stations were deployed by Civil Aerial Defense authorities (*Ziviler Luftschutz*) under the command of the Luftwaffe. As early as 1940, the Luftwaffe conscripted members of the Hitler Youth, ages 16 to 18 years, to man the guns so that troops would be freed up for the front.

German authorities, from ADOLF HITLER down, were slow to give substantial priority to civil defense, because to do so might be perceived as an indication of doubt about ultimate victory. Thus, it was late in 1943 before Germany deployed a RADAR-based system of early warning against aerial attack, despite almost daily bombing. Construction of public shelters also lagged, even as the number and intensity of air raids increased during the Allies' STRATEGIC BOMBING OF GERMANY.

On September 25, 1944, Hitler personally created the Deutsche Volkssturm, a formally established civil defense force, which, staffed largely by underage boys and overage men, was less a genuine civil defense organization than a last-stand army. All German males between the ages of 16 and 60 were liable for service, and Hitler anticipated pressing into service some 6 million to be drawn from the German workforce currently exempted from military service.

GREAT BRITAIN

A major component of British civil defense was the formation of the Local Defence Volunteers on May 14, 1940. Dubbed "Dad's Army" and soon officially renamed the Home Guard, this force reached a peak enlistment of 1,727,000 men and 31,000 women in June 1944, before it was disbanded in December of that year. The function of the Home Guard was chiefly to watch the coasts and to guard airfields and factories. However, the Home Guard was also used as a means of preparing 17-year-old and 18-year-old boys for service in the regular military. Additionally, Home Guard personnel performed a variety of civil defense duties, and some 140,000 manned antiaircraft artillery.

Another civil defense organization was the Observer Corps, which later became the Royal Observer Corps. At the peak of its strength in 1942, the organization consisted of 33,100 men and about 1,000 women. Observers performed valuable service by providing early warning of incoming enemy bombers that had managed to fly below radar coverage. Some 1,500 observer posts, manned day and night, were linked to control centers, which, in turn, communicated with Royal Air Force (RAF) airfields and greatly facilitated the dispatch of interceptor missions. When Germany began launching V-1 buzz bomb attacks, members of the Royal Observer Corps would fire signal rockets to indicate the position of each incoming rocket to aid interceptors.

As early as September 1935, the British government urged local authorities to organize Air Raid Precautions (ARP), and in April 1937, the government created the Air Raid Wardens' Service. ARP volunteers and Air Raid Wardens were responsible for enforcing BLACKOUT regulations and instructing citizens in gas-proofing procedures. They also supervised construction of covered trenches. In addition to such trench shelters and the designation of London's Underground (subway system) as a public shelter, the government distributed ANDERSON SHELTERS to be installed in the gardens of London houses. Once THE BLITZ began, ARP personnel and Air Raid Wardens participated vigorously in warning, rescue, fire-fighting, and clean-up operations.

By the end of 1940, civil defense volunteers were organized into Civil Defence (General) Service, Casualty Services, and the Fire Service. Civil Defence (General) personnel included the air raid wardens, rescue parties, stretcher bearers, and mes-

The women of Chichester, Great Britain, cheerfully display their gas masks. All sides anticipated the use of chemical weapons against civilian populations. *(Chichester Government Museum)*

sengers. Casualty personnel included ambulance drivers and first-aid providers. The Fire Service was composed of professional fire fighters as well as volunteer auxiliaries. In addition, regular policemen were equipped to perform air raid duties, and they were assisted by part-time volunteers. In all, about 1.5 million Britishers participated directly in civil defense, primarily in air-raid related activities. The air raid wardens were highly organized and operated out of designated posts. Before raids, they warned their assigned populations. During the raids, they reported bomb strikes, and they supervised the large public shelters.

ITALY

Italy did not create a formal civil defense authority or the equivalent of Germany's Volkssturm or Britain's Home Guard. Instead, large numbers of regular troops were deployed within Italy for coastal and antiaircraft (AA) defense. Even so, antiaircraft defense was mostly inadequate. Scarce AA artillery was deployed to defend the most important locations only; elsewhere, spotters were given binoculars and a telephone with which they could issue warnings and, perhaps, alert interceptor aircraft. Italian diplomats based in Switzerland, over which most Italian-bound British bomber formations flew, telephoned commanders in Italy, who sounded the air raid sirens and dispatched interceptor aircraft. The only volunteer civil defense organization active in Italy was the National Union for Antiaircraft Protection (Union Nazional Protezione Antiarea, UNPA), whose members were mostly responsible for enforcing blackout regulations and for assisting fire fighters.

JAPAN

On April 5, 1937, the Japanese government enacted an Air Defense Law, which assigned responsibility for civil defense to the governors of Japan's prefectures. Two years later, auxiliary police and fire units were created nationwide, and the Great Japan Air Defense Association and the Great Japan Fire Defense Association were created to provide training and to furnish funding to local citizens' groups. Despite these nationwide voluntary bodies, civil defense remained largely a local matter, and the Japanese government did virtually nothing to build civil defense systems until late in 1943, when Japanese authorities studied reports of the devastation of German cities. A program of public shelter construction was inaugurated, and contingency plans were drawn up for the evacuation of major cities, in particular the evacuation of children, many of whom were, in fact, moved to the country and rural villages. Some citizens were effectively *forced* to evacuate by the fire-prevention steps taken in many cities. Recognizing the highly inflammable nature of most Japanese domestic structures, authorities preemptively destroyed tens of thousands of houses to create fire breaks.

By late 1944, as American air raids increased in tempo and intensity, citizens were encouraged to join block associations and bucket brigades. Moreover, citizens were urged to take an "Air Defense Oath," by which they pledged to stand their ground in the defense of fires, even in the presence of high-explosive bombs. To adhere to such an oath was a prescription for suicide. Bucket brigades were hardly an adequate defense against the firestorms that swept cities subjected to intensive incendiary attack.

As the Japanese government and military became increasingly desperate in the final stages of the war, anticipating as inevitable a massive invasion, civilian participation in the war effort turned from civil defense to fulfilment of a Homeland Operations Plan: the active resistance to invasion. Initially, People's Volunteer Units were created, consisting of men as well as women and including school-age children, to assist the military in such civil defense activities as construction, reconstruction, evacuation, and the maintenance of public order. These units quickly became the basis for last-ditch fighting forces. On June 22, 1945, the government enacted a military service law creating the People's Volunteer Combat Corps, which recruited men from age 15 to 60 and women from 17 to 40. Because weapons were in extremely short supply, most members of the corps were equipped with nothing more formidable than bamboo staffs and bamboo spears. That the government thought of the corps as a suicide unit is apparent from the slogan attached to it: "The Glorious Death of One Hundred Million." Japan's surrender following the atomic bombing of Hiroshima and Nagasaki made an invasion unnecessary, and the People's Volunteer Combat Corps never saw action.

SOVIET UNION

In the Soviet Union, the Local Air Defense (Mestnoe PVO) had responsibility for air raid shelters, fire fighting, and chemical warfare defense. Under authority of the MPVO, local soviets organized everyone between the ages of 16 and 60 for the purposes of civil defense, and the official Soviet claim is that citizen volunteers prepared sufficient shelter resources for 20 million people. These volunteers also fought fires, provided rescue and first aid, defused unexploded ordnance, and aided in reconstruction.

In addition to civil defense volunteers operating under the MPVO, the Narodnoe Opolchenie (NO), or Home Guard, was an emergency force composed of men who had not been subject to the first call-up of conscripts and of women volunteers. In many cases, the NO was assembled and sent into battle with little or no training. Often, NO formations were absorbed into regular Red Army units. Despite their typically desperate nature, NO units were very important in the defense of Moscow and Leningrad, and 2 million men and women fought in such formations.

UNITED STATES

In the United States, civil defense was in large measure a morale-building activity. Early in the war, there was widespread public fear of sabotage by enemy agents. The Federal Bureau of Investigation (FBI) was charged with domestic counterintelligence and was anxious to avoid interference from a zealous public. Channeling popular enthusiasm and anxieties into civil defense preparedness activities was a useful means of harmlessly directing public energies. This also applied to the growing outcry for antiaircraft defenses. Rather than allocate military personnel desperately needed elsewhere, civilian volunteers were assigned various antiaircraft defense duties. Because the Axis lacked long-range bombers, there was, in fact, little danger of air raid in the United States. Nevertheless, in May 1941, President FRANKLIN D. ROOSEVELT issued an executive order creating the Office of Civilian Defense (OCD), headed by the popular New York mayor Fiorello LaGuardia, who was assisted by First Lady Eleanor Roosevelt. Once the United States actually entered the war, leadership of the OCD was assigned to James Landis. Mrs. Roosevelt's unpopular efforts to recruit African Americans for participation in the OCD resulted in her ouster, and, at its peak in 1943, some 12 million volunteers, almost exclusively white males, served. About 6 million were assigned as air raid wardens, with responsibility for carrying out air raid drills and enforcing blackout regulations. A cadre of some 600,000 OCD members were trained as aircraft spotters but became notorious for registering false alarms. Other OCD members served essentially as local ombudsmen, assisting people with wartime rationing regulations and similar war-related matters.

A special OCD operation was the Civil Air Patrol (CAP), an association of civilian pilots flying their own small planes and serving mainly as spotters in antisubmarine warfare operations off the Atlantic coast. A few CAP pilots were armed, and, reportedly, they made 57 attacks against German submarines.

Further reading: Breuer, William B. *The Air Raid Warden Was a Spy and Other Tales from Home-Front America in World War II.* New York: Wiley, 2002; MacKenzie, S. P. *The Home Guard: A Military and Political History.* Oxford: Oxford University Press, 1996; Yegorov, P. Y., N. I. Albin, and I. A. Shlyakhov. *Civil Defense: A Soviet View.* Honolulu: University Press of the Pacific, 2002.

Clark, Mark (1896–1985) *commander of the Fifth U.S. Army in the costly and protracted Italian campaign*

Dubbed the "American Eagle" by no less a figure than WINSTON CHURCHILL, Clark was an aggressive and personally courageous American com-

Lieutenant General Mark Clark on the USS *Ancon* during the Sicily Campaign *(National Archives and Records Administration)*

mander who nevertheless drew intense criticism for his leadership during the costly ITALIAN CAMPAIGN. Clark was born at Madison Barracks, Sackets Harbor, New York, into the family of a career army officer. He graduated from West Point and entered the infantry as a second lieutenant in 1917, and in April 1918 was sent to France with the 5th Infantry Division. Clark fought in the Aisne-Marne offensive. After he was wounded in June, he was assigned as a staff officer in the First Army, serving in this post during the Saint-Mihiel offensive of September 12–16 and the culminating Meuse-Argonne during September 26–November 11. After the armistice, he served in Germany on Third Army staff during the occupation.

Clark returned to the United States in November 1919 and was promoted to captain. He was posted throughout the Midwest until 1921, when he was transferred to the general staff in Washington, D.C. In 1924, he enrolled in the Infantry

School at Fort Benning, Georgia, graduating in 1925. Promoted to major in 1933, Clark graduated from the Command and General Staff School at Fort Leavenworth, Kansas, in 1935, then, like many other army officers during the depression, was assigned to command a contingent of the New Deal's Civilian Conservation Corps (CCC). He served in this capacity in Omaha, Nebraska, from 1935 to 1936, when he enrolled in the Army War College.

After graduating from the Army War College in 1937, Clark held a staff post in the 3rd Infantry Division until 1940, when he was appointed an instructor at the Army War College. Here he worked vigorously to expand and prepare the army for what he was certain was the inevitable involvement of the United States in World War II.

After promotion to brigadier general in August 1941 and then to major general in April 1942, Clark was named chief of staff of army ground forces in May. In July, he became commander of U.S. ground forces in Britain and immediately set about organizing II Corps there. Never content with a desk job, Clark planned and then personally led an extremely hazardous espionage operation to obtain intelligence on Vichy French forces in North Africa in preparation for OPERATION TORCH, the Allied North African landings.

In November 1942, Clark was promoted to lieutenant general and given command of Allied forces in North Africa under DWIGHT D. EISENHOWER. Working with Eisenhower, Clark became one of the chief architects of the invasion of Sicily (OPERATION HUSKY), which was launched from North Africa. From Sicily, Clark led the Fifth Army, as its commander, in landing at Salerno on September 9, 1943. The landing encountered heavy resistance, but Clark held out, buying sufficient time for the arrival of Allied reinforcements and for the naval action that put an end to German counterattacks during September 10–18. With the Salerno beachhead secure, Clark and the Fifth Army began an agonizing advance up the Italian peninsula from October 1943 to June 1944. In the meantime, on January 22, 1944, additional elements of Clark's forces were landed at Anzio. These troops fought their way through to Rome, which they reached on June 4.

In the advance on Rome, Clark acted largely on his own initiative, going so far as to defy the directives of his superior, British general Sir HAROLD ALEXANDER, who commanded the Fifteenth Army Group, which combined the U.S. Fifth and British Eighth Armies. Clark's enterprise meant that the American army would indeed conquer Rome, but by concentrating on this objective, Clark allowed a strategic German withdrawal. In a highly controversial command decision, Clark had opted to take a great city rather than concentrate on destroying the enemy army. The result was that the German army retreated in good order, and the Allies would therefore continue to meet resistance in Italy throughout the war.

During July–December 1944, Clark commanded the Allied advance across the Arno River and north to the German defenses known as the Gothic Line. In December, he was named to replace Alexander as commander of the Fifteenth Army Group and from this new position directed the hard-fought Allied offensive through the Gothic Line, into the Po Valley, and, as Germany's armies collapsed on every front, finally into Austria during April 9–May 2, 1945.

After Germany surrendered and the Fifteenth Army Group was deactivated, Clark was named Allied high commissioner for Austria, essentially the military governor of the country. He served in this demanding office from June 1945 to May 1947, when he was named to command of the Sixth Army. In 1949, he left this command to become chief of army field forces. This post he left in May 1952, when he was appointed the third overall U.S. commander during the Korean War, succeeding MATTHEW RIDGWAY, who had replaced General DOUGLAS MACARTHUR after MacArthur had been relieved by President HARRY S. TRUMAN. Clark remained in command in Korea until after the armistice of July 27, 1953.

After World War II, Clark wrote two popular memoirs, *Calculated Risk* (1950) and *From the Danube to the Yalu* (1954). He retired from the army in 1954 and took up new duties as comman-

dant of the Citadel, South Carolina's prestigious military academy. He served there until 1960, then retired to the suburbs of Washington, D.C.

Further reading: Blumenson, Martin. *Mark Clark.* New York: St. Martin's Press, 1984; Clark, Mark W. *From the Danube to the Yalu.* New York: Harper, 1954.

Clay, Lucius D. (1897–1978) *U.S. Army's brilliant logistics chief for Europe*

In World War II, Clay, the U.S. Army's youngest brigadier general, made his reputation not as a combat commander, but as director of material, Army Service Forces, in charge of logistics in Europe. After the war, he became the architect of the Berlin Airlift.

A native of Marietta, Georgia, Clay was born the sixth child of U.S. Senator Alexander Stephens Clay and served as a Senate page. He entered West Point in 1915 and graduated in 1918 with a commission in the Corps of Engineers. From 1924 to 1928, he taught civil and military engineering at West Point and later headed several civil engineering projects

Lieutenant General Lucius Clay *(National Archives and Records Administration)*

at the Civil Aeronautics Authority's Defense Airport Program in during 1940–41, overseeing the expansion and enlargement of 277 airports and the construction of 197 new ones.

Promoted to brigadier general in 1942, Clay became assistant chief of staff for material (Service of Supply) and then director of material, Army Service Forces. He directed the clearing and rebuilding of the badly damaged port of Cherbourg just after the NORMANDY LANDINGS (D-DAY), a monumental task that made this vital port available to the Allies. During the postwar era, on March 15, 1947, Clay succeeded DWIGHT D. EISENHOWER as military governor of Germany. The crowning achievement of Clay's career came at the commencement of the cold war, when he became the architect and chief administrator of the Berlin Airlift during 1948–49, the West's first clear victory against Soviet communist expansion in Europe. Clay retired in May 1949, just days after the Soviet blockade of Berlin had been lifted. After he returned to the United States and entered the private sector as a businessman, the city of West Berlin named a broad boulevard in his honor, Clay Allee.

Further reading: Backer, John D. *Winds of History: The German Years of Lucius Dubignon Clay.* New York: Van Nostrand Reinhold, 1983; Clay, Lucius D. *Decision in Germany.* Westport, Conn..: Greenwood Publishing Group, 1950; Smith, Jean Edward. *Lucius D. Clay: An American Life.* New York: Henry Holt, 1992.

Colmar Pocket

During the Allied advance through France following the NORMANDY LANDINGS (D-DAY) and OPERATION COBRA, which followed, elements of the German Nineteenth Army continued stubbornly to hold a bridgehead at Colmar, west of the Rhine and south of Strasbourg. By the end of 1944, this 30-square-mile so-called Colmar Pocket posed a threat to DWIGHT D. EISENHOWER's broad-front strategy of bringing all advancing units to the Rhine before launching crossings of the river at several points simultaneously. More immediately, the Colmar Pocket threatened the Sixth Army

Group under Lt. Gen. Jacob Devers, whose lines were greatly overextended. After the First French Army failed to neutralize the pocket, elements of the German Nineteenth Army advanced from their positions and staged a counteroffensive against the Allies at Strasbourg in a bid to retake the city. Although alarming, this advance offered the Allies an opportunity for an open fight, and I Corps of the First French Army, together with the 21st U.S. Corps, checked the advance. The cost to the Allies was great: 18,000 killed or wounded. However, the Germans, who refused to retreat, lost some 36,000. The Nineteenth Army virtually ceased to exist.

Further reading: Yenne, Bill. *Operation Cobra and the Great Offensive: Sixty Days That Changed the Course of World War II.* New York: Pocket Books, 2004; Zaloga, Steven J. *Operation Cobra 1944: Breakout from Normandy.* London: Osprey, 2001.

commandos

Although the term *commandos* was sometimes applied generically as a synonym for any special operations or "irregular operations" unit, during World War II it had specific application to British special forces units. In 1940, the British army raised 10 so-called Independent Companies, special forces troops to be used against the Germans in Norway. From this group, pursuant to WINSTON CHURCHILL's order to mount hit-and-run raids against the occupied coast of the European continent, battalion-size units, officially called Commandos, were formed. They were trained in small-group tactics and fought as self-contained groups. Briefly, the Commandos were renamed Special Forces battalions, but in March 1941 were once again designated Commandos, and the name remained for the rest of the war.

When they were first formed, the Commando battalions were numbered 1 through 9 and 11 and 12, each mustering 500 men. They participated in the DIEPPE RAID and other early operations. Later in the war, the Commandos were joined by a unit known only as No. 10, which was made up of personnel drawn from the governments-in-exile of nations occupied by the Nazis. Another unit, designated No. 14, was formed specifically to raid occupied Norway. And still another Commando unit, No. 30, was an interservice intelligence-gathering organization.

In addition to the army Commandos, there were a number of Royal Marine Commandos. After 1942, these were given Commando battalion numbers (Nos. 40–48) and integrated into four Special Service Brigades, which included the army and the marine Commandos. From December 1944, the name of these brigades was changed to Commando Brigades.

See also NARVIK, BATTLES OF.

Further reading: Chappell, Mike. *Army Commandos.* London: Osprey, 2001; Hunter, Robin. *True Stories of the Commandos: The British Army's Legendary Front Line Fighting Force.* London: Virgin Publishing, 2003; Thompson, Leroy. *British Commandos in Action.* Carrollton, Tex.: Squadron/Signal Publications, 1988.

"Commissar Order"

Commissars were officers of the political departments that were established within the Soviet Red Army. The function of the commissar was to indoctrinate troops politically and, even more important, to ensure that the Communist Party exercised direct control over and through the military command structure.

On June 6, 1941, about two weeks before the INVASION OF THE SOVIET UNION commenced, the WEHRMACHT high command (OKW) issued the Kommissarbefehl, or "Commissar Order." It was aimed at destroying Soviet communism by physically liquidating all who had responsibility for transmitting the actual ideology of the Communist Party and the Soviet state. In violation of international common law as well as the GENEVA CONVENTIONS, the order stipulated: "If captured during combat or while offering resistance, [commissars] must on principle be shot immediately." More broadly, the order continued: "Even if they are only suspected of resistance, sabotage, or instigation thereto . . . protection granted to prisoners of war

. . . will not apply to them. After having been segregated they are to be liquidated."

The Commissar Order was signed by General Walter Warlimont and approved by the OKW chief of staff, General WILHELM KEITEL, who was acting under the direct order of ADOLF HITLER. Early in the war, during the summer of 1941, Keitel attempted to destroy all copies of the Commissar Order, presumably to cover up evidence of what he knew to be a blatant war crime.

Further reading: Clark, Alan. *Barbarossa.* New York: Perennial, 1985; Fowler, Will. *Barbarossa: The First Seven Days.* Havertown, Pa.: Casemate, 2004; Keitel, Wilhelm. *The Memoirs of Field-Marshal Wilhelm Keitel.* New York: Cooper Square, 2000; Overy, Richard. *Russia's War.* New York: Penguin, 1998.

concentration and extermination camps

From the beginning of his regime, ADOLF HITLER used mass detention as a weapon, arresting and holding those whom he perceived as posing a threat to his power. The first of Hitler's political prisons were nothing more than improvised confinement facilities in basements, cellars, and other places. In such places, beginning in January 1933 when Hitler assumed the post of chancellor, the STURMABTEILUNG (SA), the brownshirted muscle of the Nazi party, confined those they had rounded up. In March, the SA established larger camps at Nohra, Thuringia, and Oranienburg, Prussia. At this time, the SCHUTZSTAFFEL (SS), working in concert with the Bavarian Political Police, established DACHAU, generally considered the first true concentration camp of the Nazi regime.

Before the year ended, more camps—Sonnenburg, Lichtenburg, Börgermoor, Esterwegen, and Brandenburg—were established, all in Prussia. These were quickly followed by Sachsenburg in Saxony. In May 1934, administration of the camps, which now held about 80,000 inmates, was completely assumed by the SS. SS chief HEINRICH HIMMLER assigned Theodor Ecke, who had been commandant at Dachau, to reorganize the camps. Ecke closed all the SA camps, reformed the administration of the others, and created the SS Death's Head units that served as guards. As inspector of concentration camps, Ecke was responsible for their physical administration, whereas incarcerations and releases were handled by the GESTAPO.

Under Ecke, the number of prisoners was vastly decreased, at least temporarily, and the number of camps, as of the end of 1934, reduced to five: Esterwagen, Lichtenburg, Moringen (which held just 49 prisoners, all women), Dachau, and Sachsenburg. In 1935, five new camps were authorized to accommodate those arrested in actions against communists and those judged undesirable or "antisocial," including Gypsies and habitual criminals. Beginning in November 1938, after *KRISTALLNACHT*, Jews began to arrive in substantial numbers as well. By this time, the camps had progressed beyond simple incarceration facilities and were now also used as quarters for forced labor in factories managed by the SS.

The second generation of camps included Sachsenhausen, which was opened near Berlin in July 1936. BUCHENWALD was established the next year near Weimar, whereupon Sachsenburg and Lichtenburg were closed and Dachau greatly expanded. In 1938, Mauthausen was established near Linz, as was Flossenburg. These were adjacent to stone quarries, in which prisoners were worked, often quite literally, to death. Ravensbrück was established next to accommodate a growing number of female prisoners.

Under Ecke (who was killed in action in the Soviet Union in 1943 and replaced by Richard Glücks), the camps were generally divided into five departments. The first consisted of the commandant and his staff. The second was the political department, under the direction of a Gestapo officer. The third, headed by an SS officer, oversaw the day-to-day operations of the camp. The fourth handled general administrative tasks. And the fifth was the medical department. The guards, all SS Death's Head men, were commanded separately from the rest of the soldiers at the camp.

The outbreak of war with the INVASION OF POLAND brought a rapid rise in the concentration camp population. New facilities were built at Neuengame (near Hamburg, 1940), at Stutthof (near Danzig, 1941), at Gross-Rosen (near Breslau, 1941), and at Natzweiler (in Alsace, 1941). Two camps that had been intended to serve to hold prisoners of war were converted to concentration and extermination camps: AUSCHWITZ (near Cracow, 1941) and Majdanek (near Lublin, 1941).

Early in 1942, Operation Reinhard commenced. Its purpose was to murder the Jewish population of conquered Poland, some 2,284,000 human beings. BELZEC, established in March 1942 near Lublin, was intended exclusively to kill Polish Jews. SOBIBOR and TREBLINKA were soon added. Here Polish Jews as well as Jews from other parts of Europe were murdered. In addition to these three camps, built specifically to carry out Operation Reinhard, Chelmno, Majdenek, and Auschwitz were also now used as death camps. At this point, the usual method of execution was by the introduction of carbon monoxide gas into sealed chambers.

Beginning about 1942, Germany's slave labor system expanded far beyond the original SS factories to encompass the entire German armaments and munitions industries. This spurred the establishment of a vast network of satellite camps, more than a thousand, erected near the widely dispersed factories. That the concentration camps were increasingly seen as essential to war production was made apparent by the integration of the office of the concentration camp inspector into the SS Main Office of Economy and Administration, under Oswald Pohl. The SS billed the various armaments and munitions firms for the use of the prisoners' labor, greatly enriching the SS coffers.

The INVASION OF THE SOVIET UNION produced a new abundance of prisoners beginning after June 1941. Pursuant to Hitler's infamous COMMISSAR ORDER, many thousands of Red Army officers were sent to the camps to be murdered, among them the son of JOSEPH STALIN. By 1942–43, some of the concentration and death camps were being used for medical experimentation, typically of the cruelest and most grotesquely brutal sort, often with fatal outcomes.

As the need for more space to accommodate prisoners and more facilities to murder them increased, the SS built or acquired more camps, including BERGEN-BELSEN. In 1944, not only did the number of camps and their population reach a high, the SS had developed mass extermination to its most extreme, using Zyklon-B gas at Auschwitz and Birkenau to kill Jewish prisoners at an astounding rate. The slave-labor camps also reached the apex of horror during this year, as Dora-Mittelbau, near Nordhausen, was established for the forced manufacture of components for the V-1 BUZZ BOMB and V-2 ROCKET.

At the start of 1945, the SS held 511,537 male prisoners and 202,674 female prisoners. The system, however, was beginning to collapse. Red Army troops managed to liberate some eastern camps by the summer of 1944, most notably Majdanek in July, but the Germans were generally quick to "evacuate" prisoners to camps in central Germany. This, of course, created increasingly intolerable crowding, and disease, always rampant in the camps, became uncontrollable. Many prisoners died in the course of their evacuation, either of privation, exposure, or outright murder. As the British and Americans closed in from the west, SS guards scrambled to kill more of their prisoners, presumably in an effort to leave no one behind to make witness to the horrors that had been perpetrated. Nevertheless, Buchenwald was liberated on April 11, 1945, Bergen-Belsen on April 15, and Dachau on April 30.

Many of the 6 million Jews murdered in THE HOLOCAUST were killed in the death camps of Operation Reinhard and in Auschwitz, Birekenau, Chelmno, and Majdenek. In addition to these victims, it is estimated that another 600,000 non-Jews died in the camps, the majority of them murdered.

Further reading: Abzug, Robert. *Inside the Vicious Heart: Americans and the Liberation of Nazi Concentration Camps.* New York: Oxford University Press, 1987; Allen, Michael Thad. *The Business of Genocide: The SS, Slave Labor, and the Concentration Camps.* Chapel Hill: University of North Carolina Press, 2002; Aroneanu, Eugene, comp. *Inside the Concentration Camps.* New York: Praeger, 1991; Langbein, Hermann, and Harry Zohn. *Against All Hope: Resistance in the Nazi Concentration Camps 1938–1945.* New York: Paragon House, 1994; MacLean, French L. *The Camp Men: The SS Officers Who Ran the Nazi Concentration Camp System.* Atglen, Pa.: Schiffer Publishing, 1999; Segev, Tom. *Soldiers of Evil: The Commandants of the Nazi Concentration Camps.* New York: McGraw-Hill, 1988.

See also FINAL SOLUTION, THE.

Coningham, Sir Arthur (1895–1948) *British air officer who formulated the key doctrines of close air support*

Australian born and raised in New Zealand, Coningham fought in Samoa and Egypt during World War I but was sent home in April 1916 for medical reasons. Not wanting to be out of the war, he set sail for England, where he enlisted in the Royal Flying Corps and made a name for himself as a dogfighter. By the end of the war, Coningham was a squadron commander and had earned the affectionate nickname of "Mary," a corruption of *Maori*, which reflected his New Zealand and Australian origins.

During the interwar years, Coningham promoted military aviation with a number of demonstration flights, including a spectacular east-west traversal of Africa from Cairo to Kaduna (in Nigeria) and back again. The 6,500-mile trip consumed 24 days.

On the eve of World War II, in July 1939, Coningham was named to command Fourth Group, Bomber Command. In July 1941, he was transferred to Egypt, where he took command of the unit that became the Western Desert Air Force. Coningham led a brilliant program of close air support, which was instrumental in the British victory at the second BATTLE OF EL ALAMEIN and the ultimate defeat of the "Desert Fox," ERWIN JOHANNES EUGEN ROMMEL. During these operations, Coningham formulated the doctrine and tactics of effective close air support, coordinating ground and air elements as entirely interdependent forces. So effective were Coningham's practices that they were eagerly studied and adopted by the United States in July 1943, becoming an integral part of U.S. warfighting doctrine.

After the final victory in North Africa, Coningham led Allied air forces in Sicily and Italy during 1943, then participated in the planning of the NORMANDY LANDINGS (D-DAY). Beginning during this operation, he commanded the Second Tactical Air Force and remained at the head of it through the end of the war, supplying close air and other tactical support for troops as they progressed from the beaches of Normandy to Germany and final victory. Coningham retired from the Royal Air Force after the war, in 1947, and met his death the following year in an airplane crash.

Further reading: Orange, Vincent. *Coningham: A Biography of Air Marshal Sir Arthur Coningham, KCB, KBE, DSO, MC, DFC, AFC.* Washington, D.C.: Center for Air Force History, 1992.

conscientious objectors

Following the universal conflagration of World War I, worldwide antiwar and pacifist movements developed, and it was widely assumed at the outbreak of World II that the numbers of conscientious objectors (COs), those who refuse conscription on avowed religious or moral grounds, would be legion, so large, in fact, as to have a significant impact on the war effort. This proved not to be the case. However, conscientious objectors did make themselves known in virtually all the combatant nations.

By the time of World War II, conscientious objection was a well-established tradition in Europe and America. In Europe, the Mennonites developed the first explicit and cogent policy of conscientious objection during the 16th century, and the Society of Friends (Quakers) emerged with a similar doctrine in England during the next century. Although, historically, few governments recognized the legitimacy of conscientious objection—and, in consequence, individuals who refused conscription were generally punished by law—a notable exception was 19th-century Prussia, which exempted Mennonites from military service but levied on them a military tax instead. Generally, the United States was more liberal than most other governments. The first U.S. conscription law, enacted during the Civil War, explicitly provided for alternative service in cases of conscientious objection.

In 1940, when a peacetime draft was enacted in the United States, the new selective service law included a provision for "conscientious objector status," to be conferred exclusively on members of recognized pacifistic religious sects. The law did not accept philosophical, ethical, moral, or political beliefs as a basis for securing CO status. In the United States during World War II, COs were assigned various forms of national service unrelated to the military and not controlled by the military. During the war, some 100,000 young American men (.0029 percent of those liable for conscription) were legally designated conscientious objectors and were assigned to what was officially defined as Civilian Public Service. Programs of such service were administered under strict supervision, and the men involved in them lived in camps that more closely resembled prisons than barracks or conventional civilian work camps, such as those of the depression-era Civilian Conservation Corps (CCC). About 6 percent of U.S. conscientious objectors were jailed for violating the CO provisions of the selective service laws.

In Great Britain, specially constituted tribunals granted unconditional exemptions from military service to 6.1 percent of those who identified themselves as conscientious objectors. Another 10 percent were granted CO status on condition of performing alternative service, which consisted of ordinary civilian jobs officially deemed useful to the war effort. British COs were not confined to work camps, although some (fewer than 10 percent) were imprisoned for all or part of the war. In all, about 60,000 Britons were granted legally sanctioned status as conscientious objectors. Australia, New Zealand, the Netherlands, and the Scandinavian countries had policies similar to that of Great Britain.

The Axis nations, Germany, Italy, and Japan, did not recognize the rights of conscientious objectors, nor did France, Belgium, or the Soviet Union. There are no reliable figures on the numbers of those punished by imprisonment or other sentence in these countries for attempting to maintain themselves as conscientious objectors.

Further reading: Brock, Peter. *These Strange Criminals: An Anthology of Prison Memoirs by Conscientious Objectors from the Great War to the Cold War*. Toronto: University of Toronto Press, 2004; Cornell, Julien D. *Conscience and the State: Legal and Administrative Problems of Conscientious Objectors, 1943–1944*. New York: Garland, 1973; Dasenbrock, J. Henry. *To the Beat of a Different Drummer (A Decade in the Life of a World War II Conscientious Objector)*. Winona, Minn.: Northland, 1989; Frazer, Heather T., and John O'Sullivan. *"We Have Just Begun to Not Fight": An Oral History of Conscientious Objectors in Civilian Public Service During World War II*. New York: Twayne, 1996; Goossen, Rachel Waltner. *Women Against the Good War: Conscientious Objection and Gender on the American Home Front, 1941–1947*. Chapel Hill: University of North Carolina Press, 1997; Hayes, Denis. *Challenge of Conscience: The Story of the Conscientious Objectors of 1939–1949*. New York: Garland, 1972; Sprint, Ernest C. T. *"Conchie": The Wartime Experiences of a Conscientious Objector*. New York: Cooper, 1975.

convoy system

One of the lessons of World War I was the necessity of adhering to a convoy system for overseas transport. Merchant ships traveling without protection were simply too vulnerable to attack from surface raiders, submarines, and aircraft. At its most basic, a convoy is nothing more than a collection of merchant vessels traveling under escort by warships, and all the combatant nations that had access to ocean transport used convoys during World War II. However, the Axis nations used them to a far lesser extent than the Allies. Germany used only coastal convoys. Italy used coastal convoys as well as trans-Mediterranean convoys. Japan employed a haphazard escort system, which resulted in heavy losses of merchantmen.

In contrast to the Axis, the Allies, who depended heavily on transatlantic transport, developed an elaborate system of convoys. Regular convoys were assembled at a single port, left port together, then sailed together. Operational convoys were for the movement of troopships and were generally small, consisting of four ships, typically civilian ocean liners requisitioned for troop transport, and escorted by fast surface ships. The very fastest ocean liners, most notably the British liners *Queen Mary and Queen Elizabeth*, did not travel in convoys but sailed alone. Their chief defense was speed.

At first, westbound convoys were escorted only partway across the Atlantic to a point at which their escorts would intercept eastbound ships, come about, and escort them. The conclusion of the ABC–1 Staff Agreement and the Atlantic Charter between Great Britain and the United States, however, provided U.S. Navy escorts in the west. By May 1941, bases were also established in Iceland, which enabled armed escort across the entire Atlantic. This did leave a so-called air gap in the mid-Atlantic, an area beyond the range of defensive air coverage, which was not closed until late in the war.

The inherent problem with convoys was variation in the speed of the convoy vessels. Convoys consisting mostly of fast ships could adopt a zigzag course, which was an effective evasive tactic, but slower, less maneuverable ships were incapable of such tactics and instead took evasive courses, deliberately departing from the major and most direct sea lanes in order to avoid interception by enemy surface raiders and submarines.

Early in the war, troop convoys were heavily escorted, whereas supply convoys were provided with a single escort, such as an armed merchant cruiser. As German U-boat tactics improved—and they improved rapidly—the Allies arrived at a new formula for deploying escorts. Each convoy was assigned at least three escorts plus additional escorts calculated by dividing the number of merchant ships in the convoy by 10. Thus, if a convoy consisted of 80 ships, it would be escorted by 11 armed naval vessels (3 plus 8). These might include some combination of cruisers, light cruisers, destroyers, destroyer escorts, and corvettes. The escort for large convoys often included an escort carrier, a small aircraft carrier capable of launching aircraft to furnish air cover as required.

In addition to speed and armed escort, the size of the convoy was another factor in its successful defense. By late 1942, the Allies concluded that larger convoys were inherently safer than smaller ones. This conclusion might have seemed counterintuitive, but it was borne out by analysis of loss statistics. The perimeter of an 80-ship convoy was only one-seventh longer than that of a 40-ship convoy. Therefore, 80 ships, covered (according to the Allied formula) by 11 escorts, could be defended more effectively than 40 ships covered by just seven escorts. By 1943–44, convoys routinely consisted of well over 100 ships, with one convoy, in the summer of 1944, numbering 187 vessels.

The Allies not only crossed the Atlantic and the Pacific, they engaged in extremely hazardous ARCTIC CONVOY OPERATIONS and high-loss Mediterranean convoys. Convoys across this body of water suffered losses three times the rate of Atlantic convoys, and it was ultimately decided to risk very fast merchant vessels sailing the Mediterranean alone. In sharp contrast to the situation on the Atlantic, these solo ships had a much better chance of reaching their destination than convoyed vessels.

Total losses of Allied merchant shipping from 1939 to 1945 amounted to 5,150 ships (21,570,720 tons). However, the effectiveness of the convoy system can be gauged from the ratio of losses of independently routed ships to convoyed ships. For every 80 independently routed ships sunk, 20 convoyed ships were lost.

Further reading: Burn, Alan. *The Fighting Commodores: The Convoy Commanders in the Second World War.* Annapolis, Md.: Naval Institute Press, 1999; Hague, Arnold. *The Allied Convoy System 1939–1945: Its Organization, Defence and Operation.* St. Catherines, Canada: Vanwell Publishing, 2000; Kaplan, Philip, and Jack Currie. *Convoy: Merchant Sailors at War 1939–1945.* Annapolis, Md.: Naval Institute Press, 1998; Smith, Kevin. *Conflict over Convoys: Anglo-American Logistics Diplomacy in the Second World War.* Cambridge: Cambridge University Press, 2002; United States Department of Defense. *Convoys in World War II (SuDoc D 201.38:C 73/NO.4).* Washington, D.C. Navy Department Library, 1993.

Coral Sea, Battle of the

On May 4, 1942, a Japanese invasion force commanded by Adm. Shigeyoshi Inouye left Rabaul, New Britain, bound for Port Moresby, New Guinea. Simultaneously, another Japanese force, led by the carriers *Shokaku* and *Zuikaku,* sailed into the Coral Sea, northeast of Australia. The object of these coordinated movements was an assault on Australia preparatory to an invasion of the country. Recognizing the imminent threat, and in the face of one Japanese triumph after the other, U.S. Adm. FRANK FLETCHER assumed command of a hastily assembled task force and ventured into the Coral Sea to meet the Japanese.

On May 7, Fletcher launched planes from the aircraft carriers *Yorktown* and *Lexington,* which attacked the invasion fleet north of the Louisiade Archipelago. The Japanese carrier *Shoho* was sunk, forcing the troop transports under escort to turn back. On May 8, the main body of the American force and the main body of the Japanese force approached one another. They did not, however, make a visual sighting. Instead, both launched history's first over-the-horizon attack, using aircraft to fight a naval engagement at long range and without direct ship-to-ship contact. Naval warfare was changed forever.

The battle was fierce and costly to both sides. U.S. aircraft damaged the *Shokaku* but at the cost of 33 out of 82 of the attacking craft. The Japanese, in turn, sank the *Lexington* as well as a destroyer and a tanker. They lost 43 of 69 aircraft committed to the battle. Tactically, the American side lost the battle by suffering significantly heavier losses, including that of a capital ship. Strategically, however, the Japanese were defeated. For the first time in the war, a Japanese advance had been stopped. Not only was Port Moresby saved—and, with it, Australia—but the Japanese had been driven into retreat, out of the Coral Sea. The battle set up the circumstances under which the more decisive BATTLE OF MIDWAY would be fought early the next month. A clear (albeit costly) American victory, Midway would be the indisputable turning point of the Pacific war.

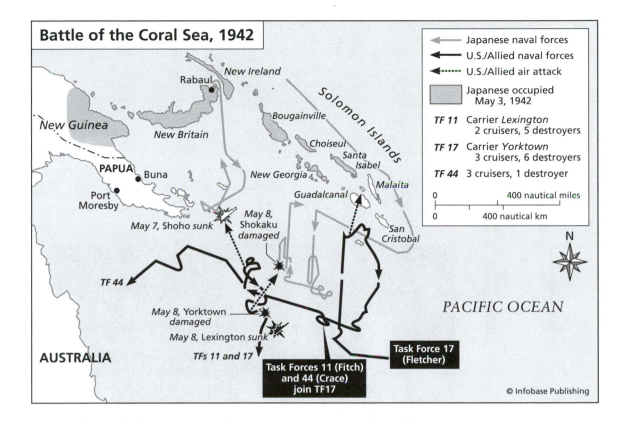

Battle of the Coral Sea, 1942

New Ireland
Rabaul
Solomon Islands
New Guinea
Bougainville
New Britain
Choiseul
PAPUA   Buna
Santa Isabel
New Georgia
Port Moresby
Guadalcanal
Malaita
May 7, Shoho sunk
May 8, Shokaku damaged
San Cristobal
TF 44
PACIFIC OCEAN
May 8, Yorktown damaged
May 8, Lexington sunk
AUSTRALIA
TFs 11 and 17
Task Forces 11 (Fitch) and 44 (Crace) join TF17
Task Force 17 (Fletcher)

→ Japanese naval forces
→ U.S./Allied naval forces
◄------ U.S./Allied air attack
Japanese occupied May 3, 1942
TF 11 Carrier *Lexington* 2 cruisers, 5 destroyers
TF 17 Carrier *Yorktown* 3 cruisers, 6 destroyers
TF 44 3 cruisers, 1 destroyer
0   400 nautical miles
0   400 nautical km
N

© Infobase Publishing

Further reading: Henry, Chris. *The Battle of the Coral Sea.* Annapolis, Md.: Naval Institute Press, 2003; Hoyt, Edwin P. *Blue Skies and Blood: The Battle of the Coral Sea.* New York: S. Eriksson, 1975; Morison, Samuel Eliot. *Coral Sea, Midway and Submarine Actions: May 1942–August 1942 (History of United States Naval Operations in World War II, Volume 4).* New York: Castle Books, 2001.

Corregidor, defense of

Corregidor is a small island, 3.5 miles long and 1.5 miles wide, located some two miles off the Bataan Peninsula. At the start of World War II, it was heavily fortified, and it was to this fortress island that Lt. Gen. DOUGLAS MACARTHUR withdrew his headquarters after Lt. Gen. HOMMA MASAHARU landed his Fourteenth Japanese Army on Luzon in December 1941. While MacArthur commanded from Corregidor, the bulk of his army forces withdrew to

the adjacent Bataan Peninsula. Ordered by President FRANKLIN D. ROOSEVELT to evacuate himself and family to Australia, MacArthur turned over his headquarters and his command to Lt. Gen. JONATHAN WAINWRIGHT on March 11, 1942.

Well before World War II, Corregidor had been dubbed the "Gibraltar of the East" and was stocked with ammunition and sufficient food to sustain 10,000 for six months. Heavily fortified, the rocklike island was pierced through with a network of tunnels, which contained a hospital, living quarters, and other facilities. Three smaller fortified islands were located nearby, together forming a fortress system that controlled Manila Bay and a superb harbor, which the Japanese desperately wanted.

Homma laid siege to Corregidor and mercilessly bombarded the island by air and with heavy artillery. The bombardment destroyed all the surface facilities on the island but left the underground systems entirely intact. In the meantime, the campaign to take Bataan proceeded much more slowly and at far greater cost than the Japanese had anticipated. However, on April 9, 1942, Bataan finally fell, giving Homma an artillery position much closer to Corregidor. From this position, his forces resumed continual barrages and incessant air raids, which leveled the beach defenses and knocked out all but three of the fortress island's guns. Corregidor's jungle was burned, the shore road pounded into the bay, and mountainsides and cliffs blasted into avalanche. Only after a full month of this

bombardment did Homma land his 4th Division on Corregidor, during the night of May 5. This force suffered stunning losses, incurring 1,200 casualties out of the 2,000 men committed to the landing. Nevertheless, once a beachhead was established, artillery and tanks were off-loaded, and an advance was made against the half-starved Filipino and American garrison of 11,000. Wainwright incurred heavy casualties and, as the assault force closed in on the tunnels of Corregidor during the morning of May 6, Wainwright surrendered. This marked the fall of the Philippines.

U.S. and Filipino soldiers surrender Corregidor to the Japanese. *(Library of Congress)*

See also BATAAN DEATH MARCH; BATAAN, FALL OF; and PHILIPPINES, FALL AND RECONQUEST OF.

Further reading: Belote, James H., and William M. Belote. *Corregidor: The Stirring Saga of a Mighty Fortress.* New York: HarperCollins, 1967; Berhow, Mark A., Terrance McGovern, and Chris Taylor. *American Defenses of Corregidor and Manila Bay 1898–1945.* London: Osprey, 2003; Morris, Eric. *Corregidor.* New York: Cooper Square, 2000.

corvettes

Designed as a coastal escort vessel, the corvette emerged in World War II as a transoceanic convoy escort ship intended for antisubmarine warfare. Small, inexpensive warships that could be quickly built, they were used primarily in the Royal Canadian Navy and the British Royal Navy, although the Royal Navy also sent some to the U.S. Navy, which reclassified them as patrol gunboats and used them for coastal duty.

The most important corvettes were those of the Flower class (so-called because all were named after flowers), 145 of which were built in Britain and 113 in Canada during 1930–42. The general specifications of the Flower class included:

Displacement: 950 tons
Length: 205 feet
Beam: 33 feet
Draft: 11.5 feet
Propulsion: two fire-tube Scotch boilers, one four-cylinder triple-expansion steam engine rated at 2,750 horsepower
Top speed: 16 knots
Range: 3,500 nautical miles
Crew: 85
Radar and sonar equipped
Armament (early): one 4-inch gun, two .50-caliber twin machine guns, two Lewis .303 caliber twin machine guns, two Mk. II depth charge throwers, two depth charge rails, and 40 depth charges
Armament (later): one 4-inch gun, one 2-pounder Mk.VIII single pom-pom gun, two 20-mm Oerlikon single guns, one Hedge-hog ASW mortar, four MK.II depth charge throwers, two depth charge rails, and 70 depth charges

A smaller class of corvette, 44 ships launched during 1943–44, was the Castle class (so called because all were named after English castles). Whereas the Flower class resembled a coastal gunboat, the Castle class looked more like a frigate or even a DESTROYER ESCORT and was better suited to transatlantic duty. The Royal Canadian and British Royal Navies operated the vessels. A single ship was transferred to the Norwegian Navy.

General specifications of the Castle class included:

Displacement: 1,060 tons
Length: 252 feet
Beam: 36.75 feet
Draft: 10 feet
Propulsion: one four-cylinder triple-expansion steam engine rated at 2,950 horsepower
Top speed: 16.5 knots
Range: 4,295 nautical miles
Armament: one 101.6 mm gun; two twin and six single 20-mm antiaircraft guns; Squid ASW mortar; depth charge launches, rails, and depth charges
Crew: 120

Further reading: Lenton, H. T. *British Escort Ships.* London: Macdonald & Jane's, 1974; Milner, Marc, and Ken MacPherson. *Corvettes of the Royal Canadian Navy: 1939–1945.* St. Catherines, Ontario: Vanwell, 1993; Williams, Andrew. *The Battle of the Atlantic: Hitler's Gray Wolves of the Sea and the Allies' Desperate Struggle to Defeat Them.* New York: Basic Books, 2003.

Coventry air raid

On the night of November 14–15, 1940, as part of THE BLITZ, German bombers raided this industrial city in the British Midlands, making use of a major advance in electronic warfare, the Pathfinder Force, KG 100, and X-Gerät radio beacon systems. Of 509 German aircraft sent against Coventry, 449 reached their target, and only one was shot down. This represented not only a major failure of Royal Air Force interceptor aircraft, but also a failure of British radio-beam countermeasures, which were designed to jam electronic guidance systems. The result of the raid was the destruction of a dozen armaments factories and most of the city's commercial center. Coventry Cathedral, dating from the 14th century, was left in ruins and became, for Britishers and the rest of the free world, a symbol of German aggression and the desperate, devastating nature of World War II. Some 380 British civilians were killed and 865 injured. The Coventry raid provided impetus to the rapid improvement of British antiaircraft defenses and electronic countermeasures.

Further reading: Fountain, Nigel. *The Battle of Britain and the Blitz: Voices from the Twentieth Century.* London: Michael O'Mara Books, 2003; Harrison, Tom. *Living Through the Blitz.* New York: Random House, 1989; Longmate, Norman. *Air Raid: The Bombing of Coventry, 1940.* London: Hutchinson, 1976.

Crete, action on

The Allies wanted to hold the island of Crete as the site of an air base from which bombing raids against the Ploesti oilfields, vital to the German war machine, could be launched. However, the demands of other fronts left Crete weakly garrisoned by just 35,000 men (British, Commonwealth, and Greek troops), poorly armed and subject to noncohesive command. Moreover, the harsh, mountainous terrain of Crete impeded defense. Artillery and air support were virtually nil.

On May 20, German paratroops of Fliegerkorps 11, under General KURT STUDENT, landed at both ends of Crete. The Allies responded by broadcasting defenders across the island, spreading them thin. For their part, the Germans had underestimated the size of the island's garrison and had to call for reinforcements from the island of Milos. The troop transports were either dispersed or sunk by British air and sea attacks. Despite this blow to the attackers, the paratroopers managed to take the airfield at Maleme, which quickly turned the tide hopelessly against the defenders.

German paratroops load into J-52s for the airborne assault on Crete. *(U.S. Army Command and General Staff School)*

On May 26, Lt. Gen Sir Bernard Freyberg, in command of the garrison, reported that his position was untenable. After securing permission to evacuate, he ordered a retreat on May 27 to Sphakia while troops at Heraklion were quickly evacuated by British warships. The defenders of the Retimo airfield were cut off and captured. In the meantime, the main force, at Sphakia, fell under heavy air attack, and the evacuation ships were pummeled. Three cruisers and six destroyers were sunk, and 17 other vessels were damaged. By May 30, the evacuation had to be aborted, leaving 5,000 men still on the island. Most of these were doomed to capture, but a small body escaped to join the Cretan resistance and were active until the German withdrawal from Crete in 1944.

After the Allied evacuation, Italian troops were sent to occupy the eastern Cretan provinces of Siteia and Lasitho while German troops held the rest of the island. Total losses at the Battle of Crete were 1,742 British, Greek, and Commonwealth troops killed, 2,225 wounded, and 11,370 captured. Royal Navy losses were some 2,000 men killed and 183 wounded. Losses to the Germans testified to the ferocity of the Allied defense: 7,000 were killed. Viewed by ADOLF HITLER as a Pyrrhic victory, the Battle of Crete persuaded him to ban further AIRBORNE ASSAULTS as too costly, and, for the rest of the war, the Germans never launched another major paratroop operation.

Further reading: Beevor, Antony. *Crete: The Battle and the Resistance.* Denver: Westview Press, 1994; Forty, George. *Battle of Crete.* Hersham, U.K.: Ian Allan, 2002; Shores, Christopher, Brian Cull, and Nicola Malizia. *Air War for Yugoslavia Greece and Crete 1940–41.* London: Grub Street, 1993; Willingham, Matthew. *Perilous Commitments: Britain's Involvement in Greece and Crete 1940–41.* London: Spellmount, 2004.

cruisers

Larger than a destroyer and significantly smaller than a battleship, the World War II cruiser combined the agility and high speed of the smaller ship with something of the range, armament, and armor of the larger vessel. It was, therefore, a ship of great versatility, used for everything from convoy escort duty, to fleet reconnaissance, to offensive operations, to amphibious fire support. Its name, appropriately enough, was derived from the era of sail, when *cruiser* was virtually synonymous with *frigate* and described a fighting ship that was smaller and more maneuverable than a ship of the line (the sail equivalent of a battleship), but still a formidable firing platform. In consequence, the cruiser-frigate became the workhorse of many navies, performing scouting duties and aggressively hunting for enemy vessels. By the end of the 19th century, early in the age of steam propulsion, the cruiser emerged as the frigate of the era.

By the beginning of the 20th century, cruisers were evolving from so-called protected cruisers, which were only partly armored with plating on their decks, to fully armored cruisers, plated on the hull. However, by World War I, the modern cruiser had become, in effect, a small battleship, displacing up to 20,000 tons and resembling a mighty dreadnought, though with limited armor in order to achieve speed. Such vessels were called battle cruisers and, while fast (25+ knots), were vulnerable because of their thin armor.

During the interwar years, the cruiser proper was revived by the Washington Treaty of 1922, which limited displacement of this vessel type to 10,000 tons, about half the size of a World War I–era battle cruiser. However, well before the outbreak of World War II, most of the signatories to the treaty had violated it by building larger cruisers. It was perceived that the function of the cruiser had changed. Aircraft carrier–launched aircraft performed the role of scouts, and submarines were seen as superior to surface ships for purposes of raiding convoys. Therefore, the cruiser mission was redefined as chiefly a firing platform, much like a battleship. The cruiser's guns were used to provide artillery bombardment in conjunction with amphibious operations and also to supply antiaircraft fire as part of the defensive component of aircraft carrier task forces. Indeed, some cruisers were built or reconfigured primarily for the antiaircraft role, bristling with many four- or five-inch rapid-fire guns.

The cruiser USS *San Francisco* enters San Francisco Bay, December 1942. *(National Archives and Records Administration)*

FRANCE

The most important French cruiser class was the La Galissonnière, which consisted of six ships, all launched during the 1930s. They were light cruisers (displacing just 7,600 tons standard and 9,120 tons under full load) capable of high speed, in excess of 35 knots. Their largest guns were six inches, and the ships of this class had nine of these, which outclassed rival vessels of the time.

The fleet of La Galissonnière cruisers saw little action in World War II. Three of the vessels were commandeered by the Allies, while the other three were scuttled during the German occupation; they had never left the port of Toulon. Two of these ships were salvaged by the Italian Navy but were subsequently sunk by Allied aerial bombardment in 1943.

General specifications of the La Galissonnière class included:

Ships: *La Galissonnière* (1933), *Jean de Vienne* (1935), *Marseillaise* (1935), *Gloire* (1935), *Montcalm* (1935), *Georges Leygues* (1936)
Displacement: 7,600 tons standard, 9,120 tons fully loaded
Length: 586 feet 3 inches
Beam: 57 feet 4 inches
Draft: 17 feet 5 inches
Power plant: geared turbines making 84,000 shaft horsepower, two shafts
Top speed: 35.7 knots
Armament: nine 6-inch guns, eight 3.5-inch guns. eight 0.52-inch antiaircraft guns, and four 21.7-inch torpedo tubes
Aircraft: accommodations for two floatplanes
Crew: 540

GERMANY

Germany had nine cruisers in World War II, including three of the *Deutschland* class, which were often called "POCKET BATTLESHIPS" by the Allies. The Germans referred to the Deutschland class vessels as *Panzerschiffe*, armored ships. Germany used its cruisers chiefly as surface raiders, preying on Allied convoys.

Displacing 12,100 tons standard and 16,200 tons fully loaded, the Deutschland class, launched between 1931 and 1934, substantially exceeded the limits of the Washington Naval Treaty. They mounted six 11-inch guns and eight 5.9-inch guns, making them a formidable firing platform, yet one that, at 28.5 knots, was faster than full-scale battleships of the day. The *Admiral Graf Spee* was lost in the Battle of the Plate River very early in the war. The *Admiral Scheer* served briefly, albeit effectively, as a surface raider. After the loss of the *Admiral Graf Spee*, the *Deutschland* was renamed *Lützow* for fear that its proud name would make it a conspicuous target and that, if sunk, it would be a severe blow to German pride and morale. Like most of the German surface fleet, it spent the greater part of the war in port. Nevertheless, both it and the *Admiral Scheer* were sunk by British bombs late in the war.

General specifications of the Deutschland class included:

Displacement: 12,100 tons standard, 16,200 tons fully loaded
Length: 610 feet 3 inches
Beam: 69 feet 11 inches
Draft: 19 feet
Power plant: eight MAN diesel engines, making a total of 56,000 shaft horsepower, two shafts
Top speed: 28.5 knots
Armament: six 11-inch guns, eight 5–9-inch guns, six 4.1-inch antiaircraft guns, eight 37-mm antiaircraft guns, 10 20-mm antiaircraft guns, and eight 21-inch torpedo tubes
Aircraft: accommodation for two floatplanes
Crew: 1,150

The other major German class of cruiser was the Hipper class, which consisted of the *Admiral Hipper* (1937), *Blücher* (1937), and *Prinz Eugen* (1938). Displacing 14,475 tons standard and 18,400 tons fully loaded, these vessels violated the Washington Naval Treaty limits even more flagrantly than the ships of the Deutschland class.

The *Admiral Hipper* was used in operations related to the invasion of Norway in 1940 and served effectively as a surface raider through 1942. At the end of 1942, however, ADOLF HITLER, concerned about the vulnerability of his surface fleet, ordered all heavy ships to port, and both the *Admiral Hipper* and *Prinz Eugen* (which had served as companion ships to the infamous battleship *Bismarck*) were captured at the end of the war. In 1945, the U.S. Navy considered commissioning the captured *Prinz Eugen* but found its machinery to be unreliable, so used it as a target ship in an atomic bomb test. As for the *Blücher*, it was sunk by Norwegian shore batteries in 1940.

General specifications of the Hipper class included:

Displacement: 14,475 tons standard, 18,400 tons fully loaded
Length: 690 feet 4 inches
Beam: 71 feet 10 inches
Draft: 25 feet 10 inches
Power plant: geared turbines making 132,000 shaft horsepower, three shafts
Top speed: 33.4 knots
Armament: eight 8-inch guns, 12 4.1-inch guns, 12 37-mm antiaircraft guns, 24 20-mm antiaircraft guns, and 12 21-inch torpedo tubes
Aircraft: accommodation for two floatplanes
Crew: 1,450

GREAT BRITAIN

At the time of World War II, the cruiser was effectively the backbone of the Royal Navy. The cruiser fleet consisted of a dozen separate classes. In addition to these were 18 other individual cruisers that fell into no particular class. The four most important classes were the County and Town classes of heavy cruisers, and the Arethusa and Dido classes of light cruisers.

The 13 ships of the County class were all launched during the 1920s and were compliant with the displacement limits of the Washington Naval Treaty. Most of these ships were used as convoy escorts, despite their inadequate antiaircraft defenses and consequent vulnerability to air attack.

General specifications of the County class included:

Ships: *Berwick* (1926), *Cornwall* (1926), *Cumberland* (1926), *Kent* (1926), *Suffolk* (1926),
Australia (1927), *Canberra* (1927), *Devonshire* (1927), *London* (1927), *Shropshire* (1928), *Sussex* (1928), *Dorsetshire* (1929), *Norfolk* (1928)
Displacement: 9,825 tons standard, 14,000 tons fully loaded
Length: 633 feet
Beam: 66 feet
Draft: 21 feet 6 inches
Power plant: geared turbines making 80,000 shaft horsepower, four shafts
Top speed: 32 knots
Armament: eight 8-inch guns, eight 4-inch antiaircraft guns, eight to 16 2-pounder antiaircraft guns, and eight 21-inch torpedo tubes
Aircraft: accommodation for one to three flying boats (depending on ship)
Crew: 660

The Town class heavy cruisers were all launched in the late 1930s and are sometimes referred to as the Southampton class. They were built to be on par with the new generation of Japanese and American cruisers and featured an impressive array of armament.

General specifications of the Town class included:

Ships: *Newcastle* (1936), *Southampton* (1936), *Birmingham* (1936), *Glasgow* (1936), *Sheffield* (1936), *Liverpool* (1937), *Manchester* (1937), *Gloucester* (1937), *Belfast* (1938), *Edinburgh* (1938)
Displacement: 10,550 tons standard, 13,175 tons fully loaded
Length: 613 feet
Beam: 63 feet 3 inches
Draft: 17 feet 6 inches
Power plant: geared turbines making 82,500 shaft horsepower, 4 shafts
Top speed: 32 knots
Armament: 12 6-inch guns, eight 4-inch antiaircraft guns, eight or 16 2-pounder guns, and six 21-inch torpedo tubes
Aircraft: accommodation for three flying boats
Crew: 850

Four Arethusa class light cruisers were launched during the 1930s, all of which served with distinction in the Mediterranean during the war. General specifications of the class included: Ships: *Arethusa* (1934), *Galatea* (1934), *Penelope* (1936), *Aurora* (1936).

Displacement: 5,250 tons standard
Length: 506 feet
Beam: 51 feet
Draft: 13 feet 9 inches
Power plant: 64,000 shaft horsepower, 4 shafts
Top speed: 32.25 knots
Armament: six 6-inch guns, eight 4-inch antiaircraft guns, eight 2-pounder antiaircraft guns, and six 21-inch torpedo tubes
Aircraft: accommodation for one flying boat (in all except *Aurora*)
Crew: 470

The Dido class were all launched after the war was under way and were built with the express purpose of providing strong anti-aircraft defense for convoys as well as serving as a firing platform to cover amphibious operations. General specifications included:

Ships: *Dido* (1939), *Euryalus* (1939), *Naiad* (1939), *Phoebe* (1939), *Sirius* (1940), *Bonaventure* (1939), *Hermione* (1939), *Charybdis* (1940), *Cleopatra* (1940), *Scylla* (1940), and *Argonaut;* the "improved Dido class" ships included *Bellona* (1942), *Black Prince* (1942), *Diadem* (1942), *Royalist* (1942), and *Spartan* (1942)
Displacement (1942): 5,770 tons standard, 6,970 tons fully loaded
Length (1942): 512 feet
Beam (1942): 50 feet 6 inches
Draft (1942): 17 feet 3 inches
Power plant (1942): geared turbines making 64,000 shaft horsepower, four shafts
Top speed (1942): 32.25 knots
Armament (1942): eight 5.25-inch guns, eight or 12 2-pounder antiaircraft guns, 12 20-mm antiaircraft guns, and six 21-inch torpedo tubes
Crew (1942): 535

ITALY

A very powerful (if somewhat obsolescent) force at the beginning of World War II, the Italian navy was badly led and essentially squandered during the war. Its 20 cruisers were divided into the Zara, Condottieri, and Capitani Romani classes.

The Zara class consisted of the *Zara* (1930), *Fiume* (1930), *Gorizia* (1930), and *Pola* (1931) and constituted the Italian Navy's heavy cruiser fleet, the ships displacing between 11,500 and 11,900 tons standard and 14,200 and 14,600 tons fully loaded. Like German ships, they exceeded the displacement limits of the Washington Naval Treaty and were, in fact, formidable vessels that, however, lacked radar and other state-of-the-art refinements. Worse, they were very poorly commanded during World War II. Three of the ships fought ineffectively in the abortive Battle of Calabria early in the war, and the *Pola, Zara,* and *Fiume* were all lost in the March 1941 BATTLE OF MATAPAN.

General specifications of the Zara class included:

Displacement: 11,500–11,900 tons standard, 14,200–14,600 tons fully loaded
Length: 599 feet 5 inches
Beam: 67 feet 7 inches
Draft: 19 feet 4 inches
Power plant: geared turbines making 108,000 shaft horsepower, two shafts
Top speed: 32 knots
Armament: eight 8-inch guns, 16 3.9-inch guns, and eight 37-mm antiaircraft guns
Aircraft: accommodation for two floatplanes
Crew: 830

The 12-ship Condottieri class consisted of light cruisers launched during the early 1930s. They were fine ships, but, again, lacked radar and, even worse, lacked competent commanders. For that matter, Italy's senior naval planners never formulated a coherent offensive strategy, so that few of the ships were actually committed to combat. Two of the most recently built of the class not only survived the war but were converted to guided-missile cruisers during the cold war.

General specifications of the Condottieri class included:

Ships: *Alberto di Giussano* (1930), *Giovanni delle Bande Nere* (1930), *Alberico da Barbiano* (1930), *Bartolomeo Colleonio* (1930), *Armando Diaz* (1930), *Luigi Cadorna* (1930), *Raimondo Montecuccoli* (1931), *Muzio Attendolo* (1933), *Emanuele Filberto Duca d'Aosta* (1932), *Eugenio di Savoia* (1933), *Luigi di Cavoia Duca degli Abruzzi* (1933), *Giuseppe Garibaldi* (1933)
Displacement: 9,195 tons standard, 11,260 tons fully loaded
Length: 612 feet 5 inches
Beam: 61 feet 11 inches
Draft: 17 feet
Power plant: geared turbines making 102,000 shaft horsepower, 2 shafts
Top speed: 33.5 knots
Armament: 10 6-inch guns, eight 3.9-inch antiaircraft guns, eight 37-mm antiaircraft guns, 10 20-mm antiaircraft guns, and six 21-inch torpedo tubes
Aircraft: accommodation for two floatplanes
Crew: 900

The Capitani Romani class were very light cruisers capable of very high speeds in excess of 40 knots. Had they been completed in time to be used effectively, they would have made highly capable surface raiders, able to outrun anything thrown against them short of air cover. However, speed was achieved at the sacrifice of armor, and, in this respect, they resembled destroyers almost more than cruisers. Their fate as combatants was largely academic, however, because four were destroyed while under construction, and five more were sunk while in the process of fitting out. Just three were actually launched (and a fourth later salvaged), but the only naval service they saw was with the postwar fleets of France and Italy.

General specifications of the Capitani Romani class included:

Ships: *Attilio Regolo* (1940), *Pompeo Magno* (1941), *Giulio Germanico* (1941), *Scipione Africano* (1941)
Displacement: 3,750 tons standard, 5,400 tons fully loaded
Length: 466 feet 6 inches
Beam: 47 feet 3 inches
Draft: 13 feet 5 inches
Power plant: geared turbines making 110,000 shaft horsepower, two shafts
Top speed: about 43 knots
Armament: eight 5.3-inch guns, eight 37-mm antiaircraft guns, eight 20-mm antiaircraft guns, and eight 21-inch torpedo tubes
Aircraft: no accommodation
Crew: 425

JAPAN

Japan's Imperial Navy relied extensively on cruisers, which it did not use for escort duty, but for attack and as firing platforms in support of amphibious operations. Particularly favored were the heavy cruisers, the most important of which were the Mogami class and the Myoko class.

The Mogami ships, four in number, were launched between 1934 and 1936 and were both heavily armed and extremely fast, achieving a top speed of 37 knots. The price for this combination of armament and speed was a paucity of armor and a very slender beam, which made for instability and poor sea keeping. Modifications shortly before the war augmented both armament and beam.

General specifications of the Mogami class included:

Ships: *Mogami* (1934), *Mikuma* (1934), *Suzuya* (1934), *Kumano* (1936)
Displacement: 12,400 tons standard
Length: 669 feet
Beam: 66 feet 3 inches
Draft: 19 feet
Power plant: geared turbines making 150,000 shaft horsepower, four shafts
Top speed: 40 knots
Armament: 10 8-inch guns, eight 5-inch guns, eight 25-mm antiaircraft guns, and 12 24-inch torpedo tubes
Aircraft: accommodation for three floatplanes
Crew: 850

The Myoko class vessels were older than the Mogami ships but were massive and durable, albeit slower than the latest generation of Japanese cruisers. General specifications included:

Ships: *Myoko* (1927), *Nachi* (1927), *Haguro* (1928), *Ashigara* (1928)
Displacement: 13,380 tons standard
Length: 661 feet 9 inches
Beam: 68 feet
Draft: 20 feet 9 inches
Power plant: geared turbines making 130,000 shaft horsepower, 4 shafts
Top speed: 33.5 knots
Armament: 10 8-inch guns, eight 5-inch guns, eight 25-mm antiaircraft guns, and 16 21-inch torpedo tubes
Aircraft: accommodation for three floatplanes
Crew: 780

UNITED STATES

No nation's navy made more extensive use of cruisers than did that of the United States, which used them equally for convoy escort, for offensive operations, and, paramountly, to support amphibious operations. The two most important classes of American cruisers that saw service in World War II were the Northampton class and the Cleveland class.

The Northampton class were products of the Washington Naval Treaty, displacing a little more than 9,000 tons standard and 12,350 tons fully loaded. They represented a significant improvement over the earlier Pensacola class inasmuch as the Northampton ships regrouped the guns and provided more accommodation space as well as generally improved seaworthiness. The ships of this class performed valiantly in the Pacific but took a beating, with three out of six badly damaged and one, the *Northampton,* sunk. The *Chester* passed through the war unscathed and remained in commission until 1960. The *Augusta* had the distinction of carrying President Franklin D. Roosevelt to his prewar epoch-making conference with Prime Minister Winston Churchill in Placentia Bay, Newfoundland, a meeting that produced the Atlantic Charter.

General specifications of the Northampton class included:

Ships: *Northampton* (1929), *Chester* (1929), *Louisville* (1930), *Chicago* (1930), *Houston* (1929), *Augusta* (1930)
Displacement: 9,050–9,300 tons standard, 12,350 tons fully loaded
Length: 600 feet 3 inches
Beam: 66 feet
Draft: 16 feet 3 inches
Power plant: geared turbines making 107,000 shaft horsepower, four shafts
Top speed: 32.5 knots
Armament: nine 8-inch guns, eight 5-inch antiaircraft guns, two 3-pounders, and eight 0.5-inch antiaircraft guns
Aircraft: accommodation for four floatplanes
Crew: 1,200

Just before and during the war, the United States embarked on an ambitious program of new cruiser construction, the Cleveland class, which ultimately consisted of 26 ships completed as cruisers, plus nine hulls converted to fast light carriers. The ships were spacious and formidable. None were lost in combat.

General specifications of the Cleveland class included:

Ships: *Cleveland* (1941), *Columbia* (1941), *Montpelier* (1941), *Denver* (1942), *Santa Fe* (1942), *Birmingham* (1942), *Mobile* (1942), *Vincennes* (1943), *Pasadena* (1943), *Springfield* (1944), *Topeka* (1944), *Biloxi* (19443), *Houston* (1943), *Providence* (1944), *Manchester* (1946), *Vicksburg* (1943), *Duluth* (1944), *Miami* (1942), *Astoria* (1943), *Oklahoma City* (1944), *Little Rock* (1944), *Galveston* (1945), *Amsterdam* (1944), *Portsmouth* (1944), *Wilkes-Barre* (1943), *Atlanta* (1944), *Dayton* (1944), *Baltimore* (1942), *Boston* (1942), *Canberra* (1943), *Quincy* (1943), *Pittsburgh* (1944), *St. Paul* (1944), *Columbia* (1944), *Helena* (1945), *Bremerton* (1944), *Fall River* (1944), *Macon* (1944), *Toledo* (1945), *Los Angeles* (1944), *Chicago* (1944)

Displacement: 10,000 tons standard, 13,775 fully loaded
Length: 610 feet
Beam: 66 feet 6 inches
Draft: 25 feet
Power plant: geared turbines making 100,000 shaft horsepower, 4 shafts
Top speed: 33 knots
Armament: 12 6-inch guns, 12 5-inch guns, eight, 24, or 28 40-mm antiaircraft guns; 10 to 21 20-mm antiaircraft guns
Aircraft: accommodation for four floatplanes
Crew: 1,425

Further reading: Friedman, Norman. *U.S. Cruisers: An Illustrated Design History.* Annapolis, Md.: Naval Institute Press, 1984; Ireland, Bernard, and Tony Gibbons. *Jane's Naval History of WWII.* New York: HarperResource, 1998; Lacroix, Eric, and Linton Well II. *Japanese Cruisers of the Pacific War.* Annapolis, Md.: Naval Institute Press, 1997; Whitley, M. J. *Cruisers of World War Two: An International Encyclopedia.* Annapolis, Md.: Naval Institute Press, 1996.

cryptology

World War II saw an explosion in the development of cryptology, the science and technology of creating and breaking codes such as those used by diplomats as well as military personnel. All the major combatant nations employed specialists in encryption and decryption, personnel who worked in what the military calls signals intelligence. The British and the Americans were particularly far advanced in signals intelligence, intercepting and breaking a wealth of coded messages. Even before the war, U.S. Naval intelligence had succeeded in breaking PURPLE (JAPANESE DIPLOMATIC CIPHER) and, during the war, broke most of the Japanese naval codes. The British, with a collection of scientists and mathematicians working at Bletchley Park, outside London, succeeded in breaking the German ENIGMA codes, fantastically complex coded messages produced with the aid of a proto-computer known as an Enigma machine.

The subjects of cryptology, signals intelligence, and code breaking in World War II are covered in the following entries: ESPIONAGE AND COUNTERESPIONAGE; GEHEIMSCHREIBER; MAGIC (JAPANESE CODE); MI5 (BRITISH MILITARY INTELLIGENCE); MI6 (BRITISH MILITARY INTELLIGENCE); NAVAJO CODE TALKERS; OFFICE OF STRATEGIC SERVICES (OSS); ORANGE (JAPANESE CODE); and ULTRA.

Further reading: Budiansky, Stephen. *Battle of Wits: The Complete Story of Codebreaking in World War II.* New York: Free Press, 2000; Gilbert, James L., and John P. Finnegan, eds. *U.S. Army Signals Intelligence in World War II (Cryptography).* Walnut Creek, Calif.: Aegean Park Press, 1998; Marks, Leo. *Between Silk and Cyanide: A Codemaker's War, 1941–1945.* New York: Free Press, 2000.

Crystal Night. *See Kristallnacht.*

Cuba

No battles took place on this island, some 90 miles off the coast of Florida, and no Cuban troops participated in combat. However, Cuban president Fulgencio Batista (1901–73) was friendly to U.S. interests—he depended heavily on American support to retain power—and was quick to join the United States in declaring war on Japan and Germany. Cuba declared against Japan on December 9, 1941, just one day after the United States, and against Germany on December 11, the day Germany declared against the United States.

For the most part, the declarations were symbolic in significance. However, Cuban authorities did work to counter Axis intelligence agents in their country. One German spy, Heinz Luning, was not only apprehended, but executed, the only Axis agent to be executed in Latin America during the war. Batista also secured passage of a conscription law and began registering men for military service in August 1942. No troops were sent overseas, however. Already the site of several U.S. naval bases and other military installations, Cuba approved the establishment of even more during the war.

Further reading: Gellman, Irwin F. *Roosevelt and Batista: Good Neighbor Diplomacy in Cuba, 1933–1945.* Albuquerque: University of New Mexico Press, 1973.

Cunningham, Alan (1887–1983) *British general defeated by Erwin Rommel in North Africa*

Far less well known than his older brother, Adm. Sir ANDREW CUNNINGHAM, Lt. Gen. Sir Alan Cunningham started the war as commander of British forces in Kenya beginning in November 1940. He preformed very effectively in EAST AFRICA in 1941, which earned him promotion to overall command of the Eighth British Army, which had been formed of British and Commonwealth personnel to oppose the forces of German general ERWIN JOHANNES EUGEN ROMMEL in North Africa. Cunningham led an offensive (Operation Crusader) in November 1941, and was promptly out-generaled by Rommel at the BATTLE OF SIDI REZEGH. When Gen. CLAUDE JOHN AYRE AUCHINLECK, British commander in chief of the Middle East, demonstrated his lack of confidence in Cunningham by intervening in Operation Crusader, Cunningham was removed from combat command and reassigned to rear-echelon administrative posts.

Further reading: Doherty, Richard. *A Noble Crusade: The History of Eighth Army, 1941 to 1945.* New York: Sarpedon, 1999; Kelly, Orr. *Meeting the Fox: The Allied Invasion of Africa, from Operation Torch to Kasserine Pass to Victory in Tunisia.* New York: Wiley, 2002.

Cunningham, Andrew (1883–1963) *British First Sea Lord and a principal naval planner of the D-day landings*

Cunningham was Britain's First Sea Lord from October 1943 and was a member of the British Chiefs of Staff as well as the Allies' Combined Chiefs of Staff. Distinguished in his contributions to the Allied war effort, his most valuable service may well have been as one of the principal architects of Operation Neptune, the sea-going phase of the NORMANDY LANDINGS (D-DAY).

At the outbreak of World War II, in September 1939, Cunningham held the rank of acting admiral and was commander in chief of the Mediterranean Fleet. An aggressive, proactive commander, he was determined to establish and maintain British naval supremacy on the Mediterranean. In November 1940, he ordered a massive air attack against the Italian fleet at TARANTO, which dealt it a crippling blow. Cunningham was a master at provoking battle on his own terms, especially against the Italian fleet at the BATTLE OF MATAPAN.

Cunningham was formally promoted to admiral in January 1941 and, from June to October 1942, headed the British Admiralty Delegation in Washington, D.C. In November, he was named Allied Naval Commander Expeditionary Force and directed the naval phase of OPERATION TORCH, the Allied landings in North Africa. Promoted to fleet admiral in January 1943, he was named commander in chief of the Mediterranean and, as Allied naval commander, directed the naval phase of the landings on SICILY in July 1943 and at SALERNO in September.

Cunningham replaced Sir Dudley Pound as First Sea Lord after Pound's death in October 1943 and played a major role in planning the Normandy landings and invasion. Even as he coordinated naval operations for OPERATION OVERLORD, he mustered the largest British fleet ever assembled—for action in the Pacific.

Cunningham was highly regarded as much for his fighting spirit, very much in the tradition of Lord Nelson and certainly of a piece with WINSTON CHURCHILL, as he was for his skill as a naval tactician and strategist. He saw the war through, then retired in March 1946. He was the elder brother of British army general Sir ALAN CUNNINGHAM.

Further reading: Pack, S. W. C. *Cunningham the Commander.* London: B. T. Batsford, 1974; Simpson, Michael. *A Life of Admiral of the Fleet Andrew Cunningham: A Twentieth-Century Naval Leader.* London: Frank Cass, 2004.

Cunningham, Winfield Scott (1900–1986) *naval commander of the defense of Wake Island*

U.S. Navy commander Winfield Scott Cunningham was in overall command of the small detachment of marines and others who heroically defended WAKE ISLAND in the days following the Japanese attack on PEARL HARBOR and general advance across the Pacific. Cunningham was born in Rockbridge, Wisconsin, and received an appointment to the U.S. Naval Academy in 1916, at the age of 16. Because of the pressures of World War I, his class graduated early, in 1919, and Cunningham was assigned to the naval transport *Martha Washington.* Subsequently, he served aboard USS *Scorpion* and USS *Whipple.* In 1923, he joined the officer complement of the light cruiser USS *Milwaukee,* then trained as a naval aviator, receiving his wings in 1925. In 1926, he transferred to the aviation unit of the battleship *Oklahoma* and also qualified for landings on the navy's first aircraft carrier, USS *Langley.* In 1935, Cunningham was assigned as executive officer of Fighting Squadron 2 on the aircraft carrier *Lexington,* and in 1936 he assembled and trained a fighter squadron for USS *Yorktown.*

Cunningham became navigator aboard USS *Wright* in April 1940. In the months and weeks before Pearl Harbor, the *Wright* supported the establishment of aviation bases on Midway, Canton, Johnston, Palmyra, and Wake Islands, transporting marines, aviation personnel, and civilian contractors to and between these valuable bases. In November 1941, Cunningham was assigned as Officer in Charge, All Naval Activities, Wake Island. On November 28, Cunningham replaced USMC major James Devereux, who continued to serve as commander of the Marine First Defense Battalion under Commander Cunningham.

From December 8 to December 23, Cunningham directed an extraordinary defense of Wake Island by the overwhelmingly outnumbered marines. The Japanese attackers lost hundreds of casualties and two battleships. Cunningham and the Wake Island survivors were made prisoners of war. However, on the night of March 11, 1942, Cunningham and others managed to escape from a Japanese prison in China, only to be recaptured. A second escape was attempted on October 6, 1944, but Cunningham was recaptured. He survived and was liberated at the end of the war, returning to the United States on September 8, 1945. Cunningham

continued to serve in the postwar navy, retiring as a rear admiral on June 30, 1950.

Further reading: Cressman, Robert J. *A Magnificent Fight: The Battle for Wake Island.* Annapolis, Md.: Naval Institute Press, 1995; Cunningham, Winfield Scott. *Wake Island Command.* Boston: Little, Brown, 1961; Urwin, Gregory. *A Siege of Wake Island: Facing Fearful Odds.* Norman: University of Nebraska Press, 1997.

Czechoslovakia

In 1938, Czechoslovakia was a democratic republic created after World War I under the terms of the TREATY OF VERSAILLES and situated strategically in middle Europe. To the west and northwest was Germany, to the northeast Poland, to the east Romania, and to the south Hungary and Austria. The nation contained valuable iron ore and coal, as well as a highly developed industrial capacity, including the famed arms manufacturer Skoda. Population in 1938 was more than 14 million, including 10 million Czechs and Slovaks, as well as 3 million Germans and small minorities of Hungarians, Poles, and Ukrainians. The Germans lived mainly along the western, northern, and southern fringes of Czechoslovakia, an area called the SUDETENLAND.

After Germany's ANSCHLUSS with Austria, Czechoslovakia became the next target of ADOLF HITLER's expansionist ambitions on the eve of World War II. The September 1938 MUNICH CONFERENCE AND AGREEMENT, which implemented British prime minister NEVILLE CHAMBERLAIN's APPEASEMENT POLICY, resulted in the cession of the Sudetenland to Germany. With the loss of this territory went the heavily fortified border, possession of which would greatly facilitate Germany's subsequent INVASION OF THE SOVIET UNION. When the Sudetenland was ceded to Germany, Poland opportunistically stepped in to seize Teschen, home of a Polish minority. At this time, too, Slovakia, the eastern portion of Czechoslovakia, effectively became a German client state, though a part of Slovakia, as well as all of Ruthenia, fell at this time to Hungary. Thus dismembered, Czechoslovakia

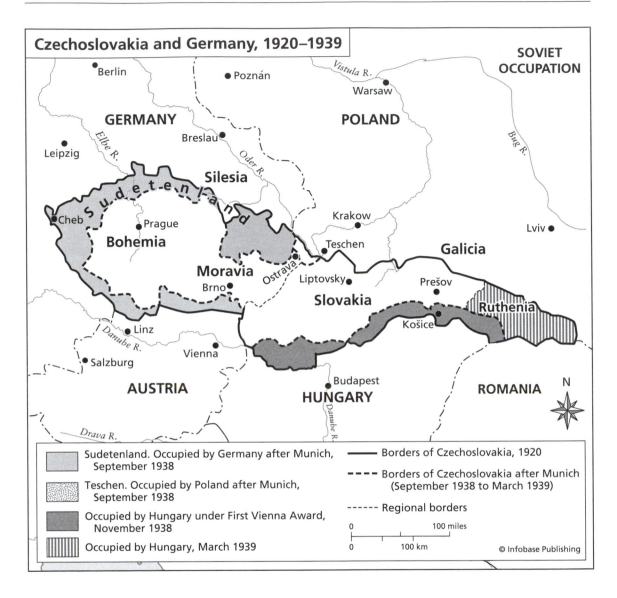

Czechoslovakia and Germany, 1920–1939

SOVIET OCCUPATION

GERMANY

POLAND

Berlin

Poznán

Vistula R.

Warsaw

Leipzig

Elbe R.

Breslau

Silesia

Oder R.

Bug R.

Cheb

Sudetenland

Prague

Bohemia

Krakow

Lviv

Teschen

Galicia

Moravia

Ostrava

Liptovsky

Prešov

Ruthenia

Brno

Slovakia

Košice

Linz

Danube R.

Vienna

Salzburg

AUSTRIA

Budapest

HUNGARY

Danube R.

ROMANIA

N

Drava R.

	Sudetenland. Occupied by Germany after Munich, September 1938
	Teschen. Occupied by Poland after Munich, September 1938
	Occupied by Hungary under First Vienna Award, November 1938
	Occupied by Hungary, March 1939

——— Borders of Czechoslovakia, 1920

– – – Borders of Czechoslovakia after Munich (September 1938 to March 1939)

------ Regional borders

0   100 miles
0   100 km

© Infobase Publishing

now consisted only of Bohemia and Moravia, and even these regions were soon invaded and occupied by the German WEHRMACHT on March 15, 1939, in contravention of the Munich Agreement. Hitler effectively annexed this region to the Third Reich as the "Protectorate of Bohemia and Moravia" under the governance of Baron Konstantin von Neurath, who, proving incompetent, was quickly replaced as *Reichsprotektor* by REINHARD HEYDRICH, a man who earned the epithet "The Butcher of Prague." The Czech government proper was no more than a shell with a figurehead president, Emil Hácha.

The Nazi occupation of the mutilated Czechoslovakia was brutal, yet less so than the Nazi regime in Poland and in the occupied Soviet Union. As elsewhere, however, Jews were singled out, rounded up, deported, and made victims of THE HOLOCAUST. Yet the occupiers were keenly concerned with exploiting the industrial productivity of the region. Therefore, they tended to make concessions to the laboring classes, whose hard work was rewarded. In this way, the basis for organized resistance in occupied Czechoslovakia was significantly co-opted. Nevertheless, a resistance movement did come about, and its boldest act was the assassination of no less a figure than *Reichsprotektor* Heydrich. This resulted in extravagantly brutal reprisals, including, most infamously, the wholesale destruction of the village of Lidice. It was not until May 1945 that a full-scale popular uprising erupted, in Prague, which aided the final advance of the Red Army.

While resistance within Czechoslovakia was neither intense nor extensive, EDVARD BENEŠ successfully established a very active Czech government in exile in London. In Great Britain, Beneš formed a Czech legion, a unit of brigade strength, consisting of 5,000 men equipped with tanks, which served in the NORMANDY LANDINGS (D-DAY) and in subsequent engagements. Three Czech fighter squadrons and one Czech bomber squadron flew with the Royal Air Force, and Czech intelligence operatives served with the British throughout the war.

In July 1941, the Beneš government concluded a treaty with the Soviet Union by which the USSR recognized the legitimacy of the government in exile and, with the United States and Great Britain, upheld its status as an Allied power. In the Soviet Union, two Czech parachute brigades and, ultimately, an entire corps (1st Czechoslovak Army Corps) served on the eastern front. A regiment of fighter pilots also served under the auspices of the Soviet air forces.

Further reading: MacDonald, Callum. *The Killing of Reinhard Heydrich: The SS "Butcher of Prague."* New York: Da Capo, 1998; Mastny, Vojtech. *Czechs under Nazi Rule: The Failure of National Resistance, 1939–42.* New York: Columbia University Press, 1971; Zeman, Z. A. B., and Antonin Klimek. *The Life of Edvard Benes 1884–1948: Czechoslovakia in Peace and War.* Oxford and New York: Oxford University Press, 1997.

D

Dachau concentration camp

Established in March 1933, Dachau was among the first of the Nazi concentration camps. It was located 12 miles north of Munich and was originally intended as a "correctional" facility for those who spoke out against the regime of ADOLF HITLER or who were for other reasons regarded as socially undesirable. Between its opening in 1933 and the end of the war in May 1945, some 225,000 persons had been inmates at the prison. Official Nazi records list 31,950 deaths, although this figure is certainly much too low. While Jews were among those incarcerated here, Dachau also housed political prisoners, including the former Austrian chancellor KURT VON SCHUSCHNIGG and various German anti-Nazi activists. Dachau was the scene of atrocities that included so-called medical experiments, the most notorious of which involved deliberately infecting inmate test subjects with malaria and also measuring the effects of immersion in cold water for long periods. The former work was supposed to contribute to developing vaccines and other measures to protect German troops against malaria, and the latter "experiments" were intended to assist pilots downed in the icy North Atlantic.

See also CONCENTRATION AND EXTERMINATION CAMPS; and HOLOCAUST, THE.

Further reading: Distel, Barbara, and Ruth Jakusch. *Concentration Camp Dachau, 1933–1945.* Dachau: Comité International de Dachau, 1978.

Daladier, Édouard (1884–1970) *French premier who reluctantly signed the Munich Pact with Hitler*

With British prime minister NEVILLE CHAMBERLAIN, French premier Édouard Daladier signed the Munich Pact of September 30, 1938, giving ADOLF HITLER the Czech SUDETENLAND. Born in Carpentras, France, Daladier was first elected to the Chamber of Deputies in 1919 as a member of the Radical Party. A vigorous politician, he served from 1924 to 1933 variously as minister of colonies, minister of war, minister of public instruction, and minister of public works. On January 31, 1933, he formed his own government, which dissolved in October. The next year, in January 1934, he formed another government, which endured a mere four weeks. In 1935, he led the Radical Party in a coalition with the Socialists and the Communists as the Popular Front, with himself as premier.

Like Chamberlain, Daladier was concerned at virtually any cost to avoid war with Germany and thus cooperated in Chamberlain's APPEASEMENT POLICY by endorsing the Munich Pact, thereby abrogating France's treaty agreement to defend the national integrity of Czechoslovakia. Appeasement, of course, failed to avert armed conflict, and Daladier led France into a war for which it had failed to prepare. In June 1940, when France fell following the BATTLE OF FRANCE, Daladier attempted a last-minute escape to French North Africa, where he intended to establish a government in exile. In

Morocco, however, agents of the VICHY GOVERN-
MENT arrested him and returned him to France.
There he was tried at Riom in February 1942. With
others who had resisted the Vichy compromise,
Daladier publicly accused HENRIE-PHILIPPE
PÉTAIN and his followers of having failed to pre-
pare for war. Vichy authorities in turn remanded
Daladier to German custody, and he remained a
prisoner of the Reich until the liberation of France
in 1945.

After the war, Daladier was again elected to the
Chamber of Deputies, serving from 1946 to 1958.
Diehard president of the much-diminished Radical
Party, he opposed the constitution promulgated by
CHARLES DE GAULLE in 1958. After the failure of
his opposition, he retired from politics and public
life.

Further reading: Daladier, Édouard. *Prison Journal
1940–1945.* New York: Perseus, 1995; Jackson, Julian.
The Fall of France: The Nazi Invasion of 1940. Oxford and
New York: Oxford University Press, 2003; Shirer, William
L. *The Collapse of the Third Republic: An Inquiry into the
Fall of France in 1940.* New York: Da Capo, 1994.

Daluege, Kurt (1897–1946) *Nazi official who perpetrated the Lidice massacre*

Daluege, among the earliest members of the NAZI
PARTY (NSDAP), established the first STURMAB-
TEILUNG (SA) unit in Berlin in 1926, then two years
later transferred to the SCHUTZSTAFFEL (SS) and
became a senior officer. He served as a member of
the Nazi delegation in the Prussian legislature in
1932 and the following year became a member of
the Reichstag. Appointed chief of the Order Police
(Orpo) in 1936, he succeeded REINHARD HEY-
DRICH in 1942 as Reich protector (military governor) of Bohemia and Moravia. He authorized the
Lidice massacre in reprisal for the assassination of
Heydrich.

Daluege was born in Kreuzburg on September
15, 1897, and fought with distinction in World War
I. Active in the FREIKORPS after the war, he joined
the Nazi Party virtually at its inception in 1922.
After forming the first SA unit in Berlin in 1926, he

transferred to the SS in 1928 and began a close
working relationship with SS chief HEINRICH HIM-
MLER. In 1936, three years after his election to the
Reichstag, Daluege was tapped by HERMANN
GÖRING as head of the Prussian police. When
Göring took control of all German police forces, he
named Daluege chief of the Orpo, the Order Police
(Ordnungspolizei). In this position, Daluege created the Kameradschaftsbund Deutscher Polize-
beamten, ostensibly a fraternal organization of
police officials, but, in fact, a body intended to
facilitate the suppression of internal revolt.

After the beginning of World War II, Daluege
became deputy to Reinhard Heydrich in the SS. In
May 1942, Heydrich was fatally wounded by Czech
assassins, whereupon ADOLF HITLER and Himmler
dispatched Daluege to Prague to replace the fallen
Heydrich as Reich protector of Czechoslovakia.
Daluege's first actions were to visit upon the Czechs
brutal reprisals for the assassination. The most
notorious of these was the annihilation of the village of Lidice, which was razed. All 173 of its male
inhabitants were summarily executed, and its 198
women were sent to a Ravensbrueck concentration
camp. On Daluege's orders, 256 other Czechs suffered death for Heydrich's assassination.

Daluege was arrested after World War II and
charged with war crimes. He was convicted by a
Czech court and hanged in Prague on October 24,
1946.

Further reading: Hilberg, Raul. *Perpetrators, Victims,
Bystanders: Jewish Catastrophe 1933–1945.* New York:
Perennial, 1993; MacDonald, Callum. *The Killing of
Reinhard Heydrich: The SS 'Butcher of Prague.'* New York:
Da Capo, 1998; Reitlinger, Gerald. *The SS: Alibi of a
Nation, 1922–1945.* New York: Da Capo, 1989.

Dambusters raid

In March 1943, the Royal Air Force (RAF) formed
617 Squadron, a heavy bomber unit flying four-
engine Lancasters, that trained for one specialized
task: to bomb and thereby breach the dams in Germany's industrial Ruhr valley. The objective was to
create flooding that would extensively damage war

industries and also that would disrupt river navigation and the supply of drinking and industrial water. Three major dams were targets: the Möhne and Sorpe, which provided much of the water supply for the Ruhr, and the Eder Dam, which was essential to maintaining the navigable waters of the Wester River and the Mittelland Canal. For this mission, the British airship and aircraft engineer Barnes Wallis developed a special dambuster bomb. Knowing that the dams were protected by nets intended to deflect conventional bombs, Wallis proposed a bouncing bomb, which would clear the nets, bounce off the water, then smash into the dam wall, but remain intact until it had sunk to a depth of 30 feet. At that point a hydrostatic fuse (like those used in depth charges) would detonate 6,600 pounds of powerful RDX explosive, ensuring that the dam would rupture catastrophically well below the water line. Concerned that the bomb would fail to travel down the dam wall to the required depth, Wallis designed a canister, or drum-shaped bomb, 50 inches in diameter and 60 inches long. He further designed a rig to mount it across the bomb bay of the Lancaster, and installed a small motor in the bomb bay that would start the canister spinning forward, so that it would indeed roll down the wall of its target.

The design was only half the requirement of the mission. The bomb had to be dropped just 60 feet above the water, so that it would bounce with sufficient force to reach the dam with the momentum required to roll down to the required depth. This called for flying skill of the most exacting and daring order.

After intensive crew training, and with the Wallis bombs installed, 19 Lancasters took off on the night of May 16–17, 1943, under the leadership of Wing Commander Guy Gibson. Eight of the aircraft were lost, but the Möhne and Eder Dams were indeed breached, bringing a massive flood. The Sorpe Dam remained undamaged. While many German citizens were flooded out of their homes, the hoped-for dislocation and disruption of industry did not occur, and the dams themselves were repaired by October. Gibson was decorated with the Victoria Cross. Although another dambusting

mission was never attempted—and the Wallis bomb was never again deployed—the 617 Squadron was retained intact for other precision bombing missions.

Further reading: Bennett, Tom. *617 Squadron: The Dambusters at War.* New York: Sterling, 1987; Cooper, Alan. *The Men Who Breached the Dams: 617 Squadron, "The Dambusters."* Stillwater, Minn.: Voyageur Press, 1993; Flower, Stephen. *Barnes Wallis' Bombs: Tallboy, Dambuster and Grand Slam.* London: Tempus, 2004; Ottaway, Susan. *Dambuster: A Life of Guy Gibson.* Barnsley, U.K.: Pen & Sword Books, 2003; Sweetman, John. *The Dambusters.* London: Little, Brown UK, 2003.

Darlan, Jean-François (1881–1942)
commander of Vichy French forces in North Africa

Darlan was an admiral in the French navy who served as deputy premier (under HENRI-PHILIPPE PÉTAIN) of the VICHY GOVERNMENT. He was in Algiers and assumed command of Vichy French forces in North Africa when the Allies invaded with OPERATION TORCH. Gen. DWIGHT D. EISENHOWER concluded a controversial rapprochement with him, securing his cooperation with the Allies in return for Allied confirmation of his appointment as high commissioner for French North Africa.

Darlan graduated from the French naval academy in 1902 and joined the French navy, commanding a naval artillery battle during World War I. By 1929, Darlan was an admiral and, as war clouds gathered in the mid-1930s, was engaged in rebuilding the French navy. Darlan was named admiral chief of staff in 1936 and in 1937 admiral of the fleet, in command of all French naval forces. With war approaching, the right-wing Darlan gave vent to his anti-English sentiments and, as the BATTLE OF FRANCE got under way, expressed his hope that Germany would win the war. Following the resignation of French premier PAUL REYNAUD on June 16, 1940, Darlan eagerly threw his support behind Marshal Pétain and the collaborationist Vichy government. Pétain named Darlan minister of the navy, and after Pétain formally concluded the armistice with Nazi Germany, Darlan ordered the French fleet to colonial bases in North Africa, ordering officers and sailors to conduct themselves in loyalty to Vichy.

In February 1941, Darlan replaced Pierre Laval as vice premier, and the aging Pétain named him his successor. At the same time, Darlan became minister for foreign affairs, defense, and the interior. In January 1942, he was appointed commander in chief of French armed forces and the high commissioner for North Africa. Fearing the concentration of so much authority in one man, Adolf Hitler pressured Darlan to yield his cabinet posts to Pierre Laval on April 17, 1942, but he remained Pétain's deputy premier and retained his military and North African posts.

When the Allied North African invasion came on November 8, 1942, Vichy forces acted in accordance with Darlan's orders and resisted, but Darlan immediately entered into negotiations with the Allies, agreed to a cease fire on November 10, and surrendered the following day. Moreover, he agreed to cooperate fully with the Allies in return for Eisenhower's confirmation and approval of his position as the chief civil and military administrator of French North Africa. Eisenhower saw an opportunity to neutralize the Vichy forces without bloodshed. Free French leader Charles de Gaulle was outraged by Eisenhower's endorsement of a collaborationist. The French resistance was similarly appalled. They regarded Darlan as a traitor. But both Winston Churchill and Franklin D. Roosevelt concurred in and supported Eisenhower's bold decision. For his part, Darlan did prepare to assist the Allies in their military operations in western North Africa. In the meantime, the panic-stricken Vichy government scrambled to give assurances to Hitler. He, however, turned a deaf ear and sent troops into the unoccupied zone of France and into Tunisia.

Darlan was not fated to exercise his newly confirmed office for long. On Christmas Eve 1942, he was assassinated in Algiers by Ferdinand Bonnier de la Chapelle, an anti-Nazi royalist. Bonnier de la Chapelle had been trained by the British Special Operations Executive (SOE) and had been a member of the French resistance. However, historians believe that he was acting on his own authority and out of personal hatred for Darlan rather than on orders of any nation or organization.

Further reading: Melton, Georges E. *Darlan.* London: Pygmalion, 2002; Verrier, Anthony. *Assassination in Algiers: Churchill, Roosevelt, De Gaulle and the Murder of Admiral Darlan.* London: Pan Macmillan, 1992.

declarations of war

World War II began on September 1, 1939, with the German invasion of Poland. Declarations of war spanned 1939 to 1945.

1. Germany invades Poland without declaration, September 1, 1939
2. Great Britain, France, Australia, and New Zealand declare against Germany, September 3, 1939
3. Canada declares against Germany, September 10, 1939
4. USSR invades Poland without declaration, September 17, 1939
5. USSR declares against Finland, November 13, 1939
6. Germany invades Denmark and Norway without declaration, April 9, 1940
7. Germany invades Holland and Belgium without declaration, May 10, 1940
8. Italy declares against Great Britain and France, June 10, 1940
9. Italy invades Greece without declaration, October 28, 1940
10. Bulgaria declares against the Allies, April 6, 1941
11. Germany invades Greece and Yugoslavia without declaration, April 6, 1941
12. Italy invades Yugoslavia without declaration, April 6, 1941
13. Germany invades USSR without declaration, June 22, 1941
14. USSR declares against Germany, June 22, 1941
15. Italy and Romania declare against USSR, June 22, 1941
16. Hungary and Slovakia declare against USSR, June 27, 1941

17. Finland declares against USSR, June 26, 1941
18. Great Britain declares against Finland, Hungary, and Romania, December 5, 1941
19. Japan declares against Great Britain and the United States, December 7, 1941
20. United States declares against Japan, December 8, 1941
21. Germany and Italy declare against the United States, December 11, 1941
22. United States declares against Germany and Italy, December 11, 1941
23. Hungary declares against the United States, December 11, 1941
24. Brazil declares against Germany and Italy, August 22, 1942
25. Bolivia declares against Germany, Italy, and Japan, April 7, 1943
26. Iran declares against Germany, September 9, 1943
27. Italy declares against Germany, October 13, 1943
28. Liberia declares against Germany and Japan, January 26, 1944
29. Romania declares against Germany, August 25, 1944
30. Bulgaria declares against Germany, September 7, 1944
31. Ecuador declares against Germany and Japan, February 2, 1945
32. Peru declares against Germany and Japan, February 11, 1945
33. Chile declares against Japan, February 14, 1945
34. Venezuela declares against Germany and Japan, February 16, 1945
35. Uruguay declares against Germany and Japan, February 22, 1945
36. Turkey declares against Germany and Japan, February 23, 1945
37. Egypt declares against Germany and Japan, February 24, 1945
38. Syria declares against Germany and Japan, February 26, 1945
39. Lebanon declares against Germany and Japan, February 27, 1945
40. Saudi Arabia declares against Germany and Japan, March 1, 1945
41. Iran declares against Japan, March 1, 1945
42. Finland declares against Germany, March 4, 1945 (stipulating that a state of war has existed from September 15, 1944)
43. Argentina declares against Germany and Japan, March 27, 1945
44. Brazil declares against Japan, June 6, 1945
45. USSR declares against Japan, August 8, 1945

U.S. president Franklin D. Roosevelt asks Congress for a declaration of war against Japan, December 8, 1941. *(Library of Congress)*

Dempsey, Miles (1896–1969) *British general*

Miles Christopher Dempsey commanded the Second British Army, the principal British element in the advance across western Europe following the NORMANDY LANDINGS (D-DAY). He was born in New Brighton, England, and received his commission in 1915, in time to fight in France during World War I. At the outbreak of World War II in 1939, he held the rank of lieutenant colonel but was in command of an entire infantry brigade in France, performing brilliant rearguard cover for the DUNKIRK EVACUATION during May–June 1940. He was rapidly promoted, and in November 1942, as a lieutenant general, Dempsey assumed command of XIII Corps, Eighth British Army, in the NORTH AFRICAN CAMPAIGN. Dempsey's corps formed the right wing of BERNARD LAW MONTGOMERY's forces in the SICILY CAMPAIGN, in July 1943. In September, it was Dempsey and his XIII Corps that led the invasion of mainland Italy across the Strait of Messina. In the remarkable span of 17 days, Dempsey led his corps some 300 miles up the Italian west coast to link up with Lieutenant General MARK CLARK's Fifth U.S. Army forces at SALERNO.

Modest, unassuming, efficient, and quietly competent, Dempsey made a stark contrast with the flamboyant and typically strident Montgomery. Nevertheless, Montgomery recognized talent when he saw it and chose Dempsey to command the Second British Army (which included Canadian and Polish as well as British units) in the Normandy invasion of June 1944. Dempsey landed on Gold, Juno, and Sword beaches on June 6, then advanced inland, capturing Caen on July 9. Dempsey was content to follow orders to batter at the German armored units, tying them down, while the First U.S. Army executed OPERATION COBRA and broke out of Normandy on July 25. Only then did Dempsey lead his army in battles at Mortain and Falaise, advancing swiftly eastward across northern France and Belgium after these engagements. After this advance, he was assigned a role in OPERATION MARKET GARDEN, Montgomery's failed and costly attempt in September 1944 to capture Arnhem, Netherlands, as a bridgehead into Germany.

It was March 1945 before Dempsey finally led the Second British Army across the Rhine. After crossing, he advanced northeastward, taking the major industrial centers of Bremen, Hamburg, and Kiel and reaching the Danish frontier by the end of the war in May 1945.

After Germany's surrender, Dempsey was transferred to the Asian theater, where he was named commander in chief of Allied land forces in Southeast Asia. He served in this post through V-J DAY and in 1946 was transferred to chief command of forces in the Middle East. He served here until his retirement in 1947.

Further reading: Badsey, Stephen. *Normandy, 1944: Allied Landings and Breakout.* London: Osprey, 1990; Ford, Ken, and Peter Dennis. *Caen 1944: Montgomery's Breakout Attempt.* London: Osprey, 2004; Ryan, Cornelius. *Bridge Too Far: The Classic History of the Greatest Airborne Battle of World War II.* New York: Simon & Schuster, 1995.

Denmark, invasion of and resistance in

Denmark hoped to be respected as a neutral in World War II, but, fearing Nazi aggression, concluded a nonaggression pact with Germany early in 1939. This isolated Denmark from the rest of Scandinavia but preserved its lucrative trade with Britain until the actual occupation of the country, which began in April 1940.

The Danes were well aware that, militarily, they could do little to resist German aggression. At the time of the occupation, in April 1940, the Danish army consisted of a mere 14,000 men, a number that included 8,000 brand new draftees. The navy manned coastal defenses and had only two major but obsolescent ships. There was no separate air force, but, between them, the Danish army and navy divided 50 obsolete aircraft.

Thanks to the anti-Hitler sabotage of German intelligence chief WILHELM CANARIS, the Danes were given several days' notice of the impending German invasion. However, although they learned of it on April 4, 1940, Danish military authorities did nothing to prepare for the attack until April 8, when Copenhagen was reinforced, as was the border with Germany. These steps were to no avail, and, beginning on April 9, the Germans easily took the country, encountering almost no resistance from the Danish army and absolutely none from the navy.

The first German troops crossed into Denmark at 4:15 A.M. By 6 in the morning, Copenhagen was occupied. In the meantime, a successful AIRBORNE ASSAULT (the first in any war) was launched south of Zealand. Effectively paralyzed, the Danish government ordered a ceasefire and accepted German occupation.

Because the Danish government cooperated with the occupiers, it was not only allowed to retain a show of neutrality, but also permitted to retain control over the day-to-day administration of government, the police, and the law courts—at least until August 29, 1943, when the rise of the RESISTANCE MOVEMENT in Denmark prompted the Germans to take over administration entirely. Until this time, however, with the Nazis triumphant on many fronts, Danish public opinion largely favored a policy of collaboration. Yet as the tide gradually turned against Germany, the collaborators became less and less collaborative. In 1942, Werner Best, a hardline Nazi bureaucrat, was sent to Denmark to wrest more compliance short of seizing complete control of the government. Outwardly, a majority of the Danish people continued to support collaboration, voting overwhelmingly in March 1943 to support Denmark's collaborationist foreign minister, Erik Scavenius. Yet the resistance movement stepped up acts of sabotage, and workers often went on strike, significantly crippling the industries that fed the Nazi war machine. The British used the BBC to broadcast propaganda, and British Special Operations Executive (SOE) agents were infiltrated into the country to help organize the resistance and coordinate with Allied intelligence requirements. As the power and influence of the underground became increasingly apparent, ADOLF HITLER intervened, formally bringing Denmark under direct German control on August 29, 1943. The Germans now moved quickly to arrest influential citizens believed to be resistance leaders and to preemptively neutralize the tiny, and thus far silent, Danish navy. Naval personnel responded by scuttling their few ships to keep them out of German hands.

The Germans called on Niels Svenningsen, a leading Danish collaborationist, to attend to the day-to-day administration of the country under close Nazi supervision. However, beginning in June 1944, Copenhagen was swept by a general strike in direct protest of German brutality. An increasing number of Danes joined the Frihedsrådet, the Freedom Council, the country's chief resistance organization (founded on September 16, 1943). The council very effectively coordinated underground activities throughout Denmark. Its leadership consisted of six Danes, each representing a major resistance group, and one British SOE agent. The council operated an underground press, which, by 1944, was publishing an astounding 254 illegal newspapers, the combined circulation of which reached some 11 million—in a country with a population of just 3.85 million.

As the NORMANDY LANDINGS (D-DAY) approached, the activities of the Danish underground focused on sabotaging railroad lines in Jutland in order to create an obstacle to reinforcement of the Atlantic coast by German troops stationed in Norway. Danish intelligence, supplied by the underground, provided vital information about the V-1 BUZZ BOMB, one of which fell on the Danish island of Bornholm during an early test flight. The underground also had spectacular success in saving some 7,000 Jews when the Germans began arresting Danish Jews in fall 1943. This large group of refugees was spirited into Sweden—and safety—during the night of October 1.

Denmark's now vigorous resistance did not escape unscathed. Indeed, the GESTAPO succeeded in rounding up many of its top leaders. Informed of this, the Allies sent 18 British Mosquito bombers and 25 U.S. Mustang fighters in March 1945 to bomb Copenhagen's Gestapo headquarters (the Shell House) in a successful effort to destroy its records and to create a diversion that allowed many prisoners held there to escape. Total numbers in the internal Danish resistance probably reached 40,000 at the movement's height. The Danish police were so thoroughly infiltrated by resistance members that the Germans disbanded the force in September 1944 and deported some 2,000 officers. Citizen patrols had to be formed to take the place of the regular police in an effort to control crime.

Danish resistance to the Nazi occupation included Danish expatriates. Henrik Kauffmann, who was in the United States during the invasion serving as Denmark's minister to the country, declared himself an independent representative of the Danish government and, in that capacity, signed a treaty with the Americans in April 1941, giving control of Greenland, a Danish possession, to the United States. The Faeroe Islands were occupied by Britain in April 1940, and the following month

Iceland, at the time a Danish colony, declared its temporary independence. British troops occupied Iceland and were subsequently relieved by American soldiers. In 1944, Iceland proclaimed its permanent independence.

The portion of Denmark's merchant marine fleet that was at sea during the invasion turned itself over to the Allies: some 230 ships and 6,000 sailors. Most joined the Allied merchant marine and suffered heroic losses as a result: 1,500 deaths and nearly two-thirds of the merchant fleet sunk. Other expatriates served aboard two Royal Navy minesweepers and other warships or in the Royal Air Force, British army, or American army. A select number joined the SOE and reentered Denmark to serve in the underground.

The surrender of the Germans to the Allies on May 4, 1945, prompted resistance leaders to seize control of Denmark on May 5. The German commander on Bornholm Island refused to give up, and the island had to be bombed (May 7–8) by Soviet aircraft and then "visited" by Soviet warships (May 9) before the diehard finally capitulated. Soviet troops remained in occupation of the island until April 1946.

In the immediate postwar years, the resistance saw to it that the most egregious collaborators were identified and arrested. In all, about 34,000 Danes were tried and received some form of judicial punishment for having collaborated with the Nazi occupation.

Further reading: Levine, Ellen. *Darkness over Denmark: The Danish Resistance and the Rescue of the Jews.* New York: Holiday House, 2000; Pundik, Herbert. *In Denmark It Could Not Happen: The Flight of the Jews to Sweden in 1943.* London: Gefen, 1998; Werner, Emmy E. *A Conspiracy of Decency: The Rescue of the Danish Jews During World War II.* Denver: Westview, 2002; Werstein, Irving. *That Denmark Might Live: The Saga of the Danish Resistance in World War II.* Philadelphia: Macrae Smith, 1967.

Desert Rats

The nickname *Desert Rats* was applied to at least three British army organizations that were instru-

mental in the NORTH AFRICAN CAMPAIGNS against the Italians and ERWIN ROMMEL's Afrika Korps. The name derives from the jerboa, a nocturnal rodent native to North Africa, which hops like a kangaroo.

The 4th Armoured Brigade, which was formed in Egypt in 1938, before the outbreak of war but after the MUNICH CONFERENCE AND AGREEMENT, has traditionally claimed to be the first British unit to have adopted the sobriquet *Desert Rats*. However, the 7th Armoured Division appropriated the name and preceded the 4th Armoured Brigade back to England in preparation for the NORMANDY LANDINGS (D-DAY). The 4th Armoured Brigade left North Africa and participated in the fighting in Italy before returning to England prior to the D-day invasion. When the 4th reached England, it discovered that the 7th was not only calling itself the Desert Rats, but had created a divisional badge featuring an image of a jerboa. Thus spurred, the 4th Armoured Brigade created its own jerboa badge. Finally, the nickname *the Desert Rats* was also often applied generally to the entire Eighth British Army to honor its combat success against the Axis forces in North Africa.

Further reading: Delaforce, Patrick. *Churchill's Desert Rats 2: The Armoured Division in North Africa, Burma, Sicily and Italy.* London: Sutton, 2002; Verney, G. L. *The Desert Rats: The 7th Armoured Division in World War II.* London: Greenhill, 2002.

destroyer escorts

The destroyer escort was an exclusively American ship type first built during World War II. Like the Japanese, American naval planners saw little need for defensive or escort ships before the outbreak of the war, but the terrible toll exacted by German submarines against Allied convoys in the BATTLE OF THE ATLANTIC demonstrated an urgent need for such warships, and a total of 565 destroyer escorts were rushed through production during the war years. That 425 of these were completed and commissioned between April 1943 and April 1944 is astounding even for U.S. wartime production capacity. Some of the mass production techniques employed to build LIBERTY SHIPS were adapted to the destroyer escorts. Large subassemblies were constructed at welding and fabrication shops across the United States, then shipped by rail to the appropriate shipyard.

Although the primary mission of the destroyer escort was convoy defense, the ship could also be pressed into attack service when necessary as the next best thing to a DESTROYER. However, destroyer escorts were contingency ships, which cost half what it cost to build destroyers and took much less time to build. They were smaller and less fully armed, but they could be put into the sea fast.

Of the 563 destroyer escorts built during and shortly after the war, 78 were built for Great Britain, six for France, and eight for Brazil. A total of 30 of the Edsall class ships were delivered to the U.S. Coast Guard. All the rest of the production went to the U.S. Navy. Originally intended for Atlantic service, a significant number also found their way to the Pacific, often in attack roles rather than the defensive role for which they had been designed. In addition to convoy defense and antisubmarine warfare, the destroyer escorts were used for shore bombardment, picket duty, surface engagements, and even troop transport.

More than a thousand destroyer escorts were ordered during the war, but almost half these orders were cancelled. The majority of the destroyer escort fleet was decommissioned and mothballed after the war, but a few were put into naval reserve duty. Some 52 ships were reactivated during the Korean War, and it was 1973 before the last of the World War II vessels was stricken.

There were six classes of destroyer escort in World War II. All classes made a top speed of 20 to 24 knots and were crewed by 12 to 15 officers and 175 to 200 enlisted personnel.

Evarts class:

Length: 289 feet 5 inches
Beam: 35 feet 1 inch
Displacement: 1,436 tons
Power plant: diesel making 6,000 horsepower

Armament: three 3-inch guns, eight K guns, one twin 40-mm antiaircraft gun, nine 20-mm antiaircraft guns, two depth charge racks, one Hedgehog, and no torpedo tubes

Buckley class:

Length: 306 feet
Beam: 36 feet 9 inches
Displacement: 1,673 tons
Power plant: steam making 12,000 horsepower
Armament: three 3-inch guns, eight K guns, one twin 40-mm antiaircraft gun, eight 20-mm antiaircraft guns, two depth charge racks, one Hedgehog, and one triple torpedo tube

Rodderow class:

Length: 306 feet
Beam: 36 feet 11 inches
Displacement: 1,450 tons
Power plant: steam making 12,000 horsepower
Armament: two 3-inch guns, eight K guns, two twin 40-mm antiaircraft guns, 10 20-mm antiaircraft guns, two depth charge racks, one Hedgehog, and two triple torpedo tubes

Cannon class:

Length: 308 feet
Beam: 36 feet 10 inches
Displacement: 1,525 tons
Power plant: diesel making 10,800 horsepower
Armament: three 3-inch guns, eight K guns, one twin 40-mm antiaircraft gun, eight 20-mm antiaircraft guns, two depth charge racks, one Hedgehog, and one triple torpedo tube

Edsall class:

Length: 306 feet
Beam: 36 feet 10 inches
Displacement: 1,490 tons
Power plant: diesel making 6,000 horsepower
Armament: three 3-inch guns, eight K guns, one twin 40-mm antiaircraft gun, eight 20-mm

antiaircraft guns, two depth charge racks, one Hedgehog, and one triple torpedo tube

Butler class:

Length: 306 feet
Beam: 36 feet 10 inches
Displacement: 1,600 tons
Power plant: steam making 12,000 horsepower
Armament: three 3-inch guns, eight K guns, one twin 40-mm antiaircraft gun, eight 20-mm antiaircraft guns, two depth charge racks, one Hedgehog, and one triple torpedo tube

Further reading: Adcock, Al, and Don Greer. *Destroyer Escorts in Action.* Carrollton, Tex.: Squadron/Signal Publications, 1997; Andrews, Lewis M., Jr. *Tempest, Fire and Foe: Destroyer Escorts in World War II.* Bishopville, S.C.: Narwhal Press, 1999; Franklin, Bruce Hampton. *The Buckley-Class Destroyer Escorts.* Annapolis, Md.: Naval Institute Press, 1999; Stafford, Edward P. *Little Ship, Big War: The Saga of DE 343.* Annapolis, Md.: Naval Institute Press, 2000.

destroyers

The destroyer emerged as a warship type at the end of the 19th century. At that time, the term *destroyer* was applied to small, fast ships used to defend battleships from torpedo boat attack. When they were

U.S. destroyer in "battle dress" camouflage *(U.S. Navy)*

first developed, in the 1890s, destroyers were, in fact, called torpedo-boat destroyers. However, by World War I, their mission had changed from that of countering torpedo boats to serving as platforms for launching torpedoes. They were also typically sent ahead of the battle fleet to serve as its eyes and ears and to defeat, using guns, enemy destroyers. Once the opponent's destroyers were neutralized, the attacking destroyers would switch from deck guns to torpedoes to attack such capital ships as battleships and cruisers.

Before the end of World War I, the submarine had evolved into the principal torpedo-launching vessel, and so the primary role of the destroyer changed again. The vessels were fitted with antisubmarine warfare systems, including hydrophones and depth charges, and were assigned to escort merchant ship convoys and battle fleets, defending them against submarine attack. This antisubmarine escort role was carried over into World War II, but the destroyer mission by that time was also augmented to include antiaircraft (AA) defense. The ships were equipped with radar and antiaircraft guns.

AMERICAN DESTROYERS

Before the United States entered World War II, the British, their convoys under devastating submarine attack, were in desperate need of destroyers. President FRANKLIN D. ROOSEVELT concluded the LEND-LEASE ACT, which traded World War I–era American destroyers for the use of British naval bases in the Western Hemisphere. Before and during World War II, the United States developed 14 major classes of destroyers.

Allen M. Sumner class. The 70 destroyers of this class represented the next evolutionary step from the highly successful Fletcher class, putting greater emphasis on antiaircraft defense. Otherwise, they shared the same power plant as the Fletcher ships but incorporated more battle-survivable twin rudders and were somewhat larger, both wider in beam and longer. Of the 70 ships of this class, five were lost to enemy action.

General specifications of the class included:

Length: 376 feet 6 inches
Beam: 40 feet 10 inches

Draft: 14 feet 5 inches
Displacement (standard): 2,200 tons
Displacement (full): 3,315 tons
Armament: six 5-inch 38 caliber guns, two 40-mm twin antiaircraft mounts, two 40-mm quadruple antiaircraft mounts, and two 21-inch quintuple torpedo tubes
Propulsion: four boilers driving two General Electric turbines, making 60,000 horsepower
Top speed: 34.2 knots
Crew: 20 officers, 325 enlisted

Bagley class. The Bagley class dates to 1934, and eight destroyers of the class were built. Although not the fastest of the U.S. destroyers deployed in World War II, the Bagley class was very stable and therefore served as an excellent antiaircraft platform. During 1942 and 1943–44, the ships were extensively modified with the addition of advanced AA systems, including six 20-mm guns, air and surface search radar, and a twin 40-mm mount. All eight destroyers of this class served in the Pacific Fleet, participating in every major engagement.

General specifications included:

Length: 341 feet 3 ⅝ inches
Beam: 35 feet 6 ⅛ inches
Draft: 12 feet 9.5 inches
Displacement (standard): 1,624 tons
Displacement (full load): 2,245 tons
Power plant: two General Electric geared turbines making 49,000 horsepower
Top speed: 37 knots
Armament (Bagley in May 1944): four 12-mm L/38 guns, two forward superfiring, two aft superfiring; two 40-mm L/56 antiaircraft guns in one twin mount; seven 20-mm L/70 antiaircraft guns; 16 533-mm torpedo tubes in four quadruple wing mounts; four K-Gun depth charges; and two depth charge tracks
Crew: eight officers, 150 enlisted

Benham class. Most of the 10 Benham class destroyers were built in 1938, and all served in the Pacific. They shared the following specifications:

Length: 340 feet 9 inches
Beam: 35 feet 6 inches

Draft: 13 feet 3 inches
Displacement (standard): 1,500 tons
Displacement (full load): 2,350 tons
Power plant: three boilers driving two Westinghouse turbines at 50,000 horsepower
Top speed: 40.7 knots
Armament: four 5-inch 38-caliber guns, two 40-mm twin antiaircraft mounts, and two 21-inch quadruple torpedo tubes
Crew: 16 officers, 235 enlisted

Benson/Gleaves/Livermore/Bristol class. The 96 destroyers of this class (which encompassed a total of four variations) were built during 1937–39 and were the backbone of the U.S. destroyer fleet from 1940 to 1942. They represented an evolutionary improvement on the Sims class, which preceded these ships but featured a general layout that was similar to the earlier generation of vessels, except belowdecks, where there was now a more efficient alternating engine room–boiler room layout. This necessitated two pipes (smoke stacks), because the boilers were now farther apart. The new destroyers also featured enhanced antiaircraft capabilities.

Ships of these classes served in every naval operation of World War II. Initially, most were deployed to the Atlantic, but as the Atlantic became less active as a battlefield in 1944–45, many were redeployed to the Pacific.

General specifications included:

Length: 348 feet
Beam: 36 feet
Draft: 13 feet 8 ¼ inches–13 feet 9 ¾ inches
Displacement (standard): 1,838–1,911 tons
Displacement (full load): 2,572–2,591 tons
Top speed: 35 knots
Armament (as launched): five 127-mm L/38 guns, six 12.7-mm L/90 antiaircraft guns in single mounts, 10 533-mm torpedo tubes in two quintuple centerline mounts, two depth charge tracks, and 10 depth charges
Crew: nine–10 officers, 182–199 enlisted

The Farragut class consisted of eight destroyers authorized in 1918 but not designed until 1931. They were highly advanced ships for their time, and all were completed by mid-1935. As Destroyer Squadron 1, all eight were present at the BATTLE OF PEARL HARBOR on December 7, 1941, and one of the class, USS *Monaghan,* depth charged and sank a Japanese "midget" submarine during the attack. During the war, some of the Farraguts fought in the Aleutians, while others served elsewhere in the Pacific.

General specifications included:

Length: 341 feet 3 inches
Beam: 34 feet 3 inches
Draft: 12 feet 4 inches
Displacement (standard): 1,365 tons
Displacement (full load): 2,255 tons
Power plant: four boilers driving two Curtis turbines for 42,800 horsepower
Top speed: 37 knots
Armament: four 5-inch 38-caliber guns, two 40-mm twin antiaircraft mounts, and two 21-inch quadruple torpedo tubes
Crew: 16 officers, 235 enlisted

Fletcher class. The 175 ships of this class constituted what most naval historians believe to have been the best class of destroyers in World War II. They were introduced in 1942 and became the mainstays of the destroyer fleet from 1943 on. They were fast and capable of absorbing heavy damage. The Fletchers fought through most of the Pacific war. They all displaced about 2,100 tons (standard) and 2,900 tons (fully loaded), making them significantly larger than any preceding American destroyers. This allowed the Fletchers increases in armament, machinery, ammunition, stores, and fuel oil. The ships were built at a fast rate, with 175 launched from 11 shipyards over a 32-month period. The Fletcher class became the most numerous class of destroyers in any nation's navy.

The Fletchers served in the Pacific during World War II and, in the postwar period, saw action in Korea and even Vietnam. Many were transferred to the navies of other nations, and the last one, *Cuitlahuac* (ex-*John Rodgers*), was not decommissioned from the Mexican Navy until 2001.

General specifications included:

Length: 376 feet 5 inches
Beam: 39 feet 7 inches

Draft: 13 feet 9 inches
Displacement (standard): 2,325 tons
Displacement (full load): 2,924 tons
Power plant: four Babcock & Wilcox boilers driving two-shaft G.E.C. geared turbines for 60,000 shaft horsepower
Top Speed: 36 knots
Armament: five 5-inch guns, four 1.1-inch guns, four 20-mm antiaircraft guns and 10 21-inch torpedoes
Crew: 34 officers, 295 enlisted

Gearing class. The 105 ships of this class were launched in the final year of the war (the lead ship, *Gearing,* on February 18, 1945), and many believe it was the most advanced destroyer to emerge from World War II. Certainly, the ships proved durable, serving with the U.S. Navy for some three decades after the war (having been modernized) and with the navies of other nations for even longer. The Gearing class was essentially the same in design as the Sumner class except for the addition of 14 more feet of length to accommodate additional fuel and antiaircraft weapons. They were the final class of U.S. World War II destroyers.

General specifications included:

Length: 390 feet 6 inches
Beam: 40 feet 10 inches
Draft: 14 feet 4 inches
Displacement (standard): 2,425 tons
Displacement (full load): 3,479 tons
Power plant: four Babcock and Wilcox boilers driving two sets of turbines generating a total of 60,000 shaft horsepower
Top speed: 34.5 knots.
Armament: three 5-inch 38-caliber twin gun mounts; five 40-mm gun mounts, ten 21-inch quintupled torpedo tubes, and two depth charge racks of Mk–6 and 7 (cylindrical) and later Mk–9 and 14 (teardrop) depth charges
Crew: 20 officers, 325 enlisted

Gridley class. Consisting of four vessels built in the mid 1930s, the ships used a hull design similar to the earlier Mahan class but featured a single pipe (smokestack). The Gridley class also mounted 16 torpedo tubes, the heaviest battery ever among American destroyers. Most important, a new power plant produced 50,000 shaft horsepower for a top speed of 42.8 knots, at the time the highest speed of any American destroyer. Although the ships served well in the Pacific, there were lingering concerns over the stability and hull strength of the class.

General specifications included:

Length: 341.33 feet
Beam: 35.4 feet
Draft: 35.4 feet
Displacement (standard): 1,589 tons
Displacement (full load): 2,405 tons
Power plant: 50,000 shaft horse power
Top speed: 42.8 knots
Armament: four single 5-inch/38 DP guns, seven single 20-mm antiaircraft guns, four .50-caliber machine guns, four quad 21-inch torpedo tubes, two depth charge racks, and 14 depth charges
Crew: 10 officers, 225 enlisted

Mahan class. The 16 ships of the Mahan class were authorized in 1934 as improved versions of the Farragut class. Two of the ships, the *Cassin* and *Downes,* were sunk at the Battle of Pearl Harbor. The rest served mainly as escorts for aircraft carriers. Except for battle losses, the ships served throughout World War II.

General specifications included:

Length: 341 feet 4 inches
Beam: 35 feet 5 inches
Draft: 13 feet 2 inches
Displacement (standard): 1,465 tons
Displacement (full load): 2,345 tons
Power plant: four boilers driving two General Electric turbines for 49,000 horsepower
Top speed: 39.2 knots
Armament: four 5-inch .38 caliber guns, two 40-mm twin antiaircraft mounts, and two 21-inch quadruple torpedo tubes
Crew: 16 officers, 235 enlisted

Porter class. Planning for what became the Porter class began in the late 1920s, as naval authorities looked for a large destroyer (sometimes called a destroyer leader) to serve in an intermediate role between conventional destroyers and light cruisers. The intended mission of these large destroyers was to use their guns to break through the enemy screen, creating a breach through which the smaller (following) destroyers would advance. The eight ships of the class were all built during the 1930s. When the ships went to war, they were modified with augmented antiaircraft armament. Three ships of the class, the *McDougal, Winslow,* and *Moffett,* served in the Atlantic during World War II, while the five other vessels served in the Pacific, mainly escorting carriers.

General specifications included:

Length: 381 feet 1 inch
Beam: 37 feet
Draft: 13 feet 9 inches
Displacement (standard): 1,850 tons
Displacement (full load): 2,840 tons
Power plant: four boilers driving two turbines for 50,000 horsepower
Top speed: 36.4 knots
Armament: five 5-inch .38 caliber guns, two 40-mm twin antiaircraft mounts, one 40-mm quadruple antiaircraft mount, and two 21-inch quadruple torpedo tubes
Crew: 16 officers, 278 enlisted

Sims class. The 12 ships of this class were authorized in 1937 and constituted the last destroyer class to be completed before the beginning of World War II. Its design was both backward and forward looking. Like earlier destroyers, the Sims class had a single fireroom and engine room instead of a pair of each, the latter innovation affording a substantial increase in survivability. Unlike previous generations, however, the class had a lengthened, 348-foot hull plus a faired sheer strake, a design feature that gave it a strikingly modern appearance for the time, as did its streamlined bridge. The ships were completed between 1939 and 1940. During the war, ships of this class operated in the Atlantic, the Mediterranean, and the Pacific. Seven survived the war.

General specifications included:

Length: 348 feet 4 inches
Beam: 36 feet

Draft: 13 feet 4 inches
Displacement (standard): 1,570 tons
Displacement (full load): 2,465 tons
Power plant: three boilers driving two Westing-house turbines for 50,000 horsepower
Top speed: 38.7 knots
Armament: four 5-inch .38-caliber guns, two 40-mm twin antiaircraft mounts, and two 21-inch quadruple torpedo tubes
Crew: 16 officers, 235 enlisted

Somers class. The five ships of this class started out as Porter class vessels but were finally built with innovative power plants that warranted assignment to a new class. The more efficient power plant allowed room for three centerline torpedo mounts. The ships were completed in 1935–36, and, during the war, all served exclusively in the Atlantic or Mediterranean, except the *Sampson,* which was later transferred to the Pacific.

General specifications of the class included:

Length: 381 feet
Beam: 36 feet 11 inches
Draft: 14 feet
Displacement (standard): 1,850 tons
Displacement (full load): 2,905 tons
Power plant: four boilers driving two General Electric turbines for 52,000 horsepower
Top speed: 39.0 knots
Armament: five 5-inch .38-caliber guns, three 40-mm twin antiaircraft mounts, and two 21-inch quadruple torpedo tubes
Crew: 16 officers, 278 enlisted

Clemson and Wickes classes. Most of the destroyers of these World War I–vintage destroyers were transferred to Great Britain in 1940.

BRITISH DESTROYERS

The Royal Navy made extensive use of destroyers in antisubmarine warfare and to escort convoys.

A-class. These 11 ships were commissioned in the early 1930s; two were built for the Royal Canadian Navy. Each ship of the class featured four to eight quad torpedo tubes, and, during the war, they were equipped with augmented antiaircraft defenses.

The class was used extensively during the war. Six were sunk.

General specifications included:

Length: 323 feet
Displacement: 1,350 tons
Beam: 32 feet
Draft: 12.2 feet
Power plant: three boilers driving two steam turbines for 34,000 horsepower
Top speed: 35 knots
Armament (as built): four 4.7-inch guns, eight 0.5-inch machine guns, and eight 21-inch torpedo tubes
Crew: 138

B-class. These nine ships essentially duplicated the specifications of the A-class with few minor modifications.

C-class. The six ships of this class were very similar to the A and B classes. All six were turned over to the Royal Canadian Navy before the outbreak of the war, save one ship, which was turned over early in the war. They were used almost exclusively as convoy escorts.

D-class. The 10 ships of this class repeated the major specifications of classes A through C.

E-class. These 10 ships were built in the mid-1930s and were larger than their predecessors. They were intended as "destroyer leaders," ships tasked with breaking through enemy screening vessels and thereby making way for follow-on attack by other ships of the flotilla.

General specifications included:

Length: 329 feet
Displacement: 1,405 tons
Power plant: geared turbines, two shafts, making 36,000 horsepower
Top speed: 36 knots
Armament: four 4.7-inch guns, eight 0.5-inch antiaircraft guns, and eight 21-inch torpedo tubes
Crew: 145 men

F class. These eleven ships repeated the E class with minor modifications.

G class. The 10 ships of the G class were all built in the mid-1930s as light destroyers with two stacks. Their general specifications included:

Length: 323 feet
Displacement: 1,350 tons
Power plant: two boilers driving geared turbines, two shafts, for 34,000 horsepower
Top speed: 36 knots
Armament: four 4.7-inch guns, two 0.5-inch antiaircraft twin mounts, and eight 21-inch torpedo tubes
Crew: 145 officers and enlisted

H and I classes: These repeated G class, except for minor modifications.

J class. The ships of the J, K and N classes were developed in response to political pressures to cut costs while producing new and more powerful destroyers. The destroyers of this class were ordered in March 1937, and the first of eight ships laid down before the end of the year. Considered formidable combatants, the ships of this class were sent into the most intensive theaters, and they suffered heavy losses.

General specifications included:

Length: 357 feet
Displacement: 1,690 tons
Power plant: two boilers driving geared turbines, two shafts, for 40,000 horsepower
Top speed: 36 knots
Armament: six 4.7-inch guns, four 2-pounder antiaircraft guns, eight 5-inch machine guns, and 10 21-inch torpedo tubes
Crew: 183 officers and enlisted

K and N classes. These essentially repeated the J class, except for minor variations.

L class. The eight ships of the L class were authorized in 1937 and were the product of revised thinking after observations made during the Spanish civil war. The new ships included heavier antiaircraft armament than previous generations of destroyers. They were also the first British destroyers to have their guns in fully enclosed mountings.

General specifications included:

Length: 345 feet
Displacement: 1,930 tons
Power plant: two Admiralty boilers driving Parsons geared turbines, two shafts, for 48.000 horsepower
Armament (typical): six 4.7-inch guns, one 4-inch antiaircraft gun, four 2-pounder antiaircraft guns, eight 0.5-inch antiaircraft guns, and four 21-inch torpedo tubes
Top speed: 36 knots
Crew: 221 officers and enlisted

M class. This class repeated the L class with minor modifications.

O class. The eight ships of this class were ordered pursuant to the First Emergency Flotilla Program announced in 1939 immediately after the outbreak of World War II. The British Admiralty recognized a pressing need for destroyers for antisubmarine warfare and for convoy escort. The lead ship of the class, the *Onslow*, was laid down in 1940, and the other seven ships were completed by the end of 1942.

General specifications included:

Length: 345 feet
Displacement: 1,540 tons
Top speed: 36 knots
Armament: four 4.7-inch guns, four 2-pounder antiaircraft guns, six 20-mm antiaircraft machine guns, and four 21-inch torpedo tubes
Crew: 175 officers and enlisted

P class. These four ships repeated the O class.

Q class. Laid down and built during the early years of the war, six of the eight ships of this class were delivered to the Australian navy.

General specifications included:

Length: 359 feet
Displacement: 1,692 tons
Power plant: two boilers driving geared turbines, two shafts, for 40,000 horsepower
Top speed: 36 knots
Armament: four 4.7-inch guns, four 2-pounder antiaircraft guns, six 20-mm antiaircraft

machine guns, and eight 21-inch torpedo tubes

Crew: 176 officers and men

R class. Repeated the Q class.

S class through W class. These classes, consisting of eight ships each, were all built under provisions of ongoing Emergency Flotilla Programs through 1944.

Their general specifications included:

Displacement: 1,700 tons
Top speed: 37 knots
Armament: four 4.7-inch guns, four 2-pounder antiaircraft guns, six 20-mm antiaircraft machine guns, and eight 21-inch torpedo tubes
Crew: 180 officers and enlisted

Z class. Essentially repeated the S through W classes, with minor modifications.

Town class. The 51 ships of the Town class were World War I–vintage U.S. Navy destroyers exchanged with Great Britain under Lend-Lease. They were extensively refitted by the British and, in the case of Royal Canadian Navy vessels, refitted in Canadian shipyards.

General specifications of the class included:

Length: 314 feet
Displacement: 1,190 tons
Armament: four 4-inch guns, four 21-inch torpedo tubes, and depth charge throwers
Crew: 190 men

Admiralty S class. The 11 World War I–era ships of this class were used at the beginning of World War II but were badly outclassed by the enemy's modern destroyers. Three of the ships were refitted as minelayers, while six others were dispatched to the Far East in 1939 as part of local defense flotillas at Hong Kong and Singapore.

General specifications of the class included:

Displacement: 905 tons
Power plant: two boilers driving geared turbines, 2 shafts, for 27,000 horsepower
Top speed: 36 knots

Armament: three 4-inch guns, one 2-pounder antiaircraft guns, and four 21-inch torpedo tubes
Crew: 90 officers and enlisted

Admiralty V and W classes. These were World War I destroyers that had been consigned to reserve duty prior to the outbreak of the war. They were pressed into service for fleet duties and convoy escort, then were relegated to escort duty as newer destroyers became available.

General specifications included:

Length: 312 feet
Displacement: 1,188 tons
Power plant: two boilers driving geared turbines, 2 shafts, for 30,000 horsepower
Top speed: 34 knots
Armament (original): four 4-inch guns, two 2-pounder antiaircraft guns, and six 21-inch torpedo tubes
Armament (as modified for fast escort duty): four 4-inch antiaircraft guns, and eight 0 .5-inch antiaircraft guns
Armament (as modified for short-range escort duty): three 4-inch guns, and one 3-inch antiaircraft gun, two 2-pounder antiaircraft guns, and three 21-inch torpedo tubes
Armament (as modified for long-range escort duty): two 4-inch guns, one 3-inch antiaircraft gun, two 2-pounder antiaircraft guns, and one Hedgehog
Crew: 134 officers and enlisted

Admiralty Modified W class. There were 15 Admiralty W class ships modified early in the war with more powerful guns.

General specifications included:

Length: 312 feet
Power plant: two boilers driving geared turbines, two shafts, for 27,000 horsepower
Top speed: 34 knots
Armament (original modification): four 4.7-inch guns, two 2-pounder antiaircraft guns, and six 21-inch torpedo tubes

Armament (as short-range escort): three 4.7-inch guns, one 3-inch antiaircraft gun, two 2-pounder antiaircraft guns, and three 21-inch torpedo tubes

Armament (as long-range escort): two 4.7-inch guns, one 3-inch antiaircraft gun, two 2-pounder antiaircraft guns, and one Hedgehog

Crew: 134 officers and enlisted

Tribal class. The 27 ships of the Tribal class were planned in 1934 as a response to the new large destroyers being built by Japan, Italy, and Germany. The first seven of the class were ordered in March 1936. Eight of the class were built during the war for the Royal Canadian Navy, and Australia built three for its own navy.

General specifications of the class included:

Length: 377 feet
Displacement: 1,883 tons
Power plant: two boilers driving geared turbines, two shafts, for 44,000 horsepower
Top speed: 36 knots
Armament: eight 4.7-inch guns, four 2-pounder antiaircraft guns, eight 0.5-inch antiaircraft machine guns, four 21-inch torpedo tubes
Crew: 190–219 officers and men

Battle class. The 18 ships of this class were conceived in 1941, largely in response to Prime Minister WINSTON CHURCHILL's request for ships to counteract German air attacks on convoys. After much design discussion, the first orders were placed in mid-1942.

General specifications included:

Length: 379 feet
Displacement: 2,325 tons
Power plant: two 2 Admiralty three-drum boilers driving Parson I. R. single reduction turbines for 50,000 horsepower
Top speed: 30 knots
Armament (original): four 4.5-inch guns, one 4-inch gun, eight 40-mm Bofors guns, six 20-mm Oerlikon antiaircraft machine guns, one .303 Vickers, two sets quadruple hand-worked torpedo tubes, with 8 torpedoes,

four depth charge throwers, two rails, and 60 depth charges

Crew: 240–288, increasing to 380 in wartime

FRENCH DESTROYERS

The French destroyers at the beginning of World War II comprised three major classes.

L'Adroit class. Of the 14 ships of this class, 10 were lost by 1942.

Their general specifications included:

Length: 351 feet
Displacement: 1,378 tons
Power plant: two boilers driving geared turbines, two shafts, for 35,000 horsepower
Top speed: 33 knots
Armament: four 5.1-inch guns, two 37-mm antiaircraft guns, four 13-mm antiaircraft guns, and six 21.7-inch torpedo tubes
Crew: 100 officers and enlisted

Bourrasque class. Of the dozen ships of this class, seven were lost during 1940 and 1942.

Their general specifications included:

Length: 347 feet
Displacement: 1,298 tons
Power plant: two boilers driving geared turbines, two shafts, for 31,000 horsepower
Top speed: 33 knots
Armament: four 5.1-inch guns, two 37-mm antiaircraft guns, four 13-mm antiaircraft guns, and six 21.7-inch torpedo tubes
Crew: 7 officers and 138 enlisted

Le Hardi class. All eight ships of this destroyer class, the largest, fastest, and most modern destroyers in the French fleet, were lost in North Africa on November 27, 1942.

Their general specifications included:

Length: 383 feet
Displacement: 1,772 tons
Power plant: two boilers driving geared turbines, two shafts, for 58,000 horsepower
Top speed: 37 knots

Armament: six 5.1-inch guns, two 37-mm anti-aircraft guns, four 13-mm antiaircraft guns, and seven 21.7-inch torpedo tubes

Crew: 187 officers and enlisted

GERMAN DESTROYERS

Type 34. In November 1932, even before ADOLF HITLER came to power, the German Navy began planning its response to the large destroyers being built by Poland and France, even though the TREATY OF VERSAILLES forbade Germany from building destroyers of this size. German planners recognized that while its navy would almost certainly be smaller than that of its opponents, the individual ships could be superior. Accordingly, the first of the new class of destroyers, called the Type 34, would be heavier, more powerful, and better armed than the preceding generation of vessels. The Type 34 became the most numerous class of German destroyers, at 16 ships, but suffered from structural flaws and poor mechanical reliability. Another weakness was a lack of adequate storage for ammunition, so that some ships ran out of ammunition in the middle of an action.

General specifications included:

Length: 390.42 feet
Beam: 37.07 feet
Displacement (standard): 2,268 tons
Displacement (full load): 3,206 tons
Power plant: 70,000 horsepower
Top speed: 38 knots
Armament: five 127-mm (5.0-in) guns in single mounts, four 37-mm (1.46-in) cannon in two double mounts, six 20-mm (0.79-in) machine guns in single mounts, eight 21-inch torpedo tubes in two quadruple mounts, four depth charge launchers with two on each side of the superstructure, and two rails fitted at stern
Crew: 325 officers and enlisted

Type 36A or Z23 Class. Whereas the Type 34 destroyers were built prior to the war, the Type 36A, also called the Z23 Class, were built during the war and were launched between 1940 and 1942. The new ships were an incremental improvement over the previous generation, providing more powerful guns and greater range.

General specifications included:

Length: 416.67 feet
Beam: 39.4 feet
Displacement (standard): 2,600 tons
Displacement (full load): 3,600 tons
Power plant: two boilers driving two turbines for 70,000 horsepower
Top speed: 36 knots
Armament: three single and one twin 150-mm gun, two twin 37-mm antiaircraft guns, five single 20-mm antiaircraft guns, and two quad 21-inch torpedo tubes
Crew: 321 officers and enlisted

Type 36B or Z35 class. The 150-mm guns of the Type 36A class proved to be disappointing performers, so the new 36B ships were designed around 127-mm main guns. They were somewhat lighter than the 36A ships but basically of similar profile.

General specifications included:

Length: 416.67 feet
Beam: 39.4 feet
Displacement (standard): 2,525 tons
Displacement (full load): 3,505 tons
Power plant: two boilers driving two turbines for 70,000 horsepower
Top speed: 36 knots
Armament: five single 127-mm guns, two twin antiaircraft guns, three quad and three single 20-mm antiaircraft guns, and two quad 21-inch torpedo tubes
Crew: 321 officers and enlisted

SP1 or Z40 class. These ships were originally conceived as "scout cruisers," vessels bigger than destroyers but smaller than light cruisers. The Allies classified them as large destroyers. Only three were built.

Their general specifications included:

Length: 498.7 feet
Beam: 47.9 feet
Displacement (standard): 4,540 tons

Power plant: two boilers driving two geared turbines for 77,500 horsepower

Top speed: 36 knots

Armament: three twin 150-mm guns, one twin 88-mm gun, four twin 37-mm antiaircraft guns, three quad 20-mm antiaircraft guns, and two quintuple 21-inch torpedo tubes

Crew: number unknown

T22 or Ebbing class. This class encompassed light destroyers with greater capability and capacity than torpedo boats.

General specifications included:

Length: 334.6 feet

Beam: 32.8 feet

Displacement (standard): 1,295 tons

Displacement (full load): 1,755 tons

Power plant: two boilers driving steam turbines for 32,000 horsepower

Top speed: 32.5 knots

Armament: four single 105-mm guns, two twin 37-mm antiaircraft guns, six single 20-mm antiaircraft guns, and two triple 21-inch torpedo tubes

Crew: 198 officers and enlisted

ITALIAN DESTROYERS

The Italian Navy sailed five major classes of destroyers, which were generally referred to as torpedo boats.

Generale class. These six ships were of World War I vintage and were quite small, although, for their size, well armed. None were employed in front-line operations because they would have been readily outclassed by virtually any modern opponent.

General specifications included:

Length: 241.1 feet

Beam: 24 feet

Displacement (standard): 635 tons

Displacement (full load): 890 tons

Power plant: two boilers driving steam turbines for 15,000 horsepower

Top speed: 30 knots

Armament: three single 102-mm guns, two 76-mm antiaircraft guns, and two twin 450-mm torpedo tubes

Crew: 105 officers and enlisted

Turbine class. Built during 1927–28, the eight ships of this class were inadequately armed with low-velocity 120-mm main guns. All were sunk early in the war, except for the *Turbine* itself, which was taken over by the Germans after the Italian capitulation. It was sunk in September 1944.

General specifications included:

Length: 304 feet

Beam: 30.2 feet

Displacement (standard): 1,090 tons

Displacement (full load): 1,700 tons

Power plant: two boilers driving two turbines for 40,000 horsepower

Armament: two twin 120-mm guns, two single 40-mm antiaircraft guns, and two triple 21-inch torpedo tubes

Crew: 180 officers and enlisted

Navigatore class. Built during 1928–30, the dozen ships of the Navigatore class were large for their day, but by the time of World War II, they were surpassed by the increasing scale of modern destroyers. They were very fast ships, but the light construction that gave them their speed detracted from their seakeeping qualities and also made them more vulnerable to enemy fire.

General specifications included:

Length: 353.5 feet

Beam: 33.5 feet

Displacement (standard): 1,945 tons

Displacement (full load): 2,580 tons

Power plant: two boilers driving two geared turbines for 50,000 horsepower

Top speed: 38 knots

Armament: three twin 120-mm guns, three single 37-mm antiaircraft guns, and two twin or triple 21-inch torpedo tubes

Crew: 225 officers and enlisted

Soldato class. This was the first of several similar classes of Italian destroyers, which began construction in 1930–32 and ended in 1937–38. These were fine ships capable of high speed although deficient in their torpedo complement.

General specifications included:

Length: 350.2 feet
Beam: 33.3 feet
Displacement (standard): 1,830 tons
Displacement (full load): 2,460 tons
Power plant: two boilers driving two geared turbines for 48,000 horsepower
Top speed: 39 knots
Armament: four or five 120-mm guns, one 37-mm antiaircraft gun, and two triple 21-inch torpedo tubes
Crew: 218 officers and enlisted

Ariete class. The Ariete class was built during the war, in 1942–43 and was definitely classed by the Italians as a torpedo boat type rather than as a destroyer. Of the 40 ships planned, only 16 were laid down, and only one was delivered to the Italian fleet.

General specifications included:

Length: 269.8 feet
Beam: 28.2 feet
Displacement (standard): 800 tons
Displacement (full load): 1,125 tons
Power plant: two boilers driving two turbines for 22,000 horsepower
Top speed: 31 knots
Armament: two single 100-mm guns, two single 37-mm antiaircraft guns, and two triple 21-inch torpedo tubes
Crew: 155 officers and enlisted

JAPANESE DESTROYERS

The Japanese entered World War II with perhaps the finest destroyers among any of the combatants, culminating in the highly advanced Akitsuki class, which were intermediate between true destroyers and light cruisers. The Imperial Navy used its large destroyer fleet in a variety of roles, from providing off-shore support for the army, to escort duty, to offensive action that took the battle to the American fleet. The major classes of Japanese destroyers included the following.

Minekaze class. Built between 1919 and 1922, the destroyers of this aging class served throughout World War II. Advanced for their time, they were outclassed by the beginning of the war but were often armed with extra depth charges and augmented antiaircraft defenses to serve as convoy escorts.

General specifications included:

Length: 336.3 feet
Beam: 29.5 feet
Displacement (standard): 1,215 tons
Displacement (full load): 1,650 tons
Power plant: two boilers driving two geared steam turbines for 38,500 horsepower
Top speed: 39 knots
Armament: four single 120-mm guns, two machine guns, and two triple 21-inch torpedo tubes
Crew: 148 officers and enlisted

Fubuki class. There were 20 ships of this class launched between 1927 and 1931. They represented at that time the cutting edge of destroyer design, and, indeed, the ships remained formidable adversaries throughout World War II. Their leading characteristic was their size, a precedent that other nations would follow, albeit mostly in ships built during the war.

General specifications included:

Length: 388.3 feet
Beam: 34 feet
Displacement (standard): 2.090 tons
Power plant: two boilers driving two geared steam turbines for 50,000 horsepower
Top speed: 37 knots
Armament: three twin 127-mm guns, two machine guns, and three triple 24-inch torpedo tubes
Crew: 197 officers and enlisted

Ootori class. These eight ships, launched during 1935–37, were in stark contrast to the prevailing Japanese philosophy of building ever larger destroyers. Designers created a very light, slender ship, then packed it with an ambitious array of armaments. The result was not entirely successful, as the ships showed poor seakeeping and even a tendency to capsize. Nevertheless, these eight vessels served through much of the war.

Their general specifications included:

Length: 289.9 feet
Beam: 26.9 feet
Displacement (standard): 840 tons
Displacement (full load): 1,060 tons
Power plant: two boilers driving two geared steam turbines for 19,000 horsepower
Top speed: 30 knots
Armament: three single 120-mm guns, one 40-mm antiaircraft gun, and one triple 21-inch torpedo tube
Crew: 112 officers and enlisted

Akatsuki and Kagero classes. These two classes were virtually identical, except that the Kagero class (18 ships) was slightly broader in the beam than the four ships of the Akatsuki class. The Akatsuki ships were launched in the early 1930s, whereas the Kagero class ships were launched between 1938 and 1941. Both were large, speedy, highly survivable combatants, but, like other Japanese destroyers, they had been designed primarily for surface combat and had to be extensively modified with weapons for antisubmarine warfare and antiaircraft defense.

General specifications of the Kagero class included:

Length: 388.6 feet
Beam: 35.4 feet
Displacement (standard): 2,035 tons
Displacement (full load): 2,490 tons
Power plant: two boilers driving two geared steam turbines for 52,000 horsepower
Top speed: 35 knots
Armament: three twin 127-mm guns, two twin 25-mm antiaircraft guns, and two quad 24-inch torpedo tubes
Crew: 240 officers and enlisted

Akitsuki class. Massive by destroyer standards, the ships of this class might, in fact, be deemed light cruisers. The guns of these dozen ships were powerful and plentiful, generally capable of a higher rate of fire than their Western opponents. These ships were formidable antiaircraft platforms, and they had room for plenty of depth charges to use against submarines. Speed, at 33 knots, was adequate.

General specifications included:

Length: 440 feet
Beam: 38.1 feet
Displacement (standard): 2,700 tons
Displacement (full load): 3,700 tons
Power plant: two boilers driving two geared steam turbines for 52,000 horsepower
Top speed: 33 knots
Armament: four twin 100-mm guns, two twin 25-mm antiaircraft guns, and one quad 24-inch torpedo tube
Crew: 285 officers and enlisted

Matsu class. The ships of this class were products of desperation. Although 28 were planned, only 17 were built during 1944–45 in an effort to make up the heavy losses suffered by the Imperial Navy. The ships were small and inelegant, designed for rapid construction from dwindling supplies of raw materials.

Their general specifications included:

Length: 328.1 feet
Beam: 30.7 feet
Displacement (standard): 1,260 tons
Displacement (full load): 1,530 tons
Power plant: two boilers driving two geared steam turbines for 19,000 horsepower
Top speed: 27.5 knots
Armament: one twin and one single 127-mm gun, four triple and 12 single 25-mm antiaircraft guns, and one quad 24-inch torpedo tube

Further reading: Koop, Gerhard. *German Destroyers of World War II.* London: Greenhill, 2003; Langtree, Christopher, and John Lambert. *The Kellys: British J, K and N Class Destroyers of World War II.* Annapolis, Md.: Naval Institute Press, 2002; Reilly, Joseph. *U.S. Navy Destroyers of World War II.* New York: Sterling, 1984; Roscoe, Theodore. *United States Destroyer Operations in World War Two.* Annapolis, Md.: Naval Institute Press, 1953; Sadkovich, James J. *The Italian Navy in World War II.* Westport, Conn.: Greenwood Press, 1994; Ward, John, and Chris Westhorp. *Ships of World War II.* Osceola, Wis.:

Motorbooks International, 2000; Whitley, M. J. *Destroyers of World War Two: An International Encyclopedia.* Annapolis, Md.: Naval Institute Press, 2000; Worth, Richard. *Fleets of World War II.* New York: Da Capo, 2002.

Dieppe raid

Originally code named Operation Rutter, the raid on Dieppe, a German-occupied French port, was launched on August 19, 1942. It was planned by the Combined Operations Headquarters of the British army in collaboration with the General Headquarters of the Home Forces, which had delegated authority to Gen. BERNARD LAW MONTGOMERY, at the time commander in chief of the Southeastern Command. Montgomery fashioned the raid into a full-scale frontal assault on Dieppe but made no provision for preparation in the form of aerial bombardment. While the raid was planned by the British, it was executed primarily by Canadian troops of the 2nd Canadian Division, commanded by Maj. Gen. J. H. Roberts, largely in response to a Canadian request for a greater role in the war. When adverse weather postponed Operation Rutter on July 7, 1942, Montgomery reconsidered the entire enterprise and ended up recommending that it be discarded altogether. Thus, Dieppe might never have happened but for the fact that Montgomery was transferred to command of the Eighth British Army in North Africa, leaving Vice Admiral Lord LOUIS MOUNTBATTEN, chief of Combined Operations, to revive Rutter as Operation Jubilee. Not only was this decision unfortunate from a tactical point of view, it presented a grave security risk, since Operation Rutter, planned then cancelled, was no longer a secret. Nevertheless, the operation went forward—and would prove disastrous.

Operation Jubilee was launched from five English ports between Southampton and Newhaven and included 4,963 Canadians, 1,075 British, and 50 U.S. Army rangers, a force far too small for an ambitious frontal assault on the port of an occupied country. Much more impressive was the naval force assembled to support the raid, 237 warships and landing craft, until one recognizes that no battleships were employed because of the difficulties of maneuvering in the English Channel. Eight destroyers were expected to lend fire support to the landings. It was a mission for which destroyers were not at all suited. Naval bombardment preparatory to a major amphibious assault requires the heavy guns of battleships or cruisers. Nor was air cover adequate, because the British declined to divert heavy bombers from the STRATEGIC BOMBING OF GERMANY. Only fighter squadrons were deployed in the hope of drawing the Luftwaffe into open battle. There was no preparatory aerial bombardment.

Although aerial reconnaissance had been thorough, it was limited to coastal defenses and did not reveal the German gun emplacements in the cliffs of the headlands. Indeed, on-the-ground intelligence was generally lacking, and very little was known about German order of battle or even basic numbers. Terrain had been superficially assessed, not from military maps or eyewitnesses, but from a collection of holiday snapshots. Thus, an inadequate force was being sent, without preparation by naval or aerial bombardment and virtually blind, against the superbly prepared defenses of a highly skilled enemy.

The raid stepped off at dawn and began with attacks along a 10-mile front against a coastal battery near Varengeville, German positions at Pourville, German positions at Puys, and the coastal battery near Berneval. The German garrisons offered a stout defense and, even worse, a German convoy in the area fired on the landing force. (This came as a surprise to the Canadians, but should not have, since the admiralty *twice* warned them of the presence of the convoy.) Because of the exchange with the convoy, the vital element of surprise, already compromised, was completely sacrificed.

The commandos succeeded in temporarily suppressing fire from the Berneval battery, and commandos also captured the Varengeville battery. But elsewhere, the landings went very badly. At Puys, the Canadians landed late. At Pourville, the Canadians landed unopposed, but many were landed in the wrong places, thereby delaying the assault on the high ground to the east. This deficit would never be corrected. By the time the unintentionally piecemeal preliminary landings were completed, the Germans had positioned strong reinforcements to repel the threat.

At 5:20 in the morning, a half-hour after the initial flank attacks, the main assault was launched by the Royal Hamilton Light Infantry, the Essex Scottish Regiment, and tanks of the 14th Army Tank Regiment. Aircraft did nothing but lay a smokescreen, and the landing of the tanks was delayed. As a result, the defenders recovered the initiative quickly, pinning down most of the assaulting troops before they could enter the town of Dieppe. When the tanks finally landed, only 15 of 27 were able to negotiate the sea wall, and these were soon blocked by German defenses.

Pinned down, the Canadians were being torn apart. However, poor communication led Roberts to assume that the assault was going as planned. Therefore, he ordered two of his floating reserves, Les Fusiliers Mont-Royal and commandos of the Royal Marines, to land, inadvertently leading them into ambush. The Fusiliers were immediately pinned down under the port's cliffs, while the commandos, literally rushing to their destruction, were saved by their field commander from total annihilation. Perceiving the true nature of the situation, he was able to turn back at least some of the landing craft before he was fatally stricken by fire from shore.

At 11 A.M. the order was given to abort the raid and withdraw from the beaches. By this time, German fire was heavier than ever, and the next four hours saw continual slaughter. By two in the afternoon, the survivors had withdrawn. Of 4,963 Canadians committed to battle, 3,367 were killed, wounded, or taken prisoner. (Miraculously, most of the wounded eventually recovered.) British ground casualties were 275, and the Royal Navy lost a destroyer and 33 landing craft and suffered 550 casualties, killed or wounded. The Royal Air Force fared very poorly, losing 106 aircraft. As for the Germans, casualties were nearly negligible: 48 of 945 aircraft and 591 men killed or wounded.

Prime Minister WINSTON CHURCHILL, who had demanded offensive action prematurely, nearly became a political casualty of Dieppe, as did Mountbatten, who endured much justified criticism. Yet while it is difficult to find much benefit in what was an unmitigated fiasco and, indeed, a tragic waste of life, the lessons of Dieppe did not go unheeded. First, the Allies took to heart the absolute necessity of providing aerial bombardment preparation and then sustained close air support for any amphibious assault. They learned the absolute necessity of overwhelming sea support. They learned the importance of securing thorough ground-based intelligence. They learned the vital importance of never compromising secrecy or sacrificing the element of surprise. Most of all, they learned that a frontal assault on Europe would require huge numbers and absolute coordination among all units. These were valuable lessons, but the fact is that they should have been learned without the fruitless sacrifices of Dieppe, which, despite lessons learned, was in no real sense a prelude to the much later NORMANDY LANDINGS (D-DAY), although a few historians and writers have suggested as much.

Further reading: Atkin, Ronald. *Dieppe 1942: The Jubilee Disaster.* New York: Macmillan, 1980; Ford, Ken, and Howard Gerrard. *Dieppe 1942: Prelude to D-day.* London: Osprey, 2003; Fowler, Will. *The Commandos at Dieppe: Rehearsal for D-day.* London: HarperCollins, 2003.

Dietrich, Josef "Sepp" (1892–1966) *key SS commander found culpable for the Malmédy Massacre*

Sepp Dietrich was one of ADOLF HITLER's inner circle, the first commander of SS Watch Battalion-Berlin, which became the SS Leibstandarte (Life Guard)-Adolf Hitler, and later the chief of Führer's Security. It was Dietrich's SS who provided a seven-man shooting party during the infamous Night of the Long Knives (June 28–29, 1934), the overthrow of the STURMABTEILUNG (SA).

Dietrich was born in Hawangen, Bavaria, and joined the German Army in 1911. He fought with distinction and valor during World War I and was one of the crew that manned Germany's very first tank. After the war, Dietrich joined the FREIKORPS and took part in the violent overthrow of Munich's local Communist regime. He soon joined the NAZI

Sepp Dietrich *(Library of Congress)*

PARTY (NSDAP) and, in 1928, enrolled in the newly formed SCHUTZSTAFFEL (SS). Rising rapidly in the SS, he became a member of Hitler's inner circle, eventually coming to work and live in the chancellery, occupying a room in Hitler's personal suite. The führer assigned Dietrich to create and command the SS Watch Battalion-Berlin, which evolved into the SS Leibstandarte (Life Guard)-Adolf Hitler. Appointed chief of Hitler's personal security force, Dietrich was assigned to provide the hit squad for the raid on the SA during the Night of the Long Knives (June 28–29, 1934). After this, on July 1, 1934, Dietrich was promoted to SS Obergruppenfuehrer, equivalent in rank to a WEHRMACHT general. Dietrich went on to develop the SS Leibstandarte into an elite combat unit, which served with distinction in the BATTLE OF FRANCE. For his role in the campaign, Dietrich received the Knight's Cross of the Iron Cross on July 5, 1940. His Leibstandarte was next expanded into a full brigade as Dietrich led it in the invasion of YUGOSLAVIA and the INVASION OF GREECE.

Commanding the 1st SS Panzer Division, Dietrich took part in the INVASION OF THE SOVIET UNION and was largely responsible for ensuring his troops'

survival during the retreat through Russia. Dietrich was in command of the SS 1st Panzer Division in Normandy during D-day and suffered profound disillusionment with Hitler when he was ordered to hold his ground rather than retreat to a more favorable defensive position. Despite this, Dietrich accepted Hitler's assignment as the spearhead of the December 1944 ARDENNES offensive. Despite his leading role in the SS, Dietrich had a reputation for avoiding the worst extremes of GERMAN ATROCITIES and even, on one occasion, protested personally to Hitler the wholesale shooting of unarmed Jewish civilians. Yet he may have shared the guilt for the MALMÉDY MASSACRE, the cold blooded murder of American prisoners of war during the Ardennes offensive. (After the war, he was found guilty of having committed an "offense against customs and ethics of war," though other high-ranking German officers came to his defense.)

Dietrich's last battle was fought in Vienna. Failing to halt the Red Army's advance into the city, Dietrich fled west and surrendered his army to U.S. general GEORGE SMITH PATTON JR. on May 8, 1945.

After a military tribunal found him guilty of complicity in the Malmédy Massacre, Dietrich was sentenced to life imprisonment. The sentence was subsequently commuted to 25 years, and Dietrich was released in 1955, after serving 10. However, a German court ordered his arrest and trial for his role in the murder of Ernst Roehm and other SA members. Sentenced to 18 months, he was released in February 1958. Eight years later, he succumbed to a heart attack.

Further reading: Messenger, Charles. *Hitler's Gladiator: The Life and Times of Oberstgruppenfuhrer and Panzergeneral-Oberst der Waffen-SS Sepp Dietrich.* London and New York: Brassey's, 1988; Weingartner, James J. *Crossroads of Death: The Story of the Malmedy Massacre and Trial.* Berkeley: University of California Press, 1979.

Dimitrov, Georgi (1882–1949) *leader of anti-Nazi resistance in Bulgaria*

A Bulgarian communist leader, Dimitrov, based in Moscow, directed anti-Nazi resistance in Bulgaria during World War II. He was born in Kovachevtsi, Bulgaria, and worked as a printer. Active in the trade union movement, Dimitrov became a prominent socialist and led the Bulgarian parliament's socialist opposition to financing World War I. In 1919, Dimitrov was instrumental in the creation of the Bulgarian Communist Party. He traveled to the Soviet Union, where he was elected to the executive committee of the Comintern (Communist International) in 1921, then returned to Bulgaria in 1923 to lead a communist uprising. When the uprising was suppressed, Dimitrov fled to Berlin in 1929 and became head of the central European Comintern.

Dimitrov came to international prominence after the burning of the Reichstag on February 27, 1933. He and other prominent communists were accused of arson. Acting as his own counsel at his trial, Dimitrov defended himself so brilliantly that he was acquitted. He left Berlin and moved to Moscow, where he was named secretary general of the Comintern's executive committee, serving from 1935 to 1943. In this role, he nurtured the development of various national popular front movements against the Nazis, suspending this activity only when JOSEPH STALIN and ADOLF HITLER concluded the GERMAN-SOVIET NON-AGGRESSION PACT. After the German INVASION OF THE SOVIET UNION, however, Dimitrov resumed his work.

Beginning in 1944, Dimitrov began directing from Moscow Bulgaria's organized resistance to the nation's puppet government. He returned to Bulgaria immediately after the war and was appointed prime minister of the communist Fatherland Front government. The following year, he masterminded the formation of the Bulgarian People's Republic.

Further reading: Dallin, Alexander, and Fridrikh Igorevich Firsov, eds. *Dimitrov and Stalin, 1934–1943: Letters from the Soviet Archives.* New Haven, Conn.: Yale University Press, 2000; Dimitrov, Georgi. *The Diary of Georgi Dimitrov, 1933–1949.* New Haven, Conn.: Yale University Press, 2003; Moser, Charles A. *Dimitrov of Bulgaria: A Political Biography of Dr. Georgi M. Dimitrov.* Ottawa, Ill.: Caroline House, 1979.

Dirksen, Herbert von (1882–1955) *Nazi diplomat*

Dirksen was a Weimar diplomat and then a diplomat in the Nazi service. Born in Berlin, he studied law and became an attorney, then an assistant judge. He served with distinction in combat in World War I, earning an Iron Cross, then joined the diplomatic service, with postings in Kiev (1918–19) and Warsaw (1920–21). He was appointed consul-general in Danzig (Gdansk) in 1923 and served until 1925, when he was appointed chief of the East European division of the Foreign Office. In 1928, he was named ambassador to the Soviet Union and served until 1933. ADOLF HITLER approved Dirksen's appointment as ambassador to Japan in 1933, and he served in that office until 1938, when he was tapped to replace JOACHIM VON RIBBENTROP as ambassador to Great Britain.

Recalled at the outbreak of World War II, Dirksen returned to Berlin and retired. Although Dirksen was a member of the Nazi Party, he was cleared in June 1947 of any complicity in war crimes. He published *Moscow, Tokyo, London,* a valuable memoir of German foreign relations during the Weimar years and the prewar years of the Third Reich.

Further reading: Dirksen, Herbert von. *Moscow, Tokyo, London; Twenty Years of German Foreign Policy.* Norman: University of Oklahoma Press, 1952.

Dissard, Marie Louise (1880–1974) *French resistance worker*

As a member of the FRENCH RESISTANCE, Dissard was responsible for arranging the return to Britain of more than 250 Allied airmen who had bailed out of disabled aircraft over France. Born in Toulouse in 1880, Dissard was 60 years old when France fell after the BATTLE OF FRANCE in 1940. She joined the resistance immediately, working under Ian Garrow, a British soldier who, having missed the DUNKIRK EVACUATION, remained in France and worked to arrange an escape route for Allied airmen over the Pyrenees. Dissard and Garrow were based in Toulouse, from which they ran operations in Paris, Marseilles, and Perpignan.

When Garrow was captured in October 1941, Albert Guerisse became head of the escape network. Dissard succeeded him when he was arrested. Because of her relatively advanced age, the GESTAPO did not suspect that she was a resistance member. This gave her considerable freedom to travel throughout France, arranging escape for airmen. Her customary procedure was to escort airmen to Toulouse, where, through the network, she arranged lodgings. From here, they were moved to Perpignan and transferred to the care of guides for the trek across the Pyrenees.

Crisis came for Dissard in January 1944 when one of the Pyrenees guides was arrested in Perpignan. In a grave breach of resistance practice, he had carried a notebook, which contained Dissard's name. Fortunately, she learned of this discovery and was able to go into hiding. She found refuge in various attics, cellars, and garages in and around Toulouse, regaining her freedom only after France had been liberated. Remarkably, all during this period of hiding and evasion, Dissard continued her work for the escape network. Of the 250-plus airmen she rescued, 110 were sent into escape even as the Gestapo was hunting for her. After the war, the U.S. government recognized Dissard's services with the nation's highest civilian award, the Medal of Freedom.

Further reading: McIntosh, Elizabeth. *Sisterhood of Spies.* New York: Dell, 1999; Weitz, Margaret Collins. *Sisters in the Resistance: How Women Fought to Free France, 1940–1945.* New York: Wiley, 1998.

dive bombers

In World War II, a dive bomber was an aircraft designed to dive against its target at a very steep angle to achieve the highest degree of accuracy. The principle was simple: Dropping a bomb very close to its target decreases the time it takes for the bomb to reach the target, and the speed of the dive provides momentum that increases the speed of the dropped bomb. Together decreased distance and increased speed reduce the effects of drag, making the path of the bomb much more predictable. The dive bomber was used for tactical rather than strategic bombing, that is, targets were such high-value individual installations as bridges, command buildings, important vehicles, and ships.

The dive bombing concept dates to World War I. No special aircraft existed then, but Royal Air Force pilots developed and practiced steep dive techniques. They were severely limited by the inherent fragility of early airframes, which could not withstand the stress of recovery from a steep dive. U.S. Marine aviators in action against Haitian and Nicaraguan guerrillas in the 1920s employed limited dive bombing techniques. Although aircraft technology advanced sufficiently in the late 1920s to allow steeper dives and safer recoveries, the U.S. Army Air Corps focused on the development of strategic bombers. The U.S. Navy, however, recognized the value of dive bombers as antiship weapons and ordered the first aircraft designed specifically for the dive bombing mission, the Curtiss F8C Helldiver.

The Helldiver was a two-seat biplane first delivered to the navy in 1928 as the F8C-1. It was powered by a 430-horsepower Pratt and Whitney radial engine and had a top speed of a little more than 140 mph, but it was sturdy, and, in 1929, the navy ordered a modified version designated as the F8C-4, which could carry a modest bomb load that could be deployed in a steep dive. (The F8C-4 Helldiver is not to be confused with the later SB2C Helldiver, a far more advanced monoplane dive bomber introduced in 1940.)

If the F8C-4 pleased the U.S. Navy, it made an even greater impact on a German military observer visiting the United States in the early 1930s. Ernst Udet, who was otherwise unimpressed by the mostly backward state of American military aircraft, purchased four F8C-4s and sent them to Germany. Luftwaffe planners immediately understood their significance. Dive bombing would allow a relatively small air force to become a potent tactical weapon, precisely what was needed to conduct BLITZKRIEG-style assaults. Inspired by the F8C-4, German designers developed the Junkers Ju 87 Stuka, destined to become the archetypal and most feared dive bomber in the world.

The prototype first flew in 1934, and various production models were produced, the most advanced of which, the Ju 87 D-1, appearing in 1941. The Stuka was extraordinarily effective against vehicles, fortifications, ships, and personnel. Against the latter, the effects were not merely physical but psychological as well. The Stuka descended at an angle of 80°, like a giant bird of prey. Sirens were fitted on its nonretractable wheel covers, so that an unearthly keening was emitted as the aircraft dived, amplifying the effect of terror and panic. Most innovative was an automatic pull-up system, which was activated upon bomb release. It ensured that the plane pulled out of its dive even if the pilot lost consciousness due to high G forces.

The Stuka was most devastatingly effective early in the war, during the INVASION OF POLAND and the BATTLE OF FRANCE, the heyday of Blitzkrieg. Once the Allies deployed even moderately advanced fighters against the aircraft, it proved highly vulnerable. Nevertheless, some 5,709 Stukas were built before the end of the war. General specifications of the Ju 87 D-1 included:

Wingspan: 45 feet 3 inches
Top speed: 255 mph
Service ceiling: 24,000 feet

The Japanese also developed dive bombers for deployment from aircraft carriers and against naval targets. The first was the Aichi D3A, code named "Val" by the Allies. The Val was among the aircraft used against PEARL HARBOR and, it was one of these planes that dropped the first bombs of the attack. A two-seat aircraft, the Val was the standard Japanese carrier-based dive bomber during the early stages of the Pacific War. Its general specifications included:

Wingspan: 47 feet 2 inches
Power plant (D3A2): one 1,200-horsepower Kinsei 54
Top speed (D3A2): 281 mph
Service ceiling (D3A2): 35,700 feet
Armament: two fixed forward-firing 7.7-mm machine guns in wings and one 7.7-mm manually aimed machine gun in rear cockpit

Bomb load: one 250-kg bomb under fuselage plus two 60-kg bombs under wings

Like the German Stuka, the Japanese Val soon proved vulnerable to enemy fighters and was replaced by the Yokosuka D4Y Suisei, called "Judy" by the Allies. Introduced in 1942, the early units were unreliable and suffered from structural problems that were catastrophic in a dive bomber. But once these problems had been solved, the Judy was a highly effective two-seat dive bomber. A total of 2,157 were built. General specifications included:

Wingspan: 37 feet 9 inches
Power plant (D4Y3, D4Y4): one 1,560-horsepower Mitsubishi Kinsei 62 14-cylinder two-row radial
Top speed: (D4Y3): 356 mph.
Service ceiling: 34,500 feet
Armament (typical): two 7.7-mm fixed forward-firing machine guns above engine and one 7.7-mm manually aimed 7.7-mm machine gun in rear cockpit
Bomb load: one 250-kg bomb in internal fuselage bay and two 30-kg bombs, one under each wing

By this time, the U.S. Navy was flying the Douglas SBD Dauntless and the Curtiss SB2C. Design on the Dauntless began in 1938, and the aircraft went into production in 1940 for the U.S. Marine Corps and the U.S. Navy. The U.S. Army Air Corps ordered the SBD-3 version in 1941, designating it A-24. However, the army made little use of the aircraft. General specifications of the final version, SBD-6, included:

Wingspan: 41 feet 6 inches
Power plant: one 1,350-horsepower Wright R–1820–66 Cyclone nine-cylinder radial piston engine
Top speed: 255 mph
Ceiling: 25,200 feet
Armament: two forward-firing 12.7-mm (0.5-inch) machine guns and two 7.62-mm (0.3-inch) machine guns on flexible mounts
Bomb load: up to 1,600 pounds of bombs under fuselage and up to 650 pounds of bombs under wings

Nearly 5,936 Dauntless dive bombers were built, but even more—some 7,000—of the Curtiss SB2C Helldiver rolled off assembly lines to join the fleet in 1943. A two-seat dive bomber, the aircraft had a reputation for being very difficult to handle at slow speeds and was initially so despised by pilots that the designation *SB2C* was said to denote "Son of a Bitch, Second Class." Nevertheless, the Helldiver was responsible for the destruction of more Japanese targets than any other aircraft. Specifications of the SB2C–4 version included:

Wingspan: 49 feet 9 inches
Power plant: one 1,900-horsepower Wright R–2600–20 Cyclone 14 radial piston engine
Top speed: 295 mph
Ceiling: 29,100 feet
Armament: two 20-mm wing-mounted cannon and two 7.62-mm (0.3-inch) machine guns in rear cockpit
Bomb load: up to 2,000 pounds of bombs on underwing racks and in fuselage bay

While the Americans, Germans, and Japanese made extensive use of dive bombers, the British never developed either overland or antiship equivalents of this aircraft. Indeed, the dive bomber as an aircraft type proved to be short lived. It disappeared after the war as the speed of level-flying aircraft increased and the vastly improved quality of computing bombsights provided great accuracy for level bombing or bomb runs from shallow angles.

Further reading: Aders, Gebhard, and Werner Held. *Stuka Dive Bombers, Pursuit Bombers, Combat Pilots: A Pictorial Chronicle of German Close-Combat Aircraft to 1945.* Atglen, Pa.: Schiffer, 1989; Smith, Peter. *Dive Bomber.* Annapolis, Md.: Naval Institute Press, 1982; Smith, Peter. *Vengeance!: The Vultee Vengeance Dive Bomber.* Washington, D.C.: Smithsonian Institution Press, 1988; Tagaya, Osamu. *Imperial Japanese Naval Aviator 1937–45.* London: Osprey, 2003; Tillman, Barrett. *The Dauntless Dive Bomber of World War Two.* Annapolis, Md.: Naval Institute Press, 1976; Tillman, Barrett, and Robert L. Lawson. *U.S. Navy Dive and Torpedo Bombers of World War II.* Osceola, Wis.: Motorbooks International, 2001.

Dobbie, William (1879–1964) *British military governor of besieged Malta*

Lieutenant General Sir William Dobbie was military governor of Malta. A profoundly religious man raised in the church of the Protestant Plymouth Brethren, he took what many considered a religious approach to leadership and has been criticized for his failure to attend to such practical matters as building adequate bomb shelters, laying up sufficient stores, and instituting effective civil defense and food rationing programs, all of which were badly needed during the SIEGE OF MALTA.

Dobbie had served in the Boer War and in World War I. Between the two world wars, he was commandant of the British School of Military Engineering.

Further reading: Bradford, Ernle. *Siege: Malta 1940–1943.* Barnsely, U.K.: Pen & Sword, 2003; Dobbie, Sybil. *Faith and Fortitude: The Life and Work of General Sir William Dobbie.* Gillingham, U.K.: P. E. Johnston, 1979; Dobbie, Sybil. *Grace under Malta.* London: L. Drummond, 1944; Holland, James. *Fortress Malta: An Island Under Siege 1940–43.* New York: Miramax, 2003.

Dodecanese campaign of 1943

Dodecanese, from the Greek, meaning "Twelve Islands," is a group of islands in the Aegean Sea off the southwestern coast of Turkey. By the terms of the 1923 Treaty of Lausanne, the islands became possessions of Italy and were thus during World War II (after which, they became part of Greece). As part of the Mediterranean Sea naval operations, battles were fought on and among these islands during 1943. Important Axis installations included Italian air bases on Rhodes (the largest and most important of the islands), an airstrip on Cos, and a seaplane base with naval shore batteries at Leros. Germany had an air base at Scarpanto.

On the very day Italy concluded a separate peace with the Allies, September 8, 1943, a British officer was parachuted into Rhodes, charged with coaxing the 30,000 men of the Italian garrison there to turn against and take prisoner the 7,000 Germans on the island. Astoundingly, the vastly outnumbered Germans preempted this by attacking the Italians, who quickly surrendered—to the Germans.

Under British general HENRY MAITLAND "JUMBO" WILSON and on orders directly from WINSTON CHURCHILL, a British brigade of infantry was dispatched to join other small units already in the area, so that by the beginning of October, some 4,000 British troops were thinly deployed across eight of the Dodecanese, as well as the island of Samos to the north of the group. Unfortunately, lack of Allied air support (which was heavily committed to the ongoing Italian campaign), prevented the outnumbered British from gaining air superiority, and, surprisingly enough, the Germans were determined to hold the islands. On October 3, they attacked the British contingent at Cos, which quickly surrendered. At this point, Wilson and others advised Churchill to order a general withdrawal from the Dodecanese. Churchill, as usual, had a grander strategic motive for wanting to hold the islands. He thought the islands could be used as a springboard to an offensive in the Balkans, which might bring hitherto neutral Turkey (a nation that pressed a claim of sovereignty over the Dodecanese) into the war on the side of the Allies. This would infuse 40 fresh divisions into the cause. Nevertheless, both his British advisers and American allies objected, albeit to no avail. Ordering that Leros and Samos be held, Churchill resolved to carry on with plans to invade Rhodes.

In November, reinforcements arrived on Leros, bringing the number of British troops there to 2,500, half of the 5,000 now deployed throughout the islands. The Germans counterattacked on November 12, quickly overrunning the still-outnumbered British. Even Churchill now saw that he had no choice but to order a general withdrawal. The entire venture had been a disaster comparable in scale, although not in ultimate effect, to the DIEPPE RAID. British losses included 4,800 men (five battalions) and heavy naval losses. Six cruisers and 33 destroyers (including 7 belonging to the

Greek Navy) had been committed to the campaign. Of these, four cruisers were badly damaged, six destroyers were sunk, and another four were damaged. Also sunk were two submarines and 10 coastal craft and minesweepers. Of the 288 British airplanes that fought, 113 were downed. German losses, in contrast, were disproportionately small: 1,184 men and 15 small landing craft.

Further reading: D'Este, Carlo. *World War II in the Mediterranean, 1942–1945.* Chapel Hill, N.C.: Algonquin Books, 1990; Horner, D. M., and Paul Collier. *Second World War: The Mediterranean 1940–1945.* London: Osprey, 2003; Whipple, A. B. C. *The Mediterranean (World War II).* Alexandria, Va.: Time-Life Books, 1981.

Dollfuss, Engelbert (1892–1934) *Austrian chancellor who vainly opposed Anschluss*

Opposed to what he saw as the impending ANSCHLUSS, ADOLF HITLER's annexation of AUSTRIA, Dollfuss, the nation's chancellor, aligned himself with BENITO MUSSOLINI in the hope of maintaining Austrian independence. Born in Lower Austria on October 4, 1892, Engelbert Dollfuss studied law at the University of Vienna and economics at the University of Berlin. With the outbreak of World War I, he served as an officer in the Austrian Army, and, after the war, as a conservative Roman Catholic, he became active in the Christian Socialist Party. Dollfuss served as secretary of the Lower Austrian Peasant Federation and, in 1927, as director of the Lower Austria Chamber of Agriculture. After a brief stint as president of the railways system in 1930, he became secretary of agriculture in 1931. With the Christian Socialists maintaining an exactly one-vote majority in the Austrian lower house, Dollfuss was named chancellor of Austria on May 20, 1932.

Dollfuss's chief concern was the worldwide economic depression, which had hit post–World War I Austria especially hard. Drawn by the promise of $9 million in loans from the League of Nations and fearful of Allied pressure, Dollfuss declined to join Germany in a customs union. This alienated him from both the German and Austrian Nazis, as well as from pro-German Austrians and Austrian socialists. Amid a public outcry against Dollfuss, the three presidents of the Austrian parliament resigned, whereupon Dollfuss suspended parliament and ruled by decree. Now in desperate need of foreign support and increasingly concerned over the threat posed by Hitler, Dollfuss turned to the Italian fascist Benito Mussolini, who at this point in his career, had by no means thrown in his lot with that of Hitler. At a meeting in Riccione in 1933, he secured from the Italian dictator a guarantee to defend Austrian independence in return for the abolition of political parties in Austria and the restructuring of the nation's constitution along fascist lines. Acting on this agreement, Dollfuss abolished the Austrian parliament in September 1933 and set about creating a fascist Austria with his "Fatherland Front," which replaced political parties. Dollfuss deployed a secret police force, with which he ruthlessly squelched opposition, and he increasingly subjugated his government to Italy.

At Mussolini's behest, Dollfuss deliberately instigated social unrest in Austria to give him an excuse for the bloody suppression of the Austrian socialists in February 1934. On May 1, 1934, Dollfuss proclaimed a new constitution in Austria, which effectively made Austria an Italian satellite. In delivering Austria to Mussolini, Dollfuss cut himself off from all domestic support. Far from saving Austria from German domination, subjugation to Italy stirred a majority of Austrians to support Hitler. This triggered an Austrian Nazi coup attempt on July 25, 1934. Although the coup miscarried, Dollfuss was assassinated. Socialism reigned in Austria for the next four years, until March 1938, when Hitler's army marched into Vienna and consummated *Anschluss.*

Further reading: Brook-Shepherd, Gordon. *Dollfuss.* Westport, Conn.: Greenwood Press, 1978; Lehr, David. *Austria Before and After the Anschluss.* Pittsburgh: Dorrance, 2000; Sweet, Paul R. "Mussolini and Dollfuss: An Episode in Fascist Diplomacy." In Julius Braunthal, ed. *The Tragedy of Austria.* London: Gollancz, 1948.

Dollmann, Friedrich (1882–1944) *German army commander*

A career army officer, Dollmann enlisted in the German army in 1899 and, during World War I, commanded an artillery battalion. He was part of the select group of officers who remained in the army during the interwar period, and he managed to continue his rise, primarily in the artillery branch. By 1932, he was a brigadier general and three years later a corps commander. By 1936, he held the rank of lieutenant general.

As commander of the Seventh German Army, Dollmann was among the leaders of the invasion of France during the BATTLE OF FRANCE in May and June 1940. Instrumental in executing the western BLITZKRIEG, he earned the admiration of no less a figure than ADOLF HITLER and was promoted to general in July 1940. During the next four years, Dollmann operated out of a headquarters in Le Mans, commanding the Seventh German Army in northern France. Its task was to defend Normandy and Brittany against any cross-channel Allied invasion. However, by the time of the NORMANDY LANDINGS (D-DAY) beginning on June 6, 1944, Dollmann's Seventh German Army consisted of just six infantry divisions manned mostly by second-rate, poorly equipped troops. The reason for this is that the best divisions stationed in France had been deployed to the area adjacent to Pas de Calais, the cross-channel passage by which German high command (and Hitler) anticipated the Allied invasion. Predictably, Dollmann's men were unable to arrest the Allied advance—at Normandy, not Calais—and after American forces overran the Cotentin peninsula and took Cherbourg (June 26), Hitler, who had once sponsored Dollmann, now threatened him (and others) with courts martial. Those around Dollmann saw that their commander was deeply shaken by Hitler's threats. He died under mysterious circumstances at his headquarters on June 28, 1944. Officially, the cause was fixed as a heart attack or a stroke, but many believe he committed suicide by poisoning.

Further reading: Carell, Paul, and David Johnston. *Invasion! They're Coming!: The German Account of the D-day*

Landings and the 80 Days' Battle for France. Atglen, Pa.: Schiffer, 1995; Isby, David C., ed. *Fighting the Invasion: The German Army at D-day*. London: Greenhill, 2000; Isby, David C., ed. *Fighting in Normandy: The German Army from D-day to Villers-Bocage*. Mechanicsburg, Pa.: Stackpole, 2001.

Dönitz, Karl (1891–1980) *chief of the German Navy*

A German admiral, Dönitz was the architect of SUBMARINE strategy and replaced ERICH RAEDER as chief of the navy during World War II. Just before committing suicide on the eve of Germany's collapse, ADOLF HITLER named Dönitz head of state, and it was Dönitz who authorized surrender to the Allies.

Dönitz was born in Grünau and joined the navy on April 1, 1910, serving on U-boats during World War I. This experience persuaded the young officer that submarines would play an increasingly important role in naval strategy. Between the world wars, Dönitz remained in service with the Reichsmarine, the diminutive navy Germany was permitted under the harsh terms of the TREATY OF VERSAILLES. Operating clandestinely, Dönitz set about building a modern submarine force, even though submarines were strictly prohibited to Germany by the Versailles Treaty.

In 1935, Dönitz was named chief of the Submarine Force and was instrumental in expanding the force, which came to dominate the German Navy. Promoted to rear admiral shortly after the start of World War II, Dönitz held a simultaneous post as flag officer in charge of the fleet's submarines. With brilliance, the admiral molded a relatively unprepared U-boat fleet into a devastating weapon, leading a highly effective campaign against Allied shipping in the North Atlantic, a campaign that threatened to strangle Great Britain. Dönitz's success encouraged him to claim greater and greater shares of German war funding, and he soon became highly unpopular with the other service chiefs and, in particular, with navy commander in chief Erich Raeder, an old-line sailor who favored surface vessels over submarine warfare. Success, however,

spoke loudest, and Dönitz gained funding as well as promotion to vice admiral in 1940 and admiral in 1942. His rise came at the expense of Raeder, whom Dönitz replaced as commander in chief of the navy on January 30, 1943. Dönitz never relinquished his direct, hands-on role as commander of the U-boat force, and it now constituted the bulk of the German fleet.

The year 1943 was, however, a turning point for Dönitz's fortunes and those of the German submarine fleet. The Allies were beginning to achieve substantial success in antisubmarine warfare, and while losses among Allied convoys were still high, they were declining, even as more and more German submarines were being sunk. In search of technological improvements, Dönitz introduced and championed the snorkel. Submarines of the day were hybrid diesel-electrics; they were propelled by an air-breathing diesel engine while surfaced, and by electric motors while submerged. The diesels continually charged the batteries that powered the electric motors, which, however, had limited endurance. The snorkel permitted shallow-depth operation of the diesel engines, thereby saving battery power and greatly extending the time submarines could operate underwater. It was an important advance, because submarines were especially vulnerable on the surface. However, by this time, the Allies had developed SONAR and hydrophone technologies, which made it easier to locate submarines underwater. For this reason, Dönitz's technological advances made relatively little impact. With each passing month, he was losing the BATTLE OF THE ATLANTIC.

Hitler named Dönitz his successor as chancellor in the will he composed on April 30, 1945, the day he committed suicide. For just over a week after Hitler's death, Dönitz conducted the government of what little was left of the Third Reich. On May 7–8, 1945, it was Dönitz who negotiated surrender to the Allies.

Admiral Dönitz was tried and convicted of war crimes at the NUREMBERG WAR CRIMES TRIBUNAL later in 1945. He was sentenced to 10 years in Spandau Prison and served his full term, gaining release in 1956. He lived out the remainder of his life quietly in a suburb of Hamburg.

A highly skilled commander, Karl Dönitz developed tactics that had a devastating impact on Allied shipping. The most important of these were WOLF PACK U-BOAT TACTICS, whereby submarines hunted in coordinated groups. He also created an extensive support network for the vessels—including seaborne tankers and submarine tenders for underway replenishment—which greatly extended submarine range. Always forward looking, Dönitz married submarine and aerial technology, developing tactics that coordinated aerial reconnaissance with submarine attacks on convoys.

Further reading: Dönitz, Karl. *Memoirs.* New York: Da Capo, 1997; Edwards, Bernard. *Dönitz and the Wolf Packs.* New York: Sterling, 1997; Padfield, Peter. *Dönitz: The Last Führer.* New York: HarperCollins, 1987.

Donovan, William (1883–1959) *leader of the U.S. Office of Strategic Services (OSS)*

"Wild Bill" Donovan headed the U.S. OFFICE OF STRATEGIC SERVICES (OSS) during 1942–45. Born in Buffalo, New York, he was trained in law and began practicing in his hometown in 1907. He served with General John J. Pershing in the Punitive Expedition against Pancho Villa in 1916 as a member of the New York National Guard. After this, he saw combat in France during World War I with the 165th Infantry Regiment. He fought with great bravery and distinction, earning not only promotion to the rank of colonel but also the Medal of Honor.

After the war, in 1922, Donovan became U.S. district attorney for western New York, then served as assistant attorney general in the Justice Department from 1924 to 1929. He returned to the private practice of law in the 1930s but never severed his many connections to both the civil government and the military. On the eve of American entry into World War II, in 1940, President FRANKLIN D. ROOSEVELT called on Donovan to outline plans for the creation of a national central intelligence service at a time when the nation had no such body. Roosevelt formally appointed Donovan coordinator of information on July 11, 1941, and on June 13 of the following year he was named chief of what was now the OSS.

The OSS was a military, not a civilian, agency. Its wartime mission was threefold: to gather foreign intelligence, to conduct propaganda and counterpropaganda campaigns, and to conduct covert actions. Donovan had OSS operatives active in all theaters of the war except for the Pacific. The Latin American nations were also, for reasons of hemispheric diplomacy, exempted.

The OSS became a valuable source of intelligence during the war, especially in Europe. It also served as the foundation for the postwar Central Intelligence Agency, an entity Donovan enthusiastically supported, though he declined to take any role in its creation or operation. Donovan remained in government service after the war, serving as ambassador to Thailand in 1953–54.

Further reading: Brown, Anthony. *The Last Hero: Wild Bill Donovan.* New York: Random House, 1982; Dunlop, Richard. *Donovan: America's Master Spy.* New York: Rand McNally, 1982; O'Donnell, Patrick K. *Operatives, Spies, and Saboteurs: The Unknown Story of the Men and Women of World War II's OSS.* New York: Free Press, 2004; Stevenson, William. *A Man Called Intrepid.* Guilford, Conn.: Lyons Press, 2000; Troy, Thomas F. *Wild Bill and Intrepid: Donovan, Stephenson, and the Origin of CIA.* New Haven, Conn.: Yale University Press, 1996.

Doolittle, James Harold "Jimmy" (1896–1993) *U.S. Army Air Forces officer and leader of the Doolittle Raid on Tokyo*

A U.S. Army Air Corps (USAAC) and U.S. Army Air Forces (USAAF) officer, Doolittle is best remembered for leading the spectacular carrier-launched DOOLITTLE TOKYO RAID early in the war. He was born in Alameda, California, and educated at Los Angeles Junior College and the University of California. He joined the Army Reserve Corps in October 1917 shortly after the United States entered World War I and was assigned to the Signal Corps, in which he served as a flight instructor through 1919. In 1920, Doolittle was commissioned a first lieutenant in the U.S. Army Air Service (USAAS) and earned national attention by making the first transcontinental flight in less than 14 hours, on September 4, 1922. Established now as a world-class flier, Doolittle was enrolled under USAAC auspices in the aeronautical science program at Massachusetts Institute of Technology. He earned a doctorate of science degree from that institution in 1925, then worked in several military aviation testing stations. Simultaneously, during 1925–30, Doolittle participated in high-profile air races as well as demonstrations of experimental aircraft. His objective was to promote aviation generally and military aviation in particular. A major breakthrough came in September 1929, when he demonstrated the potential of instrument flying by making the first ever instruments-only ("blind") landing.

In 1930, Doolittle resigned his commission to become aviation manager for Shell Oil, where he worked on the development of new high-efficiency aviation fuels. He also continued to race, claiming victories in a number of prestigious competitions, including those for the Harmon (1930) and Bendix (1931) trophies. In 1932, he set a world speed record. However, as war became imminent in July 1940, Doolittle returned to active duty as a major in the U.S. Army Air Corps. In the months following the Battle of Pearl Harbor (December 7, 1941), the American and Allied forces were in a desperate defensive position in the Pacific theater. In an effort to raise Allied morale and to force the Japanese to divert a portion of their air forces to defense of their homeland, Doolittle eagerly embraced a proposal for a bombing raid on Tokyo. With others, he planned the logistics of the raid. The formidable problem was that Tokyo was far out of range of any U.S. air bases. Aircraft carriers were not designed to launch bombers capable of the mission. Doolittle worked with navy and army air forces personnel to devise techniques for launching 16 B-25 medium bombers from the deck of the USS *Hornet*.

Doolittle personally led all-volunteer crews, who took off from the *Hornet* on April 18, 1942. All aircraft were launched successfully, but each airman understood that fuel limitations meant that no return trip was possible—and, in any case, no aircraft carrier could possibly accommodate a B-25 landing. Doolittle and his men would have to land in China, hope to evade capture, and find their way back to Allied lines. It was as close to a suicide mission as any ever undertaken by American fighting men.

The Doolittle Tokyo Raid succeeded, although, in strictly military terms, that success was modest in that the damage to Tokyo and other targets from 16 medium bombers was trivial. However, the raid on the Japanese homeland provided a morale boost of incalculable effect, and it surely did much to spur the American war effort. As planned, it also served to tie down a portion of the Japanese air

James H. "Jimmy" Doolittle *(National Archives and Records Administration)*

force to home defense, and it must have made an impact on the morale of the hitherto undefeated Japanese.

Doolittle and most of his raiders survived the action, and Doolittle was promoted to brigadier general. He was sent to England to organize the Twelfth U.S. Air Force in September 1942 and, with the temporary rank of major general, commanded the Twelfth in OPERATION TORCH, the assault portion of the Allied NORTH AFRICAN CAMPAIGN. During March 1943–January 1944, Doolittle commanded strategic air operations in the Mediterranean theater and was promoted to the temporary rank of lieutenant general in March 1944. He was given command of the British-based Eighth Air Force, which executed massive and ongoing bombing operations against Germany during January 1944–May 1945.

After V-E Day, Doolittle was transferred to the Pacific once again. With the Eighth Air Force, he provided support in the Battle of OKINAWA (April–July 1945) and the massive bombardment of the Japanese home islands.

Following the war, in May 1946, Doolittle left active duty (remaining in the reserves) and became an executive with Shell Oil. While working in the private sector, he was often called on by the government to serve as an adviser on scientific, technological, and aeronautical commissions during 1948–57. Even after he retired from Shell and the Air Force Reserve in 1959, he continued to work as a consultant, not only in matters of science and aeronautics, but in national security policy issues as well.

Doolittle is justly remembered for the Tokyo raid that bears his name. But he was even more important during the war as a high-level army air force commander, and his contributions to aviation include the testing and development of technological advances and the raising of public awareness of and support for the emerging field.

Further reading: Doolittle, James H., with Carroll V. Glines. *I Could Never Be So Lucky Again: An Autobiography.* New York: Bantam, 2001; Doolittle, Jonna Hoppes. *Calculated Risk: The Extraordinary Life of Jimmy Doolittle*

Aviation Pioneer: A Memoir. Santa Monica, Calif.: Santa Monica Press, 2005; Glines, Carroll V. *The Doolittle Raid.* Atglen, Pa.: Schiffer, 2000.

Doolittle Tokyo Raid

On April 18, 1942, with the Japanese victorious on every front, Lieutenant Colonel JAMES H. "JIMMY" DOOLITTLE of U.S. Army Air Forces (USAAF), led 16 B-25 Mitchell bombers from the deck of the aircraft carrier *Hornet* on a daring—well-nigh suicidal—bombing raid against Tokyo and other Japanese cities. The pilots knew that they could not deliver enough bombs on their targets to cause anything approaching strategically significant damage. However, in the wake of the BATTLE OF PEARL HARBOR and other American and British defeats, Doolittle and his raiders wanted to carry out a mission that would generally raise American and Allied morale, that would depress the morale of the Japanese, and that would force the Japanese to keep a large number of aircraft on patrol over the home islands rather than in combat. Doolittle and his men also knew that, difficult as it was to launch twin-engine medium bombers from the deck of an aircraft carrier, it was impossible to land them there again, and they could not carry sufficient fuel to fly to a friendly base. After the raid, they would have to land in China and hope for the best in their efforts to escape and evade capture and return home.

The origin of the Doolittle raid is obscure. Official early USAAF histories credited President FRANKLIN D. ROOSEVELT with the idea, but U.S. Fleet Commander Adm. ERNEST J. KING said that he first heard of it as an off-handed remark from his operations officer, who observed that it was possible to launch twin-engine bombers from an aircraft carrier, a prospect that made an early air attack on Japan feasible, albeit just barely. Enthusiastic about the idea, King conferred with USAAF chief General HENRY H. ("HAP") ARNOLD, who also greeted it with enthusiasm. Arnold chose Doolittle, a great pilot with formal training in aerodynamics, to organize and lead an air group to execute the mission. Doolittle decided on using the

One of Jimmy Doolittle's B-25s lifts off the deck of USS *Hornet* en route to bomb Tokyo. *(Library of Congress)*

B-25B Mitchell medium bomber, which was both modern and combat proven. Quick tests proved that it could indeed be launched from a carrier while hauling a militarily useful bomb load and sufficient fuel to strike Tokyo, then continue to airstrips in China. Once Doolittle had established to his satisfaction the technical feasibility of the mission, he set about recruiting volunteers for a top secret mission he could not at the time explain, other than to warn each prospect that it was highly dangerous. After gathering pilots and crews for 16 planes, Doolittle led a special training program for his men and oversaw necessary modifications to their aircraft.

The *Hornet,* newly launched, would carry the planes, but the mission was so secret that the carri-er's skipper, Captain MARC MITSCHER, was not briefed until just before the aircraft were loaded onto the flight deck. On April 2, 1942, the *Hornet* sailed and was joined en route by the carrier *Enterprise,* Vice Admiral WILLIAM "BULL" HALSEY's flag-ship, on April 13. The *Enterprise* would provide air cover during the approach to the launching point, which was scheduled to be reached on April 18. This position was about 400 miles off the Japanese mainland. Shortly before dawn on the 18th, how-ever, enemy picket boats were sighted much farther east than expected. Although the U.S. ships either evaded or sank the enemy craft, they had been able to transmit radio warnings. With the element of surprise hanging in the balance, Doolittle decided to launch his raid immediately, not 400 miles off the coast, but 700, which would strain fuel supply even more and quite probably prevent at least some of the aircraft from finding relatively safe haven in China.

The raiders took off, all successfully, about 8 A.M., 16 five-man crews in all. One bomber attacked Kobe, another Nagoya, and a third, slated to bomb Osaka, instead dropped its ordnance on the Yokosuka naval yard and on Yokohama. A fourth plane was forced to divert to a landing at Vladivostok. The 12 other raiders bombed Tokyo at noon. As chance would have it, the Japanese were conducting a drill, a mock air raid, at the time. This probably diluted the psychological effect of the raid, but it also provided a diversion that helped the bombers escape. No bomber was lost over Japan.

Damage inflicted was modest. Some 50 people were killed and 100 houses damaged or destroyed. The damage to the prestige and air of invulnerability that had surrounded the Japanese militarists was much more severe. Another effect of the raid was to remove official objections to the plan proposed by Admiral YAMAMOTO ISORUKU to draw out the American fleet to the area of Midway Island and deliver a fatal blow there. In fact, the BATTLE OF MIDWAY would result in an American victory that turned the tide of the war in the Pacific.

After the raid, the bombers, now critically short of fuel, either crash landed in China or were abandoned, their crews bailing out. Almost miraculously, Doolittle and 70 other mission members survived, all eventually finding their way back home. One airman was killed in parachuting from his plane, and eight were captured by the Japanese. Of this number, three were executed and one died in prison.

Further reading: Doolittle, James, with Carroll V. Glines. *I Could Never Be So Lucky Again: An Autobiography.* New York: Bantam, 2001; Glines, Carroll V. *The Doolittle Raid.* Atglen, Pa.: Schiffer, 2000; Lawson, Ted W. *Thirty Seconds over Tokyo.* London and New York: Brassey's, 2003; Nelson, Craig. *The First Heroes: The Extraordinary Story of the Doolittle Raid—America's First World War II Victory.* New York: Viking. 2002.

Dowding, Hugh (1882–1970) *head of British Fighter Command during the Battle of Britain*

Britain's air chief marshal, Hugh Dowding was also head of Fighter Command during the BATTLE OF BRITAIN. Under his leadership, the Luftwaffe was defeated in the skies above England and the nation thereby saved from invasion.

Dowding was trained as an artillery officer but became a squadron commander in the Royal Flying Corps during World War I and ended that war with the rank of brigadier general. He was then commissioned in the newly formed Royal Air Force (RAF) and served in command, staff, and training posts in Britain and Asia. In 1936, he was named commander in chief of the newly created Fighter Command and was responsible for advocating the development of RADAR and of the great Spitfire and Hurricane fighters. These technological developments would prove invaluable during the Battle of Britain.

When World War II began, Dowding fought fiercely against dispersal of fighter resources first in Norway and then in the BATTLE OF FRANCE. Slated for retirement, he extended his service and led Fighter Command in the Battle of Britain. The RAF was outnumbered by the German Luftwaffe, but Dowding conducted a campaign that leveraged superior strategy and tactics, prevailing against the Germans and, by denying the Luftwaffe air supremacy, preventing what was surely imminent invasion.

Dowding was a great husbander of resources, coordinating his fighters with ground-based radar information. Some of his subordinates believed he was too cautious. Whereas Dowding fought the battle chiefly over English skies, some advocated conducting an aerial counteroffensive farther out over the English Channel. Dowding's advancing age was cited as the reason for his replacement as commander in chief of Fighter Command on November 24, 1940. It is likely, however, that the command's failure to defend against the COVENTRY AIR RAID was the more immediate cause. Certainly, at the time, Dowding was given little enough credit for what he had accomplished in the Battle of Britain. However, over the years, the importance of his early leadership has been widely recognized.

Dowding was given other assignments, as liaison to U.S. aircraft factories and as a kind of inspector general of factories at home. He was never satisfied with these assignments and requested retirement in November 1942. The following year he was created Baron Dowding of Bentley Priory.

Further reading: Flint, Peter. *Dowding and Headquarters Fighter Command.* Shrewsbury, U.K.: Airlife Publishing, 1996; Ray, John. *The Battle of Britain: Dowding and the First Victory 1940.* London: Cassell, 2001; Wright, Robert. *Dowding and the Battle of Britain.* London: Macdonald, 1969.

Dresden air raid

The massive Allied air raid on the medieval German city of Dresden during February 13–14, 1945, was enormously destructive and highly controversial. Many historians and others have condemned it as an act of wanton and vengeful destruction, a mission with no true military purpose. Others have seen it as just another episode of the STRATEGIC BOMBING OF GERMANY, a program intended to hasten the end of the war.

Capital of Saxony, Dresden was a city of beautiful medieval architecture. Its major industry was the creation of fine china, and it had little heavy industry, even during the war. Because it was considered of negligible strategic importance, it had been largely bypassed by Allied bombers, except for a minor U.S. raid in October 1944.

In January 1945, under the direction of British air marshal ARTHUR "BOMBER" HARRIS, plans were drawn up for Operation Thunderclap to attack Berlin and other major population centers as the Soviet Red Army was closing in rapidly from the east. The idea was that the raids would make defense against the Soviet advance more difficult and that they would disrupt the flow of westward-bound refugees from that advance. It was particularly important, western Allied leaders felt, to make a demonstration of support for the Soviet effort.

The first Thunderclap missions were flown over Berlin and Magdeburg on February 3, and over Magdeburg and Chemnitz on February 6. On February 9, Magdeburg was targeted a third time. Harris had wanted to put Dresden at the top of the list, but raids against that city were delayed by adverse weather. When February 13 looked good for a night raid, Royal Air Force Bomber Command sent 796 Avro Lancaster heavy bombers and nine Mosquito fighter bombers over Dresden. Together, they dropped 1,478 tons of high-explosive bombs and another 1,182 tons of incendiaries. The combination of rubble and the intensive incendiary bombing created not merely a series of fires, but a firestorm, which engulfed the city. As if this were not bad enough, the U.S. Eighth Air Force followed up with a daylight raid on February 14 using its B-17 Flying Fortresses to multiply the already devastating destruction. As a result of the two raids, more than 50,000 civilians, including westward-bound refugees, died. Dresden lay in ruins.

Immediately after the raids, war correspondents and others raised questions as to the purpose, utility, and morality of the attacks on Dresden. Even WINSTON CHURCHILL, who had endorsed Operation Thunderclap, was appalled. "Bomber" Harris, however, voiced no doubts about the operation he had led and considered the destruction of cities perfectly legitimate in a total war.

Further reading: Knell, Hermann. *To Destroy a City: Strategic Bombing and Its Human Consequences in World War II.* New York: Da Capo, 2003; Taylor, Frederick. *Dresden: Tuesday, February 13, 1945.* New York: HarperCollins, 2004.

Dulles, Allen (1893–1969) *head of the U.S. Office of Strategic Services (OSS) in Europe*

Younger brother of JOHN FOSTER DULLES, Allan Dulles headed the OFFICE OF STRATEGIC SERVICES (OSS) in Europe during World War II, beginning in November 1942. He was born in Watertown, New York, and received a master's degree from Princeton University in 1916, then went on to a career in the U.S. diplomatic corps. In 1922, he was promoted to chief of the Near Eastern division of the U.S. Department of State. Dulles took time out to acquire a law degree, which he received in 1926, then was appointed attorney to the U.S. delegation in Peking (Beijing). Shortly afterward, he entered the private sector, joining his brother's New York City law firm.

With America's entry into World War II following the BATTLE OF PEARL HARBOR, Colonel WILLIAM DONOVAN, creator and director of the Office of Strategic Services (OSS), recruited Dulles. As Donovan saw it, Dulles was well qualified for high-level intelligence work because he had an extensive diplomatic background but was no longer part of the formal State Department bureaucracy. Donovan put Dulles in charge of an OSS office operating in Bern, in neutral Switzerland. Dulles served there from October 1942 to May 1945, coordinating the activities of RESISTANCE MOVEMENTS in Germany. Dulles was able to make contact with Fritz Kolbe, a German foreign office clerk and anti-Nazi, who transmitted to him some 1,500 top-secret foreign office cables. These were invaluable in unmasking many of Germany's spies who had infiltrated Britain and other Allied countries. Dulles also was primarily responsible for establishing an extensive intelligence network in the south of France. But perhaps his greatest coup was the role he played as a covert intermediary in negotiating the surrender of all German troops in northern Italy shortly before V-E Day.

After the war, in 1948, Dulles was named chairman of a committee that surveyed and evaluated the American intelligence establishment. He was instrumental in recommending the creation of the Central Intelligence Agency (CIA), which was formally established in 1951, with Dulles as deputy director under General WALTER BEDELL SMITH. Dulles was appointed director by President DWIGHT D. EISENHOWER two years later. Dulles presided over a number of cold war intelligence successes during the Eisenhower years and was reappointed by President John F. Kennedy. But he shouldered a large amount of the blame for the abortive and disastrous Bay of Pigs invasion of Cuba in April 1961 and in the fall of that year resigned. He then wrote widely about the field of intelligence.

Further reading: Dulles, Allen. *The Craft of Intelligence: America's Legendary Spy Master on the Fundamentals of Intelligence Gathering for a Free World.* Guilford, Conn.: Lyons Press, 2004; Grose, Peter. *Gentleman Spy: The Life of Allen Dulles.* Andover: University of Massachusetts Press, 1996; Hersh, Burton. *The Old Boys: The American Elite and the Origins of the CIA.* New York: Scribner's, 1992; Srodes, James. *Allen Dulles: Master of Spies.* Chicago: Regnery, 1999.

Dulles, John Foster (1888–1959) *U.S. diplomat*

Older brother of ALLEN DULLES, John Foster Dulles was instrumental in creating the United Nations Charter at the Dumbarton Oaks Conference, in Washington, D.C., toward the end of World War II and was also a senior adviser at the first United Nations conference in San Francisco. It was Dulles who acted as key negotiator of the definitive peace treaty with Japan in 1951. As secretary of state (1953–59) in the cabinet of President DWIGHT D. EISENHOWER, Dulles was the architect of many U.S. policies that shaped the postwar world.

Dulles was born in Watertown, New York, into a family with a long political tradition. His maternal grandfather, John Watson Foster, was secretary of state under President Benjamin Harrison, Robert Lansing, an uncle by marriage, was secretary of state under Woodrow Wilson. Educated at Princeton University, George Washington University, and the Sorbonne, Dulles joined the New York law firm of Sullivan and Cromwell in 1911 as a specialist in international law. He became senior partner in the firm in 1927. However, Dulles was never exclusively committed to the private sector, and after World War I, he served at Wilson's behest as legal counsel to the U.S. delegation to the Versailles Peace Conference. He was also a member of the war reparations commission.

Dulles was called to government service again at the end of World War II, to collaborate on the composition of the United Nations Charter. President HARRY S. TRUMAN sent him to San Francisco as a senior adviser at the opening meeting of the United Nations. When, after fruitless discussion, it became clear that a definitive peace treaty with Japan that would be acceptable to the United States would not be acceptable to the Soviet Union, President Truman and Secretary of State Dean Acheson chose not to call a peace conference for the negotiation of the treaty, but instead assigned Dulles the monumental undertaking of personally negotiating the treaty individually with each nation that had been involved in the conflict. Dulles negotiated with 49 nations, including Japan itself, and the final treaty was signed in San Francisco in 1951.

When Dwight D. Eisenhower succeeded to the White House in 1953, he appointed Dulles his secretary of state. His tenure was controversial in that he, not the president, took the firmer hand in shaping foreign policy. Dulles was directly responsible for creating the Southeast Asia Treaty Organization (SEATO) and the Central Treaty Organization (CENTO), the latter uniting Turkey, Iraq, Iran, and Pakistan in a U.S.-dominated mutual defense organization. It was as secretary of state that Dulles directed the composition of the Trieste agreement (1954), which partitioned the free territory between Italy and Yugoslavia, and the Austrian State Treaty (1955), which restored that nation's pre-ANSCHLUSS (1938) frontiers and forbade any future union with Germany.

Dulles's postwar policies were vehemently anticommunist and anti-Soviet, and he seemed almost to revel in pushing the USSR to the brink and declaring in no uncertain terms that U.S. nuclear policy was one of "massive nuclear retaliation" to any Soviet aggression. His unwillingness to compromise in the cold war earned Dulles many admirers and detractors, but President Eisenhower's confidence in him never wavered, and he awarded him the Medal of Freedom on April 15, 1959, a month before Dulles succumbed to cancer.

Further reading: Beal, John. *John Foster Dulles, 1888–1959*. Westport, Conn.: Greenwood, 1974; Goold-Adams, Richard. *John Foster Dulles: A Reappraisal*. Westport,

Conn.: Greenwood, 1974; Guhin, Michael A. *John Foster Dulles: A Statesman and His Times*. New York: Columbia University Press, 1972; Immerman, Richard H. *John Foster Dulles: Piety, Pragmatism, and Power in U.S. Foreign Policy*. Wilmington, Del.: SR Books, 1998.

Dunkirk evacuation

The German BLITZKRIEG brought the BATTLE OF FRANCE to so swift and devastating a conclusion that the bulk of the British Expeditionary Force (BEF) and other troops had no choice but to retreat to Dunkirk on the English Channel French coast near the Belgian border. German general GERD VON RUNDSTEDT expressed to ADOLF HITLER his reservations about the extremely aggressive tactics of Blitzkrieg advocate and armor commander HEINZ GUDERIAN, who was determined to push virtually the entire BEF into the English Channel. Rundstedt believed that Guderian's tanks could not do this alone and advised calling a halt to their advance until more conventional infantry divisions could catch up. Hitler agreed, Guderian's advance was halted, and a narrow window of opportunity was thereby opened for British and French troops to be evacuated from Dunkirk.

The evacuation, which has been called miraculous, was a mammoth effort (appropriately code named Operation Dynamo) between May 26 and June 4, 1940. The British Admiralty cobbled together a fleet of 693 ships, including 39 destroyers, 36 minesweepers, 77 civilian trawlers, 26 civilian yachts, and a motley assortment of other small craft, which fetched from Dunkirk 338,226 soldiers, including 140,000 French troops. The Allies were forced, however, to abandon a huge cache of heavy equipment. (Even before Operation Dynamo began, some 28,000 nonessential British personnel had been evacuated via Dunkirk.)

Although Operation Dynamo was extremely successful, it was accompanied by much confusion and friction between the British and the French. Indeed, initially, the French were not allowed to embark on the evacuation ships, and only after virtually all the British troops had been evacuated were large numbers of French troops taken off en

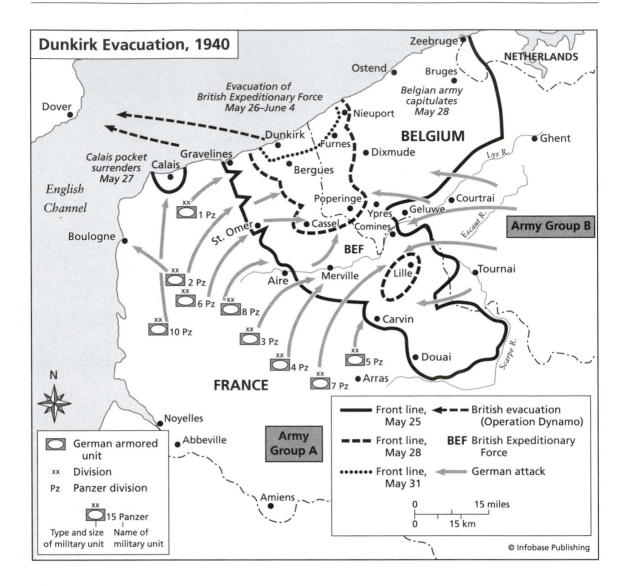

Dunkirk Evacuation, 1940

Zeebruge
NETHERLANDS
Ostend
Bruges
Dover
Evacuation of
British Expeditionary Force
May 26–June 4
Belgian army
capitulates
May 28
Nieuport
Ghent
Dunkirk
Furnes
BELGIUM
Gravelines
Dixmude
Lys R.
Calais pocket
surrenders
May 27
Calais
Bergues
English
Channel
Poperinge
Ypres
Geluwe
Courtrai
Cassel
Comines
Escaut R.
Army Group B
Boulogne
St. Omer
BEF
XX
1 Pz
XX
2 Pz
Aire
Merville
Lille
Tournai
XX
6 Pz
XX
8 Pz
XX
10 Pz
XX
3 Pz
Carvin
XX
4 Pz
XX
5 Pz
Douai
Scarpe R.
N
XX
7 Pz
Arras
FRANCE

— Front line, May 25	◄■■■ British evacuation (Operation Dynamo)
■ ■ ■ Front line, May 28	**BEF** British Expeditionary Force
••••• Front line, May 31	◄■ German attack

Noyelles
Abbeville
Army
Group A

	German armored unit
xx	Division
Pz	Panzer division

XX
15 Panzer
Type and size
of military unit
Name of
military unit

Amiens

0   15 miles
0   15 km

© Infobase Publishing

masse. On the last two nights of the operation, 53,000 French soldiers embarked. Nor was the evacuation as heroic, stoic, and orderly as it is often portrayed to have been. Officers sometimes used small arms to control panicky troops in the evacuation lines, and the sailors managing the small boats that transferred troops from shore to waiting vessels not infrequently used their oars to beat off those threatening to overload and swamp their tiny craft. It is true, however, that the greatest disorder

occurred early in the operation, as the rear echelon troops were being evacuated. The front line troops, who were the last to leave, tended to be far more disciplined, calm, and orderly.

Fortunately for Operation Dynamo, the notoriously treacherous waters of the English Channel were uncommonly calm. Nevertheless, all ships were subject to attack by Luftwaffe aircraft and by U-boats as well as by small German E-boats, the equivalent of allied torpedo boats, or PT boats. The

Luftwaffe also bombed and strafed Dunkirk itself, razing the town. Far greater casualties would have been incurred among the French and British evacuees had the weather permitted more air attacks. Moreover, the Royal Air Force (RAF) provided extensive air cover for the evacuation, and, so swift had been the German advance that the Luftwaffe had not had time to prepare forward bases. As a consequence, it experienced a severe logistical strain, which also limited air attack. Indeed, it may be argued that the tremendous smoke coverage created by Luftwaffe bombing actually worked to the Allies' advantage, screening much of the evacuation process. Nevertheless, covering the evacuation cost the RAF 177 precious aircraft—though its contribution to the effort was absolutely instrumental to its success. Prime Minister WINSTON CHURCHILL, although vastly relieved by the success of Dynamo, reported to Parliament on June 4 that "Wars are not won by evacuations." However, he was able to point out that the RAF had taken such a toll on the Luftwaffe that the air component of the operation could well be counted a British *offensive* victory.

As the evacuation proceeded, it quickly became apparent that the greatest bottleneck in the operation was in conveying evacuees from the shore to the larger vessels. On May 29, the operation was announced to the British public, and masters of small power craft, ranging from 30 to 100 feet in length, rallied to the cause, volunteering small craft and crew to transfer troops from shore to ship. The yeoman service of this fleet of "Little Ships" gave rise to what was popularly called the "Dunkirk Spirit" and did much to transform an ignominious military defeat and retreat into what was popularly perceived as a triumph. (There was much heroism in this, but, again, perhaps not always as much as popular lore suggests. At the outbreak of the war, a Small Vessels Pool was created, by which modest civilian motorized craft were registered and were to be made available for emergency military service. Nevertheless, the Rye fishing fleet and some coastal lifeboat crews flatly refused to volunteer for service in the evacuation.)

After a devastating Luftwaffe attack on June 1, during which a passenger liner and three destroyers were sunk and four other vessels severely damaged with much loss of life, daylight sailings were discontinued, and the rest of Operation Dynamo was carried out under cover of darkness. By this point, the perimeter around Dunkirk was shrinking rapidly. Admiral Sir Bertram Ramsay, in command of Operation Dynamo, ordered officers to shoot any soldiers who drew back from the perimeter without orders. At dawn on June 2, the last of the British warships retired, and the few remaining BEF personnel were evacuated aboard a civilian ferry. That night, ships did return to pick up French troops, but were unable to do so. A political uproar compelled Ramsay to dispatch more ships the following night, which managed to pluck a final 27,000 French soldiers from the port.

The importance of the Dunkirk evacuation cannot be overestimated. Operation Dynamo saved the bulk of the BEF. To have lost so many men would likely have forced Britain to negotiate peace—that is, surrender to—with the Germans. By allowing Rundstedt to delay Guderian's advance, Hitler may not have lost the war in the spring of 1940, but he certainly gave up an extraordinary opportunity to win it.

Further reading: Atkin, Ronald. *Pillar of Fire: Dunkirk 1940*. Edinburgh: Birlinn, 2001; Gelb, Norman. *Dunkirk: The Complete Story of the First Step in the Defeat of Hitler*, New York: William Morrow, 1989; Lord, Walter. *The Miracle of Dunkirk*. Conshohocken, Pa.: Combined Publishing, 1998; Patrick, Wilson. *Dunkirk (Battleground Europe Series)*. Conshohocken, Pa.: Combined Publishing, 2000.

Dutch East Indies, action in

Also called the Netherlands East Indies, this was, at the time of World War II, a vast Dutch colony in Southeast Asia encompassing Java, Sumatra, Dutch Borneo, Dutch New Guinea, Celebes, the western portion of Timor, and the Moluccas. The colony was an extraordinarily rich source of oil (concentrated in Sumatra), tin, bauxite (the ore from which aluminum is produced), and coal. The colony was densely populated by some 70.5 million persons, including a quarter million Dutch nationals (most of whom fell into Japanese hands and suffered internment under extremely inhumane conditions for the duration of the war).

After the Netherlands fell to Germany and came under occupation in May 1940, the People's Council in Batavia, Java, declared the colony loyal to the Dutch government in exile. This did not impress Japan, Germany's Axis partner, which proclaimed the region part of the so-called Greater Asia Co-Prosperity Sphere and summarily demanded a large portion of the colony's produce, as well as fishing and mining rights and access to all ports. The People's Council protested the Japanese declaration and demands, but nevertheless traded with Japan until August 1941, when the Dutch government in exile ordered the colony to cease trade and, in particular, to cut off the supply of oil. Thus, when general war broke out in the Pacific in December, the Dutch East Indies loomed as a great prize for the Japanese.

On December 20, 1941, elements of the Sixteenth Japanese Army, operating from Mindanao in the Philippines, attacked Dutch Borneo, Celebes, and the Moluccas. In a rare Japanese AIRBORNE ASSAULT, paratroops seized the Celebes airfield on January 11, then fanned out to the oilfields of Dutch Borneo and the airfields in Celebes and the Moluccas. Paratroops also preceded the Sixteenth Japanese Army's land invasion of southern Sumatra on February 16. This captured the major refinery at Palembang, Sumatra. Three days later, paratroops cleared the way for the Japanese occupation of Dutch Timor.

As would be the case throughout the war, what the Allies called the China-Burma-India theater was very meagerly provided with the means to defend itself. Colonial forces, aided in some measure by American, Australian, and British troops, put up valiant demonstrations of resistance but were overwhelmed. Particularly deficient were the Allies' air assets in the area. Most available aircraft were destroyed on the ground during raids on February 19 and 27. In the air, Japanese Zeroes easily outflew Allied fighters, and Japanese naval strength overpowered the slim Allied resources in the region.

On February 25, 1942, the ABDA (American-British-Dutch-Australian) Command, under General Sir ARCHIBALD WAVELL, considered by the Allies to have been defeated, was dissolved. The Dutch governor general took command of what forces remained, but, on March 8, after the Japanese had advanced from landing places in Java, he surrendered them. Some 93,000 troops of the Royal Netherlands East Indies Army, together with various other Allied units, became prisoners of war. Also on March 8, Japanese troops arrived in northern Sumatra from Singapore. Sumatra was completely overrun by the end of March and was being used as a staging area for the invasion of Dutch New Guinea. Here, guerrilla resistance remained fierce through October, and, in fact, the Japanese never fully subjugated Dutch New Guinea.

The vast territory that the Japanese did come absolutely to control was divided for administrative purposes between the Imperial Army and the Imperial Navy. Guerrillas throughout the region were active during the entire war and made significant inroads against the Japanese in Dutch Timor. However, attempts by the Special Operations Executive to organize and assist the guerrillas proved futile because of logistical problems (paramountly, the jungle terrain and climate) and the noncooperation or outright hostility of most of the native population, which saw the Japanese occupation as a means of evicting the long-hated European overlords. Only near the end of the war, from May to July 1945, did Special Operations Australia (SOA) forces succeed in executing amphibious operations on British Borneo, which threatened the Japanese hold on the rest of the island. The war ended, however, before the SOA had expanded its invasion.

Further reading: Allen, Louis. *Burma: The Longest War 1941–1945.* London: Cassell, 2000; Astor, Gerald. *The Jungle War: Mavericks, Marauders and Madmen in the China-Burma-India Theater of World War II.* New York: Wiley, 2004; Slim, William. *Defeat Into Victory.* New York: Cooper Square, 2000.

E

Eaker, Ira (1896–1987) *architect of the strategic bombing of Germany*

Ira Clarence Eaker, an American military aviation pioneer, commanded the Eighth U.S. Bomber Command, based in England, and led the first raids in the Strategic Bombing of Germany. He was the chief planner of the Combined Bomber Offensive, the strategic bombing collaboration of the Royal Air Force (RAF) and U.S. Army Air Forces (USAAF), which became known as the Eaker plan.

Born in Field Creek, Texas, and raised in Texas and Oklahoma, Eaker was educated at Southeastern State Teachers College (now Southeastern Oklahoma State University) and entered the U.S. Army in 1917 as a second lieutenant. In March 1918, he attended ground school at the University of Texas, Austin, and then began flight training at Kelly Field, San Antonio. After earning his wings on July 17, 1918, he was promoted to first lieutenant and sent to Rockwell Field, California, where he met Colonel Henry Harley ("Hap") Arnold and Major Carl A. (Tooey) Spaatz, with whom he developed a close working relationship that would have profound consequences for the air war in World War II.

In July 1919, Eaker assumed command of Second Aero Squadron in the Philippines, then, as captain, was reassigned in 1920 as commander of the Third Aero Squadron. Returning to the United States in 1921, he was assigned to Mitchel Field, New York, and also attended Columbia Law School. He then served on the staff of Major General Mason M. Patrick, chief of the U.S. Army Air Service (USAAS), in Washington, D.C.

One of 10 USAAS pilots chosen to make the Pan American Goodwill Flight in 1926, Eaker and his copilot were the only team to complete the entire 23,000-mile, 23-nation flight. In 1929 Eaker, with Spaatz and Elwood R. Quesada, flew a Fokker trimotor for 150 hours, 40 minutes, and 15 seconds between Los Angeles and San Diego, refueling in flight through a hose lowered from a Douglas C–1. This endurance record was unbroken for many years. In 1930, Eaker took midair refueling to the next step, flying the first transcontinental flight that relied solely on the technique. Next, in 1935, Major Eaker flew blind—relying on instruments only—from Mitchel Field, New York, to March Field, Riverside, California.

After attending the Air Corps Tactical School at Maxwell Field, Alabama, and the Army Command and General Staff School at Fort Leavenworth, Kansas, in the late 1930s, Eaker was promoted to colonel in December 1941 and to brigadier general in January 1942, when he was sent to England to form and command the Eighth Bomber Command. Eaker spearheaded the development of daylight precision bombing in the European theater and hammered out the so-called Eaker plan, which reconciled the RAF's policy of nighttime raids with the USAAF's policy of day-

Ira Eaker *(United States Air Force History Center)*

time precision bombing. The solution was for night and day raids, the British responsible for the night, the Americans for the day.

In December 1942, Eaker was assigned command of the Eighth Air Force, based in England, and was promoted to lieutenant general on September 13, 1943. The next month, he assumed command of both American air forces in the United Kingdom, the Eighth and the Ninth, then, on January 15, 1944, was assigned to command the joint Mediterranean Allied Air Forces (MAAF), taking over from British air marshal ARTHUR TEDDER. With 321,429 personnel and 12,598 aircraft, Eaker's MAAF was the world's largest air force.

On March 22, 1945, Eaker was sent to Washington, D.C., as deputy chief of the USAAF under Hap Arnold. It fell to Eaker to transmit the command from President HARRY S. TRUMAN to Spaatz, then commanding the Pacific Air Forces, to drop the atomic bomb on HIROSHIMA.

Eaker retired from the military in 1947, becoming an executive with the Hughes Aircraft Corporation from 1947 to 1957, then a corporate director of Douglas Aircraft Company. He left this position in 1961 to return to Hughes as a consultant. At this time, he took up journalism and became a nationally syndicated columnist, writing on national security matters. Eaker was also coauthor, with Arnold, of *This Flying Game* (1936), *Winged Warfare* (1941), and *Army Fliers* (1942).

Further reading: Astor, Gerald. *The Mighty Eighth: The Air War in Europe as Told by the Men Who Fought It.* New York: Dell, 1998; Copp, Dewitt S. *A Few Great Captains: The Men and Events That Shaped the Development of U.S. Air Power.* McLean, Va.: EPM Publications, 1989; Parton, James. *Air Force Spoken Here: General Ira Eaker and the Command of the Air.* Bethesda, Md.: Woodbine House, 1986.

East Africa, action in

In contrast to nearly every other front in the opening months of World War II, the action in East Africa was spectacularly favorable to the Allies. This was a result of the resourcefulness of British commanders, the remarkable work of British CRYPTOLOGY experts (who quickly broke the key Italian codes), and the timid ineptitude of the key Italian theater commander, Aimone Roberto Margherita Maria Giuseppe Savoy, duke of Aosta.

The Italians initially seized the upper hand during June 1940, moving out from their colony of Ethiopia (then called Abyssinia) to occupy Karora, Gallabat, Kurmak, and Kassala, all near the border of Sudan. Italian troops also occupied Moyale, on the border of Kenya and, in August, advanced into British Somaliland, which thereby became the first British colony to fall into the hands of the Axis. On paper, the situation looked quite desperate for the British. Against some 92,000 Italian troops and 250,000 Ethiopians under Italian arms, the British had about 40,000 colonial soldiers. British armor was almost nonexistent, and whereas the Italians had 323 aircraft available, the British commanded at most 100. What the Italians lacked, however, the British possessed in abundant quality: brilliant leadership. The duke of Aosta failed to exploit his manifest superiority of numbers and equipment and instead took cognizance only of his isolated position, far from any sources of resupply and reinforcement. Rather than act quickly and offensively against the British, Aosta hunkered down and, as a result, fell under attack by British units and by growing numbers of anti-Italian Ethiopian rebels called by the Allies "Patriots."

In October 1940, the British commanders devised a highly effective strategy for East Africa. Major General William Platt, British commander in chief of the Sudan, was assigned to lead the 5th Indian Division against Gallabat in November, then against Kassala in January 1941. The newly named commander in chief of Kenya, Lieutenant General SIR ALAN CUNNINGHAM, was tasked with taking Kismayu, also in January. In the meantime, HAILE SELASSIE, the exiled emperor of Italian-occupied Ethiopia, was assigned then-Major ORDE WINGATE as his military adviser to help him organize and prepare Patriot units.

Platt's field commander of the 10th Indian Infantry Brigade, SIR WILLIAM JOSEPH SLIM, attacked Gallabat on November 6 but was driven back by Italian air attacks. However, the Italians, as usual, failed to press their advantage and remained on the defensive. Using decrypts of coded Italian messages, Slim and others were readily able to anticipate all Italian moves and thereby quickly turned the British withdrawal into renewed multiple attacks. As the hunkered-down Italians were fending off British offensives, word of early British victories in the NORTH AFRICAN CAMPAIGNS brought panic to the Italian ranks and thoroughly demoralized Aosta, who withdrew from the Sudanese frontier, relinquishing all the advance positions he had occupied. Beginning on January 19, 1941, Platt unleashed columns to harry and pursue the retreating Italians.

After suffering heavy losses, Aosta ordered General Luigi Frusci, commander in chief of Eritrea, to hold southwest of Keren. Aosta reinforced Frusci in

terrain that greatly favored the defenders. Platt, whose forces were augmented by the 4th Indian Division, battered away at Frusci, who did not yield Keren until March 27. Asmara then fell to Platt on April 1. Although fighting would continue, the Battles of Keren and Asmara were decisive for the action in East Africa. More than 3,000 Italians were killed, as against 536 British and Indian troops.

After taking Keren and Asmara, Platt detailed forces to advance against the important port of Massawa. The six Italian destroyers that had been stationed there set sail, bound for a raid on British-held Port Said. However, British aircraft attacked them heavily, sinking four and forcing the Italians to scuttle the remaining two. Massawa fell on April 8 to a contingent of Indian and Free French troops.

With Eritrea reeling under Platt's onslaught, Cunningham struck from Kenya, using what was now a large contingent of 33,000 East African troops, 9,000 West Africans, and 27,000 South Africans. Six South African air squadrons provided close air support. Cunningham tried to incite the Patriots to rebel in the Ethiopian province of Galla-Sidamo, but the action failed to gel. Nevertheless, his forces did retake Moyale on February 18, 1941, but they did not advance beyond this point. Another attack, also launched by Cunningham, was far more successful. Beginning on February 11, two of his East African divisions advanced along the Indian Ocean coast, pushing the Italians before them. On February 14, Kismayu was captured, followed soon by Mogadishu in Italian Somaliland. Cunningham coordinated this advance with action in the interior, and all of Italian Somaliland and Ethiopia fell to the British by April 6, when the Italians evacuated Addis Ababa, the Ethiopian capital. In the space of two months, Cunningham's forces had covered 1,700 miles, pushing out or scooping up a very large portion of Aosta's command. Only 501 British and colonials were killed or wounded.

In the meantime, Orde Wingate was making spectacular use of the Ethiopian Patriots. Assigned merely to secure the province of Gojjam as a seat of command for Haile Selassie, Wingate used guerrilla tactics not only to accomplish this, but

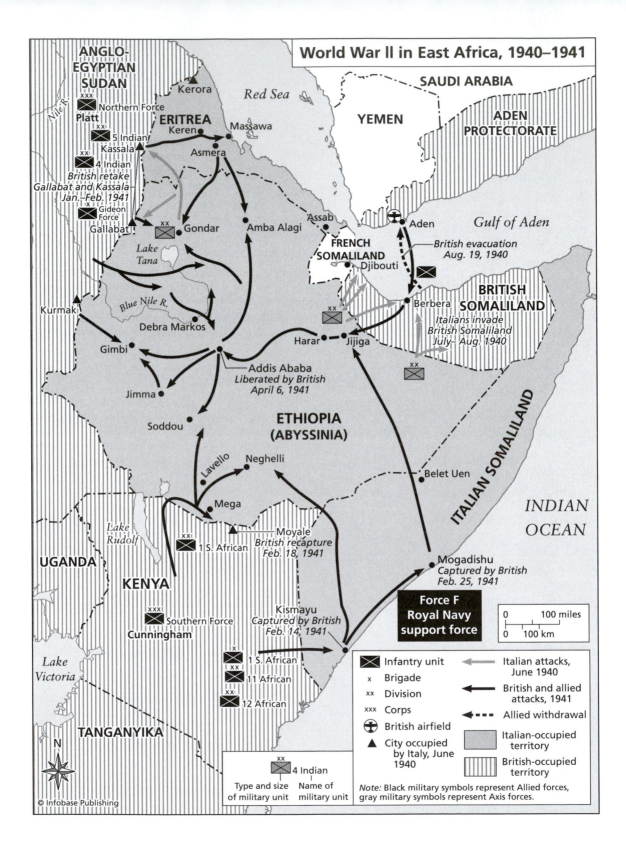

World War II in East Africa, 1940–1941

ANGLO-EGYPTIAN SUDAN

Kerora
Red Sea

Platt — Northern Force

ERITREA

5 Indian
Kassala
4 Indian
British retake Gallabat and Kassala Jan.–Feb. 1941

Gideon Force
Gallabat

Keren
Massawa
Asmera

Gondar
Amba Alagi
Assab

Lake Tana

Kurmak

Blue Nile R.

Debra Markos

Gimbi

Jimma

Soddou

Lavello

Neghelli

Mega

Moyale
British recapture Feb. 18, 1941

1 S. African

UGANDA

Lake Rudolf

KENYA

Southern Force
Cunningham

Kismayu
Captured by British Feb. 14, 1941

Lake Victoria

TANGANYIKA

N

© Infobase Publishing

SAUDI ARABIA

YEMEN

ADEN PROTECTORATE

Aden
Gulf of Aden

British evacuation Aug. 19, 1940

FRENCH SOMALILAND
Djibouti

Berbera
BRITISH SOMALILAND
Italians invade British Somaliland July– Aug. 1940

Harar
Jijiga

Addis Ababa
Liberated by British April 6, 1941

ETHIOPIA (ABYSSINIA)

Belet Uen

ITALIAN SOMALILAND

INDIAN OCEAN

Mogadishu
Captured by British Feb. 25, 1941

Force F Royal Navy support force

| 0 | 100 miles |
| 0 | 100 km |

1 S. African

11 African

12 African

☒	Infantry unit
x	Brigade
xx	Division
xxx	Corps
✠	British airfield
▲	City occupied by Italy, June 1940

→	Italian attacks, June 1940
→	British and allied attacks, 1941
◄--	Allied withdrawal
▨	Italian-occupied territory
▥	British-occupied territory

4 Indian
Type and size / Name of
of military unit / military unit

Note: Black military symbols represent Allied forces, gray military symbols represent Axis forces.

to intimidate a large-scale surrender of Italian-controlled African forces at Debra Markos on April 6. This cleared the way for Haile Selassie to return to the throne, and he entered Addis Ababa on May 5, 1941. The restoration of the emperor accomplished, Wingate rallied his small force in pursuit of the scattered Italians, taking prisoner 1,100 Italians and 7,000 Italian-controlled colonials at Addis Derra on May 20.

As Cunningham and Wingate made their spectacular gains, the rest of the British forces formed the jaws of a great pincer, which closed on Aosta's fallback position in the mountains of Amba Alagi in Eritrea. Aosta, who had relinquished all his early advantages through fear of being cut off, was now cut off indeed, and hopelessly so. He stubbornly rejected a British surrender demand on April 20, whereupon British and colonial forces began a slow series of methodical attacks and advances, forcing the Italians to withdraw behind a rapidly shrinking defensive perimeter. At last, on May 16, 1941, Aosta yielded. The war in East Africa was virtually over except for mop-up operations at Galla-Sidaamo, Gondar, and Assab, where isolated Italian units held out. These surrendered by November.

The spectacular victory against Italy forced this Axis power to relinquish Ethiopia and its other holdings in the region. They were humiliating defeats that hurt Italian morale as severely as they, in turn, lifted the morale of the hard-pressed Allies. Of more immediate strategic importance, however, the taking of the coastal regions along the Indian Ocean, Red Sea, and Gulf of Aden meant that these approaches to the Suez Canal were no longer a war zone, as defined by the U.S. Neutrality Acts then in force. as such, President Franklin Roosevelt, sympathetic to the Allied cause but inhibited by a still-isolationist Congress, could now allow U.S. merchant ships through to the Suez Canal to deliver much-needed materiel to British forces. The British and British colonial victories in this remote part of the world were thus dramatically leveraged both in terms of morale and overall strategy.

Further reading: Bierman, John, and Colin Smith. *Fire in the Night: Wingate of Burma, Ethiopia, and Zion.* New York: Random House, 1999; Buchanan, Angus. *Three Years of War in East Africa.* Westport, Conn.: Greenwood Press, 1970; Shores, Christopher. *Dust Clouds in the Middle East: The Air War for East Africa, Iraq, Syria, Iran and Madagascar, 1940–1942.* Boston: Grub Street, 1996.

Eden, Anthony (1897–1977) *British foreign secretary during most of World War II*

Robert Anthony Eden, first earl of Avon, viscount Eden of Royal Leamington Spa, served before (1935–38), during (1940–45), and after (1951–55) World War II as Britain's foreign secretary and, during the postwar years, as prime minister (1955–57). He was born in Windlestone, Durham, and saw combat during World War I. He enrolled at Christ Church, Oxford University, after the war to study Arabic and Persian, then was elected to the House of Commons in 1923. Eden was appointed undersecretary of state for foreign affairs in the cabinet of Stanley Baldwin in 1931, then lord privy seal (with special responsibility for international relations) in 1934. In 1935, he filled the specially created cabinet post of minister for League of Nations affairs, became foreign secretary at the end of that year, but resigned in February 1938 in protest of Prime Minister Neville Chamberlain's policy of Appeasement, which culminated in the Munich Conference and Agreement.

Eden returned to Chamberlain's government at the beginning of World War II, in September 1939, as dominions secretary (without a cabinet seat), and when Winston Churchill replaced Chamberlain as prime minister on May 10, 1940, he named Eden secretary of state for war. Despite this title, Eden actually served as foreign secretary from December 23, 1940 until Churchill and the Conservatives were voted out in July 1945.

Eden was a strong advocate for such key British generals as Sir John Dill, Alan Brooke, and Archibald Wavell, the latter a figure who did not always enjoy Churchill's confidence. After Wavell achieved victories in the Middle East, however, Churchill placed increasing reliance on Eden's counsel and sent him as his representative to meetings he could not attend personally. In particular,

Eden was the envoy of choice to Moscow, and Churchill ensured that he was present at all the major Allied conferences, except for the CASABLANCA CONFERENCE, from which foreign secretaries were explicitly barred.

Eden and Churchill presented a unified public presence throughout the war, but Eden was never Churchill's yes man, and he disagreed with his chief on several critical issues, including, most importantly, the status of the Polish government in exile and the role of CHARLES DE GAULLE in the Free French government and FREE FRENCH FORCES. Whereas Churchill supported the so-called Morgenthau Plan, a peace proposal that would have transformed Germany into a kind of pastoral economy, Eden vehemently opposed it, an opposition shared by HARRY S. TRUMAN after he became president. There is evidence that Eden deliberated the feasibility and advisability of unseating Churchill in 1942. Yet the pair managed to conduct a vigorous and ultimately successful wartime government, and Churchill praised Eden as his great support and "mainstay."

Eden, like Churchill, became a victim of the defeat of the Conservative government at the end of the war, but, on October 27, 1951, after Churchill and the Conservatives were returned, Eden was again appointed foreign secretary and was explicitly designated deputy prime minister. Despite his own serious illness, he succeeded Churchill as prime minister on April 6, 1955, resigning on January 9, 1957, amid the scandal of the Suez crisis but citing ill health as his reason.

Further reading: Carlton, David. *Anthony Eden: A Biography.* New York: Viking, 1981; Dutton, David. *Anthony Eden: A Life and Reputation.* London: Arnold Publishers, 1997; Rhodes, James Robert. *Anthony Eden: A Biography.* New York: McGraw-Hill, 1987; Rothwell, Victor. *Anthony Eden: A Political Biography, 1931–57.* London: Palgrave Macmillan, 1992.

Egypt, action in

Egypt was not a part of the British Empire during World War II, but it was only nominally independent of British control. By the terms of the 1936 Anglo-Egyptian Treaty, Britain claimed the right to defend the Suez Canal, a lifeline to the Far Eastern reaches of the British Empire, and the Egyptian government, in time of emergency, was obliged to give British forces control of virtually everything of military value in Egypt. Thus, Egypt was, in effect, occupied by British forces throughout the war, and its capital, Cairo, served as the headquarters for the British Middle East Command. Despite all this, Egypt's King Farouk and his prime minister, Ali Mahir, were solidly anti-British and at least mildly profascist. While they did not actively oppose the British, neither did they cooperate wholeheartedly in arresting German and Italian nationals (though these were ultimately rounded up). British pressure forced Farouk to remove Ali Mahir in June 1940, but when Italian troops invaded Egypt on September 17, 1940, at the start of the WESTERN DESERT CAMPAIGNS, Farouk violated his pledge to declare war on Italy in the event of an invasion. Instead, he held his kingdom in a state of nonbelligerency. It was left to British forces alone to drive the invaders out, which they did by June 1941.

Prime Minister Ali Mahir was replaced by Hasan Sabri, who continued to walk a fine line between nonbelligerency and the demands of the British occupiers. He died in November 1940 and was replaced by Husayn Sirry, under whom economic conditions in Egypt precipitously deteriorated. Food shortages were rampant, rationing programs failed, and Egypt was near revolt. In the meantime, the British forced Farouk to sever diplomatic relations with the VICHY GOVERNMENT, even as Axis forces closed in on the borders of Egypt. Large numbers of Egyptians, hungry and desperate, began to see in the approach of the Germans and Italians the possibility of deliverance. This prompted Sirry to resign, whereupon the British, fearful of losing the Egyptian populace to the Axis cause, demanded that Farouk name the frankly pro-British Mustafa al-Nahhas to step in and form a new government. When Farouk declined to act, the British demanded his abdication, backing up this demand with a show of force. Farouk yielded, and al-Nahhas came to power. He readily cooperated with British authorities to suppress pro-Axis activity in Cairo and elsewhere, even as ERWIN ROMMEL and his panzers crossed into Egyptian territory in 1942.

Despite the ascension of al-Nahhas, a large portion of the Egyptian population and a majority faction of the Egyptian Army remained not only anti-British but vocally pro-Axis. Fortunately, the second of the two BATTLES OF EL ALAMEIN was fought and won in November 1942, driving Rommel out of Egypt. As it became apparent that Egypt would no longer be a combat theater, relations between Britain and Egypt improved. Britain, its attention now turned to other theaters of the war, suspended its active support of al-Nahhas, whom Farouk replaced with Ahmad Mahir. Early in 1945, when the defeat of the remaining Axis powers, Germany and Japan, seemed inevitable, Mahir obtained the approval of the Egyptian parliament to declare war on these nations. Mahir was assassinated before the declaration was formalized, but it was nevertheless made on February 26, and by this means Egypt secured a place among the founders of the UNITED NATIONS. To have declared war earlier, during the Axis invasion, would have represented for Farouk capitulation to the British. Now that the Axis had been all but defeated, the declaration was actually an assertion and proclamation of national sovereignty.

Further reading: Marlow, John. *A History of Modern Egypt and Anglo-Egyptian Relations, 1800–1956.* Ann Arbor: University Microfilms International, 1981; McLeave, Hugh. *The Last Pharaoh: Farouk of Egypt.* New York: McCall, 1970; Stadiem, William. *Too Rich: The High Life and Tragic Death of King Farouk.* New York: Carroll & Graf, 1991.

Eichelberger, Robert Lawrence
(1886–1961) *U.S. field commander under Douglas MacArthur*

Serving under General DOUGLAS MACARTHUR, Robert Eichelberger led important operations against the Japanese in the jungles of the Pacific islands, including the make-or-break BATTLE OF BUNA during the NEW GUINEA CAMPAIGN. Born in Urbana, Ohio, Eichelberger enrolled at Ohio State University, studying there from 1903 to 1905 until he received an appointment to West Point. After graduating from the military academy in 1909, he was commissioned in the infantry, gaining promotion to first lieutenant in 1915 and captain in 1917. After the United States entered World War I, Eichelberger was not sent to France but was instead posted in the South and Southwest, assigned to training and staff missions. He performed exceptionally and received a promotion to temporary major and an appointment as assistant chief of staff to General William Graves's Siberian Expeditionary Force in August 1918, an arduous assignment that earned him promotion to temporary lieutenant colonel in 1919.

Beginning in 1921, Eichelberger served in the Pacific and was posted to the Philippines and Tientsin (Tianjin), China. In 1921, he was also promoted to the regular rank of major and attached to the military intelligence division of the general staff. In 1924, he was reassigned to the Command and General Staff School, Fort Leavenworth. After graduating in 1926, Eichelberger remained at Fort Leavenworth as a staff officer. He enrolled in the Army War College in 1929, graduating in 1930, then transferred to West Point as adjutant and secretary, serving in these capacities from 1931 to 1935.

Promoted to lieutenant colonel in 1934, Eichelberger was appointed secretary to the general staff in 1936. He served until 1938, when he was promoted to full colonel, and assigned command of the 30th Infantry at San Francisco. Two years later, he was promoted to the temporary rank of brigadier general and appointed superintendent of West Point. In March 1942, after U.S. entry into World War II, Eichelberger was promoted to temporary major general and assigned to command 77th Infantry Division. He then briefly commanded XI Corps, then I Corps, which was assembling in Australia for action against the Japanese. By September, I Corps was ready for combat, and Eichelberger led his troops into New Guinea at the beginning of the Allies' "island hopping" campaign against the forces of the Japanese empire. Promoted to temporary lieutenant general in October, he won a major and remarkable victory against a deeply fortified position at Buna after a hard-fought battle spanning November 20, 1942 to January 22, 1943. General MacArthur's orders to him had been to take Buna or "not come back alive." Eichelberger understood that MacArthur was in earnest.

After the victory at Buna, Eichelberger continued to command operations in the New Guinea campaign and the Battle of New Britain from January 1943 through July 1944. In September 1944, Eichelberger was made commander of the Eighth U.S. Army, which he led in its landing on Leyte Island in the Philippines, behind the Sixth U.S. Army. Eichelberger then directed operations on Luzon during January–April 1945, retaking Clark Field from the Japanese in February and, during February–March, liberating Manila. After this, he directed the liberation of the Visayas and the southern islands, including Mindanao (mission accomplished by August 15, 1945; *see* PHILIPPINES).

In July, MacArthur put Eichelberger in charge of LL Philippines operations, and on August 30, after the Japanese surrender, Eichelberger moved to Atsugi airfield, where he began preparations for the military occupation of Japan. By January 1946, he had completed the move to the Japanese mainland with his Eighth U.S. Army, which assumed responsibility for all ground forces in the nation of the defeated enemy.

Eichelberger returned to the United States in September 1948 and, in 1950, published a memoir entitled *Our Jungle Road to Tokyo*. He retired in July 1954 with the rank of general. That he never achieved the fame of many other major field commanders is something of a puzzle, since Eichelberger was a brilliant master of the tactics of jungle warfare in mountainous terrain, and the operations he led were certainly critical to the success of the island-hopping campaign.

See also LEYTE, BATTLE OF.

Further reading: Chwialkowski, Paul. *In Caesar's Shadow: The Life of General Robert Eichelberger.* Westport, Conn.: Greenwood Press, 1993; Eichelberger, Rob- ert L. *Dear Miss Em: General Eichelberger's War in the Pacific, 1942–1945.* Westport, Conn.: Greenwood Press, 1972; Eichelberger, Robert L. *Our Jungle Road to Tokyo.* New York: Viking Press, 1950; Shortal, John F. *Forged by Fire: Robert L. Eichelberger and the Pacific War.* Columbia: University of South Carolina Press, 1987.

Eichmann, Adolf (1906–1962) *SS officer instrumental in perpetrating the Holocaust*

A lieutenant colonel in the SCHUTZSTAFFEL (SS) and chief of the Jewish Office of the GESTAPO, Adolf Eichmann implemented the FINAL SOLUTION, the total extermination of European Jewry that was the HOLOCAUST. Eichmann was born in Solingen but grew up in Linz, Austria, to which his family moved. He aspired to the profession of engineering but failed in his course work toward that end. He then enlisted as a common laborer in his father's modest mining enterprise. He moved up to a sales position with an Austrian electrical contractor, then became a traveling salesman for the Vacuum Oil Company during 1927–33. He joined the Austrian Nazi Party on April 1, 1932, and when he lost his sales job in July 1933, he emigrated to Bavaria, where, like many other unemployed and disaffected young men, he became involved in a paramilitary political organization, joining the expatriate Austrian Legion. This gave Eichmann 14 months of military training, which stood him in good stead, in September 1934, when he applied for membership in the SICHERHEITSDIENST (SD), the security service headed by HEINRICH HIMMLER. Himmler assigned Eichmann to investigate "Jewish questions," and Eichmann responded by throwing himself zealously into his subject. He gained an elementary knowledge of Hebrew and Yiddish, and, to investigate the Zionist movement firsthand, visited Palestine in 1937. At this point, he may have been considering the possibility of encouraging or forcing German Jews to emigrate to Palestine.

On the eve of the ANSCHLUSS with Austria, Himmler appointed Eichmann assistant to the SD leader of the SS Main Region, Danube. Eichmann was sent to Vienna as an agent of the Gestapo to help prepare the ground for the *Anschluss*. From August 1938, he headed the Office for Jewish Emigration in Vienna, the Nazi agency authorized to issue exit permits for Jews from Austria. Later, Eichmann also handled such exit permits for Czechoslovakia and Germany itself. Eichmann became an authority on and highly efficient agent of forced emigration, in the space of 18 months sending some 150,000 Jews out of Austria. Soon, Eichmann's duties made a transition from forced emigration to forced evacuation: deportation to concentration camps.

In December 1939, Eichmann was transferred to a Gestapo office dedicated to implementing "Referat IV B4," the regulations dealing with Jewish affairs and evacuation. For the next six years, this office, headed by Eichmann, was the center for the implementation of the Final Solution. By the summer of 1941, this came to mean the creation of death camps, the development of mass execution techniques, and the organization of mass convoys that took Jews to their deaths.

The Wannsee Conference of January 20, 1942 confirmed Eichmann's role as the Jewish specialist of the Gestapo, and the master architect of the Final Solution, Reinhard Heydrich, formally assigned Eichmann to implement the Holocaust on a universal scale. In contrast to many in the Nazi hierarchy, Eichmann had no particular hatred of Jews, nor even an ideological bias against them. He was a bureaucrat, and there was nothing personal or even emotional about the mass murders he orchestrated. His objective was to accomplish the mission assigned to him. He never railed against Jews but reserved his complaints for various logistical obstacles that threatened to interfere with his schedules and quotas. He was interested only in production, the production of death on a mass scale. And, toward the end of the war, when no less a figure than Heinrich Himmler issued a "no gassing" order, presumably hoping to ameliorate what he must have perceived as the prospect of postwar charges of war crimes, Eichmann, determined to maintain "production," ignored the order.

Yet, except briefly in Hungary, Eichmann kept a low profile, and he was not widely recognized after the war. The Allies arrested him, but he was not particularly notorious. He was kept under such loose guard that he escaped from a U.S. internment camp in 1946. He fled to Argentina, where he lived quietly until May 2, 1960, when Israeli secret agents tracked him down. He had been living under an assumed name in a Buenos Aires suburb. Bypassing official—and notoriously obstructionist—Argentine channels, the agents abducted Eichmann and spirited him off to Israel. There he was arraigned and publicly tried during April 2–August 14, 1961. Found guilty of crimes against the Jewish people and crimes against humanity, he was sentenced to death on December 2, 1961, and executed at Ramleh Prison on May 31, 1962.

Further reading: Aharoni, Zvi, and Wilhelm Dietl. *Operation Eichmann: The Truth about the Pursuit, Capture and Trial.* New York: Wiley, 1997; Arendt, Hannah. *Eichmann in Jerusalem: A Report on the Banality of Evil.* New York: Penguin, 1994; Lang, Jochen von, and Claus Sibyll, eds. *Eichmann Interrogated: Transcripts from the Archives of the Israeli Police.* New York: Da Capo, 1999; Sachs, Ruth. *Adolf Eichmann: Engineer of Death.* New York: Rosen Publishing Group, 2001.

Einstein, Albert (1879–1955) *world famous and highly influential expatriate German scientist*

The most famous scientist of his time and the most important physicist since Isaac Newton, Albert Einstein created the simple equation, $E = mc^2$ that not only demonstrated the equivalence of matter and energy, but showed the tremendous quantity of energy inherent in the atomic nucleus. The insight, provided mainly by Leo Szilard, that such energy might be liberated was the theoretical basis for the atomic bomb. While Einstein did not participate directly in the war effort, the letter Szilard persuaded him to compose and send to President Franklin D. Roosevelt on August 2, 1939, prompted Roosevelt to authorize what quickly became the Manhattan Project, the all-out

American effort to create an atomic weapon before the Axis powers (especially Germany) could do the same.

Einstein was born in Ulm, Germany, in 1879 and moved with his family the following year to Munich. Young Einstein did not respond well to the strict and unimaginative German schools, but fared better in Swiss schools. He graduated in physics and mathematics from the Federal Polytechnic Academy in Zürich in 1900. He became a Swiss citizen, taught mathematics very briefly, then worked as a patents examiner in Bern. In 1905, Einstein published "A New Determination of Molecular Dimensions," which earned him a Ph.D. from the University of Zürich. This same year saw the publication of papers including "On a Heuristic Viewpoint Concerning the Production and Transformation of Light," which formed the basis for quantum theory; "On the Electrodynamics of Moving Bodies," which postulated the epoch-making special theory of relativity; and "Does the Inertia of a Body Depend Upon Its Energy Content?" which established the equivalence of mass and energy, expressing this in the equation $E = mc^2$.

Einstein was catapulted to prominence among physicists and became in 1912 a professor at the Polytechnic in Zürich. In 1914, Einstein became associated with the Prussian Academy of Sciences and lectured at the University of Berlin. He published "Foundation of the General Theory of Relativity" in 1916, arguing that gravitation is not a force, as Newton held, but a curved field in what Einstein called the space-time continuum.

While Einstein was revolutionizing the field of physics, he was also becoming a social and political activist, with an increasing commitment to pacifism, and he used his growing international fame as a scientist to publicize his social and political views. A Jew, Einstein toured the United States in spring 1921 to raise money for the Zionist Palestine Foundation Fund. He was treated as a great celebrity in the United States and conceived an affection for the country. This same year, he was awarded the Nobel Prize for Physics. Yet the heyday of Einstein's theoretical innovations was over. During the later 1920s and 1930s, he devoted as much time to the cause of

pacifism as he did to science. In 1933, after ADOLF HITLER became chancellor, Einstein left Germany and accepted appointment to the faculty of the Institute for Advanced Study in Princeton, New Jersey. He lived in Princeton for the next two decades.

In 1939, the great Danish physicist Niels Bohr told Einstein that the German physicist Lise Meitner had split the uranium atom, resulting in the conversion of its mass into energy. It was a practical demonstration of Einstein's 1905 theory. Bohr shared with Einstein his speculation that a controlled chain reaction splitting of uranium atoms could produce an explosion far greater than any conventional chemical explosive could create. The Hungarian expatriate physicist Leo Szilard, coming to this same conclusion and fearing that German scientists would produce a nuclear weapon for Hitler, persuaded Einstein to write a letter to President Franklin D. Roosevelt urging "watchfulness and, if necessary, quick action on the part of the Administration." Einstein wrote:

> In the course of the last four months it has been made probable—through the work of Joliot in France as well as Fermi and Szilard in America—that it may become possible to set up a nuclear chain reaction in a large mass of uranium, by which vast amounts of power and large quantities of new radium-like elements would be generated. Now it appears almost certain that this could be achieved in the immediate future.
>
> This new phenomena would also lead to the construction of bombs, and it is conceivable—though much less certain—that extremely powerful bombs of a new type may thus be constructed.

Einstein suggested that the president "may think it desirable to have some permanent contact maintained between the administration and the group of physicists working on chain reactions in America," and he concluded the letter on an ominous note: "I understand that Germany has actually stopped the sale of uranium from the Czechoslovakian mines which she has taken over. That she should have taken such an early action might perhaps be understood on the ground that the son of the German

Under-Secretary of State, von Weizsacker, is attached to the Kaiser-Wilhelm-Institute in Berlin where some of the American work on uranium is now being repeated." Such was Einstein's prestige that Roosevelt almost immediately authorized what soon became the Manhattan Project.

Einstein played no actual role in the creation of the atomic bomb, but his letter provided the impetus for the undertaking. After its use on Hiroshima and Nagasaki, Einstein became an eloquent voice in the quest for ways to prevent any future use of atomic weapons. He was listened to politely but largely ignored by statesmen and politicians.

Further reading: Brian, Denis. *Einstein: A Life.* New York: Wiley, 1996; Folsing, Albrech. *Albert Einstein: A Biography.* New York: Penguin, 1998; Rhodes, Richard. *The Making of the Atomic Bomb.* New York: Simon & Schuster, 1986.

Eisenhower, Dwight D. (1890–1969)
Supreme Allied Commander, Europe

Dwight D. Eisenhower was a career U.S. Army officer who desperately wanted to lead men into combat but who was destined to become a staff officer, whose strategic, logistical, and managerial aptitude caused his rapid elevation, during World War II, to the position of Supreme Allied Commander, Europe. "Ike" Eisenhower was born in Denison, Texas, and raised in Abilene, Kansas. Enrolled in West Point, he graduated in 1915 roughly in the middle of his class. When the United States entered World War I in April 1917, Eisenhower was not sent to France but was given command of a variety of stateside training missions. He quickly proved himself an extraordinarily efficient administrator and staff officer who worked very well with others and who was especially skilled at managing diverse and discordant personalities. By 1920, Eisenhower had achieved promotion to major, a rapid rise unusual for an officer who had not seen combat duty and downright exceptional in the peacetime army.

In 1922, Eisenhower was posted to Panama, returning to the United States two years later to attend the Command and General Staff School, from which he graduated at the top of his class in 1926. Clearly being groomed for high command, he graduated two years later from the Army War College. From 1933 to 1935, Eisenhower served under General DOUGLAS MACARTHUR as his chief of staff. Although Eisenhower admired MacArthur, he was disturbed by the overbearing personality and flamboyance of his boss, and it was with some degree of reluctance that he accompanied MacArthur to the Philippines, where MacArthur took charge of building—on a shoestring—an army for the defense of the islands. In 1939, Eisenhower secured MacArthur's approval to return to the United States and what he hoped would be at long last a field command. Indeed, Eisenhower's performance in massive prewar maneuvers during the summer of 1941 earned him widespread notice as well as a promotion to temporary brigadier general in September 1941. A field command was briefly

Dwight David Eisenhower *(Dwight D. Eisenhower Presidential Library)*

his, but when the United States entered World War II following the BATTLE OF PEARL HARBOR, he was recalled to Washington, D.C., as assistant chief of the Army War Plans Division under Army Chief of Staff GEORGE C. MARSHALL.

From December 1941 to June 1942, Eisenhower, who was junior to nearly 400 other U.S. Army officers, was a key figure in planning overall U.S. strategy in the war. He was promoted to major general in April 1942 and was named to command the European theater of operations (ETO) on June 25, a promotion not only extraordinary because it was, again, over the heads of more senior commanders, but also because Eisenhower had yet to see any combat in his career. What Marshall and others recognized in Eisenhower, however, was his mastery of "big picture" strategy combined with administrative talent and a high degree of leadership skill. Not least among Ike's qualities was the aura of confidence and openness he projected. This would prove invaluable not only in leading American troops, but in working with Allied commanders at the highest level. Eisenhower's genius for juggling jarring egos and inducing diverse commanders to work well together would become increasingly evident. He recognized, without prejudice, where individual strengths and weaknesses lay, and he integrated operations in ways that maximized strengths while compensating for weaknesses.

Eisenhower served as Allied commander for OPERATION TORCH, the invasion of French North Africa, in November 1942, then directed the invasion and conquest of Tunisia from November 17, 1942, to May 13, 1943. Leading green American troops in the opening phases of the NORTH AFRICAN CAMPAIGNS proved heartbreakingly difficult, and Eisenhower made a number of missteps and at least one highly controversial decision, his agreement to allow the VICHY GOVERNMENT'S admiral JEAN-FRANÇOIS DARLAN to retain nominal control of French forces in North Africa. But he learned from his mistakes, and both Marshall and President FRANKLIN D. ROOSEVELT backed him up on the Darlan decision. Ultimately, the North African Campaigns were successful, the

American forces were forged into an effective army, and Eisenhower went on to lead the next phase of Allied operations in Europe, the invasion of SICILY during July 9–August 17, 1943, followed by the ITALIAN CAMPAIGN, which got underway during September 3–October 8. In these operations, he had overall command of all Allied forces, American and British.

After the landings in Italy, Eisenhower transferred his headquarters to London, where he took charge of plans for the principal Allied invasion of Europe, OPERATION OVERLORD, the NORMANDY LANDINGS (D-DAY). For this, the climactic operation of the war in Europe, the largest, most ambitious amphibious operation ever attempted, and the operation on which the future freedom of much of the world quite literally depended, Eisenhower was appointed Supreme Commander of the Allied Expeditionary Force.

The Normandy landings took place on June 6, 1944, after which Eisenhower assumed overall command of the advance across France, which spanned July 25 through September 14. In December 1944, Eisenhower was promoted to general of the army, a five-star rank last held only by John J. Pershing, and continued to lead the masterly orchestration of titanic and disparate forces. He was a commander of commanders, his subordinates including such larger-than-life figures as OMAR BRADLEY and GEORGE S. PATTON as well as Britain's BERNARD LAW MONTGOMERY and Free France's CHARLES DE GAULLE. By continually reconciling the often differing agendas of the Allies, including the Soviet Union, Eisenhower maintained the greatest and perhaps the most difficult military alliance in history.

While Eisenhower directed a generally rapid progress through France and beyond, he responded with resourcefulness and flexibility to the stunning German counteroffensive in the ARDENNES from December 16, 1944, to January 19, 1945, which threatened to drive a wedge between British and American advancing units. Although Bradley and some others protested that the offensive was merely a feint, Eisenhower ordered the vastly outnumbered 101st Airborne Division to hold the key Belgian village of Bastogne while he directed Patton's Third Army to march to the relief of the 101st Airborne. Thanks in large part to Eisenhower's alert resolve and his refusal to succumb to what he called "victory fever," the final German offensive of the war was crushed, and the Allied advance resumed even more rapidly than before.

Eisenhower pushed his forces into Germany during March 28–May 8, then made the courageous but controversial political and strategic decision to relinquish occupation of eastern Germany and Berlin to the Soviet troops of the Red Army, while the Western allies shifted south to Bavaria to counter expected pockets of Nazi diehards. Eisenhower's decision was based partly on military considerations and partly on diplomatic ones. His objective was to destroy the German Army, not to capture German cities. He judged too high the cost of taking Berlin, and he did not want to risk letting any sizeable fraction of the German Army escape intact. Diplomatically, his decision reflected agreements made at the YALTA Conference, which included reserving Berlin for the Red Army.

After the unconditional surrender of Germany on May 7–8, 1945, Eisenhower continued to command Allied occupation forces until November, when he returned to the United States, received a hero's welcome, and replaced Marshall as army chief of staff, serving in this position from November 1945 to February 1948. Eisenhower retired from the army in February 1948 and accepted the office of president of Columbia University, serving for two years during a time in which the great university expanded and grew in prestige. In December 1950, as the cold war heated up, President HARRY S. TRUMAN recalled Eisenhower to active duty as Supreme Allied Commander Europe (SACEUR) and commander of NATO forces. Two years later, Eisenhower again retired from the army, this time to run for president on the Republican ticket. The enormously popular Ike was elected to two terms (1953–61), after which he retired to his home in Gettysburg, Pennsylvania.

Further reading: Chandler, Alfred D., Jr. *The Papers of Dwight David Eisenhower: The War Years*, 5 vols. Bal-

timore: Johns Hopkins University Press, 1970; D'Este, Carlo. *Eisenhower: A Soldier's Life.* New York: Henry Holt, 2002; Eisenhower, Dwight D. *Crusade in Europe.* Baltimore: Johns Hopkins University Press, 1997; Eisenhower, John S. D. *General Ike: A Personal Reminiscence.* New York: Free Press, 2003; Perret, Geoffrey. *Eisenhower.* Avon, Mass.: Adams Media, 1999.

embargo, U.S., on Japan

Histories of World War II and the months leading up to the Japanese attack on PEARL HARBOR frequently mention the deterioration of Japanese-American relations exacerbated by the U.S. embargo on Japan. Trade pressure was indeed used by the administration of FRANKLIN D. ROOSEVELT as an economic alternative to war to compel Japan to cease its aggression against China. Economic sanctions were part of a larger American diplomatic offensive against Japan that had been under way since the early 1930s.

Throughout the decade, the U.S. government consistently protested against Japanese actions in China, which violated treaties and international law. Yet, in a climate dominated by isolationism, the Roosevelt administration was unwilling to provoke armed hostilities with Japan. Economic pressure was frequently considered an alternative to war. However, many in the government and the military believed that a policy of imposing embargoes upon strategic exports to Japan—the raw materials Japan needed to continue its war against China—was not so much an alternative to war as it was a provocation. As the decade drew to a close, the issue of Japanese aggression became increasingly critical and, with the outbreak in 1939 of war in Europe, the fall in June 1940 of France, and the conclusion in September 1940 of the AXIS (TRIPARTITE) PACT, Japan had clearly become a direct threat to the United States.

In view of America's relative unpreparedness for war, especially a two-front war, the government grew increasingly wary of applying frankly provocative economic sanctions, desirable as it might be to cut off essential materials to the aggressor. As an alternative to outright embargo, there developed the policy of "moral embargo." On June 11, 1938, Secretary of State CORDELL HULL condemned not only Japan's aggression against China, especially the bombing of civilian targets, but also what he called the "material encouragement" of Japanese aggression. On July 1, 1938, the Department of State notified U.S. aircraft manufacturers and exporters that the government was strongly opposed to the sale of airplanes and aeronautical equipment to countries whose armed forces were using airplanes to attack civilian populations. This communication did not carry the force of law but was a moral embargo, and in 1939 it was extended to raw materials essential to airplane manufacture as well as to plans, plants, and technical information for the production of aviation gasoline. Manufacturers and suppliers generally fell into line with the moral embargo, resulting in the effective suspension of the export to Japan of aircraft, aeronautical equipment, and other materials. In addition to the moral embargo on war materiel, the U.S. government began informally discouraging the extension of credit by U.S. banks to Japan.

By the end of 1938, interference with the rights and interests of the United States and its nationals by Japanese or Japanese-sponsored agents in China became increasingly frequent, prompting a formal protest from the United States on December 31, 1938. As evidence accumulated of endangerment of American lives, the destruction of American property, and the violation of American rights and interests by Japanese authorities or Japanese-sponsored agents in China, the Roosevelt administration reconsidered formal commercial retaliation against Japan. It was decided that the 1911 commercial treaty between the United States and Japan no longer afforded adequate protection to American commerce either in Japan or in Japanese-occupied portions of China, while at the same time the operation of the most-favored-nation clause of the treaty barred retaliatory measures against Japanese commerce. Therefore, in July 1939, the administration served notice on Japan of the termination of the treaty at the end of the six-month period prescribed by the treaty. This removed, under international law, the legal obstacle to an embargo by the United States.

During 1939 and 1940, Japan and the United States conducted high-level conferences in an effort to resolve the deterioration of relations between the nations without contributing to the further conquest of China or endangering the United States. On the eve of the fall of France, Japanese authorities began to exert pressure on French Indochina, demanding under threat of force the conclusion of an agreement to provide for Japan's use three airfields and for the transit, in case of operations against China, of Japanese troops. Although the agreement was duly concluded, Japanese forces attacked Indochina and occupied several strategic points. Secretary of State Hull protested. Shortly thereafter, however, on September 27, 1940, the announcement was made of the conclusion of the Axis Treaty among Germany, Italy, and Japan.

During this period of ever-increasing Japanese aggression, the tempo of U.S. rearmament had also accelerated and required more and more available strategic materials. As a result, U.S. exports were formally limited by measures either legislative or administrative. This resulted in a further and steady decline of export to Japan of strategic materials. The Export Control Act of July 2, 1940, authorized the president, in the interest of national defense, to prohibit or curtail the export of basic war materiel. Beginning in August 1940, pursuant to the act, licenses were refused for the export to Japan of aviation gasoline and most types of machine tools. In September, the government announced that the export of iron and steel scrap would be prohibited, provoking a formal Japanese protest on October 8, 1940, which categorized the prohibition as an "unfriendly act." In view of Japanese aggression, Secretary Hull rejected this interpretation, and, despite Japanese protest, a total embargo on the export of iron and steel scrap to destinations other than countries of the Western Hemisphere and Great Britain went into effect on October 16, 1940. By the winter of 1940–41, shipment to Japan of most strategic commodities, including arms, ammunition, implements of war, aviation gasoline and many other petroleum products, machine tools, scrap iron, pig iron, iron and steel manufactures, copper, lead, zinc, aluminum, and other commodities important to any war effort, had completely ceased.

This was the U.S. embargo against Japan. It did not, of course, deter Japanese aggression but, rather, solidified the intention of Japanese militarists to seize raw materials and other resources in Asia and the Pacific and, by means of war, to force U.S. acquiescence in this policy. In the face of continued aggressive expansion in the East, President Roosevelt stepped beyond embargo by issuing an executive order on July 26, 1941, freezing Japanese assets in the United States. The order thus brought under government control all financial and import and export trade transactions in which Japanese interests were involved. With this, trade between the United States and Japan ended, and, although discussions continued at a fevered pitch, war became increasingly inevitable.

See also SINO-JAPANESE WAR.

Further reading: Toland, John. *The Rising Sun: The Decline and Fall of the Japanese Empire, 1936–1945.* New York: Random House, 2003; United States Department of State. *Peace and War: United States Foreign Policy 1931–1941.* Washington, D.C.: United States Government Printing Office, 1943; Worth, Roland H., Jr. *No Choice but War: The United States Embargo Against Japan and the Eruption of War in the Pacific.* Jefferson, N.C.: McFarland, 1995.

Enigma cipher and machine

Enigma was the name of an electromechanical cipher encryption and decryption machine used by the WEHRMACHT, the Luftwaffe, the German Navy, the Abwehr (German secret service), and the SCHUTZSTAFFEL (SS), as well as the German state railway system during World War II. The original basic design had been patented in 1919 by H. A. Koch, a Dutch inventor, and was modified and refined by a German engineer, Arthur Scherbius, in 1923. The German Army and Navy bought all rights to the machine from Scherbius in 1929, and

Workers at Bletchley Park, the British codebreaking laboratory outside of London, tend to one of the early computers used to decrypt Enigma intercepts. *(British War Museum)*

by the outbreak of World War II, all the services mentioned were using various versions of it.

At the time of its invention, development, and use, the Enigma was the most complex encryption-decryption device in use by any nation. The basic Engima machine (and there were a number of more sophisticated variants) resembled a typewriter, but, in addition to a keyboard and type keys, it had a plug board, a light board, and a set of three rotors and half rotors (called "reflectors"). The rotors could be set independently to create a library of 16,900 (26 H 25 H 26) substitution alphabets, so that as long as the message was not longer than 16,900 characters, there would be no repeated use of a substitution alphabet within any given message. Since repetition is the traditional key by which codes are broken, it seemed to the Germans that the Enigma ciphers were inherently unbreakable. Moreover, the Enigma machine added additional complications. The sequence of alphabets used was different if the rotors were started in position ABC, as opposed to ACB; there was a rotating ring on each rotor that could be set in a different position. Additionally, the starting position of each rotor itself was variable. The military version of the Enigma added yet another device, a *Stecker,* or electric plugboard, by which some key assignments (depending on the model) could be changed. Thus, even the most basic three-wheel Enigma with six plug connections generated 3,283,883,513,796,974, 198,700,882,069,882,752,878,379,955, 261, 095, 623, 685,444,055,315,226,006, 433,616,627,409,666,933, 182,371,154,802,769,920,000, 000,000 coding positions—a staggering number. Of course, complex encryption is useless if it cannot be readily decrypted by the intended recipient. The genius of the Enigma machine was that its complex combination key could be communicated to a recipient by supplying just a few values: what rotors to use, the rotor order, the ring positions (within the rotors), the starting positions of each rotor, and the plugboard settings. The Germans were so confident of the Engima that it was used by every military echelon, from high command to tactical units, including aircraft, tanks, surface ships, and submarines.

Impressed by numbers, what German cryptologists neglected to consider was that no matter how complex a coding system may be, the underlying alphabet is simple and consists of only 26 letters, some of which are used very rarely. Moreover, the fact that although the Enigma gave the impression of bewildering randomness, it was grounded in one absolute principle: No letter could stand for itself. This immediately provided a basic key for code breakers. Finally, another Achilles' heel was the absence of numbers. Engima ciphers were alphabetical, not alphanumeric. Numbers had to be spelled out. This provided yet another key, since the spelling of numbers was easily inferred from a few clues. Finally, the Germans had not counted on a final weakness of any machine-generated code: the possibility that it could be broken by another machine.

The fact was that as early as 1932, Polish cryptologists were reading some Enigma traffic, and on the eve of the war, in mid-1939, the Poles passed much of their knowledge to the French and the British. This became the basis of work done by ALAN TURING and others at Bletchley Park, the British center of cryptanalysis, which yielded the ULTRA intelligence, a great boon to the Allied war effort.

See also ESPIONAGE AND COUNTERESPIONAGE.

Further reading: Hodges, Alan. *Alan Turing: The Enigma.* New York: Walker, 2000; Kozaczuk, Wladyslaw, and Jerzy Straszak. *Enigma: How the Poles Broke the Nazi Code.* London: Hippocrene, 2004; Sebag-Montefiore, Hugh. *Enigma: The Battle for the Code.* New York: Wiley, 2001.

Photograph of a "Type B" Enigma machine *(U.S. Army Signal Corps)*

Eniwetok Atoll, Battle of

Eniwetok Atoll is located in the Marshall Islands in the Pacific. Here, on February 17, 1944, five battalions of U.S. marines and army infantry landed as part of a mop-up mission following the main battles of the MARSHALL ISLANDS CAMPAIGN. The three principal islands of the atoll, Engebi, Parry, and Eniwetok, were held by a garrison of some 3,500 Japanese. The marines and army infantry attacked and took each in succession while carrier-based aircraft made a diversionary raid on Truk Island to prevent the Japanese from launching aircraft against the landings.

Possession of Eniwetok gave the Americans a major naval anchorage and staging area for ongoing amphibious operations. It also further isolated Japanese-held islands passed over in the American "island-hopping" campaign throughout the Pacific. Without a foothold in the atoll, there was no hope of reinforcing any of these islands, including WAKE ISLAND, which the Japanese had taken at the start of the war.

Further reading: Rottman, Gordon L., and Howard Gerrard. *The Marshall Islands 1944: Operation Flintlock, the Capture of Kwajalein and Eniwetok.* London: Osprey, 2004.

espionage and counterespionage

In no previous war was intelligence, which is built in large part on espionage and defended by counterespionage, more important than in World War II. All the major combatants developed and operated significant espionage and counterespionage agencies, and the RESISTANCE MOVEMENTS within virtually all the nations occupied by the Axis had espionage as their principal activity.

ALLIED ESPIONAGE AND COUNTERESPIONAGE AGENCIES

Allied Intelligence Bureau (AIB). Established in the Southwest Pacific by Supreme Allied Commander, Pacific General DOUGLAS MACARTHUR, AIB united Australian and American intelligence officers, who coordinated the efforts not only of military intelligence and reconnaissance, but also of indigenous observers and spies. MacArthur took a hands-on approach to this bureau, preferring to rely on it rather than on intelligence supplied by Washington or even by the U.S. Navy assets in his area. AIB played a key role in the execution of MacArthur's "island-hopping" strategy, whereby Japanese-held islands were attacked selectively and others, cut off from reinforcement and resupply, left to languish. MacArthur used AIB to identify Japanese vulnerabilities and thinly held territories, against which he leveled attacks.

Bureau Central de Renseignements et d'Action (BCRA). Established by Free French leader CHARLES DE GAULLE in London (his headquarters

in exile), BCRA operated as his liaison with the French resistance and to coordinate resistance activities with those of British agents. In addition, BCRA compiled dossiers on thousands of French citizens in an effort to identify those who could be counted on to support a Free French provisional government and those who would likely oppose it when de Gaulle returned to France. The objective was to enable the rapid creation of a new government with Charles de Gaulle as its leader.

Cambridge Spy Ring. While the focus of most World War II espionage was, naturally, conducted by the Allies against the Axis and vice versa, Soviet spymasters recruited Britons at Cambridge University to spy for the USSR. Ostensibly, the motive was to promote fuller understanding between the Western Allies and the Soviets, but, in fact, the espionage was part of JOSEPH STALIN's attempt to maneuver his nation to a more advantageous postwar situation. The Cambridge Spy Ring penetrated deeply into the British as well as U.S. intelligence communities, producing such spies as Harold "Kim" Philby, Donald Maclean, John Carincross, Guy Burgess, and Anthony Blunt, known as the "Magnificent Five." Only after the war was the ring uncovered. By that time, Philby, Maclean, and Burgess had defected to the Soviet Union. Blunt, who held the government position of keeper of the queen's art treasures, was not exposed until the 1980s.

Coastwatchers. MacArthur organized throughout the South Pacific an indigenous spy network made up of missionaries and planters as well as government workers who, at great peril to themselves, observed Japanese troop movements and sent regular radio reports to Allied headquarters in Australia. The coastwatchers were also vital in rescuing downed U.S. airmen and stranded U.S. sailors, including, most famously, John F. Kennedy and the survivors of his PT-109, which had been cut in two by a Japanese destroyer in 1943.

Detachment 101. Operated by the Office of Strategic Services (OSS), Detachment 101 worked deep behind Japanese lines in Burma and collaborated with Kachin tribespeople in Burma to sabotage bridges and railways and disrupt Japanese lines of communication. The unit also rescued downed Allied aviators.

Federal Bureau of Investigation (FBI). In peacetime, the FBI had served primarily as a police agency for the enforcement of federal criminal statutes and the apprehension of federal felons. During World War II, the bureau became the central U.S. agency responsible for internal security and conducted surveillance of suspected spies and enemy aliens as well as operations to apprehend spies working in the United States.

GRU. The Glavnoye Razvedyvatelnoye Upravelenie was the primary intelligence organization of the Red Army. Early in the war, GRU agents obtained intelligence indicating that ADOLF HITLER was planning to abrogate the GERMAN-SOVIET NON-AGGRESSION PACT by invading the Soviet Union, but Stalin refused to heed these warnings. Throughout the war, GRU agents were able to penetrate to the highest levels of the German military, including the general staff. Agents also spied on the Western Allies, most notably obtaining secrets relating to the MANHATTAN PROJECT.

MI5. Military Intelligence, Division 5 was the principal British agency responsible for counterespionage and internal security. During World War II, under the leadership of Sir David Petrie, MI5 compiled a magnificent record not only for apprehending German agents operating in the U.K., but for "turning" many of them to create double agents, who fed their handlers a stream of highly destructive disinformation.

MI6. Military Intelligence, Division 6 was the principal British agency responsible for espionage. Under the leadership of Colonel Stewart Menzies, MI6 coordinated the efforts of spies in the Axis countries as well as in neutral nations, where agents infiltrated Axis diplomatic missions. It was under the auspices of MI6 that the riddle of the German ENIGMA CIPHER AND MACHINE was untangled, yielding the valuable crop of intelligence known as ULTRA.

Navy Communications Intelligence (COMINT). This U.S. Navy unit was responsible for intercepting and decrypting Japanese coded information

and maintained a series of covert listening posts throughout the Pacific for this purpose.

NKVD. The Narodny Komisariat Vnutrennikh Del combined internal security counterespionage functions with both domestic and foreign espionage. The most extensive of all Soviet intelligence agencies, NKVD was also the most feared and was ruled ruthlessly by LAVRENTY BERIA. NKVD was responsible for the Cambridge Spy Ring in England and for other espionage operations directed against the USSR's own allies. NKVD operated a subagency known as SMERSH to monitor internal security, especially signs of disloyalty within the ranks of the Soviet military.

Office of Naval Intelligence (ONI). Established in 1882, ONI grew into a large agency during World War II with responsibility for gathering intelligence as well as ensuring internal security. Virtually every U.S. Navy ship was staffed by at least one ONI officer, who provided reports on enemy harbors, fortifications, vessels, and so on. Before and during the war, ONI sent naval attachés to U.S. embassies to collect data of all kinds. The naval attachés inhabited a shadowy world between their capacity as official representatives of the United States and spies.

Office of Strategic Services (OSS). What became the best-known U.S. espionage agency of the World War II era and the direct predecessor of the Central Intelligence Agency (CIA), OSS was founded (June 1942) and led by WILLIAM DONOVAN. The OSS operated extensively in Europe as well as in the China-Burma-India theater and not only provided spies and saboteurs, but conducted exhaustive systematic analyses of published materials issued by the Axis nations in an effort to gauge enemy morale and intentions. The OSS also operated its own propaganda unit, which generated propaganda and disinformation for covert and overt distribution behind enemy lines.

Signal Intelligence Service (SIS). This was the U.S. Army's principal code-breaking agency, which cracked the PURPLE (JAPANESE DIPLOMATIC CIPHER).

Twenty Committee. Established on January 2, 1941, under MI6, this British unit specialized in "turning" German spies operating in England, so that they would become double agents who provided disinformation to Germany. As many as 120 such agents were eventually active, and they played a key role in giving German military planners the impression that the NORMANDY LANDINGS (D-DAY) would come not at Normandy, but at the Pas de Calais. Based on this disinformation (and other factors), the bulk of German defenses were transferred to the Pas de Calais sector.

ALLIED ESPIONAGE AND COUNTERESPIONAGE OPERATIONS

Bletchley Park. At this estate north of London, much of the British intelligence community was gathered. Chief among the activities here was decryption, especially of the Engima traffic.

Bodyguard. Operation Bodyguard was the codename for much of Britain's disinformation effort, especially relating to the planned invasion of France. Operation Fortitude, a suboperation of Bodyguard, was directed at deceiving the Germans into thinking that the invasion would come not at Normandy but at the Pas de Calais. Bodyguard and Fortitude created an array of decoys (including rubber tanks and plywood aircraft) to give the impression of the build-up of invasion forces opposite Pas de Calais, and it manufactured a stream of false news reports and radio broadcasts.

Bodyline. Operation Bodyline was an effort of British intelligence to monitor the progress of German rocket development. Bodyline intelligence directed bomber raids against Peenemünde, the principal site of V-1 buzz bomb and V-2 rocket development.

Jedburgh. Under Operation Jedburgh, three-man teams, consisting of U.S., British, and Free French agents, were infiltrated into France prior to the D-day invasion to gather information and to sabotage railroads and communications.

Lucy Spy Ring. The Soviets operated this highly effective espionage ring out of Switzerland, obtaining a wealth of military intelligence about German operations, including material that was indispensable in achieving the Soviet victory at the titanic tank BATTLE OF KURSK.

Red Orchestra. This ring of Soviet spies was active in German-occupied western and central Europe and provided a steady stream of information, transmitted via radio, throughout the war.

Special Operations Executive (SOE). Established on July 22, 1940, this British operation functioned mainly as a unit of agents provocateurs, whose mission was to foment rebellion in occupied Europe, especially Poland and France. The object was not to overthrow the German occupation so much as it was to force a concentration of German troops behind the lines and away from the front.

AXIS ESPIONAGE AND COUNTERESPIONAGE AGENCIES

Abwehr. Under the leadership of Admiral WILHELM CANARIS, Abwehr was the German agency chiefly responsible for espionage against foreign military operations. Canaris was a brilliant spymaster, but his ambivalence concerning Nazi brutality often caused him to sabotage his own operations or even to provide disinformation to his superiors.

B-Dienst Observation Service. This German naval service overtly and covertly observed the movements of British merchant and military vessels, providing targeting information to U-boats.

Foreign Armies East. Under the leadership of Lieutenant Colonel Reinhard Gehlen, Foreign Armies East directed military espionage against the Soviet Union. It became infamous for blunders and contributed to the ultimate defeat of German invasion and occupation forces in the Soviet Union.

Foreign Armies West. This German organization was responsible for military intelligence in the west. It performed only marginally better than its eastern counterpart, Foreign Armies East, because its agents frequently fell prey to Allied disinformation efforts, especially regarding the intended landing area of the D-day invasion.

Gestapo. The Geheime Staatspolizei (Secret State Police) was established in 1933 by Adolf Hitler as the principal agency to provide internal security. Headed by HERMANN GÖRING and later by Heinrich Müller, the Gestapo created a vast and shadowy network of internal spies and snitches aimed at ferreting out disloyalty. Often, the

GESTAPO succeeded only in creating suspicion and undermining civilian morale.

Kempeitai. Roughly equivalent to the German Gestapo, the Kempeitai was the Japanese secret police, principally tasked with identifying and suppressing internal opposition and disloyalty. Secondarily, the agency was responsible for espionage and counterespionage.

RSHA. The Reichsicherheitshauptamt, the Reich Central Security Office, was established in 1939 under REINHARD HEYDRICH and coordinated the activities of the Gestapo and the SICHERHEITSDIENST (SD), which were the intelligence and espionage units directly controlled by the SCHUTZSTAFFEL (SS). In effect, the RSHA was the central agency of German internal security.

Sicherheitsdienst (SD). The SD was created primarily to identify and suppress plots against Adolf Hitler personally and against the Nazi regime generally. Under Reinhard Heydrich, the SD often exceeded its brief and conducted espionage abroad. The SD operated as a rival agency to the Abwehr, much to the degradation of the quality of German intelligence.

SPIES AND SPYMASTERS

Many of the major spies and spymasters are treated in separate entries in this encyclopedia. *See* BERIA, LAVRENTY; BIDAULT, GEORGES; CANARIS, WILHELM; DISSARD, MARIE LOUISE; DONOVAN, WILLIAM; DULLES, ALLEN; FUCHS, KLAUS; GÖRING, HERMANN; HEYDRICH, REINHARD; and MOULIN, JEAN. In addition to these individuals, important figures in World War II espionage include:

Cicero. Working under the code name Cicero, Elyesa Bazna was a valet to Britain's chief diplomat in Turkey and supplied a large volume of intelligence to the Germans.

Garbo. Working under the code name Garbo, Juan Pujol Garcia, a Spanish national, was a double agent who supplied disinformation to the Germans. Originally, he had been recruited by the Abwehr, but he freely volunteered to work for the Allies. His false information helped mislead German military planners into anticipating the D-day invasion not at Normandy but at the Pas de Calais. Garbo earned the distinction of being awarded the Iron Cross by Germany and the Order of the British Empire by Great Britain.

Josephine. This was a code name for a person whose identity is still unknown who supplied more—and more valuable—information to Germany than any other spy. It is believed that Josephine was a Swedish naval attaché based in London.

Layton, Edwin T. Layton served throughout the war as the U.S. Navy's chief intelligence officer in the Pacific. It was Layton who supplied warning indications of the impending attack on Pearl Harbor, a warning that, however, went largely unheeded.

Martin, William. This fictitious name was applied by the British to a corpse, which was used in an elaborate and effective (if grotesque) scheme to deceive the Germans into believing that the Allies intended to invade the Balkans rather than Sicily in 1943. A briefcase with "top secret" disinformation was handcuffed to the corpse, which was released by a British submarine near the coast of Spain. The body washed ashore, the documents were discovered by a German agent (who assumed it was the victim of a U-boat attack), and the disinformation was duly transmitted to Berlin. When the story was told after the war, William Martin was dubbed "the man who never was."

Menzies, Stewart Graham. A major in the British army, Menzies was director of MI6 during the war and through 1953. He was, in effect, Britain's chief spymaster.

Rosbaud, Paul. A German who worked under the code name Griffin, Rosbaud spied for Britain, reporting important information on Germany's rocket program and on its program to develop a nuclear weapon. Thanks to Rosbaud, the Allies learned that German nuclear weapon research was stalled and lagged far behind that of the Allies.

Schellenberg, Walter. Schellenberg was the chief of foreign intelligence in Germany's RSHA.

Stephenson, William. Operating under the code name Intrepid, Stephenson was a Canadian who directed British espionage in the United States before American entry into World War II.

Further reading: Eisner, Peter. *The Freedom Line: The Brave Men and Women Who Rescued Allied Airmen from* the Nazis During World War II. New York: William Morrow, 2004; Hohne, Heinz. *Canaris: Hitler's Master Spy.* New York: Cooper Square, 1999; Holt, Thaddeus. *The Deceivers: Allied Military Deception in the Second World War.* New York: Scribner, 2004; Kahn, David. *Hitler's Spies: German Military Intelligence in World War II.* New York: Da Capo, 2000; Kross, Peter. *The Encyclopedia of World War II Spies.* Fort Lee, N.J.: Barricade Books, 2001; O'Donnell, Patrick K. *Operatives, Spies, and Saboteurs: The Unknown Story of the Men and Women of World War II's OSS.* New York: Free Press, 2004; Piekakiewicz, Janusz. *Secret Agents, Spies, and Saboteurs: Famous Undercover Missions of World War II.* New York: William Morrow, 1974; Schellenberg, Walter. *The Labyrinth: Memoirs of Walter Schellenberg, Hitler's Chief of Counterintelligence.* New York: Da Capo, 2000; Shapiro, Milton J. *Behind Enemy Lines: American Spies and Saboteurs in World War II.* New York: Julian Messner, 1978; Wires, Richard. *The Cicero Spy Affair: German Access to British Secrets in World War II.* New York: Praeger, 1999.

F

Falkenhausen, Alexander von (1878–1966) German general and military governor of occupied Belgium

Alexander von Falkenhausen began his military career before World War I as a military attaché in Japan. With the outbreak of that war, he was seconded to the Turkish Army and served with distinction in Palestine, earning the Pour le Mérite. He returned to the German Army and remained in it during the interwar years, gaining appointment in 1927 as head of the Dresden Infantry School. He retired from the regular army in 1930 and traveled to China, where CHIANG-KAI-SHEK employed him as his military adviser.

In May 1938, Falkenhausen was again recalled to the German Army. When World War II began, he was assigned as an infantry commander in the western offensive and the BATTLE OF FRANCE. With the successful occupation of Belgium, Falkenhausen was named military governor of the country and served from 1940 through 1944. He was no more brutal than most other German officials with responsibility for occupying a country, and, indeed, he was certainly less brutal than some. Nevertheless, in the course of his administration Falkenhausen committed war crimes, authorizing deportations, especially of Jews and, in reprisal for resistance activities, the arrest and execution of hostages.

Falkenhausen was not an admirer of ADOLF HITLER, and his two closest friends, Carl Goerdeler and Erwin von Witzleben, were conspirators in the JULY PLOT (to assassinate Hitler), masterminded by KLAUS VON STAUFFENBERG. Falkenhausen was removed as military governor of Belgium and arrested but was never brought to trial.

After the war, Falkenhausen was sent back to Belgium, where he was tried for war crimes. In March 1951, found guilty of having deported Jews and executed hostages, he was sentenced to 12 years of imprisonment. He was, however, released after having served a mere three weeks. He lived out the remainder of his life in obscure retirement.

Further reading: Taylor, Telford. *Sword and Swastika: Generals and Nazis in the Third Reich.* London: Peter Smith Publisher, 1980.

Falkenhorst, Nikolaus (1885–1968) German supreme military commander of Norway

Nikolaus Falkenhorst began the major phase of his military career as military attaché in Prague and Budapest during 1933–35. Recognized as a promising officer, he was named chief of staff of Third Army Group Command in 1935 and served until 1936, when he became commander of the 32nd Division. He served in this capacity until the outbreak of war, in 1939, when he was transferred to command of XXI Corps in Poland. With the conclusion of the Polish campaign in 1940, Falkenhorst, as Generaloberst (colonel general) was given command of Commanding Group XXI, Denmark-Norway, then received command of Army Norwegen in Norway. To this was added in 1941 command of Army Lapland, and in 1942 Falkenhorst was named commander in chief, Norway. He served in this capacity until 1944, when he was effectively dismissed (officially retired). Even though he was no longer in active service, Falkenhorst became a prisoner of war in 1945 and was held by a British tribunal for trial as a war criminal. As a general, he had made himself notorious for harsh treatment of prisoners of war and had, in violation of the Geneva Conventions, ordered the summary execution of British commandos. Found guilty of war crimes in 1946, he was condemned to death, but his sentence was subsequently commuted to imprisonment for 20 years.

Further reading: Kersaudy, François. *Norway 1940.* Lincoln: University of Nebraska Press, 1998; Mann, Chris, and Christer Jörgensen. *Hitler's Arctic War: The German Campaigns in Norway, Finland, and the USSR 1940–1945.* New York: St. Martin's Press, 2003.

fascism

In the narrowest sense, fascism was a political ideology and mass movement introduced in Italy by the National Fascist Party (Partito Nazionale Fascista) under the leadership of a former socialist radical journalist, BENITO MUSSOLINI (1883–1945). Mussolini took the name of his party from the Latin word *fasces,* a symbol of authority—specifically, penal authority—in ancient Rome. The Roman *fasces* was a bundle of elm or birch rods tied securely around an axe. The meaning conveyed by the symbol is one of unity (the bound individual rods) and the strength of unity (bound together, the rods are far stronger than any individual stick of wood) as well as punitive authority.

Mussolini rose meteorically in 1922, when he was elevated to the office of prime minister with virtually dictatorial powers. His ascension was the product of his own histrionically virile magnetism, the intimidation wrought by his legion of black-shirted followers, who used violent rhetoric and outright thuggery to suppress all opposition, and the intense ideological appeal of his message. All three components of the rise of Mussolini and the concomitant rise of fascism were equally important. Fascism was founded on a cult of personality, namely the strongman leader who offers himself as the hypermasculine savior of the nation. Intimidation and violence were also inseparable from fascism, which was rooted in an atavistic will to power and which fully sanctioned the forcible molding of public opinion, culture, and government. Like many other nations after World War I, Italy seemed afflicted by moral drift and economic malaise. The violence of fascism promised to sweep this away.

Finally, there was the ideology of fascism. In contrast to the political ideology most directly opposed to fascism, communism, which had an elaborately articulated theoretical structure initially established by Karl Marx and Friedrich Engels, fascism never developed a truly cohesive intellectual framework. It is most telling that during his long tenure as Italy's leader, Mussolini employed in vain a small army of historians, lawyers, political scientists, and other scholars who were charged with expressing the ideology of fascism in a great *Fascist Encyclopedia.* This work of many years was never completed. Indeed, it may be argued that fascism never had a genuine ideological core because it was nothing more or less than a means of acquiring and maintaining power. Beyond these two objectives, fascism simply melted as a political philosophy, dissolving into ad hoc assumptions, assertions, and actions all intended to preserve ruling authority. Nevertheless, fascism was characterized by certain ideological or at least quasi-ideological principles. These included:

> Opposition to all nonfascist political philosophies and forms of government, including communism, parliamentary democracy, and political or cultural liberalism
>
> An embrace of totalitarianism
>
> Corporatism: "Corporatism" proposed organizing industry, agriculture, the professions, and even the arts into trade unions controlled by a combination of the state and management;

these "corporations" would regulate all aspects of employment and would replace all other trade associations and unions; the "corporations" would, in turn, convene in a "corporatist parliament," which, ultimately, would replace conventional representative government. No fascist state, including Italy, ever fully instituted corporatism.

Equality of social status: An assertion only; in fact, fascism tended to produce oligarchy born of a more-or-less inarticulate belief in a natural social hierarchy ruled by an elite class of superior human beings.

Imperialism: Mussolini saw his destiny as the man who would resurrect the Roman Empire.

Hypernationalism and racism, and a tendency to blur any distinction between national and racial identity

Militarism and mass mobilization, including, concomitantly, the diminishment of the individual: In Germany, this was expressed in the concept of *Volksgemeinschaft* ("people's community"), the idea that individual interests must be subordinated to the good of the nation.

The idea of the fascist as the "new man," the "man of destiny"

A cult of youth and physical strength

Violence, including the scapegoating of individuals and groups

Founded in Italy, fascism or fascist-inspired movements and governments were influential in many parts of central, southern, and eastern Europe between 1919 and 1945. Fascism even had adherents in western Europe and the United States, as well as South Africa, Japan, Latin America, and the Middle East. ADOLF HITLER was certainly inspired by the example of Mussolini, and his NAZI PARTY (NSDAP) embodied the basic principles of fascism. The chief European fascist parties were disbanded and even in many places outlawed after World War II, although so-called neofascist movements have periodically emerged since.

Mussolini did not fashion fascism out of whole cloth. Various features of fascism can be found in the work of such 19th-century political theorists as Theodor Fritsch, Paul Anton de Lagarde, Julius Langbehn, Jörg Lanz von Liebenfels, Joseph de Maistre, Charles Maurras, and Georges Sorel and such scientists and philosophers as Johann Gottlieb Fichte, Giovanni Gentile, Gustave Le Bon, Friedrich Nietzsche, Vilfredo Pareto, Karl Vogt, and Ernst Haeckel. Fascism is also implicit in the work of the German operatic composer Richard Wagner and the Italian novelist and poet Gabriele D'Annunzio, who was a contemporary of Mussolini. It was Mussolini, however, who, synthesizing the disparate strands of political and philosophical tradition, gave the movement a name.

Before and during World War II, the most important fascist and fascistlike national movements included, besides Italy's Fascist Party and Germany's Nazi Party, the Fatherland Front (Vaterländische Front) in Austria, led by ENGELBERT DOLLFUSS; the National Union (União Nacional) in Portugal, led by António de Oliveira Salazar; the Party of Free Believers (Elefterofronoi) in Greece, led by Ioannis Metaxas; the Insurgence (Ustaša) in Croatia, led by Ante Paveli; the National Union (Nasjonal Samling) in Norway, which spawned the turncoat dictatorship of VIDKUN QUISLING; the military dictatorship of TOJO HIDEKI in Japan; the Falange of Spain, founded in 1933 by José Antonio Primo de Rivera, which produced dictator FRANCISCO FRANCO; the virulently anti-Semitic Falanga in Poland, led by Boleslaw Piasecki; the ultimately failed Lapua Movement in Finland, led by Vihtori Kosola; the influential Arrow Cross Party (Nyilaskeresztes Párt) in Hungary, led by Ferenc Szálasi; and the Iron Guard (Garda de Fier) of Romania, led by Corneliu Codreanu. In the west, the Cross of Fire (Croix de Feu), subsequently renamed the French Social Party (Parti Social Français), led by Colonel François de La Rocque, became the largest party on the French right between 1936 and 1938. Nor was it the only fascist movement in France between the wars. Others included Faisceau, led by Georges Valois; the Young Patriots (Jeunesses Patriotes), led by Pierre Taittinger; French Solidarity (Solidarité Française), founded by François Coty and led by Jean Renaud; the Franks (Francistes), led by Marcel

Bucard; the French Popular Party (Parti Populaire Français), led by Jacques Doriot; and French Action (Action Française), led by Charles Maurras. The VICHY GOVERNMENT of occupied France found many French fascists to serve in government and administrative roles.

In Britain, OSWALD MOSLEY's British Union of Fascists was a significant political voice up to the very outbreak of war. In Belgium, the Rexist Party, led by Léon Degrelle, made for a significant presence in Parliament. Fascists were not active in the Soviet Union, but Russian fascist organizations were founded by expatriates in Manchuria and the United States, as well as elsewhere. Nor was fascism confined to Europe between the wars. A number of fascist movements sprang up in South Africa after 1932, including the Gentile National Socialist Movement, the South African Fascists, the South African National Democratic Party (the Blackshirts), and the Ox-Wagon Sentinel (Ossewabrandwag). In the Middle East, fascist organizations were very popular on the eve of the war. These included the Syrian People's Party (the Syrian National Socialist Party) , the Iraqi Futuwa movement, and the Young Egypt movement (called the Green Shirts after their uniforms).

Japan's militaristic government during World War II certainly partook of fascist philosophy, and a quasi-fascist tradition developed in Japan almost immediately after World War I. The Taisho Sincerity League (Taisho Nesshin'kai), the Imperial Way Faction (Kodo-ha), the Greater Japan National Essence Association (Dai Nippon Kokusui-kai), the Anti-Red Corps (Bokyo Gokoku-Dan), the Great Japan Political Justice Corps (Dai Nippon Seigi-Dan), the Blood Brotherhood League (Ketsumei-Dan), the Jimmu Association (Jimmu-Kai), the New Japan League (Shin-Nihon Domei), the Eastern Way Society (Towo Seishin-Kai), and the Great Japan Youth Party (Da-nihon Seinen-dan) were merely the best known of the many pre–World War II fascist or quasi-fascist parties active in Japan.

China was swept by fascism following the Japanese occupation of Manchuria in 1931. The most important Chinese fascist party was the Blue Shirts, who allied themselves with the Kuomintang (National People's Party) under CHIANG-KAI-SHEK.

In the Americas, the Nacis were founded in Chile by Jorge González von Mareés; the Gold Shirts were active in Mexico, led by Nicolás Rodríguez; and the Revolutionary Union (Unión Revolucionaria) put into power dictator Luis Sánchez Cerro of Peru. In Brazil, the Integralist Action Party (Ação Integralista Brasileira) claimed more than 200,000 members by the mid-1930s and mounted a failed coup attempt in 1938. In the United States, the Ku Klux Klan may be seen as a fascist organization, and other pre–World War II extreme right-wing groups were also active, including the Social Justice movement founded by a vocally anti-Semitic Roman Catholic priest, Father Charles E. Coughlin. In 1942, Coughlin's publication, called *Social Justice*, was banned from the U.S. mails for violating the Espionage Act. The Catholic Church ordered Coughlin to stop making his distressingly popular radio broadcasts. A more overtly fascist organization was the German-American Bund, founded in 1933 and openly pro-Nazi and paramilitary in orientation. The organization evaporated after U.S. entry into the war in December 1941.

Further reading: Griffin, Roger, ed. *Fascism.* New York and Oxford: Oxford University Press, 1995; Griffin, Roger. *The Nature of Fascism.* New York: Routledge, 1993; Mosse, George L. *The Fascist Revolution: Toward a General Theory of Fascism.* New York: Howard Fertig, 2000; Paxton, Robert O. *The Anatomy of Fascism.* New York: Knopf, 2004; Payne, Stanley G. *A History of Fascism, 1914–1945.* Madison: University of Wisconsin Press, 1995; Sternhell, Zeev. *The Birth of Fascist Ideology.* Princeton, N.J.: Princeton University Press, 1995.

fifth column

During World War II, *fifth column* referred to subversive activities within the Allied countries. Those who constituted the fifth column were, naturally enough, called fifth columnists.

The term *fifth column* was first used during the Spanish civil war about 1936 when a Nationalist general about to attack Madrid warned Republican defenders that in addition to the four columns of troops outside the city, he had a "fifth column" inside, awaiting only the proper moment to rise up and join the fight. Thus *fifth column* came to describe any body of organized subversion harbored within a nation. Yet the fact is that the existence of a fifth column was largely the product of rumor. While it is true that some right-wing sympathizers and even outright fascists lived in most of the Allied countries, these individuals and groups never coalesced into active, let alone effective, subversive bodies. In an effort to undermine morale, German propaganda nevertheless continually played upon and sought to intensify rumors of fifth column conspiracies.

The only places in which fifth columnists may be said to have played actual and even significant roles were in Czechoslovakia's SUDENTENLAND and in Yugoslavia and Poland. In all these instances, however, the fifth column was hardly secretly subversive but consisted of ethnic Germans who would certainly have been expected to have sympathies with the Third Reich.

Further reading: de Jong, L. *The German Fifth Column in the Second World War.* New York: H. Fertig, 1973; Mac-Donnell, Francis. *Insidious Foes: The Axis Fifth Column and the American Home Front.* Guilford, Conn.: Lyons Press, 2004.

fighter aircraft

This article discusses the development and employment of fighter aircraft during World War II. For discussion of specific aircraft, *see* AIRCRAFT, BRITISH; AIRCRAFT, FRENCH; AIRCRAFT, GERMAN; AIRCRAFT, ITALIAN; AIRCRAFT, JAPANESE; AIRCRAFT, POLISH; AIRCRAFT, SOVIET; and AIRCRAFT, UNITED STATES.

In World War II, fighters were used in four major roles. They provided close-air support for ground forces and also targeted troops and equipment. (Some few fighters were specifically designed for this ground attack role and, in the U.S. Army Air Forces, were designated "attack" planes.) At sea,

The Supermarine Spitfire was one of the legendary fighters of World War II. *(Royal Air Force Museum)*

aircraft carrier–based as well as land-based fighters attacked surface ships. For the Allies, perhaps the most important fighter role was escorting large bombers on strategic bombing missions chiefly over France, Italy, Germany, and Japan. These fighter escorts defended the bombers against enemy fighters playing the fourth role of this aircraft type: interdicting bombers.

For all four roles, fighters needed maneuverability. For all but the first role, they also needed speed. For the third and fourth roles, they needed maneuverability, speed, and a high service ceiling (so that they could either accompany or attack high-altitude bombers). For the third role, in addition to all of these qualities, fighters needed range. Without adequate range, they could not escort bombers all the way to their targets and back again. The progress of fighter development in World War II was directed at producing aircraft that excelled in all four areas of performance.

World War II began at the very end of the era of the biplane fighter. While all major combatant nations entered the war with a few biplane fighters still in service, most had already produced significant numbers of low-wing monoplanes. The typical monoplane fighter had a single engine, closed canopy, and retractable landing gear. Armament included, at minimum, fixed forward-firing machine guns. Some fighters also mounted cannon (increasingly important as bombers became more thickly armored), had wing racks for rockets, and could carry a modest bomb load or a torpedo. The quest for speed produced bigger, more powerful engines, culminating in early production of JET AIRCRAFT, especially in Germany. Even Germany, however, did not produce jets in sufficient quantity to make a significant impact on the air war.

While most fighters were single-engine designs, a few significant twin-engine fighters were also produced. The first was Germany's Messerschmidt Me-110, followed by the British Beaufighter and the Mosquito (which was also used as a light bomber). The United States produced the remarkable P-38 Lighting, which not only had twin engines, but twin fuselage booms, giving it a distinctive shape that prompted German pilots to dub it the "Fork-Tailed Devil." All twin-engine designs were sometimes used as night fighters, because they were large enough to accommodate the unwieldy RADAR equipment of the World War II era. However, the United States produced a twin-engine fighter expressly designed for the night-fighter role, the P-61 Black Widow.

The middle of the war saw the introduction of the "second generation" of the era's fighters, which featured very large engines capable of producing speeds in excess of 400 miles per hour. These included Germany's Focke-Wulf FW-190, Britain's Typhoon and Tempest, and the U.S. P-47 Thunderbolt and P–51 Mustang. Japanese fighter design excelled early in the war, and for many months of the conflict the famed A6M Zero outclassed anything the United States could hurl against it. However, by the middle of the war, Allied fighter designs had pulled well ahead of Japanese aircraft, and by the time Japanese designers had created their own "second generation" aircraft, the beleaguered nation lacked the production capacity to turn these planes out in sufficient quantity to be used effectively. Indeed, as the Japanese military situation became increasingly desperate, aircraft designers became increasingly daring, turning out jet designs (building on German technology) and even rocket-propelled aircraft. None of these was produced in significant numbers. Equally critical was a shortage of pilots and an even more critical shortage of *well-trained* pilots. Beginning in October 1944, Japanese commanders were prodigally expending even this precious resource by sending pilots on one-way KAMIKAZE (suicide) attacks.

As important as fighter development was, the training of fighter pilots and the development of fighter doctrine and tactics were, if anything, even more critical to success. Early in the war, when it became clear that the Japanese Zero was easily superior to the first generation of American fighters, U.S. pilots quickly developed tactics and skills that exploited the Zero's few but significant weaknesses while playing to the strengths of such aircraft as the Curtiss P-40C. In the hands of a skilled pilot, even this obsolescent fighter could defeat the more advanced Zero.

The principal difference between the fighter tactics of World War I and those of World War II was the diminished emphasis on the dogfight, the one-on-one fighter duel. Instead, pilots, especially in Britain's Royal Air Force (RAF), were trained in tactics designed to be most effective against bombers. The object was to bring the greatest number of guns to bear on the enemy target. To facilitate this, the British adopted the Rotte, a two-aircraft formation in which one plane served as the principal attacker and the other (the "wingman") protected the attacker against counterattack. The German Luftwaffe took this a step further and developed the *Schwarme,* which used two *pairs* of fighters and was soon adopted by the RAF and, subsequently, by the U.S. Army Air Forces as the "finger four" formation (so called because, the positions of the fighters relative to one another resembled the tips of four outspread fingers). Early in the war, the Japanese favored a three-fighter formation known as the *shotai.* American pilots, beginning with the FLYING TIGERS in China, employed a "section and stinger" formation against these formations. A two-aircraft "section" would be used to lure the three-aircraft *shotai* to attack. As the two aircraft held the focus of the *shotai* pilots, the "stinger" fighter, lurking at a higher altitude, would suddenly descend in a surprise attack. By the end of 1943, the Japanese discarded the *shotai* in favor of a version of the finger four.

From the middle years of the war onward, all sides concentrated on developing antibomber tactics. The German Luftwaffe, in particular, created an impressive repertoire, including a devastating approach from beneath and behind, which relied on a specially designed upward-firing cannon mounted in the roof of the fighter's cockpit. However, the development and extensive deployment of long-range American fighters, especially the P-51 Mustang, meant that bombers would benefit from fighter escort all the way to and from their targets. The Mustangs provided highly effective defensive coverage against German fighters, regardless of the tactics employed. In the end, it was U.S. production capacity that defeated the enemy fighters. Escorts far outnumbered the attackers. Had the Luftwaffe introduced jet fighters earlier in the war and in far greater numbers, the P-51s, magnificent as they were, would have been readily outclassed. The Me-262 jet fighter, for example, could simply outrun any opponent, and the only way to shoot it down was to attempt to catch it on takeoff or landing or to force it into a dogfight, in which its poor rate of turn would render it vulnerable. Fortunately for the Allies, the jets were deployed too late and in too small numbers to allow for the effective exploitation of their manifest superiority.

Further reading: Chant, Christopher. *An Illustrated Data Guide to World War II Fighters.* New York: Chelsea House, 1997; Dean, Francis H. *America's Hundred Thousand: U.S. Production Fighters of World War II.* Atglen, Pa.: Schiffer, 2000; Donald, David. *Fighters of World War II.* New York: MetroBooks, 1998; Ethell, Jeffrey L., and Robert T. Sand. *World War II Fighters.* Osceola, Wis.: Motorbooks International, 2002; Griehl, Manfred. *German Night Fighters in World War II.* Atglen, Pa.: Schiffer, 1991; Gunston, Bill. *An Illustrated Guide to Allied Fighters of World War II.* New York: Arco, 1981; Gunston, Bill. *Illustrated Guide to German, Italian and Japanese Fighters of World War II.* New York: Arco, 1980; Ragni, Franco. *German Fighters of World War II.* Champaign, Ill.: Squadron/Signal Publications, 1984; Tillman, Bar-rett. *U.S. Navy Fighter Squadrons in World War II.* North Branch, Minn.: Specialty Press Publishers & Wholesalers, 1997.

Filipino Scouts

Filipino, or Philippine, Scouts were the closest the United States ever came to maintaining a colonial army in the manner of the British Empire. They were native Filipinos attached to the Philippine Department of the U.S. Army beginning in 1901 and up to and during World War II. Filipino Scouts were usually commanded by U.S. officers, although a very few received training and commissions from the United States Military Academy (West Point).

The first Filipino Scout units were raised in 1901 as reinforcing columns for the regular U.S. Army forces combating the Filipino insurgency in the wake of the Spanish-American War. During 1919–20, the Filipino Scout units were reorganized and given new designations as the 43rd, 45th, and 57th Infantry Regiments, the 24th and 25th Field Artillery Regiments, and the 26th Cavalry Regiment. In addition, the scouts were also formed into support units, which included coastal artillery, medical, and quartermaster formations. Though commanded chiefly by U.S. officers, the Filipino Scout units were otherwise segregated, except for the integrated Filipino-American 808th Military Police Company.

On July 26, 1941, U.S. Army Forces-Far East (USAFFE) was created and included the Philippine Department, Philippine Army (two regular and 10 reserve divisions), and the Far East Air Force (FEAF, formerly the Philippine Army Air Corps). USAFFE was headquartered at No.1, Calle Victoria, Manila, Luzon, the Philippines, under the command of Major General DOUGLAS MACARTHUR. Under the Philippine Department at the time were 22,532 troops, of which 11,972 were Filipino Scouts.

In contrast to the Philippine Commonwealth Army, which was both poorly trained and poorly equipped, the scouts were quite well trained, well equipped, and as thoroughly experienced as the regular U.S. Army troops. American commanders respected them. The Filipino Scouts fought side by side with U.S. forces during the Japanese invasion of the Philippines and suffered heavy casualties as well as shared the horrific abuses and hardships of the infamous BATAAN DEATH MARCH. Until recently, however, their contributions and sacrifices in World War II were very inadequately recognized by the U.S. military and the government. On December 16, 2003, President George W. Bush created Public Law 108–183 by signing the Veterans' Benefits Act of 2003, which extended full veterans' benefits to the Filipino Scouts if they or their beneficiaries reside in the United States as U.S. citizens or as aliens lawfully admitted for permanent residence.

See also PHILIPPINES, FALL AND RECONQUEST OF.

Further reading: Astor, Gerald. *Crisis in the Pacific.* New York: Dell, 2001; Marple, Allan D. *The Philippine Scouts: A Case Study in the Use of Indigenous Soldiers, Northern Luzon, the Philippine Islands, 1899.* Fort Leavenworth, Kans.: U.S. Army Command and General Staff College, 1983; Olson, John E. "The History of the Philippine Scouts," Available online. URL: www.philippine-scouts. org/History/history.html. Accessed on November 22, 2006; Sides, Hampton. Wollard, James Richard. *The Philippine Scouts: The Development of America's Colonial Army.* Ann Arbor, Mich.: University Microfilms, 1980. *Ghost Soldiers.* New York: Doubleday, 2001.

Final Solution

Anti-Semitism and the scapegoating of Jews for economic and other European and German national problems were integral to the rise of ADOLF HITLER and were made explicit in his autobiographical manifesto *MEIN KAMPF* (1924). Of course, these themes were hardly new or original with Hitler. Throughout Europe, anti-Semitism had a long tradition. Hitler, the NAZI PARTY (NSDAP), and the Third Reich, however, made anti-Semitism a central political and cultural crusade, which entered into virtually every law, government activity, and administrative policy. As developed by Hitler and the Nazis, anti-Semitism required, initially, purging Jews from "German" life and, ultimately, the murder, (genocide) of all

Jews who fell under German control. This was the HOLOCAUST, in which approximately 6 million Jews perished during World War II. It must be recognized that implementation of the Final Solution, the genocide of the Jews, was not merely an aspect, let alone side effect, of World War II, but was, for Germany, a cause and a war aim, for only in the context of world war and conquest could the Holocaust called for by the Final Solution be perpetrated.

The Final Solution to the "Jewish Question" grew out of Hitler's pledge to "free" Germany of Jews and Jewish influence (which Hitler deliberately confounded with Marxism and communism). Hitler conflated German nationalism with a doctrine of German "Aryanism," a heritage of superior racial purity, which the Jewish "race" threatened to pollute. He and other Nazis demonized Jews as alien, subversive, and generally dangerous. Hitler posed to the German people the Jewish Question (*Judenfrage*): What was to be done to make Germany "Jew-free" (*Judenrein*)? The initial "answer" was internal exile, the expulsion of Jews from rural Germany, from villages and small towns, and their concentration in the larger cities. The next "answer" was voluntary emigration abroad, which was encouraged (but not required) by the government. This constituted official reich policy from 1933 to the outbreak of war in 1939. While the emigration was voluntary, German law prevented Jewish émigrés from taking their property (including homes and businesses) and most of their monetary assets with them. These were confiscated by the government. Between 1933 and 1938, more than 50 percent of Germany's 500,000 Jewish citizens emigrated, despite the great material sacrifices involved. About 100,000 went to the United States, 63,000 to Argentina, 52,000 to Great Britain, and 33,000 to Palestine. What motivated this costly exodus were government-instituted programs of persecution, discrimination, economic restriction, and exclusion from professions, culminating in the government-orchestrated "spontaneous" nationwide violence and vandalism of *KRISTALLNACHT* during November 9–10, 1938. Moreover, there was virtually nothing those identified by the government as Jews could do to remove the onus of the ethnic and racial label. The NUREMBERG LAWS of 1935 defined a Jew essentially as anyone with one Jewish grandparent. Religious practice had nothing to do with this identity; it was, rather, a question of "blood," and even those who had converted to Christianity or who had been practicing Christians for years or generations were counted as Jews on the basis of a single grandparent. As defined by the Nazis, identity as a Jew trumped and voided any other national, ethnic, or religious identity.

The Final Solution to the Jewish Question, mass murder, was not openly or officially discussed before the outbreak of war. It is not known to what degree, if any, it was even contemplated prior to 1939. Between 1933 and 1938, some thousands of German citizens, chiefly opponents of the Nazi regime, were murdered in concentration camps. Of these, fewer than 100 were Jews, and their Jewishness was incidental to their execution; they were killed because they had somehow interfered with the regime, its plans, policies, and purposes.

Germany's annexation of Austria (ANSCHLUSS) in 1938 and its acquisition of the Czech SUDENTEN-LAND and, the following year, of Bohemia and Moravia as well, brought another 250,000 Jews under reich control. They were not welcome additions, and the violence of *Kristallnacht* as well as the murder of perhaps 1,000 Jews in concentration camps by 1939 were symptoms of increased intolerance. Emigration (with the material sacrifices it entailed) continued to be pushed. Of Austria's 160,000 Jews, some 100,000 emigrated. By this time, however, many nations instituted policies restricting immigration. Fewer and fewer nations welcomed Jews as refugees. Moreover, emigration to nearby European countries hardly guaranteed safety. During World War II, the Jews who had sought new homes in the western democracies of continental Europe, primarily France, Belgium, and the Netherlands, would be deported to concentration camps and, for the most part, consigned to their doom when the Nazi forces occupied these countries.

In fall 1939, the INVASION OF POLAND suddenly brought under reich control 1.5 million Jews. Of the 10,000 Polish civilians killed during the inva-

Hungarian Jews are unloaded at Auschwitz in 1944. *(National Holocaust Museum)*

sion, 3,000 were Jews, a number of them herded into synagogues and burned alive. By winter 1939, a third solution to the Jewish Question (after internal exile and emigration) was instituted: the concentration of Jews within urban ghettoes. The term *ghetto* is medieval in origin and was applied to urban neighborhoods in which Jews were traditionally concentrated and in which they practiced their trades and arts. Under the regime of the Nazi occupiers of Poland, Jews were legally restricted to very small neighborhoods within Warsaw, Łódź, and other cities, which were physically walled off from the "Gentile" quarters of the cities. Overcrowding was severe, and the food ration set at a starvation level. Those who attempted to leave the ghetto or smuggle food into it were, if caught, summarily executed. By April 1941, the ghetto system was in full operation throughout German-occupied Poland, and by early summer of that year, among the half million Jews penned into the Warsaw ghetto, the starvation rate had reached a monthly toll of 2,000. Clearly, the German occupiers were unconcerned and were probably even pleased that a means had been found to destroy a Jewish population by attrition. However, despite the horrific conditions within the ghetto, it was estimated that some 20 years would be required to complete the starvation of the population.

In the meantime, the triumph of the armies of the reich over the western democracies and in the Balkans during 1940 brought more and more Jews under reich control. In Norway, Denmark, France, the Netherlands, Luxembourg, Belgium, and Greece, Jews were forced to distinguish themselves by wearing a yellow Star of David on their clothing. This badge ensured that they would be excluded from virtually all professions and, indeed, from most desirable jobs. Additionally, they were subjected to confiscation of property and assets. At this time, however, they were generally allowed to emigrate, and many sought refuge in the neutral nations, including Switzerland, Spain, Portugal, and Turkey.

If the ghettoes of Poland were an adumbration of the fourth and "Final" solution to the Jewish Question—mass murder—the INVASION OF THE SOVIET UNION in June 1941 ushered in precisely this on an even larger and more deliberate scale. Hard on the heels of the invasion forces came special troops, the *Einsatzgruppen,* assigned to locate and murder the Jews in each Russian community through which the German Army swept. Within six months of the beginning of the invasion, perhaps a million Jews had been killed. The work of the *Einsatzgruppen* extended to eastern Poland, Lithuania, Latvia, and Estonia, as well as western Russia. Nor did the *Einsatzgruppen* have to work alone. In Lithuania and Ukraine (and sometimes elsewhere), local pro-Nazi paramilitaries and police forces carried out the murders. Romanian auxiliaries also carried out slaughters in Bessarabia, Moldavia, and areas of southern Russia.

The course of these programs of mass murder is covered in the entry on the Holocaust, but even as genocide was well under way, German authorities continued to keep many Jews alive to use as slave labor, and in Czechoslovakia, many were confined to the so-called model ghetto of THERESIENSTADT, propaganda films of which portrayed inmates working productively and apparently prospering.

After the *Anschluss,* in March 1938, the reich established a Central Office for Jewish Emigration headed by an officer of the SCHUTZSTAFFEL (SS)

named ADOLF EICHMANN. Eichmann was transferred to leadership of a new agency, the Race and Resettlement Office, which operated under the aegis of the SS. His new assignment was to create the mechanisms of the Final Solution. Indeed, it was Eichmann who coined the very term *Endlösung* in a reply to the German foreign office concerning the request of a Jew seeking to emigrate from Germany to unoccupied France. Eichmann wrote on October 28, 1941, that the application for emigration was to be denied because of the "approaching final solution of the European Jewry problem."

As Eichmann implemented it, the Final Solution mandated the location and arrest of Jews living in the occupied countries. They were to be held locally until they could be shipped, via rail, to remote CONCENTRATION AND EXTERMINATION CAMPS. Here they would be variously held, their labor exploited, and, ultimately, they would be killed; some were "selected" for murder immediately. The program was already well underway when, on January 20, 1942, under the authority of REINHARD HEYDRICH, the top-secret WANNSEE CONFERENCE was held to codify the ongoing procedures and scope of the Final Solution. By this time, the mechanics of mass murder had been largely settled on: death by asphyxiation, either using carbon monoxide generated by the redirected exhaust of prisoner transport vans or, increasingly, in specially designed mass gas chambers, which were typically disguised as shower or delousing facilities. Soon, an alternative to carbon monoxide was introduced, Zyklon-B, a prussic acid preparation originally intended as a pesticide, which produced deadly cyanide gas. Once the method of genocide had been settled on, the biggest problem remained the disposal of corpses, which was carried out mainly in large multioven crematoria located in the death camps. Run by special SS detachments, the death camps were operated far from the areas from which the Jews had been deported. After the war, Germans and others who lived near the camps improbably claimed ignorance of the operation of the gas chambers and crematoria.

Further reading: Bartov, Omer. *The Holocaust: Origins, Implementation and Aftermath.* New York and London: Routledge, 2000); Browning, Christopher R. *Final Solution and the German Foreign Office: A Study of Referat DIII of Obteilung Deutschland 1940 1943.* London: Holmes & Meier, 1978; Browning, Christopher R. *The Path to Genocide: Essays on Launching the Final Solution.* Cambridge and New York: Cambridge University Press, 1995; Browning, Christopher R., and Jurgen Matthaus. *The Origins of the Final Solution: The Evolution of Nazi Jewish Policy, September 1939–March 1942.* Lincoln: University of Nebraska Press, 2004; Goldhagen, Daniel Jonah. *Hitler's Willing Executioners: Ordinary Germans and the Holocaust.* New York: Knopf, 1996; Laqueur, Walter, and Judith Tydor Baumel. *The Holocaust Encyclopedia.* New Haven, Conn.: Yale University Press, 2001.

Finland campaign of 1944

As a result of Soviet aggression against Finland in the Russo-Finnish War during the winter of 1939–40, by which Finland was forced to cede territory to the Soviet Union, Finland subsequently allied itself with Germany and against the Soviets in what is sometimes called the Continuation War, and Finnish forces even joined in on the German invasion of the Soviet Union. After the Battle of Stalingrad, which turned the tide of the eastern front war against the seemingly unstoppable Nazis, Finland attempted to withdraw from the war. After Finnish negotiations with the Soviets broke down in February 1944, Joseph Stalin became determined to move against Finland once again and on June 9, 1944, commenced a major offensive across the Karelian Isthmus. At this stage, the Finns were in no condition to resist, in contrast to four years earlier. The Red Army rapidly achieved a breakthrough, driving the Finns back behind Viipuri. Finnish commander in chief Carl Gustaf Mannerheim reluctantly called on the Germans to provide assistance. This was obtained in return for a Finnish promise not to make a separate peace with the Soviets. The pledge given, Finland was bolstered by German troops and was able to stabilize the line of Soviet advance by August, at a position near the Finnish-Soviet frontier established at the end of the Russo-Finnish conflict in 1940. At this point, Stalin and his Red Army commanders decided that resources could be better employed elsewhere, especially since Finland had been effectively neutralized. Despite its pledge to Germany, Finland concluded an armistice with the Soviets on September 19, 1944, which formally reestablished the 1940 frontier and obligated Finland to pay heavy reparations. At that, it turned out to be a cheap forfeit. Whereas the other nations of the east that had allied themselves with Germany fell under Soviet domination after the war, Finland emerged with both its sovereignty and democratic government intact.

Further reading: Corvey, Steven Joseph. *Finland Fights for Freedom: The Russo-Finnish War and the Continuation War, 1939–1944.* Salem, Mass.: Salem State College, 1993.

flamethrower

During World War II, a flamethrower could be mounted on a vehicle, usually a tank, or carried by an individual soldier. In either of these forms, it was basically a very simple weapon that used pressurized gas, usually nitrogen, to eject a high-pressure stream of flammable liquid, usually thickened (gelled) gasoline, which was ignited either electrically or with a small explosive charge as it left the nozzle. The range of an American portable unit was about 40 yards, and flamethrowers mounted on tanks did not project a stream much farther, although the stream was both of much greater volume and of longer duration. The best portable American unit had a total duration of 10 seconds or somewhat less. Tank-mounted weapons could project 70 or 80 three-second bursts.

In their most basic form, projected-flame weapons are almost as old as warfare itself. The weapons were modernized and reintroduced in World War I, and they were adopted by the armies of all major combatant nations in World War II. They were, however, most extensively used by Japanese forces and the U.S. Marines in the Pacific. It was the British who pioneered the design of tank-mounted flamethrowers, but they were soon widely used by the Germans as well.

Flamethrowers were terrifying weapons, but they were severely limited by fuel supply and, in the case of man-portable flamethrowers, by the vulnerability of the man carrying the weapon. As the burning stream readily marked his position, he made an easy target. Once hit, the fuel canisters he carried on his back could easily explode, killing not only him but any of his nearby comrades. It was also common for a flamethrower shooter, hit by an enemy, to spin about as he fell, projecting a stream of flame behind him against his comrades. For this reason, flamethrower shooters were generally well guarded by a party of riflemen.

Further reading: Doyle, Hilary, and Peter Sarson. *Flammpanzer German: German Flamethrowers 1941–1945.* London: Osprey, 1995; Koch, Fred. *Flamethrowers of the German Army 1914–1945.* Atglen, Pa.: Schiffer, 1997; Mountcastle, John Wyndham. *Inferno: American Flame Throwers in World War II.* Raleigh-Durham, N.C.: Duke University Press, 1976.

Fletcher, Frank (1885–1973) *U.S. admiral*

Born in Marshalltown, Iowa, Frank Jack Fletcher obtained an appointment to the U.S. Naval Academy and graduated in 1906. He served on numerous ships and in may postings and acquitted himself with such gallantry during the U.S. intervention in Vera Cruz in 1914 that he was awarded the Medal of Honor. He served as commander of five destroyers, a battleship, and three other vessels.

Promoted to rear admiral in the late 1930s, he was given command of the task force sent to relieve besieged Wake Island shortly after the BATTLE OF PEARL HARBOR. Fletcher made the decision to refuel en route, an action that delayed the task force. This in itself might not have proved fatal to the mission, but Admiral HUSBAND E. KIMMEL, who had dispatched the task force, was during this time relieved of command and replaced, temporarily, by Vice Admiral William Pye, a cautious caretaker commander who decided that the task force to rescue Wake Island was too risky. He ordered

Fletcher to abort the relief. Despite a gallant stand by overwhelmingly outnumbered marines, Wake Island fell. Whether justly or not, a charge of overcautiousness was leveled at Fletcher.

Fletcher did perform with skill and distinction at the BATTLE OF THE CORAL SEA in May 1942, a tactical victory for the Japanese but also a costly strategic defeat, since the Japanese invasion fleet that had been headed for Port Moresby, New Guinea, was forced to turn back. Fletcher also performed gallantly at the BATTLE OF MIDWAY but lost his flagship early in the battle, which meant that Admiral RAYMOND SPRUANCE assumed tactical command and therefore earned credit for the victory in this hard-fought turning-point clash.

As commander of an invasion fleet, Fletcher drew considerable criticism for precipitously withdrawing his carrier forces at the Battle of GUADALCANAL in August 1942, thereby isolating the marines who had been landed there. He took a similarly cautious and conservative approach in the Eastern Solomon Islands during the Solomon Islands Campaigns later in August.

In November 1942, Fletcher was named to command of the Thirteenth Naval District and the Northwestern Sea Frontier. At the end of 1943, he was given overall command of the Northern Pacific area, but he also participated in the OKINAWA CAMPAIGN during April 1945.

After the war, Vice Admiral Fletcher was named chairman of the general board and, on his retirement in May 1947, was advanced to the rank of admiral. The destroyer USS *Fletcher* (DD-992) was named in his honor.

See also WAKE ISLAND, BATTLE OF.

Further reading: Regan, Stephen D. *In Bitter Tempest: The Biography of Admiral Frank Jack Fletcher.* Ames: Iowa State University Press, 1994.

flying boat

The World War II flying boat was a seaplane, often of twin-engine design, the fuselage of which resembled the hull of a ship. This enabled the flying boat to land on the water with the entire fuselage as opposed to skimming the water on pontoons, as with smaller floatplanes. (Flying boats also had pontoons, or floats, on their wings for added stability in water landings, but the aircraft floated on its hull.) The flying boat was designed for long-range sea patrols, antisubmarine warfare, air-sea rescue, island transport, and limited resupply work.

All major combatant nations employed some flying boats, including France, Germany, Great Britain, Italy, Japan, the Soviet Union, and the United States. The most notable aircraft included the following:

GERMANY

Blohm und Voss Bv 138. First flown in 1937, this aircraft featured twin tail booms and three engines, two at the forward end of each of the booms and one mounted above the wing, just behind the cockpit area. The aircraft was used for long-range maritime reconnaissance and saw action in the North Atlantic and in and around Norway.

General specifications included:

Wingspan: 88 ft 4.25 in
Length: 65 ft 1.5 in
Height: 19 ft 4.25 in
Power plant: three Junkers Jumo 205 D six-cylinder vertical opposed-piston engines, each rated at 880 horsepower
Top speed: 177 mph
Service ceiling (at 31,967 lbs): 16,400 ft
Maximum range: 2,670 mi
Armament: one 20-mm MG 151 cannon in bow turret, one 20-mm MG 151 cannon mounted in turret in hull tail, and one 13-mm MG 131 machine gun on open position aft of central engine; optionally, one 7.9-mm MG 15 machine gun firing through hatch in starboard side of hull.
Bomb load: three 110-lb bombs on racks beneath the starboard wing center section, or six 110-lb bombs, or four 331-lb depth charges

Blohm und Voss Bv222 "Wiking." This aircraft had the distinction of being the largest *operational* flying boat in World War II. (Another Blohm und Voss design, the Bv238, was actually the largest prototype but failed to achieve operational status.) The aircraft was designed in 1937 for the German state-subsidized airline, Lufthansa, as a commercial transport for the Berlin-to-New York run. Like practically all interwar German aircraft designs, however, it was drawn up with an eventual military application in mind. A prototype flew on September 7, 1940, and its first military flight took place on July 10, 1941. The aircraft was used in Norway as well as in North Africa and the Mediterranean, where it served as a cargo transport. Soon, armament was added to the Wiking, which then assumed a long-range maritime reconnaissance role, operating mainly from bases in France. Among the innovations added to the craft was advanced FuG 200 "Hohentwiel" search radar equipment.

General specifications included:

Wingspan: 150 ft 11 in
Length: 121 ft 4 ¾ in
Height: 35 ft 9 in
Power plant: six 1,000-horsepower Junkers Jumo 207C inline diesel engines
Top speed: 242 mph
Service ceiling: 23,950 ft
Range: 3,787 mi
Armament (Bv 222C–09): three 20-mm MG 151 cannon, one each in forward dorsal and two over-wing turrets; and five 13-mm MG 131 machine guns, one each in bow position and four beam hatches

GREAT BRITAIN

British flying boats were far more conventional than the German models, but they were also more serviceable and capable of being produced in much more significant quantities. Three designs were most important early in the war, the Saro London, Saro Lerwick, and Supermarine Walrus.

Saro London. This biplane design dated to the 1920s and featured a metal frame and a metal-skinned fuselage, but with fabric-covered wings. Already obsolescent at the outbreak of the war, it flew on marine reconnaissance and patrol missions until June 1941.

General specifications included:

Wingspan: 80 ft
Length: 56 ft 9 ½ in
Height: 18 ft 9 in
Power plant: two 920-horsepower Bristol Pegasus X nine-cylinder radial engines
Top speed: 142 mph
Service ceiling: 19,900 ft
Range: 1,740 mi
Armament: hand-held 7.7-mm Lewis machine guns, one each in open bow, open midships, and open tail positions
Bomb load: 2,000 lbs bombs, mines, or depth charges

Saro Lerwick. This aircraft was first flown in 1938 and experienced difficult stability and handling problems, which were not corrected until 1940. The planes were used for marine reconnaissance and patrol but never fully replaced the earlier Saro London.

General specifications included:

Wingspan: 80 ft 10 in
Length: 63 ft 7 ½ in
Height: 20 ft
Power plant: two 1,375-horsepower Hercules II 14-cylinder radial engines
Top speed: 216 mph
Service ceiling: 14,000 ft
Armament: one 7.7-mm machine gun in nose turret, twin 7.7-mm machine guns in dorsal turret, and four 7.7-mm machine guns in tail turret
Bomb load: 2,000 lbs bombs, mines, or depth charges

Supermarine Walrus. Like the Saro London, the Supermarine Walrus was a 1920s design and a biplane. Unlike the London, however, the Walrus proved far more durable and successful in the role at which it excelled: air-sea rescue. The venerable design flew throughout the war.

General specifications included:

Wingspan: 45 ft 10 in
Length: 37 ft 7 in

Height: 15 ft 3 in
Power plant: one 775-horsepower Bristol Pegasus VI nine-cylinder radial engine mounted centrally above the fuselage and beneath the center of the upper wing
Top speed: 124 mph
Service ceiling: 18,500 ft
Armament: one 7.7-mm machine gun in open bow
Bomb load: 500 lbs bombs or depth charges

Short Sunderland. By far the most successful British flying boat of the war, the Sunderland was modified from a 1934 design ordered by Imperial Airways for commercial transport. The military version was first flown in 1937 and was used extensively throughout the war, mainly in long-range reconnaissance and antisubmarine service.

General specifications included:

Wingspan: 112 ft 9 ½ in
Length: 85 ft 3 ½ in
Height: 34 ft 6 in
Power plant: four 1,200-horsepower Pratt & Whitney R–1830–90 Twin Wasp 14-cylinder radial engines
Top speed: 213 mph
Service ceiling: 17,900 ft
Armament: two forward-firing 7.7-mm machine guns, two 7.7-mm machine guns in bow turret, 7.7-mm machine guns in dorsal turret, and four 7.7-mm machine guns in tail turret
Bomb load: 4,660 lbs bombs, mines, or depth charges in retractable racks mounted on hull sides

ITALY

The most notable of the Italian flying boats was the Cant Z.501 Gabbiano ("Gull"), which was designed in the 1930s and was first flown in 1934. It was used widely for maritime reconnaissance, primarily in the Mediterranean. The aircraft was powered by a single engine mounted at the front of a fuselagelike nacelle, which sat atop the high monoplane wing. Behind the engine was a machine gun turret.

General specifications included:

Wingspan: 73 ft 9 ¾ in
Length: 46 ft 11 in
Height: 14 ft 6 in
Power plant: one 900-horsepower Isotta Fraschini Asso XI R2C 15 12-cylinder inline engine
Top speed: 171 mph
Service ceiling: 22,965 ft
Armament: 7.7-mm machine guns mounted, one each, in bow, nacelle, and dorsal turrets
Bomb load: 1,441 lbs bombs, mines, or depth charges

JAPAN

The two most important Japanese flying boats were Kawanishi H6K and H8K.

Kawanishi H6K. First flown in 1936, the H6K was the only long-range flying boat in the Japanese inventory when that nation went to war on December 7, 1941. The planes were used for troop transport as well as maritime patrol. Early in the war, during the great Japanese offensives, the transport role was the more important. After the BATTLE OF MIDWAY, as the Japanese were forced to assume a defensive posture, the aircraft was increasingly used for antisubmarine patrol.

General specifications included:

Wingspan: 131 ft 2 ¾ in
Length: 84 ft ¾ in
Height: 20 ft 6 ¾ in
Power plant: four 1,300-horsepower Mitsubishi Kinsei 53 14-cylinder radial engines
Top speed: 239 mph
Service ceiling: 31,495 ft
Range: 4,210 mi
Armament: four 7.7-mm machine guns, distributed in front and midships, and in two beam blisters; and one 20-mm tail cannon
Bomb load: 4,409 lbs bombs or two torpedoes (1,764 lbs total)

Kawanishi H8K. This aircraft was designed in 1938 and first flew in January 1941, but, because of stability problems in the water, it did not enter into service until early 1942. In all, only 167 of this large craft were produced before the end of the war. Despite its small numbers, it was probably the best all-around flying boat of World War II. The most advanced model, H8K2, was remarkably fast, heavily armed, and a most formidable long-range maritime patrol craft.

General specifications included:

Wingspan: 114 ft 8 in
Length: 92 ft 3 ½ in
Height: 30 ft
Power plant: four 1,850-horsepower Mitsubishi Kasei 22 14-cylinder radial engines
Top speed: 290 mph
Service ceiling: 38,740 ft
Range: 4,460 mi
Armament: 20-mm cannon in bow, dorsal, and tail turrets and in two beam blisters; and four hand-held 7.7-mm machine guns in beam hatches
Bomb load: 4,409 lbs bombs or two torpedoes (1,764 lbs total)

SOVIET UNION

The most important of the Soviet flying boats was the Beriev Be-2 (originally designated the MBR-2), which was first flown in 1931. A small, single-engine craft, the Be-2 was used in the Baltic, the Black Sea, and the Arctic seaboard.

General specifications included:

Wingspan: 62 ft 4 in
Length: 44 ft 3 ¾ in
Power plant: one 860-horsepower AM-34NB 12-cylinder inline engine
Top speed: 154 mph
Service ceiling: 19,658 ft
Range: 870 mi
Armament: one hand-held 7.62-mm machine gun in the open bow position and one 7.62-mm machine gun in a dorsal turret
Bomb load: 661 lbs bombs, mines, or depth charges

UNITED STATES

The most important American flying boat and the preeminent flying boat of the war was the Consolidated PBY Catalina, which was built in a quantity of 2,398 by Consolidated and 892 by other manufacturers under license. The aircraft was used by the U.S. Navy and by most of the Allies.

Although originally designed in 1933, the aircraft proved incredibly durable and was used in the Atlantic and the Pacific for reconnaissance, antisubmarine warfare, transport, and air-sea rescue. Painted flat black, the aircraft was also used for night raids and attacks and was, for this mission, affectionately referred to as the "Black Cat." The aircraft was tremendously stable and durable. Its engineering was so simple that it could be easily maintained in the field amid the primitive conditions prevailing on Pacific island bases.

General specifications for the PBY-5A model included:

Wingspan: 104 ft
Length: 63 ft 10 ½ in
Height: 20 ft 2 in
Power plant: two 1,200-horsepower Pratt & Whitney 14-cylinder radial engines
Top speed: 179 mph
Service ceiling: 14,700 ft
Range: 2,545 mi
Armament: two 12.7-mm machine guns in bow turret, one 12.7-mm machine gun in each beam blister, and one 7.62-mm machine gun in ventral tunnel
Bomb load: 4,000 lbs bombs, mines, or depth charges or two torpedoes

Two other important American flying boats were the Consolidated PB2Y Coronado and the Martin PBM Mariner.

Consolidated PB2Y Coronado. This four-engine aircraft first flew in 1937 but due to stability problems was not ordered by the U.S. Navy until 1940. Delivery began the following year. Configured as a transport, this large aircraft could carry 45 passengers or 16,000 pounds of freight. It also served as a medical evacuation air ambulance. Configured for long-distance patrol, it carried an impressive bomb load.

General specifications included:

Wingspan: 115 ft
Length: 79 ft 3 in

Height: 27 ft 6 in
Power plant: four 1,200-horsepower Pratt & Whitney R-1830-88 Twin Wasp 14-cylinder radial engines
Top speed: 223 mph
Service ceiling: 20,500 ft
Range: 2,370 mi
Armament: twin 12.7-mm machine guns in bow, dorsal, and tail turrets and two 12.7-mm guns in beam hatches
Bomb load: eight 1,000-pound bombs internally and four 1,000-pound bombs externally; could also carry two torpedoes externally

Martin PBM Mariner. Widely used in the Pacific theater, this twin-engine flying boat was used for patrol and for air-sea rescue; it could also be configured as a passenger transport. The prototype flew in 1937, and the aircraft entered service in 1941.

General specifications included:

Wingspan: 118 ft
Length: 79 ft 10 in
Height: 27 ft 6 in
Power plant: two 1,900-horsepower Wright R–2600–22 Cyclone 14-cylinder radial engines
Top speed: 211 mph
Service ceiling: 19,800 ft
Range: 2,240 mi
Armament: twin 12.7-mm machine guns in bow, dorsal, and tail turrets and two 12.7-mm guns in beam hatches
Bomb load: 8,000 lbs

Further reading: Creed, Roscoe. *PBY: The Catalina Flying Boat.* Annapolis, Md.: Naval Institute Press, 1986; Hoffman, Richard Alden. *The Fighting Flying Boat: A History of the Martin PBM Mariner.* Annapolis, Md.: Naval Institute Press, 2004; Knott, Richard C. *The American Flying Boat: An Illustrated History.* Annapolis, Md.: Naval Institute Press, 1979; Knott, Richard C. *Black Cat Raiders of World War II.* Annapolis, Md.: Naval Institute Press, 2000; London, Peter. *British Flying Boats.* London: Sutton, 2003; Munson, Kenneth. *Pocket Encyclopedia of Seaplanes and Flying Boats.* New York: Macmillan, 1971; Nicolaou, Stephane. *Flying Boats and Seaplanes: A*

History from 1905. Osceola, Wis.: Motorbooks International, 1998.

Flying Tigers

The *Flying Tigers* was the popular nickname of a unit of American civilian mercenary aviators in the service of China officially designated the American Volunteer Group (AVG) and led by a retired U.S. Army Air Corps captain, Claire L. Chennault. The AVG, or Flying Tigers, had its origin in the 1940–41 authorization by President Franklin D. Roosevelt of an unofficial and covert U.S. air force to fight on behalf of China in the Sino-Japanese War, which had begun in 1937. The American Volunteer Group was planned to consist of two fighter groups and one medium bomber group. By presidential directive, 100 Tomahawk II-B fighters, equivalent to the Curtiss P-40C pursuit craft, were diverted from a British order and sent to equip the two fighter groups. Also, 100 U.S. military pilots and 200 enlisted technicians, all eager to see combat action, resigned from the U.S. Army Air Corps to accept private employment as civilian mercenaries with the AVG. The first group was designated the First American Volunteer Group and put under Chennault's command. He trained his personnel in neutral Burma.

Events soon overtook the First AVG, which was not committed to combat until after the Battle of Pearl Harbor had thrust the United States into the war in December 1941. Entry into the conflict brought the cancellation of the planned second fighter group as well as the bomber group, but the First AVG continued to fly, under Chennault, as what the public came to call the "Flying Tigers." AVG pilots painted vivid rows of shark teeth on either side of the supercharged P–40's large, distinctive air scoop. Journalists saw this as a tiger's mouth, not a shark's, and christened the group accordingly. The name conveyed the aggressive spirit that was in critically short supply among the Allies during the early days of the Pacific war.

The Flying Tigers played an important role in defending Burma until the Japanese routed the Allies in May 1942. Later in the year, transferred to China, the AVG was instrumental in holding western China until reinforcements reached the Nationalist government. Always outnumbered and operating in isolation and on a shoestring, AVG fliers were nevertheless credited with shooting down 297 Japanese aircraft; 23 AVG pilots were killed or captured.

Formally disbanded on July 4, 1942, the AVG was instantly merged into the 23rd Pursuit Group of the U.S. Army Air Forces (USAAF). Only five AVG pilots immediately accepted induction into the new USAAF unit while they were in China, but many others subsequently rejoined the U.S. military.

The exploits of the Flying Tigers were so colorful, as was their irascible leader, that it is often difficult to separate mythology from fact, and, indeed, some recent historians have concluded that the record of Flying Tiger victories was inflated. Be this as it may, it is beyond dispute that the AVG was highly effective against Japanese air and ground forces during the winter of 1941–42, when the Allies could offer very little creditable opposition to the Japanese juggernaut. Their performance slowed the relentless Japanese advance and took a heavy toll in enemy aircraft and among ground forces while simultaneously doing much to lift the morale of all the Allies during a time when the news from Asia and the Pacific was unremitting bleak.

Further reading: Bond, Charles, and Terry Anderson. *A Flying Tiger's Diary.* College Station: Texas A&M University Press, 1984; Ford, Daniel. *Flying Tigers: Claire Chennault and the American Volunteer Group.* Washington, D.C.: Smithsonian Institution Press, 1991.

Foertsch, Hermann (1885–1961) *German general of infantry and military theorist*

Hermann Foertsch was born in Munich, joined the army, and rose rapidly through the ranks. He was best known as a military pedagogue and theorist, the author of a number of books on the special role of the interwar Wehrmacht and, most famously, on modern warfare. *Kriegskunst Heute und Morgen,* published in 1939, was translated into English the following year as *The Art of Modern Warfare.* Appearing as these books did at the outbreak of World War II, they provided Allied military leaders with valuable insight into the German military mind.

From 1937 to 1939, Foertsch was an instructor at the War Academy, then was made chief of staff Military District VIII (1939) and chief of staff XXVI Corps. He was temporarily retired to reserve duty in 1940 but was recalled during 1940–41 as commander of the General Staff Course, serving in Berlin. Foertsch was assigned to a field staff post during 1941–42, as chief of staff of the Twelfth German Army in Greece. He became chief of staff to SIEGMUND LIST, commander in chief Southeast, in the Balkans, serving in this capacity from 1942 to 1944 while also serving (during 1942–43) as chief of staff Army Group E, in Greece, then as chief of staff Army Group F, in Yugoslavia (1943–44).

In 1944, Foertsch was again returned to reserve duty for a time but was soon elevated to commanding officer of the 21st Division, then acting commander and commander of X Corps, all before the end of 1944. After another period in reserve, he was named acting general officer commanding the Nineteenth German Army in 1945 and held the same post in the First German Army, from which he became a prisoner of war.

Foertsch was held by the Allies from 1945 to 1948, when he faced trial for war crimes committed mainly in the Balkans. Acquitted, Foertsch lived out the rest of his life in quiet retirement.

Further reading: Foertsch, Hermann. *The Art of Modern Warfare.* New York: Veritas, 1940.

Forrestal, James (1892–1949) *U.S. undersecretary and later secretary of the navy during World War II*

James Vincent Forrestal is best remembered for his postwar appointment as the first U.S. secretary of defense (1947–49), but during World War II, as under secretary and later as secretary of the navy, his formidable administrative genius enabled him to direct the massive wartime build-up of naval forces. Forrestal was a naval aviator during World War I, then returned to civilian life as a successful executive with a Wall Street investment firm, becoming its president in 1938. In June 1940, Forrestal was tapped by President FRANKLIN D. ROOSEVELT as his administrative assistant, and in August he was named undersecretary of the navy. He was charged with overseeing and directing the huge peacetime expansion of the navy, which was gearing up for what increasingly seemed the inevitable entry of the United States into World War II. The task was a staggering one, which became even more intensive after the BATTLE OF PEARL HARBOR thrust the nation into the war.

In May 1944, with the death of navy secretary Frank Knox, Forrestal was named the new secretary of the navy and continued to direct the logistics of this mighty force. Following the war, after passage of the National Security Act of 1947, which terminated the Department of War and inaugurated the Department of Defense at the cabinet level, Forrestal was appointed to the new post. His task was nothing less than the total reorganization and coordination of the armed services. The U.S. Air Force, independent of the army, was created, and all the armed services were redesigned to function more cooperatively together, answering to a single civilian authority, the secretary of defense.

Forrestal's war work had been tireless and overwhelming, and peacetime brought no rest. On the contrary, it required the reinvention of the entire U.S. military. Exhausted and in a state of emotional collapse, Forrestal stepped down as secretary of defense in March 1949. Afflicted with severe depression, which his physicians subsequently compared to battle fatigue, the post-traumatic stress syndrome to which combat troops often fall prey, Forrestal entered Bethesda Naval Hospital. On May 22, 1949, he leaped to his death from a hospital window.

Further reading: Forrestal, James V. *Diaries of James V. Forrestal, 1944–1949, Secretary of the Navy, 1944–1947, and First Secretary of Defence, 1947–1949.* Marlborough, U.K.:

Adam Matthew Publications, 2002; Forrestal, James V. *Papers*. Washington, D.C.: NPPSO-Naval District, Microfilm Section, 1973; Hoopes, Townsend. *Driven Patriot: The Life and Times of James Forrestal*. New York: Knopf, 1992; Rogow, Arnold A. *James Forrestal: A Study of Personality, Politics, and Policy*. New York: Macmillan, 1963.

Fortress Eben Emael

Fortress Eben Emael was actually a collection of hardened defensive emplacements made of concrete and steel and carefully sited on the Albert Canal north of Liège, Belgium. As the MAGINOT LINE was intended to be the impregnable fixed defense of France, so Eben Emael, which guarded the bridges at Briegen, Veldwezelt, and Vroenhoven, was meant to be the sovereign defense of Belgium, a means of controlling the key passages from Germany into the country.

Garrisoned by 700 men, the Eben Emael defenses were state of the art and very formidable—at least if attacked conventionally, by an army approaching on the ground and from the east. During the western European BLITZKRIEG, however, the Germans did not use conventional tactics to assault Eben Emael. Instead, on May 10, 1940, 78 engineers of the Koch Assault Detachment used gliders to land on top of the fortifications. Working with hollow charges shaped to ensure that the force of the blast was directed downward, the engineers blew up some of the emplacements of the fortress complex from the roof down. Such an assault had never been anticipated by the defenders, and the buildings were quite vulnerable when approached this way. The attack effectively neutralized Eben Emael as an AIRBORNE ASSAULT was staged to take the bridges that the fortress was supposed to defend. With these secured, the main German column, the 223rd Infantry Division, attacked the rest of the fortress complex on May 11. The garrison quickly capitulated, and Belgium was soon overrun. The cost to the Germans was six men killed and 20 wounded, all belonging to the Koch Assault Detachment.

Further reading: Dunstan, Simon. *Fort Eben Emael: The Key to Hitler's Victory in the West*. London: Osprey, 2005; Mrazek, James E. *The Fall of Eben Emael*. Novato, Calif.: Presidio Press, 1991.

foxhole

In contrast to World War I, which, particularly on the western front, was a brutally static trench war, World War II was characterized by great mobility and rapid movement. When troops needed to hold a defensive position or to pause in an advance, they dug hasty defenses. A slit trench could be dug if time permitted. It held several soldiers and was often excavated in the shape of an L. More common, especially among American forces, was the foxhole. At its most basic, the foxhole was nothing more than a hastily dug pit meant to shelter one or at most two soldiers from enemy fire. Some foxholes were shallow and meant to be used by a soldier in a crouching or even prone position. If time permitted, the foxhole could be dug more deeply and became what the U.S. Marines called a "fighting hole." This type of foxhole resembled a small section of crude trench. Deep enough to accommodate one or two standing troops, it featured a rudimentary parapet on which a rifle could be rested, a dugout shelf running along the rim of the hole to serve as an elbow rest for the shooter, and a build up of earth at the bottom front of the hole to serve as a firing step. The soldier could mount the step in order to fire, then step back down for full defensive over-head-height cover. Well-constructed fighting holes also included a dug-out water sump to collect water and keep the floor and firing step reasonably dry.

The foxhole was essential to infantry tactics in World War II, but some commanders, most notably GEORGE S. PATTON JR., decried its use or, at least, its overuse, claiming that soldiers were safer (and far more effective) the faster they advanced. He pointed out that foxholes made soldiers easy targets for an artillery barrage, against which they offered little or no protection. By digging a foxhole, Patton believed, a soldier dug his own grave.

Further reading: Bull, Stephen. *World War II Infantry Tactics: Squad and Platoon*. Osceola, Wis.: Motorbooks International, 2004.

France

With GREAT BRITAIN, France was bound by treaties to come to the aid of Czechoslovakia and Poland if they were attacked. Like Great Britain, too, France was dominated by pacifist sentiment, a desire to avoid war at all cost. This was understandable, since no western European nation had suffered more destruction and loss of life in World War I than France, which, for four years, had been the principal battlefield of the western front. At the outbreak of war, France had a very large army of 5 million, believed by many (including Britain's WINSTON CHURCHILL and the Soviet Union's JOSEPH STALIN) to be the finest army in the world. Its size, however, belied a prevailing ambivalence, absence of will, and fear of a new war. War plans, drawn up in cooperation with British military commanders, were entirely defensive in nature, and the French put a great deal of faith in a strong line of defensive fortifications along the German frontier, the MAGINOT LINE. With all of its military resources, France seemed to suffer from the same malaise afflicting the other Western democracies, an attitude that in Great Britain, which spent all but the last two or three years of the decades after World War I disarming, had motivated Prime Minister NEVILLE CHAMBERLAIN's APPEASEMENT POLICY with regard to the expansionist aggression of Germany's ADOLF HITLER.

Despite the sentiment prevailing in France, French premier EDOUARD DALADIER at first objected to his ally's Appeasement Policy and to the cession of the SUDETENLAND that followed it as a betrayal of Czechoslovakia. Yet he dared not oppose Germany alone. Instead, he appealed to U.S. President FRANKLIN D. ROOSEVELT (FDR). Although FDR was sympathetic to Daladier's objection to appeasement, he knew that he would not be able to move the isolationist U.S. Congress to alter American neutrality. With Roosevelt's rebuff, hope vanished, and Daladier agreed to hand over the Sudetenland to Hitler. Yet whereas Chamberlain seemed sincerely to believe that appeasement had brought "peace for our time," Daladier understood that it made war all the more inevitable. He was, of course, correct. After the German INVASION OF POLAND, France and Great Britain honored treaty obligations to Poland, as they had not honored those with Czechoslovakia. The two nations declared war against Germany on September 3, 1939.

It is doubtful that any nation not directly attacked ever went to war with greater reluctance than France. Despite its resources, the nation and the army were suffused with defeatism. During the first eight months of the war, Germany concentrated on the eastern front, and there was so little action in the west that the French referred to the war as the *drôle de guerre*, what the British called the PHONY WAR. During this period, the majority of the French public was more concerned about communism and communist aggression than fighting Nazi Germany. The public followed the course of the RUSSO-FINNISH WAR, but of action on the Franco-German front they heard nothing concrete, only Daladier's vague promise that France, with its powerful army, would inevitably prevail and that he would not spill French blood until absolutely necessary. British policy at the end of Chamberlain's term as prime minister and, even more, during all of Churchill's, was to rally public support by conveying full and honest information to them. In contrast, the French government communicated almost nothing to the public and made very little attempt to outline war aims. Worse, the call to general mobilization had resulted in the conscription of large numbers of factory laborers and skilled workers. This had been a politically motivated policy decision to avoid the World War I complaint that agricultural workers and peasants had borne the brunt of the sacrifice. However, it meant that production of war materiel fell at precisely the moment when it was most needed. For while France had a large army and, with a population of 41.18 million (1936), a large reserve of manpower on which to draw, it was severely short on equipment, artillery, armor, and especially aircraft. Some 2 million workers had to be withdrawn from the army in order to bring production back up to an acceptable level. This succeeded mainly in producing resentment among the rural population, which had to make up the army's shortfall and contributed to the decline of the already-failing French morale.

The eight months of *drôle de guerre* could have been spent preparing the people as well as the army and mounting a massive war production drive. Instead, the government allowed policy and morale to drift and war production to flag. As a result, the BATTLE OF FRANCE, when it finally came, beginning on May 10, 1940, was lost within six weeks. Confusion reigned in the French government. Daladier resigned as premier on March 20 and was replaced by PAUL REYNAUD the following day. More aggressive than Daladier, Reynaud concluded an agreement with Britain that neither nation would make a separate peace with Germany. As France crumbled around him following the German invasion, he declared to the National Assembly that only a miracle could save France, but that "I believe in miracles." This rather mystical pronouncement could have done little to build French confidence. Belatedly, Reynaud shuffled his cabinet, moving Daladier from his post as minister of defense to foreign minister while he himself assumed leadership of defense. During the battle, he also replaced General MAURICE-GUSTAVE GAMELIN with General MAXIME WEYGAND as commander in chief, but to no avail, as Weygand's grandiose plan to attack the German advance from two directions evaporated and yielded nothing more or less than the desperate retreat to Dunkirk and the even more desperate DUNKIRK EVACUATION.

If public information and organization had been lacking during the *drôle de guerre,* these collapsed totally during the Battle of France. Rumor and panic assumed the ascendency, and some 8 to 10 million French citizens fled the cities and the east, creating a mass refugee crisis, which was exacerbated by severe thunderstorms and by the German policy of deliberately strafing and dive-bombing the fleeing civilian columns. This heightened the terror and the misery. Moreover, with the roads clogged by retreating refugees, military transportation to the front became a slow-motion nightmare.

The fall of France was both a military failure and a failure of government. A panic-stricken, demoralized population, never provided with adequate direction in the war or a vision of purpose, were, for the most part, eager to accept the salvation offered by Marshal HENRI-PHILIPPE PÉTAIN and the collaborationist VICHY GOVERNMENT.

The cautious Daladier had been replaced by the more vocally bellicose Reynaud, who believed that the French Army and the military and economic power of the French Empire (including colonies in North Africa, West Africa, Indochina, the Pacific, and the West Indies) would ultimately prevail against Germany. The sheer speed and magnitude of the German BLITZKRIEG through France revealed this confidence as a baseless illusion. Reynaud had brought out of retirement the aggressive Weygand and the gallant World War I hero of Verdun, Marshal Pétain, precisely to stiffen French resolve. As it turned out, both of these men were quickly transformed by the battle into outright defeatists. When Reynaud proposed a government in exile (in Brittany or North Africa), these men proposed armistice instead, believing that the war was already lost. Reynaud even proposed a Franco-British union, an idea that came to nothing.

In the meantime, the government itself joined the refugee exodus, withdrawing to Bordeaux. The German invaders exploited this with a propaganda campaign portraying the French as an "abandoned people." Pétain, in effect, agreed, and made a public broadcast on June 17, 1940, accusing the Third Republic, not the French military, of having failed the people. On June 22, in the very railroad car at Compiègne in which Germany had signed the armistice ending World War I, Pétain and others surrendered to Germany.

By the terms of the armistice, France was permitted to retain an army of 100,000 men, the same limit levied against Germany by the TREATY OF VERSAILLES. The country was divided into several zones of occupation, including the vast *Zone occupée,* which encompassed Paris and all of France to the English Channel and Bay of Biscay coast; a *Zone réservée,* in the east, which was reserved for future German colonization; a *Zone rattachée,* along the Belgian frontier, which was under direct German command from Brussels in occupied Belgium; and a *Zone interdite,* along the northern and western coasts and east of the Somme River, in which the German military was to exercise absolute control. The Alsace and Lorraine regions, which had been annexed to France following World War I, were returned to Germany and became part of the reich. The rest of France constituted the *Zone libre* and was ostensibly unoccupied, although the government was hardly free of German authority. It was administered from the resort city of Vichy and, therefore, was referred to as Vichy France. The fiction of Vichy sovereignty evaporated on November 11, 1942, when Germany occupied the *Zone libre*, and Italy occupied a portion of it east of the Rhone River and also the island of Corsica. Small portions of the French-Italian frontier were annexed by Italy, and a corridor between the Italian-occupied zone and the annexed territory was demilitarized. During the occupation, France was assessed an inflated and quite ruinous charge to bear the costs of occupation.

Occupied France was administered by the *Militärbefehlshaber in Frankreich,* the German Military Administration, headquartered in Paris. German troop units were quartered throughout Paris and in every major city and town, each of which was presided over by a *Feldkommandantur* (field commander). In the annexed territory, Nazi gauleiters had absolute authority. From Alsace and Lorraine, those persons considered unalterably French were forced to leave, so that the region would be effectively Germanized. Men of military age were conscripted into the German military.

The line of demarcation separating occupied from unoccupied France was strictly patrolled, and the refugees who had fled to the south (now part of unoccupied France) were forced to remain there, which gave the German administrators of the occupied zone ample time to organize the government and administration. The result was that the Vichy south was overburdened, and its government appeared chronically disorganized, inept, and inadequate, whereas the government of occupied France appeared organized and disciplined. This appearance served to encourage French collaboration with the occupiers, suggesting that French governance was inept while German rule was efficient.

There also existed in France a very significant resistance to the occupation, and by the middle of 1942, any trace of benevolence among the German administration had vanished, as the occupied zone became a frank police state governed by repression, punishment, hostage-taking, institutionalized torture, frequent executions, and extravagant reprisals for acts of the resistance. Such reprisals increased in frequency and severity following the NORMANDY LANDINGS (D-DAY) in June 1944.

The most horrific and shameful aspect of collaboration is seen in connection with the FINAL SOLUTION and THE HOLOCAUST, beginning in 1942, when the Nazi genocide of Europe's Jews was extended to France. French police and civil authorities readily, even eagerly, cooperated with the German occupiers in rounding up Jews, and French personnel staffed the intermediate concentration camps set up in France to hold Jews for deportation to the major CONCENTRATION AND EXTERMINATION CAMPS. French aid in the arrest of Jews was not confined to the occupied zone, but was common in Vichy France as well, except for those who lived in the zone occupied by Italy. Italy long resisted German demands for collaboration in the Final Solution, and in this area the Jews were protected, at least for a time.

Germany was determined to exploit France as an economic asset. Some French citizens collaborated fully in this, hoping to prosper personally and to maintain the French economy; others worked for the Germans resentfully, as a matter of survival; still others engaged in subversive activities, promoting strikes, work slow-downs, and acts of sabotage to cripple German war production as well as the general German economy. Some workers managed to divert resources and production to the resistance. While they exploited French factory production, German administrators gave even greater priority to agriculture. The administrators created a 10-year plan for the French economy and its contribution to the Third Reich. Because of labor and material shortages, as well as chronic noncooperation among many workers, the 10-year plan was largely a fantasy. Nevertheless, by 1943, 40 percent of French industrial output went directly to Germany, including 80 percent of vehicle production. The Germans siphoned off some 55 percent of all French government revenue, ostensibly to cover the costs of occupation. France became the major outside source of German imports, including industrial goods, raw materials, and foodstuffs.

An important part of the German subjugation of the French economy was control over labor. Workers in occupied France were, of course, subject to direct German control. In June 1942, the Vichy regime of unoccupied France introduced "voluntary" worker service in Germany, but on February 16, 1943, the Service du Travail Obligatoire made worker service in Germany compulsory. The law triggered widespread revolt, which, however, did not prevent the forced labor of some 600,000 French workers in Germany and even more in French-based industries and mines necessary to the German war effort. French labor built the Atlantic Wall, the line of great coastal fortresses defending the French coasts against Allied invasion.

Under the occupation, shortages were universal and increasingly severe throughout France. Despite forced labor, production levels dropped far below their prewar levels, while the cost of living rose some 270 percent. A system of rationing was introduced, limiting adults to a food intake equivalent to 1,200 calories. Black markets flourished. Vichy France continually contended with food riots. All these hardships were greatly exacerbated by Allied air raids on French industrial plants and other installations.

Paris was liberated by the Allies on August 25, 1944, and CHARLES DE GAULLE led the transition to a provisional government, building on the French Committee for National Liberation and representing, quite broadly, the interests of a number of resistance leaders. The United States and Great Britain recognized de Gaulle's provisional government on October 23, 1944.

The provisional government quickly instituted Special Courts of Justice to purge the collaborators. However, the courts were more a moderating force than instruments of vengeance. Many individuals were tried, but acquittals far exceeded convictions.

The provisional government also took charge of the resistance and the Maquis, the important rural-based paramilitary arm of the resistance, and integrated them into the regular army. This preempted the resistance leaders from becoming a disruptive force in postoccupation France. It also provided much-needed veteran manpower for the new French Army, which was fighting side by side with the British and the Americans. The provisional government acted quickly to disarm the resistance police, or *milices patriotiques,* and replaced these individuals with a regular, official police force, the Compagnies républicaines de sécurité. Even the communists were cooperative and committed to seeing the war through to its end.

Municipal elections were held at the very end of the war, during April–May 1945, and were followed by national elections in October, soon after V-E day. Right-wing ideology was soundly repudiated by the French electorate, but communism was not embraced. The Third Republic was officially at an end, and there would be an often bitter postwar struggle to shape a new government. Political stability would eventually come, however, but the collective emotional scars would remain long afterward, including a sense of shame in defeat and a growing acknowledgment of the extent of collaboration with evil, especially with regard to the Holocaust.

Further reading: Bloch, Marc. *Strange Defeat.* New York: Norton, 1999; Burrin, Philippe. *France Under the Germans: Collaboration and Compromise.* New York: New Press, 1998; Gildea, Robert. *Marianne in Chains: Daily Life in the Heart of France During the German Occupation.* New York: Metropolitan Books, 2003; Gordon, Bertram M., ed. *Historical Dictionary of World War II France.* Westport, Conn.: Greenwood Press, 1998; Jackson, Julian. *The Fall of France: The Nazi Invasion of 1940.* New York: Oxford University Press, 2003; Jackson, Julian. *France: The Dark Years, 1940–1944.* New York: Oxford University Press, 2003; Ousby, Ian. *Occupation.* New York: Cooper Square, 2000; Paxton, Robert O. *Vichy France.* New York: Columbia University Press, 2001; Poznanski, Renée, and Nathan Bracher. *Jews in France During World War II.* Waltham, Mass.: Brandeis University Press, 2002.

France, air force of

FRANCE had been a pioneering presence in the early years of aviation, and the French military had been in the forefront of aircraft development during World War I. During the interwar period, however, French military doctrine denigrated the role of the airplane, which was seen as a secondary weapon of far less importance than ships at sea and troops on the ground. At the outbreak of World War II, the French air force was nominally commanded by General Joseph Vuillemin, who had actual direct control over only the air reserve. Command of the principal air units had to be shared cooperatively with relevant ground commanders. The result was not a successful integration of land and air forces, but a paralytic confusion of command, as operational air officers were often subject to command from three or even more ground commanders in addition to Vuillemin. Moreover, because aircraft could not be deployed by a single overall commander, they were distributed thinly across the entire front during the BATTLE OF FRANCE, which made it impossible to concentrate air power where needed to repulse an enemy thrust.

The French air force suffered not only from a lack of adequate doctrine and a disastrously ill-conceived and inadequate command structure, but also from outmoded aircraft. By the outbreak of the war, French fighter aircraft were obsolete or obsolescent. The most important, the Morane 445, was 50 miles per hour slower than the main German fighter, the Me-109. Even German medium bombers nearly outpaced it. On paper, the air force had a reasonably impressive 2,200 aircraft. Of these, however, only 610 fighters, 130 bombers, and 350 reconnaissance planes were sufficiently modern to stand any sort of chance against their German opponents. At that, many were destroyed on the ground. Those that flew fell easy prey to the Luftwaffe or to antiaircraft artillery.

To the credit of the French aircraft industry, new planes were rushed into production on the eve of war. In 1938, production stood at about 40 aircraft per month. In May 1940, 500 were turned out. But the production of aircraft outpaced the training and availability of pilots. When the Battle of

France began in May 1940, Vuillemin had at his disposal only 700 fighter pilots to fly little more than 600 fighters.

Further reading: Cain, Anthony Christopher. *The Forgotten Air Force: French Air Doctrine in the 1930s.* Washington, D.C.: Smithsonian Books, 2002; Christienne, Charles, and Pierre Lissarrague. *History of French Military Aviation.* Washington, D.C.: Smithsonian Books, 1986; Ketley, Barry. *French Aces of World War II.* London: Osprey, 1999; Van Haute, André. *Pictorial History of the French Air Force.* Oxford: Allan, 1974.

France, army of

At the outbreak of war, the French army consisted of about 5 million men grouped into three broad bodies:

> The Armée Métropolitaine, a conscript force, was raised to defend metropolitan France.
> The Armée d'Afrique, garrisoned in Algeria, Tunisia, and French Morocco, consisted of segregated white European units: the FRENCH FOREIGN LEGION and the Zouaves. Additionally, it incorporated native conscripts serving in the Spahis and Tirailleurs. Finally, the Armée d'Afrique also had command control over irregular native units, including the Goums and the Compagnies Sahariennes (camel companies).
> The Troupes Coloniales, responsible for defending French colonies other than Algeria, Tunisia, and French Morocco, consisted of white-only colonial infantry and colonial artillery formations, mostly volunteer, as well as Tirailleurs, consisting mostly of conscripted natives.

Despite this tripartite division, units of the Armée Métropolitaine were sometimes used in Africa and the other colonies, and the colonial forces were sometimes brought to France. At the outbreak of World War II, in September 1939, 38 percent of the French infantry in France were Tirailleurs from North Africa. French Foreign Legion units fought in the BATTLE OF FRANCE, and the FREE FRENCH

FORCES that fought in the NORTH AFRICAN CAMPAIGNS and in the ITALIAN CAMPAIGN, as well as some of the fighting in France during 1944, included a large proportion of colonial troops.

Because of its impressive numbers, the French Army was widely regarded as the finest in the world. Despite the defeatism that prevailed in France at the outbreak of World War II, this belief was widespread in France itself, and it also bolstered the confidence of France's closest ally, Great Britain. What was not apparent in this optimistic assessment was the lack of modern armor and field artillery. Even worse, the French high command was afflicted with the same defeatism rampant in the general population and among many politicians. French war-fighting doctrine at the time relied almost exclusively on a defensive strategy, which was given literally concrete expression in the MAGINOT LINE. French military planners had closed their eyes to the lessons of the Spanish civil war, which dramatically demonstrated both the efficacy and ascendency of mobile warfare. Instead, the prevailing doctrinal assumption remained rooted in the static trenches of World War I's western front. CHARLES DE GAULLE, a mere colonel at the time, had written widely against this hidebound notion but was vigorously shunned for his efforts and criticized for his failure of military orthodoxy. Another problem was that between 1928 and 1935, the length of French conscripted military service was reduced to a single year. It was again raised to two years early in 1935, but most of the reserve that was mobilized at the outbreak of World War II belonged to the one-year group and so had little combat training, having served briefly and, at that, perhaps as much as a full decade earlier.

The French Army suffered not only from outmoded doctrine, poor morale, and inadequate training, but also from an ineffectual high command structure. At the commencement of the Battle of France on May 10, 1940, the chief of national defense and commander in chief of land forces was MAURICE-GUSTAVE GAMELIN. His most important commander in the field was Alphonse Georges. Gamelin and Georges did not see eye to eye and, in

fact, strongly disliked one another. Moreover, because of the army's unwieldy command structure, there was inadequate communication between Gamelin and Georges, yet it was Gamelin who drew up the war plans (such as they were), and it was he who had shaped the army. Many officers, therefore, perceived Gamelin as their true commander, a perception that greatly crippled Georges's effectiveness and created confusion at every level. Moreover, Georges was responsible for executing plans in which he had taken no part, in which he had little confidence, and that he understood poorly. In the face of a super-efficient German BLITZKRIEG, this mode of organization was bound to falter and crumble. And so it did.

At the outbreak of the war, the army had 94 divisions at the front or held in reserve. Of these, 63 were conventional infantry (30 regular army, the rest reserve divisions formed around a cadre of regular infantry troops and officers), seven were motorized infantry, three were "light mechanized" infantry, five were cavalry, 13 were garrison troops manning the fortifications, and three were armor divisions. The armored divisions had some 3,000 tanks, including some of high quality and many too light to be effective against superior German armor. (Strictly in terms of numbers, the Germans fielded approximately as many tanks as the French.) French artillery outnumbered that of the Germans but was, by comparison, obsolescent. Of antitank artillery, the French Army was critically short. A rush to produce more during the opening months of the war, the ominously quiet PHONY WAR, failed to make up the shortage.

Despite the grave shortage of antitank weapons, French armor and artillery should have enabled the army to acquit itself far more effectively than it did in the Battle of France. But French command deployed these resources, tanks included, in static patterns suited to the last war instead of the realities of the present conflict. This was tragically inadequate to stem the onrush of Blitzkrieg. As for the vaunted Maginot Line, the Germans merely bypassed it via Belgium. Without doubt formidable, this line of defenses nevertheless proved quite useless.

In less than six weeks, the army so many had thought the finest in Europe was crushingly defeated. After the fall of France, the armistice with the Germans reduced the French Armée Métropolitaine to 100,000 men (called the Armée de l'Armistice), the very same limit that had been imposed on Germany's forces by the TREATY OF VERSAILLES. Germany authorized the VICHY GOVERNMENT, now officially its ally, to expand the Armée d'Afrique, which quickly grew to 225,000, to participate in the Axis defense of North Africa. During the Battle of France, German forces made some 2 million French soldiers prisoners of war. Of this number, 1.6 million were transported to Germany or other parts of the expanding reich to serve as laborers. The Vichy Government created a Légion des Combattants to help care for the families of these absent men.

In November 1942, the success of OPERATION TORCH and the North African Campaigns that followed made the Armée d'Afrique available to the Allies. On November 11, 1942, therefore, German forces occupied Vichy France (the Zone libre) and immediately disbanded the Armée de l'Armistice. This induced several commanders to break with Vichy and create the Free French Forces.

Further reading: Bloch, Marc. *Strange Defeat*. New York: Norton, 1999; Gordon, Bertram M., ed. *Historical Dictionary of World War II France*. Westport, Conn.: Greenwood Press, 1998; Jackson, Julian. *The Fall of France: The Nazi Invasion of 1940*. New York: Oxford University Press, 2003; Nafziger, George F. *The French Order of Battle in WW II: An Organizational History of the Divisions of the French Army*. West Chester, Pa.: G. Nafziger, 1995.

France, Battle of

The Battle of France, spanning May 10 to June 22, 1940, was the brilliant triumph of Germany's Fall Gelb ("Case Yellow") invasion plan, which brought about the ignominious defeat of the forces of France, Britain, Belgium, and the Netherlands. At the start of the battle, the Allied and German forces looked to be evenly matched. The French army had 104 divisions available (up from 94 at the very outbreak of war eight months earlier), the British

Expeditionary Force (BEF, British forces transferred to the Continent) had 10, Belgium 22, and the Netherlands eight, for a total of 144 divisions. Germany invaded with 141 divisions. The Allies had nearly 14,000 guns against 7,378 for Germany, but much of the Allied firepower was obsolescent. Particularly lacking were antitank and antiaircraft artillery. France had 3,063 tanks, and the other Allies a few more, for a total of 3,384, many of them light tanks with inadequate firepower. Germany had 2,445 tanks, most of them more modern than the French vehicles. In terms of aircraft, the French air force had 637 operational fighters, all obsolescent, and 242 bombers. Britain had 262 very fine fighters and 135 bombers based in France, and it had another 540 fighters and 310 bombers based in England. Belgium and the Netherlands contributed a few more of each, so that the total of Allied fighters and bombers available was 1,590 and 708, respectively. Germany substantially outmatched these totals with 1,736 fighters (of which 1,220 were operational at the commencement of battle) and 2,224 bombers (of which 1,559 were operational). The German aircraft, especially the fighters, were of the most advanced type for their day and easily outclassed the French planes.

French military resources looked far better on paper than they were in reality. The army was substantial at some 5 million men, but it was poorly led by a high command that had a weak grasp of strategy, tactics, and execution and that communicated inadequately with commanders in the field. To compound these deficiencies, army commanders consistently failed to coordinate action with air commanders. Perhaps worse, the army was pervaded by an emotion of defeatism, and France's politicians had done nothing to furnish a cogent, let alone inspiring, vision of the nation's war aims. Doctrinally, the French army was also at a grave disadvantage. It had prepared for a static, defensive battle in the manner of World War I's western front. There was virtually no offensive component to this plan, and, even as defense, it was wholly inadequate to the kind of war Germany had already demonstrated in the INVASION OF POLAND: highly violent, highly mobile BLITZKRIEG.

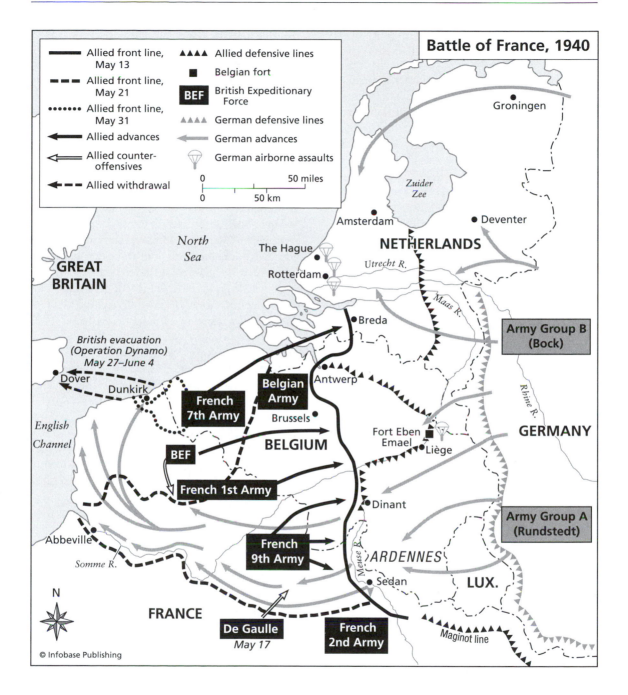

Battle of France, 1940

Legend:
- Allied front line, May 13
- Allied front line, May 21
- Allied front line, May 31
- Allied advances
- Allied counter-offensives
- Allied withdrawal
- ▲▲▲▲ Allied defensive lines
- ■ Belgian fort
- **BEF** British Expeditionary Force
- ▲▲▲▲ German defensive lines
- German advances
- German airborne assaults

0   50 miles
0   50 km

GREAT BRITAIN

North Sea

NETHERLANDS

Zuider Zee

Groningen

Deventer

Amsterdam

The Hague

Rotterdam

Utrecht R.

Maas R.

Breda

Army Group B (Bock)

Rhine R.

GERMANY

British evacuation (Operation Dynamo) May 27–June 4

Dover

Dunkirk

English Channel

French 7th Army

Belgian Army

Antwerp

Brussels

BELGIUM

Fort Eben Emael

Liège

BEF

French 1st Army

Dinant

Army Group A (Rundstedt)

French 9th Army

Meuse R.

ARDENNES

Abbeville

Somme R.

N

FRANCE

De Gaulle May 17

French 2nd Army

Sedan

LUX.

Maginot line

© Infobase Publishing

At dawn on May 10, 1940, the German WEH-RMACHT invaded the three small neutral nations of Luxembourg, Belgium, and the Netherlands. This had the effect of drawing the BEF and the Flan-

ders-based French forces to the northeast, thereby exposing the territory directly to the south, where the MAGINOT LINE, France's elaborate subterranean and semisubterranean chain of frontier forts, ended. French military planners and politicians had not wanted to offend neutral Belgium by extending the Maginot Line along its border. Besides, they believed that the thickly wooded and rugged terrain of the Ardennes was essentially impassable. This belief compounded the vulnerability of the Maginot Line. Not only was the northern end of the line left exposed so that it could be either flanked or merely bypassed by an invader, it was very thinly defended by few troops, because no one expected an invasion via the Ardennes. Yet it was precisely the Ardennes that ERICH VON MANSTEIN, the German commander with primary responsibility for executing Fall Gelb, chose as the *Schwerpunkt*, the point of concentration, for his Blitzkrieg advance. He would execute a version of the famed Schlieffen Plan, by which Germany very nearly won World War I in its first month. Breaking through the Ardennes, he would use his tanks, the panzers, to race across the great plain of France all the way to the English Channel in a great scythe that would cleave the Allied armies in two. Of course, he first had to get through Belgium, which also had a formidable system of fortresses, the most important of which, FORTRESS EBEN EMAEL, guarded the vital bridges at Briegen, Veldwezelt, and Vroenhoven, and was considered the impregnable, ultimate defense of Belgium. A daring German AIRBORNE ASSAULT quickly neutralized Eben Emael and allowed the advance into France, bypassing the Maginot Line.

Germany's Army Group B (under Fedor von Bock) was responsible for the decoy attack in the north, while Army Group A (GERD VON RUNDSTEDT), with twice the divisions of Group B and most of the armor, was poised to attack through the Ardennes. South of this *Schwerpunkt,* Army Group C (Wilhelm Ritter von Leeb) would pin down French forces at the Maginot Line. Rundstedt's panzers were under the very capable field command of HEINZ GUDERIAN, the father of German tank development, doctrine, and tactics, and ERWIN ROMMEL, who would soon emerge as one of Germany's legendary tank commanders.

While the German commanders were, for the most part, brilliant, their command network streamlined and highly efficient, and their troops among the most elite in the world, the French commanders were defeatists struggling with a poorly conceived network of command and command communication and leading demoralized, inadequately trained troops. The overall French commander, MAURICE-GUSTAVE GAMELIN, was a victim of his own conventional military mind, which made his actions perfectly predictable. He readily fell for the German decoy attack in the north. He left the sector between Namur and Sedan, the very *Schwerpunkt,* in the hands of General André Corap's Ninth Army and the Second Army of General Charles Huntziger. Most of the troops in these two forces were inexperienced and suffering from a particularly acute form of the malaise that seemed to grip all of France. These inadequate soldiers, led by two inept commanders, would feel the brunt of the Blitzkrieg. Even more useless were the 30 divisions deployed along the Maginot Line. German Army Group C would keep them in check, effectively taking them out of the battle. Making a bad situation worse, Gamelin ordered the Seventh French Army, under the very capable Henri Giraud, to rush from its position as a mobile reserve force near Dunkirk, in northwestern France on the Belgian border, to Breda, Netherlands, to support the Dutch. This had the effect of putting the most important mobile reserve force out of position for timely action when it would be needed.

As bad as the Allied deployment was on the ground, the situation was even worse in the air. Not only were the French aircraft inferior to the German, they were poorly deployed and generally misused. While the French air force did have a nominal commander, General Joseph Vuillemin, he exercised direct control over the air reserve only. Command of the principal air units was shared with the relevant ground commanders. This resulted in paralysis because operational air officers found themselves subject to command from three or even more ground commanders in addition to Vuillemin. Worse, because the aircraft were distributed among the ground units, they could not be deployed at the discretion of a single overall commander, which meant that they could not be concentrated where they were most needed. The French air asset was simply dissipated. In sharp contrast, German Blitzkrieg doctrine thoroughly integrated air assault with ground advance, and Luftwaffe pilots were keenly trained to function as part of the assault machinery. They flew precisely where they were needed, and they employed tactics that joined seamlessly with the ground assault.

Within 48 hours of breaching Eben Emael, the German invaders had overrun both Belgium and the Netherlands. At the same time, Rundstedt's tanks pushed through what had been thought to be the impassable forests of the Ardennes. Luftwaffe air cover prevented Allied air attacks against the slowly moving armored columns, and nobody among the Allies seems to have thought of mining the forest roads. Thus, by the night of May 12, seven panzer divisions had reached the east bank of the River Meuse along a front stretching from Dinant to Sedan. Astoundingly, the Allies continued to rely on intelligence estimates that were manifestly contradicted by the facts. They thought that five or six days would be required for the Germans to build up the strength necessary actually to cross the Meuse. As the Allies dithered, Guderian boldly decided to press ahead with the crossing of the Meuse on May 13, even though one of his three panzer divisions was still making its way through the Ardennes. This attack, with only three divisions, was made possible by strong air support, especially from the same Stuka dive bombers that had proved so effective in the invasion of Poland. They were true terror weapons, totally demoralizing the ground troops. Because Stukas are vulnerable to fighter attack when they dive, Me-109s kept the French fighters off. By nightfall, Guderian's troops had secured a three-mile-wide bridgehead across the Meuse. Rapid and vigorous response from the French 3rd Armored Division might have stemmed this advance, but, as usual, the unit was poorly deployed and proved ineffective. British bombers sent to destroy the pontoon bridges of the 1st Panzer Division were torn to shreds by German antiaircraft artillery. The net result was the loss of most of the British bombers, which had failed even to damage the German bridges. Allied air power

had been defeated and crushed, and the French failed to mount a creditable counterattack.

Next, Guderian and Rommel rolled through the Sedan sector as Huntziger's Second Army and Corap's Ninth melted away. Prime Minister Churchill rushed to France on May 16, only to be told that no great reserves existed with which to make a counterattack, and French premier PAUL REYNAUD pronounced the Battle of France lost. The main German thrust was toward the coast, but the French could not decide whether the objective would be the English Channel, from which an invasion of England could be staged, or Paris. Colonel CHARLES DE GAULLE led the 4th Armored Division in a spirited desperation attack near Montcornet but was repulsed.

At this point, the Germans nearly became victims of their own success: It all seemed too easy. Moreover, Guderian's panzers had moved so fast that they were far ahead of conventional infantry supporting units. On May 15 and again on May 17, they were ordered to halt so that the infantry could catch up. Both of these pauses presented the defenders with rich opportunities for counterattacks, but by this time, the Allies were so cut up and demoralized that coordinated action was impossible. Worse, the replacement of Gamelin with General MAXIME WEYGAND on May 20 accomplished nothing but to induce further delay in mounting any possible counterthrust, especially on the narrower portions of the far-extended panzer advance.

Guderian's 2nd Panzer Division reached Abbeville, on the English Channel, on May 19. This thrust had accomplished what the Schlieffen Plan of World War I had failed to do: It split the Allied forces, trapping the best French units and most of the BEF in a cul de sac that backed up against the channel. The BEF counterattacked to the south from Arras on May 21 with considerable success, but when the French failed to follow up on this, the BEF had no choice but to retreat and contract its defensive perimeter yet further. The BEF made for the port town of Dunkirk on the English Channel, where there was a very slim hope of evacuation to England.

The tanks of General PAUL LUDWIG VON KLEIST were massed against the southern perimeter of the Dunkirk pocket on May 24. Eager to push forward and bag the BEF and French units trapped there, Kleist was instead ordered by no less a figure than Adolf Hitler to halt and await the arrival of the infantry. Like the earlier halts of May 15 and May 17, this was the product of an excess of caution. It was, in fact, among the most momentous errors of World War II. While it would be an exaggeration to declare that by his halt order Hitler lost the war on May 24, 1940, it is nevertheless true that he relinquished an early opportunity either to win it outright or to compel Britain to come to favorable peace terms. As it was, Allied ULTRA intelligence intercepted and decrypted the halt order. This opened a narrow window of opportunity in which the DUNKIRK EVACUATION was launched.

The Belgians surrendered on May 28, but by June 3 the evacuation from Dunkirk was complete. A total of 338,226 Allied troops, including 140,000 French soldiers, had been saved. The "miracle of Dunkirk" gave Britain a critically needed reprieve, but there was no saving France. The rest of the battle was essentially a broad-based mopping up operation. Paris, undefended, fell on June 14. At about this time, the Maginot Line, still garrisoned by French troops who could have been used elsewhere, was taken from the rear. Declaring war against Britain and France on June 10, Italy mounted an invasion of southern France but gained little.

On June 22, 1940, the Battle of France formally ended with French signatures on an armistice concluded, humiliatingly, at a railway siding in Compiègne in the very parlor car in which Germany had signed the hated TREATY OF VERSAILLES. The immediate cost of the battle was 90,000 French troops dead and 200,000 wounded. Nearly 2 million were either taken prisoner or reported missing. German dead numbered 29,640; wounded, 133,573. Total as this victory had been, the Germans failed to provide for the most obvious follow-up: the immediate invasion of Britain, which was now at its most vulnerable. Instead, they set about occupying and exploiting France.

See also FRANCE, AIR FORCE OF; and FRANCE, ARMY OF.

Further reading: Bloch, Marc. *Strange Defeat.* New York: Norton, 1999; Deighton, Len. *Blitzkrieg: From the Rise of Hitler to the Fall of Denmark.* London: Book Sales, 2000; Gordon, Bertram M., ed. *Historical Dictionary of World War II France.* Westport, Conn.: Greenwood Press, 1998; Jackson, Julian. *The Fall of France: The Nazi Invasion of 1940.* New York: Oxford University Press, 2003; Pallud, Jean-Paul. *Blitzkrieg in the West.* London: After the Battle, 1991.

France, navy of

Like the French Army, the French Navy at the outbreak of World War II looked highly impressive on paper. With more than 660,000 tons of shipping, it was, in 1939, the fourth largest fleet in the world. In contrast to the army, it was not merely a formidable paper force, but in actuality a force to be reckoned with. Many of its ships had been built within the five years preceding the war and were state of the art except for the conspicuous absence of SONAR and RADAR. Most important, they were manned by officers and crews who were not only well trained, but largely unaffected by the defeatism so pervasive in the army. As the BATTLE OF FRANCE was lost, the French Navy successfully evacuated its warships to safe harbors. *Richelieu,* a new battleship, sailed to Dakar. *Jean Bart, Richelieu's* twin ship, was still under construction but was nevertheless sailed to Casablanca. Two veteran battleships, eight destroyers, three submarines, and other minor ships were transferred to Portsmouth and Plymouth. The modern battle cruisers (heavy cruisers) *Strasbourg* and *Dunkerque* found refuge along with six destroyers, two battleships, and a seaplane carrier at Mers-el-Kébir, a French naval base in Algeria. Another six cruisers were dispatched to Algiers. Only the French submarine fleet had taken a bad hit in combat, with 24 of 80 having been sunk. The survivors fled to Bizerta. Except for small ships at Toulon and in the French West Indies, the balance of the fleet, including a battleship, four cruisers, and three destroyers, was at Alexandria, Egypt.

The magnificent French fleet was saved—but for what? The terms of the humiliating armistice France concluded with Germany on June 22, 1940, called for the deactivation of the navy. On July 7, 1940, British admiral JAMES SOMERVILLE approached Mers-el-Kébir and gave the French commander there four choices: join the fight against Germany, be interned in the West Indies or the United States for the duration of the war, scuttle his ships in place, or suffer destruction. Admiral Marcel-Bruno Gensoul decided that French honor demanded his refusal of all options. The result was the one-sided BATTLE OF MERS-EL-KEBIR, in which three of the four capital ships harbored there were sunk with the loss of 1,297 lives. This battle caused the partial suspension of the German order to decommission all French ships. In the meantime, those French vessels in British-controlled ports were taken over by the British. Their crews were temporarily interned, then given the choice of repatriation at Casablanca or joining (indeed, creating) the Free French Navy. Most elected repatriation, but some decided to fight alongside the British.

The rest of the ships of the French Navy remained under the control of the VICHY GOVERNMENT and saw little action. After the success of OPERATION TORCH (the American landings in North Africa), in November 1942, ADOLF HITLER ordered, on November 11, the occupation of Vichy (unoccupied) France. A few days later, on November 19, he ordered the seizure of the Vichy-controlled fleet anchored at Toulon, about 80 warships, including three capital ships, the battle cruisers *Strasbourg* and *Dunkerque* and the battleship *Provence*. The seizure order was resisted, and German forces attacked the docks on November 27. The French returned fire, and during the skirmish five French submarines slipped away. Crews scuttled the rest of the fleet before the Germans could lay hands on them. With this, and except for the few ships fighting on behalf of the Allies, the French Navy of World War II came to an end.

Further reading: Le Masson, Henri. *The French Navy.* 2. vols. London: Macdonald, 1969; Auphan, Etienne. *The*

French Navy in World War II. Westport, Conn.: Greenwood Press, 1976.

Franco, Francisco (Francisco Paulino Hermenegildo Teódulo Franco Bahamonde) (1892–1975) *Spanish general, generalissimo, and fascist dictator*

Born in El Ferrol, Spain, Franco graduated from the Toledo Academia de Infantería in 1910 and was commissioned a second lieutenant. A dashing figure, his service in Spain's 1912 war in Morocco brought him quick recognition, and by 1920 he was deputy commander of the Spanish Foreign Legion in Morocco. He led the legion against Abd-el-Krim during the Riff Rebellion of 1921–26, and, in 1923, was promoted to full commander of the Foreign Legion. His 1925 assault on Alhucemas Bay led ultimately to Spanish victory in the long Riff conflict. In 1926, the triumphal Franco was jumped to the rank of brigadier general, Spain's youngest ever. Two years later, he attained the politically powerful post of director of the Academia General Militar at Saragossa during the fascist dictatorship of General Primo de Rivera. Franco was removed from leadership of the academy in 1931, when Republican forces, having overthrown the monarchy, accused him of retaining a monarchist loyalty.

Franco's removal coincided with the beginning of the turbulent years leading up to the cataclysmic Spanish civil war. Now serving in the Balearic Islands, his post from 1931 to 1934, Franco avoided involvement in the military's many conspiracies against the new republic. It was that government that recalled him in 1934 to suppress a miners' revolt in Asturias. His brutally efficient operations there earned him the respect of the conservative right wing and the hatred of the left. But it was the right that was in the ascendency, and, in 1935, Franco was named chief of the general staff, only to suffer exile the following year, when the leftist Popular Front gained a majority in the elections. Franco was assigned to a command in the remote Canary Islands.

Despite his distance from the mainland, Franco participated in the military and conservative conspiracy that erupted, on July 18, 1936, into the Spanish civil war. Once the war began, Franco flew to Morocco, where he took over the Spanish Foreign Legion garrison and airlifted a large contingent of legionnaires to Spain later in the month. During July and August, he led an advance on Madrid but was repulsed by government forces during September and October. By this time, however, the country was divided between government and Nationalist territories, and on September 29, 1936, the Nationalists established their own government, with Franco as head of state. In April of the following year, he also became leader of the Falange Party and forged a cautious alliance with fascist Italy and Nazi Germany. These two powers contributed troops, equipment, and especially aircraft to the fascist cause, so that the Nationalists ultimately prevailed against the Loyalists. After Madrid fell on March 28, 1939, the Spanish civil war ended, and Franco emerged as de facto dictator of Spain.

Like ADOLF HITLER and BENITO MUSSOLINI, Franco was ruthless in promoting his rise. Unlike them, however, he was cautious and methodical. Although he did not hesitate to outlaw all rival political parties and order the execution or imprisonment of many thousands of Loyalists, he proceeded slowly and cannily with regard to the Axis powers when World War II broke out. Both Hitler and Mussolini simply assumed that Franco would repay the support he had received during the civil war by allying with them. Instead, Franco declared Spain neutral yet, throughout the war, placated Germany by sending workers and creating the all-volunteer Blue Division (ostensibly a mercenary force) to fight for the Germans on the Russian front. Only after the tide of the war turned against Germany did Franco seriously enforce conditions of neutrality. Sensing political change in the wind, he also mildly liberalized his regime. In July 1945, after the defeat of Germany, he promulgated the Fuero de los Españoles, a bill of rights, and, in 1947, he agreed to reorganize the government as a monarchy, with himself as regent endowed with the power to choose the next king. Indeed, throughout the postwar period, Franco moderated the

outright brutality of his extreme right-wing stance, presenting himself to the world not as a fascist, but as a staunch anticommunist. During the early 1950s cold war period, he consented to the establishment of U.S. bases in Spain and, in 1955, brought Spain into the United Nations. In 1956, he renounced the imperialism of the fascist era by pulling out of northern Morocco. However, as popular unrest grew in the 1960s, Franco again became more reactionary. Yet, by this time, liberalism was too well established to allow for a full reversal into the fascist mode of the 1930s and 1940s. Franco continued to hold power until his death in 1975.

Further reading: Ellwood, Sheelagh. *Franco: Profiles in Power*. London: Longman, 2000; Grugel, Jean, and Tim Rees. *Franco's Spain*. London: Arnold, 1997; Payne, Stanley G. *Fascism in Spain, 1923–1977*. Madison: University of Wisconsin Press, 1999.

Franco-Soviet pacts

Between 1926 and 1937, the Soviet Union concluded a number of nonaggression treaties, including one with France on November 19, 1932. Three years later, on May 15, 1935, the two nations took the even bolder step of concluding a new pact, which did not merely guarantee mutual nonaggression, but gave a mutual pledge of military assistance in case of invasion by another country. For Soviet dictator JOSEPH STALIN, this was the first time he had promised to risk communist blood to aid a capitalist country. For the government of France, the pact was not only a bulwark against the expansionist aggression of Nazi Germany, it was also a means of placating left-leaning French workers. Moreover, the treaty put France's leaders in a position to rally these same workers to war not just to defend capitalist France, but the communist Soviet Union as well.

Stalin effectively abrogated both Franco-Soviet pacts by concluding the GERMAN-SOVIET NON-AGGRESSION PACT on August 23, 1939. When Germany invaded France in 1940, Stalin did not honor the 1935 Franco-Soviet pact.

Further reading: Scott, William Evans. *Alliance Against Hitler: The Origins of the Franco-Soviet Pact.* Durham, N.C.: Duke University Press, 1962.

Frank, Anne (1929–1945) *young Holocaust victim whose published diary moved the world*

Annelies Marie Frank, better known as Anne Frank, was born in Frankfurt am Main, Germany, of Jewish parents. Her father, Otto Frank, a prosperous Frankfurt businessman, realized the gravity of Nazi anti-Semitism and, in 1933, left Germany with his wife and two daughters for what he assumed would be the safe haven of Amsterdam. The German INVASION OF THE NETHERLANDS came in May 1940, and the following year, as the German occupiers instituted anti-Semitic policies in the Netherlands, Anne Frank was forced to transfer from a public school to a Jewish one. As anti-Semitism escalated to the FINAL SOLUTION in the occupied countries, Otto Frank understood that he and his family would be deported to what he assumed was a forced-labor camp. To escape this fate, Frank took his family into hiding, with four other Jews, on July 9, 1942.

They found refuge in the back room office and warehouse of Frank's wholesale food business. Christian Dutch citizens, sympathetic to the plight of the Jews, smuggled in food and other supplies at great risk to themselves. However, not all Netherlanders were so noble. Informers tipped off the local GESTAPO, which raided the Franks' hiding place on August 4, 1944. The family was sent to a local transit camp at Westerbork and thence, on September 3, 1944, to AUSCHWITZ CONCENTRATION CAMP in Poland. From here, Anne and her sister Margot were transferred to BERGEN-BELSEN CONCENTRATION CAMP in October. Their transportation to the camps had been the last from the Netherlands. Anne's mother died in January, just days before Auschwitz was evacuated on January 18, 1945. Anne and her sister succumbed to typhus, epidemic in the camps, in March 1945, shortly before Bergen-Belsen was liberated by the Allies. Alone among his family, Otto Frank survived and was liberated from Auschwitz by Red Army troops on January 27, 1945.

Even after their deportation, the Franks had not been abandoned by their Dutch friends. They found in the Franks' hiding place numerous papers and personal effects the Gestapo had failed to confiscate. They saved these, and when Otto Frank returned to Amsterdam, they gave the material to him. He discovered a diary Anne had kept during their desperate confinement. Frank edited it (to some extent bowdlerizing it), and it was published in Dutch in 1947 as *Diary of a Young Girl.* An extraordinary document, it is an intimate view of THE HOLOCAUST through the eyes of an adolescent girl, a vision the more poignant because the diary records all that interested any girl of Anne's age, including her growth into young womanhood, in addition to the terror outside Otto Frank's back room. It is a profoundly human document and a monument to the durability of the human spirit

Anne Frank *(National Holocaust Museum)*

even in the greatest adversity. "In spite of everything," Anne wrote in a particularly memorable passage, "I still believe that people are really good at heart."

Diary of a Young Girl, often called "The Diary of Anne Frank," has appeared in more than 50 languages and is certainly the most widely read document to emerge from the Holocaust. In 1995, a new English translation was published, which restored extensive material Otto Frank had expunged from his original version. The government of the Netherlands and the city of Amsterdam preserve the Frank family's hiding place, on the Prinsengracht Canal, as a museum and memorial.

Further reading: Frank, Anne. *The Diary of Anne Frank: The Revised Critical Edition.* New York: Doubleday, 2003; Lindwer, Willy. *The Last Seven Months of Anne Frank.* New York: Anchor, 1992; Muller, Melissa. *Anne Frank: The Biography.* New York: Metropolitan Books, 1998.

Free French Forces

The Free French Forces (Forces Françaises Libres) was the name applied to French citizens who fought overtly, as a military formation, against Germany and the VICHY GOVERNMENT after France fell as a result of the BATTLE OF FRANCE. The Free French Forces had its origin in a BBC broadcast of June 18, 1940, by CHARLES DE GAULLE from London to the French people. Commemorated in French history as the "Appeal of June 18," it was a call to French men and women to continue to resist the Nazi occupation. Subsequent broadcasts repeated this call, and De Gaulle, keenly aware of the power of symbols, even fashioned a Free French flag featuring the red Cross of Lorraine superimposed on the white band of the nation's tricolor. As compelling a figure as de Gaulle was, his broadcasts initially drew only some 7,000 volunteers to the Free French Forces. In addition, about 3,600 sailors joined the Free French Navy, which consisted of 50 ships that had been in British-controlled ports or had sailed to such ports at the time of the fall of France. This force operated as an auxiliary to the British Royal Navy.

The Free French Forces received a significant influx of men in fall 1940, when the French colonies of Chad, Cameroon, Moyen-Congo, French Equatorial Africa, and Oubangi-Chari broke with the Vichy Government and joined the Free French. Somewhat later, colonies in New Caledonia, French Polynesia, Saint-Pierre and Miquelon, and the New Hebrides also joined. French Indochina and the French colonies of Guadeloupe and Martinique in the West Indies remained under Vichy control.

A blow to recruitment came as a result of the BATTLE OF MERS-EL-KEBIR, a British attack on the French fleet harbored in this Algerian port, in which some 1,297 French sailors were killed. This turned many against the idea of joining the Free French Forces, which collaborated with the British. Nevertheless, de Gaulle carried on, and, in September 1941, he formally created the Comité National Français (French National Committee), the Free French government in exile. On November 24, 1941, U.S. president FRANKLIN D. ROOSEVELT conferred considerable legitimacy on the Comité National Français by extending LEND-LEASE ACT policy to it. Free French troops fought in the NORTH AFRICAN CAMPAIGNS and also against Italians in Ethiopia and Eritrea. They also fought Vichy French troops in Syria and Lebanon.

The Free French Forces existed separately from the FRENCH RESISTANCE AND UNDERGROUND MOVEMENTS until de Gaulle worked to unite them—and, indeed, all the disparate resistance movements—under his own leadership. Changing the name of Comité National Français to Forces Françaises Combattantes (Fighting French Forces), he sent resistance leader JEAN MOULIN back to France to unite the major resistance groups into one organization. This became the Conseil National de la Résistance, but complete union between the overt military (what the Allies continued to call the Free French Forces) and the covert and guerrilla-style resistance was never really achieved.

OPERATION TORCH, the Allied invasion of North Africa, prompted various French units to surrender and join the Free French. At this point General Henri Giraud presented himself as a rival to de Gaulle's leadership of the forces, but de Gaulle retained control. As the North African campaign progressed, the Free French forces grew, and in 1943, some 100,000 Free French troops participated in the Allies' ITALIAN CAMPAIGN. By the time of the NORMANDY LANDINGS (D-DAY), the Free French mustered about 400,000 troops and featured a formal military organization. The Free French 2nd Armored Division, led by General JACQUES-PHILIPPE LECLERC, landed at Normandy and, subsequently, took the lead in the Allied drive toward Paris. It was the first unit to actually enter Paris on August 25, 1944. The Free French First Army, commanded by General Jean de Lattre de Tassigny, participated in the invasion of southern France. This unit retook Alsace from the Germans, an event of powerful symbolic significance.

See also FRANCE, ARMY OF and FRANCE, NAVY OF.

Further reading: Bimberg, Edward L. *Tricolor over the Sahara: The Desert Battles of the Free French, 1940–1942.* Westport, Conn.: Greenwood Press, 2002; Maguire, G. E. *Anglo-American Policy Towards the Free French.* London: Palgrave Macmillan, 1995; Sumner, Ian, and Francois Vauvillier. *The French Army 1939–45 (2): Free French, Fighting French and the Army of Liberation.* London: Osprey, 1999; Thompson, Robert Smith. *Pledge to Destiny: Charles de Gaulle and the Rise of the Free French.* New York: McGraw-Hill, 1974.

Freikorps

Freikorps ("Free Corps") was a name applied to a number of nongovernment paramilitary groups that sprang into existence throughout Germany beginning in December 1918, immediately after the nation's defeat in World War I. The Freikorps consisted of recently discharged veterans, both enlisted men and officers, as well as an admixture of unemployed and discontented civilian youths. By the 1920s, more than 65 corps were scattered throughout the country.

Freikorps members shared an intense nationalism and reactionary conservatism. They took it upon themselves, often with unofficial sanction from the Weimar government, to put down left-wing demonstrations and uprisings in Berlin, Bre-

men, Brunswick, Hamburg, Halle, Leipzig, Silesia, Thuringia, and the Ruhr. The Freikorps often operated as right-wing terrorist organizations, and they assassinated officials and politicians identified as leftist or communist. The highest-profile assassination ascribed to the Freikorps was that of Walther Rathenau, German foreign minister, in 1922.

In the wake of the chaotic despair fueled by the TREATY OF VERSAILLES, the Freikorps nurtured the right-wing sentiments that found their most significant expression in the NAZI PARTY (NSDAP). The Weimar Republic made use of the Freikorps however it could, but the movement was suppressed as official police forces and the regular army grew strong enough to suppress leftist and other antigovernment activity. Many Freikorps members were absorbed into the rising Nazi Party, and a portion of the Freikorps survived virtually intact as the basis of the Nazi Party's strongarm STURMABTEILUNG (SA) ("Storm Troopers") organization, which was led by a former Freikorps commander, Ernst Röhm.

Further reading: Jones, Nigel, and Michael Burleigh. *A Brief History of the Birth of the Nazis: How the Freikorps Blazed the Trail for Hitler.* New York: Carroll & Graf, 2004; Jurado, Carlos Caballero, and Rameiro Bujeiro. *The German Freikorps 1918–23.* London: Osprey, 2001; Waite, Robert G. L. *Vanguard of Nazism: The Free Corps Movement in Postwar Germany, 1918–1923.* Cambridge, Mass.: Harvard University Press, 1952.

French foreign legion

The celebrated French foreign legion (Légion Étrangère) was created in 1831 by King Louis-Philippe for the purpose of patrolling and policing French colonial possessions in North Africa. Until the later 20th century, membership in the legion was restricted to foreign volunteers, who, after serving five years with good conduct, were granted French citizenship. Membership in the foreign legion has never required the swearing of an oath of allegiance to France but, rather, an oath to the legion itself, in keeping with the legion's unofficial motto, "Legio patria nostra" ("The legion is our fatherland").

Another feature of enlistment in the foreign legion is a high degree of anonymity. In most military forces, a soldier's past is a matter of detailed record; in the legion, however, it is a secret. For this reason, the foreign legion has acquired a mystique as a haven for criminals, the lovelorn, and others who seek refuge from their past. This image has been portrayed in many fictional depictions of the organization. Doubtless, some recruits have sought escape in the service, but the foreign legion is first and foremost an elite military organization, which, from the beginning, attracted chiefly professional men at arms looking for intense combat experience.

From its inception, the foreign legion was barred from serving in metropolitan France during peacetime. However, legion units were in France during World War I and World War II. In 1939, the foreign legion quickly expanded because of an influx of refugees into its ranks. Foreign legion regiments fought in the BATTLE OF FRANCE in May–June 1940. After the fall of France resulting from this battle, all German nationals serving in the foreign legion were compelled to return to their homeland. Abroad, in SYRIA, foreign legion troops fought on both sides, some joining the FREE FRENCH FORCES and others fighting on behalf of the VICHY GOVERNMENT. On the Free French side, the most celebrated foreign legion unit was the 13th Demi-Brigade, which fought in the BATTLE OF NARVIK, against the Italians in Ethiopia (Abyssinia), in Syria, and in the NORTH AFRICAN CAMPAIGNS and the ITALIAN CAMPAIGN. The unit landed in France in August 1944 and participated in the drive through that occupied country. Since 1962, with Algerian independence, French foreign legion headquarters have been maintained in France proper at Aubagne, near Marseille.

See also FRANCE, ARMY OF.

Further reading: Geraghty, Tony. *March or Die: A New History of the French Foreign Legion.* New York: Facts On File, 1987; Porch, Douglas. *The French Foreign Legion: Complete History of the Legendary Fighting Force.* New York: Perennial, 1992; Windrow, Martin, and Mike Chappel. *French Foreign Legion 1914–1945.* London: Osprey, 1999.

French resistance and underground movements

The fall of France resulting from the BATTLE OF FRANCE brought a humiliating armistice with Germany and the division of France into occupied zones and the nominally sovereign VICHY GOVERNMENT led by HENRI-PHILIPPE PÉTAIN. During the fall of France, a French army officer, CHARLES DE GAULLE, was in London, and he used his absence as an opportunity to rally the French with a broadcast appeal on June 18, 1940, repudiating Pétain, proclaiming that the war had not ended, and calling on all French men and women to resist the occupiers. De Gaulle emerged as de facto head of a Free French government in exile and leader of the FREE FRENCH FORCES, mainly consisting of French military personnel and a few ships that had evaded capture or that had not declared allegiance to Vichy. Also answering de Gaulle's appeal were French civilians still living in France who began organizing underground activities, including secret newspapers and networks for rescuing downed Allied airmen, and resistance cells, which engaged in various subversive activities, including sabotage and assassination. The terms *underground* and *resistance* are frequently used interchangeably. However, it is useful to distinguish between the essentially civilian resistance and the underground, on the one hand, and the more formally military Free French Forces on the other.

The earliest acts of resistance were mounted by secondary school students on July 14 (Bastille Day), and November 11 (the anniversary of World War I's armistice), 1940. Work-related sabotage and mass strikes began soon after in an effort to cripple production destined to serve Germany's war effort. Miners in Nord and Pas-de-Calais struck from May 27, 1941, to June 8, 1941. True armed resistance is usually said to have commenced on August 22, 1941, with the assassination of a German naval cadet, Alfons Moser. This resulted in the occupying army's promulgation of a hostage policy, whereby French citizens, randomly chosen, were subject to reprisal—that is, execution—for violence perpetrated against German or Vichy officials. Though widely posted and publicized, the hostage and reprisal policy failed to stop additional attacks. On September 3, resistance members assassinated another German officer; three days later, the military government executed three hostages. Despite this, more assassinations took place, followed by more reprisals. On September 16, Adolf Hitler directed army chief of staff general Wilhelm Keitel to order commanders in France and the other occupied countries to regard human life of little value in these territories and to act with utmost violence against the resistance. Through Keitel, Hitler suggested that 50 or 100 hostages should be executed for each German soldier killed by resistance members.

The occupiers of France fought the resistance by means of the Abwehr, Gestapo, Schutzstaffel (SS), Sicherheitsdienst (SD), and the regular army, the Wehrmacht. Vichy authorities used the collaborationist police organization known as the Milice.

Despite the increasing severity of reprisals, resistance and underground movements proliferated in France, both in the occupied zones and in Vichy territory. Members came from all walks of life and included men as well as women. Many were students, and many others were former soldiers who had managed to escape from the Germans or even joined the resistance after gaining release from prisoner of war (POW) camps. Other members were left-wing activists, including socialists and communists, who had evaded capture by the Gestapo. Resistance cells were urban as well as rural. Indeed, many hid in the forested regions of the unoccupied zones and were informally called Maquis, a word that describes the dense growth of Mediterranean shrubs and trees, suggesting the undergrowth in which this shadow army hid.

Resistance and Maquis groups typically organized themselves into small units, or cells. The risks of resistance work were great and many, not only because of the hostage and reprisal policy, but because of the interrogation methods used by the Gestapo and other authorities, which employed extreme torture. By adopting a cell structure, in which each cell was linked to another yet was also autonomous, so that no one operative had direct

knowledge of more than a few comrades, the resistance could control the damage that resulted from interrogation of members who were apprehended. Even under the worst torture, a captured resistance member would have relatively little information to give up.

One disadvantage of the cell approach to organization was that it reinforced the scattered nature of the resistance and underground. Resistance groups often failed to coordinate action, and rivalries even developed. The most important resistance groups included the following (and the list is far from complete):

Armée Secrète (AS). This group was loyal to Charles de Gaulle and was led by Charles Delestraint.

Bureau d'Opérations Aériennes (BOA). This resistance group organized clandestine air operations in northern France.

Chantiers de la Jeunesse. Ostensibly a set of youth camps, the organization actually ran assembly places for young members of the French Army who were homeless after the fall of France.

Combat. Formed in 1942 by Henri Frenay, *Combat* was one of the best known underground groups. Moderately left-wing in political orientation, it specialized in sabotage and, through its newspaper (*Combat*), in counterpropaganda. Its most famous members were the novelist Albert Camus and the philosopher Jean-Paul Sartre.

Comité d'Action Socialiste (CAS). The group was founded in January 1941 by Daniel Mayer, a member of the French Socialist Party.

Comité Départemental de Libération (CDL).

Comité Français de la Libération Nationale (CFLN).

Compagnons de la France (Companions of France). This resistance organization consisted of veterans operating in Vichy France.

Défense de la France. Sorbonne University students organized this group to publish an underground newspaper of the same name, to carry out espionage, and to operate an escape network. The group was known for producing excellent counterfeit identification papers for resistance members.

Francs-Tireur. A leftist group formed in Lyon in 1941, it published *Le Franc-Tireur,* an underground newspaper. The group was also active in the Mediterranean area.

Francs-Tireurs et Partisans (Français) (FTP or FTPF). This was the military resistance organization of the French Communist Party's *Front National (FN).*

Francs-Tireurs et Partisans de la Main d'Oeuvre Immigrée (FTP-MOI). A mostly communist resistance group composed chiefly of immigrants, FTP-MOI specialized in urban guerrilla actions.

Front Libération-Sud. This socialist group was based in Paris and published the underground newspaper *Libération.*

Musée de l'Homme. Another Paris-based group, it published an underground newspaper, covertly transmitted political and military information to Britain, and created an Allied POW escape network. After a Vichy agent infiltrated the organization, most of its members were arrested and many executed.

Organisation de la Résistance de l'Armée (ORA). The ORA consisted of supporters of Henri Giraud, rival to de Gaulle. The most famous member was François Mitterrand, who became president of France in 1981 and served until 1995.

From the beginning, Britain's Special Operations Executive (SOE), created by WINSTON CHURCHILL to foment uprising and resistance in occupied Europe, helped to supply the various resistance groups by sending weapons, radios, radio operators, and advisers. The British SPECIAL AIR SERVICE (SAS) and other British intelligence organizations also sent agents to France to work with the resistance. De Gaulle, who was reluctant to share control of the resistance with Britain (and, later, with the United States), created the Bureau Central de Renseignements et d'Action (BCRA), in effect a private intelligence organization over which he exercised direct control. On January 1, 1942, de Gaulle sent an already established resistance leader,

JEAN MOULIN, into Arles by parachute drop with two other agents and radio equipment. Setting up in Marseilles, they began a gradual and partially successful effort to coordinate the activities of the disparate resistance groups. However, the biggest boon to the resistance movement was furnished by the Germans themselves. When the occupiers initiated a forced labor draft, conscripting workers for labor in Germany, early in 1943, thousands of young men evaded the call and rushed to join the Maquis. The SOE, now together with the U.S. OFFICE OF STRATEGIC SERVICES (OSS), fostered this expansion by sending supplies and agents. In June 1943, the SOE also at last began to coordinate activity with de Gaulle's BCRA. At about this time, too, Moulin had finally persuaded the Armée Secrète, Comité d'Action Socialiste, Francs-Tireur, Front National, and Libération to unite as the Conseil National de la Resistance (CNR) under the direction of Charles de Gaulle and with Moulin as chairman. The first meeting of this united organization took place in Paris on May 27, 1943.

At first, while the British supported de Gaulle, the Americans tended to favor his rival for leadership of the Free French movement, General Henri Giraud. Fortunately, however, the CASABLANCA CONFERENCE of June 1943 produced reconciliation between de Gaulle and Giraud, who assumed joint leadership of the CNR, until de Gaulle wrested sole direction of the organization from Giraud in October 1943.

As OPERATION OVERLORD—the NORMANDY LANDINGS (D-DAY)—approached, the British and Americans worked more closely with the resistance to focus efforts on intelligence collection and sabotage against transportation and communication lines. Maquis and other resistance members destroyed railway tracks, bridges, and even trains. General de Gaulle organized a new London headquarters for the Forces Françaises de l'Intérieur (FFI), which he put under the command of general Marie-Pierre Koenig. The FFI worked with the SOE and OSS on Operation Jedburgh, creating three-man teams that consisted of one French and one American or British agent, plus a radioman, which were infiltrated into France to work directly with the resistance in order to intensify and direct sabotage efforts prior to D-day. In all, some 87 Jedburgh teams were infiltrated. Among the information communicated to the resistance groups was a set of code words that would be broadcast over the BBC to alert operatives to the commencement of the Normandy landings. Upon hearing these broadcasted code words, the resistance groups intensified their sabotage, derailing trains, blowing up ammunition dumps, and attacking isolated German garrisons. Other operatives observed German troop movements and defensive preparations, communicating these developments to the Allies as they happened.

The activities of the resistance were important to the success of the Allied invasion, and the resistance continued to work with the Allies as they advanced across France. Resistance cells were highly active as the Allied columns closed in to liberate Paris in August 1944. As the troops approached, resistance members disrupted German defenses with grenades, acts of sabotage, and sniper activity. Known collaborationist leaders were quickly rounded up and, often, summarily executed. The show of resistance force persuaded most of the Paris police force, hitherto at the mercy of the occupiers, to join the movement.

The liberation of Paris was the high-water mark of the French resistance. Paris was officially liberated on August 25. Three days later, Charles de Gaulle gave the order to stand down the Free French Forces as well as the resistance organizations. He invited those who still wished to fight to join the new regular French Army.

Further reading: Aubrac, Lucie. *Outwitting the Gestapo.* Lincoln: University of Nebraska Press, 1994; Aubrac, Raymond. *The French Resistance: 1940–1944.* Paris: Hazan, 1997; Johnson, Michael. *French Resistance.* New York: Routledge, 1996; Marnham, Patrick. *Resistance and Betrayal: The Death and Life of the Greatest Hero of the French Resistance.* New York: Random House, 2002; Rougeyron, Andre, and Marie-Antoinette McConnell. *Agents for Escape: Inside the French Resistance, 1939–1945.* Baton Rouge: Louisiana State University Press, 1995; Schoenbrun, David. *Soldiers of the Night: The Story of the French Resistance.* New York: Dutton, 1980; Weitz, Margaret Collins. *Sisters in the Resistance: How Women Fought to Free France, 1940–1945.* New York: Wiley, 1998.

Fritsch, Werner von (1880–1939) *German general and victim of Hitler's treachery*

Werner von Fritsch was born in Benrath, Germany. He served as a staff officer during World War I and remained in the interwar army, achieving promotion to lieutenant general and the post of commander in chief of the army in February 1934. Fritsch was highly respected by fellow officers, but he, in turn, was contemptuous of ADOLF HITLER and was often heard to disparage him. He was especially outraged by Hitler's treacherous purge of Ernst Roehm and the STURMABTEILUNG (SA) in the "Night of the Long Knives" massacre in June 1934.

As he became aware of Fritsch's doubts about Nazism, his disparagement of himself, and the objections he raised to many of his military plans, Hitler became determined to gain personal control of the army. He assigned HEINRICH HIMMLER to investigate Fritsch secretly. Himmler apparently persuaded Hans Schmidt, a male prostitute, to claim that he had had a sexual relationship with Fritsch. Himmler presented this "information" to Hitler, who, on January 24, 1938, confronted Fritsch with the claims. It quickly became apparent to Fritsch that no one in the senior command was willing to step forth to support him against the trumped-up charges. He therefore yielded, on February 3, 1938, to Hitler's demand that he resign. It was subsequently discovered that Schmidt had lied and, in a military trial, Fritsch was exonerated. Nevertheless, Hitler declined to reinstate him as commander in chief of the army. Fritsch was, however, recalled to the army at the outbreak of the war, and he returned to his former regiment as its honorary colonel. He was killed in the attack on Warsaw on September 22, 1939, during the INVASION OF POLAND.

The Fritsch affair had a lasting effect on the army command's relationship with Hitler and the Nazi inner circle. Although his fellow officers had not supported him, the failure of Fritsch's reinstatement turned a number of important commanders against Hitler and the Nazi regime. Most important among these was Admiral WILHELM CANARIS, head of the Abwehr intelligence organization, who deliberately sabotaged certain aspects of the German intelligence effort in order to embarrass Hitler. Others, including Colonel-General Hans Oster, Field Marshal Erwin von Witzleben, and General Karl Heinrich von Stuelpnagel, actively conspired to bring about Hitler's overthrow. Their alienation began with outrage over the framing and subsequent treatment of Fritsch.

Further reading: Parssinen, Terry. *The Oster Conspiracy of 1938: The Unknown Story of the Military Plot to Kill Hitler and Avert World War II.* New York: HarperCollins, 2003; Plant, Richard. *The Pink Triangle: The Nazi War Against Homosexuals.* New York: Owl Books, 1988; Welch, David. *The Hitler Conspiracies: Secrets and Lies Behind the Rise and Fall of the Nazi Party.* London and New York: Brassey's, 2002.

Fuchs, Klaus (1911–1988) *German-born British physicist and Soviet spy*

Born in Rüsselsheim, Germany, Klaus Fuchs was educated at the Universities of Leipzig and Kiel, where he studied physics and mathematics. An enthusiastic member of the German Communist Party beginning in 1930, he fled Germany after ADOLF HITLER was named chancellor and the Nazis came to power in 1933. Immigrating to Great Britain, he earned a Ph.D. in physics from the University of Edinburgh. At the outbreak of World War II, he was briefly interned by the British government as an enemy alien, but his credentials as a physicist earned him a place on what became the joint Anglo-American project to create an atomic bomb. He carried out research at the University of Birmingham and in 1942 became a British citizen.

Despite his new citizenship, Fuchs remained a committed communist, and he began passing information on the top-secret atomic bomb project to the Soviet Union. In 1943, Fuchs was sent to the United States to work at Los Alamos, New Mexico, the central laboratory of the MANHATTAN PROJECT and the very epicenter of World War II nuclear weapons development. His work here provided him with a comprehensive view of the atomic bomb project, so that he moved beyond the theoretical appreciation he had had in Birmingham to practical knowledge of actual design. This he passed on to the Soviets. It was information so valuable that most scientists and historians believe it gave the Soviets at least a year's head start on developing their own atomic bomb shortly after World War II.

During the war, Fuchs's espionage remained undiscovered. He returned to England at the conclusion of peace and rose to chair the physics department of the British nuclear research center at Harwell. In 1950, however, Fuchs's espionage activities were at last uncovered, and he was arrested. He soon confessed to having passed information to the Soviet Union since 1943. Found guilty, Fuchs was sentenced to 14 years in prison but was released in 1959 for good behavior. Immediately after his release, he traveled to communist East Germany, where he was granted citizenship and named deputy director of the Central Institute for Nuclear Research at Rossendorf. He expressed absolutely no regret for his espionage and was lavishly honored by the East German Communist Party as well as by its state-controlled scientific establishment.

Further reading: Feklisov, Alexander, and Sergei Kostin. *The Man Behind the Rosenbergs, by the KGB Spymaster Who Was the Case Officer of Julius Rosenberg, Klaus Fuchs, and Helped Resolve the Cuban Missile Crisis.* New York: Enigma Books, 2004; Moss, Norman. *Klaus Fuchs: The Man Who Stole the Atom Bomb.* London: Grafton, 1990; Williams, Robert Chadwell. *Klaus Fuchs, Atom Spy.* Cambridge, Mass.: Harvard University Press, 1989.

Funk, Walther (1890–1960) *economic minister of the Third Reich and president of the Reichsbank*

Walther Funk studied economics at the Universities of Berlin and Leipzig, worked for a time as a journalist, then joined the German Army in 1914, at the beginning of World War I. Discharged in 1916 as unfit for service, he was hired in 1922 as editor of the *Berliner Boersen Zeitung,* the most influential financial and economic daily in Germany. He joined the NAZI PARTY (NSDAP) early in its existence and, in 1931, was chosen by ADOLF HITLER as his economic adviser. Funk became Hitler's liaison with Germany's top industrialists, and he was instrumental in forging the economic partnership between the Nazi Party and the German financial-industrial sector.

In 1938, Funk was appointed minister of economic affairs in the Third Reich, but, in reality, he had almost no autonomy, answering directly to HERMANN GÖRING, whose control of the reich's "four-year plan" was absolute. On January 20, 1939, while continuing to retain his ministerial post, Funk was appointed president of the Reichsbank, a position of considerably more importance. He was instrumental in the economic planning for the INVASION OF THE SOVIET UNION and took part in planning the economic aspects of the ongoing persecution of the Jews. He also played roles in all other Nazi economic depredations throughout the war.

Funk was arrested by U.S. forces in May 1945 and was held for indictment by the NUREMBERG WAR CRIMES TRIBUNAL. Indicted on August 29, 1945, he attempted to present himself as, in reality, a minor figure in the Nazi hierarchy, an assertion that was corroborated by fellow defendant Göring. This notwithstanding, the tribunal found him guilty of war crimes, crimes against the peace, and crimes against humanity. He was sentenced to life imprisonment on October 1 but was released on May 16, 1957. He lived out the rest of his life in retirement in West Germany.

Further reading: James, Harold. *The Deutsche Bank and the Nazi Economic War Against the Jews: The Expropriation of Jewish-Owned Property.* Cambridge and New York: Cambridge University Press, 2001; James, Harold. *The Nazi Dictatorship and the Deutsche Bank.* Cambridge and New York: Cambridge University Press, 2004; Overy, R. J. *The Nazi Economic Recovery 1932–1938.* Cambridge and New York: Cambridge University Press, 1996; Overy, R. J. *War and Economy in the Third Reich.* Oxford and New York: Oxford University Press, 1995.

G

Gamelin, Maurice-Gustave (1872–1958)
general in command of all French forces at the outbreak of World War II

Paris-born Maurice-Gustave Gamelin graduated from Saint-Cyr, the French military academy, in 1893 and, at the outbreak of World War I, in August 1914, served as a staff officer, operations section, under French commander in chief Joseph Joffre. He remained a highly placed staff officer throughout most of the war but was given field command of a division before it ended.

After the armistice, Gamelin was appointed to head a military mission to Brazil, serving there from 1919 to 1925, when he was appointed chief of staff to General Maurice Sarrail, who commanded all French forces in the Levant. In 1926, Gamelin succeeded Sarrail, serving in the Levant through 1930. He was elevated to army chief of staff in 1931 and vice president of the Supreme War Council as well as army inspector general in 1935. In 1938, Gamelin was named chief of staff for national defense, effectively becoming the commander of all French forces.

As chief, Gamelin directed the French mobilization at the outbreak of World War II, in September 1939, and he was in command during the BATTLE OF FRANCE, which began on May 10, 1940. Gamelin was neither better nor worse than most of the rest of the senior French command, which, unfortunately for France, meant that he was a mediocrity, dedicated to the status quo. He had done nothing to streamline and rationalize the complex, cumbersome, and counterproductive command structure of the French Army. He had done nothing to address deficiencies of training and the even graver deficiencies of morale. He had denigrated the value and the role of air power. He had done little to address shortages of adequate antiaircraft and antitank weapons. With the rest of the French high command, he had blindly assumed that a second world war would, of necessity, be a repetition of the first—fought as static combat from trenches—and he therefore operated only according to a defensive plan, which proved disastrously inadequate to stem the German invasion BLITZKRIEG.

During the opening moves of the invasion, Gamelin blundered into the German trap, sending mobile forces into Belgium to meet the expected advance there. Instead, the main panzer thrust came through the Ardennes, which Gamelin (and others) had considered impassable. Stunned, Gamelin dithered in response and was dismissed by Premier PAUL REYNAUD, who replaced him with the more aggressive, albeit superannuated, MAXIME WEYGAND on May 19.

On September 6, 1940, Gamelin was arrested on charges of having been responsible for the military defeat of France. Gamelin never accepted the charges and refused to testify at his trial. He was imprisoned in France, then deported to BUCHENWALD CONCENTRATION CAMP by the German occupiers in the spring of 1942. He was held at Buchenwald and then at Itter, from which he was liberated by U.S. troops in May 1945. He returned to France and, between 1946 and 1947, published his three-volume memoir, *Servir*.

Further reading: Alexander, Martin S. *The Republic in Danger: General Maurice Gamelin and the Politics of French Defence, 1933–1940*. Cambridge and New York: Cambridge University Press, 2003; Bloch, Marc. *Strange Defeat*. New York: Norton, 1999; Gordon, Bertram M., ed. *Historical Dictionary of World War II France*. Westport, Conn.: Greenwood Press, 1998; Jackson, Julian. *The Fall of France: The Nazi Invasion of 1940*. New York: Oxford University Press, 2003; Young, Robert J. *In Command of France: French Foreign Policy and Military Planning, 1933–1940*. Cambridge, Mass.: Harvard University Press, 1978.

Charles de Gaulle with Henri Giraud *(National Archives and Records Administration)*

Gaulle, Charles de (1890–1970) *most important leader of the Free French during the Nazi occupation*

De Gaulle was the military and political leader of the FREE FRENCH FORCES and the French government in exile during World War II. After the war, he was the moving force behind the creation of France's Fifth Republic.

De Gaulle was raised in an intensely nationalistic family and was educated at the Military Academy of Saint-Cyr. He joined an infantry regiment under Colonel HENRI-PHILIPPE PÉTAIN in 1913 and quickly made an impression with his intelligence and initiative. With the outbreak of World War I, he also proved himself a courageous officer, participating in the defense of Verdun, in which he was wounded three times. De Gaulle was captured by the Germans and served two years and eight months in a prisoner of war camp, making five valiant, though unsuccessful, attempts to escape.

After World War I, De Gaulle served as a member of a military mission to Poland, then became an instructor at Saint-Cyr. He underwent two years of special training in strategy and tactics at the École Supérieure de Guerre, the French war college, and upon his graduation in 1925 was promoted by

Pétain to the staff of the Conseil Supérieur de la Guerre, the Supreme War Council. It was a most prestigious appointment.

Now a major, De Gaulle served during 1927–29 in the army occupying the Rhineland. During this period, he became alarmed by the danger he believed Germany continued to pose. After his Rhineland assignment, he served for two years in the Middle East, then, as a lieutenant colonel, served for four years as a member of the secretariat of the Conseil Supérieur de la Défense Nationale, the National Defense Council. While serving in the field as well as in staff posts, De Gaulle also turned his attention to the formulation of military theory and doctrine. In 1924, he wrote a study of the relation of the civil and military powers in Germany, "Discord Among the Enemy." He also lectured on the subject of leadership, publishing these lectures in 1932 as *The Edge of the Sword*. Two years later, he published a study of military theory, *The Army of the Future*, developing in this work the idea of a small professional army based on a high degree of mechanization for maximum flexibility and mobility. This was, in fact, German policy between the wars, but it was directly opposed to the defensive, static strategy favored in France and embodied most dramatically in the MAGINOT LINE. Never content to allow his ideas to be taken as merely academic, de Gaulle appealed directly to political leaders in an attempt to persuade them to his point of view. This provoked great discord with de Gaulle's commanders and senior officers, including Marshal Pétain himself, who protested de Gaulle's right to publish a historical study titled *France and Her Army*. De Gaulle prevailed, and the work was published in 1938.

When World War II began, de Gaulle was put in command of a tank brigade of the Fifth French Army. He was quickly promoted to the temporary rank of brigadier general in the 4th Armored Division—it was the highest military rank he was to hold—and proved himself a very able tank commander. He was named undersecretary of state for defense and war on June 6 by French premier PAUL REYNAUD, who sent him on several missions to England to explore ways in which France might continue to prosecute the war against Germany. De Gaulle remained in England after the Reynaud government fell and was replaced by the collaborationist VICHY GOVERNMENT of Marshal Pétain, de Gaulle's former military mentor.

On June 18, 1940, de Gaulle broadcast from London his first appeal to the French people to resist Germany. As a result of this and subsequent broadcasts, a French military court tried de Gaulle in absentia, found him guilty of treason, and sentenced him on August 2, 1940, to death, loss of military rank, and confiscation of property. De Gaulle responded by throwing himself with even greater energy and determination into organizing the Free French Forces as well as a shadow Free French government in exile. It was an extraordinary, audacious undertaking; for de Gaulle was all but unknown outside French military circles. Even the people of France did not recognize him as a political figure. All that sustained him in this enterprise was his self-confidence, his strength of character, his natural ability to lead, and his conviction that the French nation must not be allowed to perish.

Throughout the war, until the liberation of France, de Gaulle continued to broadcast. From exile, he directed the action of the Free French Forces and other resistance groups in France. He worked closely, though not always smoothly, with the British secret services in this effort. Indeed, as his relations with the British government and military became increasingly strained, de Gaulle moved his headquarters to Algiers in 1943 and became president of the French Committee of National Liberation. He served at first under General Henri Giraud but skillfully engineered Giraud's ouster and emerged as sole leader of the committee. It was de Gaulle, not Giraud, who headed the government in exile and marched into Paris on September 9, 1944, after its liberation.

De Gaulle led two successive provisional governments as the war wound down and in the immediate postwar period. However, on January 20, 1946, he suddenly resigned over a dispute with the political parties forming the coalition government. He opposed the Fourth French Republic as too likely to repeat the errors of the Third Republic and, in 1947, formed the Rally of the French People (Rassemblement du Peuple Français, RPF), which won 120 seats in the national assembly in the 1951 elections. Soon growing dissatisfied with the RPF, de Gaulle severed his connection with it in 1953, and it disbanded in 1955. De Gaulle retired for a time and, during 1955–56, wrote three volumes of memoirs.

When insurrection broke out in Algiers in 1958 and threatened to bring civil war to France itself, de Gaulle was brought back to the national limelight as prime minister designate and, on December 21, 1958, was elected president of the republic. He served for the next 10 years amid much turbulence, controversy, and opposition from the nation's left-wing political leaders. After his retirement, he continued writing his memoirs but died of a heart attack the year after he left office.

Further reading: Cogan, Charles G. *Charles de Gaulle: A Brief Biography with Documents*. New York: St. Martin's Press, 1995; De Gaulle, Charles. *The Complete War Memoirs of Charles De Gaulle*. New York: Carroll & Graf, 1998; Williams, Charles. *The Last Great Frenchman: A Life of General De Gaulle*. New York: Wiley, 1997.

Gazala, Battle of

The Battle of Gazala (May 26–June 17, 1942) was a prelude to the disastrous British defeat at the BATTLES OF TOBRUK. Gazala did much to enhance and render virtually legendary the reputation of the German commander ERWIN ROMMEL, and the battle foiled British hopes of driving Rommel out of Libya before the commencement of the Allies' NORTH AFRICAN CAMPAIGNS. Rommel's victory also demonstrated, yet again, the inadequacy of static tactics versus the tactics of mobility in World War II. The Eighth British Army, at the time commanded by Lieutenant General NEIL RITCHIE, was deployed in an elaborately conceived defensive line, the Gazala Line, west of Tobruk. Ritchie had grouped his assets in "boxes," tactical strong points, along the line, parceling out his armor accordingly. This manner of deployment meant that armor was treated as a static asset instead of a highly mobile one, an error that made it difficult to mass the tanks as needed and that therefore contributed greatly to the British defeat.

Thanks to ULTRA decrypts, Ritchie was well apprised of Rommel's intention to attack, but he had no idea of where the attack would come. With his customary genius for rapid mobility, Rommel threw his Italian troops against the Gazala Line in a frontal assault while his main panzers swung rapidly around Bir Hakeim, the southern end of the Gazala Line. This put Rommel into position to flank and roll up the British line. The problem with mobile warfare, however, is always one of supply, and Rommel moved so far so fast that his supply lines were stretched very thin. Worse, his own intelligence had failed him, having grossly underestimated British strength. British armor was also more formidable than in the past, thanks to the addition of the new American Grant tank.

Thus, on May 29, 1942, after a pitched armor duel, Rommel's flanking attack was checked. He withdrew to an area soon dubbed "the Cauldron," a move Ritiche misinterpreted as a mere disengagement. This prompted Ritchie to hold off making a counterattack. It was a fatal excess of caution, for Rommel used the lull in the battle to regroup and to reestablish his lines of supply. This quickly accomplished, he launched a new assault at Bir Hakeim and, on June 10, forced a breach in the Gazala Line there. Now, belatedly, Ritchie did counterattack, forcing Rommel back to the Cauldron, which Ritchie started to encircle. Instead of assuming a defensive posture, however, the always aggressive Rommel counterattacked in turn, creating a bulge, or salient, in the Gazala Line at the defensive "box" code-named Knightsbridge. This brought about the dissolution of the Gazala Line and forced an opening to Tobruk.

The theater commander CLAUDE JOHN AYRE AUCHINLECK ordered Ritchie to set up a new defensive line, but it was to no avail, and Rommel pushed through to Tobruk, which fell on June 21. As a result of Gazala and Tobruk, both Ritchie and Auchinleck were subsequently relieved by British high command.

Further reading: Atkinson, Rick. *An Army at Dawn: The War in Africa, 1942–1943.* New York: Owl Books, 2003; Harrison, Frank. *Tobruk: The Birth of a Legend.* New York: Sterling, 2003; Mitcham, Samuel. *Rommel's Greatest Victory.* Novato, Calif.: Presidio, 2001.

Geheimschreiber

A German word meaning "secret writer," *Geheimschreiber* was the name of a cipher machine that produced an encrypted punched tape, which could be fed through a teleprinter for transmission via radio lines. The transmitting stations had first been detected by British intelligence in 1940, and by 1942 most had been identified. Interception and decryption operations began in mid-1942 and presented an even greater challenge than decrypting messages produced by the more famous ENIGMA CIPHER AND MACHINE because the Geheimschreiber used more encryption rotors: 10 as opposed to the three to five rotors of the Enigma. Indeed, it required the invention of some of the first practical computers—an experimental machine dubbed "Heath Robinson," followed by the more celebrated "Colossus I" and "Colossus II"—to perform the work. Colossus II is considered by some historians of computer science to be the first genuine fully electronic computer. It came on line on June 6, 1944, the very day of the NORMANDY LANDINGS (D-DAY), and was invaluable in its yield of important intelligence through the end of the war in Europe. Geheimschreiber decrypts were code named "FISH" by the Allies.

Further reading: Copeland, Jack. *Colossus: The First Electronic Computer.* Oxford and New York: Oxford University Press, 2005; Cragon, Harvy G. *From Fish to Colossus: How the German Lorenz Cipher was Broken at Bletchley Park.* Dallas: Cragon Books, 2003; Haufler, Hervie. *Codebreaker's Victory: How the Allied Cryptographers Won World War II.* New York: New American Library, 2003; Sale, Tony. *The Colossus Computer 1943–1996: How It Helped to Break the German Lorenz Cipher in WW II.* Cleobury Mortimer, Shropshire, U.K.: M & M Baldwin, 1998.

Geiger, Roy (1885–1947) *U.S. Marine Corps general*

A native of Middleburg, Florida, Geiger graduated from John B. Stetson University in 1907 and practiced law for less than a year before enlisting in the U.S. Marine Corps (USMC) in November 1907. In less than two years, he was commissioned a 2nd lieutenant, then was promoted to 1st lieutenant in 1915 after having served at sea and in the Caribbean, the Philippines, and China. In 1917, Geiger was promoted to captain and became the fifth USMC officer to complete aviator training. After the United States entered World War I, Geiger, now a major, commanded a squadron of the 1st Marine Aviation Force in France.

After World War I, Geiger served in Haiti as commanding officer of the 1st Aviation Group, 3rd Marine Brigade, from 1919 to 1921. He was transferred to Quantico, Virginia, in 1921 and graduated from the army's Command and General Staff School in 1925. In 1929, he graduated from the Army War College. From 1929 to 1931, he commanded Aircraft Squadrons, East Coast Expeditionary Force, stationed at Quantico, then was made officer in charge of aviation at Marine Corps headquarters in Washington, D.C., serving there from 1931 to 1935.

Promoted to lieutenant colonel in 1934, Geiger commanded Marine Air Group One, 1st Marine Brigade, from 1935 to 1939, when he was sent to the Navy War College. Following graduation in 1941, he was promoted to brigadier general and given command of the 1st Marine Air Wing, Fleet Marine Force, in September. After the BATTLE OF PEARL HARBOR and U.S. entry into World War II, Geiger assumed command of the air wing on Guadalcanal as soon as the island was captured from the Japanese (September 1942–February 1943). Promoted to major general, Geiger returned to Washington as director of the marine Division of Aviation. He served in this post from May to November 1943, when he succeeded Gen. ALEXANDER VANDEGRIFT as commander of I Amphibious Corps (later redesignated III Amphibious Corps). He led this corps in the retaking of Guam, in the MARIANA ISLANDS CAMPAIGN, from July 21 to August 10, 1944, then commanded at the BATTLE OF PELELIU from September 15 to November 25.

Roy S. Geiger *(United States Marine Corps)*

Geiger next took part in the Okinawa Campaign (April 1–June 18, 1945), beginning with the landing. Geiger's corps was attached to the Tenth U.S. Army, commanded by General Simon B. Buckner. After Buckner was killed in battle, Geiger assumed command of the Tenth Army until the arrival of General Joseph A. Stilwell on June 23. Geiger's brief tenure was the only occasion on which a USMC officer commanded a U.S. field army.

In July 1945, Geiger was named to command Fleet Marine Force, Pacific. His next command came after the war, in November 1946, when he was assigned to a post in Washington. Geiger fell ill a few months after his arrival in Washington, however, and died the next year. A grateful Congress posthumously awarded him the honorary rank of general in July 1947.

Further reading: Willock, Roger. *Unaccustomed to Fear: A Biography of the Late General Roy S. Geiger, U.S.M.C.* Princeton, N.J.: Privately printed, 1968.

Geisler, Hans (1891–1966) *German Luftwaffe general*

Hans Geisler's military career began in the German Navy, which he entered on April 1, 1909. During World War I, he served mainly as an air observer in the naval aviation branch, transferring to the newly formed Luftwaffe on September 1, 1933. Geisler commanded X Fliegerkorps during the Invasion of Norway in 1940, the Luftwaffe element of the entire invasion. Air support was crucial to the success of German operations in Norway, and Lieutenant General Geisler was awarded the Knight's Cross for the part he played in the Norwegian Campaign. He continued to command X Fliegerkorps until August 23, 1942, then retired from active duty on October 31, 1942, with the rank of *general der flieger* (general of the air force).

Further reading: Kersaudy, François. *Norway 1940.* Lincoln: University of Nebraska Press, 1998; Mann, Chris, and Christer Jorgensen. *Hitler's Arctic War: The German Campaigns in Norway, Finland, and the USSR 1940–1945.* New York: St. Martin's Press, 2003; Petrow, Richard. *The Bitter Years; The Invasion and Occupation of Denmark and Norway, April 1940–May 1945.* New York: William Morrow, 1974.

Geneva Conventions

The Geneva Conventions of 1929 were, at the time of World War II, the latest chapter in a long history of attempts to regulate wartime behavior by codifying the rules of appropriate and humane military conduct. Historians believe that the earliest recorded attempt along these lines is found in the writings of the sixth-century B.C.E. Chinese general, strategist, and military theorist Sun Tzu. As early as 200 B.C.E., in ancient India, the Hindu *Law Code of Manu* introduced the concept of war crimes. In 1625, the Dutch jurist and theologian Hugo Grotius (1583–1645) wrote *On the Law of War and Peace*, which concerns the treatment of civilians in time of war. During World War II, references to the "Geneva Convention" usually cited the convention dealing with the treatment of Prisoners of War (POW). However, the first "Geneva Convention," concluded in 1864 under the sponsorship of the International Red Cross, was an international agreement on certain standards and procedures to protect the sick and wounded in wartime. Ever since this convention, the International Red Cross has taken a role in drafting conventions and in monitoring compliance.

In 1899, at the instigation of Czar Nicholas II of Russia, an international conference was convened at the Hague, Netherlands, to institute arms limitations as a first step toward eventual international disarmament. Ultimately, the Hague Conventions (1899) failed to address arms limitations, but they did include provisions for impartial arbitration as an alternative to war. And they provided declarations against the use of asphyxiating gases and expanding ("dum-dum") bullets as inhumane weapons. A second conference in 1907 produced the Hague Conventions (1907), which more fully defined the procedures, institutions, and apparatus for peaceful international arbitration and also produced a Convention on Prisoners of War, which codified rules of treatment already generally accepted and in practice. It was not until the 1925

Protocol for the Prohibition of the Use in War of Asphyxiating, Poisonous or Other Gases, and of Bacteriological Methods of Warfare that a comprehensive international ban on poison gas and "germ warfare" was concluded.

In 1929, at Geneva, the most detailed conventions thus far were concluded concerning the treatment of prisoners of war and of the wounded: Convention Relative to the Treatment of Prisoners of War and Convention for the Amelioration of the Condition of the Wounded and Sick in Armies in the Field. Both of these conventions would be renewed and expanded after World War II, in 1949.

That none of the belligerents used poison gas as a combat weapon in World War II may or may not be attributed to compliance with the 1925 Geneva Protocol for the Prohibition of the Use in War of Asphyxiating, Poisonous or Other Gases, and of Bacteriological Methods of Warfare. The fact is that the use of chemical warfare, marginally effective in the trenches of World War I, would have been even less effective on a mobile battlefield. Moreover, chemical warfare is notoriously difficult to control and can be as deadly to those who use it as to those it is used against. It is most likely these reasons, and not the Geneva Protocol, that discouraged its use in World War II. The Allies did fear that the Japanese, in particular, would employ BIOLOGICAL WARFARE (BW), as they already had in the SINO-JAPANESE WAR. However, BW was of negligible significance in World War II, again most likely because it was impractical and difficult to control, a danger to attacker as well as defender.

Japan was not a signatory to the 1929 Geneva Protocol prohibiting the use of poison gas and biological warfare; nor did it subscribe to the 1929 Convention Relative to the Treatment of Prisoners of War. All of the other major combatants in World War II, including the United States, Great Britain, and Germany, were signatories to the protocol and the convention.

The essence of the Geneva Convention on prisoners of war is set out in the preamble to the document: "in the extreme event of a war, it will be the duty of every Power to mitigate as far as possible the inevitable rigors thereof and to alleviate the condition of prisoners of war." Another key provisions is given in Article 2 of the convention:

> Prisoners of war are in the power of the hostile Government, but not of the individuals or formation which captured them. They shall at all times be humanely treated and protected, particularly against acts of violence, from insults and from public curiosity. Measures of reprisal against them are forbidden.

In addition, the convention lays down minimum requirements concerning conditions of capture; evacuation of POWs from combat zones; sanitation, food, shelter, and other requirements for POW camps; POW labor rules; the right of POWs to communicate with their families and certain other persons; rules regulating discipline, punishment, and prisoners' relations with authorities; rules regulating parole and release; and the application of POW status (and, therefore, POW rights) to certain civilians ("Persons who follow the armed forces without directly belonging thereto, such as correspondents, newspaper reporters, sutlers, or contractors, who fall into the hands of the enemy, and whom the latter think fit to detain, shall be entitled to be treated as prisoners of war, provided they are in possession of an authorization from the military authorities of the armed forces which they were following"). Prisoners were obligated to furnish their captors with no information other than their name and rank; Allied prisoners also volunteered their serial identification numbers as well. Interrogation was permitted, but torture or other punishment (including withholding food, medical attention, or other rights guaranteed by the convention) was prohibited. Prisoners were given the right to report abuses to prison camp authorities without fear of reprisal. They were also given the right to report abuses to representatives of the International Red Cross, who made periodic visits to inspect the camps. The convention itself was to be publicly posted inside the camp and available for examination by all prisoners.

The 1929 Convention for the Amelioration of the Condition of the Wounded and Sick in Armies in the Field, subscribed to by all major combatants except Japan, addressed provisions for the treatment of wounded and sick prisoners of war. Each party to the convention agreed to provide care to all enemy wounded under its control on a par with the treatment provided to its own soldiers. Medical formations and establishments were to be accorded noncombatant status. Medical personnel, including medical corps troops and civilian volunteers, were to be considered immune from attack and were to be allowed to function as medical personnel in the event of their capture. Although military medical buildings and vehicles were subject to capture, they were also to be clearly marked and, therefore, immune from destructive attack. The familiar red cross marking was specifically prescribed as universal. Finally, signatories to the convention also agreed to provide for burial of enemy dead and to furnish lists of wounded and dead to officials on the opposite side.

In general, the Western Allies abided by the Geneva Conventions and Protocols. The Soviets often did not and were highly abusive of German POWs in particular, many of whom were mistreated during their captivity and were not released until months, even years, after the cessation of hostilities. German treatment of POWs varied widely. Prisoners from the Western nations were generally treated much better than Soviet POWs (who were often starved and even deliberately murdered). Western Allied air personnel, who were confined in camps administered by the Luftwaffe, generally received more humane treatment than ground troops, who were held in camps administered by the army. The Geneva Conventions provided a legal basis for prosecution of war crimes by the postwar NUREMBERG WAR CRIMES TRIBUNAL and at the TOKYO WAR CRIMES TRIALS.

See also BATAAN DEATH MARCH; and MALMÉDY MASSACRE.

Further reading: The Avalon Project at Yale Law School. "Convention Between the United States of America and Other Powers, Relating to Prisoners of War; July 27, 1929," Available online. URL: www.yale.edu/lawweb/avalon/lawofwar/geneva02.htm. Accessed on November 22, 2006. Eig, Larry M. *The Geneva Convention Relative to the Treatment of Prisoners of War*. Washington, D.C.:

Congressional Research Service, Library of Congress, 1991.

German-Japanese-Italian Pact

Germany, Japan, and Italy concluded the AXIS (TRIPARTITE) PACT in September 1940, among other things in the hope that it would intimidate the United States by the prospect of a two-front war and thereby discourage it from continuing its move away from neutrality and toward the Allies. Instead, the pact drove the administration of President FRANKLIN D. ROOSEVELT even closer to partnership with WINSTON CHURCHILL's Britain. When Japan ended the last pretense of U.S. neutrality at the BATTLE OF PEARL HARBOR on December 7, 1941, prompting a U.S. declaration of war the next day, ADOLF HITLER and BENITO MUSSOLINI reaffirmed the Axis alliance by declaring war on the United States on December 11 and simultaneously concluding the German-Japanese-Italian Pact, an agreement for the joint prosecution of the war. The brief document stated common war goals, namely victory over Great Britain and the United States, to be followed by the "closest cooperation [among Germany, Japan, and Italy] with a view to establishing a new and just order along the lines of the Tripartite Agreement." Most important, the three Axis partners agreed to make no separate peace with the United States and Great Britain. Italy, of course, did just that on September 8, 1943, and Germany surrendered on May 7–8, 1945. Japan did not capitulate until August 15 of that year, formalizing the surrender on September 2.

Further reading: Phillips, Charles, and Alan Axelrod, "Agreement among Germany, Italy, and Japan on the Joint Prosecution of the War." In Charles Phillips and Alan Axelrod, eds. *Encyclopedia of Historical Treaties and Alliances*. New York: Facts On File, 2001. Vol. 2, pp. 597–598.

German resistance to Nazism

From the perspective of the Allies fighting ADOLF HITLER, Nazi Germany seemed a nation gripped in monolithic totalitarianism, a population of virtual robots. In fact, allegiance to Hitler and Nazism was by no means universal among Germans, and *Widerstand,* the collective name given to the resistance movements in Nazi Germany, was active throughout the war. The extent of this resistance may be gauged in part by recognizing that between 1938 and 1945, there were no fewer than 17 attempts to assassinate Adolf Hitler, all efforts of *Widerstand.* The July 20 Plot, the final assassination attempt masterminded by army officer CLAUS VON STAUFFENBERG in 1944, was the product of a network of conspirators. Following the failure of the plot, nearly 5,000 suspects were captured and executed. Many historians have dismissed this mass judicial slaughter as a symptom of Hitler's paranoia. More likely, most of those apprehended were actually involved in anti-Hitler or anti-Nazi resistance, if not direct accessories to the July 20 Plot. Certainly, their deaths brought most resistance activities to an end within Germany.

Black Orchestra (*Schwarze Kapelle*) was the name the GESTAPO gave to nearly all organized opposition to Adolf Hitler. The Black Orchestra included aristocrats, diplomats, and senior army officers. The American OFFICE OF STRATEGIC SERVICES (OSS) communicated with some elements of the Black Orchestra, principally General Ludwig Beck (former head of the *Truppenamt,* the clandestine prewar general staff) and Carl Goerdeler (former mayor of Leipzig) via Hans Bernd Gisevius, German vice consul in Zurich, Switzerland. Gisevius was in direct contact with ALLEN DULLES, OSS chief in Zurich. The most important groups and plots of the so-called Black Orchestra included:

The Halder Conspiracy: On the eve of war, WEHRMACHT officer Fritz Halder plotted a coup d'état to overthrow the Hitler regime. It failed to materialize.

Operation Spark: General Henning von Treskow, one of Hitler's commanders in the ill-fated INVASION OF THE SOVIET UNION, plotted to assassinate Hitler and then stage a coup to overthrow the Nazi regime.

The Kreisau Circle (Kreisauer Kreis): This group of anti-Nazi Germans consisted mainly of members of the German nobility who met at the Kreisau estate of Helmuth James Graf von Moltke for the purpose of formulating an alternative to Nazism. Formed before the outbreak of the war, the idea of the Kreisau Circle was to create a Christian society centered around small communities. Members reached out to other resistance groups and also attempted to alert people outside Germany to the threat of Nazism. During the war, beginning in 1943, the group worked more aggressively to foment an outright coup d'état. In January 1944, however, Gestapo agents arrested Moltke. His circle dissolved, although some associated with it participated in the July 20 Plot.

White Rose Society (Die Weisse Rose): This group of five Munich students published and distributed six inflammatory anti-Nazi leaflets from June 1942 to February 1943. Hans Scholl and his sister Sophie were the leaders of the group, which also included Christoph Probst, Alexander Schmorell, and Willi Graf. A professor, Kurt Huber, joined late and drafted the final two leaflets. All of the White Rose men were war veterans who had fought on the French and Russian fronts. They were revolted by German atrocities on the battlefield and as part of THE HOLOCAUST. They and the other White Rose members wanted to overthrow Hitler and steer Germany away from nationalism entirely. They advocated a federated Europe based on the Christian moral principles of tolerance and justice. Their leaflet campaign was intended to stir the German intelligentsia to oppose the Nazi regime. Early in 1943, the members of the White Rose were arrested and tried for treason. All five original members were executed, and others accused of having aided the White Rose were sentenced to prison terms ranging from six months to 10 years.

Edelweiss Pirates (Edelweissspiraten): This group emerged in western Germany during the late

1930s in rebellion against the regimentation of the Hitler Youth movement. Members, between the ages of 14 and 18, were, in effect, dropouts from Nazi society who left school to avoid membership in the Hitler Youth and who evaded reich labor service and military service. The Edelweiss Pirates were in large measure a social organization whose members hiked and camped together. Members were neither spies nor saboteurs, but they were social protesters nevertheless. The Gestapo dealt with them harshly, sometimes sending members to concentration camps or prison. On October 25, 1944, by order of HEINRICH HIMMLER, 13 members were publicly hanged in Cologne. Yet the Edelweiss Pirate movement endured to the very end of the war. They have never been officially recognized as a resistance movement.

Red Orchestra (Rote Kapelle): Red Orchestra was the name given by German counterespionage authorities, mainly the Abwehr, to a Soviet-sponsored espionage and resistance ring in Nazi-occupied Europe and in Germany proper. The name was derived from the fact that Moscow-based intelligence agents referred to the radio transmitters of operatives as "music boxes" and called the operatives themselves "musicians."

Leopold Trepper, an agent of the Soviet NKVD, organized underground operations in Germany, France, the Netherlands, and Switzerland. Red Orchestra agents infiltrated the German government, military, and even the Abwehr itself. So dangerous was the Red Orchestra that German counterespionage agents created the Red Orchestra Special Detachment (Sonderkommando Rote Kapelle) specifically to target it. Trepper's agents were mostly procommunist Germans, many of them highly placed in the government and military: Harro Schulze-Boysen was an intelligence officer for the German Ministry of Air, Arvid Harnack held a position in the Ministry of Economics, Margarete Harnack worked in the Office for Race Policy,

Horst Heilmann was an army cryptologist, Gunther Weisenborn was an executive with the German national radio system, Herbert Gollnow was a military counterintelligence agent, and Johann Graudens was an aircraft manufacturer. Red Orchestra agents reported on German troop concentrations and movements, aircraft and other armaments production, and fuel shipments.

In 1942, Abwehr agents were able to get a fix on radio transmissions from Johann Wenzel, a Red Orchestra agent in Belgium. Arrested, he turned double agent, and, through him, German counterintelligence arrested Schulze-Boysen and his wife on August 30, 1942. Harnack and his wife were rounded up in September. More followed, and the entire network was soon undone, its operations halted by spring of 1943.

See also BONHOEFFER, DIETRICH.

Further reading: Dulles, Allen Welsh. *Germany's Underground: The Anti-Nazi Resistance.* New York: Da Capo, 2000; Fest, Joachim. *Plotting Hitler's Death: The Story of German Resistance.* New York: Owl Books, 1997; Hoffmann, Peter. *The History of the German Resistance, 1933–1945.* Montreal: McGill-Queen's University Press, 1996; McDonough, Frank. *Opposition and Resistance in Nazi Germany.* Cambridge and New York: Cambridge University Press, 2001.

German-Soviet Non-Aggression Pact

On the eve of World War II, the Western democracies took considerable comfort in what they were confident was the implacable opposition of Soviet communism to German Nazism. JOSEPH STALIN was the polar opposite of ADOLF HITLER, and as long as Hitler had reason to fear the Soviets in the east, he would never venture to begin a war with the west.

This optimistic view of European politics relied too heavily on Stalin's idealism, which, it turned out, was a nonexistent commodity. While Nazism was indeed the ideological antithesis of communism, Stalin, the pragmatist, decided that a guarantee of nonaggression with his rival would put the Soviet Union in a powerful position with respect to the capitalist democracies while protecting the nation against German expansion. Finally, in the short run, a nonaggression pact would give the Soviet Union necessary leeway for some expansion of its own, at the expense of Poland and Finland. Stalin therefore approached Hitler with the proposal that they conclude a Nazi-Soviet nonaggression pact, guaranteeing that neither nation would act militarily against the other. For his part, Hitler, who had his own designs on the east, most immediately Poland, and who sought to neutralize the FRANCO-SOVIET PACTS, was eager to treat with his ideological adversary.

The German-Soviet Non-Aggression Pact, also known as the Hitler-Stalin Pact, was concluded on August 23, 1939, at Moscow. It stunned the world, especially Western politicians and the Western intelligentsia, many of whom were apologists for Stalin, excusing his many "excesses"—purges and the lethal programs of agricultural collectivization—on ideological grounds.

The treaty with Germany was one of several nonaggression pacts the Soviet Union had signed with other powers, but this one went beyond merely declaring nonaggression. It was linked to a trade agreement that had been concluded a few days earlier, on August 19, by which Germany exported manufactured goods to the USSR in return for raw materials essential to its war production. Unknown to the outside world, the nonaggression pact included a secret protocol providing for the German-Soviet partition of Poland. The secret protocol also cleared the way for the Soviet occupation of the Baltic states.

The pact gave Hitler leave for the INVASION OF POLAND, which started World War II. Stalin also claimed a piece of Poland, and, thanks to the pact, was free to fight the RUSSO-FINNISH WAR to annex portions of that country. For the USSR, the pact had much graver consequences as well. It lulled Stalin into trusting Adolf Hitler, a trust that proved disastrous when, on June 22, 1941, Hitler unilaterally abrogated the nonaggression pact with the INVASION OF THE SOVIET UNION.

Further reading: Leonhard, Wolfgang. *Betrayal: The Hitler-Stalin Pact of 1939.* New York: St. Martin's Press, 1989; Phillips, Charles, and Alan Axelrod, "Agreement among Germany, Italy, and Japan on the Joint Prosecution of the War." In Charles Phillips and Alan Axelrod, eds. *Encyclopedia of Historical Treaties and Alliances.* New York: Facts On File, 2001, vol. 2, pp. 533–534; Read, Anthony. *Deadly Embrace: Hitler, Stalin and the Nazi-Soviet Pact, 1939–1941.* New York: Norton, 1988; Roberts, Geoffrey K. *Unholy Alliance: Stalin's Pact with Hitler.* Bloomington: Indiana University Press, 1990.

Germany

Beginning in 1933, the identity and fate of Germany, as well as its role in creating World War II, were bound up with the leadership of a single man, ADOLF HITLER. He brought to Germany a cult of personality and injected the nation with a myth of racial superiority that (according to the myth) destined the German people to dominate Europe and, indeed, the world. Hitler rose in a Germany that was desperately ready to receive such a myth. Defeated in World War I (for which it had been in large part, although by no means solely, responsible), Germany was subjected to the relentlessly punitive TREATY OF VERSAILLES, which eviscerated its military (limiting the army to 100,000 men, eliminating the air force, and greatly restricting the navy), imposed ruinous financial reparations, ended its monarchy, stripped away its modest colonial empire, and forced it to assume complete moral responsibility for the war. The terms of the treaty exacerbated the postwar instability of Germany, suddenly without an emperor and struggling to create a democracy amid the competing forces of communism, socialism, and FASCISM, the latter a form of government newly emerged in postwar Italy. Politically adrift, Germany fell (like much of Europe) on economic hard times, which were destined to grow worse as the 1920s became the 1930s and worldwide depression set it.

Yet Germany was, in some respects, more fortunate than its primary adversary in the Great War so recently ended. All the combatant nations had lost a great portion of the flower of their young man-

Expansion of Nazi Germany, 1933–1939

Expansion of Nazi Germany, 1933–1939

- Germany, 1933
- Saar region, 1935
- Rhineland, 1936

Territory annexed
- 1938
- 1939

© Infobase Publishing

hood, but France, with Belgium, had the added misfortune of having been the major battlefield of the western front. Nominally victorious, France emerged from World War I deeply ravaged. Germany, in contrast, though defeated, was superficially unscathed. Whereas France looked like a beaten country, Germany appeared whole. Moreover, while the German conscript army had suffered horrific casualties, the army's professional, volunteer core was very much intact, whereas

France and the other great European democracy, Britain, were intensely war weary, afflicted, as it were, by a kind of demoralizing malaise. Their joint victory notwithstanding, Britain and France were resolutely determined to avoid any more wars. In contrast, at its heart, Germany remained a military power.

The poverty and the chaos throughout much of postwar Germany were undeniable, of course, and the democratic government imposed on Germany by the Treaty of Versailles seemed woefully incapable of bringing order, economic recovery, and an alternative to the encroachment of communism. Paramilitary groups, especially the FREIKORPS, had already formed, consisting mainly of discontented World War I veterans. These groups performed vigilante duty as well as the forcible suppression of socialist and communist activity. They and much of the general populace were ripe not just for strong leadership, but for the leadership of a fascist strongman. Hitler offered Germany its destiny, a destiny far superior to what the Allies had dealt to the nation in the Treaty of Versailles. Hitler also offered an enemy: an amalgam of democrats, socialists, communists, and Jews who had collectively betrayed Germany in World War I, depriving it of the military victory it had earned and that it deserved. The Jews were especially demonized, not merely as a political and economic threat, but as a threat to German racial purity and identity and, therefore, to the fulfillment of German destiny.

After he had assumed the post of chancellor of Germany, Hitler did introduce a significant measure of economic prosperity to the nation as he geared up industrial production for war. At first, he did this clandestinely, in covert defiance of the Treaty of Versailles, but, as it became apparent that the Western democracies lacked the will to oppose him, he became increasingly open, even brazen. War was the object of Hitler's political and cultural plan for Germany. He spoke of the necessity—again, in fulfilment of the national destiny—of acquiring LEBENSRAUM (living space), which, of course, meant conquest, and that, in turn, required war. As plans for the FINAL SOLUTION to the Jewish question evolved into the policy of genocide known to history as THE HOLOCAUST, the Nazis' dedication to anti-semitism also required war, for killing on the scale required by the Final Solution could hardly be carried out in time of peace.

By the end of the 1930s and the INVASION OF POLAND, which began World War II on September 1, 1939, the German government, culture, and economy were driven by the monolithic machinery and mythology of Nazism. This does not mean that the Nazis lacked opposition, but the opposition was largely suppressed by the apparatus of what had become a police state, including extensive and sophisticated systems for generating propaganda (under the brilliant direction of Propaganda Minister JOSEF GOEBBELS) and military and civilian policing authorities (especially the GESTAPO, SCHUTZSTAFFEL [SS], and SICHERHEITSDIENST [SD]). Internal solidarity was achieved in large measure through a policy of racial mythology and racial purity, so that the distinction between national and racial identity was blurred. Jews, Slavs, and other "mongrel races" were to be purged from the reich. Also to be purged were those judged antithetical to Nazi society, including homosexuals, the mentally retarded, those with serious physical disabilities, and persons with hereditary diseases. "Purging" might mean involuntary relocation from one part of the reich to another (internal exile), ostensibly voluntary foreign emigration, or something even worse. Mandatory sterilization was instituted for those judged to have hereditary defects. Later, a large-scale euthanasia program for children as well as adults was instituted. As for the Jews and other proscribed political, ethnic, social, and racial groups, mass murder was the ultimate fate. The objective of the effort to achieve racial and national homogeneity was *Gleichshaltung* (regimented conformity) and *Volksgemeinschaft* (subjugation of the individual identity to the collective identity of "the people," and of individual well-being to collective well-being), The German economy was also tightly controlled, but this was achieved mainly through a mutually profitable partnership between the government and German industrialists and financiers, the most prosperous of whom were Nazi Party members.

As it was poised for war in 1939, Germany encompassed 226,288 square miles of territory and had a population of 79.5 million. During the war, at the height of its success, the so-called Greater German Reich included 344,080 square miles and encompassed a population of about 116 million. By the time it went to war, Germany, devoting its full economic effort to war-related production, had eliminated the unemployment of the depression and had a workforce of 24.5 million men and 14.6 million women in addition to some 300,000 foreign workers. At the outbreak of war, the armed forces mobilized more than 4.5 million men. As demands for military manpower grew, labor shortages became critical, and, during the course of the war, German labor was increasingly performed by slaves, including PRISONERS OF WAR (POW) and the forced labor of civilians from the conquered and occupied countries. By 1944, Germany had 7.1 million foreign workers, including 5.3 million civilians subject to forced labor and 1.8 million POWs. All worked under the most appalling conditions. Yet another source of forced labor were the CONCENTRATION AND EXTERMINATION CAMPS. Originally built as part of the police state apparatus to confine political dissidents and social undesirables, the camps became during the war a vast network of confinement from which few emerged alive. Able-bodied inmates, even among those marked for eventual death, were often tapped for slave labor. By 1944, the inmate labor rolls had swelled to about 300,000, many of them assigned to work in subterranean aircraft factories. Inmate labor was regulated directly by the SS, which billed factory owners a profitable fee for each laborer supplied.

The government of Nazi Germany was a paradoxical combination of the absolute personal authority of Adolf Hitler (the "Führer," absolute leader) and a bewildering maze of administrative bureaucracies at the national as well as local levels. Hitler operated without any constitutional check, and loyalty to the German nation was intended to be synonymous with personal loyalty to Hitler. Officially, Hitler was head of state, leader of the Nazi Party, and supreme commander of the military. The principal bureaucratic structure was organized under five chancelleries, which administered policy as set down or personally approved by Hitler. Additionally, the Greater German Reich (at its height in 1941) was divided into 42 *Gaue*, or party districts, each headed by a gauleiter (regional party leader), and 39 state entities (consisting of *Reichsgaue*, *Länder*, and Prussian provinces), plus 18 military districts. The five chancelleries not-

withstanding, regional leaders generally had direct access to Hitler if they required it on occasion.

Nazi Germany was, on its surface, a highly legalistic society. At the beginning of the war, there were 2,199 law courts, which were administered by 198 higher courts. There were also supreme civil courts, military courts, special courts, and the people's court, the last two with jurisdiction over political crimes. The courts did not dispense justice but, rather, aided the police and other authorities in serving state security as that was defined ultimately by HEINRICH HIMMLER, head of the SS and given by Hitler virtually unlimited police powers. The courts had no authority over the police. Among the most serious yet generalized offenses was *Wehrkraftzersetzung*, subversion of the war effort, a crime that could consist of just about anything police officials or the courts determined. Laws abounded in Nazi Germany, but the rule of law was nonexistent. All authority, all privileges (for there were no rights), all sanctions, and all policies flowed ultimately from the person and fiat of Adolf Hitler, who could justifiably have said, with France's Louis XIV, "I am the state."

See also GERMAN RESISTANCE TO NAZISM.

Further reading: Burleigh, Michael. *The Third Reich: A New History.* New York: Hill & Wang, 2001; Burleigh, Michael, and Wolfgang Wippermann. *The Racial State: Germany 1933–1945.* Cambridge and New York: Cambridge University Press, 1991; Evans, Richard J. *The Coming of the Third Reich.* New York: Penguin, 2004; Fischer, Klaus P. *Nazi Germany: A New History.* London: Continuum International Publishing Group, 1996; Grunberger, Richard. *The 12-Year Reich: A Social History of Nazi Germany 1933–1945.* New York: Da Capo Press, 1995; Kershaw, Ian. *The 'Hitler Myth': Image and Reality in the Third Reich.* Oxford and New York: Oxford University Press, 2001; Peukert, Detlev J. K. *Inside Nazi Germany: Conformity, Opposition, and Racism in Everyday Life.* New Haven, Conn.: Yale University Press, 1989; Peukert, Detlev J. K. *The Weimar Republic.* New York: Hill & Wang, 1993; Shirer, William L. *The Nightmare Years: 1930–1940.* Boston: Little, Brown, 1984; Shirer, William L. *Rise And Fall of the Third Reich.* New York: Simon & Schuster, 1990.

Germany, air force of

The Luftwaffe, a branch of the German WEHR-MACHT, had been created by the Nazi regime prior to World War II in defiance of the TREATY OF VERSAILLES, which barred Germany from having an air force. Moreover, the air arm was headed by HERMANN GÖRING, a World War I flying ace and a career military aviator, but also a member of ADOLF HITLER's innermost circle. As a Nazi creation presided over by a high-ranking Nazi, the German air force enjoyed a kind of privileged status among the branches of the German military. This was a dramatic contrast with the Allied powers, in which the air force was typically regarded as a kind of military stepchild, second to the army and navy. Indeed, Hitler, who, throughout the war, placed great faith in "wonder weapons," saw the air force as just such a weapon, the sovereign means of achieving his territorial ambitions and one that was even more important than the army and far more important than the navy. Hitler intended to use the air force as an offensive weapon, which would reach out to intimidate his neighbors. For this reason, he allocated extensive resources to the Luftwaffe in an effort to build it up from post–World War I nonexistence to a force that would overmatch the air arms of France and Great Britain.

Hitler emphasized the production of large numbers of advanced aircraft, and he achieved just that. However, the production was devoted almost exclusively to single-engine fighters and twin-engine light or medium bombers. These were short-range aircraft designed for short wars, and they were incapable of the long-range strategic bombing that might have been of great use, possibly even decisive, in the campaigns against Great Britain and the Soviet Union. The almost complete absence of long-range strategic bombers in the Luftwaffe was another key contrast with the air forces of Great Britain and the United States, which put great emphasis on four-engine heavy bombers.

The absence of heavy bombers was not the Luftwaffe's only serious deficiency. Göring presided over an unnecessarily complex and redundant command structure, which was not rationalized until the creation of the Luftwaffe High Command late in the war, in the middle of 1944. By this time, the Luftwaffe had been hobbled by procurement problems, which a unified command would have done much to solve. Such a command would also have been able to shift the make-up of the Luftwaffe from the offensive force that had entered the war to the defensive force required in the war's endgame. Göring exercised personal and sometimes capricious control of the Luftwaffe, and because he was an intimate of Hitler, the führer did little or nothing to keep him in check. Göring proved to be a singularly poor personnel manager who interposed between himself and the airmen in the field a layer of staff officers combining inexperience with a desire to please their chief, often at the expense of the hard realities. The result was that Göring continually received the overly optimistic reports of yes men. As the Luftwaffe increasingly yielded air superiority and then air supremacy to the Allies, Göring seemed simply to give up on his leadership responsibilities, and, by late 1944, the air arm fell under the personal direction of Hitler, who was quite incapable of managing it.

In terms of operations, the Luftwaffe was organized into *Luftflotten,* or air fleets (the equivalent of U.S "air forces"), which, in turn, were divided into *Fliegerkorps* (flying corps), and, below this, *Fliegerdivisions.* Within each *Fliegerdivision* were *Geschwader,* or groups, including *Kampfgeschwader* (bomber groups), *Jagdgeschwader* (fighter groups), *Nachtjagdgeschwader* (night fighter groups), *Stukageschwader* (dive bomber groups), *Zerstoerergeschwader* ("destroyer" groups, mainly consisting of twin-engine Me-110 night fighters), and *Lehrgeschwader* (training formations). Each *Geschwader* consisted of three or four *Gruppen* (groups), divided into three or four *Staffeln* (squadrons), normally consisting of a dozen aircraft each. At the outbreak of the war, in September 1939, the Luftwaffe operated 302 *Staffeln* with 2,563 aircraft.

In addition to operating aircraft offensively, the Luftwaffe was also responsible for antiaircraft defense. This included dispatching fighters to meet incoming enemy bombers and manning ground-based antiaircraft artillery. The Luftwaffe also maintained Germany's early warning network, including observers, RADAR installations, and radar operators. Under Luftwaffe command were some 100,000 women who served in air warning units and communication units and who operated home-based antiaircraft artillery. The Luftwaffe also had full responsibility for AIRBORNE ASSAULT through its *Fallschirmjäger,* or parachute division. Finally, in an effort to retain surplus Luftwaffe personnel, Göring created no fewer than 21 conventional ground-troop divisions. Despite his best efforts, however, Göring was compelled to relinquish control of these to the army in November 1943. Most of these troops were inferior to the regular army forces, but the famed Hermann Göring Panzer Division, an all-volunteer unit, was a notable elite exception.

To the great consternation and discouragement of the Allies, war production seemed little harmed by the costly STRATEGIC BOMBING OF GERMANY. Indeed, aircraft were turned out at a remarkable rate, even well into 1944, by which time many factories had been moved into hardened underground facilities manned by slave labor drawn from CONCENTRATION AND EXTERMINATION CAMPS. Increasingly scarce, however, were pilots, especially seasoned pilots, and even less readily available was fuel. That shortage compounded the trained pilot shortage, since the Luftwaffe could not afford to expend much fuel on "mere" training missions. Many Luftwaffe officers were eager to develop JET AIRCRAFT, which were operational late in the war. Jets so thoroughly outperformed the long-range Allied fighters (such as the P-51 Mustangs), which escorted B-17 and B-24 bombers on their incessant raids into the homeland, that it was believed they might be sufficient to turn the tide of the air war. However, the jets were introduced too late and in too small numbers to make a significant impact, and the Luftwaffe continued to disintegrate until the end of the war.

Further reading: Bekker, Cajus. *The Luftwaffe War Diaries: The German Air Force in World War II.* New York: Da Capo Press, 1994; Brown, Eric. *Wings of the Luftwaffe: Flying German Aircraft of the Second World War.* Shrews-bury, U.K.: Airlife Publishing, 1993; Corum, James S. *The Luftwaffe: Creating the Operational Air War, 1918–1940.* Lawrence: University Press of Kansas, 1997; Corum, James S., and Richard R. Muller. *The Luftwaffe's Way of War: German Air Force Doctrine, 1911–1945.* Mount Pleasant, S.C.: Nautical & Aviation Publishing Company of America, 1998; Hayward, Joel S. A. *Stopped at Stalingrad: The Luftwaffe and Hitler's Defeat in the East, 1942–1943.* Lawrence: University Press of Kansas, 2001; Homze, E. *Arming the Luftwaffe: The Reich Air Ministry and the German Aircraft Industry 1919–1939.* Lincoln: University of Nebraska Press, 1976; Isby, David C., ed. *Fighting the Bombers: The Luftwaffe's Struggle Against the Allied Bomber Offensive, As Seen by Its Commanders.* London: Greenhill, 2003.

Germany, army of

Germany's principal ground forces consisted of the army (which reached a peak strength of 6.55 million men in 1943), the WAFFEN-SS (which peaked in 1945 at 830,000 men), and several thousand men in the field (ground troop) divisions of the Luftwaffe. The term *WEHRMACHT* is often mistakenly used as a synonym for the German Army. *Wehrmacht,* which means "defense power," was actually the collective term for *all* the German armed forces, and, as an institution, the Wehrmacht took the place of a war ministry or war department. ADOLF HITLER exercised direct control over the Wehrmacht and, therefore, over all of the armed forces. By the time of World War II, soldiers, sailors, and airmen of all ranks swore an oath of personal loyalty to Hitler, not to Germany. (Officers had been required to swear the personal loyalty oath since 1934.)

At the outbreak of World War II in 1939, the army, called in German *das Heer,* had grown rapidly into a force of 3.74 million men, mostly conscripts, who were organized around a core of highly professional officers and veteran noncommissioned officers. The TREATY OF VERSAILLES that ended World War I permitted Germany a 100,000-man army. The German military used this severe limitation to its advantage, building a *Führerheer,* or leader army, of highly trained officers and enlisted men as a cadre around which a much larger conscript army could, in very short order, be raised. Thus, at the outbreak of World War II and through most of the war, the German army was highly skilled, very disciplined, and quite well equipped. It was a most formidable force, with many extraordinary, even legendary, commanders. The traditions of the peerless Prussian Army endowed the modern German Army with an excellent staff-officer echelon, which greatly facilitated the execution of high command orders. Officers in the field were uniformly of a high level, and, contrary to the notion that the German Army was inflexible, field officers were given great latitude in operational decisions. Moreover, officers at every level were groomed for leadership and were taught never to regard themselves as mere functionaries. This autonomy and commitment to leadership was brought to bear in the execution of *Auftragstaktik,* or mission-oriented tactics, which produced a high degree of efficiency.

Army high command, the Oberkommando des Heeres (OKH), was, at the outbreak of war, headed by Field Marshal WALTHER VON BRAUCHITSCH, whom Hitler dismissed in December 1941 as the INVASION OF THE SOVIET UNION faltered. From this point on, Hitler, who already had direct charge of the Wehrmacht, assumed personal command of the OKH as well. It was an act of supreme hubris, which, to the good fortune of the Allies, proved highly destructive to the army as well as to the overall war strategy. Indeed, as the war progressed, relations between Hitler and his top generals deteriorated. The OKH became a shell. Hitler's word was final, and by the middle of the war, he rarely listened to his generals, but simply gave commands.

The main fighting force of the army was Field Army, which, at its peak strength, was divided into 11 army group commands controlling 26 armies. These, in turn, were built of divisions. At its peak, Germany fielded 31 panzer ("armored") divisions, 13 motorized divisions (later called panzer grenadier divisions), 2 cavalry divisions, 176 infantry divisions, 11 Jäger (light infantry) divisions, 10 mountain divisions, 50 Volksgrenadier divisions (low-grade infantry divisions made up mostly of the remnants of shattered regular divisions), one air-landing division, four coastal defense divisions, and six security divisions (which provided security for military installations). The Field Army had no separate artillery divisions because artillery was integral to all divisions except for the security divisions, which needed no artillery component.

The German Army entered the war with equipment that was as good as, and often markedly superior to, that of the Allies. However, shortages became increasingly acute as the war progressed, and the army came to rely heavily on captured materiel and equipment, which was often of poor quality and mismatched with German ammunition and other equipment. Mobile warfare (the BLITZKRIEG) was an essential feature of German war-fighting doctrine, but, even from the beginning, the army faced a chronic shortage of transport vehicles and relied extensively on horses to draw artillery and supply wagons. This increasingly impaired mobility.

For all its attention to efficient command structures internally, the army was hobbled by strained and awkward relations with the Luftwaffe and the Waffen-SS. At their best, the army and the Luftwaffe cooperated closely in executing Blitzkrieg tactics, but when it came to defense, there was often conflict, since the Luftwaffe was responsible for antiaircraft artillery and even fielded its own (generally mediocre) ground troops. With the Waffen-SS, relations were even more difficult. In the early phases of the war, Waffen-SS units were poorly disciplined yet better equipped than the army. This generated resentments and jealousies. As the war progressed, the Waffen-SS gradually earned a reputation as elite troops, and cooperation with the army was often much better. However, the SS *Einsatzgruppen* (police battalions) always remained problematical. These were the SS troops assigned to carry out missions of terror against civilian populations, especially on the eastern front, and including the execution of the infamous COMMISSAR ORDER and some of the atrocities associated with the FINAL SOLUTION and THE HOLOCAUST. Many in the regular army were appalled by these activities, though few made complaints about them. Of greater concern was the army's lack of authority and control over the SS *Einsatzgruppen.*

Despite grave problems—the inept military leadership of Hitler, shortages of supply, friction with other services—the German Army was a fiercely effective force, and this was true even very late in the war, as the BATTLE OF THE ARDENNES (BATTLE OF THE BULGE) and the BATTLE OF BERLIN attest. Casualties were staggering. Between September 1, 1939, and January 1945, 1,622,561 German Army personnel had been killed in action (another 160,237 died of other causes), 4,145,863 had been wounded, and 1,646,316 were missing.

Further reading: Buchner, Alex. *The German Infantry Handbook.* Atglen, Pa.: Schiffer, 1991; Davies, W. J. K. *German Army Handbook.* New York: Arco, 1984; Mitcham, Samuel W. *Hitler's Legions: The German Army Order Battle, World War II.* Chelsea, Mich.: Scarborough House, 1985; Pimlot, John. *Wehrmacht: The Illustrated History of the German Army in World War II.* Osceola, Wis.: Motorbooks International, 1997; Thomas, Nigel. *German Army 1939–1945: Blitzkrieg.* London: Osprey, 1998; Thomas, Nigel. *German Army 1939–45: Eastern Front 1943–1945.* London: Osprey, 1999; Thomas, Nigel. *The German Army in World War II.* London: Osprey, 2002; Williamson, Gordon. *German Army Elite Units 1939–45.* London: Osprey, 2002.

Germany, navy of

The German Navy, or Kriegsmarine, was a highly modern force in World War II, having been built up pursuant to the provisions of the Anglo-German Naval Treaty of 1935, which generally abrogated the naval restrictions that had been imposed by the TREATY OF VERSAILLES. The 1935 treaty allowed Germany a surface fleet 35 percent the size of the British surface fleet and 45 percent that of the British submarine fleet. Moreover, the treaty gave Germany the option of reducing surface tonnage to the point at which one-to-one parity was permitted between the British and German submarine forces. ADOLF HITLER's assumption at the time

of the treaty was that he would go to war with the Soviet Union and France, not Great Britain. Therefore, he embarked on a program of surface ship construction. By 1938, however, war with Great Britain seemed increasingly likely, and Hitler was well aware that the British surface fleet greatly outnumbered that of Germany. Grand Admiral ERICH RAEDER advocated the building of more surface ships, and while he had to admit that the German surface navy would never equal that of the British, he also believed that the bulk of the British fleet would have to be deployed in foreign waters, leaving only the Home Fleet for the Kriegsmarine to contend with, a plausible mission. Sharply differing from Raeder was Admiral KARL DÖNITZ, commander in chief of the Kriegsmarine's U-boat force. His advice was to develop the U-boat fleet as a weapon to be used against British shipping, thereby starving the island nation into submission. This, in fact, was destined to become the principal German naval strategy, but at the beginning of 1939, Raeder's point of view prevailed, largely because he had successfully argued that antisubmarine warfare had become so sophisticated that U-boats would not prove nearly as effective as they had in World War I.

Raeder's Plan Z, approved by Hitler in January 1939, called for the construction of a very large surface fleet, to be completed by 1944. At the outbreak of war, however, on September 1, 1939, the Kriegsmarine was far outnumbered by the British and the French fleets. It consisted of two battleships, three pocket battleships, one heavy cruiser, six light cruisers, 21 destroyers, 12 torpedo boats, and 57 U-boats. In contrast to the navies of the other World War II powers, the Kriegsmarine did not have its own air arm, in deference to HERMANN GÖRING's edict that all aircraft were to be controlled by the Luftwaffe. While it is true that a single aircraft carrier, the *Zeppelin,* was laid down, it was never completed, and it is likely that any aircraft launched from it would have been operated by the Luftwaffe.

One indisputable advantage the Kriegsmarine enjoyed was a cadre of excellent commanders, from the top down, and the luxury of relative freedom from the meddling of Hitler, who saw himself as a land-based warrior and tended to leave naval matters to the experts. Naval high command was the Oberkommando der Marine (OKM) headquartered in Berlin. Reporting to the OKM were Naval Group Command East, Naval Group Command West, Naval Station North Sea, and Naval Station Baltic. Two additional naval stations controlled coastal defense and training. The fleet was distributed as required among these commands. It was divided into the High Seas Fleet, the Security Forces, and the U-boat Fleet. The High Seas Fleet encompassed all major surface ships. The Security Forces controlled coastal defense, convoy escorts, antisubmarine forces, and minesweeping forces. The U-boat Fleet experienced explosive growth during the war and became the dominant arm of the Kriegsmarine.

On December 31, 1942, a British ARCTIC CONVOY OPERATIONS convoy reached the Soviet Union. Enraged that the Kriegsmarine had allowed this to happen, Hitler forced the resignation of Grand Admiral Raeder, who was immediately replaced as navy commander in chief by Admiral Dönitz. Once in charge, Dönitz began implementing his U-boat strategy, and by early 1944, the U-boat fleet reached peak strength at 445 vessels. (More than 1,100 U-boats were commissioned during the war, but, as effective as they were in sinking Allied tonnage, they experienced a terrible rate of attrition.) After the successful conclusion of the BATTLE OF FRANCE, Dönitz moved U-boat headquarters to Paris and then to Lorient, on the French Atlantic coast, so that he could closely supervise U-boat bases. By the middle of the war, the German Navy was effectively a submarine force, its capital surface ships confined to home ports for fear of being lost to overwhelming Allied sea power.

For many months of the war, Dönitz's vision for the U-boat was amply vindicated, as the submarines took a terrible toll on Allied shipping. However, Dönitz had not—and could not have—envisioned the will and productivity of the United States, which rapidly turned out vast numbers of LIBERTY SHIPS faster than the U-boats could sink them. Even worse, improvements in the CONVOY SYSTEM and the development of SONAR and other increasingly sophisticated tools of antisubmarine warfare inexorably turned the tide against the U-boats. Their losses, always high, became overwhelming.

Further reading: Jackson, Robert. *Kriegsmarine: The Illustrated History of the German Navy in World War II.* Osceola, Wis.: MBI Publishing, 2001; Showell, J. P. *German Navy in World War Two: An Illustrated Guide to the Kriegsmarine, 1920–1945.* Annapolis, Md.: Naval Institute Press, 1979; Showell, J. P. *The German Navy in World War Two: A reference Guide to the Kriegsmarine, 1935–1945.* London: Arms & Armour Press, 1979; Stern, Robert C. *Kriegsmarine: A Pictorial History of the German Navy, 1935–1945.* Carrollton, Tex.: Squadron/Signal Publications, 1979; Tarrant, V. E. *The Last Year of the Kriegsmarine: May 1944–May 1945.* Annapolis, Md.: Naval Institute Press, 1994.

Gestapo

An acronym for Geheime Staatspolizei ("Secret State Police"), *Gestapo* was the name of the political police of Nazi Germany. This agency operated within the country to root out and eliminate opposition to the government and the Nazi Party, and, outside the country, in the occupied territories, Gestapo agents were responsible for suppressing RESISTANCE AND UNDERGROUND MOVEMENTS and for directing and to a large extent executing the mass arrest of Jews pursuant to the FINAL SOLUTION.

The Gestapo had its origin on April 26, 1933, when HERMANN GÖRING, at the time minister of the interior for Prussia, assumed personal control of the political and espionage units of the regular Prussian police, built them up with a large cadre of Nazis, then consolidated and reorganized the units as the Gestapo. At about the same time, HEINRICH HIMMLER, chief of the SCHUTZSTAFFEL (SS), and his principal lieutenant, REINHARD HEYDRICH, did the same with the Bavarian police and then with the police forces of the other German *Länder* ("states"). In April 1934, ADOLF HITLER gave Himmler command over Göring's Gestapo, and, two years later, on June 17, 1936, Himmler was appointed *Reichsführer* in charge of the state police. Thus, Himmler came to control both the SS and the Gestapo. He assigned command of the Gestapo to Gruppenführer Heinrich Müller and joined the Gestapo to the Kriminalpolizei ("Criminal Police") within a newly created organization, the Sicherheitspolizei (Sipo, or "Security Police"). In 1939, the SS was extensively reorganized, and Sipo was combined with the Sicherheitsdienst (SD) ("Security Service"), the SS intelligence department, to create the Reichssicherheitshauptamt ("Reich Security Central Office") commanded by Heydrich. The consolidation of these various forces did not submerge the Gestapo, which retained a high profile throughout the war years, but it did create confusion, competition, and duplication of effort among the agencies. Doubtless, this was less a bureaucratic misstep than a deliberate attempt to add a layer of security by causing one agency continually to look over the shoulder of another.

The Gestapo had virtually limitless power, including the authority of preventative arrest. Its actions were outside the conventional judicial system and could not be appealed through the courts or, indeed, to any authority. Gestapo agents swept up political dissidents, social undesirables, uncooperative clergy, "dangerous" intellectuals, homosexuals, and, of course, Jews. These individuals were customarily "deported" to concentration and extermination camps. Working in conjunction with the SS, the Gestapo was also responsible for the suppression of resistance and partisan activities in the occupied territories. Gestapo agents were charged with executing reprisal actions against civilians in the occupied territories as a means of suppressing the resistance. Gestapo agents were also attached to the SS Einsatzgruppen that followed closely behind the regular German Army in Poland and Russia, their mission to round up and summarily murder Jews as well as others deemed undesirable. Adolf Eichmann was a Gestapo officer, who headed Bureau IV B4, which was responsible for the mass deportation of Jews from occupied countries to the death camps of Poland.

Further reading: Butler, Rupert. *The Gestapo: A History of Hitler's Secret Police 1933–45.* Havertown, Pa.:

Casemate Publishers & Book Distributors, 2004; Butler, Rupert. *An Illustrated History of the Gestapo.* Osceola, Wis.: Motorbooks International, 1993; Johnson, Eric A. *Nazi Terror: The Gestapo, Jews, and Ordinary Germans.* New York: Basic Books, 2000.

Gibraltar

A rocky projection from the coast of southern Spain, Gibraltar became a British colony in 1704 and, from the end of the Battle of France to 1943, was the only toehold left to the Allies on the European continent. Some 25 miles of tunnels and subterranean chambers were excavated into the rock, which furnished warehouse space, munitions storage, living quarters, and military headquarters for the Allies. It was from such a bunkerlike headquarters on Gibraltar that General Dwight David Eisenhower directed Operation Torch, the Allied landings at the commencement of the North African Campaigns. Some 600 aircraft operated from an airstrip at Gibraltar to provide close air support for Operation Torch.

Gibraltar functioned as the base for the Royal Navy's small fleet designated Force H and for the British Naval Contraband Control Service, which boarded and searched neutral shipping. Gibraltar was also vital to the convoy system as the point at which many convoys assembled and started their journeys. During the Siege of Malta, that island was sustained by supplies convoyed from Gibraltar. Gibraltar also functioned as a way station for Allied airmen who had been shot down and were either evading capture or had escaped from captivity.

Gibraltar was variously targeted by the Italians and the Vichy French. However, Spain's dictator, Francisco Franco, blocked a German attempt to capture the base because he saw such an operation as a threat to Spanish neutrality. Not wishing to alienate a friendly fascist "neutral," Adolf Hitler reluctantly withdrew plans for attack.

Further reading: Bradford, Ernle. *Gibraltar: The History of a Fortress.* New York: Harcourt, 1972; Jackson, Sir William G. F. *The Rock of the Gibraltarians: A History of*

Gibraltar. Madison, N.J.: Fairleigh Dickinson University Press, 1988.

Gideon Force

Formed by then Lieutenant Colonel ORDE WINGATE in January 1941, the Gideon Force operated under the direction of the British Special Operations Executive (SOE) to help restore emperor HAILE SELASSIE to the throne of Ethiopia, which was occupied by Italy. Comprised of 50 British officers and 20 British noncommissioned officers in charge of 800 members of the Sudan Frontier Battalion and 800 Ethiopian (Abyssinian) troops, the Gideon Force fought a daring guerrilla campaign and succeeded not only in establishing Haile Selassie in a base at Gojjam, Ethiopia, but also in escorting him to the very capital of the country, Addis Ababa, and returning him to power. This small guerrilla force was instrumental in forcing the Italians to lose their grip on Ethiopia.

Further reading: Bierman, John, and Colin Smith. *Fire in the Night: Wingate of Burma, Ethiopia, and Zion.* New York: Random House, 1999; Mockler, Anthony. *Haile Salassie's War: The Ethiopian-Italian Campaign, 1935– 1940.* New York: Random House, 1985.

gliders

In World War II, gliders, light, nonpowered aircraft, were used to transport AIRBORNE ASSAULT troops as well as limited supplies and equipment, including vehicles, tanks, and artillery. To reduce weight, gliders were constructed with wood or with fabric covering a wooden or tubular steel framework. They were designed to be towed by transport aircraft or, in some cases, by modified bombers, then released near their target area. Gliders could be towed singly or in pairs. They generally did not require improved runways for landing, but merely a flat, level landing area, and typically one much shorter than that required for powered aircraft. This flexibility, along with motorless silence, simplicity of construction, and low cost of production were great advantages of gliders for inserting troops and supplies behind enemy lines. Their disadvantages were, however, daunting. Unpowered flight time was limited, and gliders were far more subject to weather and wind hazards than were conventional aircraft. Gliders were fragile, and landings were often rough. Although nominally reusable, most glider flights in combat were one way because, typically, the craft was damaged on landing, especially on unimproved fields. Gliders were slow and incapable of evasive action; they were therefore vulnerable to ground fire, even from small arms.

The Soviet Union employed gliders in military operations during the 1930s, but only as a means of air-dropping supplies. Germany was the only Axis power to use them during World War II for airborne assault and troop insertion, and the aircraft was used with especially spectacular success in the assault on FORTRESS EBEN EMAEL during the invasion of Belgium on May 10, 1940. Axis gliders were also used in the Balkans during the INVASION OF GREECE and in the ACTION ON CRETE. The daring guerrilla tactician OTTO SKORZENY made gliders a part of his remarkable rescue of BENITO MUSSOLINI after the dictator's downfall.

The most important German glider was the DFS 230, the first "assault glider" used by any air force in the war. It was capable of transporting 10 troops with a total of about 606 pounds of equipment and could be towed by light aircraft at 130 mph. Weighing just 1,896 pounds empty, it had a wingspan of 68 feet, 5.7 inches and a length of 36 feet, 10.5 inches. Instead of wheeled landing gear, the DFS 230 featured a skid mounted on spring shock absorbers, which enabled it to land without even a rudimentary runway.

The small size of the DFS 230 was both an advantage and a liability. It could insert small numbers of troops almost anywhere and with great stealth, but its carrying capacity was very limited. The Germans, therefore, designed the Messerschmidt Me-323 Giant, a 24-ton unpowered aircraft that could carry 200 troops fully equipped. It required three aircraft for towing, although the Germans also experimented with a specially designed towing aircraft, the Heinkel He 111Z, which consisted of two He 111H medium bombers welded together at the wing, so that they combined the power of four engines. A pilot and flight crew were required in each fuselage. Two hundred of the Me-323 Giants were built but were never satisfactorily deployed.

On the Allied side, both the British and the Americans employed gliders for assault. They were used in OPERATION HUSKY and the subsequent SICILY CAMPAIGN as well as in the NORMANDY LANDINGS (D-DAY). Some 2,500 gliders were employed in the ill-fated OPERATION MARKET GARDEN (BATTLE OF ARNHEM). In the Pacific theater, the CHINDITS used them to land behind Japanese lines in the BURMA CAMPAIGN.

The most important British glider was the Airspeed Horsa, a large aircraft capable of transporting 25 troops or about 7,500 pounds of cargo. Constructed of wood, the aircraft was designed to be built, at least in part, by the British furniture industry, and a total of 3,633 were turned out. Weighting 7,500 pounds empty and with a wingspan of 88 feet and length of 67 feet, the big Horsa had a maximum towed speed of barely 100 miles per hour. The wheeled landing gear could be jettisoned in flight if rough landing conditions required a belly skid. The Horsas were extensively used in the Normandy landings and other operations.

The only U.S. glider deployed in combat during World War II was the Waco CG-4A Hadrian, which was produced in a spectacular quantity of 12,393. With a wingspan of 83 feet 8 inches and a fuselage length of 48 feet 3.75 inches, the Hadrian could carry 15 soldiers or such equipment as a Jeep or a 75-mm field piece plus crew. The Hadrian, which weighed just 3,790 pounds empty and could carry more than 5,000 pounds, was typically towed by C-47 Skytrain transports. It was used extensively in the Normandy landings and in later European operations and was being prepared for use in the invasion of Japan, an operation made unnecessary by that country's surrender in August 1945.

Further reading: Esvelin, Philippe. *D-day Gliders.* Bayeux, France: Editions Heimdal, 2001; Lowden, John L. *Silent Wings at War: Combat Gliders in World War II.* Washington, D.C.: Smithsonian Institution Press, 2002;

Mrazek, James E. *The Fall of Eben Emael.* New York: Random House, 1998; Nowarra, Heinz J. *German Gliders in World War II.* Atglen, Pa.: Schiffer, 1999; Richlak, Jerry L. *Glide to Glory.* Cobham, U.K.: Cedar House, 2002.

Goebbels, Joseph (1897–1945) *Nazi minister of propaganda*

Joseph Goebbels was the mastermind who crafted the ongoing propaganda campaign that was indispensable in selling ADOLF HITLER, the NAZI PARTY (NSDAP), the Nazi regime, and Nazi war aims to the German people. He was born in the Rhenish town of Rheydt, the son of a factory clerk. Highly intelligent, Goebbels earned a doctorate in philology from Heidelberg University in 1922, having been exempted from World War I service because of a clubfoot. Goebbels had literary and journalistic aspirations, but, much as Hitler had been frustrated in his youthful aspiration to become an artist, Goebbels found no market for his works. After he befriended a group of early Nazis in 1924, Goebbels drifted into National Socialist politics,

Joseph Goebbels, Adolf Hitler's minister of propaganda *(Library of Congress)*

and when it was discovered that he was a talented public speaker, he was named gauleiter (district leader) of the Nazi Party in Elberfeld, where he was given the job of editing the biweekly *National Socialist* magazine.

The Nazi Party was, understandably, poorly supplied with intellectuals and writers of ability. Although the dark-featured, clubfooted Goebbels hardly fit the "Aryan" Nazi mold, he rose quickly within the party, and Hitler appointed him gauleiter of Berlin in 1926. This was an important assignment, since the party, having established itself in Bavaria, had no real presence in the capital. Goebbels rapidly built up the Nazi organization in Berlin while expanding his journalistic career on behalf of the party by editing a new magazine, *Der Angriff* ("the Assault"). In 1928, Hitler recognized his prodigious abilities as a communicator by appointing Goebbels propaganda director for the party. Goebbels set to work not merely to promote the Nazi political agenda, but to create around Hitler a powerful cult of personality, which imbued Hitler with the "Führer myth," transforming his image into that of a combination savior, messiah, and infallible leader. Goebbels's propaganda program went far beyond the printed page. He developed speeches and radio broadcasts, and he orchestrated and choreographed vast ritualistic party convocations, demonstrations, rallies, and celebrations. It was Goebbels who introduced the universal Nazi salute and salutation, *"Heil Hitler!"* No person other than Hitler himself was more responsible for the creation of the führer's public persona.

When Hitler rose to the office of chancellor in 1933, he created a Ministry for Public Enlightenment and Propaganda at the cabinet level, with Goebbels as its minister. Goebbels was also named president of the Reich Chamber of Culture, which gave him control not only of the print press and radio, but also the stage, cinema, literature, music, and the other fine arts. Goebbels also enlarged his brief to encompass education, especially at the high school level, which became an important institution for dissemination of propaganda. Goebbels was more than sufficiently intelligent to exercise his extraordinary authority sparingly, and, in fact, he regulated the various media and arts with a surprisingly liberal hand. He understood that he was, in effect, a salesman and that his wares consisted of Adolf Hitler and National Socialism, and he understood that nothing dulls the appeal of merchandise like enforced repetition. He therefore integrated propaganda into the stream of general culture and took care to avoid smothering the media and the arts. Moreover, he worked with creative writers, artists, and especially filmmakers to produce propaganda that was entertaining and even aesthetically appealing. He did not want to coerce, but to seduce.

Many within the party hierarchy were jealous of Goebbels's power, and by the late 1930s, his critics had made inroads into his domain that lessened his influence. Goebbels also allowed his personal life to compromise his political existence when a romantic affair with a Czech movie star became widely known and created a scandal in outwardly prudish Nazi society. He managed to salvage his career but was not highly influential in the lead up to World War II, a conflict he did not believe wise. Once the war began, however, he carved out a fresh niche for himself by developing propaganda directed toward Germany's enemies for the purpose of undermining their morale. He developed broadcasts to be beamed to Polish and French soldiers, and he planted rumors concerning FIFTH COLUMN (subversive) activities in the Allied nations. He also created for such generals as ERWIN ROMMEL myths of invincibility, much as he had done for Hitler during the dictator's rise. Among Goebbels's best-known creations were Axis Sally and Lord Haw Haw. Axis Sally was an American named Mildred Gillars who lived in Germany and whom Goebbels hired to broadcast propaganda to American troops. (After the war, Gillars was convicted of treason and sentenced to 12 years of imprisonment; she was paroled in 1951.) Lord Haw Haw was an American-born Englishman named William Joyce who joined the British Fascist Party in 1923 and, in 1933, the British Union of Fascists. In 1937, he founded the pro-Nazi British National Socialist League, then fled Britain in 1939 and went to work in Germany for an English-language radio station. As Lord Haw Haw (a name he appropriated from an earlier German propaganda broadcaster, usually identified as Norman Baillie-Stewart), Joyce broadcast propaganda intended to erode the morale of British as well as American troops. (Although Joyce was naturalized as a German citizen in 1940, a postwar court ruled that his allegiance was still to the Crown because he held a British passport. Found guilty of high treason, he was hanged in 1946.)

Goebbels's efforts at subverting Allied morale had little effect, and he did not again come into his own as a master propagandist until the tides of the war turned against Germany. As bad news came out of North Africa and the Soviet Union, Goebbels launched his most elaborate and far-reaching campaigns. He was not merely a censor or a liar, but, rather, a shaper of popular interpretation. He continually presented himself before the German public to present a vision of inevitable, destined victory in spite of defeats and setbacks. If his earlier merchandise had been Hitler and the Nazi Party, his new product was hope, which he built up by references to historical example on the one hand and the imminence of future salvation on the other: Goebbels repeatedly invoked the emergence of a new "wonder weapon," which would surely reverse the fortunes of war yet again. In contrast to other highly placed Nazis, who retreated from the public as defeat was piled upon defeat, Goebbels continually thrust himself into the forefront.

As the perimeter of Nazi conquest shrank in the final months of the war, Goebbels turned his attention to rallying the homefront for a final stand, advocating what he called total war. When the attempted assassination of Hitler failed on July 20, 1944, Goebbels took charge of the situation in Berlin and suppressed the incipient coup d'état there. This earned from Hitler a grandiose appointment as Reich Plenipotentiary for Total War, making Goebbels the third most powerful figure in the Third Reich, behind Hitler and Heinrich Himmler. Yet, by this time, it was an empty appointment. Goebbels remained by Hitler's side to the bitterest of bitter ends. He served as witness to the marriage of Hitler and Eva Braun in the Führerbunker on April 29, 1945. On the next day, before taking his life and that of his bride, Hitler named Goebbels chancellor of the reich. It was an office in which Goebbels served barely a day. On May 1, 1945, in the bunker beneath the streets of besieged Berlin, Goebbels and his wife administered poison to each of their six children then took their own lives.

Further reading: Goebbels, Josef. *The Goebbels Diaries, 1942–1943.* Westport, Conn.: Greenwood Publishing Group, 1970; Reuth, Ralf Georg. *Goebbels.* New York: Harvest/HBJ, 1994; Roberts, Jeremy. *Joseph Goebbels: Nazi Propaganda Minister.* New York: Rosen Publishing Group, 2001.

Gomułka, Władysław (1905–1982) *leader of Communist underground in Poland*

Władysław Gomułka was born near Krosno, Poland, to a Socialist oil field worker and his wife. Gomułka joined the Socialist youth movement, then, in 1926, became a member of the clandestine Communist Party of Poland. He worked as a professional union organizer and, during the 1930s, organized strikes throughout Poland. Arrested in 1932, he was sentenced to four years of imprisonment but was released in 1934 because of his poor health. He left Poland for Moscow, where, during 1934–35, he studied at the International Lenin School. Returning to Poland, he resumed revolutionary agitation in Silesia. Arrested again in 1936, he was sentenced to seven years of imprisonment, a fortuitous incarceration that allowed him to escape execution when Joseph Stalin dissolved the Communist Party of Poland in 1938. Gomułka was released, however, during the invasion of Poland in September 1939 and participated in the defense of Warsaw. He then moved to the Soviet-occupied portion of the country and found work in a paper mill in Lvov.

With the invasion of the Soviet Union and outbreak of war between Germany and the USSR in 1941, Gomułka resumed his Communist political activities, organizing the Communist underground in and around Krosno. He moved to Warsaw in July 1942 and became district secretary and a member of the Central Committee of the Polish Workers' Party. Working within this organization, he planned and executed attacks against the Nazi occupiers. When the party's secretary general was arrested in November 1943, Gomułka took over, wrote the party's ideological manifesto, and established the National Home Council, which became the basis for Communist domination of the provisional government after the liberation of Poland. In January 1945, Gomułka was appointed deputy premier of the provisional government, and in June, after the surrender of Germany, he was given responsibility for the administration of all Polish lands now recovered from Germany.

During the postwar years, Gomułka ruthlessly rose to dominate Polish politics, clashed bitterly with Stalin, was stripped of all power, and was imprisoned. In 1954, a year after Stalin's death, he was released, and began his rise anew. He served as first secretary of the Central Committee of the Polish Communist Party from 1956 until 1970, when he was forced into semiretirement.

Further reading: Korbonski, Stefan. *Fighting Warsaw: The Story of the Polish Underground State, 1939–1945.* New York: Hippocrene, 2004; Peszke, Michael Alfred. *The Polish Underground Army, the Western Allies, and the Failure of Strategic Unity.* Jefferson, N.C.: McFarland, 2004.

Gona, Battle of

Gona is located on the northern coast of Papua New Guinea, and, during the New Guinea Campaign, it was a Japanese stronghold. On November 16, 1942, a combined Australian and American force attacked Gona through a miserable tropical swamp in an effort to reduce this position. Gona was very well defended, the Japanese having established an 11-mile-long perimeter along the beachhead. Two regiments of the 32nd U.S. Division attacked the nearby village of Buna and Cape Endaiadere, while two brigades of the 7th Australian Division hit Gona village, then, in concert with

another regiment from the 32nd U.S. Division, attacked Sanananda Point.

The defense of Gona was far fiercer and the defenders far more numerous than had been anticipated. The battle was protracted over two months and exacted a significant cost. The Japanese made their last stand at Sanananda Point on January 21, 1943. When the Allies took that, the Battle of Gona was at last ended.

See also Buna, Battle of.

Further reading: Eichelberger, Robert L. *Dear Miss Em: General Eichelberger's War in the Pacific, 1942–1945.* Westport, Conn.: Greenwood Press, 1972; Eichelberger, Robert L. *Our Jungle Road to Tokyo.* New York: Viking Press, 1950; Mayo, Lida. *Bloody Buna: The Campaign That Halted the Japanese Invasion of Australia.* Newton Abbot, U.K.: David & Charles, 1975; Shortal, John F. *Forged by Fire: Robert L. Eichelberger and the Pacific War.* Columbia: University of South Carolina Press, 1987; Vader, John. *New Guinea: The Tide Is Stemmed.* New York: Ballantine, 1971.

Göring, Hermann (1893–1946) *Nazi Reichsmarschall (imperial marshal) and head of the Luftwaffe*

Hermann Göring was born at Rosenheim, Bavaria, the son of a former cavalry officer who had also served as German consul-general in Haiti. Göring enrolled at the Karlsruhe Military Academy in 1905 then attended the main cadet school at Lichterfelde beginning in 1909. After graduating in 1912, he was commissioned a lieutenant in the 112th Infantry but soon transferred to the air service. When World War I began in 1914, Göring served with distinction as an officer-observer then trained and qualified as an officer-pilot in October 1915. Shot down before the end of the year, he was badly wounded and did not return to duty until 1916, when he resumed flying and compiled a superb record. He was promoted to squadron commander in May 1917, and, after the death of Germany's most celebrated air ace, Baron Manfred von Richthofen, he succeeded to command of Richthofen's squadron in July 1918 and led it with distinction, emerging himself as an air ace.

Hermann Göring, Luftwaffe chief *(San Diego State University)*

Göring was demobilized after the November 11, 1918, armistice with the rank of captain and found immediate employment as a test pilot for the Dutch Fokker aircraft manufacturing firm and the Swedish Svenska Luftraflik. He left these positions in 1920 and, the following year, enrolled at Munich University. While in this city, Göring met ADOLF HITLER and joined the fledgling NAZI PARTY (NSDAP). He was appointed to command the party's paramilitary STURMABTEILUNG (SA) and was a participant in the abortive Munich (Beer Hall) Putsch of November 9, 1923. Göring was seriously wounded in the melée that resulted from the collapse of the Putsch. Although arrested, he escaped and found refuge in Austria. He did not return to Germany until 1927 and, the following year, won election to the Reichstag as a Nazi.

In 1932, with the Nazi Party dominant on the German political scene, Göring became Reichstag president. After Hitler was made chancellor of Germany in 1933, he appointed Göring Reichsminister, minister of the interior, Prussian prime minister, and air commissioner. Thus, Göring became the second most powerful man in German government. Göring quickly created a secret police force, the GESTAPO, and ordered construction of the first concentration camps,

intended to hold political dissidents and other political and social undesirables. The camps were turned over to HEINRICH HIMMLER in April 1934, and, later that year, Göring was appointed master of the Reich Hunt and Forest Office. Remarkably, he proved to be an enlightened environmentalist, who created wildlife preserves and introduced game laws and forest-management reforms that are still in use in Germany today.

Göring's interest in natural resources did not interfere with the continuation of his ruthless program of eliminating enemies and dissidents. At Hitler's behest, he played a major role in the violent purge of the SA during the "Night of the Long Knives" (June 30, 1934). Nor did he neglect the renewal of Germany as a military power. As Reichsminister for Air and commander of the Luftwaffe, Göring directed, in contravention of the terms of the TREATY OF VERSAILLES, the covert creation and organization of what would become, in many respects, the world's most advanced and powerful air force. In 1936, he also assumed the office of director of the four-year plan, with absolute authority in matters of the German economy. He undertook the reorganization of state-owned industries under the umbrella of the Hermann Göring Works during 1937–41. In 1939, Hitler formalized Göring's status as the second most powerful man in the Third Reich by designating him his successor and conferring on him the title of Reichsmarschall.

The INVASION OF POLAND elevated Göring to even greater stature, as his Luftwaffe proved itself to be a critically effective arm of BLITZKRIEG. But Göring's reign as Hitler's favorite did not last long. Despite Germany's triumph in the BATTLE OF FRANCE (May–June 1940), the Luftwaffe was unable to interdict the DUNKIRK EVACUATION and prevent the salvation of Anglo-French forces (May 28–June 4, 1940). The fact is that Hitler's order halting the advance of HEINZ GUDERIAN's panzers was primarily responsible for the escape of the cornered British and French, but it is also true that if the air force had destroyed the Allied armies, the way would have been clear for OPERATION SEALION, the never-realized invasion of Britain. The next failure was the BATTLE OF BRITAIN (August 1940–May 1941). Göring's original plan was to attack Royal Air Force (RAF) bases, destroying aircraft on the ground and thereby neutralizing the RAF as a fighting force. Instead, he acquiesced in Hitler's decision to bomb major cities. This strategy not only failed to break the British will to fight, it allowed the RAF an opportunity to mount a formidable defense against the Luftwaffe, which the RAF ultimately forced from British skies. This ended the threat of a German invasion, kept Britain in the war, and, in the long run, doomed Germany to defeat.

Toward the end of 1942, Göring made another serious strategic blunder. As the Sixth German Army was reeling under the twin forces of the Russian winter and the relentless hammering of the Red Army at Stalingrad, Göring vowed to resupply the troops by air. Lacking sufficient numbers of transports and long-range escorts, however, the Luftwaffe failed miserably during November–December 1942, and the decimated Sixth German Army surrendered to the Soviets. With that, the war on the Soviet front, which had begun in unalloyed triumph, turned irreversibly against Germany.

The failure on the eastern front destroyed Hitler's confidence in Göring, who then descended into outright corruption, embezzling government funds and looting the art treasures of conquered nations. He erected for himself a kind of palace, which he decorated with the spoils of war. As the military fortunes of Germany continued to disintegrate, Göring lived his life in increasing dissipation and became a morphine addict. (He had been introduced to the drug when it was used to treat the pain of the injuries suffered in the 1923 Putsch.) As Göring lost the faith of Hitler, so he lost that of the German people. Early in the war, Göring had joked that he would change his name to Meier (a common German name) if a single bomb ever fell on Germany. By 1944, with bombs raining upon German cities day and night, the people regularly referred to him by that most derisive epithet.

For all practical purposes, Göring's power had come to an end. This fact was driven home to him in April 1945, when he volunteered to succeed Hitler, who was holed up in the *Führerbunker* beneath the streets of Berlin. In response to the offer, Hitler summarily stripped Göring of all his offices, then charged him with high treason. On Hitler's orders, Göring was placed under arrest and confined at Berchtesgaden, Hitler's mountain retreat, on April 23. When Berchtesgaden was overrun by American troops, Göring surrendered to them. He was charged with war crimes at the Nuremberg Tribunal. Found guilty, he was sentenced on October 1, 1946, to be hanged. Before the sentence could be carried out, however, he committed suicide by swallowing a capsule of cyanide he had secreted in his rectum.

Further reading: Buckley, William F., Jr. *Nuremberg: The Reckoning.* New York: Harcourt Brace, 2003; Butler, Ewan. *Life and Death of Hermann Goering.* Cincinnati, Oh.: F & W Publications, 1990; Mosley, Leonard. *Reich Marshal: A Biography of Hermann Goering.* New York: Doubleday, 1974; Overy, Richard. *Goering.* New York: Barnes & Noble Books, 2003; Ramen, Fred. *Hermann Goering: Hitler's Second in Command.* New York: Rosen Publishing Group, 2001.

Gothic Line

The Gothic Line was the name the Germans originally conferred on their strong series of defenses in the Apennines of Italy. Running from north of Lucca on the west coast of the Italian peninsula to south of Pesaro on the east coast, the Gothic Line was a formidable objective during the ITALIAN CAMPAIGN. It was not breached until September 1944.

In June 1944, ADOLF HITLER renamed the Gothic Line the Green Line, and the Allies generally referred to it as the Pisa-Rimini Line. However, these defenses continue to be known to history as the Gothic Line.

Further reading: Botjer, George F. *Sideshow War: The Italian Campaign, 1943–1945.* College Station: Texas A&M University Press, 1996; Kaufmann, J. E. *Fortress Third Reich: German Fortifications and Defense Systems in World War II.* New York: Da Capo Press, 2003.

Great Britain

As World War II approached, Britain was at the center of an empire that, although it was about to enter its twilight, covered a quarter of the globe. At the outbreak of the war, the United Kingdom, encompassing Great Britain and Northern Ireland (the six northeastern Irish counties that remained part of the United Kingdom after the creation of the Irish Free State in 1922), had a population of only 47,700,000, but the territory and peoples tied to Britain were vast. These included the dominions of Canada, Australia, New Zealand, and South Africa, since 1931 having the status in international law of independent nations that shared the same monarch with Britain (in the World War II era, King George VI). Also in Africa, Southern Rhodesia functioned as a self-governing British colony. India had been agitating for full independence since early in the century but was, at the outbreak of war and throughout the war, governed by a viceroy who worked closely with a secretary of state for India within the British cabinet. The viceroy directly governed about two-thirds of the Indian subcontinent, the rest being governed by Indian princes who were, in effect, political clients of the viceroy and of Britain. Beyond the dominions and India were the far-flung colonies, which were variously governed, some closely by the Crown, others more directly by their own legislatures. Added to these constituents of the British Empire, all of long standing, were the recent additions of the League of Nations mandates. These were territories entrusted to the governance of Britain under the Treaty of Versailles following World War I. They had formerly been parts of the German or Turkish Empires. In addition to British mandates, various Pacific territories were mandated to Australia and New Zealand, and Southwest Africa (formerly a German colony) was mandated to South Africa. Finally came the British protectorates, the most important of which at the outbreak of World War II was Egypt. Legally and nominally independent, Egypt was, in fact, a British client state, which meant that Britain had the right to garrison the country. With Egypt, Britain shared a protectorate over Sudan.

The British took comfort in their empire, believing that it gave them control over a vast portion of the world. In fact, it is unlikely that the nation would have prevailed in the conflict without its empire, whose troops and resources were invaluable in World War II. By the same token, the vastness of the British realm and of British interests was also a heavy burden of responsibility in the war. Nor did the Crown take into account the precarious political status of much of the empire. The king's declaration of war on September 3, 1939, was simply assumed to bind India and the colonies. In fact, while many Indian troops participated in the war, the high-handed assumption that India was bound by Britain's declaration brought the issue of Indian independence to a head, and, in 1947, shortly after the war ended, India became independent. As for the dominions, Canada, Australia, New Zealand, and South Africa, King George VI's declaration did not legally bind them, but their participation was taken for granted. All declared war within days after the British declaration. Ireland remained neutral.

Like its closest ally, France, Great Britain between the wars was suffused with a kind of national malaise compounded of economic depression and an urge to avoid a new war at all costs. Unlike France, it was the British government that took what it perceived as positive steps to avoid such a war. This amounted to sometimes unilateral disarmament as well as attempts to establish a parity of arms among nations. Under Prime Minster Stanley Baldwin, British pacifism produced a state of collective denial, as the government closed its eyes to German and Italian aggression, the rise of Nazism, and the build-up of German arms and the military. Under Baldwin's successor, Neville Chamberlain, Great Britain began to prepare for war by increasing its domestic arms production, but Chamberlain simultaneously adopted an active Appeasement Policy, hoping to satisfy Adolf Hitler's aggressive expansionism by not contesting his claim to the Czech Sudentenland. The policy, of course, turned out to be disastrous, effectively encouraging Hitler's greater and wider aggression. However, it was not as craven as it appeared on the surface to be. Although a military build-up had begun in Britain, Chamberlain recognized that the nation was woefully unprepared for war, and he hoped that appeasement would buy time to build up a credible defense against the two nations generally believed to offer more menace than Germany: Italy and Japan. In the meantime, Hitler's aggression notwithstanding, Chamberlain regarded military action against Germany as preventive war, and he refused to engage in it.

The opposition, whose most eloquent and committed spokesman was WINSTON CHURCHILL, saw appeasement for the disaster that it was and urged, first, preparedness and, later, military action. In the end, it was the German INVASION OF POLAND on September 1, 1939, that brought a British declaration of war against Germany. By that time, Germany was fully mobilized, and both Britain and France were in far weaker positions than they had been at the time of the German ANSCHLUSS of Austria and the annexation of the Sudetenland. Moreover, as in France, widespread pacifism continued to pervade the civilian population of Britain, and the government was not unanimous on the necessity of war, with a sizable faction advocating a settlement with Hitler.

While war raged on the eastern front, the period from September 1939 to April 1940 was static in the west and so quiet that the British dubbed it the PHONY WAR. Britain had hardly roused itself from the severe unemployment of the Great Depression, yet enlistment rates remained low and pacifism high. It was not until the failure of the NORWEGIAN CAMPAIGN that the war began to hit home. That military disaster resulted in the removal of Chamberlain and the elevation of Churchill as prime minister. On the very day that Chamberlain resigned, May 10, 1940, BELGIUM and the NETHERLANDS were invaded, and the BATTLE OF FRANCE commenced. This quickly brought an end to the Phony War, and Churchill began to raise the collective war will of the nation with speeches and broadcasts of unparalleled eloquence and vigor. Britain suffered one major defeat after another and was under imminent peril of invasion, saved only by the slim Royal Air Force (RAF) victory in the BATTLE OF BRITAIN. U.S. entry into the war following the BATTLE OF PEARL HARBOR on December 7, 1941, brought new hope, as did BERNARD LAW MONTGOMERY's success against ERWIN ROMMEL in the NORTH AFRICAN CAMPAIGNS. Despite disastrous defeats at the hands of the Japanese, the defeatism of the Phony War and the anxiety that had followed the fall of France were replaced by a wildly overoptimistic confidence in an early victory, which soon gave way to a grim but resolute determination to prevail, no matter how long it took.

Britons endured serious food shortages and THE BLITZ, which killed some 43,000 civilians and injured another 139,000. Beginning in January 1942, they also endured the presence of thousands of American GIs. While the Anglo-American alliance was extremely effective, it was not always smooth, and despite a very real mutual affection between the American and British peoples, there was also significant friction between the American troops and the British population. Britishers said that there were just three things wrong with Americans: they were "overpaid, oversexed, and over here."

Whereas France had failed miserably to mobilize its people for war, Great Britain mobilized a greater percentage of its citizens than any other nation in World War II. At the peak of military service, 22 percent of the population were in the armed forces and another 33 percent were directly involved in civilian war work. In addition, many thousands more worked as CIVIL DEFENSE volunteers. ERNEST BEVIN, head of the Ministry of Labor, exercised central control over civilian manpower resources, and citizens were required to register for mandatory assignment in the workforce. Men over 41 were liable for such service (younger men were liable for military service), as were women between the ages of 18 and 60. Unemployment vanished, and, as in the United States, women assumed a major role in war production, working in virtually every industry except coal mining. A Women's Land Army (WLA) was created, ultimately 80,000 strong, to organize women for agricultural work.

Although, early in the conflict, war production was criticized as inefficient, it soon rose to a very impressive height. For instance, whereas British firms had turned out 3,000 military aircraft in 1938, they produced 15,000 in 1940, 24,000 in 1942, and 26,500 in 1944. Some 52 major combat vessels were launched in 1940, 114 in 1942, and 76 in 1944. While high employment brought prosperity, strict rationing severely limited what one could purchase, but many people made up for personal food shortages by planting vegetable gardens in whatever spaces they could find.

As much as any other factor, the failure of French morale had brought about the collapse of that country before the German onslaught. In Great Britain, the onset of war and the Phony War were likewise characterized by problems of public morale, but the ascension of Churchill and the imminence of invasion rapidly coalesced the public will. If Hitler had hoped to break the British war will by bombing London and other cities, he badly misread the British public. If anything, the Blitz served to unite Britons all the more and strengthen their resolve to see the war through to total victory.

Further reading: Brown, Mike. *The Wartime House: Home Life in Wartime Britain, 1939–1945.* London: Sutton, 2001; Chamberlin, E. R. *Life in Wartime Britain.* London: Chrysalis Books, 1985; Freeman, Roger A. *Britain: The First Colour Photographs: Images of Wartime Britain.* London: Blandford Press, 1995; Millgate, Helen D. *Got Any Gum Chum?: GIs in Wartime Britain, 1942–1945.* London: Sutton, 2002; Paynter, Barbara. *The Grass Widow and Her Cow: An Enchanting Account of Country Life in Wartime Britain.* London: Robson Books, 1998; Tames, Richard. *Life in Wartime Britain.* London: B. T. Batsford, 1993; Webley, Nicholas. *A Taste of Wartime Britain.* London: Thorogood, 2003.

Great Britain, air force of

The Royal Air Force (RAF) came into being in 1918 and was an independent force on an equal footing with the Royal Navy and the army. Its civilian head was the secretary of state for air, who presided over the Air Council. The top uniformed officer was the chief of the air staff. Until May 1940, there was also, on the Air Council, an air member for development and production, but this position was obvi-

ated by the creation of a separate Ministry of Air Production. In 1941, this ministry was reintegrated into the Air Council and was headed by the controller of research and development.

Operationally, the wartime RAF was divided into Bomber Command, Fighter Command, Coastal Command, Reserve Command, and Training Command. Training Command subsequently absorbed Reserve Command but was itself divided into Flying Training Command and Technical Training Command. Before the war ended, more commands were added: Army Co-Operation Command, Balloon Command, Maintenance Command, and Ferry Command (responsible for delivering aircraft from factories to combat units). In practice, Coastal Command was under the control of the Admiralty, and Fighter Command assumed control of all homeland air defense, including antiaircraft artillery. Each RAF command was organized into groups, which were in turn divided into squadrons. Fighter groups also featured a "fighter wing," which was intermediated between the group and squadron level.

The RAF was supplemented by the Royal Auxiliary Air Force and the Royal Air Force Volunteer Reserve. Also, the air forces of the dominions, Australia, New Zealand, Canada, and South Africa, were incorporated into the RAF, as were elements of the air forces of nations that had been invaded

A Spitfire on the assembly line *(National Archives and Records Administration)*

and occupied by the Germans: Czechoslovakia, Belgium, Netherlands, France, Norway, and Poland. Although these elements were absorbed into the RAF, they were often permitted to retain their unique identity by forming into national legions or squadrons. Women also played a role in the RAF through the Women's Auxiliary Air Force (WAAF) and Princess Mary's RAF Nursing Service. The RAF drew many of its ground personnel, especially RADAR operators, plotters, and radio communications monitors, from the WAAF.

The British army, navy, and air force all drew on conscription for personnel. However, all RAF aircrews were volunteers, many of them trained through the British Empire Air Training Scheme, in which the dominions participated extensively. Indeed, the time-consuming training of aircrews, especially pilots, was the chief factor limiting the effectiveness of the RAF—a far more limiting factor than aircraft production.

The RAF numbered 193,000 men at the outbreak of war in September 1939 and peaked at 992,000 in September 1944. The WAAF had 17,400 women in September 1940 and peaked at 180,300 in September 1943. RAF losses included 69,606 killed, 6,736 missing, 22,839 wounded, and 13,115 taken as prisoners of war.

See also AIRCRAFT, BRITISH.

Further reading: Armitage, Sir Michael. *The Royal Air Force.* London: Weidenfeld & Nicholson, 1990; Armitage, Sir Michael. *The Royal Air Force: An Illustrated History.* London: Orion, 1993; Cormack, Andrew. *The Royal Air Force, 1939–45.* London: Osprey, 1990; Fitzsimons, B. *RAF: A History of the Royal Air Force.* London: Book Sales, 1983; Freeman, Roger A. *The Royal Air Force of World War Two in Colour.* London: Arms & Armour, 1993; Price, Alfred. *Britain's Air Defences 1935–45.* London: Osprey, 2004; Terraine, John. *A Time for Courage: The Royal Air Force in the European War, 1939–1945.* New York and London: Macmillan, 1985.

Great Britain, army of

The British army was controlled by the secretary of state for war, presiding over the Army Council.

Its highest uniformed officer, who sat on the Army Council, was the chief of the Imperial General Staff. The other uniformed council members included the adjutant-general (with responsibility for personnel matters), the quartermaster general (logistical head), the vice chief of the Imperial General Staff (who was responsible for operations, plans, intelligence, and training), the deputy chief of the Imperial General Staff (responsible for organizing for war), and the master general of ordnance.

Operationally, the army was divided into the Regular Army and the Territorial Army. The Territorial Army, primarily a conscript force, was originally conceived as a homeland force but in time of war was mobilized to fight alongside the much smaller Regular Army, originally a volunteer professional force. Like the other services, the army received the bulk of its personnel through conscription. At the outbreak of the war in September 1939, the total strength of the army was 897,000. It peaked in June 1945 at 2,920,000. The basic organizing element in the army was the regiment, many of which were organizations dating to the 17th century, and they typically reflected regional organization. The British army encouraged soldiers to identify closely with their regiments in order to acquire and maintain esprit de corps.

Functionally, the army was divided into teeth arms, supporting arms, and service arms. Teeth arms were combat units and included the Royal Armoured Corps (mechanized units largely formed from the traditional cavalry), the Royal Tank Corps, and the infantry. A Reconnaissance Corps was raised in June 1940 and was integrated into the Royal Armoured Corps in January 1944.

There were three supporting arms: The Royal Artillery manned all the army's artillery, including antiaircraft and coastal artillery. A special unit of this arm, the Royal Maritime Artillery, provided gun crews for merchant vessels. The Royal Engineers were historically referred to as sappers. They were responsible for mine laying and clearance, demolition, and building of all kinds, including bridges, camps, airstrips, and so on. Conduct of the military postal system also fell to the engineers.

The Royal Corps of Signals took charge of communications of all kinds.

The principal service arms included the Royal Army Service Corps, the Royal Army Ordnance Corps, and the Royal Army Medical Corps. The Royal Army Service Corps conveyed supplies to troops in the field, from food to ammunition. The Royal Army Ordnance Corps took charge of stores, from clothing to weapons. The Ordnance Corps also had charge of repair and maintenance of weapons and weapons systems until 1942, when this function was taken over by the newly created Royal Electrical and Mechanical Engineers. The Royal Medical Corps was, of course, responsible for all medical functions. Additionally, the service arm included the Royal Army Chaplains Department, the Corps of Military Police, the Royal Army Pay Corps, and so on.

Women played an important role in the army through the Auxiliary Territorial Service (ATS), which was formed in 1939. In addition to clerical and communications duties, ATS women also managed many antiaircraft installations. At its peak in 1943, the ATS numbered 212,500 women. In addition to the ATS, the army also relied heavily on Queen Alexandra's Imperial Nursing Service and the Territorial Army Nursing Service.

At its peak, the army had 11 armored divisions, 34 infantry divisions, and two airborne divisions. During the war, 144,079 lost their lives, 33,771 went missing, 239,575 were wounded, and 152,076 were made prisoners of war.

Further reading: Bevis, Mark. *British and Commonwealth Armies 1944–45.* Solihull, U.K.: Helion, 2004; Brayley, Martin J. *The British Army 1939–45: The Far East.* London: Osprey, 2002; Brayley, Martin J. *British Army 1939–45: Northwest Europe.* London: Osprey, 2001; Davis, Brian L. *The British Army in WW II: A Handbook on the Organization, Armament, Equipment, Ranks, Uniforms, Etc. 1942.* London: Greenhill, 1990; French, David. *Raising Churchill's Army: The British Army and the War Against Germany 1919–1945.* Oxford and New York: Oxford University Press, 2001; Jeffreys, Alan. *British Army in World War II: The Far East 1941–45.* London: Osprey, 2005; Jeffreys, Alan, Kevin Lyles, and Jeff Vanelle. *British Infantryman in the Far East, 1941–45.* London: Osprey, 2003; Place, Tim Harrison. *Military Training in the British Army 1940–1944: From Dunkirk to D-day.* London: Frank Cass, 2001.

Great Britain, navy of

The British standing army was always small in peacetime. In both world wars, a large conscript force was quickly raised around the core of the professional regular force. The Royal Air Force (RAF) was similarly expanded at the outbreak and in the course of World War II. The Royal Navy, however, was always large, a war-fighting force that was also intended to keep the peace. Above all other branches of arms, the navy was the instrument by which the Crown maintained its empire. At the outbreak of World War II, the Royal Navy (RN) was the most powerful force in the Atlantic.

The Admiralty was the war ministry with control over the navy. At its head was the Admiralty Board, consisting of the First Lord—a civilian cabinet member—and the First Sea Lord, a uniformed officer who also served as chief of naval staff. The Second Sea Lord had responsibility for manning and recruiting; the Third Sea Lord (Controller of the Navy) for ship building, repair, and dockyards; the Fourth Sea Lord for supplies and naval hospitals; and the Fifth Sea Lord for the Fleet Air Arm. The First Sea Lord had control of operations, which he exercised through the vice chief of the naval staff, who, in turn, was aided by three assistant chiefs. The Royal Navy was apportioned geographically into the North Atlantic Command, the South Atlantic Command, the China Station, the America and West Indies Station, and the East Indies Stations. In addition to these global commands were six home commands: Orkney and Shetlands, Rosyth, Nore, Dover, Portsmouth, and Western Approaches. Whereas the global commands had fleets that included great capital ships, the home commands were furnished with defensive forces, including destroyers, minesweepers, and torpedo boats. Western Approaches also controlled escort ships responsible for the escort of convoys. Deployable among these commands were the resources of three fleets: the Home Fleet, the Mediterranean Fleet, and the Eastern Fleet (later expanded and called the British Pacific Fleet). These fleets were organized into numbered squadrons (in the case of cruisers and larger vessels) and flotillas (in the case of destroyers and smaller vessels). Submarines operated independently as needed. The Royal Navy also had a Combined Operations organization, which managed amphibious operations in conjunction with the army and the RAF, and which had at its disposal the Royal Navy's fleet of landing craft. During the war, the Admiralty assumed control of the warships of the navies of the Commonwealth nations and also of those belonging to several governments in exile.

The Royal Navy was staffed by the Royal Navy proper, the Royal Navy Reserve, and the Royal Naval Volunteer Reserve. Royal Navy personnel were the officers and men of the regular standing navy. The Royal Navy Reserve consisted of experienced sailors, officers and enlisted personnel who had either previously served in the Royal Navy or who were merchant navy officers. The Royal Naval Volunteer Reserve (RNVR) were officers who volunteered for service during the war or who were conscripted and commissioned during the war. Many of the officers who served aboard the escort fleets were RNVR personnel.

Functionally, the Royal Navy was divided into specialized branches, including the Seaman's Branch (Executive Branch), which encompassed general operational naval personnel, and an Engineering Branch, a Medical Branch, a Supply Branch, an Instructional Branch, a Paymasters Branch, and a Chaplains Branch. The most important of the specialized branches was the Fleet Air Arm, which had responsibility for aircraft operating from aircraft carriers.

As in the other services, women played an important role. The Women's Royal Naval Service (WRNS—called "Wrens") had been created late in World War I, was suspended at the end of that war, then reactivated in 1939. Wrens performed shore duties only, including communications, RADAR operations, plotting, and clerical work, thereby freeing men for shipboard and other combat-related duties. Women also staffed Queen Alexandra's Royal Naval Nursing Service.

The Royal Navy exercised direct control over the Royal Marines. Traditionally, the Royal Marines served aboard RN ships to enforce order and to assist in manning guns. Between the wars, their role was theoretically expanded to include amphibious strike operations and the defense of naval installations overseas. However, this expansion was not put into practice until World War II was under way. Royal Marines served in several special forces roles as COMMANDOS.

The strength of the Royal Navy stood at 180,000 men at the outbreak of war in September 1939 and peaked at 783,000 in June 1945. The Royal Navy lost 50,758 men killed, 820 missing, 14,663 wounded, and 7,401 taken as prisoners of war.

For Royal Navy ship types and approximate numbers, *see* SHIPS, BRITISH.

Further reading: Gray, Edwyn. *Operation Pacific: The Royal Navy's War Against Japan, 1941–1945.* Annapolis, Md.: Naval Institute Press, 1991; Jackson, Robert. *The Royal Navy in World War II.* Annapolis, Md.: Naval Institute Press, 1998; Levy, James. *The Royal Navy's Home Fleet in World War II.* London: Palgrave Macmillan, 2003; Thompson, Julian. *The Imperial War Museum Book of the War at Sea: The Royal Navy in the Second World War.* Osceola, Wis.: Motorbooks International, 1996; Warlow, Ben. *The Royal Navy in Focus in World War II.* Liskeard, U.K.: Maritime Books, 2003; Worth, Richard. *Fleets of World War II.* New York: Da Capo, 2002.

Greece, invasion of

The invasion of ALBANIA, Greece, and YUGOSLAVIA instigated a Balkan campaign fought by Greek, British, and Yugoslav forces. Italy invaded Albania in April 1939, more than a year before BENITO MUSSOLINI took his country into World War II. Much as ADOLF HITLER had done with the SUDETENLAND, Mussolini gave assurances that the invasion would stop with Albania and that he had no intention of invading Greece. The Allies, France and Great Britain, did not take this disclaimer at face value but responded to it with pledges to defend the sovereignty of Romania and Greece. It was a response that moved Italy squarely into the German camp as the two nations concluded the PACT OF STEEL. Yet even after Italy declared war against the Allies on June 10, 1940, Mussolini continued to assert his intention not to invade Greece. However, on October 28, 1940, claiming that Greece had in its relations with Great Britain forfeited its status as a neutral, Mussolini moved troops from Albania into Greece.

The Italian dictator did not anticipate much resistance. France had already lost the fight for its life, and, with British forces preoccupied with home defense and Mediterranean Sea naval operations, he had no reason to believe that Great Britain would be in any position to honor its earlier pledge of aid. Accordingly, the invasion force was understrength, and it was quickly brushed aside by Greek resistance, which was bolstered by five Royal Air Force (RAF) squadrons providing close air support. On November 14, the Greeks turned the tables on the Italians, staging a counteroffensive that drove them back into Albania. British bombers braved miserable weather to bomb Italian port facilities and communications as the Greeks advanced against Valona.

As Italy reeled under this humiliating counteroffensive, German planners, recognizing the need to secure the Romanian oilfields and also to protect the southernmost flank of the planned INVASION OF THE SOVIET UNION, decided to stage their own invasion of Greece. In January 1941, Germany began a troop build-up in Romania, a nation now aligned with the Axis. Luftwaffe units were also dispatched to Bulgaria. In the meantime, German diplomats fruitlessly attempted to intervene in the ongoing combat between Greece and Italy. Despite success against the Italians, the Greek position was increasingly vulnerable as the Greek-British alliance faltered under mutual suspicions. Nevertheless, on March 9, 1941, when the Italians launched a new offensive against Greece, this time with 28 divisions, they were again repulsed. But a new problem developed as Yugoslavia officially joined the Axis on March 25, a move that provoked an antifascist coup against the Yugoslav

government. This reinvigorated the Greek-British alliance, and Commonwealth troops were rushed to the Greek front from the Middle East, along with more RAF units. All of this would have been more than a match for the Italians, but, on April 6, 1941, the Luftwaffe attacked Belgrade, and, simultaneously, General SIEGMUND LIST led the Twelfth German Army from Bulgaria into Yugoslavia and Greece. On April 8 and 10, combined German, Italian, and Hungarian forces invaded Yugoslavia. Belgrade fell on April 12, and the nation surrendered on April 17.

The process of Yugoslavia's defeat freed up List's 40th Corps to advance from southern Yugoslavia into Greece, outflanking the troops holding the Aliakmon Line there. Simultaneously, List's 18th Corps plowed through the Metaxas Line and took Salonika on April 9. British general MAITLAND WILSON pulled his forces back to a new defensive line on April 10, then, on the 14th, withdrew all the way to Thermopylae. Greek general Alexandros Papagos, fearing a total collapse of Greek Army morale, delayed withdrawal from the Albanian front, and when he finally did order it, on April 12, List was sufficiently far advanced to isolate the Greek forces from their British and Commonwealth allies. New Zealand troops scored a small triumph against List's 18th Corps at Olympus Pass on April 14, but the situation was ultimately hopeless. On April 21, the British decided to cut their losses and withdraw from Greece altogether, whereupon the Greek Army surrendered.

The evacuation of British and Commonwealth forces was hard fought but successfully completed during the night of April 30–May 1. As for Greece, the Communist Party (KKE) there organized disparate guerrilla bands into a fairly well coordinated resistance, which, by September 1941, developed into the National Liberation Front (EAM), a left-leaning group, but by no means completely communist. In December, the EAM created the National People's Liberation Army (ELAS) as its military arm. ELAS forces organized themselves in the mountains and were joined there by members of the National Republican League (EDES) as well as a few smaller resistance groups. British Special

Operations Executive (SOE) operatives were parachuted into Greece to work with Greek guerrilla fighters in a program of sabotage, which, despite severe German reprisals, was highly effective. Especially hard hit were Greece's already tenuous rail lines, which the guerrillas effectively denied to the occupiers through incessant and often spectacular acts of sabotage. However, relations between the SOE and the guerrillas were often strained. When the Germans withdrew from Greece in October 1944, ending the occupation, Georgios Papandreou, the Greek prime minister, ordered the guerrillas to disband. ELAS refused, and the nation that had just been delivered from German occupation now tottered on the brink of civil war. The British brought in more troops, but a low-level war erupted between ELAS and Greek government forces in December 1944. It did not end until February 1945 with a truce. Outright civil war did erupt in the years following World War II, and it was only by means of British and then, even more important, American military and economic aid that a communist takeover was averted and the government secured by 1949.

Further reading: Bitzes, John G. *Greece in World War II: To April 1941*. Manhattan, Kans.: Sunflower University Press, 1989; Catherwood, Christopher. *The Balkans in World War II: Britain's Balkan Dilemma*. London: Palgrave Macmillan, 2004; Condit, Doris M. *Case Study in Guerrilla War: Greece during World War II*. Washington, D.C.: Special Operations Research Office, American University, 1961; Leary, William M. *Fueling the Fires of Resistance: Army Air Forces Special Operations in the Balkans During World War II*. Honolulu: University Press of the Pacific, 2004.

Groves, Leslie (1896–1970) *U.S. general who headed the Manhattan Project*

Born in Albany, New York, Leslie Richard Groves enrolled at the University of Washington for one year and then the Massachusetts Institute of Technology for two years before entering West Point, from which he graduated in 1918. Commissioned a second lieutenant in the Army Corps of Engineers,

Major General Leslie Groves confers with J. Robert Oppenheimer. *(U.S. Department of Energy)*

he was enrolled at the Engineer's School, Camp Humphreys (now Fort Belvoir), Virginia, from 1918 to 1920 and again in 1921, absenting himself from his studies while serving briefly in France during World War I. After graduation, Groves was assigned to engineering units in San Francisco, Hawaii, Delaware, and Nicaragua before he was transferred in 1931 to the Office of the Chief of Engineers in Washington, D.C. Promoted to captain in October 1934, he was sent to the Command and General Staff School, Fort Leavenworth, Kansas, from which he graduated in 1936. He graduated from the Army War College in 1939, then was assigned to the general staff in Washington.

Promoted to major and temporary colonel in July and November of 1940, Groves was attached to the Office of the Quartermaster General and then to the Office of the Chief of Engineers. In this latter post, he was given responsibility for building a number of army construction projects, including, most notably, the Pentagon, which was completed under Groves's close supervision in a mere 18 months.

After finishing the Pentagon, and with World War II underway, Groves hoped to be given a combat assignment but was instead put in charge of a project code named Manhattan Engineer District: the MANHATTAN PROJECT. Promoted to temporary brigadier general, Groves found himself in charge of a titanic undertaking, easily the biggest scientific, industrial, and engineering enterprise any nation, in peace or war, had attempted up to that time. His mission was to oversee research, design, and fabrication of an atomic bomb. Virtually limitless resources were put at his disposal, but the enormous enterprise had to be conducted in absolute secrecy. Moreover, because it was believed that German scientists were also working on an atomic bomb, the Manhattan Project was a race against time and the enemy. Should the Germans get to the bomb first, the consequences for the world would be disastrous.

Groves had to supervise a highly volatile combination of scientists, military personnel, and civilian industrialists. Most of the research was carried out at Columbia University in New York, the University of Chicago, and, finally, at Los Alamos, New Mexico. Plants for the manufacture of fissionable radioactive material—the bomb's explosive material—were established at Oak Ridge, Tennessee, and at the Hanford Engineer Works near Pasco, Washington. Groves administered some $2 billion in funds, mostly through blind appropriations that were totally in his control. Groves worked closely with the brilliant physicist J. ROBERT OPPENHEIMER, who served as scientific director of the project. While the two men were polar opposites in temperament, intellect, and cultural orientation, they developed a highly effective working relationship, and, on July 16, 1945, a nuclear fission bomb was successfully detonated in a test at Alamogordo, New Mexico. Two more devices were prepared for use in combat and were deployed at HIROSHIMA, Japan, on August 6, 1945, and at NAGASAKI on August 9. Within days, the Japanese surrendered, and World War II came to an end.

Having been promoted to temporary major general in December 1944, Groves went on after the war to head the U.S. atomic establishment that he had been instrumental in creating. He left this post in January 1947 to become chief of the U.S. Army's Special Weapons Project and was promoted to temporary lieutenant general in January 1948. He left the army for civilian life in February and took a position as vice president of the Sperry Rand Corporation, which he held until his retirement in 1961.

Further reading: Norris, Robert S. *Racing for the Bomb: General Leslie R. Groves, the Manhattan Project's Indispensable Man.* South Royalton, Vt.: Steerforth Press, 2002; Rhodes, Richard. *The Making of the Atomic Bomb.* New York: Simon & Schuster, 1986.

Guadalcanal Campaign (Battle of Guadalcanal)

The Guadalcanal Campaign was a six-month epic of violence played out on land, sea, and in the air, beginning in August 1942 and ending in January 1943. The next major campaign after the fall of the Philippines, the Guadalcanal Campaign was costly to both sides but, in conjunction with the BATTLE OF MIDWAY, constituted the turning point of the war in the Pacific. From the twin defeats at Midway and Guadalcanal, Japan would never recover.

The battle was joined because U.S. Admiral ERNEST J. KING targeted Guadalcanal as a means of

Destroyer Squadron 12 maneuvers off Savo Island during the Guadalcanal Campaign. *(U.S. Navy)*

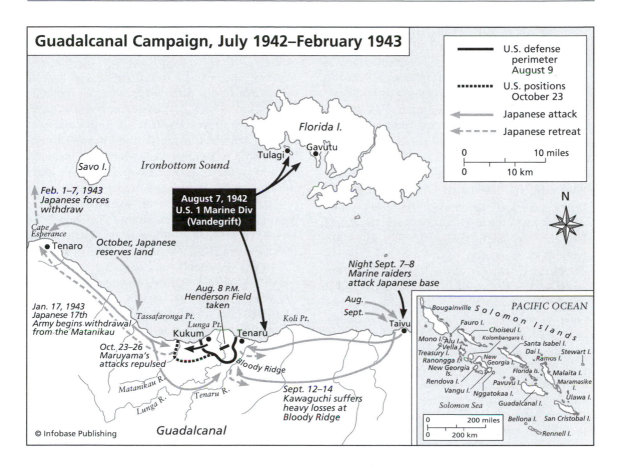

Guadalcanal Campaign, July 1942–February 1943

checking a Japanese thrust intended to cut off Australia. Steamy and overgrown with tropical jungle, Guadalcanal is 90 miles long and 25 miles wide, one of the Solomon Islands in the South Pacific. Intercepted radio messages indicated that the Japanese were going to use the island as an air base from which to intercept U.S. convoys bound for Australia. On August 7, 1942, King landed the 1st Marine Division on Guadalcanal in a surprise assault that quickly seized the all-but-completed Japanese airstrip. This triumph was short lived, however, as a Japanese naval task force on August 9 surprised and defeated an Allied screening force off Savo Island. The attack so alarmed U.S. Admiral FRANK FLETCHER, who was in tactical command of the Guadalcanal operation, that he withdrew his aircraft carriers, forcing partially unloaded troop

transports to withdraw as well. This left the marine contingent on Guadalcanal isolated, at least until August 20, when the so-called Cactus Air Force, a mixed group of mostly U.S. Marine aircraft (19 fighters and 12 torpedo bombers), arrived to operate from the captured airfield, now dubbed Henderson Field. Other air units would later join this small force and proved highly effective against Japanese naval forces. For the time being, however, the Japanese enjoyed superiority in the seas around Guadalcanal. The Cactus Air Force prevented daytime assaults against the island, but the Japanese were able to land troops, who were supplied and reinforced by destroyers operating at night, the so-called Tokyo Express.

Repeatedly over the next three months, Japanese land forces engaged the marines, who, thanks to the growing presence of aircraft, were adequately furnished with resupply and reinforcement. Each side built up troop strength on the island. By November 12, there were 30,000 Japanese fighting 29,000 Americans. By the beginning of December, Japanese numbers had been reduced to 25,000, and American troop strength peaked at 40,000, including two marine divisions and two army divisions. The Japanese had erred early on by making conservative, piecemeal attacks, which the marine forces, isolated though they were, managed to repulse. Having thus lost the momentum, the Japanese were never able to regain it, although Henderson Field was repeatedly threatened over the entire course of the campaign.

Ultimately, decisive victory at Guadalcanal was won at sea. On August 24, the U.S. Navy blocked an attempted major landing while suffering a tactical defeat. Revenge for these losses came in the nighttime Battle of Cape Esperance during October 11–12, when a task force under Rear Admiral Norman Scott attacked a Japanese bombardment force under Rear Admiral Goto Aritomo, which was tasked with shelling the marines and landing more reinforcements. Thanks to advanced surface RADAR, Scott detected the Japanese force and was able to sink one Japanese heavy cruiser and a destroyer. Scott's task force also damaged another heavy cruiser and, in the course of the engagement, killed Goto. The next day, two more Japanese destroyers were sunk. American losses included one destroyer sunk and damage to three other ships.

Despite the victory at Cape Esperance, the first successful night action for the U.S. Navy in the Pacific war, and despite the salutary effect on the marines, Admiral CHESTER A. NIMITZ remained dissatisfied with the generally cautious approach of South Pacific theater commander Robert L. Ghormely. He relieved Ghormely and replaced him with the hyperaggressive Vice Admiral WILLIAM A. "BULL" HALSEY. At the Battle of Santa Cruz on October 26, Halsey lost the carrier *Hornet* and 74 aircraft but destroyed 100 Japanese planes. Next, during November 12–15, in the massively destructive sea engagement known as the Battle of Guadalcanal, the U.S. Navy prevailed, albeit at a heavy

cost. On the night of November 12–13, six U.S. Navy ships were sunk versus three Japanese vessels, including, however, one battleship. On the next morning, the Japanese lost a cruiser and suffered severe damage to three others. On the night of November 13–14, the Japanese lost another battleship and a destroyer, while the Americans sacrificed six destroyers and incurred severe damage to one battleship. The Japanese troop transports had to be beached to disgorge their troops, and those ships were bombed and destroyed during the day.

The sea and air Battle of Guadalcanal was the culmination of the Guadalcanal Campaign and persuaded the Japanese (despite victory at another nighttime sea battle, Tasafaraonga, on November 30) to cut their losses and evacuate their troops from Guadalcanal. Fighting continued in a more desultory fashion, but, early in January, despite what was now Allied air and sea superiority, the Japanese managed to evacuate some 13,000 men, who were ferried by night in barges to waiting destroyers.

While the American victory at Guadalcanal was decisive, it was marred by the missed opportunity to destroy the Japanese ground forces completely. Nevertheless, Japanese casualties were devastating: about 30,000 men killed and 680 aircraft plus 24 warships lost. American losses included some 5,000 sailors and 2,500 marines, soldiers, and airmen killed, as well as 615 aircraft and 25 ships lost.

See also PHILIPPINES, FALL AND RECONQUEST OF.

Further reading: Frank, Richard B. *Guadalcanal: The Definitive Account of the Landmark Battle.* New York: Penguin, 1992; Griffith, Samuel B. II. *The Battle for Guadalcanal.* Champaign: University of Illinois Press, 2000; Hersey, John. *Into the Valley: Marines at Guadalcanal.* Lincoln: University of Nebraska Press, 2002; Tregaskis, Richard. *Guadalcanal Diary.* New York: Modern Library, 2000.

Guam, Battle of

This article discusses the fall of Guam to the Japanese on December 10, 1941. The battle to retake the island is discussed in MARIANA ISLANDS CAMPAIGN.

Guam, in the Pacific, is the largest of the Mariana Islands. It was ceded to the United States as a result of the Spanish-American War in 1898 and was put under the administration of the U.S. Navy. At the outbreak of the war in the Pacific, Guam was unfortified and was defended by no more than 430 U.S. Marines and 180 native Chamorro guards, all under the command of Captain George McMillan, U.S. Navy, the military governor of the island. The Japanese landed 5,400 troops on Guam on December 10, 1941, and engaged McMillan's vastly outnumbered command for three hours before the captain surrendered the island. The only reason that the small band of defenders held out even for three hours was the difficult terrain of the island, which greatly favored defenders over attackers. A total of 17 marines and Chamorros were killed in the battle. Only one of the Japanese invaders died.

The loss of Guam was a serious blow to the American presence in the Pacific. In 1941, Guam possessed the only adequate freshwater supply in all the Marianas, and it provided the best harbor. It would serve as an important advance base for whoever held it, and the Japanese, recognizing its value, garrisoned it with some 19,000 troops.

Further reading: Rogers, Robert F. *Destiny's Landfall: A History of Guam.* Honolulu: University of Hawaii Press, 1995; Rottman, Gordon. *Guam 1941/1944: Loss and Reconquest.* Osceola, Wis.: Motorbooks International, 2004; Rottman, Gordon. *US Marine Corps Pacific Theater of Operation, 1941–43.* London: Osprey, 2004.

Guderian, Heinz (1888–1953) *German panzer general*

Heinz Guderian was born at Kulm (Chelmno) into the family of a Prussian army officer and was sent to the cadet school in Karlsruhe, which he attended from September 1900 to April 1903. Guderian moved on to the main cadet school at Gross Lichteffelde, from which he graduated in December 1907. The following year, on January 27, Guderian entered the 10th Hannoverian Jäger as a second lieutenant. During 1913–14, he attended the Kriegsakademie (War College), and,

at the beginning of World War I, in August 1914, Guderian was assigned command of a radio station. By April 1915, he had been advanced to assistant signals officer for the Fourth German Army. He served in this post through April 1917, when he moved through a variety of staff posts, culminating in an appointment to the Great General Staff in February 1918, the assignment he held until the armistice.

Following the war, Guderian participated in FREIKORPS operations in Latvia during March–July 1919 as chief of staff of the Iron Division. He then was chosen for retention as one of a small cadre of 4,000 officers of the 100,000-man Reichswehr, the diminutive army permitted Germany by the TREATY OF VERSAILLES. In January 1922, Guderian was assigned to the Inspectorate of Transport Troops in the so-called Truppenamt, code name for the German General Staff, a body that had been proscribed by the Versailles treaty. During 1922–24, Guderian served in a transport battalion in Munich, then became an instructor in tactics and military history on the staff of 2nd Division during 1924–27. He returned to the Truppenamt during October 1927–February 1930 and, during this time, was briefly seconded to a Swedish tank battalion. Later, during 1930–31, given command of a motor transport battalion, he reorganized it as a provisional armored reconnaissance battalion. This was the first fruit of work he had begun in 1921, planning for the creation of tank (panzer) forces.

In October 1935, Guderian left the staff post to assume command of the 2nd Panzer Division at Würzburg. The following year, he was promoted from colonel to major general and, in 1937, gained international attention in military circles with his *Achtung! Panzer* (*Attention! Armor*), a compact book into which he had distilled his highly advanced theories of mechanized warfare.

During 1937–38, Guderian commanded XVI Corps, comprising three panzer divisions. During ANSCHLUSS, he led the 2nd Panzer Division through Linz to Vienna (March 12–13, 1938). At the outbreak of World War II, he led XIX Panzer Corps in the INVASION OF POLAND (September 1–October 5, 1939), providing a devastating demonstration of the role of armor in BLITZKRIEG by advancing with great speed from Pomerania across the Polish Corridor, on September 4, to capture Brest-Litovsk during September 16–17. Reinforced, the XIX Corps was next placed under Panzer Group Kleist for the campaign in France. Guderian and his unit were in the vanguard of the BATTLE OF FRANCE on May 10, 1940, crossing the Meuse River at Sedan and reaching the English Channel coast on May 19. Guderian had led the panzers through the forest of the Ardennes, which the French considered impassable and, therefore, had failed to defend adequately.

Guderian and his panzers raced across France and outran the conventional infantry units participating in the invasion. The panzers were closing in on British and French troops at Dunkirk, forcing them back against the English Channel, when Guderian was ordered to halt on authority of ADOLF HITLER. Hitler and his top advisers feared that Guderian would be counterattacked, and they wanted him to wait for an infantry build up. The delay allowed the British and French to be evacuated, thereby saving the British Expeditionary Force from annihilation. By stopping Guderian, Hitler had sacrificed a probable opportunity to force Britain into a negotiated peace.

With the fall of France, Guderian's XIX Corps was on the Swiss frontier near Basel, and, by November 1940, was expanded into 2nd Panzer Group. It became part of Field Marshal Fedor von Bock's Army Group Center during the INVASION OF THE SOVIET UNION, which stepped off on June 22, 1941. During the invasion, Guderian's 2nd Panzers, along with the 3rd Panzer Group, encircled Soviet forces at Minsk on July 10. They went on to surround Smolensk and to capture Roslavl during July 12–August 8, 1941. From these victories, Guderian was sent south to coordinate operations with the 4th Panzer Group of Field Marshal GERD VON RUNDSTEDT's Army Group South in a massive maneuver to encircle 600,000 Red Army troops in the "Kiev pocket," which was accomplished during August 21–September 6.

Guderian's next offensive push, on the Soviet capital of Moscow, was stalled by a combination of early winter weather and increasingly formidable Soviet resistance during October 23–November 7, 1941. Deeming his situation desperate, Guderian sought permission from higher command to withdraw from exposed positions around Tula during December 5–26. By way of response, he was summarily relieved of command and replaced by General Gunther von Kluge on December 26, 1941. Following this, Guderian fell ill and was out of action until February 1943, when he was recalled to duty as inspector general of panzer troops. By this time, however, the magnificent panzers had been badly mauled at the BATTLE OF STALINGRAD, and Guderian set about the task of rebuilding German armor. In this effort, he worked closely with Reich Armaments Minister ALBERT SPEER to increase and accelerate tank production.

On July 21, 1943, Guderian replaced General Kurt Zeitzler as army chief of staff, but, as the war was coming to an end, Hitler dismissed Guderian on March 28, 1945. He was held under arrest by the Allies for several months after the German surrender but, unlike many other top generals, was not charged with war crimes. Today, he is recognized as one of the pioneers in the doctrine of armored warfare.

Further reading: Guderian, Heinz. *Achtung! Panzer.* New York: Sterling, 1999; Guderian, Heinz. *Panzer Leader.* New York: Da Capo, 2001; Higgins, George A. *The Operational Tenets of Generals Heinz Guderian and George S. Patton, Jr.* Carlisle, Pa.: U.S. Army Command and General Staff College, 1985.

Gustav Line

The Gustav Line was a chain of German defensive positions northwest of Naples during the ITALIAN CAMPAIGN. It was set up originally as a fallback defense behind the much lighter Bernhardt Line, which ran from a position near Minturno, northwest of Naples, along the Garigliano River, through the mountains, and to the east coast at Fossacesia. The Gustav Line also served to cover the gap between the western end of the Bernhardt Line near Minturno. The most prominent strong point along the Gustav Line was Monte Cassino, scene of the extremely destructive and bloody BATTLES OF CASSINO.

The completion of the Gustav Line effectively incorporated the Bernhardt Line, so that the entire series of fortified positions was referred to as the Gustav Line. With the Hitler Line, running from Terracina on Italy's west coast, to Monte Cairo, the Gustav Line was often called the Winter Line by the Allies who battered long and hard against it.

Further reading: Hapgood, David, and David Richardson. *Monte Cassino: The Story of the Most Controversial Battle of World War II.* New York: Da Capo, 2002; Lamb, Richard. *War in Italy 1943–1945: A Brutal Story.* Da Capo, 1996; Parker, Matthew. *Monte Cassino: The Hardest-Fought Battle of World War II.* New York: Doubleday, 2004.

H

Hahn, Otto (1879–1968) *German scientist credited with the discovery of nuclear fission*

Born into the family of a Frankfurt glazier, Hahn studied chemistry at the University of Marburg, earning his doctorate in 1901. He served briefly in the military, then taught at Marburg before moving to London in 1904. Here he worked at University College with the British scientist Sir William Ramsay. The two men studied phenomena associated with radioactivity, and, in the course of this work, Hahn discovered the existence of a new radioactive substance, radiothorium, a breakthrough that, with Ramsay's help, earned Hahn a post on the faculty of the University of Berlin. Before beginning his duties there, Hahn worked briefly with the British physicist Ernest Rutherford in Montreal, then, once in Germany again, collaborated with the brilliant Austrian physicist Lise Meitner. In 1911, Hahn and Meitner took their work to the newly opened Kaiser Wilhelm Institute for Chemistry at Berlin-Dahlen, where Hahn headed the department of radiochemistry. This would become the nexus of German research on radioactivity and, ultimately, on nuclear fission, the basis (among many other things) of atomic weaponry.

During World War I, Hahn was attached to a military regiment and served his country as a specialist in chemical warfare, including the production and use of poison gases. Following the armistice, he and Meitner returned to atomic research. In 1934, Hahn began studying the recent work of the Italian physicist Enrico Fermi, who had observed that bombarding uranium with neutrons produced a number of radioactive substances, which Fermi theorized were artificial elements similar to uranium. Hahn and Meitner, assisted by the chemist Fritz Strassmann, reached a different conclusion. In the midst of this work, however, in 1938, Meitner, a Jew, fled Germany to escape Nazi persecution, and Hahn carried on with Strassmann. At length, the two concluded that bombarding uranium with neutrons produced (among other products) the element barium. The only possible interpretation of this phenomenon was that the uranium atom had split into two lighter atoms. Conventional chemical theory held that atoms were irreducible and that one element could not, therefore, be converted to another. Hahn and Strassmann had demonstrated that atoms can be "split" (made to undergo fission) and that the result was the creation of atoms of a different, lighter element. After Hahn sent a report of the work to Meitner, she and her nephew Otto Frisch proposed an explanation of the process they called nuclear fission.

Even before World War II began, Hahn and other scientists (most notably WERNER HEISENBERG) were assembled under authority of the German government to study military applications of the discovery. During the war, Heisenberg led scientists in a more focused effort to develop a fission weapon. Vague but menacing reports of Hahn and

Heisenberg's work in this direction alarmed scientists outside Germany, including the Hungarian expatriate LEO SZILARD, who prevailed upon the most famous physicist of the era, ALBERT EINSTEIN, to endorse a letter to President FRANKLIN D. ROOSEVELT apprising him of German work on a fission weapon and advising that the government sanction a nuclear research effort in the United States. As it turned out, German progress toward an atomic bomb was hampered by inadequate government support and, possibly, scientific errors (or even Heisenberg's deliberate misdirection), so that there was relatively little danger that ADOLF HITLER would have obtained a weapon before the end of the war. As for Hahn, who had shown willingness during World War I to work on poison gas weapons, he seems to have been motivated by nothing more than a desire to be allowed to continue his work.

After the war ended, Hahn and other German nuclear scientists were taken to England. While there, Hahn learned that he had been awarded the Nobel Prize for 1944. The news that the United States had actually developed and used atomic weapons against Japan came to him as a profound shock. Hahn returned to Germany and was elected president of the Max Planck Society for the Advancement of Science (formerly the Kaiser Wilhelm Society). He also became an outspoken public advocate of banning both the further development and testing of nuclear weapons.

Further reading: Hahn, Otto. *Otto Hahn: A Scientific Autobiography.* New York: Scribner's, 1966; Hoffmann, Klaus. *Otto Hahn: Nobel Prize and Atom Bomb.* New York: Springer-Verlag, 2001; Shea, William R. *Otto Hahn and the Rise of Nuclear Physics.* Dordrecht, Netherlands: Kluwer Academic Publishers, 1983; Walker, Mark. *German National Socialism and the Quest for Nuclear Power, 1939–1949.* New York and Cambridge: Cambridge University Press, 1992.

Halsey, William "Bull" (1882–1959) *U.S. admiral in the Pacific theater*

William "Bull" Halsey was born in Elizabeth, New Jersey, the son of a naval officer. He graduated from the U.S. Naval Academy at Annapolis in 1904 and was commissioned an ensign in 1906. Halsey sailed with Admiral George Dewey on the world-circling cruise of the Great White Fleet from August 1907 to February 1909. He subsequently attended torpedo school at Charleston, South Carolina, and was assigned duty aboard destroyers and torpedo boats before being given command of the destroyers *Flusser* in 1912 and *Jervis* in 1913. The latter vessel he commanded during the occupation of Veracruz (April–October 1914) and left it in 1915, when he was attached to the executive department at the Naval Academy. Halsey was promoted to lieutenant commander in August 1916, and, with American entry into World War I, was assigned command of two destroyers, the *Duncan* and *Benham,* performing convoy escort duty from a base in Queenstown, Ireland. After the armistice, Halsey commanded destroyers in the Atlantic as well as the Pacific through 1921, when he was transferred from sea duty to the Office of Naval Intelligence.

In 1922, Halsey was named naval attaché in Berlin and, subsequently, became attaché in Norway, Denmark, and Sweden. He returned to sea duty in 1924 aboard destroyers in the Atlantic, then transferred to the battleship *Wyoming* as executive officer during 1926–27. Promoted to captain in February 1927, he was given command of the

Admiral "Bull" Halsey (center) attends a party for officers aboard the USS *Saratoga,* 1943. *(National Archives and Records Administration)*

Reina Mercedes (IX-25), the post ship at Annapolis, which had been captured from the Spaniards in 1898. In 1930, Halsey assumed command of Destroyer Squadron 14, serving until 1932, when he enrolled in the Naval War College (graduated 1933) and the Army War College (graduated 1934).

Seeing the future of naval warfare in carrier-based aviation, Halsey, at the age of 52, completed flight training at Pensacola, Florida, in May 1935 and assumed command of the aircraft carrier *Saratoga* that July. Two years later, he returned to Pensacola as commander of the Pensacola Naval Air Station. After promotion to rear admiral in March 1938, he took command of Carrier Division 2, followed by command of Carrier Division 1 in 1939. Halsey was promoted to vice admiral in June 1940 and was assigned to command Aircraft Battle Force as well as returning to command of Carrier Division 2. He was at sea with the carriers *Enterprise* and *Yorktown* during the BATTLE OF PEARL HARBOR on December 7, 1941. This fortuitously saved the carriers from destruction, and he used them in the months that followed to raid outlying Japanese islands in the Central Pacific (January–May 1942). He also worked with U.S. Army Air Corps colonel JAMES H. DOOLITTLE in carrying out the DOOLITTLE TOKYO RAID, launching 16 B-25 bombers from the carrier *Hornet.*

Late in May 1942, Halsey fell seriously ill and was compelled to turn command over to RAYMOND AMES SPRUANCE. His illness caused him to miss the turning-point BATTLE OF MIDWAY on June 4, 1942. However, by October, Halsey was returned to active duty and was tapped by Admiral CHESTER A. NIMITZ to replace Robert L. Ghormley as commander of South Pacific Force and Area. Suffering a tactical defeat in his first engagement, at Santa Cruz (October 26–28) during the GUADALCANAL CAMPAIGN, he nevertheless scored a critical strategic victory by maintaining station off Guadalcanal, thereby preventing Japanese reinforcement of its invasion force on the island. During November 12–15, Halsey defeated the Japanese at sea off the island, then commanded naval support efforts for the capture of the rest of the Solomon Islands.

During the BOUGAINVILLE CAMPAIGN, he commanded sea operations that isolated the key Japanese base at Rabaul, rendering it vulnerable during the ensuing BATTLES OF RABAUL.

Named commander of Third Fleet in June 1944, Halsey directed landings at Leyte in the Philippines (October 17–20, 1944) from his flagship, the battleship *New Jersey.* He faltered here by allowing himself to be decoyed into pursuit of the remnant of the Japanese carrier force off Luzon on October 25, 1944. Although he sank four Japanese vessels in this action, he left San Bernardino Strait covered only by a weak force of escort carriers and destroyers, which were attacked by Admiral Takeo Kurita's significantly superior Central Force. Despite being both outnumbered and outclassed, the Americans managed to repulse the attack in the Battle of Samar (October 25). In the meantime, Halsey dashed back to San Bernardino Strait to reinforce the beleaguered detachment in an operation that became known as "Bull's Run." This incident, however, stained Halsey's reputation, and he suffered an additional reverse when his Third Fleet, supporting amphibious operations in the Philippines, was stuck by a typhoon that sank three destroyer escorts in December. Despite this, Halsey went on to sweep through the South China Sea, destroying massive amounts of Japanese tonnage during January 10–20, 1945.

Halsey turned over command to Spruance, then returned to sea-going command during the last stages of the OKINAWA CAMPAIGN (May–June 22, 1945) and the raids against the Japanese home islands during July and August. Japan's formal surrender took place aboard Halsey's new flagship, the battleship *Missouri,* in Tokyo Bay on September 2.

In November, Halsey turned over command of Third Fleet to Admiral Howard Kingman, was promoted to fleet admiral the following month, and was assigned to special duty in the office of the secretary of the navy until he retired in April 1947. In civilian life, Halsey held a number of executive and advisory positions in business, but he also was repeatedly compelled to defend his actions during the Philippines campaign. Despite this, "Bull" Halsey was greatly loved by the public and is remembered as one of the U.S. Navy's heroic commanders.

See also PHILIPPINES, FALL AND RECONQUEST OF.

Further reading: Halsey, William F., and J. Bryan III. *Admiral Halsey's Story.* New York: Da Capo Press, 1976; Potter, E. B. *Bull Halsey.* Annapolis, Md.: Naval Institute Press, 2003.

Harris, Sir Arthur Travers "Bomber"
(1892–1984) *British air marshal*

Sir Arthur Travers, first Baronet Harris, was born at Cheltenham, Gloucestershire, and was educated at Sittingbourne. His first military service was with a Rhodesian regiment in Africa from 1914 to 1915, when he transferred to the Royal Flying Corps and served in Europe on the western front. After World War I, Harris briefly flew with the Home Defense Command of the Royal Air Force (RAF), then transferred to service in India and the Middle East in 1919. He served in foreign posts until about 1936, when he became a member of the RAF planning staff in England.

At the outbreak of World War II, in September 1939, Harris was commanding officer of Bomber Group 5. Within less than a year, he was named deputy chief of the Air Staff, serving in this capacity from 1940 to 1941. In February 1942, Harris was appointed chief of Bomber Command and set about reevaluating British bomber performance. In contrast to U.S. Army Air Forces doctrine, which espoused precision daylight bombing, Harris advocated area bombing, targeting large industrial areas with incendiary and high-explosive bombs in an effort to disrupt German industry. Working closely with Prime Minister WINSTON CHURCHILL, Harris also departed from American doctrine by advocating nighttime raids beginning in summer 1943. Harris argued that area bombing did not require daylight and that the night sky offered more protection from fighters and antiaircraft fire. The nighttime strategy also allowed for better coordination with the American effort, achieving round-the-clock bombardment. While the Americans continued a regime of precision bombing by day, Harris employed area bombing by night.

Although his aggressiveness was widely admired, Harris was also criticized for two of his policies. First, area bombing caused excessive collateral damage, to the point that many considered it deliberate terrorism against civilian populations. Second, neither area bombing—nor, for that matter, precision bombing, nor the combination of the two—succeeded in greatly crippling German industry. Much manufacturing, especially aircraft production, was moved underground and remained fairly immune to the bombing, despite its unrelenting intensity. Harris was especially criticized for the DRESDEN AIR RAID of February 13–14, 1945, which created a tragically devastating firestorm that killed tens of thousands of civilians, destroyed a showplace medieval city, and yet served little military purpose. Harris retired after the war and was created baronet in 1953.

See also STRATEGIC BOMBING OF GERMANY.

Further reading: Neillands, Robin. *The Bomber War: Arthur Harris and the Allied Bomber Offensive 1939–1945.* London: John Murray, 2001; Probert, Henry. *Bomber Harris, His Life and Times: The Biography of Marshal of the Royal Air Force Sir Arthur Harris, the Wartime Chief of Bomber Command.* London: Greenhill, 2001; Saward, Dudley. *Bomber Harris: The Story of Marshal of the Royal Air Force Sir Arthur Harris, Bt, GCB, OBE, AFC, LLD, Air Officer Commanding-in-Chief, Bomber Command, 1942–1945.* London: Time Warner Books, 1990.

Heisenberg, Werner (1901–1976) *physicist who led German atomic bomb research in World War II*

Born in Wurzburg, Germany, Werner Karl Heisenberg was awarded the Nobel Prize in Physics in 1932 for his pioneering work in quantum mechanics. He may be even better known for his 1927 "uncertainty principle," which has implications not only for physics but for the broader field of philosophy as a definition of the absolute limit of knowledge of the physical world. In addition, Heisenberg worked in the areas of the hydrodynamics of turbulence, the nature of the atomic nucleus, the nature of ferromagnetism, cosmic rays, and elementary particles. During World War II, he was the leader of German scientists at work on transforming the principle of nuclear fission into a nuclear reactor and, ultimately, a nuclear weapon.

Heisenberg was at the forefront of 20th-century physics and was an original thinker as well as a great synthesizer of the work of Niels Bohr and ALBERT EINSTEIN. He studied physics at the University of Munich in company with the remarkable Wolfgang Pauli and under the tutelage of Arnold Sommerfeld. Receiving his doctorate in 1923, Heisenberg followed Pauli to the University of Göttingen, where he studied under Max Born. In 1924, he continued advanced studies with Niels Bohr at the Institute for Theoretical Physics in Copenhagen. Heisenberg reinterpreted Bohr's atomic model to produce a new model that involved a radical revision of quantum theory and created an entire new discipline: the quantum mechanics of atomic systems. This, in turn, gave rise to what Heisenberg termed matrix mechanics, a field of inquiry that led to a new understanding of mechanics on the subatomic level and, in 1927, to the formulation of the uncertainty principle, an elegant mathematical statement of the theoretical limitations of observation, measurement, and knowledge. Heisenberg demonstrated that, at the subatomic level, the measurement of the position and the momentum of an atomic particle could not be determined precisely because the measurement of one necessarily affects the measurement of the other. In effect, Heisenberg had described the ultimate "graininess" of the universe, the level beyond which knowing was simply and absolutely impossible.

From 1927 to 1941, Heisenberg taught at the University of Leipzig. During most of World War II, he served as director of the government-funded Kaiser Wilhelm Institute for Physics (today known as the Max Planck Institute of Physics) in Berlin. Heisenberg was not an overt or vocal opponent of Nazism. Although he was privately opposed to Nazi ideology and policies, he was nevertheless publicly silent concerning them. During the war, he worked with OTTO HAHN to develop a nuclear

reactor, which was a project preparatory to the development of nuclear weapons. Heisenberg's role in this work has long been problematical for historians as well as scientists. Some believe that Heisenberg, the leader of the Nazi atomic bomb effort, earnestly tried to produce a weapon, but failed. Others believe that he deliberately misled government overseers, effectively sabotaging the work, and that he never intended to give ADOLF HITLER an atomic bomb. These individuals further suggest that, as director of the Kaiser Wilhelm Institute, Heisenberg operated to save the lives of Jewish scientists and others who had fallen afoul of the Nazi regime. They further suggest that Heisenberg remained in Germany and at least apparently served the Third Reich in an effort to preserve German science from total destruction during the war. The most recent evidence suggests that Heisenberg did, in fact, work in earnest on a nuclear reactor and even on a nuclear weapon but failed because of a combination of theoretical errors and lack of technical resources. The full truth may never be known, however, and, as was the case during and immediately after the war, Heisenberg will probably always have his detractors and defenders.

After the war, Heisenberg created and became director of the Max Planck Institute for Physics and Astrophysics at Göttingen, then moved with the institute to Munich in 1958. He continued pursuing highly advanced work in theoretical physics and mathematics, and he became a vocal international advocate for the peaceful use of atomic energy.

Further reading: Cassidy, David C. *Uncertainty: The Life and Science of Werner Heisenberg.* New York: W. H. Freeman, 1993; Powers, Thomas. *Heisenberg's War: The Secret History of the German Bomb.* New York: Da Capo, 2000.

Hess, Rudolf W. (1894–1987) *deputy Nazi Party leader*

A merchant's son, Hess was born in Alexandria, Egypt, and saw service in the German Army during World War I. After the armistice, he attended the University of Munich and there became involved in the beginnings of the Nazi Party (NSDAP) in 1920. Working closely with Adolf Hitler, he became a member of his inner circle and was part of Hitler's failed 1923 "Beer Hall Putsch." Although Hess made his way to Austria after this coup attempt, he turned himself in and was incarcerated at Landsberg Prison, where he collaborated with Hitler, also held there, on the latter's autobiographical manifesto, *Mein Kampf*. This earned Hess the post of Hitler's private secretary.

In 1932, following the defection of certain left-leaning party members, Hitler assigned Hess to reorganize the party leadership. This he did with great effectiveness and, in April 1933, was appointed deputy party leader. With the ascension of Hitler as chancellor of Germany, Hess entered the cabinet, and, in 1939, Hitler formally proclaimed Hess to be second to Hermann Göring in the line of succession as party leader and führer.

Hess's rise in the Nazi Party and Nazi governing regime was the result of his intense, even dog-like, loyalty to Hitler rather than to his own intelligence or political talent, both of which were manifestly limited. Indeed, Hess garnered little respect from others in the party, and by the late 1930s and beginning of World War II, his influence in both the party and the government rapidly diminished as others, more sophisticated politically and diplomatically, gained power. In a rare flash of initiative but with little forethought and with neither the knowledge nor approval of Hitler, Hess embarked on a one-man mission to Britain for the purpose of negotiating peace between the two countries. His hope, apparently, was that in a single stroke, he might restore his place within the Nazi hierarchy.

On May 10, 1941, Hess flew from Augsburg and parachuted into Scotland bearing a proposal, of his own invention, that Britain give Germany leave to pursue its war aims on the continent and that it return all former German colonies to the reich in exchange for Germany's pledge to keep hands off the British Empire. It was, of course, an absurdly Quixotic mission, and no British government official dignified the proposal with a response. Instead, Hess was taken into immediate custody as a pris-oner of war. Even Hitler disavowed the act as that of a person suffering from "pacifist delusions."

Held through the duration of World War II, Hess was remanded to the Nuremberg War Crimes Tribunal after the war and tried for war crimes. Found guilty, he was sentenced to life imprisonment, a sentence he served in Berlin's Spandau Prison. From 1966 until his death in 1987, the hapless Hess was the only inmate there.

Further reading: Bird, Eugene K. *The Loneliest Man in the World: The Inside Story of the 30-year Imprisonment of Rudolf Hess.* London: Secker & Warburg, 1974; Iles, Greg. *Spandau Phoenix.* New York: Signet Book, 1994.

Heydrich, Reinhard (1904–1942) *SS deputy who was a key perpetrator of the Holocaust*

Reinhard Tristan Eugen Heydrich was born in Halle, Germany, into a highly cultivated musical family. Heydrich's father was the headmaster of a musical conservatory and a prominent Wagnerian tenor. From his father, Heydrich received both a musical education (he played the violin at a professional level) and indoctrination into the cult of Richard Wagner, whose music informed the philosophy of Adolf Hitler and the racial mythology of Nazism. Despite his ideological pedigree, Reinhard Heydrich would be dogged throughout his career by shadowy rumors, apparently unfounded, of Jewish ancestry.

In 1919, Heydrich joined the Freikorps, then entered the German Navy in 1922 with a commission as an officer. In 1931, he was discharged for misconduct after he refused to marry a shipyard official's daughter with whom he was conducting a sexual liaison. Once out of the navy, Heydrich joined the Schutzstaffel (SS) and met SS chief Heinrich Himmler. Greatly impressed with young Heydrich, Himmler assigned him to organize the Sicherheitsdienst (SD), the SS "Security Service," which Heydrich helped to fashion into a ruthlessly efficient intelligence and surveillance organization. With Hitler's elevation as chancellor of Germany in 1933, Heydrich was named chief of the political department of the Munich police. He used this position to bring the political departments of all German police forces under the control of the SS and Heinrich Himmler. This catapulted Heydrich into the top levels of the SD. However, Heydrich also recognized that he was unlikely to advance beyond Himmler. Appointed SS chief for Berlin in 1934, Heydrich took full operational charge of the SD as well as the criminal police and the GESTAPO in 1936, after Himmler was appointed chief of all German police forces.

Heydrich used his new positions so aggressively that he earned the sobriquet *Der Henker,* "the Hangman." He not only played a key role in the 1938 purge of the German Army high command, but also masterminded a program of disinformation that helped to incite JOSEPH STALIN to purge the Red Army, an action that greatly weakened the Soviet officer corps on the eve of World War II. Heydrich's position as chief of the Gestapo gave him virtually unlimited powers of arrest. He was one of the architects of KRISTALLNACHT in November 1938, and he saw to it that this government-sanctioned outburst of anti-Semitic violence occasioned the round-up and imprisonment of thousands of Jews. This marked the beginning of THE HOLOCAUST.

In 1939, Heydrich was appointed head of the Reichssicherheitshauptamt ("Reich Security Central Office"), which expanded his police administrative authority to encompass all security and secret police in the Third Reich. It was Heydrich who set up the faked Polish attack on a German radio transmitter at the frontier town of Gleiwitz, which served as the pretext for the INVASION OF POLAND that started World War II on September 1, 1939. Early in the war, Heydrich collaborated with ADOLF EICHMANN in organizing the FINAL SOLUTION, the systematic genocide of all European Jewry. This process began with deportation of Jews from Germany and Austria to Polish ghettos, then continued with the killing of Soviet and Polish Jews by SS Einsatzgruppen, "deployment groups," Heydrich organized to follow the conquering Nazi armies, round up the Jews in occupied territories, and kill them.

Despite the Einsatzgruppen, Heydrich apparently did not initially conceive a plan to kill all European Jews. His object was to remove them completely from German life, which, he believed, would soon encompass the life of all Europe. He first planned to accomplish this removal by confining Jews to reservations established to contain them, and he next proposed the deportation of all European Jews to Madagascar. When these plans appeared manifestly unfeasible, the only choice left, he believed, was genocide, and, on July 31, 1941, HERMANN GÖRING personally authorized Heydrich to carry out the Final Solution. This led to the WANNSEE CONFERENCE of January 20, 1942, chaired by Heydrich, at which top regime authorities were charged with creating the logistics of genocide.

In addition to a leadership role in the German secret police agencies and as architect of the Final Solution, Heydrich, as of September 1941, served as Reichsprotektor (governor) of Bohemia and Moravia, the former Czechoslovakia. He ruled with an iron hand, making extensive use of terror, torture, and mass executions to "pacify" the Czech population and suppress RESISTANCE MOVEMENTS. On May 27, 1942, two resistance operatives, members of the Free Czech movement, hurled a bomb at Heydrich's car and fired shots at him as he was driven through the streets of Prague. The supremely arrogant Heydrich assumed that his measures of extreme repression had extinguished any and all resistance, and thus he was not accompanied by armed escorts. Severely wounded in the assault, Heydrich died on June 4. This triggered horrific SS reprisals throughout the former Czechoslovakia, including the infamous massacre of Lidice.

Further reading: Barwick, James. *The Hangman's Crusade.* London: Macmillan, 1980; Calic, Edward. *Reinhard Heydrich: The Chilling Story of the Man Who Masterminded the Nazi Death Camps.* New York: Morrow, 1984; MacDonald, C. A. *The Killing of Reinhard Heydrich: The SS "Butcher of Prague."* New York: Da Capo, 1998; Whiting, Charles. *Heydrich: Henchman of Death.* Barnsely, U.K.: Leo Cooper, 1999; Williams, Max. *Reinhard Heydrich: Enigma.* Shropshire, U.K.: Ulric, 2002.

Higashikuni Naruhiko (1887–1990) *Japan's general commander of defense*

Born in Kyoto, the ninth son of Prince Kuni Asahiko and the court lady Terao Utako, Higashikuni Naruhiko was likewise a prince who secured permission from Emperor Meiji to start a new branch of the imperial family. Higashikuni graduated from the Imperial Military Academy in 1908 and the Army War College in 1914. Like other high-ranking members of the Japanese military, Higashikuni also received schooling in the West, at the École Supérieure de Guerre in Paris from 1920 to 1922. He then returned to Japan and rose rapidly through the ranks. As a general officer, he commanded the 5th Infantry Brigade (1930–34) and the 4th Army Division (1934–37). At the outbreak of the SINO-JAPANESE WAR, he took command of the Military Aviation Department (1937–38) and then of the Second Army in China (1938–39).

In 1939, Higashikuni was elevated to the Supreme War Council and, upon Japan's entry into World War II, became commander of the Home Defense Command. In 1944, after the U.S. victory in the BATTLE OF SAIPAN, Higashikuni conspired with a group of fellow nobles and members of the imperial family to remove General TOJO HIDEKI, who had been effectively the military dictator of Japan, from the office of prime minister. This did not, however, alter the course of the war.

Even before Japan formally surrendered, Higashikuni was named the nation's 43rd prime minister on August 17, 1945. He served only to October 9, 1945, at just 54 days, the briefest tenure of any Japanese prime minister. In October 1947, Higashikuni Naruhiko forfeited his title as well as his membership in the imperial family during the U.S. occupation with its many attendant reforms. He turned to a series of merchant enterprises, all of which failed, then became the chief priest of a new religious order, which was quickly banned by U.S. occupation authorities. After this, he became a Buddhist monk and lived in religious retirement to the remarkable age of 102.

Further reading: Bix, Herbert P. *Hirohito and the Making of Modern Japan.* New York: HarperCollins, 2001; Dower, John W. *Embracing Defeat: Japan in the Wake of World War II.* New York: Norton, 2000; Ienaga, Saburo. *The Pacific War, 1931–1945: A Critical Perspective on Japan's Role in World War II.* New York: Random House, 1979.

Himmler, Heinrich (1900–1945)
Adolf Hitler's chief lieutenant in the Third Reich

Heinrich Himmler was born in Munich, the son of a Roman Catholic schoolmaster. Himmler was trained in cadet officer school toward the end of World War I but never saw service. After the armistice, he enrolled in a technical school, from which he received a diploma in agriculture, then went on to work as a fertilizer salesman and as a chicken farmer while also becoming increasingly active politically. He joined several right-wing paramilitary organizations loosely affiliated with the FREIKORPS. As a member of Ernst Röhm's Reichskriegsflagge ("Imperial War Flag"), he was a participant in the "Beer Hall Putsch" of November 1923 and joined the NAZI PARTY (NSDAP) two years later. An early favorite of ADOLF HITLER, Himmler quickly ascended through the party ranks, gaining election as a deputy to the Reichstag in 1930. Even more important, Hitler appointed him Reichsführer (leader) of the SCHUTZSTAFFEL (SS) in 1927, which was at the time Hitler's personal corps of bodyguards. At its inception, the SS was under the control of the STURMABTEILUNG (SA), but Himmler seized the opportunity to expand this elite corps so that it soon rivaled its nominal parent organization. By 1933, SS membership reached 53,000.

By the time Hitler became chancellor of Germany on January 30, 1933, Heinrich Himmler was a very powerful man. The new chancellor named him chief of the Munich police and shortly afterward commander of all German police units outside Prussia. This, combined with his SS leadership, gave Himmler almost absolute police powers throughout Germany. He established DACHAU CONCENTRATION CAMP in March 1933, the first such camp created in the Third Reich.

In April 1934, Himmler further consolidated his control of Germany's policing structure with his appointment as assistant chief of the GESTAPO (Secret State Police) in Prussia. Two years later, he assumed total command of all Germany's police agencies. Before this, however, he saw to the elimination of the only real threat to his power, the SA. It was Himmler who persuaded Hitler that Ernst Röhm and his followers were a danger to the party, and it was Himmler who planned and saw to the execution of the "Night of the Long Knives," the June 30, 1934, purge in which the SA was eliminated. The purge not only gave Hitler final and complete control of the Nazi Party, it left the SS as the only armed branch of the party. Under Himmler, it became second only to the German Army as the most powerful armed force in Germany. Himmler saw to it that the SS obtained absolute police powers, not only in Germany but with the commencement of the war within all the occupied territories as well. The SS also oversaw security, espionage, and counterespionage activities, although in these areas it often conflicted with such agencies as the Abwehr under Admiral WILHELM CANARIS.

Himmler built up the SS in three significant ways. In 1931, he created the SS Race and Settlement Office (SS-Rasse und Siedlungsamt), in which Nazi anti-Semitism was thoroughly institutionalized and most policies of the FINAL SOLUTION initially formulated, as well as other aspects of the racial basis of Nazism. In 1939, Himmler established the WAFFEN SS, a complete army existing parallel to and outside the control of the WEHRMACHT. By the end of World War II, the Waffen SS was 800,000 strong and included troops from occupied countries. An elite force, the Waffen SS was highly effective and fanatically loyal to Himmler and Hitler. Finally, during the INVASION OF THE SOVIET UNION, Hitler delegated Himmler to administer all conquered Soviet territory and to do so with the goal of totally eliminating the Soviet system. To accomplish this, Himmler created the SS Einsatzgruppen ("deployment groups"), which followed close behind the advancing army and saw to the murder of local Soviet political leaders pursuant to Hitler's COMMISSAR ORDER and to the mass murder of Jews.

Heinrich Himmler *(Library of Congress)*

In addition to organizing the SS Einsatzgruppen, Himmler was responsible for perpetrating much of THE HOLOCAUST by establishing CONCENTRATION AND EXTERMINATION CAMPS in German-occupied Poland. These camps were not only the site of genocide, they also were the source of slave labor for the German war machine. The SS charged German war industries a fee for each worker it provided and thus became a profit center for the Third Reich even as it supplied labor for war production.

In 1943, Himmler added the title of minister of the interior and plenipotentiary for reich administration to his other duties. In addition to his continued expansion of the Waffen SS, he consolidated his absolute control of all German intelligence as well as oversight of the armaments industry. Having created a massive slave labor operation, Himmler sought to establish a war industries empire solely controlled by his SS. This brought him into direct conflict with ALBERT SPEER, Hitler's appointed minister for armaments and war production. Himmler plotted, abortively, the assassination of his rival in February 1944.

As the German war effort became increasingly desperate in 1944, Himmler also created and controlled the Volkssturm ("People's Storm Troop"), a conscript home guard army of overage men and underage boys. At the very end of the war, Himmler created the secret Werewolf force, a guerrilla army that would (he hoped) carry on the fight even after the conventional forces had been defeated. Additionally, Himmler assumed personal command of two conventional army groups with disastrous results.

Like Hitler, Himmler descended into profound mental instability as the war became hopeless. During the closing months of the conflict, he was in a state of nervous collapse, and Hitler marginalized him within what little order was left of the Nazi regime. In April 1945, Himmler secretly made overtures through Count Folke Bernadotte of neutral Sweden to offer surrender terms to the Allies, and he also approached the Allies more directly with a proposal that he be permitted to succeed Hitler as head of state and join the western Allies in turning the war *against* the Soviet Union. Himmler also ordered a halt to the mass slaughter in the death camps, apparently as a gesture to appease the Allies. (The order went unheeded.)

Himmler's overtures were rebuffed, but word of them reached Hitler, who summarily stripped Himmler of all his offices and ordered his arrest. This Himmler evaded by disguising himself as a private, and he also hoped in this way to escape capture by the advancing Allies. He was, however, taken prisoner by the western Allies after the German surrender. While in captivity in Lüneburg, Heinrich Himmler killed himself by swallowing a cyanide capsule on May 23, 1945.

Further reading: Breitman, Richard. *The Architect of Genocide: Himmler and the Final Solution.* Danvers,
Mass.: University Press of New England, 1992; Goerman, Robert A. *Himmler's War.* Frederick, Md.: Publish America, 2002; Hale, Christopher. *Himmler's Crusade: The Nazi Expedition to Find the Origins of the Aryan Race.* New York: Wiley, 2003; Mansson, Martin. *Heinrich Himmler: A Photographic Chronicle of Hitler's Reichsführer.* Atglen, Pa.: Schiffer, 2001; Padfield, Peter. *Himmler: Reichsführer-SS.* New York: Sterling, 2001; Shirer, William L. *Rise and Fall of the Third Reich: A History of Nazi Germany.* New York: Simon & Schuster, 1990; Smith, Bradley F. *Heinrich Himmler: A Nazi in the Making, 1900–1926.* Washington, D.C.: Hoover Institution Press, 1971.

Hiranuma Kiichiro (1865–1952) *Japanese statesman and militarist*

Baron Hiranuma Kiichiro was one of Japan's leading right-wing militarists who, in 1924, founded Kokuhonsha, which became a hotbed of the Japanese militarism that would lead first to aggression against China and the SINO-JAPANESE WAR, then, ultimately, to Japan's involvement in World War II. Hiranuma's official government post was minister of justice (1923), but he exerted his greatest influence as head of the Kokuhonsha, which attracted the most powerful military, business, and political figures in the country. This resulted in Hiranuma's elevation in 1926 to the vice presidency of the privy council, the inner circle of Japanese government. It was Hiranuma who drove Japan's withdrawal from the League of Nations as well as its abrogation of the Washington Naval Treaty, which had limited the expansion of the Japanese Imperial Fleet. Hiranuma also encouraged the signing of the ANTI-COMINTERN PACT, immediate precursor to the AXIS (TRIPARTITE) PACT.

In February 1936, an abortive military coup d'état catapulted Hiranuma to the presidency of the privy council, and in 1939, he became prime minister, resigning later that year to protest the GERMAN-SOVIET NON-AGGRESSION PACT. However, he continued to serve as president of the privy council and was named home minister in 1940. In these posts, Hiranuma was unflagging in his advocacy of all-out war, and even after Japan had clearly suffered military defeat, he supported the call of Tojo Hideki to fight to the last Japanese man and woman.

After the surrender of Japan, Hiranuma was arrested and tried in 1946 in the Tokyo War Crimes Trials. Found guilty, he was sentenced to life imprisonment but was released in 1951.

Further reading: Bix, Herbert P. *Hirohito and the Making of Modern Japan.* New York: HarperCollins, 2001; Dower, John W. *Embracing Defeat: Japan in the Wake of World War II.* New York: Norton, 2000; Hendrix, Henry J. *The Roots of Japanese Militarism.* Annapolis, Md.: Naval Postgraduate School, 1994; Ienaga, Saburo. *The Pacific War, 1931–1945: A Critical Perspective on Japan's Role in World War II.* New York: Random House, 1979; Sunoo, Harold Hakwon. *Japanese Militarism, Past and Present.* New York: Nelson-Hall, 1975.

Hirohito (1901–1989) *emperor of Japan*

Hirohito Michinomiya was born at the Aoyama Palace in Tokyo and received an education befitting a future emperor at the Peers' School and at the Crown Prince's Institute. A scholarly young man, Hirohito developed an intense interest in marine biology, a subject on which he became an internationally recognized authority and the author of a number of books in the field. Despite his sheltered upbringing, Hirohito was an urbane figure who became the first Japanese crown prince to travel abroad when he toured Europe in 1921. When he returned to Japan, he was named prince regent because his father, the emperor Taisho, suffering from mental illness, had stepped down from the throne. Hirohito married the princess Nagako Kuni in 1924 and, upon the death of his father, ascended the Chrysanthemum Throne of Imperial Japan on December 25, 1926.

The honorific name conferred on the reign of Hirohito was Shxwa, or "Enlightened Peace." This designation would prove supremely ironic, as Hirohito, head of the Japanese state, would bear personal responsibility for his nation's aggressive actions first against China and then, in World War II, against other subject peoples as well as the Allied

nations. His ultimate responsibility notwithstanding, it is by no means certain just how to gauge Hirohito's actual role in the war. Most historians believe that Hirohito personally opposed going to war with the Allies and the United States in particular, but that his paradoxical position as an emperor of modern Japan, in principle absolute and supreme in his authority but in practice subject to the will of ministers, advisers, and the military, gave him little latitude in preventing the war. Yet even while conceding the precarious position Hirohito occupied, a significant number of historians suggest that Hirohito did, in fact, actively participate in planning for the expansion of the Japanese empire

Emperor Hirohito *(Library of Congress)*

beginning as early as 1931. At the very least, he never acted to oppose the rise of right-wing militarists in the Japanese government, and his silence may (the historians argue) be taken as a token of his tacit approval.

While Hirohito *reigned* before and during World War II, he did not *rule*. Subject to the Meiji Constitution of 1889, his political and administrative prerogatives were limited, and most actual power was delegated to a variety of ministers. This notwithstanding, Hirohito was revered as a god on Earth, and he might well have brought moral pressure to bear in preventing the war. As it was, during the conflict, he made appearances among the troops astride a white horse and exhorted them to render the supreme effort in battle. Perhaps all that can be said for certain about Hirohito and World War II is that he could do little to counter the will of the militarists in the government, but he did not do even what little was available to him, and in his appearances before the troops, he was unambiguously martial.

Hirohito did finally assert himself in August 1945, after the atomic bombings of HIROSHIMA and NAGASAKI. Whereas a substantial contingent of diehard militarists, both in the military and in the government, advocated fighting the war to the finish—that is, to the death of the last Japanese man and woman—Hirohito risked provoking a coup d'état by siding with the ministerial faction that advocated surrender, and he recorded a radio broadcast to the Japanese people announcing Japan's acceptance of the Allied terms. Broadcast on August 15, 1945, it was the first time the emperor's subjects had heard his voice. Whatever role Hirohito had played in bringing about the war, whether by acts of commission or omission, it is indisputable that he was instrumental in ending the war.

In the immediate postwar weeks and months, Hirohito neither sought nor received any guarantee of immunity from prosecution for war crimes. Many in the Allied nations, especially Australia and the United States, believed that he should stand trial. However, the administration of HARRY S. TRUMAN favored permitting Hirohito to remain on the throne, albeit subject to the authority of Supreme Allied Commander General DOUGLAS MACARTHUR, who was head of the government of military occupation. Hirohito, apparently anxious only to see to the welfare of his people, closely cooperated with MacArthur and thereby promoted the generally harmonious and highly effective administration of the occupation government. In a radio broadcast on January 1, 1946, Hirohito sought to pave the way for the institution of true democracy in Japan by explicitly repudiating the traditional divine status of Japan's emperors. This made it possible for the government and the people to accept a new constitution, drafted chiefly by MacArthur and other U.S. occupation officials, which made Japan a constitutional monarchy on the Western model.

If Hirohito had had great titular power but little actual power before and during the war, he now relinquished even the appearance of absolute authority by acknowledging that sovereignty lay not with the emperor but with the democratic will of the people. Nor did Hirohito acknowledge this merely in the letter of the new law. He sought to promote a genuinely democratic spirit by making himself publicly accessible to an unprecedented degree and was frequently seen and heard in public. Even more astoundingly, his oldest son, Crown Prince Akihito, married a commoner, Shoda Michiko, in 1959, ending a 1,500-year tradition of the insular imperial family. In 1971, Hirohito became the first reigning Japanese emperor to travel abroad when he made a tour of Europe. Four years later, he made a state visit to the United States. The imperial succession was preserved, however, as Akihito ascended the throne upon the death of his father in 1989.

Further reading: Behr, Edward. *Hirohito: Behind the Myth.* New York: Vintage, 1990; Bix, Herbert P. *Hirohito and the Making of Modern Japan.* New York: HarperCollins, 2001; Gluck, Carol, and Stephen Graubard. *Showa: The Japan of Hirohito.* New York: Norton, 1993; Hoyt, Edwin P. *Hirohito.* New York: Praeger, 1992; Keene, Donald. *Emperor of Japan.* New York: Columbia University Press, 2002; Large, Stephen S. *Emperor Hirohito* *and Showa Japan: A Political Biography.* New York and London: Routledge, 1997; Manning, Paul. *Hirohito: The War Years.* New York: Bantam, 1989; Osanaga, Kanroji. *Hirohito: An Intimate Portrait of the Japanese Emperor.* New York: HarperCollins, 1976.

Hiroshima, atomic bombing of

Hiroshima, a Japanese city and manufacturing center of some 350,000 people about 500 miles from Tokyo, was the target of the first militarily operational atomic bomb. A product of the vast MANHATTAN PROJECT, the bomb, dubbed Little Boy, had been delivered to an airfield on the captured Pacific island of Tinian by the cruiser *Indianapolis.* The bomb was loaded aboard a B-29 that had been specially modified to accommodate the nearly 8,000-ton, 9-foot-9-inch device. Its explosive yield, derived from the implosion of a uranium-235 core, was 12.5 kilotons, that is, the equivalent of 12.5 kilotons of conventional TNT. Of course, the explosion is only one aspect of the lethality of an atomic weapon. The bomb yielded tremendous heat and radioactivity, including lethal radioactive contamination in the form of fallout.

Hiroshima had been selected by a U.S. target committee because it had not yet been bombed by U.S. Army Air Forces. The city's pristine condition would not only allow the Allies to assess the effect of the bomb, it would also vividly demonstrate that effect to the Japanese. The bomb was dropped from the *Enola Gay,* the B-29 piloted by Colonel PAUL TIBBETS, at 8:15 (local time) on the morning of August 6, 1945. Deployed by parachute, it was detonated (by design) at 1,885 feet above ground level in order to achieve the maximum effect of the blast. All wooden buildings within a 1.2-mile radius of the point of detonation (the hypocenter) were destroyed. Reinforced concrete structures were destroyed within 1,625 feet of the hypocenter. A total area of 5 square miles was largely incinerated, and 62.9 percent of the city's 76,000 buildings were entirely destroyed by blast or fire. A mere 8 percent escaped substantial damage. The immediate death toll among those located within three-quarters of a mile of the hypocenter was 50 percent. The one-

year death rate, through August 10, 1946, from the Hiroshima blast was 118,661. Another 30,524 persons were considered severely injured, and 48,606 were considered slightly injured. Nearly 4,000 citizens of Hiroshima went missing and have never been accounted for. Of the approximately 350,000 persons believed to have been in Hiroshima at the time, 118,613 were confirmed uninjured through August 10, 1946. In addition to the civilian deaths, it is believed that about 20,000 military personnel died as a direct result of the bombing.

The longer-term effects of radiation exposure included elevated rates of genetic and chromosome damage and birth defects (including especially stunted growth and mental retardation) of some children born to parents who survived the blast. Surprisingly, greatly increased rates of cancer, anticipated as a result of the attack, did not materialize.

The bombing of Hiroshima did not elicit an immediate offer of surrender from the Japanese, and, on August 9, 1945, a second B-29, *Bock's Car,* dropped a second bomb, "Fat Man," against NAGASAKI.

Further reading: Goldstein, Donald K., J. Michael Wenger, and Katherine V. Dillon. *Rain of Ruin: A Photographic History of Hiroshima and Nagasaki.* Dulles, Va.: Potomac Books, 1999; Hersey, John. *Hiroshima.* New York: Vintage, 1989; Hogan, Michael J., ed. *Hiroshima in History and Memory.* New York and Cambridge: Cambridge University Press, 1996; Takaki, Ronald. *Hiroshima: Why America Dropped the Atomic Bomb.* Boston: Back Bay Books, 1996.

Hitler, Adolf (1889–1945) *founder of Nazism and dictator of Germany*

Adolf Hitler's biographers typically remark on the utterly undistinguished background of this most infamous of modern dictators. He was born on April 20, 1889, in Braunau am Inn, Austria, but was raised mainly in Linz, the son of a minor customs official. Alois Hitler, his father, was of illegitimate birth and used his mother's maiden name, Schickelgruber, until 1876, when he took the name Hitler. During World War II, the Allied mass media

Adolf Hitler *(Library of Congress)*

its only hint of direction provided by a growing racial hatred focused primarily on Jews. Drawing on a long-standing central European heritage of anti-Semitism and on his own understanding of German-Nordic mythology (heightened by a passion for the powerfully mythologizing music of Richard Wagner), Hitler formulated a world view in which Jews were seen as a political and even genetic threat to the Germanic—or "Aryan"—race.

In 1913, Hitler moved from Vienna, Austria, to Munich, Germany, apparently to avoid conscription into the Austrian Army. Despite this effort, he was recalled to Austria in February 1914 for examination for military service, only to be rejected as unfit, his years of financial struggle having rendered him underweight and physically frail. Nevertheless, the outbreak of World War I in August 1914 suddenly rejuvenated Hitler, who rushed to enlist in the 16th Bavarian Reserve Infantry (List) Regiment. Service in the war transformed the drifter into a rigid and militaristic nationalist. Although he never advanced beyond the rank of corporal, his service in combat was distinguished. He volunteered for the particularly hazardous duty of front-lines runner (messenger) and was decorated four times, receiving the Iron Cross 1st Class on August 4, 1918, a rare honor for an enlisted man. Hitler was seriously wounded in October 1916, and he was gassed toward the end of the war. Although he did not advance into the officer corps, Hitler decided to remain with his regiment after the armistice, through April 1920. In the postwar army, he served as a uniformed political agent and joined the German Workers' Party in Munich in September 1919. Soon, his political ambitions eclipsed his military interests, and, beginning in April 1920, he went to work full time in the propaganda section of the German Workers' Party. It was a desperate and heady time for German politics. The TREATY OF VERSAILLES, which ended World War I, brought economic ruin and collective national humiliation. The chaos and hard times of postwar Germany made the nation ripe for a Communist revolution, which proved abortive. Hitler seized on the unrest around him and, by August 1920, was

frequently made derisive use of *Schickelgruber* in place of the name *Hitler*. Alois Hitler was, by all accounts, a dense and brutal father who criticized what he considered his son's dreamy and effeminate nature. An indifferent student, young Adolf Hitler left secondary school in 1905 without obtaining a graduation certificate. His ambition was to become an artist, but his drawings and watercolors, while competent, were passionless and unoriginal. They twice failed to gain him admission to the Academy of Fine Arts in Vienna, and his being thwarted in this way seems deeply to have hurt him. Nevertheless, after the death of his mother, who, in contrast to his father, had doted on him and whom he both idolized and idealized, Hitler went to Vienna, hoping, even without an academy education, to make a name for himself as an artist. He managed from 1907 to 1913 to eke out a living by painting advertisements, postcards, and the like, but his existence was marked by drift, instrumental in transforming the German Workers' Party into the Nazionalsozialistische Deutsche Arbeiterpartei, or NAZI PARTY (NSDAP). Hitler forged an alliance with a former army staff officer and FREIKORPS activist, Ernst Röhm, which gained him sufficient support to be elected president of the Nazi Party in July 1921.

Hitler proved to be a dynamic political agitator and accomplished street-corner orator. He identified Germany's problem as the Treaty of Versailles and Germany's enemies as the Allied nations that had forced the unjust and disgraceful treaty on Germany, the German democratic leaders who had accepted the treaty, the Communists, and, most of all, the Jews (whom he often identified with the Communists). With an inflated sense of his own influence, Hitler, on November 8–9, 1923, mistakenly decided that Bavaria (and, ultimately, all of Germany) was ripe for his revolution. He instigated and led the Munich "Beer Hall Putsch," an attempt at a coup d'état against the Bavarian government. Premature, the uprising was quickly quashed, and Hitler was arrested, tried, and convicted of treason. Unwilling to make a martyr of Hitler, authorities handed down a light sentence of five years in quite comfortable accommodations at Landesberg Prison, near Munich. Here he wrote his political memoir-manifesto, MEIN KAMPF (My Struggle), a crude and long-winded but effective work in which he expressed the political philosophy of Nazism and proclaimed his eternal opposition to Jews, Communists, liberals, and exploitive capitalists the world over. In Mein Kampf, Hitler sought to bring about the rebirth of German racial purity and exulted in the unstoppable national will. Hitler envisioned a Germany risen, phoenixlike, to become the dominant power in the world, a Germany that would successfully claim LEBENSRAUM—"living space"—in central Europe and Russia. Adolf Hitler was released from prison, having completed Mein Kampf and having served only nine months of his sentence. He set about consolidating his grip on the party and increasing its numbers. It was during this period that he was joined by the men who would lead Germany into a policy of atrocity and total war: World War I air ace HERMANN

GÖRING, propaganda master JOSEPH GOEBBELS, political terrorist HEINRICH HIMMLER, and anti-Semitic journalist JULIUS STREICHER. With the onset of a worldwide economic depression in 1929, the political climate ripened further for the growth of the Nazi Party, and Hitler forged an alliance with the Nationalist Party headed by industrialist Alfred Hugenberg. The Nazis now increased their number of Reichstag seats from 12 to 107, thereby becoming the second largest party in Germany. To promote and ensure the rise of his party, Hitler and Röhm developed the STURMABETEILUNG (SA), or Brownshirts, the party's thuggish paramilitary arm, which quite literally beat down the opposition in the streets of Germany.

In 1932, Hitler ran against World War I hero Paul von Hindenburg for the presidency of the German republic. Although Hitler came in second, his party polled 37 percent of the vote and gained a total of 230 Reichstag seats, making it the largest single party represented. Hindenburg clearly detested Hitler, but he could hardly ignore him, and on January 30, 1933, he appointed him Reichskanzler (reich chancellor), effectively Germany's prime minister. At last, Hitler had a position of great legitimate power, and he rapidly overshadowed the old and ailing Hindenburg. When fire destroyed the Reichstag on February 27, 1933, an arson the Nazis had covertly arranged, Hitler gained a pretext for legally abolishing the Communist Party and rounding up for imprisonment its principal leaders. This was followed, on March 23, 1933, by the Enabling Act, which granted him four years of unalloyed dictatorial powers as Hindenburg receded into the status of figurehead.

Pursuant to the Enabling Act, Hitler set about dismantling all German parties, save for the Nazis. He purged Jews from all government institutions and brought all government offices under the direct control of the party. Then he turned to the ranks of his own party. On June 30, 1934, during the Night of the Long Knives, Hitler directed the round-up and, ultimately, the murder of Ernst Röhm and hundreds of other SA members and Nazis who posed a threat to his absolute domination of the party. In August, Hindenburg died, leaving Hitler not merely to assume the functions of the presidency, but to replace the title and concept of *president* with that of *Führer,* supreme leader, of the new government, the Third Reich.

Hitler replaced the SA with the SCHUTZSTAFFEL (SS), the Blackshirts, under the leadership of Himmler, who was subordinate to no one but Hitler alone. The SS and the new secret police, the GESTAPO, created a system of concentration camps to which, at first, political enemies were consigned. Soon, this system developed into a vast complex of CONCENTRATION AND EXTERMINATION CAMPS, which would become the places of confinement and murder of some of the 6 million Jews killed in THE HOLOCAUST. Racial persecution, purging, and, ultimately, genocide were key aspects of Hitler's vision for Germany, and, at his behest, in 1935, Nazi-affiliated German jurists created the NUREMBERG LAWS, which deprived Jews of citizenship and authorized the policy of persecution that eventuated in the FINAL SOLUTION.

Throughout his rise and the process of consolidating his power, Hitler combined outright terror and police state tactics with a highly sophisticated program of propaganda orchestrated by minister of propaganda Joseph Goebbels. Hitler also presided over the general economic recovery of depression-era Germany by ramping up industrial production in order to rearm the nation in defiance of the Treaty of Versailles. Hitler created a Luftwaffe (air force) under Göring, remilitarized the Rhineland (in 1936), and built up the army as well as the navy. He gambled that the western democracies, Britain and France, war weary and pacifistic, would do nothing to oppose his violation of the Versailles terms. His gamble paid off even beyond his expectations.

During the period of his earliest rise to power within the fledgling Nazi Party and through his rise in German government, Hitler turned an admiring eye on BENITO MUSSOLINI, since 1922 the fascist dictator of Italy. In 1936, Hitler concluded with Italy and with militaristic Japan the ANTI-COMINTERN PACT, which foreshadowed the 1939 PACT OF STEEL between Hitler and Mussolini and the 1940 AXIS (TRIPARTITE) PACT among Germany, Italy,

and Japan. Having met no resistance from the democracies after remilitarizing the Rhineland, Hitler took the next step in his aggressive expansion of Germany in March 1938 when he invaded and annexed Austria in the ANSCHLUSS. After this, he persuaded Great Britain's prime minister, NEVILLE CHAMBERLAIN, to acquiesce in German annexation of the Czech SUDETENLAND, followed by the takeover of virtually all Czechoslovakia.

Chamberlain persuaded his French counterparts that allowing Hitler to gobble up Czechoslovakia, a nation both Britain and France were bound by treaty to defend, would "appease" German expansionism. Of course, appeasement only whetted the führer's appetite for more. With an eye on Poland, he shocked the world by concluding the GERMAN-SOVIET NON-AGGRESSION PACT with his ideological antithesis, Soviet dictator JOSEPH STALIN, on August 23, 1939. The very next month, on September 1, taking as pretext a trumped-up Polish "attack" orchestrated by propaganda minister Goebbels, Hitler invaded Poland and started World War II.

The INVASION OF POLAND and the BATTLE OF FRANCE put Hitler in control of most of the European continent. Of the western democracies, only Great Britain held out against him, and, at this point, Hitler, always eager to assert what he considered his military genius, blundered. First, he issued orders that allowed the British Expeditionary Force to escape destruction in France (DUNKIRK EVACUATION), then, instead of preparing for an invasion of Great Britain, Hitler misdirected the Luftwaffe in attacks on English cities, sparing the British Royal Air Force, which, during July–October 1940, prevailed in the BATTLE OF BRITAIN, thereby denying Hitler air supremacy in British skies and forcing him to abandon OPERATION SEALION, his plan to invade the British Isles. Nevertheless, during the rest of 1940 and into 1941, Hitler's armies came to control territory from North Africa to the Arctic and from France to central Europe. In April 1941, Hitler's armies invaded the Balkans, occupying Yugoslavia and Greece, and on June 22, 1941, Hitler summarily abrogated his nonaggression pact with Stalin with the INVASION OF THE SOVIET UNION. As in the west, BLITZKRIEG tactics made rapid and devastating gains that were accompanied by barbarities and atrocities on a massive scale, including those pursuant to the Final Solution and the COMMISSAR ORDER, whereby local Soviet leaders were massacred as they were encountered. However, the Russian winter and the resistance of the Russian people and the Red Army, dogged and heroic, slowed and then stopped Hitler's forces, first at the BATTLE OF MOSCOW in December 1941, then, during the winter of 1942–43, at the BATTLE OF STALINGRAD. It was at Stalingrad that the tide of war on the eastern front turned, devastatingly, against the Germans.

In the meantime, the BATTLE OF PEARL HARBOR on December 7, 1941, brought the United States into World War II. This was a contingency for which Hitler had never really planned, although, with characteristic arrogance, he did not hesitate to declare war against the United States on December 11, 1941. It would take some time for the military forces of the United States to have an effect on Germany, but by 1943, the tide had turned not only in Russia, but elsewhere. Germany had lost North Africa, and Mussolini had been deposed after the Allied invasion of Italy. American and British bombers were pummeling German cities by day and by night. The situation reached its crisis for Germany with the NORMANDY LANDINGS (D-DAY) on June 6, 1944. Now Hitler was menaced from the east, south, and west.

The Allied invasion of France drove Hitler to make increasingly desperate and irrational demands of his military, and a significant cadre in the German officer corps turned against the führer. In the best known of no fewer than 17 attempts on Hitler's life, KLAUS VON STAUFFENBERG, a highly decorated officer who had suffered grievous wounds, masterminded a plot to assassinate Hitler at his military headquarters known as Wolf's Lair. On July 20, 1944, a bomb planted in the building exploded as scheduled, but Hitler, remarkably, survived, although slightly injured and more seriously affected emotionally. The July 20 Plot moved Hitler to make a general purge, and some 5,000 officers and others were arrested, many of them executed.

The war, in any real military sense, had been lost, but from December 16, 1944, to January 1945,

Hitler committed his last reserves to a final offensive, the BATTLE OF THE ARDENNES (BATTLE OF THE BULGE). His hope was to divide the advancing Allied forces and retake what was now a key Allied port and supply depot at Amsterdam. The Ardennes offensive caught the Allies completely by surprise and precipitated a harrowing struggle, which nevertheless ended in a crushing defeat for the Germans. With the last credible German resistance destroyed, the Allies advanced on the German heartland. As the Soviet Red Army began the BATTLE OF BERLIN, Hitler retreated to the Führerbunker, a hardened underground command shelter beneath the streets of the German capital. From here, he attempted to direct a suicidal resistance to the last German man and woman. His intention, it seemed clear, was to see Germany destroyed with him.

On April 29, 1945, as the Battle of Berlin drew rapidly to an end, Hitler married his mistress, Eva Braun, who occupied the bunker with him. In his last will and testament, Hitler appointed Admiral KARL DÖNITZ to succeed him as head of state, and, on April 30, Hitler and his bride committed suicide, Eva Braun by taking cyanide, Hitler, apparently, by a combination of cyanide and gunshot. Dönitz hastily concluded the surrender of Germany and what Adolf Hitler had frequently called the "Thousand-Year Reich."

Further reading: Bullock, Alan. *Hitler and Stalin: Parallel Lives.* New York: Vintage, 1993; Giblin, James Cross. *The Life and Death of Adolf Hitler.* New York: Clarion Books, 2002; Hitler, Adolf. *Mein Kampf.* New York: Mariner Books, 1998; Kershaw, Ian. *Hitler, 1889–1936: Hubris.* New York: Norton, 1999; Rosenbaum, Ron. *Explaining Hitler: The Search for the Origins of His Evil.* New York: Perennial, 1999; Toland, John: *Adolf Hitler: The Definitive Biography.* New York: Anchor, 1991; Victor, George. *Hitler: The Pathology of Evil.* Dulles, Va.: Potomac Books, 1999.

Hitler Youth

The Hitlerjugend, Hitler Youth, was founded in 1922 as part of the NAZI PARTY (NSDAP) movement, a kind of party auxiliary for youths aged 14 to 18. Beginning in 1929, the Hitler Youth also came to include an organization for girls, aged 14 to 18, called the League of German Maidens (Bund deutscher Mädel). In 1931, the age range of the Hitler Youth movement was extended, downward through the German Young People (Deutsches Jungvolk), for boys between 10 and 14, and the Young Maidens (Jungmädelbund) for girls of the same ages. For young women, 18 to 21, the range was extended upward through an organization called Faith and Beauty (Glaube und Schönheit). At 18, young men customarily left the Hitler Youth for six months with the State Labor Service, followed by service in the German military. By the time of World War II, the Hitler Youth had become closely associated with the Schutzstaffel (SS), whose combat arm, the Waffen-SS, had a special Hitler Youth (Hitlerjugend) Division.

Hitler Youth was a means of indoctrinating German youths into the Nazi German way of life generally and, more particularly, to prepare them for military service. The organization was regarded as central to the Nazi program and to German patriotism. It was seen as so indispensable to the continuation of the Nazi regime that branches of the Hitler Youth were quickly established in all countries occupied by Germany during World War II. Additionally, Hitler Youth served as a means of toughening up boys and young men for military service. The organization came under the directorship of Baldur von Schirach (1907–74) in 1931 and grew during this period to a membership of 7.7 million by 1939. Hitler Youth became an official organization of the state in 1933, and membership became compulsory in 1940. In that year, Artur Axmann (1913–1996) was appointed to replace Schirach, who became governor of Vienna.

Under Axmann, the Hitler Youth became the dominant force in German schools. Children were made members of a Hitler Youth Patrol Service (*Streifendienst*), a junior version of the security police. They were encouraged to spy on adults, including their parents, and to report any apparent subversive or unorthodox activity they might detect. At the age of 12, boys were trained in the use of military rifles and even machine guns. At 14, they attended a month of military training camp.

Beginning in 1943, 15- to 17-year-old Hitler Youths were pressed into service manning antiaircraft artillery defenses throughout Germany. They also participated in civil defense work, including fire fighting and even some police functions. They were encouraged to capture or kill shot-down Allied airmen who parachuted into Germany.

As World War II in Europe drew to a close and Adolf Hitler inducted overage men and underage boys into service in the Volkssturm (home guard), Hitler Youth members were committed to front-line combat, especially in the Battle of Berlin. Very few survived. In the most desperate action of all, Heinrich Himmler recruited Hitler Youth for membership in the Werewolves, a proposed (but never activated) guerrilla organization that was to carry on the fight even after the surrender of Germany.

Further reading: Kater, Michael. *Hitler Youth.* Cambridge, Mass.: Harvard University Press, 2004; Koch, H. W. *The Hitler Youth.* New York: Cooper Square, 2000; Metelmann, Henry. *A Hitler Youth: Growing Up in Germany in the 1930s.* London: Spellmount Publishers, 2004; Rempel, Gerhard. *Hitler's Children: The Hitler Youth and the SS.* Chapel Hill: University of North Carolina Press, 1991.

Hoare, Samuel (1880–1959) *British foreign secretary who proposed an ignominious settlement of Italian claims in Ethiopia*

The elder son of Sir Samuel Hoare, Hoare was educated at Harrow and Oxford and entered Parliament for Chelsea in 1910. He served as an officer during World War I and, after the war, from 1922 to 1929 (except for a brief interval of Labour Party rule), was minister of air. Hoare was instrumental in building the Royal Air Force (RAF).

In 1931, Hoare became secretary of state for India, serving until 1935, when on June 7, he became foreign secretary. In response to Benito Mussolini's invasion of Ethiopia, Hoare developed with Pierre Laval of France the Hoare-Laval Plan for the partition of Ethiopian territory

between Italy and Ethiopia. Widely seen as an ignominious surrender both to aggression and to fascism, the Hoare-Laval proposal drew such criticism
that Samuel Hoare stepped down as foreign secretary on December 18, 1935.

Hoare returned to government in June of the
following year as first lord of the admiralty. With
the ascension of NEVILLE CHAMBERLAIN as prime
minister, Hoare was appointed home secretary in
May 1937. Typifying the faction of Chamberlain's
government that favored an APPEASEMENT POLICY
toward ADOLF HITLER's Germany, Hoare was both
instrumental in formulating the MUNICH CONFER-
ENCE AND PACT and in defending it. When WIN-
STON CHURCHILL replaced Chamberlain as prime
minister in 1940, Hoare's role in the inner circle of
government as well as in Parliament ended. He was
appointed wartime ambassador to Spain and
served until 1944, when, as viscount Templewood,
he retired from public life and turned to writing.

Further reading: Cross, J. A. *Sir Samuel Hoare: A Political Biography.* London: Jonathan Cape, 1977; Hoare,
Samuel. *Nine Troubled Years.* Westport, Conn.: Greenwood Press, 1976.

Ho Chi Minh (1890–1969) *leader of Vietnamese anti-Japanese guerrilla resistance in World War II*

Most Americans know Ho Chi Minh as the first
president of the Democratic Republic of Vietnam
(North Vietnam) and America's opponent during
the Vietnam War. However, during World War II,
this popular Vietnamese political figure collaborated with the U.S. OFFICE OF STRATEGIC SERVICES
(OSS) in guerrilla operations against the Japanese
occupiers of Vietnam.

Ho Chi Minh was born Nguyen That Thanh
(and was also called Nguyen Al Quoc) in the village
of Kim Lien, where his father was an impoverished
scholar. Raised in poverty, Ho was educated at the
grammar school in the ancient city of Hue and
went to work for a time as a schoolmaster before he
enrolled at a technical institute in Saigon. He left
Vietnam (then called French Indochina) in 1911 to
work as a cook, first on a French ocean liner and
then at a London hotel. With the end of World War
I, he moved to France, where he became a socialist
and a Vietnamese nationalist. During the 1919
Paris Peace Conference ending World War I, he
petitioned for civil rights in French Indochina, and
when he was rebuffed, he became sufficiently radicalized to found the French Communist Party. He
traveled to the Soviet Union to study revolutionary
methods and joined the Comintern, the Moscow-
based organization dedicated to the dissemination
of communism worldwide. Ho was assigned to do
no less than bring communism to East Asia. In
1930, he founded the Indochinese Communist
Party and lived for the rest of the decade in the
Soviet Union and China.

With the outbreak of World War II, Ho Chi
Minh returned to Vietnam, where, in 1941, he
organized the Communist-controlled League for
the Independence of Vietnam, or Viet Minh, which
became the focus of the resistance movement
against Japanese occupation. During the war,
despite a period of imprisonment by the anti-
Communist Nationalist Chinese in 1942–43 (during which he adopted "Ho Chi Minh"—He Who
Enlightens—as his name), Ho formed a relationship with the OSS, which helped him to develop a
Vietnamese guerilla movement to fight the Japanese. After the war, this very network would become
the core of Communist resistance, first to the
return of French colonial domination and then to
American efforts to overthrow the North Vietnamese regime during the Vietnam War.

On September 2, 1945, after the Japanese surrender in World War II, Ho Chi Minh proclaimed
the independence of the Democratic Republic of
Vietnam and became its first president. For the
next quarter century, he served as president of a
divided, embattled people. Ho led the Viet Minh in
eight years of guerrilla warfare against French colonial forces from 1946 to 1954. With his top general,
Vo Nguyen Giap, he decisively defeated the French
at Dien Bien Phu in 1954, then turned to 15 years
of battle against the anti-Communist South Vietnamese regime. Beginning about 1959, the United
States became involved in this struggle, first in a

military advisory capacity and, eventually, as a major combatant. By 1969, about 500,000 U.S. troops were fighting in Southeast Asia.

Ho Chi Minh did not live to see the withdrawal of American forces from Vietnam and the nation's unification under a Communist government. Indeed, his active role in the war against the south decreased beginning in 1959 as his health declined.

Further reading: Druiker, William J. *Ho Chi Minh: A Life.* New York: Theia, 2001; Ho Chi Minh. *Selected Writings 1920–1969.* Honolulu: University Press of the Pacific, 2001; Lacouture, Jean. *Ho Chi Minh: A Political Biography.* New York: Random House, 1968.

Hodge, John (1893–1963) *U.S. general*

John Hodge was instrumental in the GUADALCANAL CAMPAIGN, the NEW GEORGIA CAMPAIGN, the BOUGAINVILLE CAMPAIGN, the BATTLE OF LEYTE, and the OKINAWA CAMPAIGN. Hodge was born in Golconda, Illinois, and was educated at Southern Illinois Teachers College (now Southern Illinois University) and the University of Illinois before U.S. entry into World War I prompted him to enroll in a reserve officer's training program at Fort Sheridan, Illinois, in 1917. He emerged from the program by the end of the year with a commission as a second lieutenant and served in France during the war and in Luxembourg during the occupation. Promoted to captain in 1920, Hodge was an instructor in military science at Mississippi State University from 1921 to 1925. He graduated from the Infantry School at Fort Benning, Georgia, in 1926 and spent the next three years in Hawaii. In 1934, Hodge graduated from the Command and General Staff School, then went on to the Army War College, from which he graduated in 1935. Next, he took the entire course offered by the Air Corps Tactical School and, on graduation in 1936, was attached to the general staff as a major.

Hodge was promoted to lieutenant colonel in 1940 and joined the staff of VII Corps at the beginning of 1941. In December, he was promoted to temporary colonel and became chief of staff of VII

Corps. Promoted to brigadier general, he was made deputy commander of the 25th Infantry Division in June 1942 and first saw combat in the closing phases of the Guadalcanal Campaign.

In April 1943, Hodge was promoted to major general and, the next month, was assigned to command the Americal Division. After a brief interval reorganizing U.S. forces on New Georgia during July and August 1943, Hodge returned to the Americal Division, which he led in amphibious operations on Bougainville during December.

Transferred to the Southwest Pacific in April 1944, Hodge commanded XXIV Corps of Sixth Army, which he led in a landing on Leyte at Dulag on December 10. Hodge captured Ormoc and Limon on Leyte and saw the fighting through to the end. He was then sent to Okinawa, fighting there from April 1945 to June 21, the culmination of the campaign. As the Okinawa Campaign closed, Hodge was promoted to lieutenant general and, with the Japanese surrender, was dispatched to Korea to command U.S. occupying forces. Hodge left Korea in 1948, after the republic was formed. He returned to the United States to command V Corps at Fort Bragg, North Carolina, then, in June 1950, was named to command Third Army at Fort McPherson, Georgia. In May 1952, Hodge was named chief of Army Field Forces and, in July, promoted to general. He retired the following year.

Further reading: Frank, Richard B. *Guadalcanal: The Definitive Account of the Landmark Battle.* New York: Penguin, 1992; Gailey, Harry A. *Bougainville, 1943–1945: The Forgotten Campaign.* Lexington: University Press of Kentucky, 2003; Griffith, Samuel B. II. *The Battle for Guadalcanal.* Champaign: University of Illinois Press, 2000; McGee, William L. *The Solomons Campaigns, 1942–1943: From Guadalcanal to Bougainville—Pacific War Turning Point.* St, Helena, Calif.: BMC Publications, 2001.

Hodges, Courtney (1887–1966) *U.S. general*

Courtney Hodges commanded First Army in Europe and earned a reputation as a solid, if conservative and conventional, field commander. He was born in Perry, Georgia, and gained admission to West Point in 1904. He fared poorly in academics and decided to withdraw in 1905. Determined to serve in the U.S. Army, he enlisted in 1906 as a private and earned his commission three years later. Hodges served on several stateside posts and in the Philippines. He was part of the punitive expedition General John J. Pershing led against the Mexican social bandit Pancho Villa in 1916–17, then, as a major, was sent to France during World War I. Hodges fought with the 6th Infantry Regiment at Saint-Mihiel and at the Meuse-Argonne, then served with the occupation forces after the armistice.

In 1920, Hodges returned to the United States and taught at the institution from which he had dropped out, West Point, until 1924. After graduating from Command and General Staff School in 1925, Hodges taught at the Infantry School during 1925–26 and at the Air Corps Tactical School from 1926 to 1929. From 1929 to 1933, he was a member of the Infantry Board at Fort Benning, then graduated from the Army War College in 1934.

Hodges was posted to Washington state and the Philippines during 1934–38 and was promoted to brigadier general in April 1940. In October of that year, he was named to command the Infantry School at Fort Benning. In May 1941, he was promoted to major general and assigned as chief of infantry in Washington, D.C. When that post was abolished in the reorganization of the army on March 9, 1942, Hodges was assigned to create the Training and School Command at Birmingham, Alabama. In May, he was assigned command of X Corps, and, after promotion to lieutenant general in February 1943, he was named commander of the Southern Defense Command, which encompassed Third Army.

Hodges led Third Army to England in January 1944, then, relinquishing the Third Army to Lieutenant General GEORGE S. PATTON, JR., became deputy commander of First Army, serving under OMAR BRADLEY. With Bradley's subsequent assignment to command Twelfth Army Group, Hodges assumed command of First Army, which he led across northern France during August and September 1944. His troops were the first U.S. troops to enter Paris and, in September, the first to cross the SIEGFRIED LINE. In November, Hodges was in command during the Battle of Hürtgen Forest. After this bitter struggle, he found himself the chief target of the German offensive in the BATTLE OF THE ARDENNES (BATTLE OF THE BULGE) during December 1944–January 1945. After the Ardennes offensive was crushed, Hodges led his First Army across the Rhine at REMAGEN BRIDGE on March 7, 1945, and his soldiers were the first to link up with Soviet Red Army units that had advanced from the east.

In April, Hodges was promoted to general and began preparations to lead First Army to the Pacific theater, where it was to form part of the force that would invade the Japanese home islands. The surrender of Japan obviated this, and Hodges returned to the United States, where he commanded First Army at Fort Bragg, North Carolina, then at Governor's Island, New York. He retired from the army in March 1949.

Further reading: Astor, Gerald. *A Blood-Dimmed Tide: The Battle of the Bulge by the Men Who Fought It.* New York: Dell, 1998. Hechler, Ken. *The Bridge at Remagen: The Amazing Story of March 7, 1945—The Day the Rhine River Was Crossed.* New York: Ballantine, 1978; MacDonald, Charles B. *A Time for Trumpets: The Untold Story of the Battle of the Bulge.* Harper Perennial, 1997. Toland, John. *Battle: The Story of the Bulge.* Lincoln: University of Nebraska Press, 1999.

Hoepner, Erich (1886–1944) *German general who plotted against Adolf Hitler*

Born in Frankfurt, Germany, Erich Hoepner joined the German Army, fought in World War I, then joined the FREIKORPS after the war. He subsequently rejoined the regular army, attaining the rank of major general by 1938. As commander of the 1st Light Division, he participated in the invasion of CZECHOSLOVAKIA and the INVASION OF POLAND, having succeeded HEINZ GUDERIAN as head of the 16th Army Corps in March 1939. In 1940, Hoepner participated in the BATTLE OF FRANCE, then took part in the INVASION OF THE SOVIET UNION as commander of the Fourth Panzer Army. He led his troops against Leningrad (St. Petersburg) before being transferred to Army Group Center, where he fought under GUNTHER VON KLUGE in the BATTLE OF MOSCOW.

Hoepner advanced to within 20 miles north of Moscow by December 5, 1941, but met with a fierce counterattack by the Red Army. Under this onslaught, he retreated to preserve his army, despite ADOLF HITLER's standing order forbidding retreat. The führer relieved Hoepner of command, eliciting an unusual series of protests from senior commanders throughout the army. While this did not persuade Hitler to reinstate Hoepner, he was permitted to retire with full pension rights. Not mollified by this gesture, Hoepner conspired in 1944 with KLAUS VON STAUFFENBERG in the "July 20 Plot" to assassinate Hitler. When the plot miscarried, Hoepner was among some 5,000 conspirators who were arrested. Subjected like many others to a public show trial, he was convicted of treason and hanged at Ploetzwnsee Prison on August 8, 1944.

Further reading: Dunn, Walter S. *Heroes or Traitors: The German Replacement Army, the July Plot, and Adolf Hitler.* New York: Praeger, 2003; Fitzgibbon, Constantine. *To Kill Hitler: The Officers' Plot July 1944.* London: SPA Books, 1994.

Hollandia, Battle of

Hollandia was the colonial administrative center of Dutch New Guinea's northern coast. The Japanese took possession of it in April 1942 and set up a naval and air base. General DOUGLAS MACARTHUR saw Hollandia as the first obstacle to be overcome in his campaign to retake the Philippines. He deployed elements of the "Alamo Force," the U.S. 24th, 32nd, and 41st Infantry Divisions under Lieutenant General ROBERT LAWRENCE EICHELBERGER to retake Hollandia. Acting on ULTRA intelligence, MacArthur was able to prepare the

way for Eichelberger's landings at Hollandia and Aitape (125 miles to the southeast) on April 22, 1944, by thoroughly destroying Japanese air power in the region. By the time the Fifth U.S. Air Force under Lieutenant General GEORGE KENNY had completed its mission, only 25 undamaged aircraft were left to the Japanese. Eichelberger's landings were virtually unopposed.

Eichelberger brought to bear combined forces of 80,000 ground troops and 217 ships, all fighting about 500 miles from the closest Allied base. The operation was a perfect example of MacArthur's "island-hopping" strategy, for it bypassed Wewak and Hansa Bay, which were defended by the Eighteenth Japanese Army. Because commanders on these isolated islands did not know whether they would be attacked, they were forced to maintain forces there. Their response to the Hollandia landings was, therefore, delayed.

Eichelberger's troops seized all Japanese airstrips in and near Hollandia within three days of the landings, and, on June 6, the entire area had been secured. It was July 10, 1944, before the Eighteenth Japanese Army finally arrived to counterattack. They did so at Aitape but were completely deprived of the element of surprise because further ULTRA decrypts had given Eichelberger plenty of time to deploy the 11th U.S. Corps under Major General Charles Hall to defend the area of the landing at the Driniumor River. This battle was especially hard fought and dragged on until August 25. Although the Japanese did punch through Hall's lines at one point, they spent their army against his corps, and the Japanese Eighteenth lost 9,000 men killed out of the 20,000 who had landed at Aitape. The entire Hollandia action is an example of the successful exploitation of intelligence based on intercepted and decrypted coded communications and must be considered one of the most successful U.S. operations in the Pacific war.

See also PHILIPPINES, FALL AND RECONQUEST OF.

Further reading: Drea, Edward J. *Defending the Driniumor: Covering Force Operations in New Guinea, 1944.* Fort Leavenworth, Kans.: Combat Studies Institute, U.S.

Army Command and General Staff College, 1984; Drea, Edward J. *MacArthur's ULTRA: Codebreaking and the War Against Japan, 1942–1945*. Lawrence: University Press of Kansas, 1992.

Hollywood and World War II

At the time of World War II, Hollywood was recognized as the world's cinematic dream factory and the international center of film production. The U.S. government was eager to harness the power of Hollywood to win hearts and minds, to lift public morale, and to help build the public war effort. Overwhelmingly, the people of Hollywood, from the executives to the directors, writers, and actors, were enthusiastic about "doing their part" to win the war. A highly active and influential government agency, the Office of War Information (OWI), was created, which monitored and advised producers in all the mass media but nowhere more vigorously than in the film industry. Even in the exigencies of war, the OWI lacked censorship authority, but it wielded, often with a heavy hand, its strong moral authority, reviewing scripts as well as finished films and always putting to them a single overriding question: How will this help win the war? (It must be noted that while the OWI did not have *direct* censorship authority, it communicated with another agency, the Office of Censorship, which could prevent the release of a movie to the foreign markets, which were vital to Hollywood's bottom line.)

Hollywood movies generally aimed at conveying three principal messages. First, that Allied leaders, military brass, and field commanders were highly skilled and courageous and were moved by the most selfless of motives. Second, that the American fighting man was an ordinary Joe, an individual, who, when duty called, invariably proved capable of extraordinary heroism. Third, that the Allied nations, despite differences with Americans, were populated by decent, courageous people who wanted the same freedoms Americans enjoy. Particularly important was transforming the popular American image of the British from a stuffy, somewhat effete people into

effective, courageous, and friendly brothers in arms. Even more difficult was converting the Soviets from an image of godless communists and enemies of capitalism into gallant, freedom-loving, life-loving allies. Hollywood also sought to overcome long-standing American racial prejudice against the Chinese, although efforts to do so (as in the 1944 *Dragon Seed*) typically seem condescending and patronizing by today's standards. The most popularly successful portrayals of the Allied nations were films focusing on Great Britain, most notably *Mrs. Miniver* (1942), which celebrated the spirit of the British people even under the worst hardship and which is still capable of moving audiences today.

Neither the government nor the film industry wanted to produce war films exclusively, and, during the war, films were made on all the usual subjects. However, movies focusing on the American homefront were especially popular, as were combat action films. Interestingly, directors were often at pains to portray a degree of economic, ethnic, and racial harmony on screen that did not exist on the real-life homefront or in the military. *Bataan* (1943), for example, portrayed racially integrated combat units, whereas the U.S. military was actually segregated. Despite such manipulation of the truth, most Hollywood depictions of combat strived for some semblance of realism. Heroes were plentiful, but hollow, pompous patriotism was out. The message was that in the armed forces of a democratic people, anyone could be, and *had* to be, a hero.

Throughout the war, depictions of the enemy were typically superficial and without humanity. Nazis were evil and treacherous, as were the Japanese, who were also often portrayed as physically grotesque. While Hollywood often painted the Japanese in broad racist strokes, more care was taken to separate the German people from the Nazis. The former were capable of decency and were, in fact, as much victims of the Nazis as other conquered peoples throughout Europe.

By 1944, production of war films began to wane significantly. Those war films that continued to be produced were often more sophisticated and complex than the earlier fare. Especially notable late in the war was *The Story of G.I. Joe* (1945), based on the hard-bitten, intensely human front-line journalism of ERNIE PYLE. Here was a glimpse of war that was short on idealism and optimism but suffused with fear, pain, hardship, and decidedly grim determination. The early postwar years saw a resurgence of light escapist films but also movies that tackled the problems of postwar society and the difficulties many soldiers had in readjusting to civilian life. The enduring classic among these is *The Best Years of Our Lives* (1946), which follows the return of an infantry sergeant, an Army Air Forces captain, and a sailor. All are emotionally scarred, and the young sailor returned home having suffered the loss of both hands. (He was played by Harold Russell, a veteran who had actually lost both hands.)

In addition to producing war-related commercial entertainment films, Hollywood also pitched in for the war effort by providing facilities and expertise to produce military training films for the armed forces and what must be described as propaganda films for military personnel and civilians, the most famous of which was the distinguished *Why We Fight* series directed by Frank Capra. Hollywood experts were also tapped as consultants for various combat photography assignments and for the design and operation of movie equipment for reconnaissance applications. Hollywood set designers were even consulted in matters of camouflage and decoy design. Many high-profile film stars volunteered for combat service, including, most notably, Clark Gable and James Stewart, both of whom joined the Army Air Forces.

Further reading: Chambers, John Whiteclay II, and David Culbert. *World War II, Film, and History.* New York and Oxford: Oxford University Press, 1996; Dick, Bernard F. *The Star-Spangled Screen: The American World War II Film.* Lexington: University Press of Kentucky, 1996; Hoopes, Roy. *When the Stars Went to War: Hollywood and World War II.* New York: Random House, 1995; Koppes, Clayton R., and Gregory D. Black. *Hollywood Goes to War: How Politics, Profits, and Propaganda Shaped World War II Movies.* Berkeley: University of California Press, 1990.

Holocaust, the

Holocaust is a derivation of the Greek word *holokauston*, which, in turn, is a translation from Hebrew *'olah*, or burnt sacrifice. The word reflects the ultimate fate of those killed in German CONCENTRATION AND EXTERMINATION CAMPS, cremation. In modern usage, the Holocaust is sometimes referred to by the Hebrew word *Shoah*.

As discussed in the FINAL SOLUTION, the Holocaust was the product of ADOLF HITLER's extreme anti-Semitism as it was manifested in the policies of the NAZI PARTY (NSDAP). For Hitler and the Nazis, purging the Jews from German life, and, ultimately, from Europe and the rest of the world, was necessary to the advancement of the German people. Jews were deemed *Untermenschen* ("subhumans"), and, therefore, a menace to the German, or Aryan, "race," which aspired to the status of *Ubermenschen* ("supermen"). Hitler became chancellor of Germany on January 30, 1933. On April 1, he instituted a nationwide boycott of Jewish businesses, which was followed, days later, by the removal of Jews from the civil service, and, days after this, by restrictions on Jewish attendance at schools and universities. More restrictions and persecutions were forthcoming, as were legal racial definitions of Jews and Aryans in the NUREMBERG LAWS of 1935. These laws became the basis of a multiplying series of anti-Jewish regulations and legislation. The first major instance of state-sanctioned mass violence against Germany's Jews came on the night of November 9, 1938, KRISTALLNACHT, a national riot that burned or damaged more than a thousand synagogues and more than 7,500 Jewish businesses and that resulted in the arrest of about 30,000 Jewish men, who were sent to concentration camps.

Throughout the 1930s, the German government encouraged the emigration of Jews, albeit at the cost of confiscation of all real property and most other wealth. The volume of Jews leaving Germany was so great that many countries set limits on Jewish immigration. Moreover, German aggressive expansion, including the ANSCHLUSS with Austria and the annexation of the SUDETENLAND and most of the rest of CZECHOSLOVAKIA,

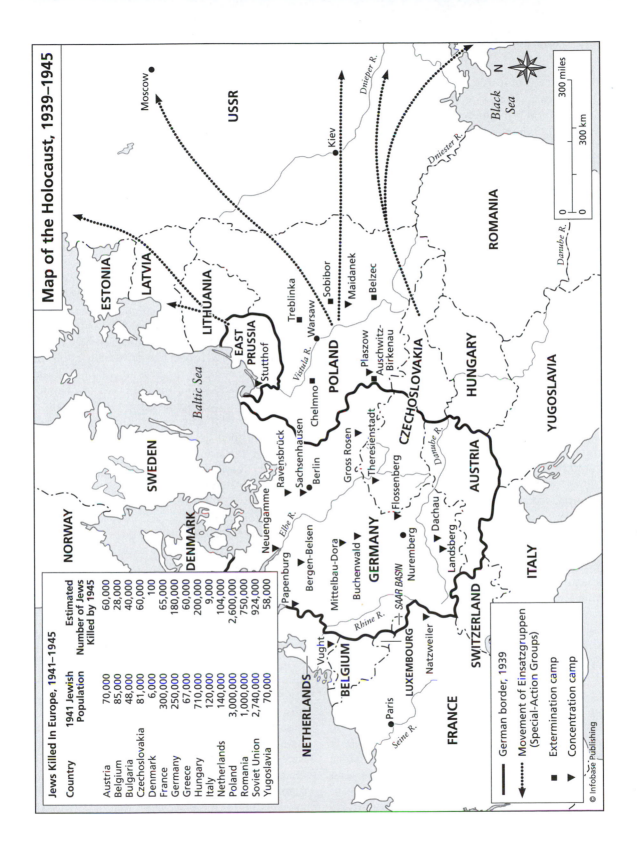

Map of the Holocaust, 1939–1945

Jews Killed In Europe, 1941–1945

Country	1941 Jewish Population	Estimated Number of Jews Killed by 1945
Austria	70,000	60,000
Belgium	85,000	28,000
Bulgaria	48,000	40,000
Czechoslovakia	81,000	60,000
Denmark	6,000	100
France	300,000	65,000
Germany	250,000	180,000
Greece	67,000	60,000
Hungary	710,000	200,000
Italy	120,000	9,000
Netherlands	140,000	104,000
Poland	3,000,000	2,600,000
Romania	1,000,000	750,000
Soviet Union	2,740,000	924,000
Yugoslavia	70,000	58,000

Legend:

— German border, 1939

···· Movement of Einsatzgruppen (Special-Action Groups)

■ Extermination camp

▶ Concentration camp

© Infobase Publishing

N

300 miles

300 km

USSR
ROMANIA
Black Sea
Moscow
Kiev
Dnieper R.
Dniester R.
Danube R.
ESTONIA
LATVIA
LITHUANIA
EAST PRUSSIA
Stutthof
Treblinka
Warsaw
Sobibor
Maidanek
Belzec
POLAND
Chelmno
Plaszow
Auschwitz-Birkenau
CZECHOSLOVAKIA
HUNGARY
YUGOSLAVIA
AUSTRIA
Vistula R.
Baltic Sea
SWEDEN
NORWAY
DENMARK
Neuengamme
Elbe R.
Ravensbrück
Sachsenhausen
Berlin
Gross Rosen
Theresienstadt
Flossenberg
Danube R.
Dachau
Landsberg
Nuremberg
SAAR BASIN
Buchenwald
Mittelbau-Dora
GERMANY
Bergen-Belsen
Papenburg
Rhine R.
Natzweiler
SWITZERLAND
ITALY
FRANCE
Paris
Seine R.
LUXEMBOURG
BELGIUM
NETHERLANDS
Vught

brought even more Jews under the control of the Third Reich. The INVASION OF POLAND, which started World War II on September 1, 1939, brought in many more. Mass emigration was no longer a viable means of purging Germany and its conquered lands, and while the Nazi officers charged with dealing with the "Jewish question," most notably REINHARD HEYDRICH and ADOLF EICHMANN, went so far as to suggest a mass shipment of Jews to Madagascar, the only "practical" solution came to seem mass murder: genocide.

The first major intermediate step toward this genocide was the creation of some 400 ghettos throughout occupied Poland, to which all of nation's Jews were confined. Overcrowding (the largest ghetto, in Warsaw, occupied a mere 2.4 percent of the city's area but held 30 percent of the city's population) and starvation rations ensured that malnutrition and disease would begin the process of mass murder. The ghetto system also consolidated the Jewish population in Poland so that the people could be readily controlled, policed, and, ultimately, prepared for "deportation" to the concentration and extermination camps. Before this began, however, the systematic killing of Jews was first implemented as part of the INVASION OF THE SOVIET UNION, beginning in June 1941. Some 3,000 men of special SCHUTZ-STAFFEL (SS) units known as Einsatzgruppen ("deployment groups") followed close behind the vanguard of the German invading forces. Their assignment was to round up and summarily execute Jews, Gypsies, and, pursuant to Hitler's COMMISSAR ORDER, Soviet commissars (local political leaders). Often, the Einsatzgruppen personnel worked closely with local police as well as anti-Semitic local civilians to accomplish their mission. The most infamous atrocities occurred at Babi Yar, near Kiev, Ukraine, where 33,771 Jews were killed on September 28–29, 1941; in the Rumbula Forest near Riga, Latvia, where some 28,000 Jews were murdered on November 30 and December 8–9; at Ponary, outside Vilna (now Vilnius), Lithuania, during the summer of 1941, where more than 70,000 Jews were killed; and at Ninth Fort, near Kovno (now Kaunas), Lithuania, on October 28,

where 9,000 Jews were killed, including some 5,000 children. Historians believe that Einsatzgruppen killed more than 1 million people, the vast majority Jews, all by shooting.

Despite the staggering numbers killed in the Soviet Union, it was decided that shootings on such a massive scale were both impractical and too public. (Indeed, when the Red Army counterattacked in the Ukraine, the Germans hastily attempted to dig up the mass graves of those slaughtered, so that the bodies could be burned and the evidence of the atrocity thereby destroyed.) Therefore, on January 20, 1942, Reinhard Heydrich convened the WANNSEE CONFERENCE to begin the implementation of an efficient and more secretive mechanism for genocide. What followed was the construction of death camps in Poland, to which Jews and others were transported, usually by rail, in box cars or cattle cars, for mass execution. The first camp dedicated to extermination was at Chelmno, Poland, which used mobile gas vans to kill victims. The condemned were packed into the vehicles, which had their exhaust rerouted into the cargo area, so that the victims were asphyxiated by the time they reached crematoria or other places of disposal. Later, in other camps, permanent gas chambers were built. They were connected directly to crematoria, so that the dead could be efficiently moved from the gas chambers to the ovens. In effect, the Nazis had created factories for the production and disposal of corpses. The process was made even more efficient when carbon monoxide was replaced by Zyklon-B, a cyanide gas agent intended for use as a powerful pesticide.

The most notorious of the death camps was AUSCHWITZ EXTERMINATION CAMP, in Poland. A complex of three camps, Auschwitz represented the ultimate in the German system of high-volume death. Prisoners were received at Auschwitz I, the prison camp, and were "selected" (underwent Selektion). Some, including pregnant women, young children, the old, the disabled, and the sick, were selected for immediate murder and were sent directly to Auschwitz II—Birkenau, the death camp. Others were held at Auschwitz I, and still others sent to the slave-labor camp, Auschwitz

III—Buna-Monowitz. The *Selektion* was administered by SS physicians.

Slave labor was an important resource for German war production as well as an important source of income for the SS. However, the slave laborers, like those held in the prison camp proper, were underfed, poorly clothed, inadequately sheltered, and deprived of medical care. Most succumbed to privation or were simply worked to death. The sick and infirm among them were periodically culled through an ongoing program of *Selektion.*

Camps such as Auschwitz and Majdanek combined the slave labor function with extermination. Other camps, including Belzec, Treblinka, and Sobibor, were dedicated exclusively to mass murder. There were six specialized extermination camps, all in German-occupied Poland.

A total of 21 German-occupied countries were affected by the Holocaust. Most were helpless to defend their Jewish populations. In some countries, locals actively collaborated with German authorities in rounding up Jewish victims. In HUNGARY, which entered the war as a German ally, Jews were variously persecuted, but, as a matter of national sovereignty, the Hungarian government refused to allow their deportation to camps. When Germany invaded Hungary on March 19, 1944, Nazi authorities acted vigorously to confine Jews to ghettos and then, beginning on May 15, 1944, to deport them to Auschwitz: 438,000 in 55 days. ROMANIA, another German ally, assumed responsibility for murdering its own Jews during most of the war, whereas BULGARIA, yet another ally, willingly allowed Macedonian and Thracian Jews to be deported to camps, but the government met with popular resistance when it attempted to deport Jews living in Bulgaria proper. The VICHY GOVERNMENT of France was notoriously cooperative in extending the Holocaust to French soil, as were officials in occupied France.

Other occupied countries resisted collaborating in the Holocaust. Although it was an early key German ally, ITALY refused to persecute, arrest, or deport its Jewish population until Germany occupied northern Italy after BENITO MUSSOLINI was overthrown. The people of Denmark, which was occupied early in the war, actively resisted the Holocaust and managed to save most of their nation's Jewish population first by harboring Jews and then by covertly sending them to neutral Sweden by sea during October 1943.

While much of the story of the Holocaust presents a horrifying picture of collaboration in mass murder, or apathy in the face of it, there were heroes. The Swedish diplomat Raoul Wallenberg worked successfully in Hungary to prevent the deportation of the last of that nation's Jews. Even in Poland, which had a long history of popular anti-Semitism and where, under German occupation, aiding Jews was a capital offense, the Zegota (Council for Aid to Jews), financed by the London-based Polish government in exile, hid Jews and provided them with sustenance and forged documents. France, overwhelmingly shameful in its treatment of Jews during the Holocaust, also had its protectors of Jews. The Huguenots (French Protestants) of Le Chambon-sur-Lignon turned their village into a refuge and safe haven for some 5,000 Jews. By no means did all Germans, even some members of the Nazi Party, support the Final Solution. The most famous and effective protector of German Jews was OSKAR SCHINDLER, a party member who sheltered large numbers of Jews under the guise of employing them as slave labor.

While the question of why so many became accomplices in mass murder is profoundly troubling, many historians and others have also asked why the Jews themselves failed to mount effective resistance against the Holocaust. In fact, there *was* widespread resistance in the ghettos (most notably manifested in the WARSAW RISING), in the countryside, and even in some of the death camps. But large-scale resistance was probably impossible. Jews had no access to arms, they typically lived among anti-Semitic populations and were forsaken by their own governments, and they were slow to recognize, comprehend, or even believe the enormity of the Nazi policy against them. Moreover, the German system of collective reprisal, whereby an act of resistance by one or two individuals would be met with the random killing of perhaps hundreds uninvolved in the act of resistance, discouraged a general uprising in most cases.

The closing months of the war brought some hope to the Jews, especially those in the camps. However, in an effort to conceal Nazi crimes against humanity, German camp officials increased the pace of the killing. They also evacuated prisoners from the Polish camps and marched them, under deplorable conditions, into Germany. Prisoners who faltered along the way were summarily shot.

By the start of 1945, Allied armies were beginning to liberate the concentration camps, both in the east and in Germany itself. Liberation did not necessarily bring salvation, since many prisoners were so malnourished and ill that they were beyond saving. At Bergen-Belsen concentration camp, for example, 28,000 prisoners died *after* the camp was liberated.

In all, some 6 million Jews perished in the Holocaust. For those who survived, there was very little, if anything, to return to. Their wealth and property had been confiscated and their communities razed. Many lived for an extended period in displaced-persons camps. However, the horrors of the Holocaust did provide strong impetus to the Zionist movement, which received both British and American support for a Jewish homeland in British-administered Palestine. The end result was the creation of the state of Israel in May 1948. Additionally, liberalized postwar immigration laws in the United States opened this country to many Jews and other refugees. As the full truth of the horrors of the Holocaust became widely known, the Nuremberg War Crimes Tribunal received widespread support, and many SS members and other Nazi officials were indicted and tried not simply for war crimes, but, for the first time in history, for "crimes against humanity." Some of the most notorious criminals associated with the Holocaust, however, either escaped prosecution or evaded it for a long time. Adolf Eichmann was not apprehended, tried, and executed until 1961. Klaus Barbie, the "butcher of Lyon," was not brought to justice until 1987.

Further reading: Bartov, Omer. *The Holocaust: Origins, Implementation and Aftermath.* New York and London:

Routledge, 2000; Browning, Christopher R. *Final Solution and the German Foreign Office: A Study of Referat DIII of Obteilung Deutschland 1940–1943.* London: Holmes & Meier, 1978; Browning, Christopher R. *The Path to Genocide: Essays on Launching the Final Solution.* Cambridge and New York: Cambridge University Press, 1995; Browning, Christopher R., and Jurgen Matthaus. *The Origins of the Final Solution: The Evolution of Nazi Jewish Policy, September 1939–March 1942.* Lincoln: University of Nebraska Press, 2004; Goldhagen, Daniel Jonah. *Hitler's Willing Executioners: Ordinary Germans and the Holocaust.* New York: Knopf, 1996; Laqueur, Walter, and Judith Tydor Baumel. *The Holocaust Encyclopedia.* New Haven, Conn.: Yale University Press, 2001.

Home Guard

On May 14, 1940, the British government announced the creation of the Local Defence Volunteers, a military organization consisting of volunteer men overage for regular military service. Immediately dubbed "Dad's Army," it was subsequently officially renamed the Home Guard and, at its peak in 1943, consisted of 1,784,000 men. A smaller number of women joined as well, with female enlistment reaching 31,000 in 1944. Early on, the Home Guard was haphazardly uniformed, equipped, and trained, its personnel serving mainly as lookouts along coasts and over such facilities as war plants and airfields. Beginning early in 1940, Home Guard service was made compulsory, and late in 1942, the Home Guard was manned not only by the overage, but by the underage as well. Boys, ages 17 and 18, served in the Home Guard as a means of preparing for service in the regular army. By the middle of 1943, the average age of a Home Guard battalion had dropped to 30. Before the Home Guard "stood down" in December 1944, it was performing a wide variety of duties, including manning antiaircraft installations.

See also CIVIL DEFENSE.

Further reading: Carroll, David. *The Home Guard.* London: Sutton, 1999; Longmate, Norman. *The Real Dad's Army: The Story of the Home Guard.* London: Arrow Books, 1974; MacKenzie, S. P. *The Home Guard: A Mili-*

tary and Political History. Oxford and New York: Oxford University Press, 1995.

Homma Masaharu (1887–1946) *Japanese general who commanded the Philippine invasion*

Born in Sado, Japan, into the family of a wealthy landowner, Homma graduated in 1907 at the top of the Army Academy and was sent to the prestigious Army War College in 1915. He served during World War I as an observer with the British forces in France and, in 1925, was appointed Japanese resident officer in India. He left this assignment in 1930 when he was named military attaché in London. Homma's education and experience Westernized him to a greater degree than his fellow officers. Homma commanded Japanese forces at Tientsin, China, in 1939, then, in December 1941, just days after the BATTLE OF PEARL HARBOR began World War II in the Pacific, Lieutenant General Homma led the invasion of the Philippine Islands. His assignment was to take the islands within 50 days, but the heroic resistance of the Filipino and American forces on the Philippines made the campaign much longer and far more costly. Although he was ultimately successful, Homma was recalled to Japan in August 1942 and was not given another command assignment.

Homma surrendered to American forces in Tokyo on September 14, 1945, and was indicted as a war criminal, charged with responsibility for the BATAAN DEATH MARCH, along with other atrocities in the Philippines. Homma's defense was based on his claim that, far from ordering the Bataan Death March, he had never even heard of it. This availed not at all with a U.S. military commission that tried him. Convicted, Homma was executed by firing squad at Los Baños, Luzon, Philippines, on April 3, 1946.

Further reading: Falk, Stanley L. *Bataan: March of Death.* New York: Jove Books, 1985; Knox, Donald. *Death March: The Survivors of Bataan.* New York: Harvest Books, 2002; Taylor, Lawrence. *A Trial of Generals: Homma, Yamashita, MacArthur.* South Bend, Ind.: Icarus Press, 1981.

General Homma in prison and awaiting trial in Tokyo *(Harry S. Truman Presidential Library)*

Honda Masaki (1889–1964) *Japanese general*

After graduating from the Japanese Imperial military academy, Honda Masaki was commissioned in the Japanese army and, by 1940, held command of the 8th Division. At the outbreak of World War II, he was appointed head of the Military Education Branch Armored Department, serving in this post until 1943, when he was named to command of the Twentieth Army. In April 1944, Honda was assigned to command the Thirty-third Army in Burma, his chief mission to hold at bay Chinese forces in north Burma. In January 1945, Honda was commanded to hold a north-south line from Lashio to Mandalay to check the advance of U.S. general JOSEPH STILWELL and his combined U.S.-Chinese troops, who were about to reopen the Burma Road, China's major supply artery. As Honda moved against Stillwell, British generals WILLIAM SLIM and Frank Messervy attacked him. Honda retreated through southern Burma, leaving Rangoon vulnerable. British forces recaptured the Burmese capital on May 3, 1945.

Honda Masaki survived the war and died in Japan in 1964.

Further reading: Dupuy, Trevor N. *Asiatic Land Battles: Allied Victories in China and Burma.* New York: Franklin Watts, 1963; Hogan, David W. *India-Burma (The U.S. Army Campaigns of World War II).* Carlisle, Pa.: Army Center of Military History, 1991; Webster, Donovan. *The Burma Road: The Epic Story of the China-Burma-India Theater in World War II.* New York: Farrar, Straus and Giroux, 2003.

Hong Kong, fall of

At the outbreak of World War II in the Pacific, Hong Kong was a British Crown colony, densely populated over about 400 square miles by 1.4 million persons, virtually all of them Chinese. British military planners understood well that Hong Kong was vulnerable to attack and invasion from the Japanese-occupied Chinese mainland. The 12,000-man British garrison was instructed to hold out as long as possible in the event of an attack, pending the arrival of Chinese forces under CHIANG KAI-SHEK (Jiang Jieshi). Inasmuch as Japanese spies had been active in Hong Kong for many years and had provided Japanese military command with highly detailed information concerning the island's defenses and its troop dispositions, the standing order was little more than wishful thinking. A small garrison could not hold out for any significant length of time against an invasion of any substance.

The British deployed their main defensive line three miles north of Kowloon in the so-called Leased Territories on the Chinese mainland. Three battalions of Scots and Indian troops were deployed much too thinly along the line. Three battalions, including two Canadian battalions, were deployed

on the island of Hong Kong itself. A kind of home guard was also present on the island, consisting of poorly equipped locals who manned artillery and antiaircraft defenses. Sea support included nothing more than a destroyer, eight motor torpedo boats (the Royal Navy equivalent of the American PT boat), and four obsolescent gunboats. A mere seven outmoded aircraft constituted the available air forces. All of this small, motley, and inadequate garrison force was under the command of Major General Christopher Maltby.

The attack on Hong Kong came with terrible swiftness on the day after the BATTLE OF PEARL HARBOR opened the Pacific theater of World War II. The assault began with an air attack that quickly destroyed, on the ground, all seven British aircraft. This was quickly followed by an overland invasion: The 38th Division of the Twenty-third Japanese Army under Lieutenant General Sano Tadayoshi crossed the Sham Chun River and poured into the Leased Territories. By nightfall, Maltby had been forced to withdraw entirely from the Kowloon mainland and consolidate his position on Hong Kong island.

Sano kept the pressure on Maltby, who completed his withdrawal by December 13. Once this operation had been accomplished, Sano launched relentless air attacks against the business district of Victoria and against the British naval assets in port. Sano ordered his men across to the island on December 15, but, to his chagrin, they were initially repulsed. On December 18, however, Japanese forces landed in strength along a line between North Point and Aldrich Bay. Moving inland, they drove a wedge between the forces of the defenders. The motor torpedo boats that had survived the initial air attacks turned their attention to the Japanese troop transports, but were suppressed by overwhelming Japanese air superiority.

Despite heavy British losses, Sano's progress was much slower than either he or the Japanese high command had anticipated. Indeed, on December 20, Sano was compelled to halt his general advance to regroup, and it was not until Christmas Eve that the preponderance of Japanese numbers finally prevailed. With supplies and ammunition exhausted, Maltby asked for a cease-fire on Christmas day. That evening, the British governor of Hong Kong formally turned the colony over to Sano's superior, Lieutenant General Sakai Takashi, commander of the Twenty-third Japanese Army.

British military losses were about 4,400 killed or wounded, among them 800 Canadian dead. The Japanese took much heavier-than-expected casualties: 2,754 killed or wounded. Except for a handful of British and Commonwealth troops who managed to escape, the rest of the garrison became prisoners of war for the duration, and all Western residents of Hong Kong were interned.

Further reading: Greenhous, Brereton. *C Force to Hong Kong: A Canadian Catastrophe.* Toronto: Dundurn Press, 1997; Roland, Charles G. *Long Night's Journey into Day: Prisoners of War in Hong Kong and Japan 1941–1945.* Waterloo, Ontario: Wilfrid Laurier University Press, 2001; Snow, Philip. *The Fall of Hong Kong: Britain, China, and the Japanese Occupation.* New Haven, Conn.: Yale University Press, 2004; Whitfield, Andrew J. *Hong Kong, Empire and the Anglo-American Alliance At War, 1941–45.* London: Palgrave Macmillan, 2001.

Hopkins, Harry (1890–1946) *Franklin Delano Roosevelt's emissary and adviser*

Born in Sioux City, Iowa, Harry Hopkins traveled far from his background as the son of a rural harness maker when he became an innovative and influential social worker in New York City during the 1920s. In 1931, during the Depression, then-governor of New York FRANKLIN DELANO ROOSEVELT appointed Hopkins executive director (later chairman) of the New York State Temporary Emergency Relief Administration, a relief agency Governor Roosevelt had created. Greatly impressed by Hopkins, FDR established a close working relationship with him, and when Roosevelt was elected to the presidency, he took Hopkins with him as the first director of the Federal Emergency Relief Administration.

A crusading liberal, Hopkins encouraged FDR to introduce a wide range of relief and reform programs, including, most important, the Works Progress (later renamed Work Projects) Administration (WPA), of which he became director. Under Hopkins's leadership, the WPA quickly evolved into a massive and massively ambitious program. In the meantime, Hopkins himself became an increasingly influential adviser to the president, who appointed him secretary of commerce in 1938. Afflicted by poor health, including stomach cancer, Hopkins tempered his personal political ambitions and threw himself even more vigorously into the role of adviser and confidant.

After FDR was elected to his third term in 1940, Hopkins resigned as secretary of commerce but continued in his advisory role. With the commencement of World War II, while the United States maintained its official neutrality, FDR called on Hopkins to be his eyes and ears in London and Moscow. It was to a significant degree Hopkins's strong personal impression of the character and resolve of British prime minister WINSTON CHURCHILL that moved him to recommend to Roosevelt that the British be given every support possible (short of an outright declaration of war). Hopkins was instrumental in fostering the close personal and political relationship between FDR and Churchill and was thus instrumental in creating the Anglo-American alliance essential to victory in the war.

In 1941, the president appointed Hopkins director of the LEND-LEASE program, and he also served on the powerful War Production Board and the Pacific War Council. These official appointments notwithstanding, Hopkins's most important role remained as FDR's confidant and adviser. Hopkins was on call 24 hours a day, seven days a week. He even took up full-time residence in the White House.

Hopkins's labors on behalf of the war effort were truly heroic, especially given his deteriorating health and increasingly frail condition. He survived the president to arrange, on behalf of HARRY S. TRUMAN, the POTSDAM CONFERENCE, traveling for the purpose—and for the last time in his career—to

Moscow in April 1945. It is a testament to Hopkins's straight-talking, frank skills as a communicator that he was highly esteemed by the diverse likes of Roosevelt, Churchill, and even JOSEPH STALIN. In 1946, Hopkins finally succumbed to the cancer that had long afflicted him.

Further reading: Hopkins, June. *Harry Hopkins: Sudden Hero, Brash Reformer.* New York: St. Martin's Press, 1999; McJimsey, George T. *Harry Hopkins: Ally of the Poor and Defender of Democracy.* Cambridge, Mass.: Harvard University Press, 1987; Sherwood, Robert E. *Roosevelt and Hopkins.* New York: Enigma Books, 2001; Wills, Matthew B. *Wartime Missions of Harry L. Hopkins.* Bloomington, Ind.: Authorhouse, 2005.

Horii Tomitaro (1890–1942) *Japanese general*

Lieutenant General Horii Tomitaro was one of the Imperial Army's most highly regarded field commanders. He fought in the SINO-JAPANESE WAR beginning in 1938 as commander of the 12th Independent Regiment then, from 1940 to 1941, as the general officer in command of the 55th Division. After the outbreak of World War II in the Pacific, Horii essentially created the elite South Seas Detachment, made up of six of his own handpicked battalions, mountain artillery, and engineers. He led this unit in the NEW GUINEA CAMPAIGN, including a planned attack on Port Moresby by way of Buna and Gona. His plan was to storm through Buna and Gona while follow-up forces established a well-fortified beachhead between the two villages.

The assault on Port Moresby failed, and among the Japanese casualties was Horii Tomitaro. It was a major command loss for the Imperial Army.

See also BUNA, BATTLE OF; GONA, BATTLE OF; and PORT MORESBY, DEFENSE OF.

Further reading: Mayo, Lida. *Bloody Buna: The Campaign That Halted the Japanese Invasion of Australia.* Newton Abbot, U.K.: David and Charles, 1975; Vader, John. *New Guinea: The Tide Is Stemmed.* New York: Ballantine, 1971.

Horthy de Nagybánya, Miklós (1868–1957) *fascist dictator of Hungary*

Born into an aristocratic family, Miklós Horthy enrolled in the Austro-Hungarian naval academy at Fiume when he was 14. He served as aide-de-camp to the Austrian archduke Francis Ferdinand from 1909 until the archduke was assassinated at Sarajevo in 1914, the event that precipitated World War I. During that conflict, Horthy proved himself an able and courageous naval commander, successfully running the Allies' blockade of the Adriatic. He rose quickly during the war, achieving the rank of admiral in time to assume responsibility for the transfer of the Austro-Hungarian fleet to Yugoslavia in October 1918.

Postwar Hungary writhed under the brutal oppression of the Communist regime of Béla Kun. Counterrevolutionary forces based at Szeged, Hungary, called on Horthy, who enjoyed the status of a national hero, to organize an army to march on Budapest and overthrow Kun. Horthy led the advance in November 1919, and it proved sufficient to intimidate Kun into fleeing. In January 1920, a conservative, right-wing Hungarian parliament voted to restore the monarchy and, on March 1, named Horthy regent. To the astonishment of the parliament, Horthy blocked King Charles IV's bid to regain the throne and, instead, continued to serve as de facto head of government. Horthy governed in this manner from 1921 to 1931, when Hungary, hit hard by the worldwide Depression, found itself assailed by Bolshevism once again. In this climate of crisis, Horthy assumed increasingly personal control of the Hungarian government and prevailed on parliament to vote him the power of absolute dictator in 1937.

Horthy both distrusted and personally despised ADOLF HITLER, but he saw an alliance with this most powerful of right-wing leaders as an essential defense against the encroachment of a Communist takeover. For this reason, at the outbreak of World War II, Hungary entered the hostilities on the side of Germany. It was an alliance Horthy instantly regretted, and he set to work in an effort to extricate his nation from actual involvement in the war. This increased the friction between his regime and

Hitler, and Horty was forced to step down. Abducted by German agents in 1944, Horthy was not liberated until the German surrender in May 1945.

With Hungary now dominated by the Communists, Horthy sought refuge in Portugal, which had been a neutral power in World War II. He lived the rest of his life in the town of Estoril.

Further reading: Fenyo, Mario D. *Hitler, Horthy, and Hungary: German-Hungarian relations, 1941–1944.* New Haven, Conn.: Yale University Press, 1972; Horthy, Nicholas [Miklos]. *Admiral Nicholas Horthy's Memoirs.* Rochester, N.Y.: Simon Publications, 2001.

Hoth, Hermann (1891–1971) *German general*

Born in Neuruppen, Germany, to the family of an army medical officer, Hoth joined the German army as a youth and saw service throughout World War I. He remained in service during the interwar years, steadily advancing in rank, and in 1935 assumed command of the 18th Division at Liegnitz. In November 1938, he was promoted to lieutenant general and assigned command of 15th Motorized Corps. He led this corps in the INVASION OF POLAND on September 1, 1939.

After the conclusion of Polish operations, Hoth was transferred to the West and participated in the BATTLE OF FRANCE, leading his forces through the Ardennes all the way to the English Channel, then sweeping around into Normandy and Brittany. The success of this spectacular drive earned him promotion to general on July 19, 1940.

Transferred again to the east, Hoth was given top command of Panzer Group 3 during the INVASION OF THE SOVIET UNION. His forces took Minsk and Vitebsk, then headed toward Moscow. He was transferred again, in October 1941, to command the Seventeenth German Army in action in the Ukraine. In January 1942, however, his army absorbed the brunt of a massive Red Army counterattack, and he pulled back his forces. Despite this, Hoth was advanced in June 1942 to succeed ERICH HOEPNER as commander of the Fourth Panzer Army. In this capacity, he participated in the ill-fated siege of Stalingrad as well as in the titanic contest of armor at the BATTLE OF KURSK in July 1943.

Beaten back at Kursk, Hoth withdrew in good order to advantageous defensive positions, but this retreat, at last, earned the wrath of ADOLF HITLER, who recalled Hoth to Germany in November 1943. From this time on, he was relegated to service with the reserve.

At the NUREMBERG WAR CRIMES TRIBUNAL, Hoth was found guilty of having committed war crimes in the Ukraine. Sentenced on October 27, 1948, to 15 years in prison, he was released after serving six, and he devoted the rest of his life to writing military history.

Further reading: Carruthers, Bob, and John Erickson. *The Russian Front 1941–1945.* New York: Sterling, 2000; Von Mellenthin, F. W. *Panzer Battles.* London: Trafalgar Square, 2002.

Hoxha, Enver (1908–1985) *leader of the Albanian Communist Party*

Enver Hoxha was born in Gjirokastër, Albania, the son of a cloth merchant. He had an excellent education at a French lycée and at the American Technical School in Tiranë, the Albanian capital. A superb student, he earned a state scholarship in 1930 to the University of Montpellier, France, and served from 1934 to 1936 as a secretary at the Albanian consulate general in Brussels. While there, he studied law before returning to Albania in 1936 as a teacher. He was removed from this position in 1939 after Italy invaded Albania because he would not join the newly created Albanian Fascist Party. After leaving teaching, he opened a tobacco shop in Tiranë, which he transformed into the headquarters of the local communist cell. Following the German invasion of Yugoslavia in 1941, exiled Yugoslav communists supported Hoxha in founding the Albanian Communist Party (later called the Party of Labor). During the war, Hoxha served as the first secretary of the party's Central Committee and was political commissar of the Army of National Liberation. Hoxha held the office of prime minister of Albania after the country was liberated in 1944. He served until 1954, but remained first secretary of the Central Committee of the Party of Labor for life. In effect, this made him dictator of Albania for life.

Further reading: Instituti i Studimeve Marksiste-Leniniste. *History of the Party of Labor of Albania.* Tiranë: Naim Frashri, 1971; Pollo, Stefanaq. *The History of Albania: From Its Origins to the Present Day.* London: Routledge and Kegan Paul, 1981.

Hull, Cordell (1871–1955) *U.S. secretary of state during most of World War II*

Born and raised in rural Overton county, Tennessee, Hull studied law and became interested in Democratic politics. He gained election to the House of Representatives in 1907 and served for 22 years, from 1907 to 1921 and from 1923 to 1931. He was elected to the U.S. Senate in 1931 but left in 1933, when he was appointed secretary of state by President FRANKLIN D. ROOSEVELT. In keeping with the spirit of FDR's New Deal, Hull called for the lowering of high protectionist tariff barriers, arguing that they put the brakes on the development of badly needed foreign trade. His advocacy of this policy earned him national as well as international acclaim. Hull was also instrumental, during the 1930s, in improving relations between the United States and Latin America, promoting and implementing FDR's "Good Neighbor Policy." This created a sentiment of hemispherical solidarity, which was especially gratifying after the outbreak of World War II, when the entire hemisphere stood together against Nazi German aggression.

Hull was an opponent of the so-called Japanese Monroe Doctrine, a policy that would have given Japan leave to dominate China. Hull's foreign policy increasingly aligned the United States with China and against Japanese imperialism. Although this was undoubtedly the just and morally correct policy, it led to an ultimately cataclysmic deterioration of relations between Japan and the United States.

Even during the war, Hull began planning for the postwar world by laying the foundation for what would become the United Nations. At the Moscow Conference of Foreign Ministers in 1943, Hull secured a pledge from all the major Allied nations to continue a key aspect of the alliance after the war to create a world organization for the maintenance of international peace and security. Not only did this achievement earn from FDR the epithet of "father of the United Nations," it earned Cordell Hull the Nobel Prize in 1945.

In failing health, Hull resigned as secretary of state after Roosevelt was elected to his fourth term in 1944. He published his extraordinarily illuminating autobiography, *Memoirs of Cordell Hull,* in 1950.

Further reading: Gellman, Irwin F. *Secret Affairs: Franklin Roosevelt, Cordell Hull, and Sumner Welles.* Baltimore: Johns Hopkins University Press, 1995; Hull, Cordell. *The Memoirs of Cordell Hull.* New York: Macmillan, 1950; Roberston, Charles L. *The American Secretary of State: A Study of Office under Henry L. Stimson and Cordell Hull.* Ann Arbor, Mich.: University Microfilms, 1960; Utley, Jonathan G. *Going to War with Japan, 1937–1941.* Knoxville: University of Tennessee Press, 1985.

Hump, the

The Hump was an air supply route flown by the U.S. Air Transport Command from Dinjan, India, to Kunming, China, a distance of 500 miles over treacherous mountain ridges as high as 15,000 feet. The Hump route began operation in July 1942 after the fall of Burma and the consequent closure of the Burma Road. For most of the war, it was the only military means by which the Allies supplied China.

Transport aircraft flew over the Patkai, Kumon, and Santsung Mountains, near the maximum ceiling of the fully loaded aircraft and usually in very poor weather characterized by icing and turbulence. During part of the year, the monsoon was also a major hazard. "Flying the Hump" was some of the most hazardous air duty in the war. Typical of the losses were those suffered in the single month of January 1945, when 44,000 tons of supplies were lifted at the cost of 23 major mishaps, which claimed 36 lives. In total, airlift operations transported 650,00 tons of supplies into China using the services of 22,000 military personnel and about 47,000 civilians, mostly laborers. About 300 transport aircraft were active in operations.

Further reading: Ethell, Jeff, and Don Downie. *Flying the Hump in Original World War II Color.* Osceola, Wis.: Motorbooks International, 2004; Spencer, Otha C. *Flying the Hump: Memories of an Air War.* College Station: Texas A & M University Press, 1994; Webster, Donovan. *The Burma Road: The Epic Story of the China-Burma-India Theater in World War II.* New York: Farrar, Straus and Giroux, 2003.

Hungary

It is a commonplace that the TREATY OF VERSAILLES created the conditions that made Germany ripe for the rise of ADOLF HITLER. Less well recognized is that the Treaty of Trianon, a document related to the Treaty of Versailles, dismembered Hungary (which was split off from Austria) and created a sense of deep injustice that threw that country into the Axis embrace at the outbreak of World War II. Pre–World War I Hungary had a population of some 21 million. After the war, it was reduced to under 8 million. Worst of all, some 3 million Magyars, ethnic Hungarians, were cut off from their homeland as a result of the Treaty of Trianon. Thus, Hungary was highly receptive to Hitler, who promised an alliance that would regain what Hungary had lost. Moreover, for most Hungarians, fascism seemed preferable to communism. Better to risk domination by Germany than to be swallowed up by the Soviets. Finally, Hungary experienced a surge of anti-Semitism in the years preceding World War II, which took the form of resentment against the perceived growing influence of the Jewish community. Among everything else Hitler seemed to offer, his anti-Semitism was very much in harmony with the prevailing Hungarian sentiment.

Hungary gravitated toward the Nazi regime from the beginning, as early as 1933. Hitler rewarded this growing allegiance in 1938, when, following the annexation of the SUDETENLAND, he forced the cession of southern Slovakia to Hungary. After all of CZECHOSLOVAKIA had been partitioned, Hitler additionally parceled out to Hungary Carpathian Ruthenia in 1939. The next year, Germany pressured another ally, ROMANIA, to deliver northern Transylvania to Hungary. As a result of these cessions, many Hungarian leaders were eager to join the Axis formally as a full military ally; but even those who had their doubts were willing to press forward with the alliance because they feared that failure to do so would result in Romania's reclaiming what it had ceded. When Hungary gave the armies of Hitler free passage through its territory for the INVASION OF YUGOSLAVIA in April 1941, it was rewarded with yet more Magyar-occupied territory. The acquisition of so much territory, combined with the continuing fear of communism, prompted Hungary to seize on a provocation—the bombing of the northern Hungarian town of Kassa, which may well have been the work of German provocateurs rather than Soviets—to declare war, on June 27, 1941, against the Soviet Union, which had been invaded by Germany days before.

Hungary was valuable to the Axis for its strategic geographic location, as well as for its resources, including livestock, wheat, corn, and for textile manufacture, flax. The country was also rich in bauxite, manganese, and oil, all highly prized wartime commodities. Indeed, oil would become increasingly important in the course of the war and motivated Germany's occupation of Hungary beginning in March 1944. Although Hungary was primarily an agricultural nation, important industries developed rapidly during the war, and Hungary became an important producer of ammunition and aircraft.

In some ways, this most attractive prize was waiting to be seized. In 1920, the Hungarian parliament restored the monarchy, yet the king was not welcomed back to the throne, and Admiral MIKLÓS HORTHY DE NAGYBÁNYA was installed instead as regent. Horthy was strongly right wing and an enemy to communism; however, an even more radically right-wing group, known as the Arrow

Cross movement, gained great power in parliament and was instrumental in propelling the nation into the Nazi sphere. The alliance took Hungary to war with all of Germany's enemies, including, ultimately, Great Britain and the United States, in addition to the Soviet Union. Hungary's valuable agricultural and mineral wealth, as well as its crossroads geographical position, made it a target for aerial bombardment and for ground battle. With the nation now in the thick of the fighting, even the right wing began to see that Hungary's involvement in the war was a disaster. Government support for the German war effort faltered as officials desperately searched for an exit strategy. Hitler would have none of this, however, and on March 19, 1944, he sent German forces to occupy an increasingly reluctant Hungary. A puppet government was set up, through Horthy, under General Döme Sztójay, who suppressed anti-Nazi agitation in the country and contributed a new army to the war effort. Up to this time, Hungarian authorities, while zealous in their persecution of Hungarian Jews, stoutly resisted their deportation beyond Hungary's borders. Now the SCHUTZSTAFFEL (SS) was given free rein to round up the Jews and send them to the CONCENTRATION AND EXTERMINATION CAMPS. Between March and July 1944, about 438,000 were deported, almost all to their deaths.

Despite Hungary's anti-Semitism, it was in part the fate of the Jews—and Romania's decision to leave the Axis for the Allied cause—that prompted Horthy to defy the Nazis. He ordered an immediate halt to the deportations and on August 29, 1944, appointed a new government under General Géza Lakatos. Even more boldly, he made a separate peace with the Soviet Union, concluding a preliminary armistice on October 11. This triggered the Arrow Cross to rise up and remove Horthy in a coup d'état. A new government under Arrow Cross leader Ferenc Szálasi assumed power, but by this time Nazi domination of Hungary was rapidly coming to an end. The Soviets backed a new provisional government, which was created at Debrecen on December 21–22, 1944.

Hungary was more important to the Germans for its agricultural and mineral goods, as well as for its strategic location, than for its military. The nation entered the war with about 216,000 ill-equipped infantry troops, two brigades of cavalry, and another two motorized brigades. Armor was obsolescent and motor transport in critically short supply. German pressure resulted in the raising of a "Second Army," which consisted of about 250,000 men, including some 50,000 slave laborers, most of them Jews. This force was used in the Ukraine, where, vastly outclassed by the Red Army, it suffered severe casualties and disintegrated entirely soon after it was attacked south of Voronezh on January 12, 1943. This disaster convinced the Hungarian government to avoid fighting as much as possible. The German occupation of the country was largely in response to this reluctance. During the occupation, a newly reorganized Hungarian force was fielded between April and October 1944, but proved predictably ineffective and was increasingly riddled with mass defections to the Soviet side. After the fall of Budapest in mid February 1945, a few diehard Hungarian units retreated with the Germans into Austria.

The Hungarian resistance movement was late to develop, sparse when it did, and, ultimately, ineffective. The British SPECIAL OPERATIONS EXECUTIVE (SOE) sent no fewer than six missions into the country after March 1944, but none was productive. When a Committee of Liberation was formed in November 1944, armed resistance began, but was soon crushed after the committee's key members were betrayed to the GESTAPO.

Further reading: Eby, Cecil D. *Hungary at War: Civilians and Soldiers in World War II.* State College: Pennsylvania State University Press, 1998; Lackó, Miklós. *Arrow-Cross Men, National Socialists, 1935–1944.* Budapest: Akadémiai Kiadó, 1969; Pierik, Perry. *Hungary, 1944–1945—The Forgotten Tragedy: Germany's Final Offensives During World War II.* Amsterdam: Aspekt B V Uitgeverij, 1998.